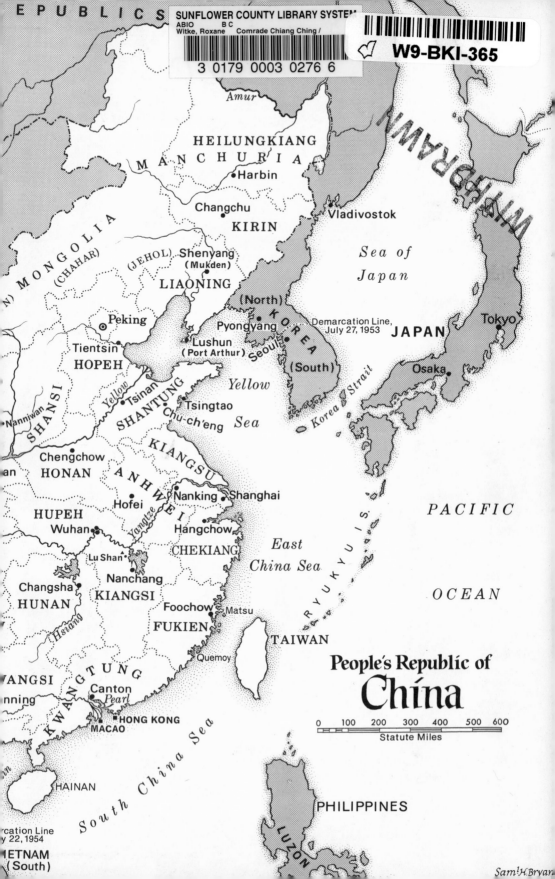

EPUBLICS

Amur

HEILUNGKIANG

MANCHURIA

• Harbin

• Changchu

KIRIN

• Vladivostok

Sea of Japan

MONGOLIA
(CHAHAR)

(JEHOL)

Shenyang
(Mukden) •

LIAONING

(North)

KOREA

Demarcation Line,
July 27, 1953

JAPAN

• Tokyo

N) MONGOLIA

⊚ Peking

• Tientsin

HOPEH

Lushun
(Port Arthur) •

Pyongyang •

Seoul •

(South)

• Osaka

SHANSI

Yellow

Tsinan •

SHANTUNG

Chu-ch'eng •

• Tsingtao

Yellow

Sea

Korea Strait

PACIFIC

• Nanniwan

Chengchow •

HONAN

KIANGSU

ANHWEI

• Nanking

• Shanghai

an

HUPEH

Wuhan •

Hofei •

Yangtze

Hangchow •

CHEKIANG

East China Sea

OCEAN

Lu Shan ▲

Nanchang •

Changsha •

HUNAN

KIANGSI

Foochow •

• Matsu

Hsiang

FUKIEN

TAIWAN

Quemoy •

ANGSI

KWANGTUNG

Canton •
Pearl

nning

HONG KONG ■
MACAO •

South China Sea

People's Republic of
China

| 0 | 100 | 200 | 300 | 400 | 500 | 600 |

Statute Miles

HAINAN

PHILIPPINES

LUZON

cation Line
y 22, 1954

IETNAM
(South)

Sam H. Bryan

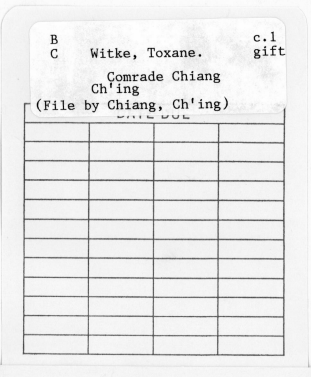

COMRADE
CHIANG CH'ING

廬山漢陽峰

江上有奇峰，鎖在煙霧中，
尋常看不見，偶爾露崢嶸。

江青攝詩贈

張特克夫人

一九七二年八月四二日

"Han Yang Peak at Lu Shan"

Poem, probably written by Mao Tse-tung in the early 1960's when he produced several comparable pieces.

"Soaring at riverside, the wondrous peak
  Locks herself in river mist
  And shows no morning glow.
  Suddenly her majesty is bared."

COMRADE
CHIANG CH'ING

◇ ◇ ◇

Roxane Witke

B
C
C1

Little, Brown and Company   Boston · Toronto

FIRST EDITION
T 04177

The author is grateful to the following publishers, individuals, and agents for permission to quote from previously copyrighted materials:

Little, Brown and Company, for excerpts from *Khrushchev Remembers* by Nikita S. Khrushchev. Translated from the Russian and edited by Strobe Talbott; introduction by Edward Crankshaw. Copyright © 1970 by Little, Brown and Company.

Curtis Brown, Ltd., for excerpts from *Report from Red China* by Harrison Forman. Copyright © 1972 by Harrison Forman.

The Seabury Press, for the poem "A Letter to Lady Tao Ch'iu" from *The Orchid Boat: Women Poets of China*. Translated and edited by Kenneth Rexroth and Ling Chung. English translation copyright © 1972 by Kenneth Rexroth and Ling Chung.

Simon & Schuster, Inc., and Penguin Books Ltd. for the poem "The Immortals" from *Mao Tse-tung* by Stuart Schram. Copyright © 1966, 1967 by Stuart Schram.

Penguin Books Ltd. for excerpts from *The Story of the Stone, Vol. 1: The Golden Days* by Cao Xueqin. Translated by David Hawkes. Copyright © 1973 by David Hawkes.

Willis Barnstone, for "Militia Women" and "Written on a photograph of the Cave of the Gods" from *The Poems of Mao Tse-tung* translated by Willis Barnstone and Ko Ching-po. English translation copyright © 1972 by Bantam Books Inc.

Random House, Inc., for four lines from "Surgical Ward" from *Collected Poems* by W. H. Auden. Copyright 1945 by W. H. Auden.

Oxford University Press, for four lines from "Reply to Kuo Mo-jo" by Mao Tse-tung. From *Mao and the Chinese Revolution*, translated by Michael Bullock and Jerome Ch'en. Copyright © 1965 Oxford University Press.

Note: Transliteration of Chinese words used in this book conforms to the Wade-Giles system, unless convention is otherwise.

Library of Congress Cataloging in Publication Data

Witke, Roxane.
  Comrade Chiang Ch'ing.

  1. Chiang, Ch'ing. 2. Statesmen — China —
Biography. 3. Women — China — Biography. 4. China
— Biography. 5. China — History — 1900–
I. Title.
DS778.C5374W57   951.05'092'4 [B]   77-935
ISBN 0-316-94900-0

*Published simultaneously in Canada
by Little, Brown & Company (Canada) Limited*

PRINTED IN THE UNITED STATES OF AMERICA

For Alexandra

Acknowledgments

I want to thank The Johnson Foundation of Racine, Wisconsin; the Joint Committee on Contemporary China of the Social Science Research Council and the American Council of Learned Societies; and the National Endowment for the Humanities for the time granted to me by their generous support. The East Asian Research Center of Harvard University provided an excellent collegial atmosphere for two years. Stanford University and the State University of New York at Binghamton were understanding of the demands of my research. Among the friends and colleagues to whom I am the most indebted for inspiration, judgment, and critical readings are Larned G. Bradford, John K. Fairbank, Tsi-an Hsia, Michael Ipson, Donald R. Kelley, Donald W. Klein, John W. Lewis, Andrew J. Nathan, John S. Service, Ezra F. Vogel, and Frederic Wakeman, Jr. A special credit is owed to my small daughter, who used to wonder when Chiang Ch'ing was coming to dinner.

Roxane Witke

January 1977

List of Illustrations

Unless otherwise noted, the illustrations appear through the courtesy of Chiang Ch'ing. The New China News Agency photographs are also courtesy of Chiang Ch'ing.

Frontispiece: "Han Yang Peak at Lu Shan"

Between pages 220 and 221

Chiang Ch'ing, Yao Wen-yuan, and the author, at the Great Hall of the People. NEW CHINA NEWS AGENCY PHOTOGRAPH

Chiang Ch'ing, Shen Jo-yun, the author, Hsu Erh-wei, and Yao Wen-yuan. NCNA PHOTOGRAPH

At a roast duck dinner in the Great Hall of the People. NCNA PHOTOGRAPH

Assemblage with Chiang Ch'ing and the author. NCNA PHOTOGRAPH

Chiang Ch'ing on a veranda in the orchid park. PHOTOGRAPH BY THE AUTHOR

Chang Ying in her new black skirt. PHOTOGRAPH BY THE AUTHOR

Shen Jo-yun. PHOTOGRAPH BY THE AUTHOR

Yü Shih-lien. PHOTOGRAPH BY THE AUTHOR

The mirthful raconteur. PHOTOGRAPH BY THE AUTHOR

Maps

Chronology

	General	Chiang Ch'ing
1900	Boxer Rebellion and Eight-Power Invasion to relieve Boxer siege of the Peking legations.	
1911	Revolution of 1911 against the Manchu dynasty. Establishment of the Republic.	
1914		*March. Born in Chu-ch'eng, Shantung province.*
1916	Opening of warlord era, lasting twelve years.	
1919	May Fourth Movement.	
1921	Chinese Community Party (CCP) founded.	
1925	May 30. University students demonstrating for Chinese workers are fired on by Britain's police.	
1926	Chiang Kai-shek leads Nationalist forces on the Northern Expedition lasting until 1928.	
1927	The Kuomintang (KMT) purges itself of the CCP after four years of collaboration.	*Moves with her mother to Tientsin.*

General (cont.)	*Chiang Ch'ing (cont.)*
1928 Mao Tse-tung starts a guerrilla movement in southeastern China.	
1929	*With her mother, moves from Tientsin to Tsinan. Matriculates at Shantung Provincial Experimental Art Theater.*
1931 September 18. The Mukden Incident: Japan invades the Northeast.	*Goes to Tsingtao, becomes a university student and an itinerant actress. Joins the League of Left-Wing Dramatists and the League of Left-Wing Writers.*
1932 January 28. Japanese attack Shanghai. December 12. USSR establishes relations with Nanking (KMT) government.	*Joins the Anti-Imperialist League.*
1933	*February. Joins the CCP in Tsingtao. In the summer sails to Shanghai.*
1934 October. The Red Army's Long March begins, ending a year later in the Northwest.	*Performs with the Shanghai Work Study Troupe. Teaches at a workers' night school, and pursues the underground branch of the CCP in Shanghai. Is seized and imprisoned by the KMT.*
1935 The CCP's August First Manifesto promulgates a united front policy with the KMT; not reciprocated by the latter. August. Tsunyi Conference establishes Mao as first among equals in the CCP. December Ninth student movement, sparked at Peking University, spreads nationwide.	*February. Released from prison; resumes acting career. Joins National Salvation associations.*
1936 December. Sian Incident: Chiang Kai-shek arrested and agrees to accept the United Front with the CCP.	*As Lan P'ing, extends her acting career to left-wing films for two years.*

	General (cont.)	Chiang Ch'ing (cont.)
1937		*July. Departs Shanghai, soon under siege.*
	August 13. Japanese invasion of Shanghai begins a full-scale Sino-Japanese War.	*August. Reaches Yenan; is admitted to the Party School and the Lu Hsun School and Academy; undergoes six months of military training.*
1938		*Acting and teaching at Lu Hsun Academy. Begins living with Mao.*
1939		*Six-month tour of duty at Nanniwan. For the next eight years she is mainly Mao's companion and secretary.*
1942		*May. Participates in the Yenan Forum on Literature and the Arts, in which Mao sets forth proletarian cultural standards for all.*
1942–1944	Rectification Campaign: Mao-centered thought reform throughout Yenan's revolutionary institutions.	
1945	August. Japan surrenders.	
1946	Spring. The Marshall mission of reconciliation fails. The KMT-CCP civil war is reopened.	
1947	March 13. The Northwest Campaign under Mao begins, continuing until June 12, 1949.	*Serves as political instructor for the Northwest Campaign.*
1949	October 1. The People's Republic of China (PRC) is founded.	*March. Is sent to Moscow and Yalta for medical cure, returning in the fall. Is made a member of the Sino-Soviet Friendship Association.*
	The Nationalists under Chiang Kai-shek retreat to Taiwan.	
	Mao visits USSR, December 16–March 4, 1950.	

	General (cont.)	Chiang Ch'ing (cont.)
1950	The Korean War begins, ending in 1953. Land reforms continues; marriage reform begins.	*Spring. Participates incognito in land reform in East China.* *Is appointed director of the Cinema Department of the Propaganda Department and launches condemnation of the film* Inside Story of the Ch'ing Court. *Spring through summer. Leads the Wu Hsun investigation.*
1951		*Fall. Her second episode of incognito land reform, which includes marriage reform in the environs of Wuhan.*
	Winter. Three Antis Movement against corruption, waste, and bureaucratism.	*Winter. Is forced to resign her post as chief of the General Office of the Party's Central Committee. Again becomes Mao's secretary and remains so through the 1950's.*
1952		*Returns to Moscow, staying until the fall of 1953. Is mostly bedridden for the next six years.*
1954	February. The Kao Kang and Jao Shu-shih purge begins, and Hu Feng's defiance of the CCP is joined by other Shanghai-bred writers.	*Engineers Marxian debates over the novel* Dream of the Red Chamber.
1955	Mao counterattacks Hu Feng and the literary dissidents.	
1956	May. Mao issues the statement, "Let One Hundred Flowers Bloom."	*Still not cured by Chinese doctors, who diagnose her illness as cancer, is returned to the Soviet Union against her will.*
1957	January. Chou En-lai travels in the Soviet Union and generally in Asia. February. Mao's speech "On the Correct Handling of Contradictions among the People" repeats the One Hundred Flowers slogan, making a cal-	*Home again.*

General (*cont.*)	Chiang Ch'ing (*cont.*)

culated bid for criticism by the people and the Party.

June. Beginning of the Rectification (Anti-Rightist) Campaign against those who criticized the Party during the Hundred Flowers period.

1958　Spring. The Great Leap Forward begins.

Summer. The people's communes are under way.

December. Mao resigns as Chairman of the PRC, yielding to Liu Shao-ch'i, who is recognized as his successor.

1959　July. P'eng Te-huai criticizes Mao at Lu Shan. He is dismissed as national defense minister and is replaced by Lin Piao.

July. Hastens to Lu Shan, then leaves with Mao for Hangchow, and independently for Shanghai. Begins physical rehabilitation and the exploration of Shanghai's unreconstructed cultural world.

1960　Effective end of Sino-Soviet amity.

1961　The Central Committee admits that the 1960 agricultural production figures as projected by Mao's Great Leap Forward have not been met.

Is preoccupied with a class analysis of the performing arts.

1962

With the mayor of Shanghai, K'o Ch'ing-shih, begins her attack against feudal and bourgeois conventions in art and literature.

Spring. Drafts the May Sixteenth Circular.

September. Report of the Tenth Plenum of the Eighth Central Committee, including Chiang Ch'ing's May Sixteenth Circular. The "spirit of

General (cont.)	*Chiang Ch'ing (cont.)*
the Tenth Plenum" affirms the ideological priorities and class struggle basic to cultural revolution.	
1963 The Socialist Education Campaign begins, a three-year exercise in emulation of the People's Liberation Army (PLA) and in nationwide class struggle.	*December. Seeks background for* The Red Detachment of Women *on Hainan island.*
1964	*June and July. Peking Opera Festival. Makes her first public speech. Continues opera and ballet reform behind the scenes, while stimulating other arts festivals.* *October. Appears with Mao on National Day and on other great occasions.* *December. Elected to the National People's Congress.*
1965 Offensive of the Cultural Revolution begun.	*Organizes the critique of Wu Han's* Hai Jui Dismissed from Office, *presented in Yao Wen-yuan's name in November.*
1966 February Outline. P'eng Chen's resistance to the attack on Wu Han. May 18. Lin Piao's "notorious counterrevolutionary speech" at Hangchow.	*February. Directs the Forum on the Work in Literature and Art in the Armed Forces in Shanghai. Appointed cultural adviser to the army by Lin Piao.* *Drafts second May Sixteenth Circular, dismantling the February Outline. Cultural Revolution Group of the Central Committee is convened with Ch'en Po-ta as head, and Chiang Ch'ing and Chang Ch'un-ch'iao as his deputies.*
June 13. All university instruction is suspended by the Central Committee.	*Becomes secretary of the Standing Committee of the Politburo.*

General (cont.)	*Chiang Ch'ing (cont.)*
	July 18. Mao's private letter to her discloses misgivings about Lin Piao. July 20. Returns to Peking and takes a stand at Peking University.
August 1–12. Liu Shao-ch'i and Teng Hsiao-p'ing are degraded. August 8. The Sixteen-Point Decision. August 18. The first Red Guard parade at the Gate of Heavenly Peace opens "mass mobilization."	
	November. Is named adviser to the PLA on cultural work, thereby clinching her full censorial control over the arts.
December. Workers are told to carry the Cultural Revolution struggles into the factories.	
1967 The January Storm begins in Shanghai, accompanied by "anarchist" tendencies. The Shanghai Commune is established. February. The February Countercurrent, a revisionist reaction to the January Storm, is launched. Revolutionary committees are gradually established nationwide. February and March. Counterattack by leftists calling for Great Alliances. April. Wang Kuang-mei's trial at Tsinghua University.	*January. Appointed adviser to a reorganized PLA Cultural Revolution Group.*
	May. Heads a subgroup of the Cultural Revolution Group, which is re-

General (cont.)	Chiang Ch'ing (cont.)
	sponsible for controlling the nation's literature and arts. *Having addressed groups and rallies for almost a year, presides over the Peking Rally commemorating the twenty-fifth anniversary of Mao's Yenan talks. Popular acclaim makes this occasion the zenith of her personal cult.*
July–August. The Wuhan Mutiny and the Ultra-Left offensive. Attacks against PLA. September. Ultra-Leftism quelled, gradually bringing order through February 1968.	
1968 February–July. The rightist countercurrent reappears. Revolutionary committees proliferate, becoming a new order of governance by the end of the year.	
1969 Ninth Party Congress, where a new Party constitution names Lin Piao "Comrade Mao Tse-tung's close comrade-in-arms and successor."	*April. Is elected to the Politburo. Contends with Lin Piao over the next two years.*
1970 September. Struggle against Lin Piao's attempt to seize power at Lu Shan.	
1971 September 12. Lin Piao reportedly crashes over Outer Mongolia.	*Winter. Among the designers of the national campaign against Lin Piao. Throughout the mid-1970's continues to revise revolutionary operas, ballets, and musical compositions introduced in the 1960's. Releases film versions of some.*

General (cont.)	Chiang Ch'ing (cont.)

1972   February. President Nixon's visit reopens Sino-American relations. Issue of the Shanghai Communiqué.
Summer. Anti–Lin Piao propaganda is under way.

Entertains President and Mrs. Nixon. August 12. Meets with the author in Peking.

August 25–30. Continues talking with the author secretly in Canton.

1973   January. Antonioni's invited film report on China is denounced.
Fall. Announcement of the campaign against Confucius as a continuation of the campaign against Lin Piao.

September. Hosts Philadelphia Orchestra.

1974   Vilification of the Shansi opera *Three Visits to Peach Mountain* exonerates Liu Shao-ch'i.
Spring. Attack against the "bourgeois music" played by the Philadelphia Orchestra in Peking and Shanghai the previous September.

January. Celebration of the first decade of the model revolutionary theater she authorized.

July. Is extolled as an "expounder of Mao Tse-tung Thought" for her superstructural achievements.
September. Entertains Imelda Marcos and draws national attention to her utopian brigade at Hsiao-chinchuang.

Reversal of the negative verdict on the first Legalist emperor and on empresses in Chinese history.

1975   January. At the Fourth National People's Congress, Chou En-lai outlines economic modernization; Teng Hsiao-p'ing becomes vice-chairman of the Central Committee.

	General *(cont.)*	Chiang Ch'ing *(cont.)*
		March. Speaks out on foreign policy. September. With Teng Hsiao-p'ing and Hua Kuo-feng, attends an agricultural conference at the model Tai-chai Brigade.
1976	January. Death of Chou En-lai spells political demise of Teng Hsiao-p'ing, who becomes the object of a new anti-rightist campaign said to be instigated by Chiang Ch'ing. April. T'ien-an-men Incident. July. A series of disastrous earthquakes, mainly in North China. September 9. Death of Mao Tse-tung. October 7. Hua Kuo-feng proclaimed Mao's successor as Party Chairman, and inheritor of his other military and state posts.	*October. Arrested with Wang Hung-wen, Chang Ch'un-ch'iao, and Yao Wen-yuan — the Gang of Four. A nationwide campaign against them and their followers continues into* 1977.

Contents

COMRADE
CHIANG CH'ING

Prologue

If you want knowledge, you must take part
in the practice of changing reality. If you
want to know the taste of a pear, you must
change the pear by eating it yourself.
— Mao Tse-tung, "On Practice"

The month after the death of Mao Tse-tung on September 9, 1976, his widow Chiang Ch'ing and three other senior leaders — Yao Wen-yuan, Wang Hung-wen, and Chang Ch'un-ch'iao — who had risen to power by advocating Mao's principles of cultural revolution were arrested by self-proclaimed successors and labeled enemies of the Party and the state. In following weeks masses by the millions thronged the streets of Peking, Shanghai, and other cities, accusing this "Gang of Four" of attempts to assassinate Hua Kuo-feng, the man who had succeeded Mao as Party Chairman, and to usurp highest Party and state authority. Marchers in Shanghai carried effigies of Chiang Ch'ing, her neck decorated with a hangman's noose and banners bearing her name in huge ideographic characters drawn to look like bones. Early in October Hua reportedly informed the Politburo of the Central Committee that Chiang Ch'ing had tried to augment her power by a series of unauthorized actions, including an extraordinary weeklong interview with an American woman scholar in the summer of 1972. She was charged with using these interviews "to establish a cult of herself," and with betraying personal affairs and Party secrets to a foreigner. Cartooned wall posters over the next month vilified her as an "empress" and a "traitor." Some showed photographs of Chiang Ch'ing and the "American woman scholar" — myself — conducting interviews. What once was her prerogative had become her punishment.

Chiang Ch'ing is the fourth and final wife of Mao Tse-tung, once the most influential and durable revolutionary leader of the modern world. At the time of our interviews and while I was writing this book, she was, regardless of the Chinese government's restrained publicity about her, the most powerful woman in the world. In our conversations she spoke far less of being Mao Tse-tung's wife than of her thirty-year struggle to become a leader in her own right. Even during and after the Cultural Revolution of the 1960's when she was at the pinnacle of the political structure, her tenure was precarious. The reasons for that instability are demonstrated subtly but emphatically in her reconstruction of the past. During the first decade of those thirty years she was largely unnoticed; during the second and third she was bound by her status as the wife of a revolutionary leader in a society that was, and still is, largely patriarchal, though less so than before. Not until the fourth decade, when Mao's vitality waned and left him more a symbol than an active leader, did she stride to the fore.

Though one of the top echelon, she found herself unrecognized by the world. From time immemorial in China the goal of any man of talent has been to make a name in history. Chiang Ch'ing is among the very few women in Chinese history to have the same aspiration. This book is evidence of her bid for historical recognition, of her attempt to record her past as she alone knows it, and to be remembered in the future for her beliefs and accomplishments.

Of course, Chiang Ch'ing took a great risk in seeking such individual publicity. By soliciting a book of personal history she was defying the phasing of the Communist era. From the late 1930's through the middle 1940's, years when the Chinese Communists, then based in Northwest Yenan, were young and enthusiastic rural revolutionaries of little or ill repute, the ruling Kuomintang (KMT) sought to neutralize their challenge by denying them access to the outside world. The Communists circumvented this by entrusting judicious versions of their personal histories to some daredevil journalists who had been able to reach their base areas. Such foreign guests — the most memorable was Edgar Snow — would, it was hoped, present sympathetic portraits of these struggling revolutionaries to the non-Chinese world.

The era of commissioning individual biographies ended with the Communists' consolidation of rule over China at midcentury, when they began their totalistic reconstruction of the land and the people, and entered into formal diplomatic relations with foreign powers. Although China of the 1970's was still controlled largely by the same group of men as in the Yenan days, they promoted more aggressively than ever the Marxian notion that the masses make history. Armed with confidence accrued from nearly a quarter century of rule, the leaders invited thousands of foreigners to visit China, fully expecting them to be astonished by the transformations and to report favorably and extensively on the liberated masses to the rest of the world.

A strict Chinese Communist, Chiang Ch'ing would not openly contest that axiom that the masses make history and so should have histories written about them. Yet she could not forget that when she was still living in Mao's shadow in Yenan, she had missed the opportunity to make her name and accomplishments known abroad. Thus, in the summer of 1972, when she was riding the crest of the Cultural Revolution she had inspired, she seized the chance to convince me (I had been commissioned only to report on China's female masses) and hence the world of her solo struggle to become a leader and compete with others for portions of Mao's role after his death.

To convey her message, often she had to be indirect. Her political talent, like that of past Chinese rulers, was complemented by artistic and literary skills. On the back of one of the art photographs she gave me, this one of Han Yang peak in the Lu Shan range (see the frontispiece), she copied what is most certainly an unpublished poem by Mao. (The style and substance match other poems of his of the early 1960's.) In the tradition of poems that are ostensibly about nature but actually about politics, he compares her to a wondrous peak that is usually locked in river mist (the Chiang of Chiang Ch'ing means "river"). Only rarely — and here may be the motive for her presentation — is her "majesty" bared.

i

"Let me dissect myself before you," Chiang Ch'ing proposed. She went on to reveal each event in her life with emotional candor and ideological virtuosity. The metaphor of "dissection," a constant in her consciousness and a leitmotif in her narrative, she borrowed from Lu Hsun, the twentieth century's greatest protest writer and a man she idolized. Her dissections, like his, were always double-edged: self-dissection and dissection of others. In looser translation for the masses, these terms became self-criticism and criticism of others, the daily litany of revolutionary life.

Chiang Ch'ing's dissections in our interviews exposed a plethora of contradictions and conflicts. Among the most arresting were the ambivalence of her personal insecurity and the firm front with which she faced the public, the paradox of her stance as a persistent adversary in a community of supposed comrades, and her ruthlessness in the service of a faith in the revolution's ultimate beneficence. Mao's recognition of Marx, that dialectic is the "algebra of revolution," has governed Chiang Ch'ing's emotional and ideological life. From childhood she thrived on conflict. The Marxian dialectic she absorbed in adolescence reinforced her willful and combative temperament. Those patterns were confirmed by her experience as a radical agitator against the repressive government of Chiang Kai-shek. Marriage to the prince of bandits, which gave her status in the revolutionary vanguard, might have satisfied her heart and mind, but the course of events, Mao's separate sense of the main chance, and her personal ambitions determined otherwise.

Chiang Ch'ing's life, the revolution, and hence this book are thus riddled with contradictions, some puzzling and others illuminating. The daily language of Marxism-become-Maoism focuses mainly upon the epic conflicts between classes (landlords versus peasants, capitalists versus workers, bourgeoisie versus proletariat), and most foreign observers of China are content with such gross polarities. But other more familiar and easily believable conflicts also express revolutionary consciousness. Among them are tensions among the leaders, between the leaders and the led, between the sexes, among generations, between public and private domains, between intellectual liberalism and political orthodoxy, and between the "strong" and "weak" sides of human nature. Although Chiang Ch'ing's formal pronouncements were uttered within Marxian typologies, her life story indicates that other conflicts were equally significant and psychologically more immediate.

All in all, the life she described was lonely and harsh, devoid of trust and tenderness save for a few familial and comradely attachments. After the children brought up by her and Mao were grown, and Mao lurched ahead on his rash political course, marked by withdrawals and self-absorption, she was left isolated as never before. In her middle years she faced the choice of aging obscurely or vying for a place in the community of leaders, where she would have to survive by her own wits. Thus, starting in the early 1960's, she threw herself into a cultural revolution. In so doing, she developed her own political style, one that was deliberately dialectical and tactically friendly, but fundamentally antagonistic. Gradually she perfected the art of eliciting absolute loyalty from confidants and advisers, who in turn coordinated those beneath them throughout the political system. But her enjoyment of their loyalty was always edged by fear of betrayal. No more than Mao could she afford qualms about abandoning or even publicly disgracing comrades whose political utility had expired. In a world where the notion of serving all the people takes priority over serving individuals, no friendship was impervious to judgments of "class stand." Because of her lofty political standards, she spoke of — indeed, "dissected" — far more enemies than friends.

As early as 1934, when she was an aspiring young film actress, she was am- bivalent toward the masses, even then the ultimate subject and object of all radical political appeal. Would they rush upon her, pressing her with flowers? Would they murder her? Or would they so shame her that she would be driven to suicide? Almost always, I discovered, her personal obsessions were tied to politics. A prime example is her long story of persecution, partly imagined, partly real, by the cultural commissar Chou Yang and his phalanx of talents, men against whom she harbored grudges for three decades until she acquired sufficient power to destroy them. Personal vengeance fused to Mao-serving pol- itics drove her to demand a cultural revolution against their obstinate "revision- ist" ideology, one that appears to us to be considerably more liberal than hers and Mao's.

Ever present in her consciousness was uncertainty of Mao's support of her grandiose projects, especially as he became more the retired philosopher than the reigning king. The anxiety that runs like a red thread through her narrative is less a paranoid than a justified response to Mao's impetuosity. After repudiat- ing his first wife, a mere peasant foisted upon him by his parents, he married and then abandoned his second wife, an intellectual who had borne him three sons; she was executed by the Kuomintang in retaliation for his Communist ag- itation. The third wife, who lost her mind during the harrowing Long March, was committed to a Chinese asylum after a long exile in the Soviet Union. About his two designated successors, Liu Shao-ch'i and Lin Piao, Mao sud- denly changed his mind, and destroyed both of them in their prime. In the face of such actions how could Chiang Ch'ing as a wife or a political helpmeet feel the least secure?

ii

Without acting the anthropologist and perceiving Chiang Ch'ing in all her complexities operating in her own milieu, one may miss the rationales of her life. Such facile labels as "radical," "ultra-leftist," or even "paranoid" meagerly convey the dimensions of her personality or of the revolution to which she among millions was committed. When a society is more prone to declaim what ought to be than to disclose what is, the necessary task of reconstruction of realities is not easy.

Contemporary China is moved as much by the pull of tradition as by the push of revolution. Central to political dynamics anywhere is the relation between the leaders and the led. The philosopher Confucius, a teacher of ethical and political precepts adhered to more or less for twenty-five centuries, compared the ruler's effect upon the people to the pressure of wind over grass. Through inner virtue and outer action, through words and deeds, rulers stood as models for their people, who yielded to their largely moral force.

Not always wittingly perhaps, but from the very beginning of their movement, the Communist leaders drew upon the same notion, then broadened it to encompass entire constituencies. The "leading comrades" (as the top-echelon leaders call themselves) serve as models of virtue and activity for the people. To encourage popular response, individuals from the masses are rewarded for yielding to the moral force from the center. The most worthy persons from the masses are set up in turn as local models. The process of emulation is extended to the fundamental arenas of control — the family, the school, and work. But throughout the political structure, policy implemented at the lowest levels emanates from the top.

Who then governs and who makes history? Leaders already at the top and freshly drawn from the masses, as implied by Confucian tradition? Or mainly the masses, as Marx taught and the Chinese Communists affirm? Chiang Ch'ing, like the regime she came to stand for, spoke and acted within both traditions. And she lived at both ends of the social spectrum, if at neither agreeably.

Being female trapped her in a constant dilemma. A child of the masses, she rejected her family, learned through acting the art of winning people over, and fought her way to the peak of revolutionary power. Her marriage to Mao, which confirmed her achievement, seemed to set her at the head of a new society in which men and women are said to be equal. But in actuality she was forced to dwell in the shadow of a great man, excluded from the councils of the leaders, and cut off from the masses, who were beginning to change history. In her middle years she broke away from the Chairman's dominance by using other powerful men and the performing arts to restore her ties to the masses. Only they offered her the political legitimacy and security possible for a life of perpetual revolution.

For Chiang Ch'ing the burden of living only among the masses had been intensified by the determination of the ruling Nationalist government of the 1930's to destroy malcontents, especially political radicals like herself. Added to that was sexual disadvantage, the traditional disdain for girl children and the denigration of legitimate actresses and film stars. Linking destinies with Mao Tsetung in the liberated Northwest provoked other prejudices: one against younger women who displace older wives, and another against wives of leaders who seek separate status and direct relations with the people. A self-promoted leader of the 1960's, she ran into conflict with still another tradition and nearly universal assumption: that the authority in the arts is the natural right of men. In the course of the Cultural Revolution she took command over the supremely important cultural sphere, which in contemporary China transmits political ideology and thus determines the consciousness of the people. More than any woman of her time, she made the Nietzschean leap over her generation and lived increasingly by the Faustian conviction that there was no art she could not master, no science she could not know, no realm she could not conquer.

A spontaneous rebel in childhood, Chiang Ch'ing became a woman of extremes. As she adopted a Marxian political consciousness, she deplored the middle position. In the society around her she detested the middle class. In the drama brought under her control she swept the "middle characters" (those not representing class extremes) from the stage. All projects she carried to the end regardless of consequences. Something was not true to her unless it hurt — herself, another, or a social class. Her perpetual risk-taking, arduously wrought sense of the past, and improvisational style of cultural revolution showed her to be in conscious rebellion against certain cloying pieties of Communist politics and against the old-fashioned bureaucratism that excludes women and youth from the exercise of power and responsibility.

Although in her male-dominated society she had every reason to be a feminist, she was not one in the usual sense. Occasionally she remarked on difficulties faced by Chinese women and on changes in their status (she made no comment on women's condition in the West). But she almost never complained, though it had often been true, that men in particular and in general had thwarted her right to an opinion and rise to power. Her reasons for reticence were mainly ideological. In a Marxian review of China's past, the feminist movement belonged to the bourgeois-democratic stage of development. Thus the Chinese Communist Party expounded the doctrine that women under socialism should abandon the sex struggle, join the class struggle, and battle alongside their proletarian brothers against common oppressors: landlords, capitalists, and imperialists. Whenever Chiang Ch'ing vented spleen against men in our interviews, she assailed their "revisionist" and "counterrevolutionary" schemes, only rarely their "male supremacy." To have claimed loudly that the Communist leadership was studded with male chauvinists would have called into question the success with which the present regime has reached the socialist stage, and would have violated the traditional and revolutionary notion that the leaders are virtuous models to be emulated by all the people. Nor, for the most public and personal reasons, could she fault her husband. Chairman Mao, above all, presented himself to the masses of women as their personal champion, the leader who filled them with pride by saying, "Women uphold half the sky."

Chiang Ch'ing should be remembered as a person of extraordinary courage, as a woman leader in a time of transition, and as a leader in the revolutionary avant-garde. She was a remnant of the feudal era, when rulers married power-less but beautiful and talented women, some of whom eventually managed to wield power behind the throne, though only rarely from the throne itself. Successive stages of the nation's liberation catapulted few women to top positions. But the Cultural Revolution made the poor, the young, and the female eligible for more extrafamilial status than before. Although Chiang Ch'ing's route to power was matrimonial in its first step, the autonomy she won subsequently beckoned other women to political authority regardless of their husbands or family connections.

Had Chiang Ch'ing's political career been grounded in the material side of the revolution — in advancements in agriculture, industry, or science — my labor of historical reconstruction would have been far easier. Few challenge the argument that increasing and equalizing food production and distribution, for example, must be a primary national goal in a vast country given to periodic famine. But by the time Chiang Ch'ing clambered up the control tower of the revolution, the economy was supervised by men who had long held power. Others were entrenched as the guardians of political truth — ideology.

However, the nonmaterial side — what in Marxian language constitutes the "superstructure" — most attracted Chiang Ch'ing. As Mao knew all along, the greatest challenge of revolutionary leadership was to manipulate the human mind, to motivate the ignorant and the educated alike to turn their backs on centuries-old values in the new name of proletarian class interest. Moral as well as instrumental problems of revolution and questions of the uses and abuses of propaganda have been pondered as much by China's leaders as by their observers, as Chiang Ch'ing's narrative discloses. In sum, though, we know far less about the leaders' private contemplation of alternatives than about their public resolutions.

Ideology is often said to be in isolation, and foreign journalists and political analysts regard the "ideologues" or "radicals" as being in a separate camp. Yet ideology is also vitally connected to resolving the material concerns of life in China. This connection between ideas and action obsessed Chiang Ch'ing, whose major work was the management of human motivation. How, for example, could peasants and workers be provoked to break the habits of generations by overthrowing their social superiors (landlords, capitalists, and the like), who in reality might have appeared more paternalistic than tyrannical in their eyes? How could millions of young people be driven to violate the fundamental

Confucian precept of filial piety, the notion that the wisdom of age should never be questioned but dutifully followed? How could women learn to stand up to men when their customary groveling might have been more comfortable than shouting the men down? How could people who for centuries had followed ancient ways of producing things be made to innovate in order to meet unprecedented production goals? How could the new producers be stimulated more effectively by spiritual than material incentives?

Answers to such questions lay in reforming the language of motivation and the system of rewards and punishments with a single-mindedness more extreme than any known to human history. In that superstructural industry pushed relentlessly in the 1960's, Chiang Ch'ing emerged as a chief engineer flourishing blueprints designed by none other than Chairman Mao. In their world, encompassing the public sense of both the present and the past, she, Mao, and their supporters tolerated no countervailing authority or power.

"A great writer is, so to speak, a second government of his country," wrote Solzhenitsyn in *The First Circle*, years before he defected. Because the tsarist tradition was heavily modified by European notions of liberty and liberalism, the Soviet Union has been forced to tolerate a more or less permanent community of dissenters. But China's autocratic imperial tradition was largely untouched by such ideas before it was inherited by the one government of Mao Tse-tung. Millions of supporters drowned out stray voices of dissent, which were first raised during the transitional liberal challenge of the equally autocratic Chiang Kai-shek. Writers who failed to support Mao's government were suppressed, destroyed, or "saved" by programmed thought reform.

Under Mao's rule the freedoms of conscience, expression, and the press, by which we in our culture claim to live, were condemned as bourgeois, reactionary, and counterrevolutionary. As Chiang Ch'ing shifted from fighting one central government (of the Nationalists of the 1930's) to defending another (that of Mao Tse-tung), she became the anima of the spiritual realm, the doyenne of the superstructure, the chief of national syndication of a proletarian culture. The assumption was that insofar as the central government is truly "of the people," a "second government," whether of the left or right, is absolutely not needed.

Chiang Ch'ing and Mao, one deposed, the other dead, will inevitably be compared as persons and leaders. Commitment to the cause was mutual, though contrast of talent and strategy was striking. Chiang Ch'ing's conversation and prose lacked the ideological virtuosity, the broad grasp of the historical past, the mellowness, pungency, and poetic flights, the detachment and the intimations of the absurd that occasionally softened Mao Tse-tung's lacquered image. Chiang Ch'ing learned to live far more in the public domain and to submit her political career to the test of practical success. All told, the story of her life and assessments of its effects may be the more important contribution to history than the judgments she has rendered to the Chinese people and through this book.

Comrade Chiang Ch'ing, as all knew her in China, had a special magic, which I experienced up close but found dissipated by distance and missing from her writings. Regardless of her age, she exhibited the special attractiveness — some might call it sexiness — inherent in great power. Her formidable monologue was paced by theatrical swerves of mood, from fury to tenderness to hilarity, like the public face of the Cultural Revolution she guided. The "star quality" that marked her political leadership was not simply the residue of a brief acting career long past, but appeared to be rooted in a consciousness of her place in history and was as persuasive in private as before the masses. Her personal vibrancy illuminated and reflected the people's sense of their own colossal national drama.

iii

This book is "authorized" only insofar as Chiang Ch'ing expressed her desire that it be published. Never did she ask to see the manuscript before publication. Our first meeting, in Peking, caught me off guard, toting a notebook but too spellbound to think to use it. She touched upon a wide range of subjects, some lightly and others vigorously. The transcripts of that interview, handed to me nearly two weeks later, were, as she explained, edited for "accuracy and discretion" by Premier Chou En-lai, Yao Wen-yuan (chief among Chiang Ch'ing's literary collaborators), and "some other leading comrades" (the reference did not exclude Mao). As I anticipated, some shocking remarks about Lin Piao's travesties and their deleterious effects upon her psychic and physical health had been struck from the official record, though not from my memory. Upon her request such details do not appear in this book.

At subsequent meetings I took notes constantly, despite Chiang Ch'ing's assurance that I would be supplied with transcripts like the first ones. These would, she said, be based on tape recordings supplemented by the notes of one or more official scribes; or, to cover most of the times when we were mobile, on scribes' notes alone. Regardless of their efficiency and my confidence in Chiang Ch'ing's power to carry out her word, I prepared my own record, which covered most of what she said and included my own observations of her — what she looked like, how she moved, her settings — and of the participation of others. My notes would suffice if need be, or could be compared with the promised transcripts — the political editings by Chou and other leaders would have intrinsic interest.

For more than a year after my return to the United States in 1972, Chiang Ch'ing and I exchanged numerous books and photographs, two feature films, and various messages through the diplomatic channel provided by the Chinese ambassador to the United Nations, Huang Hua, and his wife, Ho Li-liang. However, the question of the delivery of the rest of the transcripts hung in the balance for some months. From time to time I received reports that their preparation in two languages (Chinese and English, as the first had been) was onerous, but that they would be forthcoming. Finally, in May 1973 I was informed by Ho Li-liang on behalf of the ambassador and their comrades that the record of our conversations had been judged "too long and complicated" to be issued as an official report of their Party or government. I was free, she assured me (and both she and the ambassador repeated the injunction on other occasions), to publish the first transcript (whose substance was deeply entangled in the fuller story Chiang Ch'ing subsequently told me) and to publish from my own notes. I should not prepare a "biography" (to do so would violate the Marxian axiom that the masses, not the leaders, make history, and the Chinese Communist notion that Mao is the sole font of truth and wisdom) but write a history of the revolution "from Chairman Mao's point of view," allowing a chapter or two for Chiang Ch'ing.

"But I did not meet Chairman Mao and so was not informed of his point of view," I responded.

"You may read his works," Ho Li-liang said.

Many had, indeed many *foreigners* had, I told her, but to the Chairman's personal perspective I could add little that was new, and that would necessarily come from what Chiang Ch'ing had told me. I understood then that they had received orders to nullify Chiang Ch'ing's original commission to me to publish in full her "point of view."

Being denied all but the first transcripts was distressing at first, then became intriguing as I found myself faced with obvious contradictions and conflicts of interest among the Chinese leaders. The subtle anxiety I perceived in their unrelaxed hospitality toward me in their New York Mission was, I knew, only the outward sign of far more profound and complex fissures. Those were always screened from the Chinese public by summary remarks and ukases from Chairman Mao. But in the long run their decision not to deliver an official version of Chiang Ch'ing's discourses liberated me as the author of this book. Instead of being expected to function merely as Chiang Ch'ing's mouthpiece, I could report what she said, but evaluate that with outside sources and include my own interpretations. Inevitably, conflict among the leaders would become part of the story. Had Chiang Ch'ing, for example, who had promised the transcripts all along and had never failed to act upon her word while I was in China, suddenly decided *on her own* not to authorize them? Or was that decision rendered by Mao or provoked by others who possibly resented her flounting the rules of revolutionary anonymity, running on for days about herself, revealing cutthroat behavior among the leaders, tossing off opinions distinct from Mao's or otherwise not corporately shared?

Such imponderables only reinforced my determination to follow the dictates of the voluminous materials Chiang Ch'ing had provided. My preparation of the book was not kept secret from the Chinese delegation to the United Nations, and their anxiety about it seemed to heighten as time passed and as some of the substance of Chiang Ch'ing's conversations with me (and objections from on high) apparently were made available to them from Peking. Finally, in January 1974, Ho Li-liang (who had recently spent three months in Peking) urged me once again not to publish a full biographical account, or as I preferred to call it, "a history of the revolution largely from Comrade Chiang Ch'ing's point of view." Ho asked me whether I recalled the "May Communiqué" (in May 1973 she and Huang Hua had warned me against writing a biography) and offered financial incentive to comply with their directive. Naturally, I refused. Out of respect for Chiang Ch'ing's original wishes and for history, which I felt should not be denied that unique record, I continued with the project.

What some high Chinese officials sought to suppress, their American counterparts were as eager to know. Representatives of Secretary of State Kissinger's office, the CIA, and the FBI asked me directly and indirectly, through friends and associates, for complete copies of the transcripts and my personal notes. I declined to provide them for two reasons. First, no representative of the Chinese government in China had attempted to use me as a conduit of political information of the U.S. government, and no issues of national security were involved. Second, as a historian who had gone to China representing no one but herself, I felt no obligation to submit my raw materials to others before testing them myself for accuracy and discretion, and preparing a book which would make intelligible to the general public Chiang Ch'ing's extraordinary life and its implications in revolutionary history.

After I returned from China and spent a year at Stanford and two years at Harvard, the fact of my interviews with Chiang Ch'ing, though only selections of the substance, became known in academic circles and to those of the public to whom I had spoken about her life, her comrades, and China as a whole. Starting in the late fall of 1975, when the usual jockeyings for advantage among the aging and dying, as well as among upcoming leaders, were having more than the usual public effects, fragments of remarks I had made privately or publicly about the interviews were seized upon by China Watching journalists whose business it is to call the ups and downs of Chinese leadership. Among scattered reports was one that her indiscretions with a foreigner and revelations of Chairman Mao's "secret strategies" had caused her decline and fall, then obviously an exaggeration in view of her subsequent frequent appearances and the survival of her principles of leadership. During the public disgrace of Chou En-lai's presumed heir, Teng Hsiao-p'ing, the next spring, travelers through Canton observed wall posters denouncing Chiang Ch'ing (thought to be the anima behind the Anti-Rightist Movement) for having solicited a biography that disclosed inner Party workings and cited "personal affairs embarrassing to Mao." Similar speculations, including irresponsible reports of the theft of parts of my manuscript from my Harvard office* and their delivery to Acting Premier Teng Hsiao-p'ing, who allegedly passed them on to Mao, proliferated internationally the next spring.

Such speculation about Chinese rulers and the perils of their private foreign contacts is integral to Chiang Ch'ing's story. A persistent theme of her reconstruction of the past is how, throughout her life, she had been plagued by the sorts of gossip to which women who strive for political effect inevitably are subject. She once remarked to me, with concern, that she hoped my close personal contact with her and my writing about her would not make me vulnerable to comparable slander.

Chiang Ch'ing's mercurial moods, her shifting back and forth from the personal to the public, from candor to propriety, and from her own opinions to Mao's orthodoxy, have made interpreting her human and historical significance uncommonly difficult. To direct and indirect quotations of her in this book are added my observations of her as a person and raconteur. When necessary, her recollections are put in the historical perspective gained from documentary sources. Her gratuitous flatteries — part of her political style — have been eliminated. The difficulty of bringing forth an integrated view of her past, a task which she as host, narrator, and model for her people, could not accomplish on her own, has been heightened by the foreignness to us of Chinese culture, including the sexual taboos from which even a most revolutionary woman is not liberated. Added to that are problems of translation (literal translation of Chinese does not always make literate English) and of the rigidity of Marxian terminology, which has come to govern so much of the Chinese people's daily life and perceptions of the world.

Had the Chairman or the Central Committee wanted a purely promotional work about Chiang Ch'ing, they could have concocted one themselves and

---

* Details of occasions of theft, in which no unique materials were lost, have never been discussed by me publicly or in print.

circulated it in languages of their choice. A lightly edited report by me of interviews that have the character of narrated memoirs would have served no one in the long run, least of all Chiang Ch'ing, whose view of the world requires interpretation. A journalistic tissue of sensational and snap judgments — a collision of her culture and class and mine — would have coarsened the evidence and left unexplored the tortured avenues of personal and historical events she had risked her fortunes to reveal. Instead, I chose to present her in the style which the experience of being with her seemed to demand — complementing her narration and my close observation of her person and her world with distanced judgments. For I was, as she remarked confidently several times, not a journalist but a historian.

1.

◇ ◇ ◇

Encounter

I have never told another foreigner about
my own past. You are the first one I have
told because I heard you wished to know
about it.
— Chiang Ch'ing, August 12, 1972

My trip to China evolved unexpectedly from the dramatic reversal in
Sino-American relations that was started in the summer of 1971 after more
than twenty years' commitment to "nonrecognition." That peculiar doctrine
was grounded in our Cold War dread of Communism, a political ideology
whose unique Chinese embodiment still eluded us. Our principled ignorance
was matched by China's historical self-absorption, now vaguely eased by a
Marxian world view that legitimized ritual vilification of imperialist super-
powers; from the Chinese Communist perspective the United States government loomed peerless. At a magic moment born of *Realpolitik*, our programmed hostility turned to eagerness to negotiate. Secretary of State Henry
Kissinger's furtive approach to Premier Chou En-lai was followed by President
Nixon's celebrated journey to Peking. As we watched that historic encounter on
television, we began to reassess our strange blend of enthusiasm and antagonism toward the ways in which the leaders of revolutionary China had marshaled the energies of more than eight hundred million people against the
dominance of their past.

Reversals were swift. The People's Republic of China was admitted to the United Nations in the fall, and the skillful arm of Chinese cultural diplomacy was extended to America. Our people's thirst to experience the "real" China suddenly seemed insatiable. Unlike many colleagues who rushed to apply for visas and to impose themselves upon the Chinese Embassy in Ottawa, I made no such move. Growing up during the Cold War in the 1950's had convinced me that the social and intellectual history of modern China, the subject of my teaching and research of the 1960's, would remain "academic" — beyond personal involvement.

Chance and caprice ended that disengagement. In the late fall of 1971 I made a routine trip to New York to attend the Modern China Seminar at Columbia University. That night I checked in at an unpretentious hotel, the Roosevelt. As I scanned *The New York Times* in the lobby after breakfast the next morning, I was distracted by the sweep of a hard-edged human formation — ramrod figures, eyes beamed ahead, short hair exactingly trimmed, high-collared tunics of marine blue. Unmistakably the Chinese delegation, freshly arrived from the People's Republic. These officials were stationed temporarily on the fourteenth floor, and I had been occupying the same hotel without savoring the wonder of coincidence.

With a few moments to spare before my next engagement, I sped to the elevator and pushed 14 with no more conscious motive than to discover whether these austere emissaries of Peking were cleaving to the culinary tradition I had known five years earlier in Taiwan. Were they consuming a typical North Chinese breakfast of coarse pancakes and crullers, perhaps cozying their teapots on the hotel's antiquated radiators?

The doors parted to the faces of two huge policemen and a costumed bellhop. "Identify yourself," one officer demanded. I did. "Purpose?" I was saying something fatuous about being intellectually involved with China when I caught sight of a pajamaed Chinese figure peering curiously around a door. I called over to him colloquially, *"Ni-ch'ih-le ma?* [Have you eaten?]" and asked how he and his countrymen were getting along in an American city. Alarmed, he disappeared. From a flurry behind the door emerged a slender man clad in a short-sleeved shirt and baggy trousers. "I'm Liu," he said nervously as he escorted me to a small room. We sat down. He offered me tea and cigarettes, both Chinese products. In spurts of Chinese, French, and English we began a gentle conversation about shifts in Chinese diplomacy, the possibility of student exchange ("remote"), and the likelihood of developing a community of ideas between the Chinese and American peoples. The conversation was speculative, but on both sides noncommittal. Chairman Mao's name was not mentioned.

When I left, with Mr. Liu's quietly tendered invitation to return some day, the bellhop leaped into the elevator after me. On the descent he said smartly, "You think I'm a bellhop, but I'm really a detective. Not only that, I'm a student at John Jay University. If you're really the professor you say you are — and I have my doubts — why not correct my term paper on ecology?" His proposition dangled in the air as I made a beeline for the streets, and finally lost him after running some blocks thick with pedestrians.

That bizarre meeting served to remind me of what vision distorted by the Cold War and the pains of scholarship had nearly forced me to forget: that Communists are people who can speak and behave in ways other than what are admitted by the strident ideology with which they choose to go into print.

By the time I returned to New York on another academic mission some weeks later, the Chinese had settled into their converted hotel on West Sixty-sixth Street. There they had begun to buffer themselves more effectively against maverick Americans. With a few hours to spare I decided to pay a return visit, not so easy to do now, for it took some twenty telephone calls. Among the mis-connections was one answered by the United Nations office (about to be re-moved) of the Republic of China (Taiwan), from which an infuriated male voice snarled, "The Communist bandits don't live here!"

Dimes later I was put in touch with an associate of Mr. Liu's, Ho Li-liang, a counselor to the Mission and the wife of Ambassador Huang Hua, the Mission's chief representative and for years the highest-ranking Chinese serving abroad. She urged a visit that afternoon. In our conversation, which swung from Chinese to French (at that time French was her major language of diplomacy), we were joined by Kao Liang, then second secretary to the Mission. Kao Liang was robust and high-spirited, speaking only Chinese. From our discussion it emerged that they had learned through their own devices that modern Chinese feminism was the subject of a book I was preparing for publication, an enterprise that had familiarized me with the rebellious adolescence of many of their present "veteran revolutionaries." They had also found out that I had been the co-author of a sixteen-volume digest of untranslated personal reminiscences by revolutionaries, *The Red Flag Waves.*[1] In commenting on that collection they warned me that the thought of some of the contributors, among them fallen comrades, "contained errors." They were also curious about a piece of investigative work I had done on their Chairman's earliest essays, one I called "Mao, Women and Suicide in the May Fourth Era."[2] As we discussed dilemmas of women in socialist revolutions, with Ho Li-liang assuring me that if only women would join in the proletarian class struggle they would be the equals of men, I mentioned that upon my return to Berkeley in the fall of 1967, after a two-year study tour in Asia and Europe, I had read news reports of Chiang Ch'ing and was fascinated by her. This once-elusive wife of Mao Tse-tung was suddenly lording it over the national scene, assailing old men and their establishments. I could not resist setting aside all other work in order to write up her story, a project that proved nearly impossible. For up to the time of the Cultural Revolution, which had flared publicly in 1966, her person and whatever political role she might have played had been all but ignored by the Communist press. Such reticence at the center opened the gates to rash speculation by the China Watchers, who were astonished and titillated to see a Chinese woman wielding power.

Added to the chorus were garrulous old Chinese gentlemen who claimed, sometimes in print, to have known this reborn star in the old days when she was neither a great beauty nor any great shakes as an actress, but notoriously temperamental and always a loner.[3] Common to such reminiscences were predictable sexual motifs: movie star romances and broken hearts strewn along her path to power. Not only the accuracy but also the relevance of such information was dubious. What if the subject of all these tales were a man who suddenly had soared to power? Could speculative, sexually biased gossip fabricated by fawning or furious women suffice as a reliable source for a biography of him? Six weeks of soaking in such slime disgusted me. I threw it all in a back file and did not review it until months after I had met the lady in question.

Aroused and angered by my reports of Chiang Ch'ing's unjustly sleazy image abroad, Ho Li-liang conceded that Chiang Ch'ing was an "original revolutionary," but I should not dwell on her past. Why not study younger women comrades, especially those promoted to the Central Committee in recent years? Would I mind if she and Kao Liang wrote a letter to Peking on my behalf, requesting that I visit China to study revolutionary women and culture? Only by seeing the country with my own eyes and talking with people directly could I avoid the pitfalls of writing "academically," on the basis of erroneous or undesirable documents in foreign libraries.

Of course I would not mind. Nor did I take her proposition seriously. I simply returned to teaching at the State University of New York at Binghamton and to rewriting my intellectual history of Chinese feminism of the 1920's. Some weeks later Kao Liang telephoned me, his voice shrill with excitement. The Chinese People's Association for Friendship with Foreign Countries (the arm of the government that deals with nations with which China does not have formal diplomatic relations) had invited me to visit China "as an individual" whenever convenient that summer. All expenses in China would be paid. No, it was not necessary to visit Ottawa, Kao told me. Just send the passport — a new one cleansed of evidence of previous trips to Taiwan. A few days later the passport was returned, visa attached, in a plain brown envelope.

i

On the eighteenth of July I flew to Hong Kong and at the Kai Tak airport was greeted by "our friends," affable agents of the Friendship Association who delivered me to an inconspicuous hotel. The next morning the chief of these friends, Mr. Lai, and two others covertly accompanied me by train across the Kowloon Peninsula to the town of Shumchun, the border station between Hong Kong and the People's Republic. There I stood on the brink of a civilization I knew only historically and could scarcely imagine in present human realities. On research tours years earlier I had caught glimpses from Hong Kong hilltops and the offshore islands of Quemoy and Matsu of what we once dubbed "Red China." The people so distanced were mere calligraphic traces against long blurred stretches of landscape. Up close now, the scene was still unreal. To the blare of revolutionary music I turned my back on Kowloon, crossed the Lowu Bridge and faced ahead a storybook image of timeless China: cheerful workers and peasants in the foreground, neatly tended fields in the middle ground, and rising green hills in the background. Under the glare of the morning sun that first glimpse of the real had the surreal impact of a Peter Max cartoon.

From Shumchun I continued by train to Canton, where I was put in the charge of two female members of the local Friendship Association, one young and the other middle-aged, both intensely hospitable. After a siesta (their custom forced upon my eagerness — I could only pretend to sleep) and a splendid southern-style dinner, I continued by air to Peking. But en route our supercautious pilots reported ominous weather and decreed an unscheduled overnight stop in Chengchow, memorable as the center of the tobacco industry. Denied our baggage, we spent a sweltering night on rattan beds in a proletarian-palatial but ramshackle guesthouse, and completed the flight in the morning.

At the airport I was met by the Peking contingent of the Friendship Association. As we drove down one of the verdant, willow-lined roadways radiating from the capital, I chatted with the three representatives who were to be my regular companions for the next six and a half weeks: Yü Shih-lien, a seasoned interpreter in her mid-thirties; Ch'en Wen-chao, an interpreter in training, in his early thirties; and a second woman, Ch'en Ming-hsien, whom we conventionally called Lao Ch'en (Venerable Ch'en) because she was senior to us — in her early forties. Although the age difference between my two younger companions and Lao Ch'en was less than a decade, that decade marked a generational break. The former were total products of the Communists' politically disciplined educational system. Lao Ch'en, however, had been exposed to the

semi-Western liberal education which the triumph of Communist Party orthodoxy had destroyed. Although she spoke no English, her broader knowledge
and subtler sensibilities eased our communication and thus, I believe,
smoothed the important turns of my visit.

Soon after settling into the Peking Hotel I was asked to draw up an itinerary
and to submit a list of persons I wished to interview. The scheme of the journey, which included major sites and cities, was of the ordinary; the interviews I
suggested ranged from the expected to the seemingly impossible, including one
with this book's subject, a pro forma courtesy toward China's most prominent
woman and authority on revolutionary culture. At that time I had not the least
expectation, and because of her intimidating reputation, no desire to see her.

Within three weeks I had done the grand tour of Peking, imperial and revolutionary; flown to the Northwest, where I visited Sian, the ghost capital of the
magnificent T'ang dynasty (A.D. 618–960); and to Yenan, a shantytown refurbished as a shrine to the cult of Mao Tse-tung and to the CCP (Chinese Communist Party). At each stop the interpreters arranged for me to meet both men
and women of varying ages, whose means of livelihood had been transformed
since the revolution. With a few memorable exceptions, these carefully selected exemplars of the new social order had discarded their private stores of experience, or had reorganized them along now-orthodox lines of political ideology. To one such as I was and am, bred on an individualist ethic and used to
the intellectual yeastiness of academia, their perpetual political litany was distressing. Always I had to remind myself that they were not simply trying to
prove something to me, but were rather convincing themselves that certain
new systems of belief were now "right" and the old ones "wrong." In such
largely programmed communications, generations made a difference. Richness
and candor of recollection were usually a function of seniority and status.
Older women who had survived the political trials of the founders' era proved
tough and resilient in arguments on established topics, especially in system-
atized accounts of how the revolution was won. A few had a quick, even earthy
sense of humor. But almost none, by virtue of their revolutionary credentials,
would answer questions of an unorthodox political nature. Intellectual adventures of any sort between our separate classes and cultures were out of bounds.
Younger women, who had grown up in the relative calm that has prevailed
since mid-century, were far less confident in recounting experiences and rendering judgments, even on familiar matters, than the older women. Paradoxically, fresh-faced girls sounded staid and stale beyond their years. Yet their
simple recitations of the Party line provided compelling evidence of their leaders'
power to determine admissible thought and to control public behavior.

The very simplicity of most reports about the bad past and good present, about iniquitous Liu Shao-ch'i (Mao's first discarded heir apparent) and marvelous Mao, impelled me to tell my companions, who were responsible for the success of my work, that if they expected foreigners to want to read my accounts of women in China, our focus would need to shift. Instead of dealing exclusively with these "typical" members of the masses, whose averageness made them uninteresting to foreigners, would it not be better for me to meet some unusual individuals — whose names at least were known abroad — and show how they had developed with their times?

The suggestion took, for during the third week of my journey the level of the interviews gradually rose; so did the mutual challenge. During half-day or full-day meetings with historians, doctors, and performing artists — the majority were women — inexorably I found myself in the position of being the only opposition to their ideological orthodoxy, relentlessly argued. Tired and thirsty for intellectual game, I occasionally found myself playing devil's advocate (that is, revisionist or defender of the disgraced Liu Shao-ch'i), the only alternative to being flattened politically and intellectually into the simple line they advocated.

ii

In the evening of August 11 my companions, more fluttery than usual, announced that the next morning Teng Ying-ch'ao (the revolution's chief affirmative-action officer for women and the wife of Premier Chou En-lai) and K'ang K'o-ch'ing (the warrior wife of Chu Te, the founding father of the Red Army) would discuss with me the origins of the women's movement. That perfect convergence of the main line of my research and the focus of their lives was unnerving, to say the least.

I fled down the long flights of the hotel stairs and plunged into the nocturnal heat of the barely illuminated central square of the Gate of Heavenly Peace. There invisibly I joined the masses milling until the early morning hours. A snatch of sleep, and I was up for the nine o'clock interview at the Foreign Ministry. Teng Ying-ch'ao and K'ang K'o-ch'ing had been joined by other women leaders, though clearly the latter were of secondary importance to the two revolutionary matriarchs. A delicate woman in her late sixties, Teng Ying-ch'ao flourished a swift wit and generous humor. That morning she began to reflect on crises of the past fifty years, all told from the scarcely known women's side of the revolution.

My head heavy with these stirrings of the past, I returned to the Peking

Hotel, for the first time aching to indulge in a Chinese siesta. I was intercepted by Yü Shih-lien, which puzzled me, because that was the time of day when she and the other guides were usually dozing.

In hushed tones Yü said, "Some younger comrades might visit you in your room this afternoon."

"Who?"

"I'm not sure," she replied evasively. A few moments later she reappeared at my door to announce that it was *likely* that "younger comrades" would visit me. "You'd better straighten your things and I'll order a service of better tea and fresh cups."

As I neatened papers and books on the desk, trays of tea, mineral waters, and a pyramid of fresh fruits were delivered. Yü returned, her eyes sparking in excitement. "They're on their way. And it seems that they were sent by Comrade Chiang Ch'ing!"

At three sharp two formidable young women, stunningly attractive in the austere revolutionary style, halted at my door. Hsu Erh-wei and Shen Jo-yun shook my hand, introducing themselves with the cordial officiousness of high-level Party workers. I greeted them in Chinese and they replied in excellent English, which they spoke with an upper-class British accent.

"Comrade Chiang Ch'ing wants you to know her political thoughts," Shen began. "She has instructed us to read to you summaries of four major speeches she made during the Cultural Revolution."

"Why so pressing?" I asked, wondering.

"We have no idea," they replied with smiles, and set to work.

For two and a half hours, interrupted only once to sip tap water from saucerless cups, they read in impromptu English translation the text of a long rambling speech delivered by Chiang Ch'ing to the Forum on the Work in Literature and Art in the Armed Forces in February 1966.[4] Her bold, ten-point directive called upon the PLA (People's Liberation Army) to take the initiative in waging cultural revolution against survivals and revivals of the "black line of the 1930's" (when China's proletarian and bourgeois arts and international leftist culture first flourished) and in creating a new revolutionary culture to serve the workers, peasants, and soldiers.

My role, they let me know, was not just to listen dutifully, but to write furiously in the Communist fashion. If my pen ceased to move during rhetorical or repetitive passages, one or both of them stared at it until I resumed writing.

"Why not let me read these texts in the original on my own time?"

"Because Comrade Chiang Ch'ing instructed us to read them to you."

My hunch then, confirmed upon my return to America when I could investigate the records of Chiang Ch'ing's speeches, was that the original printed versions, most of which have restricted circulation in China, contain comradely references to Lin Piao, Ch'en Po-ta, and other pilots of the Cultural Revolution, who were later dismissed from the ranks of the revolutionary elect.

So they continued reading and I recording until five-thirty, when Yü signaled to them through a crack in the door. Immediately, they scooped up their black plastic cases (status bag of officials) and Chiang Ch'ing's uncensored speeches, and bade a brisk farewell. Excited and impatient, Yü told me that I had better get cleaned up. But I was exhausted from the long morning with women makers of this extraordinary social order and from writing at white heat all afternoon. So I told Yü that I would dine quietly that night, write up my thoughts, and retire early for a change.

"You cannot do that," she replied tartly.

"Why not?"

"Because it is *possible* that Comrade Chiang Ch'ing will have time to see you this evening. So hurry!"

Within moments "possible" changed to "probable," and then to "positive." No clue was given about the nature, location, or purpose of such a visit. I strove to be sensible and to rid my mind of previous images of Chiang Ch'ing, mostly disagreeable. Only once had I seen her in person, from the distance of four tables at a banquet in the Great Hall of the People that celebrated, on August 1, the forty-fifth anniversary of the founding of the PLA. She had marched in stiffly with the other leaders and had been seated at midpoint at the "high table" of revolutionary patriarchs, including Chu Te and Tung Pi-wu, both waxy and skeletal octogenarians. Drably uniformed in gray, she conversed scarcely at all with her brilliantly costumed dinner companion, Madame Sihanouk of Cambodia, who smiled and chattered vivaciously, not in the least discouraged by Chiang Ch'ing's dour expression. I also remembered new clips of Chiang Ch'ing turned out in baggy military fatigues and a rakish cap, haranguing the masses during the Cultural Revolution. An earlier impression came from a photograph of the early 1960's which had the aura of the 1950's; evidently embarrassed, she smiled fiercely at the camera.

"Twenty minutes to go!" Yü said as she hurried me out of the sweat-soaked shirt and trousers I had worn since five that morning. A quick plunge into a bath of cold water, a double dose of pills to stop the onslaught of a massive headache, and I was zipped into the one of my two travel dresses Yü had chosen, saying, "Better the black than the red."

The hospitality of the Chinese is legendary, I reminded myself as our car honked its way down Ch'ang-an Boulevard. So is their skill in controlling guests by indulging their interests and tastes, then catching them off guard. As the car drew up to the broad staircase leading to the Great Hall of the People, where the leaders conduct major political affairs and entertainments, it was obvious that what seemed to be tentative plans for the evening actually concealed a carefully orchestrated happening. Because Chiang Ch'ing had issued one of her rare invitations to a foreigner, and in this case one whose role was hers to determine, the media were mobilized to create the aura of officiality. Photographers from Hsin Hua, the Party news agency, flocked to the car, flashed pictures, and ground away on television cameras as we ascended the stairs. At the main hall nods and names were swiftly exchanged with various members of Chiang Ch'ing's following, which included Mao Tse-tung's reputed niece and Vice-Foreign Minister Wang Hai-jung. We passed through more chambers and were brought to a pause in a large vestibule bleached by artificial lights. A throat cleared and a voice rising in pitch announced that Comrade Chiang Ch'ing was in the next room, "nearly prepared."

iii

The door opened and Chiang Ch'ing swept in, arm extended, smiling widely. Clutching my hand, she gazed searchingly into my eyes. Our hands dropped, but eyes stayed riveted upon one another for what seemed an eternity — two minutes, perhaps — before further words were exchanged.

"You're younger than I thought," she observed.

"Older than I look," I said, hoping she would not be disappointed.

She laughed and said she was aging, about to be sixty. I resisted saying that she looked far younger than her years, for even in the revolutionary era, age still carries the advantage of seniority. During the next flurry of remarks, she scrutinized my face, hair, dress, and high-heeled sandals unabashedly, making no effort to hide her curiosity. I was equally curious, but I trust I was less obtrusive in making my assessments.

Chiang Ch'ing was wearing the brown plastic-topped and bowed glasses I had noticed on her in pictures since the early 1960's. Her fine, olive complexion glistened in the heat. Her nose and cheeks were fully sculpted and similar in their set to Mao's. The flesh-colored moles at the tip of her nose and lower right corner of her mouth were more decorative than disfiguring.

Drawing up her full five feet five inches, she claimed to be quite tall (as most Shantung people are). When she stood up against me and fell short several inches, she mocked a frown at the unfair advantage of my shoes. Slim and small-boned, with sloping shoulders and a narrow waist, she moved with exceptional suppleness and grace. Her delicate hands, tapered with what the classical poets used to call "bean-thread fingers," gestured with liquid motions.

Her dress was conservative — pearl-gray trousers and a matching tunic jacket over a tailored white silk blouse. Like almost everyone in China, she wore plastic sandals, though hers were unusual in being white. They matched a white plastic handbag quite suited to our own proletarian culture. The style, cut, and quality of her costume, like Teng Ying-ch'ao's, were better articulated than the average. Along the edges, though, her clothing, like Teng's, was slightly shabby. Upon eminent shoulders, cultivated signs of proletarianism?

Standing uneasily at Chiang Ch'ing's left elbow was Yao Wen-yuan, whom she introduced enthusiastically as one who had performed loyal literary service since the early stages of the Cultural Revolution. A man of medium build with round shoulders and a bullish, balding skull, Yao was attired in a tunic suit of the lightweight fabric of pearl gray reserved for top-echelon leaders. Of the men present, he alone wore the typical worker's cap, which has a soft crown and a narrow visor. Wearing high-gloss plastic shoes, he shifted restlessly from one foot to the other, repeatedly taking his cap off and putting it on as others talked. In that first encounter he projected the officious bearing of one who had never wasted any of his years. Younger than Chiang Ch'ing by more than a decade, he was clearly subservient to her and always swiftly responsive to her conversational initiatives.

She led us to a reception room where we lapsed into a scattered conversation on history and literature, each making valiant (or vain!) efforts to comment on the other's culture. Small talk was left in the Mandarin Chinese we both spoke, but the business of the evening's discussion — her past life, present work, and various opinions — was rendered in English through interpreters who turned out to be Shen Jo-yun and Hsu Erh-wei, Chiang Ch'ing's redoubtable emissaries of the afternoon. It was at this point, in the intensity of an encounter which was more alive and less predictable than any I had had in China, that I mentioned to Chiang Ch'ing that I had completely forgotten to take notes. She assured me then that all was being recorded on tape and by note-takers and would be cleared by other leading comrades before being issued to me in Chinese and English transcripts.*

The room was furnished in the unassertive interior design of revolutionary China — outsized and overstuffed armchairs, nondescript side tables and coffee tables, and light wooden chairs which were moved about to accommodate

---

* That transcript is the source of most of the direct quotation from Chiang Ch'ing in this book, except what is drawn from documentary sources and is so indicated. During subsequent meetings I took notes continuously of what she said, and that, paraphrased, forms the basis of her story.

aides and interpreters. Highly aromatic tea was served in lidded celadon mugs, gross versions of a Sung dynasty prototype. Apart from a small piece of red yarn wrapped around the handle of Chiang Ch'ing's cup and an electric call button folded in a small towel on her side table, her effects were indistinguishable from the rest.

Dinner for ten, ourselves and eight aides, was served at a round table in another spacious room. I was seated at Chiang Ch'ing's left, and on my left was Yao Wen-yuan. The menu was built on the classic theme of Peking duck — my favorite, I commented. That she knew, she said, smiling broadly. As new dishes appeared, she was quick to point out the unusual seafood and vegetarian dishes and their composition, and to make certain that I ate the (edible) flowers. When the roast duck's extremities and innards arrived thinly sliced and arranged exquisitely on a platter, Yao Wen-yuan's chopsticks dove for the severed tongue, which he poked into my mouth. I swallowed and thanked him, but refrained from commenting that never in my life had I tasted anything quite so like a piece of rubber band.

That evening was the only time I met Yao Wen-yuan. Since Chiang Ch'ing was both the host and main subject of discussion, facing her inevitably meant turning my back to him. But that was less awkward than the fact that he was the only Chinese during my visit who refused to comprehend my admittedly less-than-perfect use of his language. When I addressed him he threw up his hands in frustration and summoned an interpreter: "*T'a shuo-ti shen-ma! T'a shuo-ti shen-ma!* [What did she say! What did she say!]." Because he was from Shanghai — and his voice still boomed in the commandeering style of its unreconstructed society — my American-accented Mandarin, the standard pronunciation based on the Peking dialect, may have been hard for him to grasp. Or did my refusal to force all thought into the usual ideological jargon offend him?

The remains of the first courses were cleared away by fresh-faced girls as more buxom young women carried in enormous platters of caramel-colored roast duck for the guests to admire. They retreated behind screens where they deftly dismembered the birds, skin from flesh and flesh from bones, reserving the carcass for the soup that would be served as the next-to-last course. While this performance went on, I commented to Yao Wen-yuan that just recently I had visited the China-Cuba Friendship People's Commune, where I observed the entire cycle of duck farming.

"Force-fed ducks," Yao assured me.

"Yes, and I even photographed the final stage of engorgement, where the 'specialist' crams the duck's beak over the feed pipe."

"You too like to take pictures!" Chiang Ch'ing remarked. "That is something I have in common with you. I like to take pictures."

Then we compared notes on what would photograph well around Peking. Whereas I focused upon human subjects — men and women moving sinuously in the ancient exercise *t'ai-chi ch'üan* or singing old opera against the resounding palace walls at dawn — she preferred nature.

"Have you taken any pictures of clouds over Peihai Park at sunset?" she asked. I had not. "I am not good at taking pictures," she continued, "but I have taken one of that scene that I can give you."

Later she would admit to taking an inordinate number of pictures, around ten thousand in recent years. But she had destroyed three or four thousand, and there were still more to weed out, especially those lacking in artistic or historical value.

"Why take photographs in such staggering numbers?"

"Just to temper myself!" That phrase, which she used often, was her shorthand for self-discipline and striving always to do better.

One of Premier Chou's solicitudes, she said, changing the subject, was to advise her on which foreign guests she should receive. When Edgar Snow's wife, Lois Wheeler Snow, came to Peking in September 1970, a reception for her had to be arranged on extremely short notice. Chiang Ch'ing was at home napping when the summons came to attend, and with no forewarning she was at a loss to think of a suitable gift to take to the guest of honor. On her part, Mrs. Snow was thrown into such confusion that she accidentally gave Chiang Ch'ing the gift she had intended for Vice–Foreign Minister Ch'iao Kuan-hua!

"Did you ever meet the Snows?" she asked.

I had not, though I had read much of what Snow had written, which we briefly discussed. I had, however, been in correspondence with his former wife, Nym Wales, who had interviewed China's leading women revolutionaries in the late 1930's.[5]

"His present wife is also very friendly to China. If you should meet her, please convey to her and her whole family my regards and my hope that she will come again. When you become China's friend you may also visit us frequently. So long as I am still living, I will certainly receive you."

Mention of the future and mortality changed her mood to seriousness. Glancing at other faces at the table, she said, "A dialectical materialist can well understand the law of birth, old age, sickness, and death. It is possible to maintain one's political youth, but it is very difficult to ensure perpetual health. Now I admit I am old."

Picking up her sudden shift of mood, Yao Wen-yuan began reciting:

The aged steed that lies in the stable
Aspires to race a thousand miles;
The hero in his evening years
Never lets droop his noble ideal.

"These lines by Ts'ao Ts'ao are very good," Yao observed.

"The other lines of the poem are also not bad." Chiang Ch'ing continued:

Though long may live the Sacred Turtle
There is a time it has to die.
The Flying Snake on mist arises,
At last to dust it has to turn.

"Still four more lines follow upon these," she noted, but warned, "this is naive materialism":

It's not with Heaven alone that rests
The fullness or abridgment of life.
By keeping peace of mind and body
One will secure longevity.

That poem turned Chiang Ch'ing's thought to the relation between longevity and physical well-being. As her life story would reveal, she had long been plagued by sickness and had come to regard disease and personal enemies as parallels—challenges to the will to survive biologically and politically. Her chopsticks flicking over a fresh array of dishes, she commented, "I have been resting recently. But for your sake I have come today. I have been in poor health and have not been sleeping well lately. I require medical care and rest as well as physical exercise."

"What sort of exercises do you do?" I asked.

"Swimming, riding, walking, and gardening," she replied as she dipped her hand into her pocket and withdrew a handful of jasmine blossoms homegrown at Chung-nan-hai (site of the Mao family residence within the former imperial palace in Peking). As she pressed those pungent white blossoms into my palm, her face mirrored my surprise and delight. "And I grow some Chinese medicinal herbs," she added. "I grew the jasmine myself. Besides this I grow various vegetables. I have managed also to raise a plot of rice which is almost this high now" (she held her hands apart a foot or so, one above the other). "I have planted a cotton patch. All this helps me relax mentally and physically.

"We export jasmine flowers," she continued with evident national pride.

"We also do tea farming in Kiangsu, Chekiang, Kwangtung, and Shantung."

Like many foreigners I was fond of jasmine tea, I said, though my favorite was chrysanthemum tea.

"Chrysanthemum tea is good for the eyesight. Growing chrysanthemums is a sideline occupation. They are cultivated in large areas of the country. Have you seen China's tree peonies?"

"I have seen some, but mainly from Ming dynasty paintings or photographs—only rarely in real life."

"I can show you some photos. I have cultivated some; they can also serve as a kind of herb medicine." Spacing her thumb and forefinger a couple of inches apart, she said, "A piece of bark from the root, about this length, can last a pharmacy four to five months. It's very expensive."

"What does it cure?" I asked.

"I am not a traditional Chinese doctor, so I don't know. There is also the herb peony. Both its roots and flowers are used for medicinal purposes. Of course all that I grow I give over to the state.

"I have chronic trouble with my upper respiratory organs," she continued with the same matter-of-factness. "That has given rise to problems in the urinary system. In the past, whenever I had a fever, I took antibiotic injections. Recently, however, I have taken lotus stalk, which is effective for urination. Now I am taking lotus stalk four times a day and feeling much better."

Impressed by these personal disclosures, I asked how lotus stalk was taken. She explained: "You boil it in water for fifteen minutes, then drink the solution like tea. It has a light fragrance. I have not suffered any such major illness since 1969. When some medical scientists were asked to make an analysis of the lotus stalk, they were only able to isolate a certain kind of lotus alkaloid. But eating the alkaloid alone is of no use, for the lotus stalk has many other properties. I believe that in the future medical scientists will be able to carry out further research on its composition. Now take the white day lily [tuberose]. Its blossom resembles a hairpin; it is intensely fragrant; and snakes shun it. The entire plant can be used as medicine. Up to now medical scientists have not been able to analyze its composition. Thus medical science lags far behind the requirements of daily life. If American scientists are interested, they certainly can do research in this area. Because you and we occupy the same latitude on opposite sides of the globe, what we can grow here you also can grow where you are. Have you seen the lotus flower?"

"Yes, most recently at the Garden of Harmonious Interests of the Summer Palace."

"All those at the Summer Palace are red lotus."

"And those at the Purple Bamboo Park are white," Yao Wen-yuan added.

"The Chinese people have always said that all parts of the lotus are valuable," she continued. "Nothing goes to waste. What we were eating as an appetizer was lotus root of the white type. The root of the red-blossomed lotus cannot be prepared this way. The white variety can be taken only as a staple food. Lotus plants flourish south of the Yangtse River where cultivation of the lotus is a common sideline occupation for peasant families."

At that moment, among the late courses of the meal a creamy lotus porridge arrived with white jasmine blossoms floating on the surface of each guest's bowl. Chiang Ch'ing explained: "This so-called 'rock-sugar lotus-seed porridge' has millet as its basis. My hometown produces this kind of millet. Millet is much more nutritious than rice. Then eggwhite and fat are added to the dish."

Chiang Ch'ing's running commentary on the dishes' nutritional and medicinal properties also reflected her pleasure in knowing that the food was delivered from all parts of the country to her cosmopolitan table in the capital. Of the first dessert course, wedges of a pink-tinged and fine-textured melon I had not seen before, Chiang Ch'ing remarked, "This is Hami *kua*, a melon from Sinkiang province," and went on to mention, "We have four million seven hundred thousand Uighurs in Sinkiang now" (the Uighurs are a politically useful minority who have buffered China from the Soviet Union). I found the melon extraordinarily delicious and said so. Someone must have remembered, for on subsequent evenings at the Peking Hotel perfectly ripened Hami melons were served without my ordering them.

Chiang Ch'ing's moods changed swiftly. When she noticed that she had spilled some duck sauce on her trousers during dinner, she flung her arms up with laughter, exclaiming that she was as messy as a child. Upon the arrival of the final dessert course, the closest approximation of the Peach of Immortality of Taoist legend I shall ever see, she quizzed me mischievously, "Before you came to China did you conjure up mental pictures of us as demons with three heads and six arms?"

"Not quite. But I fully expected that while I was here I would be called at least once by the old sobriquet 'foreign devil.' I've been disappointed."*

"Your hair's not too long and your skirt's not weirdly small," she commented and laughed lightly. Later I would discover a musicality and sometimes an edge to her laughter.

"The masses all recognize me and surround me wherever I go," she declared at another point in the conversation. "Once I decided to stroll around the Summer Palace, but forgot that it was Children's Day. Suddenly I was surrounded by thousands and couldn't escape.

"The less seen, the more marvel; the more seen, the less marvel," Chiang

* The expectation was fulfilled later on a Shanghai street.

Ch'ing sparkled in rhyme. "When I go out in my car, I must have not just one but two opaque windows rolled up. Otherwise the masses will discover me, call out, and run after the car. That problem is most extreme when Chairman Mao goes out. The moment someone notices, the masses surge after his car. When Premier Chou goes out the masses clamor for his attention and flock around to shake his hand."

From dinner that evening we moved on to the T'ien-ch'iao Theater, arriving an hour late for a command performance of *The Red Lantern*, the first opera that Chiang Ch'ing had reformed in order to meet the proletarian political standard she enforced upon all the arts during the Cultural Revolution.

At the end of the opera Chiang Ch'ing made a triumphant exit and led the way to a private vestibule where we sank into a huge sofa. Once the din of the departing audience was closed off by the door, she looked at me intently, saying, "I hope you will be able to follow the road of Edgar Snow and the road of Mrs. Snow." *

"A formidable example!" I responded, terrified by the challenge, but understanding that the real issue between us was trust.

"People might say that we have brainwashed you," she teased. "Are you afraid?"

"No, I'm not. Such cleansing would be impossible."

"After all," she said, "President and Mrs. Nixon have been here. If I can accompany President and Mrs. Nixon, why can't I accompany you? You can run for the presidency!"

She turned then to the more serious question of my present role. I was the first foreigner to whom she had divulged portions of her past, she said, and responded next to my question about publishing the interview: "You may publish it. But you must realize that I have not treated you as a correspondent but as a good friend. First I must ask the Premier to check over the transcript of our meeting. What I have told you this evening is the truth. Clearly, we [she and the Communist leaders] have traveled a tortuous and difficult road. Even though I am going on sixty now, I am still determined to preserve my political youth."

Would she have more to say on the meaning of "political youth" and other aspects of her life? I asked.

"There is no more time on this occasion. Next time you come to China we

* Edgar Snow was the only writer, Chinese or foreign, to whom Mao gave personal account of his early years. Snow included it in *Red Star Over China* (New York, 1938; rev. ed., 1968). Lois Wheeler Snow had just prepared *China on Stage* (New York, 1972), a book of translations and descriptions of the revolutionary ballet and opera authorized by Chiang Ch'ing. Though the former book encompasses a far richer panorama than the latter, both are marked by general excellence, enthusiasm for the CCP, and in the main, absence of adverse political criticism.

will talk again. In the meantime I will give you some mementos. Though an ill-qualified amateur photographer, I have taken some pictures which I will give you as souvenirs. Perhaps this is just 'showing off in the presence of an expert.' I have no good ones with me now. I took some pictures of militia women, but 'certain people' removed the good ones. When I go back home to Chung-nan-hai I shall rummage around."

As we made our farewells in the theater, which was nearly empty except for members of her entourage, I was asked to leave first to allow her to return unobserved through the night.

iv

Though I had no expectation of seeing Chiang Ch'ing again, her image, provocative and mercurial, had stubbornly implanted itself in my imagination. To convey to others a fair sense of her past, the narrow shafts of light she cast on her largely obscure early life and growing involvement with historical forces were inadequate, more tantalizing than clarifying. She was only one woman of four hundred million. Yet I suspected that her unique experience — a fusion of the everyday with the extraordinary — carried clues to understanding fundamental dilemmas of women and power in revolutionary China.

The morning after the first evening with Chiang Ch'ing I resumed discussions with Teng Ying-ch'ao and other women leaders. Our talks continued for four successive mornings. Like her husband, Chou En-lai, Teng commanded an extraordinary range of information and spoke persuasively on ideological matters in a language richer than political jargon. Born in 1904, she was senior to Chiang Ch'ing by only a decade. In generational terms, though, the difference was greater. Teng belonged to the first generation of Communists who, as Mao's peers, had been active in the movement since the early 1920's. Chiang Ch'ing belonged to the second generation of revolutionaries, some of whom had made contact with the Communist Party in the White Areas in the early 1930's, but who did not make contact with Mao's revolutionary core in the Red Areas until late in that decade. Individually liberated from old social thralldoms, Teng and Ts'ai Ch'ang, the wife of Li Fu-ch'un and a revolutionary in her own right, along with some other women of the founding generation, devoted their lives to the monumental task of politically awakening, organizing, and revolutionizing China's women. Teng's unequivocal and unapologetic sense of primary responsibility to the special problems of women and her habit of association with women in all political contexts set her apart from Chiang Ch'ing, whose feminism had been more privately pursued and whose high political ambition demanded that she not characterize her life fundamentally as a struggle for sexual equality.

Yet I did not lose touch with Chiang Ch'ing. Each afternoon following my talks with Teng Ying-ch'ao, the emissaries Hsu Erh-wei and Shen Jo-yun came to my room to continue reading from Chiang Ch'ing's speeches. Both top-flight interpreters, Hsu and Shen were no mere linguists or bureaucratic functionaries. Valued as much for their sterling politics as for their gilded tongues, they served also as interpreters of culture. Shen Jo-yun's engaging personality, clean good looks, linguistic expertise, political sensitivity, and air of cool professionalism would have guaranteed her success in any society. Her unusual gifts made all the more remarkable her strict adherence to the hard proletarian course—though that was rewarded by growing publicity and power. In the mid-1960's she studied in London for a year and a half until called back, along with almost all Chinese Communists living abroad, to take part in the Cultural Revolution. In 1972 she accompanied China's table tennis team on its opening diplomatic mission to the United States. In the summer of 1972 she served Chiang Ch'ing on the most sensitive missions. Later that year she returned to the United States as the personal interpreter of Vice-Foreign Minister Ch'iao Kuan-hua. In 1974 she was promoted to a staff position in the Liaison Office in Washington.

After my surprise rendezvous with Chiang Ch'ing, Shen began to drop in on me at odd hours of the day and night. Besides the political readings, she delivered hitherto-unpublished photographs of Chiang Ch'ing and Mao in Yenan in the 1940's,* some art photographs in color, a set of porcelain pandas (from the famous Ching-te-chen kiln, though the product had fallen off since imperial days), and other mementos of Chiang Ch'ing's life. In her art photographs, which were of landscapes and flowers, both favorite subjects of traditional Chinese painting, I was tempted to see a technological updating of the brush-work of the former mandarin class. Such versatility in the fine arts, combined with an esoteric fascination with horticulture, obsession with self-medication, pride in physical skills, and official patronage of the theater, linked her in cultural ways to China's imperial tradition. Likewise Mao, the venerable Red Army leader Chu Te, the Faustian Kuo Mo-jo, and other senior revolutionaries wholly dedicated to a proletarian ethos continued to practice and publish as classical poets. However, less lofty comrades and the generations educated under them were barred from that high tradition. And like their imperial predecessors, no present leader, Chiang Ch'ing included, would profess to be more than an amateur, no matter how exceptionally skilled. On examining her photographs I noted with amusement that dedications were written on

* See the first picture section.

the back in red pencil, the proletarian updating of the vermilion ink always used for the signature of the emperor.

Through Shen's mediation Chiang Ch'ing playfully tested my photographic expertise. In portraits of tree peonies she had cultivated from seed, had she used natural or artifical lighting? What time of day were the photographs taken? What was the source of atmospheric moisture? Enjoying the game, I submitted my guesses to Shen, who returned the next day with the correct answers and a report of Chiang Ch'ing's delight when she discovered where her clever artistry had thrown off my judgment. I guessed natural illumination by morning sun when Chiang Ch'ing, aided by her bodyguard, had actually employed an elaborate artificial lighting system at dusk. And I presumed that the jewellike drops of water on petals were the result of natural precipitation, when she had actually flicked water from her fingers onto the petals just before shooting.*

My five days in Shanghai, which began late in the third week of August, were managed by an amplified contingent of guides. To my Peking regulars were added five more women and a man from Shanghai, all figures in the arts, sciences, and management of foreigners. Surely that official aggrandizement was the result of Chiang Ch'ing's first intervention in my visit, an event reported with a picture in the *People's Daily*. In Shanghai there was the usual exposure to revolutionary miracles, including acupuncture anesthesia used on conscious women cheerfully undergoing uterine surgery. Nerve blockage plus political hypnosis; still that seemed magical. Ts'ai Ts'ui-an, the youngest daughter of the famous liberal educator Ts'ai Yuan-p'ei, related sotto voce a richly detailed and nonideological history of her father's life and her own. Some youngish women writers confessed to the anguish and near impossibility of writing to "serve the people" in accordance with the standards of stringent simplicity set by the Cultural Revolution. Of these Shanghai female personalities the one best promoted by the regime as an exemplary "new woman" was Wang Hsiu-chen, a textile worker who by her mid-thirties was elected to the Party's Ninth Central Committee in 1969 and again to the Tenth Central Committee in 1973. Being turned into a political star had not corrupted her modesty. But her vigorous account of her past, like so many others short of the highest echelons of power, had more the quality of a set script than of memories retrieved by personal preference.

Most importantly, our visits drew us into Shanghai's cultural realm, which was understood to be Chiang Ch'ing's territory, of which Yao Wen-yuan was a local guardian. A day's visit to the home of the controversial modern writer Lu Hsun ended in literary arguments resumed later with Chiang Ch'ing. A discus-

* See the first picture section.

sion of the great eighteenth-century novel *Dream of the Red Chamber* with the battle-hardened literary critic, Professor Liu Ta-chieh of Fu-tan University, would also be picked up later by her. Opera and ballet performances and interviews with their troupes were arranged through Yao Wen-yuan.

Late in the afternoon of the twenty-fourth we returned from an exhaustive interview with dancers liberated from ballet classicism under Chiang Ch'ing's aegis. As we were driven against the sun setting hazily over Shanghai's low, industrial silhouette, my companions looked to Lao Ch'en, who strove to be calm as she announced, bursting with excitement: "We have learned that Comrade Chiang Ch'ing has made a secret flight to Canton, where she is reflecting on her life and the revolution. She will meet you again one or two times. All the questions you have raised about her in recent days will be answered. You will fly there tomorrow on a plane dispatched from Peking. We must emphasize that the journey is *secret*, not to be known to anyone except those of us who accompany you."

Were we going to be transported to a mythical kingdom (or queendom?) where women's will reigns? I asked myself silently as I struggled for a sense of reality. A moment later we all collapsed into laughter over the surface rationality of our journey's emerging mission, absurd and marvelous. There was no denying, though, that beneath this natural progression of events was the inviolable seriousness of Chiang Ch'ing's decision to develop her story.

The next afternoon our Shanghai contingent came to the airport to see us off. Yü, Lao Ch'en, and I were ushered onto a field deserted by all but one great silver jet. Its sole passengers, who had flown in from Peking — Chang Ying, a prominent figure in propaganda affairs; the interpreter Shen Jo-yun; and T'ang Lung-ping, a vice-chief of protocol and now the only male member of our mission — emerged smiling and waving at the door.

The aircraft's spacious and well-designed interior was far from the Chinese ordinary. Chang Ying and I were directed to the forward cabin, which was equipped with writing and dining tables, electronic fittings, and a full-sized bed covered with delicately embroidered silk sheets and a matching pillow of pale pink and white. Isolated there, Chang Ying and I reminisced on her adventures as a cub reporter in Chungking in the late 1930's before she migrated to Yenan, the Communist base area where her path first crossed Chiang Ch'ing's. In her sterner mode as propaganda chief she responded to my free-wheeling appreciation of Lu Hsun's intellectual versatility with the strict Party line, which cherished only glimmers of his Communist spirit. Though obviously loyal to authority, her thinking was flexible, and our ideological misfittings did not lessen mutual respect or the luxuries of our situation. As we argued amiably, two spectacularly pretty PLA girls delivered plates of roast duck, various sweetmeats, freshly steamed buns, exquisite fruits, ice cream, liquors, beer and wines.

Disarmed by the Chinese wine, I yielded to Chang Ying's urge to rest in advance of the unknown awaiting us in Canton. She withdrew to the main cabin. The silk sheets made a sensuous contrast to the rigorous proletarianism of waking hours. As I slipped from consciousness, a female attendant unfurled pale curtains. I slept until aroused by the gentle voice of the copilot who was hovering over me as he described in precise figures of time and space our descent over the Canton delta.

"Comrade Chiang Ch'ing is prepared!" These words were the summons to leave the guesthouse, where we had been waiting, and begin the drive to Chiang Ch'ing's villa. At dusk our cars honked their way through the chaotic Canton traffic, human and animal. Night fell as we moved into the outskirts, where sharp swerves on bumpy roads defied a sense of direction. Leading to Chiang Ch'ing's villa was a narrow winding road flanked by deep bamboo groves. In them young PLA guards, bayonets glinting, were partially hidden. The villa, a rangy, single-story modern building, stood in quiet reserve, surrounded by tropical gardens: climbing bougainvillea, hibiscus in hot colors, pink-tinged lotus blossoms floating on reflecting pools, redolent magnolia, jasmine, and ginger blossoms, the pulsating screams of cicadas, and the atonal descant of birds.

The interior of the villa was spacious but its decor was neutral, relieved only by vases of brilliant blue and gold irises and occasional scrolls — all contemporary, but none socialist-realist or expressly political. Here, thousands of miles from the northern capital, where she was burdened by government formality and personal rivalry, Chiang Ch'ing was softer and more relaxed. She was wearing a superbly tailored shirtwaist dress of heavy crepe de chine, with a full pleated skirt falling to midcalf, a style evocative of our early 1950's. The white plastic sandals and handbag of Peking remained, though its handle now had one oddly tattered square of terry cloth tied around it.

"Are you nervous in my presence? You should not be."

"No." In fact, I was far less nervous than at our first encounter. I began to take notes. Responding to the fierce heat and humidity, I rolled my shirtsleeves back above the elbows.

"You're too hot," she observed and motioned to an aide to turn on the air conditioning, which groaned into operation, held to a low roar for a few moments, then expired suddenly.

Reconstructing the circumstances behind our first meeting nearly two weeks earlier, she said that Premier Chou had asked her if she wanted to see me. He told her that I was "young and enthusiastic for China" and had been recom-

mended by John S. Service after my discussions began with the UN Mission.*
Though not a Communist, I was judged to be a "strong supporter of the
Chinese people and of all revolutionary people." Although she had been about
to fly off on another mission, she decided then to stay behind to meet me.
Why? To have done otherwise would have made her look arrogant or conceited. Besides, she could not dissociate herself from the responsibility she felt
toward the Chinese people. She also knew that I had already seen Big Sister
Teng (Teng Ying-ch'ao), and that Teng and I had begun searching discussions.
In great haste she had arranged for me to see some operas, assuring me that
there had been no time for elaborate preparations. Then she had agonized over
what she should give me. She laughed now when she thought of how all that
terrible anxiety and rushing about had made her perspire profusely. Certainly,
she did not know me well, yet she had formed a good impression that first
evening in Peking. After we parted, she had begun to speculate more carefully
about the nature of my work, and had decided the "primary construction" (she
used the term without explaining what it meant exactly) of a series of interviews
she would give, knowing that they would result in publication.

Four or five days ago she arose at dawn to fly to Canton. Why Canton? For a
vacation from the routine work of government and for medical treatment. She
slept and ate better when she was free of the pressures of Peking. Within a few
days her memory, which had failed her intermittently in recent months, returned to normal. Lest I conclude mistakenly that this was her usual way of
spending time, she assured me that routinely she devoted herself to "serious political matters," and stated emphatically, "I cannot endure trifles." She and I
would not waste our time on trifles.

Shortly before my arrival, she addressed some fifteen hundred people
and had reported to a group of officials on the current situation. Apart from
those engagements, her real motive was to see me, but she emphasized that our
meeting must be kept secret. If the masses in Canton and its environs learned
of her continuing presence, of her closeness to them, they would become terribly excited. And if they discovered her actual purpose, which was to talk with
a foreigner, they would be mystified. Therefore, apart from her, the members
of her entourage, and my companions, I was, until my departure at the
end of August, to be incommunicado.

Edgar Snow, she continued, had the advantage of time for long exploratory
talks with Chairman Mao, Premier Chou, and other revolutionaries of the
older generation who were working in the Northwest in the late 1930's. Thus

* Service had been a member of the U.S. Dixie Mission to Yenan in the mid-1940's. His candid
reports about life among the young Communists he found there won him the State Department's
obloquy, since reversed, and the unbroken admiration of the Chinese Communists.

far, the oldest I had talked to was Teng Ying-ch'ao. During the May Fourth Movement (1919) she was fifteen; Chiang Ch'ing was then but five and too young to comprehend that cataclysmic event. Chiang Ch'ing conceded that Teng Ying-ch'ao's revolutionary history was longer than hers; but, she pointed out, hers had been "broader" because it had not been restricted to women's affairs.

When she and the other leaders were working in the Northwest (1937–1947) their common goal was to support the views of Chairman Mao. Because of her special vantage point in those years (she and Mao were married in 1939), she would be able to discuss the Yenan period in more salient detail than Teng Ying-ch'ao was capable of doing. Though she herself did not participate in the Long March from the Central Soviets to the Northwest in the mid-1930's, her account would cast retrospective light upon that. In general she would concentrate on events that she personally witnessed. But nothing would be imposed upon me. If I did not care for military affairs she would skip over that. Since the bourgeoisie was always "armed to the teeth," the Chinese could not go without arms. The Chinese do not want wars, she insisted. But there is a difference between just and unjust wars. They never wage unjust wars against others. Her brow relaxing, she said she had no intention of rambling on dogmatically.

Smiling, she reached for a slender gold-brocaded box, from which she lifted a small fan carved delicately in sandalwood. Fingering it fondly, she said she had used it for many years. One side of the silk covering was hand-painted with pink plum blossoms. The other side was inscribed with Mao Tse-tung's poem "Winter Clouds" (*Tung-yun*), dated December 26, 1962, his birthday of seventy *sui* (the traditional Chinese method of calculating age by counting the day of birth as the first birthday). The poem reads:

> *Winter clouds snow-laden, cotton fluffs flying,*
> *None or few the unfallen flowers.*
> *Chill waves sweep through steep skies,*
> *Yet earth's gentle breath glows warm.*
> *Only heroes can quell tigers and leopards*
> *And wild bears never daunt the brave.*
> *Plum blossoms welcome the whirling snow;*
> *Small wonder flies freeze and perish.*

As I skimmed Mao's lines she assured me that this was not an original sample of his handwriting. The Chairman's calligraphy is a work of art, and his grass style (cursive script) is famous, on a par with Wang Hsi-chih's.* Should anyone think that he had a chance to possess an original piece of the Chairman's calligraphy, he would risk his life fighting for it. Gesturing widely, she turned to show off the large reproduction of Mao's bold, sometimes erratic calligraphy that hung on the wall behind us. Returning to the fan, she said she had ordered one for me which would arrive shortly, though for the time being I could use this one. Moments later she decided to give it to my daughter. "Her name?"

"Alexandra."

"Why did you choose a Russian name?" she challenged. I said something about the Russians, among others, borrowing from the Greeks, though that did not seem to interest her.

She reached then to lift circlets of white jasmine and miniature white orchid blossoms from porcelain saucers on the table, dipped her fingers into a bowl of water and splashed drops onto the petals. That pretty ritual opened all future evenings in her company. Occasionally, in the course of conversation, she passed out loose blossoms to the women in attendance. As the fans fluttered intermittently for hours into the night, the pungency of the flowers, mixed with the heavy scent of sandalwood, enveloped us and slowly filtered to all corners of the room.

"How should we proceed?" she asked invitingly. Since I was most curious to see how she would choose to present matters, I said that as director of cultural events she should keep that initiative. And I knew how different this would be from interviewing a Western or partly westernized leader, who would expect a series of questions, including contentions, from me. Moreover, I had, by now, been with her long enough to realize that my American-inspired interests were tangential if not irrelevant to the innermost dynamics of her life and the revolutionary history of China.

Her life story was long, anguished, and romantic, she began dreamily. "But don't just write about me," she added hastily. Speaking as a Marxist she recommended that her life story be set against the background of the revolution as a whole. When one takes into account the panorama of revolutionary experience, the role of any one person seems very small. And her role has been very tiny, she said firmly.

I should feel free to disagree with her and argue; that would not harm our friendship, which would remain. Her sole request was that I not distort her meaning. I had no intention of praising or blaming her, I replied, hoping

* The most famous calligrapher in Chinese history, who lived from 321 to 391. His work has been described as "light as floating clouds, vigorous as a startled dragon."

thereby to disengage myself from the didacticisms of both Confucian and Communist historians. My prime goal was to convey accurately what she said and a sense of her personality that only direct encounter could convey. Quoting Lu Hsun, she said that although she would criticize others, she would always criticize herself more severely. One must never be self-satisfied. She hoped that my unique experience of China would not make me conceited. No matter how extraordinary one's life, one must remain modest.

She surmised, and smiled knowingly as she did so, that I wanted to learn more about her personal life. For that reason we would begin with warfare, for the principles of warfare contain clues to the life she had waged and to the dynamics of the revolution as a whole. If I were uninterested, she would not press military history upon me. Yet, she guaranteed, her presentation would not be dry. Then we would move on to personal history, beginning with childhood.

By then it was nine in the evening. With a later break for dinner and a shift to another room for fresher air, she talked continuously until three-thirty in the morning. As the hours passed, her own energy level mounted, and she seemed not to mind that her listeners became enervated, even drowsy, from physical inertia in relentless heat, where the only activity was her monologue.

Each evening Chiang Ch'ing drew her narrative to a close only on the repeated insistence of her bodyguards and nurses and on intermittent signals from her two personal physicians, who paced the floor or observed her quietly from remote sections of the room. Besides these guardians of her person, our company regularly included Hsu Erh-wei and Shen Jo-yun, who spelled each other as interpreters; Vice-Minister of Propaganda Chang Ying; Vice-Chief of Protocol T'ang Lung-ping (the only man in her political entourage); and my two companions Yü Shih-lien and Lao Ch'en. With them I exchanged occasional glances and smiles, though they sustained almost absolute silence in Chiang Ch'ing's presence—a contrast to their usual volubility.

The second evening we moved to a larger villa (though Chiang Ch'ing continued to live in the first), one with more rooms that could be used in succession as the sultry southern air grew stale. Each of these cavernous rooms was identically equipped with towels — small and large, dry and wet, hot and cold — that we used to revive ourselves, tea service, cigarettes, bowls of dried fruits, writing equipment, stationery, microphones on low tables, and other recording devices. The pattern of our interviews, which continued for six days, was to start in the early evening, break for a late dinner, and continue discussion until the early morning. Once we had an additional session in the late morning and another that afternoon. Thus, as Chiang Ch'ing proceeded in the imperial proletarian style she saw as her prerogative, she gave me, often digressing and rambling, the story of her life in revolution.

PART ONE

◇ ◇ ◇

COMING OF AGE

2.

◇ ◇ ◇

Escape from Childhood

> I have some memories, but fragmentary in
> the extreme. They remind me of the fish
> scales scraped off by a knife, some of which
> stick to the fish while others fall into the
> water. When the water is stirred, a few
> scales may swirl up, glimmering, but they
> are streaked with blood, and even to me
> they seem likely to spoil the enjoyment of
> connoisseurs.
> — Lu Hsun, "In Memory of Wei Su-yuan"
> (1934)

Chiang Ch'ing entered the world as Li Chin in March 1914. She would
not reveal the exact date of her birth because, she said, she did not want the
masses to celebrate her birthday. Her first home was in Chu-ch'eng, a city of
some 80,000 persons on the south bank of the Wei River, about fifty miles
from the cosmopolitan port city of Tsingtao in Shantung province. Vulnerably
situated between the Gulf of Chihli and the Yellow Sea, Shantung was one of
the first provinces to fall prey to foreign imperialism. In 1860 the coastal city of
Chefoo was ceded to France. In 1898 the port of Wei-hai-wei was leased to the
British and the Tsingtao Peninsula to Germany. The year of Chiang Ch'ing's
birth, which saw the opening of World War I, Japan appropriated the German-
held areas of Shantung as a foothold from which the whole of China ultimately
could be drawn into the swelling Japanese Empire. In the years of her childhood the nagging military presence of Japan with its supportive colonial in-
stallations engendered throughout the province a chronic instability punctuated
by bloody crises.

Despite the lengthening shadow of imperialism, the province could boast an impressive revolutionary legacy. During the Taiping and Boxer rebellions of the middle and late nineteenth century Shantung, long riddled with bandits, produced major forces, and also a fair share of fighters for the Revolution of 1911, of which the casualties were remembered as martyrs. Shantung was the diplomatic *cause célèbre* of the nationalistic May Fourth incident of 1919. Nine years later its capital, Tsinan, was the site of the Tsinan Incident, which violently ushered in a new era of Sino-Japanese military confrontation.

Living standards in Shantung, China's second largest province and a densely populated one, were abysmal, a condition amply reflected by Chiang Ch'ing's childhood memories. In ordinary times commoners ate but one or two full meals a week, and the incidence of intestinal disorders and slow death from malnutrition was high. Famines wiped out vast numbers. But in a material sense Chiang Ch'ing's native Chu-ch'eng county was better off than most, and its cultural and educational offerings were comparatively rich. After the fall of the last dynasty a new modern system of education was advanced. During the great waves of student migrations in the first two decades of the twentieth century, Chu-ch'eng exported more students to Japan, Europe, and America than any other Shantung county. Although Chiang Ch'ing was not among them, she eventually fell under the foreign-tinged influence of some who returned as teachers, writers, Kuomintang reformists, and radical conspirators.

Chiang Ch'ing first delved into her childhood the night of our dinner in Peking. She began cautiously, cleaving to well-worn political guidelines — not all Communist — by referring summarily to the pains of the "old" society, the general perfidy of the landlord class, and nationalistic resistance to varieties of foreign imperialism. Later she continued more freely, with minimal ideological restructuring.

i

"Since you are eager to know about my past, I can tell you briefly," she began. "I grew up in the old society and had a miserable childhood. Not only did I hate the landlords of China, but I also felt a spontaneous sense of resistance against foreign countries, because foreign devils from both the East and the West used to bully us. We did not have enough food and clothing. Foreigners looked down on us and called us 'the sick man of the Orient.' "

Li Chin was the first of several names she would use before taking Chiang Ch'ing, her name in the community of Communism. She had numerous brothers and sisters — how many she would not say — the youngest of them at least a dozen years older than she was. (If there was a conscious motive for her vagueness about numbers and names of family members and subsequently of friends, it was probably to protect the survivors from public attention, investigation, or recrimination during periodic political struggles.) Her father was an "old man" of about sixty when she was born. Though her mother was over forty, Chiang Ch'ing remembered her as being much younger than her father and showing far greater tenderness. Her father started out in life as a carpenter's apprentice and eventually became the owner of a handicraft workshop that specialized in making wheels (for the famous squeaking wheelbarrows of Shantung). "Because we were poor and had little to eat, my father was always beating or cursing my mother." Such behavior earned him the sobriquet *ma-jen i-shu-chia*, an artist in insulting others. He beat the children whenever he felt the urge, but when he savagely attacked the mother all the children rallied around her, trying their best to protect her.

Some of his rages were unforgettable. At the time of the Lantern Festival, which falls on the fifteenth day of the first lunar month, numerous lanterns had been put up by a host of landlords. Seemingly maddened by this display of wealth beyond his reach, Chiang Ch'ing's father seized a spade and tore after her mother, striking her first on the back, then on the hand, breaking her little finger. When Chiang Ch'ing threw herself in front of her mother to shield her, her own mouth was struck and a tooth broken. As Chiang Ch'ing described this violent scene, which left her mother's finger crippled, she lifted her upper lip with her index finger to show where the baby tooth had been broken. As an ideological afterthought she remarked, "At first I thought that all men were no good because of the way my father bullied mother and us children. Actually, it was grinding poverty that made him act as he did." Whatever his reasons, this incident seems to have been the last straw for her mother. She strapped Chiang Ch'ing to her back and the two fled, never to return. Though only a small child, Chiang Ch'ing added mysteriously, from that point on she began to learn to grope her way in the dark, then to walk alone at night.

A landlord in Chu-ch'eng county who had a wife and several concubines but still no male offspring asked Chiang Ch'ing's mother to join his family as a servant. Chiang Ch'ing refused to go with her at first, but later agreed. She remembered her mother as being surrounded by lots of people from then on. Her mother's motive in joining the household may have perplexed Chiang Ch'ing, for she justified it in the following terms: "My mother had gone out to work so that I might be able to go to school. Yet I was able to complete that stage of primary school only because tuition and books were free. But even then I often went hungry or ate cold meals, which gave rise to a chronic gastrointestinal condition." She remembered vomiting after forcing down coarse cold pancakes given her by relatives to relieve her hunger pangs, and being nauseated for long periods. Since childhood, she said, she has suffered from digestive problems.

As a child she was never given new clothes or real girls' clothes to wear (she spoke here with a discernible tone of resentment). All were hand-me-downs from a brother. Her hair was always dressed in two pigtails, which invited trouble. In the family her mother worked for, one of the landlord's little girls made it her business to mock Chiang Ch'ing's curious appearance. Once when the child was in a taunting mood, she yanked at Chiang Ch'ing's hair. Furious, Chiang Ch'ing pushed her away with all her might. There followed a terrible scene. Members of the household rushed to the other child's defense. The upshot: Chiang Ch'ing's mother was let go.

Her mother soon found another position, this time in the home of a "bankrupt landlord" whose loss of fortune meant there was almost nothing to eat. One night when Chiang Ch'ing was left alone in the room she shared with her mother, driving rain poured through the dilapidated window frame, which lacked a paper covering. With only a small oil lamp to provide illumination, Chiang Ch'ing, who had nothing to do, sat motionless for hours on the *k'ang* (the broad stone bed typical of northern Chinese homes) awaiting her mother's return. When the rain stopped at dawn, the mother reappeared. Astounded to find her in the same upright position in which she had left her, the mother burst into tears and cradled Chiang Ch'ing in her arms. She offered Chiang Ch'ing a biscuit but the child was too exhausted to eat more than one bite. The mother could eat none at all and quietly pocketed the precious bit of food for them to share later.

"When I was only five or six, I learned to walk in the dark in search of my mother." She repeated this fact several times, leaving her listeners wondering just what her mother's nocturnal employment was. The image of her wandering alone in the dark became a motif of her childhood recollections. Other people, Chiang Ch'ing went on to say, fear that when they walk in the dark they will encounter devils, ghosts, or gods; she had never had such fears. But there was one thing she did fear: wolves.[1] For years she lived with the lingering terror that they would track her down and eat her. The unsettling thought of wolves reminded her of another time when she was staying at a certain Ch'en village where everyone, like her family, was surnamed Li. Having had but one meal that day, she was driven by hunger pangs to wander out into the alleys in search of her mother. The sparsely populated village was infested with dogs. Suddenly she was attacked by a pack of ravenous dogs and one bit her on the leg. Lifting the hem of her dress, she showed us the faintly discernible scars just above her ankle. Alerted by the dogs' barking, her mother arrived on the run, swept Chiang Ch'ing up into her arms, and carried the child home on her back, tears streaming down the mother's face.

As a result of her mother's change of position to the bankrupt landlord's establishment, Chiang Ch'ing was admitted to another primary school in Chuch'eng. Her entry was sponsored by a scholar named Hsueh Huan-teng, who was prominent in the May Fourth era (which promoted education for the poor and for girls as well as boys) and was later a professor at the Peking Women's Normal School (the avant-garde of Chinese-administered higher education for women). When she enrolled in the primary school, Professor Hsueh gave her a new name, Yun-ho (Cloud Crane), as suitable for one of her height and slenderness. County-run, the school had been established mainly for landlords' daughters, with a few girls like herself — daughters of laboring people — included "for show." Too poor to buy a uniform, Chiang Ch'ing wore any clothes she could get, most of them castoffs from boys. The other children found her appearance ludicrous. One of her dilapidated shoes revealed her big toe, which they scornfully called her "big brother"; her heels, mocked as "duck's eggs," protruded at the other end.

She was subjected to similar sarcasm by an "aunt" and a "niece" in the household of her mother's employer (the aunt and niece were probably relatives of the employer, not blood relatives of Chiang Ch'ing's). Once she flew into a rage at their mockery and struck the aunt on the breast. Both women howled in self-pity but did not fight back. Why? Because she (Li Chin) was too small, she explained. Horribly upset by the incident, she dashed to school and announced to the principal that she would quit school and run away. To her amazement, he received her sympathetically, dried her tears, and told her she should not allow such things to bother her. All that mattered was that she study hard and persist in her schoolwork. She relented. In time her teachers grew to respect her, and some even became fond of her.

But school engendered other antagonisms. The course she most hated was *hsiu-shen* — self-cultivation in Confucian morality.* One day when she was daydreaming in this class, the teacher became enraged and dragged her to the toilet, where he hit her five times with a board. (That particular teacher, she remarked, was known to have also beaten the daughter of her mother's employer.) After class, he seemed apologetic and came to make peace with her. She became involved in other conflicts, though, and was dismissed from school after one semester. She then vowed, as she remembered now, never again to let

---

* Literally, cultivation of the self, *hsiu-shen* came to mean something like self-discipline or self-abnegation. In classrooms before the Chinese Communist Party took over education, *hsiu-shen* was systematically invoked to make the young conscious of their lowly place and responsive to authority.

anyone bully her. Thus her experience of primary school ended abruptly in the fifth year.

The world has often marveled at how long the Chinese have been a "civilized" people, Chiang Ch'ing commented skeptically. From childhood she has known the depths of their barbarism. It was customary in the Shantung she once knew for the local bullies to decapitate their countrymen and display the freshly severed heads on the city wall to terrify the local populace. When she saw this as a child, she fell ill and realized that "people have no hearts." When her mother knew that such bloody events were scheduled for a time when she would be away, she asked neighbors to cover the child's eyes. Even with her eyes blindfolded, Chiang Ch'ing could visualize the awful carnage.

Other images of violence were indelible in her earliest memory. Chu-ch'eng county was a fertile area. Yet each year at harvesttime local bandits and even some landlords plundered other people's crops. Those caught in the act were imprisoned, and some were executed by rifle or broadsword. Two military officers in the Chu-ch'eng area regularly checked the prisons and decided who should die. As a child listening to the sounds of the city, Chiang Ch'ing learned to read the rifle reports resounding against the high brick city wall; from the number of shots she surmised how many had died. Her curiosity aroused, one day she made a walking tour of the long city wall. She learned that the officers, in the course of their daily inspection of the prisons, often killed a dozen or more people, including some who were obviously innocent. Why were the innocent destroyed? The policy of the military governors, whose first concern was their own security, was to open the city gates just a crack at dawn and to lock them tightly at dusk. Because they feared that aliens and other unidentified people might cause trouble, intruders were shot on sight. Through cautious observation she learned that the executions were carried out at the Little East Gate. It was situated near a suspension bridge that swayed as one walked across it. The swaying gave her a sinking feeling, but she was not frightened because the place she lived in was built on a cliff and she was used to heights.

She remembered wondering why some people should want to kill others. Still more perplexing was the public enthusiasm for such events. When the time came for scheduled executions at Chu-ch'eng, the "rich people" viewed the spectacle from high on the city wall. She knew the scene to be sharply impressive. Red tassels fluttered from the broadswords used to decapitate the victims. The prisoners filed in, each one wearing a placard on his back. Even when she did not watch the executions but only listened, she understood the sound of hands clapping. Each round of applause signaled a death. And she knew that those who clapped loudest were the rich.

"Once I saw heads hanging," she continued. In those days she and members of her family were living between the inner and outer walls of the town of Chu-ch'eng, while she attended a school inside the walls. As she was returning home from school one day, her attention was drawn to the sound of an odd gait. She looked up. Approaching her was an old man bearing a shoulder pole with two men's heads, one dangling from each end, still dripping blood. Stunned, she turned away blindly, ran home, threw her books on the floor, and collapsed in bed, where she sank into a high fever. "I think this is enough to show you something of my childhood," Chiang Ch'ing said calmly.

ii

Chiang Ch'ing grew up in perilous times that left a permanent stamp of threat and uncertainty on her consciousness. From the early 1920's on, the rise of warlordism and imperialism, which threatened the integrity of the nation, and the growth of urban industrialism in the treaty ports of Shanghai and Tsingtao pricked the political consciousness of the young May Fourth generation. Communist and Nationalist Party agents, seeking to promote revolution by stirring up urban insurrection, made clandestine contact with workers in foreign-owned factories, disseminated Marxian propaganda, and fomented strikes protesting the physical abuse of laborers, long hours, the employment of children, and deplorable dormitory conditions. When strikes broke out against Japanese-owned cotton mills in Tsingtao and Shanghai, the Japanese responded by arresting "radicals," many of them students. The most shocking confrontation of the 1920's took place in Shanghai on May 30, 1925, when university students and others demonstrating on behalf of Chinese workers exploited by Japanese- and British-owned factories were fired on by Britain's police. News of that bloody clash touched off an intense public response, which spread to Tsingtao and other Chinese cities.

In the late 1920's thousands of Japanese, defending long-term Shantung interests, were stationed in Tsinan and Tsingtao. Although Chiang Ch'ing did not elaborate upon this phase of China's political history, it left its mark on her. In the spring of 1928, when she was just fourteen, Nationalist forces led by Chiang Kai-shek and the warlords Feng Yü-hsiang and Yen Hsi-shan launched the second stage of the Northern Expedition to complete the unification of China. Japan immediately dispatched an expeditionary force to protect the interests of the thousands of Japanese residents of Tsinan and to obstruct the northward march of the Nationalist forces. On May 2, Chiang Kai-shek moved his headquarters to Tsinan to forestall the Japanese troops. During the first week of May, Japanese and Nationalist forces coexisted in Tsinan in an uneasy truce disrupted by communications and numerous small incidents. Then on May 7 Chiang Kai-shek pulled out most of his troops and resumed his northward march. The troops he left behind fell to the Japanese occupiers, who carried on a reign of terror for almost a year. Administering the city through Chinese underlings, the Japanese suspended freedom of the press and of public assembly and slaughtered Chinese citizens suspected of sympathy with Chiang Kai-shek's cause.[2] Chiang Ch'ing mentioned these crises in passing because they impinged on her life.

After the last Manchu emperor was overthrown (1911), Chiang Ch'ing went on, the military governor Ch'u Yü-p'u eventually took command of Chihli province (later Hopeh), which included Peking, the capital. In 1927 she and her mother moved to Tientsin, to live with an elder sister who was married to a minor official serving under Ch'u Yü-p'u and other northern warlords. She remembered 1927 as the year in which "Chiang Kai-shek betrayed the revolution. I was only thirteen or so. I had to do all the housework — mopping the floor, cleaning the rooms, shopping and going to the pawnshops. But that [physical labor] also tempered me. Still, I wanted very much to continue school. But tuition in all the schools there was so high that I could not afford it. Besides, my brother-in-law lost his job." Later that year — she remembered the time as close to the arrival of the Northern Expedition (which reached Tientsin on June 6, 1928) — she decided to leave home, hoping to become a worker in a a Chinese cigarette factory; in those days cigarettes were still being rolled by hand, and the work was done mostly by children. But her brother-in-law forbade her to go despite the straitened circumstances that had forced him to pawn almost all the family's belongings. He told her that working in a place like that would turn her into a "little bureaucrat" (an epithet she did not explain). Though vexed by his opposition, she deferred to his wishes. In 1929 he and her sister moved to Tsinan, Shantung's provincial capital, taking Chiang Ch'ing and her mother with them.

Located in western Shantung just six miles from the Yellow River, Tsinan was a leisurely two-hour journey from Confucius' holy mountain, Tai Shan. Tsinan had been a vital cultural center since the Ming dynasty, when its inner city wall, replete with impressive gates and towers, was erected. The city's outer wall dated from the Manchu dynasty, by which time Tsinan served as the civil service examination center for Shantung province. When Chiang Ch'ing moved there the city's population exceeded four hundred thousand, and its internal transportation system and external rail connections were the best in the province. Public education, which had been stimulated by reformism of the early twentieth century, was excellent, for there were over two hundred elementary schools, plus several high schools and colleges, including Cheeloo University.[3] Throughout the educational system, intellectual life was shaped by a modern-thinking faculty, of which a high proportion were members of the Kuomintang.[4] The city's racial composition had been complex since the late nineteenth century, when the municipal government opened the city to foreign residents, primarily Europeans and dominantly Germans. But the city's most recent immigrants were the Japanese, some five thousand strong by the time Chiang Ch'ing arrived.[5]

Since the Ming dynasty, Tsinan had been renowned for its theaters, in which, contrary to the custom prevailing elsewhere in China, some of the performers were women. In this historic cultural center Chiang Ch'ing found her vocation as an actress. Her studies began at the Shantung Provincial Experimental Art Theater, a kind of boarding school. As was standard in Republican China, tuition and living expenses were provided by the government, and in return, graduates were usually obliged to work for an unspecified period as theater apprentices.

"In 1929 I was admitted to the Shantung Provincial Experimental Art Theater at Tsinan. This was an art school, where I studied mainly modern drama but also some classical music and drama. I was only fifteen then. The school provided free tuition and meals and an allowance of two yuan [about sixty U.S. cents] a month.* Because the school preferred to enroll graduates of junior and senior high schools and even university students, I did not technically qualify for admission. I was accepted only because the school had too few girls. I studied there only one year, but I learned a lot. I studied everything that came my way. I got up before daylight and tried to learn as much as possible." Not only did she read extensively in dramatic literature and learn to sing traditional opera and perform modern drama, but she was introduced to a variety of musical instruments. Among them was the piano, then an exotic instrument in China, which she studied for three months. Although her teacher was fond of her, he was a tough disciplinarian. To regulate the tempo of her playing, he struck her wrist with sticks, a pedagogical technique she deplored. With so little training she never got beyond the scales and basic exercises.

Chiang Ch'ing's class had only three girls, of whom she was the youngest. The other two, along with the rest of the school's students, looked down on her because of her threadbare clothes. The director's wife, Yü Shan, who had been a student at the First Girls' Normal School in Tientsin (where Teng Ying-ch'ao, the wife of Chou En-lai, had also studied), was the sister of one of these two girls.[6] She was a "reactionary" who bullied Chiang Ch'ing endlessly. But

---

* A yuan, or Mexican yuan dollar, was divided into 100 cents. In 1929–1930, one yuan was worth about thirty U.S. cents.

Chiang Ch'ing held her ground and managed to play pranks of her own on the other girl students. Now, over forty years later, she recalled one with pleasure not unmixed with spite, to which she freely admitted.

The school was situated in an old Confucian temple whose rooms were stifling in summer. After classes the students often went to the huge main hall to cool off. Chiang Ch'ing remembered vividly the gigantic statue of Confucius that stood in the center of the hall. He wore an enormous hat with bead screens in front and behind; flanking him were seventy-two sages, his disciples. One sweltering evening Chiang Ch'ing retired to the hall and collapsed in an old rattan chair. The two other girl students sauntered in and demanded that she get up and arrange chairs for them. Chiang Ch'ing decided to comply in her own fashion. First she offered to hold up the lamp to assist them, then she moved two chairs into the hall for their use. As they proudly sat down, she slipped out the door with the lamp, slammed the gate behind her and fled. Isolated in that blackened and eerie chamber, the girls screamed, begging to be rescued.

Several boy students ran to console them. As soon as the boys found lanterns, they set out into the night to track down Chiang Ch'ing and "teach her a lesson," as she put it. She had run as fast as she could into some tall bushes beside a stream, where they could not find her. But the girls knew that eventually she would have to return to the room they all shared, and they would get even. When she thought they were asleep, she slipped back into the room, tunneled into bed, and pulled the mosquito netting closely around her. They knew, however, that she was terribly ticklish. When she saw fingers poking menacingly through the netting, she screamed in her turn. The angry girls tried to force her to promise never to do such a wicked thing again. "That depends," she hedged.

There was also much good that they shared. To act in the plays, Chiang Ch'ing first had to master the Peking dialect, the standard Mandarin lingua franca for all official and cultural communications throughout China. Her own dialect was that of Shantung province, specifically the local dialect of her birthplace. The other students roared with laughter at her clumsy efforts — they were already fluent in the Peking dialect. Nevertheless she persisted, she recalled with less resentment than pride in achievement, and one of her schoolmates coached her and listened patiently to her practice recitations.

Once the school mounted an experimental production of *Tragedy on a Lake*, a "bourgeois drama" by the noted playwright T'ien Han, founder of the South China Drama Society, an innovative and highly influential drama group of that era. The student who was the sister of the director's wife was assigned the lead, a rotating part that Chiang Ch'ing performed on Mondays, when the audience usually was small. As was her style, she threw herself entirely into the part, thus moving the audience to tears. Their response caused tears to pour from her own eyes — the effect of following the "naturalist" school of acting (as she explained later, naturalism was eventually repudiated by the Communist regime). When she was removing her makeup after the show, the director of the school and her teacher strode into the dressing room to commend her performance and hail her promise as a tragic actress. Overwhelmed by their praise, she dissolved into tears again and dashed from the dressing room. Despite this incident, which she recaptured as melodrama, she remembered the general aura of this period with vexation. "As a matter of fact, I was insulted everywhere in Tsinan," she added without further elaboration.

"The school was closed down when Han Fu-ch'ü, a warlord of the Northwestern Army, came to Tsinan.[7] I joined some of the school's teachers and students in organizing a touring theatrical group that went to Peking. I left without telling my mother, only mailing her a letter at the railway station just before the train pulled out.

"That year [1930] I was only sixteen, and life in Peking was very hard indeed. I was so poorly equipped that I did not even have any underclothes. Although I had taken my family's best quilt with me, I still shivered with cold because its cotton wadding was worn thin from age. That season in Peking there were heavy sandstorms and the nights were dismal. I had not yet come to know politics. I had no notion of the significance of 'Kuomintang' and 'Communist Party.' All I knew was that I wanted to feed myself and that I adored drama.

"Then in the early spring of 1931 I went to Tsingtao." (She vividly recalled the initial impact of Tsingtao: chill fog and salty sea breezes at the harbor. How strange it was, she remarked, that although her hometown Chu-ch'eng was less than fifty miles away, she had never laid eyes on the ocean before.) "My former teacher [Chao T'ai-mou], a fellow townsman who used to be director of the Experimental Theater in Tsinan, now had become dean of Tsingtao University, serving concurrently as professor in the Literature Department. Through these connections he arranged my admission to Tsingtao [now Shantung] University."

Chao T'ai-mou's invitation tempted her, but she felt uneasy about moving to the wholly unfamiliar environment of Tsingtao. To encourage her, he promised to establish on her behalf an art department (presumably dramatic arts, though she did not say so) at the university, and offered to pay her travel expenses to Tsingtao. Her classmates from the Experimental Art Theater urged her to accept. Finally she agreed. (Though she went to the university, it seems she never matriculated.) "Actually, he [Chao] belonged to the Reformist Group of the Kuomintang. His views on literature and art were close to those of Hu Shih.* I was once appreciated by the bourgeoisie," she added with a smile. "There was a time when members of Hu Shih's group, which included people like Liang Shih-ch'iu and Wen I-to, tried to win me over to their side.† Wen I-to was one of my teachers at Tsingtao University. I audited many of his lectures.

"Our greatest teacher by negative example was Japanese imperialism. After the September 18, 1931, incident at Mukden, our three northeastern provinces [Manchuria] were seized by the Japanese imperialists. That we could not tolerate. We could not become slaves to a foreign nation. As for myself, I too felt compelled to resist Japanese aggression." By that time, the whole of China was surging up in a high tide of national democratic revolution. Many students went on strike or petitioned government authorities, and the workers supported them. The movement engaged a broad spectrum of the people.

"Aroused by the situation, I said to my teacher [Chao], 'I want to join the petitioning.' He shot back, 'You want to make trouble, too?' I was dumbfounded and could scarcely say anything. So I turned and left, knowing full well that he was greatly displeased with me. I walked alone to the hills and wandered in the woods,‡ deeply perplexed by what he meant when he said that the students' patriotic movement was 'troublemaking.' When at last I realized his views were wrong, I decided to join the League of Left-Wing Dramatists [a Communist front organization] in Tsingtao.

"At Tsingtao University, there were mass student boycotts of classes and examinations. Under these circumstances, I refused to accept any more assistance from my teacher. So I joined the university staff as library clerk. My job was to write out cards. At the same time, I continued to audit classes. Each month I earned thirty yuan [about nine U.S. dollars] and sent ten to my mother. Because the cost of living at Tsingtao was very high, the twenty yuan remaining was not enough for me. For you see, I was not only supporting myself, I had to help out other comrades. We had to pay out of our own pockets the costs of

* The leader of American-trained intellectuals. After 1949 he was the chief liberal spokesman on Taiwan.

† Liang had been trained at Harvard and Columbia and had translated all of Shakespeare's works into Chinese.

Wen I-to was a highly regarded poet who was famous also as the leftist leader of the China Democratic League. Yao Wen-yuan, who was present during that first evening's conversation, interjected matter-of-factly: "Wen I-to was assassinated by Chiang Kai-shek's thugs in the latter stage of the democratic revolution because of his participation in the progressive anti-Chiang Kai-shek movement. Chairman Mao spoke highly of him in an article written in August 1949."

‡ Among the sensitive of her generation, such a trip was also a metaphor for emotional retreat, which is included in her meaning.

staging plays calling for National Salvation* — no one helped us with money. When we took our performances to factories or to the villages, the people welcomed us and helped us, but they too were hard up. At that time, I did not know that liberation must be won by the poor. Only later, after I joined the Party, did I learn from other comrades that so naive an understanding would not do, that one must serve the proletariat."

The university was but one dimension of Chiang Ch'ing's life at Tsingtao. Soon after she arrived there in 1931, she and some fellow dramatists (the "comrades" mentioned above) set up the Seaside Drama Society. Its purpose was less artistic than political: to make theatrical propaganda against the Japanese at schools and factories and in the rural areas.[8] After performing in the city at the height of the New Year festivities, the troupe left for the countryside with the purpose of spreading news of the soviet districts being developed by the Chinese Red Army in Kiangsi. In 1931 knowledge of the Red Army leaders and the emerging way of life in the soviets was scant, and their forces did not yet seriously threaten the security of the Nationalist regime. Even so, public mention of the soviets' existence was risky. To avoid arrest by Kuomintang agents who had infiltrated the countryside, the Seaside Drama Society decided to become less conspicuous in this Japanese-occupied territory by dividing into small units, which made their way separately into the rural areas.

On that first plunge into the countryside they encountered poverty far beyond imagination. There was almost no food to buy and public restaurants and inns were practically nonexistent. The sensation of gnawing hunger she mentioned repeatedly. Being forced to go for long periods with nothing to eat sapped their morale.

The first village they reached was Lao-shan-wan, a few miles up the coast from Tsingtao. When the actors arrived, the villagers were shocked by the men's Western-style suits and the women's mandarin-collared, slit-skirted dresses, which were customarily worn in the cities of Republican China. Upset by their intrusion the villagers presented them with a silver dollar, apparently to speed them on their way. Moreover, the outraged villagers accused them of coming there just for fun rather than to give a serious performance. Thus the troupe's propaganda had no noticeable effect. In those years, Chiang Ch'ing added with the advantage of hindsight, they knew nothing of the "summing-up experience," by which political workers trained in Communist methods immediately follow up a performance or work session with a collective assessment of the performers' good and bad points.

As they prepared to leave Lao-shan-wan, the villagers recommended that

* National Salvation (*chiu-kuo*) was a term popularly used from the 1920's through the 1940's to refer to all organized patriotic efforts to "save the nation" from the Japanese.

they go to Wang-ko-chuang, a larger village with several inns situated just a few miles down the coast from Tsingtao. There Chiang Ch'ing was assigned to work with children. Since by then the Japanese had taken over the entire coastal area around Tsingtao, Chiang Ch'ing established rapport with the children by teaching them anti-Japanese songs. The children responded readily, having already been alerted by their parents to the viciousness of "Western and Eastern devils." The children took to her, and a few invited her to visit their homes. Though obviously gratified by this recollection, she noted that other members of the troupe enjoyed as great a success as she did.

During the troupe's few days in Wang-ko-chuang, Chiang Ch'ing gradually became attuned to local ways, and the peasants took a liking to her. They singled her out from the group, she recalled with pleasure, and begged her to sing their favorite arias from the Peking opera. Even then she was not a devotee of the Peking opera, yet to please them she obliged. After a while they would join in, singing in the local operatic style. Once the troupe gained the people's confidence, they introduced political messages into the songs and skits. Such innovations went over best with the younger peasants. Yet how astonished they were when the players began to tell them about life in the soviet areas (still mostly based on secondhand reports), especially the communal ownership of food and clothing.

Most of the Seaside Drama Society's political work was still in the experimental stage. One of the trial performances given at Wang-ko-chuang was the original version of *Lay Down Your Whip*. [9] This one-act play set to song and instrumentation, about Manchurian refugees living under Japanese occupation, was an example of street theater that became a highly popular encapsulation of the national defense theme in the 1930's. Since the original version had flaws, Chiang Ch'ing did not want the score circulated. When some local musicians tried to get a copy from her, she quickly tucked it into her pocket, slipped away from the gathering, and ran straight to the graveyard, where she hid it under a tombstone.

The audience at Wang-ko-chuang included a good many soldiers, who obviously liked the troupe's performance. Warming to their praise, Chiang Ch'ing agreed to spend time with three of them. As they were chatting about political affairs, the soldiers kept stressing the virtues of cooperation between the Chinese Communist Party and the Kuomintang, a notion that seemed implausible to her even then. She and they parted amicably despite their political differences, the soldiers insisting that she accept some gifts for herself and her friends as a token of appreciation for their cultural work. That evening she returned to the inn laden with bounty: cotton quilts, the steamed cabbage famous in that area of Shantung, and the steamed bread popular in North

China. Only later did she discover that among the soldiers she had spoken with that day were some who had taken part in the Shanghai Uprising of 1927 — which had resulted in the Kuomintang's bloody purge of the Communist Party from its ranks — and that a branch of the Communist Party had been established in Wang-ko-chuang before their arrival. She was never in touch with that branch; her first contact with the Party was made later, in the city of Tsingtao.

After several days at Wang-ko-chuang, the players prepared to leave. Some of the villagers urged Chiang Ch'ing to stay, and she was touched by their hospitality, but the players had to move on. Whenever they took to the road in those out-of-the-way places, their cash ran out and their hungry stomachs growled. On one occasion, penniless as usual, they all piled onto a bus. Some hours later the driver halted at a bus stop on a narrow mountain road and demanded their fares. They tried to convince him they would pay when they reached their destination, but he objected loudly and would have left them stranded had not some local people rescued them by putting up the fare. That embarrassing meeting between "poor" mountain folk and "rich" urban intellectuals made a sharp impression on Chiang Ch'ing. Not long afterward she explored the social implications in a long article published in Tsingtao.

Mention of that article, written in 1931, reminded Chiang Ch'ing of a more recent incident. During the Cultural Revolution, the "Lin Piao clique" (Lin Piao was celebrated as her major political helpmate until the fall of 1971) commissioned two groups of people to search for materials that could be used against her (in the power struggle). One, which had previously been known as the May Sixteenth Group, [10] amassed all sorts of information about her past in order to embarrass her. This May Sixteenth Group demanded of Chou En-lai that he personally search for articles Chiang Ch'ing had written years before, including the one composed when she was a member of the Seaside Drama Society in Tsingtao in the early 1930's. Under their pressure, Chou complied, but his search failed to uncover anything. Besides the article that had appeared in Tsingtao, another that eluded them was called "My Open Letter," which had appeared some years later in the Shanghai newspaper *Ta-kung pao*. After a momentary hesitation in her narrative, Chiang Ch'ing corrected her earlier remark: actually, Chou had managed to track down a piece she had written for a women's magazine. Having written it so long before, Chiang Ch'ing had all but forgotten it. When she was questioned about this, her interrogators accused her of having written it just to make money. She confounded them by agreeing! Living a hand-to-mouth existence, she had done that article *only* to make money.

iii

In the Republican era it was not unusual for a poor student to attend university classes as an auditor, doing the same work as a regular student but barred from the right to a degree. In this capacity Chiang Ch'ing came into contact with renowned professors, not only at Tsingtao University, but later at Peking University and at universities in Shanghai. As an auditor at Tsingtao University, she gained her first exposure to intellectuals as personalities and as fresh sources of ideas. Although she would later repudiate open-ended academic inquiry, at the susceptible age of seventeen she was exhilarated by the free play of thought in a university environment.

She had not thought back on her Tsingtao experience for years, Chiang Ch'ing confessed, and reconstructed events elliptically. Because of her varied experience in drama, she was intensely interested in literature, ancient and modern, and in trying her hand at writing (as was popular among educated and idealistic young people of her generation). The first teacher she recalled was Wen I-to, who taught courses in T'ang poetry, in the novel and drama, and in the history of Chinese literature. The second was Yang Chen-sheng, author of the novel *Jade Gentleman* (1925) and at that time president of Tsingtao University. With him she studied creative writing, and got to know him better than Wen I-to. She also attended the classes of Fang Ling-lu, a woman writer who, to the best of her recollection, was then serving as chairman of the Literary Association of Chekiang. Chiang Ch'ing remarked that Wen I-to, Yang Chensheng, and Fang Ling-lu had all studied in the United States, and that Yang and Fang were still alive at the time of Liberation in 1949.

The names of her other teachers escaped her now. What she remembered best were impressions of her own first literary efforts. She wrote her first short story in a course taught by Yang Chen-sheng, who enthusiastically praised it for being very much like the work of the celebrated woman writer Hsieh Ping-hsin. A great admirer of Ping-hsin (the pen name by which she was best known), Chiang Ch'ing was overwhelmed by the comparison. A subsequent story did not fare as well. Though Yang rated it the best in the class, he had one criticism to make. "Miss Li," he said, "your robber is too genteel. When he curses a person he uses the expression 'Drop dead' [*k'ai-ssu*]. Now that's refined language — not rough enough for a robber." Humiliated by this criticism, she never returned to his class.

In the summer of 1931 Chiang Ch'ing wrote a play entitled "Whose Crime?" about a young revolutionary who lived with his sickly mother. When the police failed to find him they seized his mother in his stead. Eventually the son was arrested and the mother died. Reference to the plot of her play reminded her of the name of her playwriting teacher, Chao Ping-o, with whom she also had a distressing exchange in the early fall. He commended her style, but expressed bewilderment at the political ambiguities in the text. He asked her bluntly whether her "revolutionaries" belonged to the Communist Party or the Kuomintang. Still desperately ignorant of the substantive differences between the two and frustrated with embarrassment, she retorted, "*You* tell *me* what's the difference between the Chinese Communist Party and the Kuomintang!" His sharp laughter at her sophomoric response showed her he thought her a fool. Yet he liked the play well enough to urge her to expand it from one act to three. The play was not all that important, she said; what mattered was that his needling aroused her curiosity. Although during the Seaside Drama Society's tour she had made some simple propaganda for the soviets, she began to wonder now just what were the ideological differences between the Communist and Kuomintang parties. "From that point on, I began to observe."

That fall the usual calm of university life was shattered by the Mukden Incident of September 18, 1931: Japanese troops marched on Manchuria. In the heat of that crisis she was still ignorant of the meaning of "reformism" * and its relation to the Kuomintang. Although she and others like her had assumed that these "Nationalists," so heavily concentrated in the universities, were patriots who valued their country's integrity above everything else, they were wrong. She now perceived that these respected reformists were not really determined to resist Japanese aggression at all costs. When in the heat of the reaction to the Mukden Incident she declared herself openly for resistance, they criticized *her* for being a troublemaker. With Chao Ping-o's sarcasm still ringing in her ears, she wandered by herself into the woods outside Tsingtao to mull over what he had said. It dawned on her that Chao had to be a member of the Kuomintang, the "Nationalist" Party that was not following the hard line of resistance. When students at the university began to make trouble for her, she surmised that they too had to be working for the Kuomintang. After that she accepted no more help from Chao Ping-o, and set out on her own course.

The reception room in which Chiang Ch'ing and I were talking was hugely proportioned; yet the August evening in Canton, where Chiang Ch'ing amplified on her childhood, was so sultry that the air began to close in on us. She

* "Reformism" indicates a complex of attitudes held more or less by intellectuals, including some college professors, who identified either tacitly or actively with the KMT from the late 1920's onward. Such reformists were known to support the spread of literacy to the masses and the adoption of Western standards of public and higher education, sometimes to tolerate Japanese imperialism, and above all to deplore social violence and class warfare. The last two points were the ones which most separated them from the Communists.

proposed that we change to another room. Standing up, she stretched her limbs pleasurably, adjusted and smoothed her dress, and led the way. The room to which we moved was comparably grand. Seating arrangements, tables, writing and recording equipment, refreshments, and the full service of hot, cold, wet, and dry towels were set up exactly as they had been in the first room. We sat down and she resumed her narrative.

She had also studied with the writer Shen Ts'ung-wen, who taught fiction at Tsingtao University. As his student, she gradually got to know him. He lived with a sister named Shen Chou-chou, who often invited Chiang Ch'ing to visit their home. Openly impressed with her literary talent, Shen sought to improve her style by having her write a story a week. He was in earnest, she thought, but she never made the effort. From her perspective as a poor student, the Shen family seemed rich.[11] When Shen's sister, seeing that Chiang Ch'ing needed money, offered to pay her for knitting Shen a sweater, she refused. Later she learned that Shen Chou-chou had studied at the French Missionary School in Peking, an elitist institution where tuition was high — five or six hundred silver yuan a term.

Summing up the cultural significance of her Tsinan, Peking, and Tsingtao years, Chiang Ch'ing said that she had spent one year (1929–1930) at an arts academy and two years (1931–1933) in the "upper strata of culture," meaning the intellectual circle of Tsingtao University and the cultural circle of the Seaside Drama Society. In those years she developed a love of novels and poetry. She also enjoyed foreign poetry in translation, reading most extensively in "old foreign poetry," though she observed that most poetry is not translatable and so cannot be genuinely understood by foreigners. When she was young, she said, she composed verse that she considered publishing and also wrote essays, some of which were published. But in the 1930's she decided that writing poems and essays was far less important than actively making revolution. As for formal education, in all she had had but eight years, including five years of primary school. Her real learning, like Mao's, was "social education," education in the school of experience. And in 1933 that was just beginning.

3.

◇ ◇ ◇

From Party to Prison

Revolution is a bitter thing, mixed with filth
and blood, not as lovely or perfect as poets
think. It is eminently down-to-earth, involving many humble, tiresome tasks, not
as romantic as poets think.
— Lu Hsun, "Thoughts on the League of
Left-Wing Writers" (1930)

Orestes: You don't see them, you don't —
but *I* see them: they are hunting me down,
I must move on. — *Choephoroi*.
— T. S. Eliot, "Sweeney Agonistes"

Nineteen thirty-three, the year Chiang Ch'ing joined the Communist
Party, was cardinal in her life, and thus in the presentation of her story. For
her as for thousands of disaffected youths of her generation who had abandoned
family and had found religious celebration drained of meaning, joining the
Party became the chief rite of passage to maturity. But like the others who were
striving to learn, to support themselves, and to live unnoticed in the cities
ruthlessly governed by the Kuomintang, Chiang Ch'ing would find continuity
of Party membership hard to sustain, mainly because its underground character
made its network hard to trace. When she secretly joined the Party in Tsingtao
she had little idea of its organizational structure, or of who else, beyond her
immediate circle of comrades, belonged to it. Even less did she perceive what
Marxism — a foreign doctrine as yet poorly grasped by Chinese Communists — would come to mean in her country. And being a girl in a world still
dominated by men made her all the more vulnerable.

The Chinese Communist Party had been founded in Shanghai twelve years
earlier by a dozen youngish men, as angry with the world as ambitious for its

transformation. On orders from Moscow the CCP and its natural rival, the KMT, collaborated from 1923 to 1927 against warlordism, hoping thereby to bring about a reunited and regenerated nation. The inexorable split between the two parties occurred in the spring of 1927, when the chief of the KMT, Chiang Kai-shek, launched a massive attack against the Communists' underground control in the cities, which he sought to rule unchallenged. The final rupture came in April with the bloodbath in Shanghai, where the Communists' labor organization and their potential for urban insurrection had been the strongest.

The split between parties engendered still another division, one between the CCP's rural and urban factions. In 1928 Mao and Chu Te, self-styled followers of the Central Committee, assembled their rudimentary Red Army at Ching-kang-shan in Kiangsi province. But the urban faction dominated the Central Committee and disdained the unorthodox notion that naive peasants could be mobilized to revolutionize land control on their own authority. In the late 1920's this faction was guided by Li Li-san, a polemicist and labor organizer trained in Moscow. From his Shanghai station he picked up the pieces of the Communist organization shattered by the KMT purge of the spring of 1927 and for three years mounted costly urban insurrections. At the same time he aspired to launch from Shanghai a "revolutionary upsurge" by Red Army forces in the countryside that would assault the industrial centers, thereby bringing them under Communist domination. Another young radical, Ch'ü Ch'iu-pai, a prolific writer on political and literary theory, led the CCP for a year, starting in the difficult summer of 1927. He also miscalculated the revolutionary potential of the cities; both men seemed to forget that China was barely industrialized, overwhelmingly rural, and profoundly conservative. Nor had either realized the extent to which the rural revolutionaries would establish separate ways and ignore urban directives. Such blunders on the part of the Shanghai faction only made its leaders and their radical followers all the more vulnerable to the KMT's Gestapo-like secret police, who flushed known or suspected Communists out of their front and underground organizations, hounded them off the streets, imprisoned some, and executed others. Defeated in their attempt to implement a classic Marxian formula in China, these young idealists dispersed from Shanghai around 1933. Some retreated to Kiangsi province in the southeast, where Mao and Chu Te had already established a Red base. Others sought refuge with patrons in Moscow. Even after the dissolution of the urban apparatus, debates over the correct method of revolution for China continued among men of great dreams. Should China's Communist leaders aim at urban or rural targets? Should well-traveled urban intellectuals or rural-based men of the military present themselves to the world as CCP theoreticians and spokesmen? Should Party affiliates continue to risk working in the divided White

Areas or should they congregate in the Red Areas? Not until 1935 did the Central Committee's ideological orientation shift from Russian to Chinese. At the Tsunyi Conference held in August at a station of the Long March Mao Tse-tung emerged first among equals in a new collective leadership.

These monumental historical changes began when Chiang Ch'ing was in her midteens, and struggling to survive on her own, as few girls of that day tried to do, without the support of parents or siblings, husband or in-laws. Town-bred and city-bound, she knew next to nothing about rural China, by now peppered with hidden cells and bases of revolutionary action. When Japan's aggression against China's territorial integrity at Mukden in 1931 impelled her to examine her world skeptically for the first time and to act the patriot when to do so bordered upon subversion, elsewhere Mao Tse-tung and Chu Te were setting a new stage of history. Banking on their youth, a cult of willpower, and a talent for quickening the popular resentment born of poverty and oppression, they led their outlawed troops to the hills of Kiangsi, for centuries a haven for bandits. There Mao became Chairman of the First All-China Soviet government, its fledgling capital at the town of Juichin, which became transformed under occupation. In Shanghai in 1931 Ch'ü Ch'iu-pai was removed from the Politburo and from urban Communist power by the collective leadership of the Twenty-eight Bolsheviks, a sobriquet for the Moscow-trained Chinese youths who came home in the late 1920's. At that point they were fully confident that the Comintern, through their agency, could guide China along a shortcut to a new national integrity consonant with international communism. From 1931 to 1935, the years of Chiang Ch'ing's political arousal and Party initiation, the Twenty-eight Bolsheviks were led by Wang Ming — as Ch'en Shao-yü was known in the community of communism. Although Wang Ming remained with the Comintern in Moscow most of that time, his Bolsheviks reached the limits of their urban power in China, while more diffuse political developments went on in the countryside.

The actualities of life in the urban underground are almost impossible to reconstruct. No Chinese historian has dared to record that period objectively and comprehensively, and most survivors have taken what amount to vows of silence. Their motives have been political in traditional and revolutionary ways: to protect old associates from recrimination for behavior now judged to be unorthodox, and to preserve certain myths about the origins and early history of the Party that were flattering, or at least not offensive to Mao.

One of these myths was that money could not sully relations between comrades or that one could not buy one's way into the Party. But as Chiang Ch'ing revealed, membership often carried a price tag to be paid in cash, or in the case of a woman, even in sexual favors. Also subject to payment were help in making contact with other comrades, silence in tight spots, and even services to be rendered in the future. One is left wondering how different all this was from the proverbial "squeeze" of the past.

Of most importance, though, were the psychological effects of life in fragmented radical communities striving to sustain links to the Party's crippled urban wing. The fragility of ties between such neophytes as Chiang Ch'ing and the elusive and not always reliable overlords of the Communist underground in cities harshly ruled by the KMT bred in her and other Communists of her generation a peculiar and lasting complex of attitudes and behavior. Always they were on guard, tense, expecting some kind of attack. They became habitually cautious, suspicious, adept at subterfuge. They were alternately dependent and rebellious. Occasionally, they committed flamboyant acts to call attention to themselves and to alarm the world.

i

Looking at me expectantly, Chiang Ch'ing asked the obvious: "Do you want to know how I joined the Party?"

In her discussion of her two years in Tsingtao she had been leading up to this question. The answer would establish for the public record a hitherto hidden event in her life history. She was still a semistudent, a floundering actress, and a fledgling writer when she made contact with Party members through the gradual widening of her intellectual horizons. During the time she studied drama at Tsinan, she regarded the theater as a source of income and a way of acquiring culture, she said. But after reaching the far more modern and vigorous coastal city of Tsingtao early in 1931, fitfully but progressively she broke away from that youthful naiveté (as she saw it now) and gave increasing attention to analyzing political events and to forging political associations. She pursued her studies and her acting career concurrently.

During most of her two years at Tsingtao her political concerns were drivingly nationalistic. The two events she remembered most vividly were the Mukden crisis of September 18, 1931, and the Japanese attack on Shanghai on January 28, 1932. When news of those challenges to China's integrity reached Tsingtao, she joined the young radicals who demanded that the Nationalist government exert a tougher policy of resistance to Japan. Soon she suspected that the professors whom she revered on academic grounds, and once respected as "reformists," were actually in sympathy with nonresistance. Moreover, as she had explained earlier, they were antagonistic to her daring to publicize the view that their country had to be defended. Through a series of incidents, she realized that she could no longer depend on them as mentors of any sort. Their political conservatism and seeming unwillingness to take risks forced her to be independent and to search out a more sympathetic community. She found the most radical, the Communist Party.

Painstakingly, she forged a new network of affiliations. By winning the confidence of those in the outer circles of the Party she was gradually able to work inward. In 1931 she joined the Tsingtao branches of the League of Left-Wing Dramatists and the League of Left-Wing Writers, and the Anti-Imperialist League the next year. All were in some degree Communist front organizations about which she would eventually have more to tell me. To support herself she served as a check-out clerk in the library at Tsingtao University, an easy job that enabled her to do lots of "serious reading" in a collection far richer than any she had known. In off-hours she read her "first Marxist-Leninist work," Lenin's *State and Revolution*, which aroused her interest in other socialist classics available in Chinese translation.

When Chiang Ch'ing had described her job, I commented on the obvious parallel between her and Mao, who, twelve years earlier, had spent a year in just such a lowly post in the library of Peking University. Both seized the opportunity to devour books at hand and remembered best their first exposure to the fundamental works of Marx and Lenin. Within a year or so both joined the Chinese Communist Party. "I cannot be compared to the Chairman," she responded categorically. "He has done much work of many kinds, while I have only done a very little work among students, peasants, and workers, and for a period in the army, during the Liberation War."

In Tsingtao the political situation was "murky." Because of "traitorous activities" by some (Comintern-controlled) Party members the Party's branch organization in Tsingtao was partly dissolved in the early 1930's. Without a regular underground organization, management of the induction of new members was more idiosyncratic than ever. Each membership petition was handled individually, leaving much to the vagaries of dominant personalities.

In late 1932 Chiang Ch'ing was introduced to Li Ta-chang, then secretary of the Tsingtao Party organization, who later became the leading Party representative from Szechwan, China's largest province. She added that he had suffered brutally during the Cultural Revolution. While presenting her case to Li Ta-chang, she pressed him to tell her why her introduction to the municipal Party organization had been so long delayed. For months she had tried to make the right contacts, but all her efforts had been in vain. Embarrassed, he had no explanation, though she suspected that there was one. What was the prejudice against her?

Although Li Ta-chang was barely in his twenties, already he had achieved among the young radicals a reputation as a professional revolutionary. He set up, on her behalf, a series of surreptitious encounters designed to lead her safely to Party headquarters without arrest or other reprisal from the Nationalist government.

Early in 1933 a day was arranged for three Communist Party members to make a seemingly casual encounter with Chiang Ch'ing on the streets of Tsingtao. She was instructed to walk along a specified route in the company of a male student. They were to cling close to one another as if they were lovers, but to proceed cautiously, to be on the alert for spies and agents, and to watch for the agreed-upon signals. The scheme worked, and she was delivered over to men directly representing the Party. Her case was prepared, and by February she became a member.[1]

The conspiratorial intrigues that finally won her membership toughened her attitudes and also, it seemed, began to change her appearance. That spring, she remembered, some friends who knew nothing about what was happening to her in a political way started calling her by the nickname Erh Kan-tzu, literally Two Stalks, because her legs were skinny and she strutted about on them in brave style. She had lost weight because she was subsisting on very little, eating almost nothing, just two *shao-ping* (wheat-flour pancakes common to North China) a day. When student friends asked her how she managed to survive on so little, she told them a white lie, that she was taking meals with relatives. The normal thing would have been for her to eat at the university dormitory, but that would have cost her eight yuan a month, money she could ill afford. And she cut corners in other ways, such as purchasing third-class tickets to the theater, when her preference was to sit in the first-class section.

Why was she so concerned about saving money? "To pay off Li Ta-chang!" she responded brightly, refusing to elaborate, but implying that for her at least there was a price on Party membership.

ii

Later that spring Chiang Ch'ing fell in with the hundreds, soon thousands, of members of the new left generation of writers, artists, and dramatists who were drawn ineluctably from other towns and cities to Shanghai. This Paris of the East, Moscow of the Orient, and Mecca of modern Chinese culture thrived on accessibility to the substance and spirit of Western civilization, but failed to convey its unique blend of cosmopolitanism to the rest of China. To an actress aspiring to the national stage as much as to a young revolutionary attracted to the center of political action, Shanghai was an irresistible magnet. But the longer memories of political radicals were also still stinging from the Nationalists' purge of Shanghai's Communist ranks in 1927, and their vision of that city was stained with the blood of the "revolutionary martyrs" executed by the thousands for suspected Communist associations. That political rupture ushered in the "reign of White Terror." From then on the ruling KMT was served by gangs, secret agents, and military police. Paradoxically, that very polarization of political interests, combined with the buffer zones of the British International Settlement and the French Concession, where the law of extraterritoriality theoretically made Chinese immune to arrest, rendered life on the left somewhat less dangerous than in Nanking or Peking, for example. There Nationalist rule was more comprehensive and less vigorously opposed.

Chiang Ch'ing was both excited and frightened on the day of her departure from Tsingtao. Some friends accompanied her to the dock to see her off. There they introduced her to a young man (whose name she would not reveal in our conversation) to serve as her companion on the voyage south to Shanghai, an arrangement which perplexed her, though she did not protest. This first ocean voyage made her horribly seasick. Although she could climb a mountain "like a tiger," she had no talent for the sea and would never develop any. The voyage was a nightmare of nausea and vomiting. Desperately out of control, she turned to others, including her designated companion, for help. How useless that was!

To augment her troubles, her relationship to her male companion was precarious. He learned through their conversation that in Shanghai she expected to be met at the pier by another male friend, a former schoolmate. When she betrayed some uncertainty about that arrangement, he boldly proposed that the two of them spend the first night together in Shanghai at a hotel. Outraged by his presumptuousness, she declined firmly and knew then that he was "no good." Somewhere in Shanghai was a boardinghouse for women, she assured him. She would go there directly if her friend failed to meet her. She would hire a taxi or rickshaw to take her there. He persisted, changed tactics, and offered to find appropriate accommodations for her if she would advance him fifteen yüan. She rejected that too. When they docked, she scanned the crowd for the face her of friend and was so relieved to find him that she ran straight to his side. They fled to his car and sped away so fast (she blushed at the recollection) that her luggage was accidentally left behind on the dock.

The night of her arrival in Shanghai she ran into another friend, who belonged to a drama society with Russian connections. (She interrupted her account here to mention that the Soviet Union had recently established diplomatic relations with the Nanking government [on December 12, 1932]). The drama society was currently producing a "progressive show" on rural China. He invited her to have a snack with him at the Sincere Company, then the biggest department store in Shanghai.* As they ate, the calm of the restaurant

* After Liberation renamed the Number One Department Store.

was pierced by a shrill female voice coming from the street. "What's that?" she asked in alarm. "Just a prostitute soliciting customers," was his reply. Such was her first taste of Shanghai's famous street life. (She laughed as she remembered it.)

That evening's conversation would have profound effects upon her next four years in Shanghai, she continued reflectively. There she first learned about the newly formed Spring and Autumn Drama Society, already a major force in the left-wing theater movement.[2] This was led by the dramatist T'ien Han, who concurrently headed the League of Left-Wing Dramatists. He was probably not aware of the fact that she had joined the league's Tsingtao branch in 1931, the year of its founding, she mused in our conversation. In those days T'ien Han was not yet a "defector," she said in oblique reference to the defamation campaign against him launched under her aegis during the Cultural Revolution. Yet his various cultural and social affiliations with the Communist Party (he had joined it in 1931)[3] led her to believe that if she could meet him and win his confidence he would put her in touch with the headquarters of the Shanghai Party organization, thereby enabling her to sustain continuity in her membership.

Since she was already a Party member, why should making the Shanghai contact have been so difficult? I asked.

She explained that owing to Wang Ming's line, the structure of the Party organization in Shanghai had been progressively undermined, and by the mid-1930's was dissolved almost completely. Thus open and direct contact among members of branch organizations in other towns and cities was impossible. In her words, "We were lucky to survive as 'water flowers,'" by which she meant that migrant members, such as herself, floated like flotsam. Leaving Tsingtao, she said, meant leaving her precious Party identity behind her, for in the city of Shanghai claims to previous Party affiliation were meaningless until new personal connections could be forged with members of the Shanghai organization. She was sure that T'ien Han, as head of the League of Left-Wing Dramatists, could help her. In those days he was an elusive character, and she started out to find him without the faintest idea of where he lived. Nor could she forget that under the White Terror her search for such a prominent and well-connected leftist was made at the risk of her life.

Thus, Chiang Ch'ing spent the first few days in Shanghai tracking down T'ien Han and other leading figures in the Spring and Autumn Drama Society. Seeking directions of people and establishing communication of any sort were extremely difficult because her native Shantung dialect and the Peking dialect she had mastered for the stage bore no relation to the Shanghai dialect — that too she would have to learn. Her circuitous route to the hideout entailed close calls with spies and narrow escapes from arrest, which she sketched with relish and a storyteller's flair for dramatic action. How intensely she recalled her youthful anxiety as she stood before men who were both eminent playwrights and formidable politicians and explained who she was and what she hoped to accomplish in Shanghai. She wanted to be introduced to T'ien Han, she said, because she understood that he was not only chief of the Spring and Autumn Drama Society but also influential in the Party circles with which she had to make contact. Her sincerity and earnestness must have come across, for they set up the procedure for introduction.

In the course of following their directions she learned that T'ien Han was the elder of two brothers. The younger brother, T'ien Hung, known by his cohorts as the Bad Man, was assigned to her case. He attached himself to her in ways she would find increasingly distasteful. As instructed, he offered to take her to meet his elder brother, who avoided government reprisal by moving continuously among his several homes. T'ien Hung led her first to a house that turned out to occupied by his mother. The address she could not recall, but she remembered that the mother, an impressive woman, received her graciously. She invited Chiang Ch'ing to remain with them for a few days and to tell them everything about herself. With no other real choice, Chiang Ch'ing complied but spoke warily. She told them only what they needed to know: the names of some Party members she had known in Tsingtao (some of them betrayed the Party in later years, she added ruefully). The act of speaking the names of familiar comrades working elsewhere in the Party network earned her credibility with T'ien Han's family.

A few days later T'ien Han, Chou Yang, and Yang Han-sheng * paid Chiang Ch'ing a visit. They reported that the Central Committee, which they represented, was familiar with the conditions of the Party's Tsingtao organization and had decided that she should be allowed to make contact with the Shanghai Party organization through the proper channels. (Such action, it seemed, was preliminary to renewal of her full membership.) Next she was questioned about the work she would do for the Party. Knowing her to be an actress, they gave her the choice of performing either on the stage or in films. Cultural work was important to the cause, she agreed, but she rejected both options and announced that she wanted to do "mass work at the grassroots level," which meant that she was not obsessed by fame but preferred to make propaganda that would bring her in touch with the people on an informal, daily basis. Her response must have surprised them (she judged now with amusement), for they would have expected the reverse. Still, they came to an agreement and signed her up with one of several proletarian drama groups, the

---

* Actually, she called the last two men by the aliases they used in the 1930's — Chou Ch'i-ying and Hua Han respectively — when they were dominant personalities in the left-wing drama movement.

Shanghai Work Study Troupe led by the playwright and producer Chang Keng, a man with whom she would have difficulties.

A school of general education as well as the performing arts, the Shanghai Work Study Troupe reflected the educational philosophy and social concerns of Chang Keng's colleague, T'ao Hsing-chih. The troupe's name had been given by T'ao, a man Chiang Ch'ing would always admire. In those years T'ao, best known as an educator, was as famous as Wen I-to, though neither was a CCP member. When Chiang Ch'ing knew T'ao he was over forty and his regard for idealistic young people, herself included, was paternalistic. She used to be among those he "loved and protected," she said.

The Shanghai Work Study Troupe was located at Ta-ch'ang, an area now serving as an airfield for metropolitan Shanghai, not far from another group, the Shan Hai Drama School, which T'ao Hsing-chih ran himself. Tuition-free, the Shanghai Work Study Troupe attracted students from the economically and culturally depressed industrial and farming communities nearby. Its curriculum included night courses and other supplemental forms of education for women, shop assistants, and others who had missed an early chance for an education. From the beginning T'ao Hsing-chih took an active interest in the school, visited it frequently, and felt keenly responsible for its survival. If the school ran short of funds or some students did not have enough to eat. T'ao and some of the teachers took it upon themselves to go out and raise the needed money.

With evident fondness and respect, Chiang Ch'ing went on to say that T'ao was a man of broad learning and one with a philosophic cast of mind, a quality apparent in the significance of his given name and the way he changed it. His original given name was Chih-hsing, literally "knowledge-action," an allusion to the Neo-Confucian philosopher Wang Yang-ming (1472–1529), whose formula *"chih hsing ho i"* ("knowledge and action combined") advocated intuitionism. T'ao's original given name meant "only after you know can you act." But in his maturity he reversed the characters to Hsing-chih, literally "action-knowledge," thereby reversing the sense to "only after you act can you know."*

Inspired by the democratic educational philosophy of John Dewey, who lectured in China during the May Fourth era, T'ao Hsing-chih continued his studies in America, an experience which made him "liberal-minded." Upon his return to China he became an indefatigable supporter of a form of popular education that was tuition-free and also provided free room and board — an outgrowth of the Mass Education Movement originated by his colleague James Yen.

---

* A philosophic distinction implicit in John Dewey's experimentalism, which T'ao Hsing-chih studied; in Neo-Confucian philosophers of the Ming dynasty, whose ideas remained vital in modern minds; and in the Communists' stress on the realization of ideology in action.

When Chiang Ch'ing first knew T'ao he had been director of Yu-ts'ai, a free primary school in Chungking that had an excellent reputation. Some years earlier (in 1927) T'ao's name was publicized in connection with the Hsiao-chuang Experimental Village Normal School, which he had established near Nanking. The Hsiao-chuang School "specialized in free thought," according to Chiang Ch'ing, which meant that any politics was acceptable, a principle which the KMT feared and deplored. Beginning in 1927, the year the KMT rose to dictatorial power, numerous students from that school, including some Communist Party and Youth League members, were arrested for their public flaunting of democratic and anarchic convictions. Finally in 1930 the government closed down the school and rounded up its students and faculty for detention. Such suppression of an unconventional educational institution was sensationalized journalistically at both ends of the political spectrum. Being a young radical, Chiang Ch'ing was also profoundly moved by the stories of brave youths who sang the "Internationale" right in the faces of their jailers and refused to be bullied by them.

Since T'ien Han was responsible for assigning her to the Shanghai Work Study Troupe, he considered himself in a position to exercise control over all aspects of her life. Accordingly, he appointed his younger brother T'ien Hung (Bad Man) to accompany her to classes and to report on everything she did. She found this frustrating and unbearable. Besides, T'ien Hung meddled in her work and showed unwelcome signs of being enamored of her. Finally, she dashed off a letter to T'ien Han in which she described in detail how insufferable his little brother had become and asked that other work be found for him.

In those days the younger brother and all other intimates of T'ien Han called him Lao Ta, literally Old Big, or more loosely Number One, because he was the first son of the T'ien family. But the name also fitted because it belonged (less exclusively then she claimed) to the argot of bandits and hooligans. (She said this with obvious delight and with spite toward a man against whom she avenged herself in later years.) How did *she* learn bandit language? From her political work with people of the lowest social strata, who "enlightened" her vocabulary with underworld expressions. But her real introduction to bandit argot dated from the early 1950's, when she was working incognito in the rural areas. There she picked up all sorts of underworld terms, including the code names of the first nine members of a hooligan gang. The person called Old Big was at the top.

Despite her exposé of Bad Man T'ien Hung to Old Big T'ien Han, the former's personal attachment to her could not be shaken. Nor did it take her long to realize that his intrusiveness was also an act of political interference under the ultimate control of T'ien Han, whose methods were insidious. Originally she had sought out T'ien Han in order to get in touch with the branch Party organization in Shanghai; now the reverse was happening. T'ien Hung was using devious tactics to prevent her making contact with other members who, in future, could possibly shield her against government reprisal. Without those vital links, but already known in some circles to be involved in leftist operations, she was left to "drift in dangerous waters." Inexorably, it became known that she was floundering without the protective environment of the Communist underground organization. Some people she once counted as friends now refused to open their doors to her. They realized that a person in her position was destined for arrest, in which event they also would suffer.

Through her acquaintance with T'ien Han she was introduced to Liao Mo-sha, another member of the League of Left-Wing Dramatists. A struggling writer, Liao was "still all right in those days" (an indirect reference to his subsequent and devious criticism of Mao's regime through journalism, an offense that ultimately caused his downfall). She also commented that Liao's wife had a famous father but did not give his name. In the early 1930's Liao was quite poor. He and his wife lived in wretched circumstances, occupying the garret of a house belonging to someone else. When Chiang Ch'ing first got to know them, the wife was pregnant. Ostensibly because Chiang Ch'ing was still searching for the headquarters of the Party organization, Liao Mo-sha invited her to come live in his home, perhaps to test her politics and character. With no better place to go, she accepted. Their living quarters were so cramped that she had to sleep upon a tiny table. Their constant bickering, focused now upon her because she was the outsider, was aggravating and exhausting; sleep was almost out of the question.

During her involvement with Liao and his wife she began exploring the intellectual community centered at Ta-hsia, the popular name of Shanghai University. There she began to audit classes. From the early 1930's through the December Ninth demonstrations of 1935,* its political coloring continued to be "far to the left," hence expressive of the Russian-linked Wang Ming line. Whenever students and faculty members mounted demonstrations, numerous young Communists and Youth League members were rounded up by the KMT authorities. With the cresting of the wave of student protest during the December Ninth demonstrations, "hordes of followers of the Wang Ming line held aloft the red flag." She emphasized that most of those arrested were CCP members.

The weather turned hot and muggy when she started attending classes at Ta-hsia. She remembered the pleasant sensation of wearing only the lightest clothing. Making friends among the students came slowly. Being an actress, from

* A massive student movement on a par with the May Fourth Movement of 1919 and the Cultural Revolution of 1966. All were initiated at Peking University. For an analysis of men and events, see John Israel and Donald W. Klein, *Rebels and Bureaucrats: China's December 9ers* (Berkeley, 1975).

out of town, and noticeably involved in various left-wing causes undermined the confidence of others in her. As she attempted to establish herself in the Ta-hsia community, one of her first moves was to disentangle herself from Liao Mo-sha and his wife, for she was finding her association with him personally as well as politically compromising. To do this she had to get hold of money quickly. She called on a female classmate whom she knew to be reasonably well off. The girl received her graciously, which surprised her inasmuch as she was used to rebuff. When she steered the conversation around to asking for a loan of twenty yuan, the girl hesitated a moment and mumbled something about having just paid her university tuition and being short of cash. Nonetheless, she did lend the money, which Chiang Ch'ing pocketed and went directly to Liao Mo-sha's garret. She intended in turn to lend it to him because she knew he both needed and wanted it (her account, which was evasive here, implied that she was "purchasing" his silence for her sudden withdrawal). As he took the cash she announced that she was moving out and asked him to return the money soon. (Here she interrupted her narrative to say indignantly that to date she had never received so much as a penny from him).

Regardless of Liao, she had to pay back her classmate as soon as possible. How could she manage? She did have some other modest sources of income, among them part-time teaching of Chinese at several middle schools in Shang-hai. She was paid by the hour, though she could not recall what the rate was. Her only major expense in Shanghai was for transportation — to her classes, teaching assignments, theater performances, and other missions around the city. So she was able to save something and to return the twenty yuan to her girl friend within a reasonable time. What an enormous relief that was, more than the girl, who knew nothing of her underground entanglements, could have anticipated. Liao Mo-sha had no further claim upon her, and she resolved never to have any more dealings with members of the League of Left-Wing Dramatists (a resolution soon to be broken) — least of all those whom she saw as obstructing her access to the key members of the Party who could give her what she most wanted: renewed membership in Shanghai.

iii

For leftists of all ages and various occupations in the 1930's, political demonstrations became a way of life. Organized groups could publicize their views on national issues and petition the government with greater inpunity than isolated individuals could. In 1933, Chiang Ch'ing recalled, the ease with which demonstrators maneuvered was greater than it was in the years following. In August, by which time she had begun teaching, she represented a group of suburban women schoolteachers and joined a small group of students and workers who marched down to the wharf to welcome Lord Marley of the British Labour Party and Paul Vaillant-Couturier of France (editor of *L'Humanité* and a Communist). They had arrived to attend the Anti-War Conference to be held in Shanghai during the first week of September.[4] Accompanied by two brass bands, the welcoming Chinese waved red flags and set off firecrackers to honor these eminent spokesmen for their "anti-imperialism."

University-inspired demonstrations were enormously different from those conducted along the broad avenues of Shanghai. Her recollection of the simple elements of a university environment — professors, students, classes and the continual play of ideas — was far less vivid than that of imminent arrest and riot. As she remembered it, in 1933–1934 the Party organization in Shanghai, and thus at Ta-hsia, was still an expression of Wang Ming's leftist line, and the political orientation of the CCP Youth League was still more leftist than Wang Ming. Because of this and other divergencies in political stance among the Party members themselves, she could not automatically count such associates as friends.* However uneasy they were as comrades, still all were together in living under the threat of the KMT, which sought to dissolve organized resistance by infiltrating the student community with Blue Shirts (a militaristic youth corps often called fascist and compared to Hitler's Black Shirts and Mussolini's Brown Shirts), spies, agents, and counteragents, all covertly armed. There, and in Shanghai at large, distinction between enemies and friends was difficult to ascertain.

Soon Chiang Ch'ing joined friends in demonstrations throughout the Shanghai area to further the cause of national resistance. On the anniversary of the KMT's rebellious Nineteenth Route Army's surprise defense of Shanghai against the Japanese on July 18, 1932, she and a boy about her age went out to raise money for the army. Moving about Shanghai, they met other resisters, including a group of men who were literally laying their lives on the line for the cause. As she stared at those grim figures stretched over the railway tracks, a gesture of ultimate defiance of the government's tolerance of Japanese penetration, she suspected that some were members of the Red Army then located in the Central Soviet Districts † (possibly a reference to members of the Nineteenth Route Army, which had set up a People's Revolutionary Government in

---

* During the early 1930's she and her Communist urban friends were generally oriented toward the Wang Ming line, which dominated the cities. She would not repudiate that until after 1937, when she adopted Mao's "centrist" position which rejected both Wang Ming and the Youth League that was, allegedly, still more to the left.

† The CCP's original base area and first formal state government established in Juichin, Kiangsi province, in November 1931. Activities of the next three years included guerrilla-style defense, harshly enforced land reform, promulgation of draft laws, and experimentation in revolutionary culture.

Foochow in November; their bid for a united front with the Communists stationed in the nearby Central Soviet Districts was rejected).[5]

Frequent participation in street demonstrations clued her into their system. With little forewarning a student leader would announce the time and place of demonstration. Supporters would arrive swiftly from all quarters, align themselves, issue slogans and demands, and disperse before they could be caught by police and plainclothesmen. Exhilarated by her memories of youthful defiance of authority and capacity for heroic action — her own not excluded — she remarked several times that such demonstrations were always conducted at the risk of one's life. But the demonstrators had no choice. How else could they assert their values and raise money for their causes? In such enterprises she and her radical comrades enjoyed the support of the League of Left-Wing Educators, to which their liberal patron, T'ao Hsing-chih, and other sympathetic figures belonged.

More extensively and perhaps more reliably, she remembered demonstrations in commemoration of Japan's invasion of Manchuria in 1931 (the Mudken Incident). For left-wing students and radicals in general that series of demonstrations added up to a tumultuous fall. Secret agents of the KMT and traitors to the CCP seized prominent members of the Communist Youth League and claimed that they belonged to "their own people." Determined not to become "pawns of the enemy," these victimized Youth League members swore that they would rather die for their cause than survive as cowards. In a public show of strength they chanted, "Destroy the jade rather than keep the tile intact" (resistance at all costs), and "Better left than right!" However she admired them, Chiang Ch'ing was frightened by their example. After that, she said, she chose her demonstrations more judiciously.

She decided to renew her efforts to establish contact with the underground Party organization. To be sure, her stratagem, which was to join the ranks of the massive demonstrations commemorating the Mukden Incident, was risky, but her hope was to capture the attention of some sympathetic Party members and impress them with her valorous commitment to the Communist cause. It worked! Her calculated conduct in the demonstrations won over certain of the leaders, who then motioned her to step up and serve as the secret marshal of the column.

Now in the vanguard, she was put to further tests. One of the leaders of the demonstrations asked her to look after two women workers who had just joined the ranks. When she first met them, she realized that she had never seen them before. (Here she related her original impressions more candidly than usual.) She was astonished to find that these women workers were much better dressed than she. How could that be? They obviously had no family burdens, no one else to support. Her own situation was not the same. (She did not elaborate on this statement, and one wonders whether she was implying that she was supporting her mother, a husband, a lover, or simply comrades.) Though she herself was not handsomely dressed, her costume was different from that of the ordinary woman worker. An actress and a student intellectual, she did not maintain the proletarian style, even for political reasons. Yet the people who counted in this demonstration were not offended by her theatrical appearance, however outlandish in that setting. They had, after all, chosen her to be their leader.

The afternoon of the demonstrations (September 18) Chiang Ch'ing played in a benefit performance of *Babies' Murder*, a drama adapted from a Japanese film and addressed to the issues of the day. The money raised by the performance was to be delivered to workers on strike at the British-American Tobacco factory. As usual, several classes of tickets were available. The ordinary ones cost only twenty or thirty cents apiece, while the expensive ones ranged from five to ten yuan each. Since the house was not sold out, the troupe's indefatigable patron, T'ao Hsing-chih, bought out the expensive tickets just to support the players and the workers' cause.

That particular performance of *Babies' Murder* was one she would never forget. The day's events had driven the playgoers and the performers, among them other demonstrators, to a high pitch of excitement. Usually when she was onstage she paid little attention to audience reaction, but this time she closely watched movements within the audience. Because of the protest nature of the play, members of the audience no less than the performers themselves would be liable to punishment. And that afternoon arrests were made. Right after the final curtain the actors evacuated the theater by the back door and ran swiftly to catch up with the demonstrators.

When everyone had dispersed at the end of the demonstration, Chiang Ch'ing was left stranded, exhausted, and famished. She searched her purse for carfare, but found none, which meant that she also could not pay for a meal. Then she remembered that nearby some White Russians ran a small restaurant, in which they served a marvelous borscht. She knew the old man who owned it and was confident that he would give her a free meal for the asking. The moment she entered the restaurant she realized that some diners who had attended that afternoon's performance were amazed to see her because they assumed that she too had been caught by the police right after the show. But now they hailed her as Li Yun-ho, the actress whose reputation was established by her performance in a variety of roles. (She seemed quite oblivious to the self-flattery implied in what she had just said.) Someone must have told the proprietor that T'ao Hsing-chih, a man whose liberalism he could support, had courageously stood up in the audience to commend her performance, for that evening the old Russian treated her to a superb meal.

When she arranged to take part in the anti-Japanese demonstration the next day, a woman was assigned to guide her to its beginning point. But for reasons of her own, the woman abandoned her along the way. Frightened that others would think that she was reneging on her responsibility for the demonstration, Chiang Ch'ing rushed to the neighborhood of Nei-sheng-chia, where still there was no one she knew, then continued to another area, which she found completely surrounded by mounted policemen, all of them Sikhs representing the British colonial government. Skirting that dangerous area, she persisted in her search as unobtrusively as possible. By chance she met a male friend who told her that the demonstration had been relocated at Peking West Road, the main thoroughfare used for demonstrations. On her way there she ran down Ai-wen-i Street, where she found no one, then continued the pursuit until she was brought up short by the sight of a group of distinguished-looking gentlemen, all "men of letters," standing in the street. Their unusual presence among ordinary people alerted her that the demonstration was nearby.

Recollection of that chase through the streets left Chiang Ch'ing emotionally drained, her last words uttered in a near whisper. She fell silent for some moments, then regained her voice. The talk about her childhood the previous evening had so agitated her that she had had to take sleeping pills to calm down. Carelessly, she had overdosed herself and had collapsed on the floor. Her nurse found her there, lifted her up, and carried her to bed. She laughed as she told me about it. Now, on this evening, her robust young bodyguard Hsiao Chiao, a nurse, and a doctor were more vigilant than before; they moved about the room observing her moods and watching for signs of exhaustion. Hsiao Chiao was planning to make her retire at midnight, Chiang Ch'ing remarked teasingly and laughed again. The laughter suggested that he would be (as he was) hard put to have his way. This imminent battle of wills cheered her, for she stood up, untied her silk belt, and strode about the room, the belt ends dancing at her hips as she walked.

Among the people she recognized on the fringes of the demonstration was a young boy who had once been a student of hers and was now a member of the Student Corps. He was carrying a parcel, perhaps a weapon or handbills, that was bound to arouse suspicion. Just then a mounted Sikh policeman caught sight of him, raised his truncheon in the air, leaned sideways from his galloping horse, and struck the parcel out of the boy's arms. Stunned by the blow, the boy momentarily lost his balance, then recovered and ran away. Enraged by the Sikh's brutality, Chiang Ch'ing's first impulse was to run after the boy and care for him. But that would have been foolhardy, for she too might have been struck down. So as not to draw attention to herself, she ambled by a dress shop and pretended to be studying the latest fashions in the window. Because her eyes had to be focused on the display, she could observe only partially what was going on around her. Soon a middle-aged woman she knew as Lao Wang (Venerable Wang), who had spent a year or so doing grassroots political work in Shanghai, walked up and stood quietly by her side. Picking up her signal, Chiang Ch'ing followed her down Ai-wen-i Street near the Ni-tseng Bridge. Suddenly they sensed that police were on their trail. Chiang Ch'ing motioned her to go on alone, for being less well known than Chiang Ch'ing, she could maneuver more safely among the police. Chiang Ch'ing cautiously made her way back to the school where she was teaching.

Although she was not a member of the Central Committee of the Party or of the Provincial Committee (or even of the Shanghai Party branch organization), her reputation as a Communist revolutionary was growing. Notoriety meant that she should take special precautions during demonstrations. If asked to join the "flying meetings," which were swiftly organized and as swiftly dispersed, she assessed conditions carefully before accepting. Would her life be as useful in jail as it could be if she remained free to do cultural work? (She expressed this and other anxious speculations in a flurry of circuitous reasoning in which willingness for self-sacrifice, determination to survive, and a craving for fame were all subtly reconciled.)

Among left-wing political and cultural organizations survival depended on developing effective ways of behaving and communicating — ones which drew the least attention from the police. Chiang Ch'ing and her friends debated endlessly just what tactics were most successful. The complex social and political composition of the area where she worked was not easily sorted out by outsiders, and that surface opaqueness made underground communication all the more viable, but always with precaution.

In that fall she received a letter folded lengthwise, with her acquired name, Yun-ho, the two characters meaning Cloud Crane, inscribed on top.* But the character *ho* of Yun-ho was altered, leaving only the "bird" element on the right; the left side of the character had been eliminated — a matter of security. Such tactics were not unusual in the White Areas, where people changed their names for political camouflage as well as for more common personal and professional reasons. The letter itself was an exercise in indirection. Its sender commiserated with her because she supposedly had been bitten by a mad dog, was hospitalized, and was still recuperating. Those bizarre words concealed the

* In the early 1930's she was still going by the name Li Yun-ho, which retained her family name Li. But among friends, she said, she was known simply as "Ho."

real message, which she understood to say that her life was in danger and that she must leave the area immediately.

How maddening that secret command was to her then! From the time of her arrival in Shanghai her primary goal had been to establish confidence with people who could put her in touch with the branch organization of the CCP. Rival groups of left-wing organizations, among them certain grating personalities, had long plied her with advice, much of it contradictory. By now, one of these organizations, the Revolutionary League, had shifted far to the left, "even more to the left than the Party center" (still set by Wang Ming's line). The Youth League and other youth and student organizations had also been "coopted by the left," as she put it. Now these ultra-leftist groups were pressing her and certain of her friends who were not so left-leaning to get out of town, not caring really where they went. Informed of her plight and personal turmoil, the League of Left-Wing Educators reinforced the order that she leave the area immediately. At first she resisted because Shanghai, apart from her political and professional interests, was the only place where she had close personal ties. In the end she yielded and moved to Peking.

In her recollection, the White Terror in Peking was as brutal as it had been in Shanghai. Tensions were heightened by the presence of the Third Regiment of Shanghai, which was stationed both in Peking and Tientsin to protect the interests of the Kuomintang government. Isolated and more vulnerable than ever before, she attached herself to Peita (Peking University) as an auditor. Here in this third academic environment (after Tsingtao and Shanghai universities) she drifted toward the social sciences, the field in which the Marxian theoretician Li Ta was one of Peita's most popular teachers. Whenever he lectured on political science students from all over the campus slipped into the classroom; she was often among them.

At Peita she had scarcely any money. Her income (source undisclosed) was only seven yuan a month. After the rent was paid, only four cents remained for each meal. Peita, where Chairman Mao once worked, was the most famous of all the colleges and universities in the country. Even an auditor like herself could learn a lot there from attending lectures and reading. She also managed to get a card that granted her access to the Peking Municipal Library. For several months she spent the better part of her days there, reading from its extraordinarily rich collection, all the while sustaining herself on flat bread and boiled water.[6]

In her episodic narration, that austere self-image of girl scholar was set off by another, more girlish one. Her face flickered with laughter as she described how during that Peking retreat she first attempted to ride a bicycle. After several nasty spills she got the knack. When young, she was clumsy in a lot of ways, she admitted, and her sense of balance was poor. In cycling as in everything else willpower pulled her through.

iv

Chiang Ch'ing's return from Peking to Shanghai in the spring was secretly arranged by the Party organization of the League of Left-Wing Educators. The transition was fraught with higher personal drama than the simple fact implied. The league's sponsorship meant that after more than a year's dangerous suspension her contact with the Party was restored. Thanks to subtle guidance by the Educators' League and infiltration by other leftist groups, over recent months many sectors of the Shanghai school system had come under control of the CCP, "fallen into our hands," as she put it.

The Party assigned her to teach in a night-school program for women workers, one which was concurrently directed by the Shanghai branch of the Young Women's Christian Association. Though "enlightened" with respect to this labor program, the YWCA was "intensely reactionary" on most other scores. Certainly she showed no interest in its Christian spiritual foundation.

Chiang Ch'ing's service on behalf of both Christianity and Communism appears contradictory and calls for more historical explanation than she provided. In 1927, when Chiang Kai-shek betrayed his Communist collaborators, most trade unions operated by the Communists were shattered and subsequently had to be replaced by others, which either lacked political power or were efficiently controlled by the KMT. That shift of labor orientation combined with the worldwide economic crisis and the transfer of the CCP Central Committee to Kiangsi meant that as of 1932 the few Communist labor organizers holding on in Shanghai had to forge other ties. Besides infiltration of KMT organizations, options were few.[7] But prominent at this time were reputable, modern reformist Christian institutions experienced in the labor world. In the gathering urban crisis of the 1930's both the YWCA and the YMCA had become deeply involved in industrial welfare, and in their industrial missions abroad. On the Chinese front these were concentrated in Shanghai, where organized exploitation of human labor was most intense and extensive. From the KMT's vantage point, their foreign and Christian origin enhanced the government's prestige at a time when the KMT was seeking a positive international profile. Consequently, the YWCA and YMCA were the only nonofficial organizations in Shanghai that could openly engage in patriotic and other reformist activities without courting government opposition.[8]

The administrators of the YWCA's Shanghai branch wisely assigned Chinese women as well as foreign personnel to responsible positions. Probably recom-

mended by the Educators' League and known to have some teaching experience in Shanghai, Chiang Ch'ing was among those appointed. Services offered
the women workers, naive peasants in the main, ranged from social clubs and
recreation to investigation and improvement of working conditions in factories
to instruction in reading and writing and basic medical care. The YWCA also
underwrote campaigns to boycott Japanese goods, produced anti-Japanese
plays, and scheduled lectures and discussions on patriotic themes.[9]

These progressive YWCA activities converged with others sponsored by more
radical agencies, among them the League of Left-Wing Educators and its
counterparts for writers and dramatists, and the CCP. These latter, of course,
were concerned not only with literacy and patriotism, but also with developing
among workers of both sexes the proletarian class consciousness they believed
would overthrow the capitalist and imperialist classes both within and beyond
China.

The industrial labor world to which Chiang Ch'ing was relegated in 1934
was alien to all her previous experience. She was quick to point out that assignment to the working class did not mean that she would perform physical labor
with the women. She was a teacher, a comprehensive role that included living
with the women workers in her charge. Behind that arrangement, she said, was
the YWCA. After she had worked there for some time, the YWCA extended
her duties to visiting workers' families and gathering information on their living
conditions. Those private excursions into the domestic lives of others she truly
enjoyed. Later she was sent to investigate health clinics and small factories that
were beyond the normal reach of the foreign reformist agencies.

After becoming proficient in investigating and reporting on small factories,
she moved on to larger ones, usually foreign-owned though managed by Chinese. Entree was difficult because the managers feared that unfavorable reports by
outside observers, coupled with subtle political provocation of workers to unite
in making anti-Japanese propaganda, would disrupt production, which was
their only real interest. Working conditions were at best ancillary to their concerns. Of all her activities inspired in part at least by the YWCA, she found the
visits to the factories, small and large, the most absorbing.

Whatever obstruction and abuse she suffered in carrying out her assignments
were offset by the comprehensive authority she came to exercise over the workers' lives outside the factories. They were housed in what she called "dormitories," usually cheap clapboard houses that the KMT had turned over to the factories to be used for workers detached from their families. Men and women
were segregated, and all aspects of their lives were rigidly controlled.

The dormitory assigned to Chiang Ch'ing was one located in the factory district. She occupied a small room of her own at the back. The front rooms were
used as classrooms, and the women slept several to a room in the space remain-

ing. She chided herself now for being naive and inefficient when she began. For example, she allowed teaching preparation to erode far too much of her time at a point in her life when she was also acting and politicking. She spent long hours preparing lessons and correcting her students' written work, with the result that she scarcely slept at all and often worked to the brink of exhaustion. Weariness and frustration were the overwhelming sensations she remembered of that phase of her life.

Yet her trials were negligible compared with those of the women workers. The majority of her students came from the large textile mills, most of which were owned by the Japanese but managed by Chinese.[10] The rest labored in the British-owned cigarette factories, especially the British-American Tobacco Company. Work began at six in the morning, she recalled. To arrive in time, the women in her dormitory had to arise at four in the morning and walk in the dark through the city streets to the factories. Working conditions at the British-American Tobacco Company were "hellish." The highest wage earned by women workers was seventeen or eighteen yuan a month. Child labor was routine, and the children earned next to nothing. In summer when the air was intensely humid all the windows were closed, creating an internal steam bath. In winter they were flung open. Why? Because the owners feared that comfortable workers would become sluggish. So they used the summer's heat and the winter's bitter cold to control the work force. The toilets in the huge cigarette factories were so filthy that the mere sight of them made her retch.

The cigarette factories were barely equipped: rows of crude wooden benches and that was all. In the hope of being assigned seats in the morning, the children, whose jobs were not guaranteed, had to queue up the night before and wait huddled in line all night. Those lucky enough to get seats were forced to work for hours without respite, continuously rolling cigarettes and putting them in boxes. ("Just what I aspired to do as a child!" she remarked and laughed.)

To illustrate the tenor of life in a cigarette factory, she cited the case of a "rich man's daughter." Why a rich man should choose to send his daughter into notoriously brutish conditions she did not explain. Clearly, the girl was ambitious. To be sure of a seat the next morning she queued up very early the evening before. But the labor contractor, who was in charge of contract workers, wanted to put the person he was sponsoring ahead of her in the line. Standing defiantly, the rich girl would not budge. So the contractor simply grabbed her by the shoulders, dragged her across the floor, and kicked her down a flight of stairs. Her body lay crushed and motionless at the bottom of the staircase; she died soon after. After witnessing incidents like these, workers were easily mobilized, Chiang Ch'ing noted quietly.

In addition to workers from cigarette factories, her students included women from the small Chinese-owned and -operated sock factories located in the neighborhood. There the wage scale was even more disgraceful than at the cigarette factory. The highest wage earned by a sockmaker was twelve yuan a month, and that was far above the average. Exploitation of the workers was limitless. If the needle of a knitting machine broke, the worker responsible for that machine was forced to pay one yuan to replace it. One of her students happened to break eight needles in one month. After she began paying up the penalties, she had nothing left for room and board or for supporting the family with whom she no longer lived. Her exploitation by the management was compounded by the fact that she never was able to pay outright the full penalty (and by implication was made to suffer other personal abuse). At the time, Chiang Ch'ing said, she herself was earning so little that she was in no position to help the girl.

However vulnerable those women were to the vagaries of factory management, they were still better off than the contract workers, with whom she also dealt.[11] To keep various factories freshly stocked with laborers, labor contractors, or "supply men" as they were also called, made regular trips to the countryside to recruit peasants whom they brought back to perform cheap labor in the cities. The tactics of the supply men were most unscrupulous. To tantalize peasants, ignorant and poverty-stricken, they described Shanghai as an earthly paradise where even the simplest peasant could make a pile of money. Hopelessly gullible and desperate to survive, older peasants sold their children and other family members into the contract system. The "paradise" to which they were seduced in Shanghai was plain "hell." Factory hours were incredibly long. Between shifts the workers were confined to tiny rooms no bigger than a cage. Given only a meager ration of gruel and water, they all suffered from malnutrition. Many died.

Chiang Ch'ing found that not only was the KMT hostile to her political work, but rival leftist groups were jealous of her success. While she was serving as a teacher of women factory workers, the Shanghai-based CCP leaders and the Youth League, which was made up of ambitious young radicals loosely affiliated with the CCP, competed to win over the masses and promote their ideas.

Once she began to make some headway in reducing illiteracy and in propagandizing — what she called grassroots work — certain Youth League members tried to ingratiate themselves with her, hoping thereby to coopt credit for her success. It was evident to her that they had learned that the Party organization of the League of Left-Wing Educators was protecting her work, and that they resented that superior connection. One day a Youth League member caught her by surprise, appearing unannounced at her back room in the women's dormitory. He may have tried to rape her, or start a fight, for she spoke of the meeting in evasive terms. What was clear was that he was overbearing in his efforts to win her over personally and politically. She held her ground and let him know that she refused to become involved in "their style of politics . . . words which saved me," she said. Once rid of him, she went ahead with organizing her followers for the annual street demonstration to commemorate the Mukden Incident.

In the city at large, of course, the principal enemy was the KMT, whose security forces wore multiple disguises. Experience made her increasingly wary and clever at evading them. (She spoke here with obvious pleasure at the recollection.) In those days it was quite common for KMT police, who were eager to increase their score of victims, to raid buses at random. When she caught sight of policemen flagging down a bus on which she and fellow workers were traveling, she used one of several tactics to avoid identification and possible arrest: She tried to get off as fast as possible and be out of sight by the time they began their search. Or, if she managed to get off the bus but still could not avoid an encounter, she spoke to them with great courtesy; mollified, they would let her go. But if she was trapped on a bus that was being thoroughly searched and there was no easy exit, she would prepare herself to be tough and defensive. And if she was interrogated by police at a time when she was carrying sensitive political documents, she would behave so obnoxiously that they would be thrown momentarily off balance and allow her to pass.

Despite her example and her explicit teaching, the women in her night school were less clever at disguising their political activities. Through their own carelessness, several fell into the hands of members of the Communist Youth League who abused them verbally and physically. Such affronts to her students she took personally. Perhaps because they were only vaguely literate, they were insensitive to the dangers of having seditious materials in their possession. She remembered vividly one incident. While she was teaching she suddenly noticed that some of the girls had brought political handbills to the class, one that was supposed to be devoted to literacy and general education. Infuriated by their negligence, she dramatized their error by setting the handbills ablaze before their eyes. After all the handbills were reduced to ashes she ordered the girls to go to the kitchen and boil kettles of water. Even the female cook, who scarcely knew what was going on in the house, was drawn into this extracurricular lesson. Working together they scooped up all the charred fragments of the handbills and plunged them into the boiling water, which destroyed the last material traces of their secret political operations in the service of the Party.

Her routine in those days was to teach two classes: one in the morning for the women who had worked the night shift at the factory, and the other in the evening for the day-shift workers. Since she never taught in the afternoon she was free to pursue other activities then. One evening she got home late and worked in her room, correcting her students' homework until four in the morning, when she finally went to bed. The night-shift workers returned just before dawn. As was their custom, they removed their shoes at the door and tiptoed through the house in their stocking feet so as not to disturb their teacher. Since the room she occupied was poorly ventilated, she sometimes left the door open a crack for better air. That morning the sound of their footsteps on the stairs was clumsier than usual, amplified by the noise of objects bumping against walls. Puzzled, she opened her door wider and saw the women passing by in single file. Ordinarily, they carried only small boxes of work materials which they transported routinely to and from the factories. But this time each had her arms around a big bundle that Chiang Ch'ing could not identify. Alarmed, she ordered them to go straight to their rooms for an inspection.

How could she act so peremptorily, she asked herself now, mildly surprised at her own behavior. Because Teacher Li, as they called her, enjoyed such high prestige among the worker students that she exercised her will upon them as she saw fit. They treated her well, she said without embarrassment. And they appreciated her appearing to be less embroiled in the political scene than she in fact was, for they were no more eager for punishment than she was. As for those mysterious bundles, she ordered them all opened up. The women began fumbling around with them, slowly unpeeling the wrappers. Impatient, she pushed them aside and broke them open herself. She discovered that they had taken handbills — printed evidence of their political work — and wrapped them in newspapers, a ploy they thought made the handbills inconspicuous. "What a stupid job!" she shrieked. On the spot she made them take the packages apart, separate out the handbills, which were valuable, and throw out the newspapers, which were bulky and eye-catching. When they transported sensitive materials to and from the factories, they should carry only the smallest parcels, she instructed them sternly. An even better method with the handbills would be to tuck them into an umbrella. That way, should a worker be searched en route, she could immediately discard the handbills and claim in all innocence that she was only carrying an umbrella.

The security of persons involved in the simplest chores of handbill distribution among the working masses was more delicate than she could manage single-handed. Moreover, her own safety was involved. Chiang Ch'ing often reminded her charges that if any one of them sensed that she was being trailed on the return journey to the dormitory, she should not come directly back, but should reroute herself to the home of another woman worker, or slip into a shop so as to throw the enemy off her track. Even with that understanding, the unscheduled absence of any worker always made her uneasy.

One night, when several failed to return from work at the regular time, she could not sleep for fear that they might have run into trouble. Eventually all of them arrived except two, who turned up several hours later. Convinced they were being followed, they had done what she had told them to do: slipped into the homes of some co-workers and then resumed the trip back when the way seemed clear. That episode, and the fact that another Youth League member, presumably jealous of her work as the first one had been, had tracked her down to her residence, demonstrated that the place was no longer safe for her. So she packed up her belongings, borrowed some money, and rented space in another house.

iv

After her move to another neighborhood, she went out to mail a letter one day and on the way came across an old friend from Tsingtao, whose striking appearance and spanking white uniform she vividly described. In the course of their conversation he told her that he was working as a cashier at the Shanghai post office, which was within the International Settlement. But it was also evident that he belonged to some sort of left-wing organization and that working with the post office was just a façade. How glad he was to see her, he remarked over and over again. Would she be interested in his work and give him some cooperation? Would she help him by delivering messages to people in the schools where she taught? Confused and frightened by his advances, she said something to the effect that she had "not yet made contact with the Party organization," hoping that would discourage him. Of course that was a lie, she acknowledged, but one uttered in self-defense.

She reported the encounter to the Party organization of the Educators' League, which then advised her on how to proceed should they meet again. Some days later she took a walk through Tsao-fen Park — one built by foreigners, she commented drily, but she could enter because she had purchased a season ticket. There she ran into her friend a second time. On the instructions of the Party organization of the Educators' League she handed him a letter, though she was uncertain of its contents. They exchanged a few words and she told him that they should not meet again. He seemed to understand the constraint under which she was operating, yet he obviously did not want to lose touch with her. A few days later he sent her a copy of the left-wing publication *World Knowledge*. Once again they met at Tsao-fen Park, and still he pressed her with favors, this time inviting her for a meal. Worried, she declined, saying that she did not have the time. To distract him from her usual route she left the park in another direction, one which bordered upon a residential district. There she ran into a girl friend whom she had first known as a clerk in Tsingtao. The girl invited Chiang Ch'ing to her room to talk. Not daring to delay,

Chiang Ch'ing refused the invitation and sped ahead on foot because there was no bus service to her destination.

As she took leave of the girl the calm of the street was suddenly shattered by men's voices shouting and cursing some distance behind her. She glanced back and saw two men chasing someone in her direction. Another man screamed at them, "You stupid pigs!" A moment later she felt two figures close behind her. Turning to face them, she noticed in a flash that one man was dressed as a worker and the other as a merchant — agents' disguises. They seized her before she could say anything and held her firmly between them. "Kidnapped" for the first time in her life, she was furious! It made no difference to them, she told them angrily, that kidnapping was an outright violation of the foreign law of extraterritoriality which should have rendered Chinese immune to arrest by Chinese officers in that street. Impassive and brusque, they escorted her to a police station. Since there was no matron on duty, they could not search her body as was usual. Without undressing her, all they could find was the copy of *World Knowledge* she was carrying, and that in itself was not incriminating.

Although there was insufficient reason to detain her at the police station, her captors were still determined to get her out of the city (forced exodus from the city was one of the KMT's easier solutions for "troublemakers"). Frightened at the thought of being stranded in unknown territory, she told them that she would never be able to find her way out of the city in the black of night. Nor was she suitably dressed for such a journey, she added. Unmoved by her protests, they sought to speed her departure by taking from their odd supplies a gaudy Chinese gown made of velvet, one that she would never have worn ordinarily. While they looked in another direction, she put it on, but covered it with her own plain, foreign-style dress, over which she wore a wool knit waistcoat. Surreptitiously, from the undergarments she left behind, she slipped her most precious and most incriminating document — the secret application form from the Party organization — which she tucked into the corner of her waistcoat. Thus strangely costumed, she made her departure from the police station and plunged into the night.

Like other terrifying incidents in her life, this nocturnal flight from the city was described by Chiang Ch'ing in terms that were alternately surreal and grotesque. She walked quickly, running whenever she could. As she passed through neighborhoods, undoubtedly cutting a bizarre figure, there were other attempts to waylay her. She escaped. Soon she reached the city limits, with the countryside just ahead. Breathless and weary, she sped down the road. Suddenly rough hands seized her from behind and pinned her down. With all her might she struggled to break away but failed. "I'm being kidnapped!" she screamed over and over again at the top of her lungs. That was in vain, for beyond the city limits there was no one to hear her or come to her rescue. She had assumed that her captors were police, but when she studied them more closely she saw that they too were dressed in the civilian style of secret agents. With no hope of escape, she tried to gain some leverage in the situation by appearing to be outraged. She admonished the men for behaving like brutes toward a woman. Her words had some effect, for one man eased his restraint of her and made some fatuous gestures of chivalry. As they proceeded along the dark road, she took advantage of the slight leeway he offered. Pretending to trip, she tumbled off the roadway, intentionally leaping into a paddy field. Before the men regained control of her, she slipped her secret document, the application form from the Shanghai Party organization, out of the corner of her waistcoat. As fast as possible, she stuffed it into her mouth, chewed it vigorously, and swallowed. The sensation of paper passing into her system was peculiar to say the least. Yet she knew that she had destroyed all visible evidence of that incriminating affiliation.

After pulling her back into the road, the agents escorted her to the district police station, where they locked her behind bars. From her cell she overheard them telephone to report that they had caught a suspect, an achievement which, they felt, justified their requesting the use of a private car with a black license plate, a more prestigious vehicle than an ordinary taxi, which bore a white plate. But all cars were small then, Chiang Ch'ing added parenthetically.

As she sat idle in her cell, it soon dawned on her that she was being detained not for her own sake, but because of a presumed connection with persons regarded as prime public enemies by the KMT. The Nationalist government, she explained, set high prices on the heads of public enemies. An enterprising secret agent could earn a great deal of money as well as prestige by rounding up a suspect whose confessions and associations might ultimately enable him to capture a public enemy and reap the reward.

What fruitful affiliation might they have thought she had? Obviously, it had to be with the most notorious Communist, Wang Ming, chief of the so-called Twenty-eight Bolsheviks, who had returned briefly, in 1930–1931, from training with the Comintern in Moscow to take over the CCP Central Committee. By the mid-1930's (she hastened to point out for present political reasons), Wang Ming was proven a "renegade" from the CCP.* Despite his faults, his followers dominated the Communist apparatus of Shanghai. To save her own skin now, she could not reveal any links to him or to organizations influenced

---

* Throughout his career Wang Ming remained loyal to Stalin, who naturally valued his respect for the Comintern, which was under his aegis in Moscow, and thus favored him over Mao, who insisted upon a more independent Chinese course. Among Wang Ming's policies which most rankled Mao were his "adventurism" and "putschist" methods in the cities, which resulted in the fragmentation of underground Party organizations. Wang Ming, for his part was contemptuous of Mao's methods of guerrilla and mobile warfare and of his establishment of rural base areas far beyond the reach of the cities that were dominated by the KMT.

by him. Least of all could she show herself to have been embroiled in urban insurrection or labor organization — tactics basic to Wang Ming's strategy.

When she was interrogated she tried to cast an illusion of innocence over what, presumably, they had observed: her presence in the park and her rendez-vous with a young man — apparently an informer. (She had evidently been under constant surveillance.) It was her habit to wander in Tsao-fen Park (a common trysting place for leftists who assumed that foreign extraterritoriality protected them from Chinese arrest) only because she loved to watch the children playing there. And now she had to get back to her regular work of schoolteaching. Her story must not have been convincing. Still held under suspicion, she was transferred from the district police station to the municipal police station in the city. Exasperated to be put back behind bars, she laughed to remember how she sneered at her captors, "You ought to spend your time catching real Communists!"

v

Her olive skin glistening from the unremitting heat of the late evening become an early morning, Chiang Ch'ing said, "So I was once kidnapped and detained for eight months by the Kuomintang," a phase of her past she had never before revealed.* Her facial expressions betrayed contradictory emotions: frustration at her senseless confinement and amusement at the human ironies of life in the congested quarters of a women's prison.

Among the inmates — all political offenders rather than criminals — was an experienced Communist who gave her some excellent advice. Sizing up Chiang Ch'ing's appearance, the woman told her that her short hair style made her look like a radical. The woman herself wore long pigtails just to give the appearance of backwardness. She pretended to be an illiterate and was quite good at playing the fool. Chiang Ch'ing thought over what the woman had said and worked at faking an air of unenlightened stupidity. When the other in-mates broke out into revolutionary songs, Chiang Ch'ing stubbornly sang Pe-king opera! (For her, even in those days, that was *really* backward, she ex-claimed with a ripple of laughter.) No matter how obtuse she tried to be, though, the police were unshakable in their determination to investigate her revolutionary connections. Their persistence, she later learned, was triggered by a "woman traitor" among the prisoners, who tipped off the police by telling them that Li Yun-ho (Chiang Ch'ing) was not so naive as she pretended.

Among the political offenders was a woman worker who had been detained

* Possibly because over the years some comrades had been suspected or accused of collaborating with the enemy or becoming its agent as a consequence of incarceration by the KMT.

in that prison for eight months by the time Chiang Ch'ing arrived. Her story, Chiang Ch'ing said, was typical of many good comrades who were duped by Party renegades. In this case the renegade was a prison official dubbed Hei Ta-han (literally, Big Black Chinese, a nickname drawn from bandit argot and applied here to a man whose badness lay in betrayal of the CCP), a man formerly associated with the "erroneous leftist line" of the Wang Ming group. Born in Anhwei province, Hei Ta-han became a Communist and served on the Kiangsu Provincial Committee of the CCP. In the course of political work in Shanghai he was arrested. Within two hours he betrayed the Party by joining the KMT secret police, but he still pretended to be a good Communist. As a secret KMT agent he became involved in a case that made him the model of infamy in leftist circles. There was a certain woman comrade he knew and was determined to destroy. For days he pursued her, finally tracking her down to the French Concession, where she was living in relative political immunity. He won her confidence and told her that her identity had been revealed to the authorities; her life was in grave danger; she should move her household immediately and take all her Party documents with her.

That was a cruel ploy, Chiang Ch'ing reported bitterly, for the woman was a card-carrying comrade who chose to live in the French Concession because she assumed that the law of extraterritoriality would protect her from the Chinese police. No matter. Hei Ta-han persuaded her to leave, and as soon as she reached the border of the Concession the police surrounded her and dragged her screaming to the police station. The official news release on her arrest maintained that she had "voluntarily" displayed her Party documents to her captors, Chiang Ch'ing added sardonically.

After she was thrown into the prison which Hei Ta-han dominated and Chiang Ch'ing shared, he tried to make love to the woman, who knows with what success. Around that time he married another woman, whom he betrayed when he started chasing still another. A renegade and an infidel, he was also a sadist who punished his wife for no reason at all. Once he forced her to lie flat on the ground, set bricks under her ankles, and plopped his huge bulk on her legs. Her knees were fractured, leaving her crippled for life.

The woman comrade whom Hei Ta-han had tricked into arrest was stripped of her Party documents and was thereby stranded from the Party organization, which might have protected her. The police in the prison exerted great pressure upon her to write a confession of her Communist affiliations. She refused, and continued to refuse under torture. The renegade Hei Ta-han eventually stepped in and wrote one for her.

As for Chiang Ch'ing, her greatest difficulty was to maintain some link with the outside world. Her lingering hope was that someone would come forth to speak on behalf of her innocence. How else could she be released? She wrote a letter to the workers' night school where she had been doing some part-time teaching and asked for a character witness. She waited weeks for a reply, but none came. Nor did she receive replies to messages sent to prison inmates. The only result of her attempts to communicate within and beyond the prison walls was to draw attention to herself, for soon the prison officials subjected her to further grueling examinations.

Through a series of connections not clear to her at the time, she learned that the Party organization "had not forgotten her." Acting anonymously, it sent her a quilt, bread, and some money. The police seized the money. The bread passed through the rough hands of prison officials and reached her as a heap of crumbs. Only the quilt arrived intact.

Soon another lot of newly arrested women arrived. As Chiang Ch'ing glanced over them, she was astonished to recognize among them five or six of her former students. Through the prison grapevine she learned that the Party had commissioned two of them to deliver the money, bread, and quilt to her. Their pouting expressions betrayed their resentment of her; they suspected that their handling of her relief packages was the incriminating act that had led to their arrest. Infuriated that these women should be punished unfairly, Chiang Ch'ing demanded the right to speak to the prison administrators. Flanked by guards who led her to the main office, Chiang Ch'ing stood before the administrators and denounced them loudly: "You failed to catch real comrades! Nor do you know how to catch real women! You've only nabbed a few girls who were kind enough to send me a blanket.. Why don't you shoot me?" Swelling with rage, Hei Ta-han struck Chiang Ch'ing across the face. She was stunned and barely able to keep on her feet. He swore at her in foul language. She shot back, "How dare you curse me!"

Overhearing that exchange, her former students became extremely upset, Chiang Ch'ing recalled. To assure her that they were *not* resentlful of her they denied up and down that she had anything to do with their arrest, and guessed they had been picked up because they had participated in political demonstrations. While they were trying to calm each other down, Chiang Ch'ing's attention was diverted to the narrow window through which a funeral procession was coming into view. Suddenly it was apparent that they were observing the funeral of a Communist woman worker murdered in the course of her political activities. Hei Ta-han also noticed the procession and his eye flickered cruelly for a moment. Then his facial expression changed to one of great, though insincere, magnanimity. Pompously, he announced to his fellow agents, attendant police, and prisoners that he did not intend to take advantage of the Communists' funeral procession by making still another series of arrests. He explained in a voice devoid of irony that the jail was too full of women prisoners now to absorb any more.

Reinstalled in her cell, Chiang Ch'ing began to coach some of the other women prisoners on how to respond to interrogation. Whenever possible they should say something innocuous like, "Oh, we were just watching the processions!" But they were hopelessly clumsy. One who was arrested for carrying handbills was among those illiterates who were oblivious to the libelous nature of their materials. In Chiang Ch'ing's notably detached recollection, the other prisoners were overly emotional. After she had been there a while, she noticed that if one woman wept, the whole group broke into a chorus of tears. To test this, Chiang Ch'ing told one of her former students — one who still looked up to her as her teacher — to start crying. Obediently, the woman did, and the whole jail burst into tears. The mass wailing was extremely vexing to the prison guards, who invariably were men and were usually younger and less callous than the prison authorities. One of the most unstable guards always carried a whip and threatened to lash out at anyone who cried. Just hearing that threat frightened a few women to tears. Soon everyone was sobbing, even some of the guards.

When the new detainees came up for examination, each was interrogated separately. That experience was as agonizing for those waiting as for those under question. Eventually, most of the women detained more recently than Chiang Ch'ing were released. But why not Chiang Ch'ing? Because, she explained, there was no one to stand witness on behalf of her "political innocence." Before one of her students was scheduled for release, she motioned her aside and told her to report to the Party organization that she had no one to defend her and that without absolving testimony she would never be freed. She also advised the girl to assure the Party organization that her *true* identity was still undiscovered by the prison personnel.

If the girl carried out her instructions, nothing came of them. As a last resort Chiang Ch'ing decided to use foreign connections because she knew that prison officials were frightened to receive foreigners on their premises. She told another former student who was about to be released to arrange for a foreigner from the YWCA to come and guarantee her. That worked. A foreigner arrived, testified to her innocence, and she was released.

After leaving jail Chiang Ch'ing did not return to her former residence for fear of implicating the others. Instead, she moved in with a friend. Early February 1935 was the time of the lunar New Year celebration, and her own life began a new cycle.

4.

◇ ◇ ◇

Left Wing to Stage Center

> Whether men or women, they can become neither
> sagelike in virtue and wisdom nor utterly wicked and
> evil. Their uncommon intelligence and vitality place
> them above ten thousands of men, but their eccentric
> heretical unconventionality places them below these
> ten thousands. If born to high rank and wealth, they
> become romantics obsessed with love, and if born to
> bookish families of modest means, they become her-
> mits and proud scholars. Even if born to poverty and
> lowliness, they would rather achieve distinction as
> actors and courtesans than submit to the fate of being
> menials and servants, to be ordered about by the
> vulgar.
> — Ts'ao Hsueh-ch'in, *Dream of the Red Chamber*

Shanghai of the 1930's became a glittering but ominous legend by
midcentury. The city was more cosmopolitan than any since the flourishing of
Ch'ang-an, capital of the T'ang dynasty. In the eighth and ninth centuries
tradesmen and missionaries, Buddhists in the main, streamed in from Central
and South Asia, rapidly diversifying the life of the Middle Kingdom. A millennium later, when Chinese imperialism was waning, the port of Shanghai was
drawn into the Unequal Treaty system, by which European and American
merchants and Christian missionaries, moving on separate tracks, sought respectively to profit from China materially and to save it spiritually. Commercial
expansion inspired new social and intellectual differentiations. The most westernized of all Chinese cities, Shanghai became the center of modern education, publishing, and journalism, and of vigorous experimentation in the performing arts.

Chiang Ch'ing's recollections of her Shanghai days reveal in subtle ways the
contrasts between foreigners and Chinese, rich and poor, reactionaries and rad-

icals, capitulationists and patriots — the extremes of institutionalized inequalities of wealth and power. For underdogs like her life could be agonizing.

In the early 1930's the foreign population of Shanghai was about fifty thousand out of a total of some three million. Chiang Ch'ing seemed only peripherally aware of the foreigners as persons. In her recollections none is counted among her acquaintances or friends, or enemies for that matter. Still, in the larger urban panorama, they were powerfully immanent, segregated by their own preference — and to their advantage — in the International Settlement and the French Concession, where they lived in foreign-style mansions surrounded by idyllic parks and racecourses. They entertained themselves with their own orchestras, ballet companies, and movie houses, and their bookstores purveyed books and periodicals filled with news of other worlds. To the young Chinese striving to educate themselves out of ancient ways, the foreigners' lavish cultural trappings were alluring intellectually, but could also be politically dangerous or demeaning.

Foreign commercialism in Shanghai brought to life a new class of Chinese capitalists, men of ambition who learned to play national and world markets while serving as the financial underpinning of the KMT regime. If the foreigners were living in Shangri-la, this new semi-independent business class was living on borrowed time, for the Communism that was just over the horizon would not tolerate free enterprise or its cultural commodities.

Yet in the 1930's Hollywood found a profitable market in the business class and in its sons and daughters who were moving into a revolution of rising expectations. Celluloid images of glamorous men and women in other societies stimulated a demand for obvious symbols of urbanity — the cocktail bar, Parisian fashions, international cuisine, ballrooms, taxi and "social" dancing, crooners like Bing Crosby, whose popular songs were dubbed "yellow music" by China's cultural puritans, and, inevitably, street after street of brothels that included such exotics as White Russian women and a fair share of massage parlors. The material pleasures, exotic entertainments, and social advantages afforded to the urban nouveaux riches dulled the edge of their political conscience. Their neglect of the have-nots, who vastly outnumbered them, and their willingness to profit from foreign investors scheming for the political dominance of China, made them easy targets of the politically conscious left. Concern for the helpless masses so lacking in direction, and determination to fight for national integrity, were shared by the adversaries of the Kuomintang. But the most radical writers, teachers, demonstrators, and actors gave high priority to investing China's greatest natural resource, the impoverished masses, with a proletarian class consciousness which they expected to serve as the cutting edge of revolutionary transformation.

For all the revolutionary rhetoric, these new voices from the left were acting within two central historical traditions. The first was the duty of the scholar-gentleman, a position articulated by the neo-Confucian school, which flourished in the Ming and Manchu dynasties (1368–1911), to forgo cynical denial of a troubled world or Taoist retreat from it. Rather, the privileged should devote themselves to the welfare of the whole. In the 1930's a comparable sense of public responsibility was shown by politically conscious writers, artists, teachers, and actors who were determined to "awaken the masses," as they put it in their jargon, and to promote their interests against those of a selfish and self-serving oligarchy. In their ardent rhetoric against foreign threat, the leftists of the 1930's were following a second historical precedent: rebellion against foreign rule. The barbarian Mongols were overthrown by the founders of the Ming dynasty, which restored native rule. When the Ming's power of self-defense declined after three centuries, China fell to the Manchus in 1644. Then, after 267 years, the Manchus in their turn were overthrown — by forces allied with Sun Yat-sen. And now, in the 1930's, the succeeding generation of young nationalists would resist the Japanese.

New to the twentieth century was a proliferation of means of communication. The force of polemic written literature of all political stripes tion was intensified by broader literacy and more numerous and widely distributed publications. Radical voices were further amplified by politicized theater and film. Innovation in the theater began during the last Manchu decade and accelerated under the Republic. The dominant mode of traditional Chinese theater has been loosely translated as "opera." Though subject to local variation and continual evolution within each separate school, the Chinese opera generally featured simplicity of plot, absolute stylization of character, formal pantomime, spectacular acrobatics, shrill song, and weak orchestration. Except in certain local and modern variants, all the roles were played by men. When the Chinese looked abroad for new ideas, they bypassed our nominal counterpart, the grand opera, because they recognized that its musical and vocal complexity and inflated style were bound to fail in cultural translation. Instead, they were drawn to our spoken drama, in which the words alone carried the meaning and which offered fascinating new plots, new characters, and new philosophical concepts.

Chinese tastes in foreign theater evolved briskly, but were arrested too soon by the triumph of the Communist regime. In 1907 a group of Chinese students in Tokyo formed the Spring Willow Society. Their maiden performance (with an all-male cast) was a Chinese version of *La Dame aux camélias* (Dumas fils's novel was already a *succès fou* in Chinese translation).[1] Western drama caught on quickly with the young, who were eager to act in new roles. The decade of the 1920's in China, the only period that was consciously "modern" without later cultural or political regrets, was marked by vast translation projects. Ibsen,

Strindberg, Eugene O'Neill, G. B. Shaw, and Oscar Wilde headed the list. Concurrently, imitative and innovative Chinese playwrights fashioned their own spoken dramas, using both historical and contemporary themes. By the mid-1920's, Hung Shen, Ts'ao Yü, Ou-yang Yü-ch'ien, and T'ien Han had achieved national renown. Their works would entertain four decades of progressives, until the strict proletarian ethos of the Cultural Revolution put an end to them.

As an actress in her teens, Chiang Ch'ing cut her teeth on this modern repertory, as well as on the traditional one. Then the chance that China might succumb completely to Japan's expansive imperialism forced the avant-garde writers to reconsider the "art for art's sake" doctrine, which had reigned in the less troubled 1920's. The aesthetic dalliance with foreign ways so coveted by that first culturally liberated generation was abruptly ended in the early 1930's. New voices on the left, more certain of their goals than the means of achieving them, struggled to write in a plain popular style that could arouse the masses to "save the nation."

In a society given to association and organization at every level of governance, the formation of "left leagues" was a natural political consequence. On the surface these were professional organizations of writers, dramatists, teachers, journalists, critics, and so forth, and they were known to attract generally young men and women of the left, though not necessarily members of the Communist Party. Like other young radicals, Chiang Ch'ing desperately needed to belong to groups just to survive. She was first swept up in this rapidly shifting complex of left leagues in Tsingtao in 1931 when she joined the League of Left-Wing Dramatists, which was formed that year from the merger of scores of small theater groups. The main ones were the Shanghai Art Theater, founded the year before, when it produced Romain Rolland's *The Game of Love and Death* and a stage version of Erich Maria Remarque's *All Quiet on the Western Front,* and the South China Drama Society, established by the mercurial playwright T'ien Han. From the beginning the League of Left-Wing Dramatists possessed a contemporary and international character. Like the Theater Guild, the Laboratory Theater, the Federal Theater, and the Theater Collective in the United States in the 1930's, it promoted the theater as a vehicle for political messages.

Spurred by the urgency of wartime conditions, the new theater branched out in various directions. Street theater and its rural analogue, such as Chiang Ch'ing took part in when she was a member of the Seaside Drama Society in Shantung, became routinized, eventually to be adopted by the Communists on a mass scale. More formal proletarian dramas in the style of Gerhart Hauptmann and Bertolt Brecht were produced in the cities by amateur and low-budget repertory groups. She also took part in those and eventually acted in the professional theater, which was pitched toward the intellectuals and the cultural consumers of a burgeoning capitalist class. On this commercial stage the "great bourgeois dramas" of Gogol, Ostrovsky, Strindberg, and Ibsen posed questions about the human condition, fomenting a libertarian cultural revolution which would be scotched by Chiang Ch'ing in the 1960's.

In China of the early twentieth century, actresses were still an anomaly, particularly in the professional theater; they fared better in the amateur theater which was less commercial. Traditional opera was for the most part monopolized by actors, some of whom specialized in female roles. They achieved realism by hobbling around on tiny stilts, which signified the symbol of feminine beauty — bound feet. But the dominance of actors was not universal throughout China. In Canton, from earliest times, both men and women appeared on the operatic stage, and in Chekiang province the opera was actually monopolized by women, who also took men's roles. A Chekiang native, the writer Lu Hsun, used to remark on how fond men were of the all-girl shows.

Whatever the position of actresses vis-à-vis actors, both were looked down on socially. Even in cosmopolitan Shanghai of the 1930's they were lumped together with butchers, criminals, vagrants, and prostitutes, though the best of them circulated with the new and rising commercial class. Throughout our interviews Chiang Ch'ing was on the defensive about her social position in those days, though her anxieties were expressed mainly in political terms.

In the early 1920's the noted playwright and director Hung Shen, once a Harvard student, was the first to insist upon the use of actresses on the modern stage.[2] The trend toward using actresses in amateur and experimental theater picked up under T'ien Han's tutelage. His influential South China Drama Society founded in Shanghai in the middle 1920's was the forerunner of both the Shantung Experimental Art Theater of Tsinan, where Chiang Ch'ing first matriculated in 1929, and of the League of Left-Wing Dramatists. Both were among the first drama groups to make the use of actresses artistically acceptable, though public opinion was slower to come around. A sad irony of Chiang Ch'ing's story was that she never managed to reconcile her personal distaste for T'ien Han (on his part, he disliked her as much as she did him) with his professional accomplishments: he began the "small stage movement" designed for amateurs, and the modern drama repertory, which first won her public attention.

i

"In the 1930's Shanghai was rife with artists' associations," Chiang Ch'ing declared of the left leagues, whose functions included protection of modern artists from the KMT's crude censorship of unorthodox books, their destruction of avant-garde art, suppression of innovative films, and curtailment of liberal education. Each league had its own "political coloring," which was as much an expression of the personalities of the leaders as of the ideology espoused. By the mid-1930's there were the leagues of Left-Wing Writers, Educators, Dramatists, among others, as well as the Socialist League. Eventually all were linked to the Left-Wing Cultural Federation, which was headed by the playwright Yang Han-sheng, a man she first met in late 1933 when he was among the leaders of the League of Left-Wing Dramatists. Although these various leagues were organizationally separate, the network of personal ties among members, whose ranks included members of the Communist Youth League, was intricate and confusing to outsiders.

Upon release from prison around the time of the lunar New Year in 1935, she quickly resumed her acting career. For the first time she began to enjoy true acclaim, she said. Several left-wing groups began sending emissaries through the underground to make contact with her and to establish ties. Although she was not then a full-fledged Shanghai Party member in the card-carrying sense, the fact that the left leagues sought her out demonstrated their recognition of her as a person of "revolutionary character." They had become aware of her, she stressed with the fervor of one striving to dissolve contrary belief. Now they vied with one another to win her talent over to their side. They must have recognized that no matter how innocuous the plays, films, and other activities she had been engaged in may have seemed on the surface, in essence they were revolutionary.

In the early months of 1935 she was still suffering from the effects of her long sojourn in jail, where lack of food and medical attention had left her physically weakened. During confinement her menstrual periods had ceased and had not resumed, and in the afternoons she suffered from chills and fever. Those medical facts were transmitted to the Shanghai Party organization, which offered to send her to a resort area in Chekiang province to convalesce in a gentler climate. She refused, though, because she wanted above all to regain touch with the cultural life of Shanghai. Still, it was several months before she could work at a normal pace.

During the New Year celebrations the Stage Association, then under the direction of T'ien Han, gave her a free ticket to their production of his play *Song of Return to Spring* — their gesture of congratulations for getting out of jail. She was delighted to go but had nothing warm to wear — all her winter clothes had disappeared while she was in prison. She was cold most of the time, she said, and attributed that to being physically run-down as well as to lack of clothing. She solved the dilemma by borrowing an overcoat from a friend, and with ticket in hand made her way to the Golden City Theater. She chose an expensive balcony seat from which she could enjoy the full sweep of the performance.

Several days later, during the New Year celebrations, she went to see another play. Her anecdote about it had nothing to do with the performance but was told for the purpose of revealing that certain key Communist leaders had no idea that she too was a Communist. As she sat waiting for the curtain to go up, she idly watched people pass in front of her. Her eye was suddenly attracted by a familiar face, a woman strikingly attired in handsome shoes, a black fur coat, and eyeglasses. Known then as Ch'ing-shu,* she was the wife of a "well-known person" and, it was said, had just returned from the Hung Lake soviet. She apparently did not notice that Chiang Ch'ing was in the theater that evening. A few months later she learned that Chiang Ch'ing belonged to the League of Left-Wing Dramatists, but she was still unaware that Chiang Ch'ing was also a Communist (as self-perceived and originally validated in Tsingtao).

Later that spring she returned by train to Peking and for several weeks floundered about unprotected by Party organizations. She resumed auditing Li Ta's lectures at Peking University and passed long hours reading in the Peking Municipal Library. During that Peking interlude she learned that T'ien Han and some other prominent leftists had been arrested in February for their presumed Communism.[3] She remembered how afraid she was that their arrest would adversely affect her own political career, for they had dominated the League of Left-Wing Dramatists, her sponsoring organization.

At that time the Nationalist government was so anti-Communist that just attending Soviet films was dangerous (Chiang Ch'ing laughed incredulously at the recollection). Once, when she went to see a Soviet film in Peking, she had to slip out a side door right after the show was over to avoid scrutiny by the government officers stationed at the main entrance. As she reached the street, she ran into T'ien Hung (Bad Man), the younger brother of T'ien Han, who had pursued her the year before. She carefully reported to the Party organization of the Educators' League that she had seen him (and others) there.

Suddenly she received a message from the Educators' League which asked her to return to Shanghai and promised that she could have the part of Nora in *A Doll's House*. That excited her, for Nora was a role she adored. When she arrived in Shanghai her sponsors in the League invited her to join a distinguished group of actors who specialized in modern drama. In subsequent weeks they produced several plays by Ibsen, Ostrovsky's *The Tempest*, and Gogol's *The Inspector General*, in which she played the heroine. She also performed in a stage version of Dickens' *A Tale of Two Cities*. The original novel, which she

---

* Perhaps an approximation of the woman's given name. Chiang Ch'ing may have meant Meng Ch'ing-shu, the wife of Ch'en Shao-yü, alias Wang Ming. Since he eventually became a political enemy of Chiang Ch'ing's, she may have wanted to avoid explicit reference to the wife.

knew in translation, was better than the play, she admitted. Although the views expressed in the novel were "reactionary," she considered the book valuable as a source of historical knowledge.

As for her portrayal of Nora,* the newspapers and journals gave her rave reviews, but she wondered whether her acquaintance with some of the important people in the Shanghai cultural world had not influenced the critics. Only Chang Keng, who had been her director two years before in the Shanghai Work Study Troupe and who was now a prominent figure in the Shanghai branch of the Party organization, adversely criticized her acting style — he called it "too naturalistic." [4] A rigidly conventional man, he would never have been able to appreciate *her* conception of Nora's personality, for she had chosen to represent Nora as a woman *rebel*. In so doing, she went beyond Ibsen's original conception of the character, and in her judgment improved upon it. The audience clapped thunderously in response to her characterization. (She added matter-of-factly that in those days it was rare for an audience to applaud any performer. It is now imperative in revolutionary opera.)

As a work of art, *A Doll's House* lacks a satisfactory resolution, she continued. Lu Hsun once gave a speech which became an article titled, "What Will Nora Do After She Leaves?" [5] Lu Hsun was one of many who speculated on how Nora could manage to survive after she left home. Would she just become some sort of "public exhibit"? Could she ever find a job? Lu Hsun explored these and other questions relating to the emancipation of women.

ii

Performing the great modern dramas on the Shanghai stage won Chiang Ch'ing new prominence. For the first time in her life she began associating with famous actors and actresses, and the name of Li Yun-ho (her stage name at that time) became widely known. Although performing for demanding and responsive audiences afforded her great pleasure, the material conditions of actors' lives in general were abysmal. Rampant inflation caused a sharp rise in all production costs. In contrast to the simple management of the low-cost proletarian theater, which was once her specialty, this commercial world suffered from greedy theater owners who charged exorbitant rents. For example, if a performance earned five hundred yuan, half that amount had to be paid to the theater owner just for the privilege of using his facilities.

While financial burdens were shared more or less equally by the performers, her own sufferings were compounded by her sensing that other members of the troupe looked down upon her. Why should they scorn her? Probably because,

* See the first picture section.

as fairly a-political members of a cultural elite, they suspected that her leftist activities might make them guilty by association. And they surely recognized, she added in candor, that her acting skill fell short of extraordinary. Their visible contempt so upset her that she could never relax in their presence or even sleep at night. How she remembered the anguish of tossing for hours on her bed! To win the admiration of her peers, at least professionally, she channeled the overflow of nervous energy into bouts of private rehearsal. When insomnia possessed her she got up and recited scripts deep into the night. Even now she heard faint echoes of those years — the low purr and staccato rhythm of the tailor at his sewing machine in the room on the floor below. Thus through her own efforts more than formal coaching she developed the special skills demanded for modern drama. Most important was the development of a voice to represent normal conversation from the stage, for such vocal control was far more subtle than the shrill song of the old opera or the stridency of impromptu propaganda plays. As her reputation in theatrical circles mounted, people who used to despise her began currying her favor. She smiled with ironic detachment as she remembered this.

After completing their European repertory, this distinguished amateur group with which she was now associated presented a series of "famous democratic nationalist plays" — all of them Chinese and all written on contemporary themes. During the run of this second series a splinter group organized the Nineteen Forties Society. Why did they call themselves that in the 1930's? Because they fancied themselves in the avant-garde, a decade ahead of their time! One of the first plays they put on (in November 1936, at the famous Golden City Theater) was Hsia Yen's *Sai Chin-hua.* The title was the name of the notorious beauty of the Boxer era who became the mistress of a German general. Chiang Ch'ing was furious at seeing a Chinese actress portray the despicable Sai, a woman who, in her opinion, had prostituted the cause of Chinese nationalism. Her outspoken opinion of Sai so enraged the other members of the Nineteen Forties Society that they actually threatened to *kill* her, she declared, her voice shrill with emotion.[6]

Even though the director Chang Keng had criticized her acting, Chiang Ch'ing continued, he was attracted to her, and his pursuit of her damaged her politically. By 1935 he and one Hsu Mao-yung had risen to prominence in the Communist Party leadership in Shanghai. Chang Keng, in fact, was the director of the municipal Party organization. In the absence of rivals he came to regard Shanghai as his personal territory. Admittedly, she said, her memory of Chang Keng was bitter because she had experienced his incorrigible male supremacism. As she became better known as an actress and was seen with him, he bragged around Party circles that she "belonged" to him. "She's my girl, so don't touch," he would say. (Here she gave a groan of contempt and said how much she loathed him.) Yet she managed to keep him at bay. She would never consent to his taking her home in the evening after any of the political meetings they attended, no matter how often he begged for the privilege. Once he had the audacity to propose marriage to her. She refused him flatly. Obviously he lost face. In retaliation he forbade the League of Left-Wing Dramatists, over which he had jurisdiction in his capacity as director of the Shanghai Party organization, to have further contact with her. To make matters worse he spread the false rumor that she was a Trotskyite.

Chang Keng's vengeful behavior took its toll on her own political work. For example, early in March 1935 (could she have meant 1936?) she organized an amateur production in the theater of a hotel, to celebrate International Women's Day, which falls on March 8. She had instructed the other participants to meet on the seventh at the hotel for last-minute preparations and a rehearsal. She arrived according to schedule, but no one else appeared. They had left her in the lurch (had Chang Keng canceled the arrangements out of pique?), and she was desperate because by then almost all the tickets had been sold, most of them to workers whom she could not disappoint. Her faithful friend T'ao Hsing-chih had bought a few.

After a frantic search, the group of actors was pulled together and the show was put under quick rehearsal. That day she was suffering from a high fever, but there was nothing to do but ignore it. While singing a duet she suddenly realized that the stage properties had not yet been delivered. As soon as the rehearsal was over, she set out in a feverish delirium to buy some substitutes, but as she left the theater she slipped and fell downstairs. She was not hurt, fortunately, but while she was pulling herself together someone came up to her and announced that it was impossible for the show to be given in the theater of that hotel. She was panic-stricken! At the last moment the situation was saved by the intervention of the niece of Huang Shao-hsiung, a senior official of the ruling Kuomintang, who offered to sign a document which would allow them to give the show. Once the arrangements were completed Chiang Ch'ing went backstage to lodge a protest against the malicious boycott of the performance she had arranged.

Thrown into an emotional crisis by all the problems of production, she burst into tears during the performance and sobbed so uncontrollably that she could not remember her lines, nor could she hear the prompter. But that unscheduled passage in the play must have been moving (she recalled it with wonder even now) because the audience wept right along with her. Frantic to restore order, one of the other actors pretended to be drunk and struck her across the back just to bring her to her senses. That did the trick and the show continued more sedately. By the end of the play she was so weak that she could scarcely move, and her temperature had risen to over 104 degrees. As it developed, the low-grade infection she had been harboring turned into pneumonia. Friends immediately took her to a hospital, where she recuperated for several days.

iii

The year 1935 was pivotal for China and the rest of the world. The menace of Hitler and Mussolini could no longer be ignored. And in East Asia, aggressive Japanese militarists were planning an invasion of China from their base in Manchuria. The Communist world, which was then centered in Moscow, reacted by convening the Seventh Comintern Congress. Moscow's order to China was simple: set aside all political differences to resist the international fascist tide. But the execution of the order was unimaginably difficult. China was suffering both from a profound and long-standing inertia and from civil strife, generated by the warlords and by the conflicts between the KMT and the Communists. Moscow addressed the comrades in the cities, where the nationalist and revolutionary ground swell was most in evidence. Still in the shadow, Mao Tse-tung and the Red Army were making the Long March from Juichin in the Southeast to Yenan in the Northwest. Who realized at the time that their experiment in rural revolution, despite Moscow's neglect, would become the most successful in the history of the world?

Chiang Ch'ing's reflections on 1935 were still of the urban revolutionary scene. The political climate of the first half of the year she described as being in a state of "disequilibrium." Policy directives from Moscow induced organizational changes that shattered discipline among the ranks of self-proclaimed leftists. Although the League of Left-Wing Dramatists was still intact when she returned to Shanghai in 1935, its membership had changed considerably over the past four years. In late July the new leaders of the Dramatists' League called a meeting for the first of August. Chiang Ch'ing attended. At the open session the leaders presented the August First Manifesto, which had been drafted in Moscow by Wang Ming (then embroiled in the Seventh Comintern Congress). The manifesto called for the abolition of the Revolutionary League, and in its stead the establishment of the Association of Various Circles for National Salvation. The overall purpose was to call on all leagues and parties to set aside sectarian goals and make National Salvation the common focal point of the worldwide struggle against fascism.[7]

The manifesto was not only a major turning point in Chinese Communism, but also one that would have a profoundly divisive effect upon the literary world. The promulgation of a united front policy meant that the Communist Party organization in Shanghai could exert even less control than before over its subsidiary organizations. As for Chiang Ch'ing, through Chang Keng's vengeful actions in the autumn of 1935 she was cut off once more from the Party organization, though she managed to sustain ties with other leftist groups. Among these were the Film Association for National Salvation, in which she was prominent, she said; the Women's Association for National Salvation; [8] and the League of Friends of the Soviet Union. They were but a few of the many new associations designed to implement a united front among previously contending parties, leagues, and other political groups. But their names were deceptive, she cautioned. Although nominally left-wing, the leaders of most of them were "traitors, renegades, or special agents" (hyperbolic, surely, but to what extent is indeterminable). She knew of some members of the Revolutionary League, which was supposed to be pro-Communist, who were actually anti-Communist. Soon, though, the Revolutionary League was dissolved by the League of Left-Wing Dramatists, which was acting on the authority of the August First Manifesto drafted in Moscow.

Although the Association of Various Circles for National Salvation was called into existence in August 1935, it was slow to coalesce; in Chiang Ch'ing's recollection, it was not fully organized until after she left Shanghai for Yenan two years later. What actually happened was that the left leagues survived more or less over the next couple of years, though the leaders became increasingly conservative and the members continued to be made up of revolutionary young people very like herself.

How could "genuinely" revolutionary young people prove their merit? One way, she explained, was to claim previous Party affiliation, but in the White Areas the reliability of such a claim was complicated by the problems of sustaining membership once acquired (as exemplified in her own case) and by false claims of others to membership. In those days one had to operate from the assumption that an individual's claim to Party affiliation might be false (in Yenan hers was suspected). Indeed, many of the leftist organizations of the early and middle 1930's boasted a Party affiliation they did not in fact have. Still, some genuinely left-wing young people were attached to those nominally left-wing organizations. Judgments of a person's revolutionary character must always be made with the utmost discrimination, she cautioned. For example, the Party theoretician Ai Szu-ch'i was a truly good comrade, though some others have judged him to the contrary. So also was Lin Chi-lu, who was falsely criticized. Lin, who became a classmate of hers at the Party School in Yenan, later worked in Sinkiang, where he was "martyred" at the same time as the Chairman's youngest brother, Mao Tse-min.

Some members of the "false" left leagues made a specialty of assassinating the character of any talented person they saw as a rival. The writer Lu Hsun, himself an idiosyncratic leftist, was a major target, though the same campaigns were extended to others, herself included. Gossips and journalists vilified her with all sorts of vulgar names and political slander. (She spoke angrily here, but did not give details.) She was able to endure only because she was confident that the masses, if not the people who pretended to speak for them, stood behind her. The masses sensed that even when she performed in bourgeois dramas or was otherwise visibly active in the "upper strata" of culture, she was concurrently engaged in genuinely revolutionary work.

Among others prominent in the "upper strata of culture" were the so-called Seven Gentlemen (Shen Chün-ju, Chang Nai-ch'i, Tsou T'ao-fen, Li Kung-p'u, Sha Ch'ien-li, Wang Tsao-shih, and Shih Liang, a woman),[9] a coalition of journalists and other professionals leading the National Salvation movement. They were somewhat older than the "revolutionary young people" with whom she associated, she said. Simply because they were known to be members of the Executive Committee of the All-China Federation of National Salvation Associations, the KMT attacked them for their leftist and "Communistic" activities, though not one was a Communist. They were arrested in November 1936, just one month before Chiang Kai-shek was detained in Sian [10] and was forced to adopt the aggressive National Defense policy that the Seven Gentlemen had demanded earlier. Even so, the Seven Gentlemen were not released from their Soochow prison until the Sino-Japanese War broke out in July 1937, which was when Chiang Ch'ing left Shanghai for Yenan. She was not, of course, as famous as the Seven Gentlemen, but (she spoke defensively here) she too was recognized "by all the revolutionary workers," even though she could not manage to know all of them. Among the non-Communist leftists, the Seven Gentlemen were the most notable, yet there were others, actually younger, who eventually migrated from Shanghai to Yenan. There, on their own word alone, they claimed (falsely) to represent the Party organization of the White Areas.

A judgment of her own case, to be made in Yenan, was not simple because the multifaced nature of her work was misleading to outsiders. Persecution (by the Party hierarchy, presumably) of her as an individual, combined with an increasing alienation between the leftist leadership and the masses they purported to guide in Shanghai, had a "stratifying" effect upon her activities there after 1935. Being a teacher and a member of "genuine" left leagues during her first two years meant that she was, in the contemporary jargon, "doing mass work at the grassroots level." But after the program of forging a united front got under way, the Party organization in the Dramatists' League became her major protector, taking over from its counterpart in the Educators' League. Correspondingly, her professional status changed. The Dramatists' League, which had wide associations in the performing arts world, now took the initiative in reassigning her to the "upper strata" — among truly distinguished actors, playwrights, critics, and writers who were relatively unconstrained by left leagues and other antigovernment organizations. That promotion from the proletariat (or from the intellectuals who worked for it) to the world of sophisticated urban entertainment made her vulnerable to new personal and professional demands. Film impresarios started plying her with contracts. She spoke with anxiety here and returned only later to a discussion of her life as a film actress.

By late 1935 the Communist community in Shanghai was rent by rivalries and defections. It was thus dangerously isolated from the main force of the Communist movement, by then in the throes of establishing itself in the Northwest. The Central Committee, led by Mao Tse-tung, had arrived there in October 1935, after a year on the Long March. What, she asked rhetorically, could those leaders of rural revolution have known of the true nature of most of the left-wing organizations in Shanghai of the 1930's? After she arrived in Yenan she would discover that they were totally ignorant of the reactionary politics practiced by most of these self-styled left leagues. The realities of the Shanghai situation were not revealed to them until the eve of the Cultural Revolution, when she finally arranged for the truth to come out. (How could the senior leaders have been kept in the dark so long?)

iv

Standing head and shoulders above all groups of young and not-so-young leftists and civil rights leaders of the 1930's was one man, Lu Hsun. In Chiang Ch'ing's reflections of the modern era Lu Hsun was as much her cultural hero as Mao Tse-tung was her political hero, though the lines between cultural and political issues are always blurred in Chinese Communist eyes. She plainly admired these two above all others, and quoted them more frequently. For the ideological goals she set forth during the Cultural Revolution and continued to support through the mid-1970's, during our interviews she presented through a judicious choice of examples — many far-fetched — a surprising sense of the two men's mutual awareness and deep respect.

Chiang Ch'ing launched into a meandering discourse on Lu Hsun about midnight one evening. Although the members of her entourage periodically wilted and revived themselves with hot tea and alternating compresses of cold and hot, then damp and dry, towels, Chiang Ch'ing's energies were unflagging. The sweltering heat intensified by the bright artificial lighting caused beads of perspiration to sparkle on her forehead. Without breaking her monologue, she occasionally slipped her hand into her white plastic pocketbook, withdrew a green and white plastic comb, and streaked it over the top of her short-cropped hair to smooth the crown.

Of Lu Hsun's background she said that even as a youth he was "opposed to

Confucianism." During the years before the May Fourth Movement of 1919, part of which he spent studying in Japan, he became a "radical bourgeois democrat." In the mid-1920's political persecution by the northern warlord government drove him from his teaching post at the Peking Women's Normal School, where he had become embroiled in a controversy over the appointment of a reactionary woman president (Yang Yin-yu). In 1926 he accepted a teaching post at Amoy University in the South; the next year he moved to nearby Canton, where he became chairman of the Department of Literature at Sun Yat-sen University. He arrived in Shanghai in 1927, a pivotal point in the nation's political history. There he began to call himself a "tide watcher," and for the next three years he watched people. Then he stopped merely observing people and seized the pen as a weapon. [11]

Lu Hsun was still in Shanghai when she arrived there in 1933. White Terror was rampant. Underground units of the Party organization were frequently invaded, and sometimes several units were struck on the same day. Although Lu Hsun was never a member of the Party, he tried to protect those of his friends who were. To illustrate: General Ch'en Keng of the Red Army was injured during the encirclement campaigns in the Central Soviet Districts, and went to Shanghai for treatment in 1933. When Lu Hsun learned of his arrival he invited him to his home and got to know him. [12] Ch'en Keng and another Red Army commander, Hsieh Fu-chih, lived for some time under the protection of Lu Hsun's home. The writer and former Party leader Ch'ü Ch'iu-pai [13] was also an intimate of Lu Hsun's. But that was before he turned "renegade," she added sharply.

Even in her youth, when Lu Hsun's oddly delivered meanings were too subtle for her to grasp, she still revered him. She regularly read his informal essays called "Random Talk" and other pieces he wrote for the literary supplement of the Shanghai newspaper *Shen pao*. Knowing just what pieces were his was tricky because he kept signing himself under different pen names just to confuse the political authorities, who were determined to silence him. Eventually, she learned to identify his pieces by his style.

Was Lu Hsun aware of her person, I asked her? When she was living in Shanghai someone once told her that Lu Hsun had watched her perform on the stage, she replied with a faint blush. She was *told* that, she emphasized. She did not know it as a fact.

In the mid-1930's she was only a minor person who did not appreciate Lu Hsun fully. But she learned later that Chairman Mao had long since been aware of Lu Hsun's brilliance as a social observer and writer. When the Chairman was in the Northwest he devoured whatever articles by Lu Hsun he could get his hands on. Wherever he went, he was always on the lookout for more of Lu Hsun's works. After reading Lu Hsun's essay called "My Open Letter," the

Chairman discussed it with Chou En-lai and declared, "This person has real integrity!"

After she became the Chairman's wife (her usual way of referring to that quantum jump in status), she learned to her surprise that participants on the Long March had carried quite a few books with them, including works of Marx and Lenin. In later years many of those books were stolen by people who recognized their unique historical value. She managed to recover a few of the volumes that bear notes by the Chairman in his own calligraphy. She emphasized how valuable those books had become.

After the Red Army reached northern Shensi in 1935, the Party sent someone to make contact with Lu Hsun, hoping to protect him and draw him to their cause. At first that person looked for him in Shanghai, where they knew his life was in danger; he could not be found. The search was expanded nationwide, but to no avail. Had the Chairman managed to get Lu Hsun out of Shanghai into the Communist base areas, she hypothesized confidently, he would not have succumbed to illness so easily, dying in October 1936. Bolstered by the Party, he would have lived longer.

The Party's search for Lu Hsun began when the "struggle between the slogans" burst out, she said with reference to a famous dispute generated by Wang Ming's directive from Moscow. By then the Central Committee of the CCP had adopted Chairman Mao's line on the arts, which was epitomized by the slogan "People's Literature for National Revolutionary War." * The slogan, she pointed out, demonstrated a proletarian class character as well as the spirit of resistance to Japan. Wang Ming's opposing slogan was merely "National Defense Literature." But since every class could be said to favor national defense, Wang Ming's slogan had, she claimed, none of the specific class character essential to Marxist analysis. Lu Hsun accepted Chairman Mao's slogan and fought hard for it. The self-styled "left-wingers" — left in name but right in essence — jointly opposed Lu Hsun on this point. Led by Chou Yang, T'ien Han, Yang Han-sheng, and Hsia Yen (the Four Villains),[14] their promotion of Wang Ming's slogan was "really just political prostitution on the order of Sai Chin-hua," who served as the mistress of a German, or of Shih Ta-k'ai, the "big landlord who wormed his way into the Taiping Rebellion" (1850–1864). Both Sai and Shih were "one hundred percent anti-Communist traitors," Chiang Ch'ing declared indignantly, undeterred by the fact that their careers antedated the founding of the Chinese Communist Party by two and seven decades respectively.

Lu Hsun was a man of decided ways, Chiang Ch'ing continued. For ex-

* Mao had appropriated Lu Hsun's slogan, "People's Literature for National Revolutionary War," which actually was introduced by the writer Hu Feng in his article, "What Do the People Demand from Literature?" (reprinted in *Chung-kuo hsien-tai wen-hsueh shih ts'an-k'ao tz'u-liao* [Reference materials on the history of contemporary Chinese literature; Peking, 1960], 565–566).

ample, he was never one to give gifts. Somewhere he wrote that if you treat guests to the best things they will curse you. In spite of that, when he learned that Mao Tse-tung was leading the Red forces to the Northwest, he sent ham and other foodstuffs to ease their journey. As it happened, his gifts must have been lost or stolen, for they never arrived.

Unusual though he was, Lu Hsun must be judged from the viewpoint of historical materialism. Seen in that context, he was a "radical bourgeois democrat." He observed his political surroundings for three or four years. Then when he felt he knew the lay of the land, he rose up and fought until the day he died. The Chairman, who closely followed Lu Hsun's career, honored him as a "most courageous standard bearer." [15]

Some years ago certain heretofore-unknown manuscripts of Lu Hsun's were found, Chiang Ch'ing said as she showed me a photostatic copy of a letter penned by Lu Hsun, which had just been flown down from Peking to Canton to illustrate her point. Here, Lu Hsun said something to the effect that he had studied the Kuomintang's reactionary posters for several months now; they curse *everyone* but the Four Villains. [16] This and other passages prove that Lu Hsun was a keen observer, for in those days she and others like her only *sensed* that the Four Villains and their followers were not good people. Although she had to deal with such people, she had not yet seen the depths of their evil. Why? Because she lacked Lu Hsun's keenness of observation, his sense of detail. She was very young then, yet she knew intuitively that those men, the very ones who inhibited her contact with the Party center, were wrong.

Lu Hsun's "observations" were not only passive: he did not keep his views bottled up in himself. He criticized others sincerely and "gave tit for tat," as she put it. Inevitably his sharp tongue and combative pen won him numerous enemies.

In the years after she married Chairman Mao, Chiang Ch'ing befriended Lu Hsun's widow, Hsu Kuang-p'ing. "She told me that when the two of them went out, they dared not walk together on the same side of the street, but walked on opposite sides. So if the KMT should get one, the other would survive. That's the kind of life we all led in those days. Anyone who spoke up for resistance against Japanese imperialism could be arrested."

Lu Hsun's prestige in Shanghai ran high, not only among artists and intellectuals, by whom he was best known, but also among the "broad masses of workers and peasants." They sensed that he knew their plight and encouraged fledgling authors to write on their behalf. When Lu Hsun died in October 1936, working-class people thronged to his funeral procession. The demonstration was enormous and conducted in the spirit of political defiance. "I marched at the forefront of the funeral procession," Chiang Ch'ing recalled glowingly. "We sang almost all the revolutionary songs of those days save for the 'Internationale.' Had we sung that, surely we would have been arrested. We marched four abreast, arm in arm."

The artists, writers, and intellectuals who had followed Lu Hsun during his lifetime flocked around him when he died. Although he exerted a "tremendous influence" over Ting Ling, Hsiao Chün, Hu Feng, and others, their images are overblown in the historical record. Those "clever persons masqueraded as left-wing figures, but in reality were special agents of the KMT enemy," she reported bitterly (tantamount to calling John Steinbeck a John Bircher).

As for the Four Villains, she continued rapidly, in the mid-1930's they claimed to represent the Party organization, but they only perverted its principles. Those pseudo-Communists, as well as representatives of the KMT government, persecuted Lu Hsun and fought against him relentlessly, mainly through devices of literature and journalism, right to the day he died. Lu Hsun's vitality declined in the climate of persecution enveloping all Communist Party members and sympathizers in the 1930's. She speculated once again that had the Chairman, or even she and the Chairman, managed to get him out of Shanghai into the base areas, he would have lived longer. Of course he was never a member of the Party. But for people like him Party membership was unnecessary. She and the Chairman considered him a "non-Party Marxist."

Frowning in annoyance, Chiang Ch'ing said that she learned that when I was in Shanghai the week before, I was unconvinced of the sense in which Lu Hsun should be considered a Communist. She turned to Chang Ying and told her to give me a copy of Lu Hsun's letter of reply to a Trotskyite, written in 1936.[17] Immediately, Chang Ying produced a photographic copy of the Chinese original. "Read this," Chiang Ch'ing said to me. "Then you'll grasp the sense in which Lu Hsun was a good Communist."

Under her scrutiny I scanned the letter and later read it carefully. In it Lu Hsun commends Mao Tse-tung's down-to-earth approach to revolution as opposed to the high theory of the Trotskyites, and criticizes those who would "attack the proposal of Mao Tse-tung and others to unite against Japan." The letter was introduced during the Cultural Revolution as study material for political leaders, then was circulated widely at the start of the propaganda campaign to make Lu Hsun the intellectual centerpiece of an official CCP history of Shanghai in the 1930's. Among the major contributors to this continuing project of historical revisionism was Lu Hsun's widow, Hsu Kuang-p'ing, who wrote in 1967, at the height of the Cultural Revolution when Lu Hsun's rivals of three decades earlier were being destroyed: "Under the Kuomintang White Terror [Lu Hsun] cast personal safety to the winds and openly declared that he considered it a great honor to be one of Chairman Mao's comrades. At that time, Lu Hsun and Chairman Mao were separated by vast distances, but Lu

Hsun's heart was with Chairman Mao, beating with Chairman Mao. For Lu Hsun, our great leader Chairman Mao was the reddest sun in his heart."

To grasp correctly Lu Hsun's several positions in the political debates of the 1930's Chiang Ch'ing recommended my reading Lu Hsun's letter of reply to Hsu Mao-yung,[18] which would clarify the argument between Lu Hsun's slogan, "People's Literature for National Revolutionary War," and Chou Yang's support for Wang Ming's "National Defense Literature." All the latter meant, she reiterated, was that anything goes, regardless of class character, so long as the Japanese are ritually berated. To understand Lu Hsun's political and historical views and his judgment of the way people dealt with one another in Shanghai, one should read "On the Anti-Japanese United Front," "On Confucianism," and "People's Gossip Is a Fearful Thing." [19] All these essays recapture the unique historical circumstances by which the entire leftist community, herself included, was persecuted by the manipulation of public opinion.

Lightly touching my arm, Chiang Ch'ing nodded across the room to a wide table, which the aides had just stacked high with some twenty thick volumes hand-bound in red. *"The Complete Works of Lu Hsun* in the original 1938 edition," she announced delightedly, adding that the edition was rare now. Even her aides, specially commissioned, could not easily locate this collection in bookstores or private collections. This work was a gift to me to commemorate mutual interest in Lu Hsun and to demonstrate the Communist Party's abiding receptivity to the totality of his writings. One must always read Lu Hsun in the original edition, she cautioned. Why so? Because in the 1950's and 1960's the Four Villains, and the publishers who cooperated with them, prepared reprint editions which altered parts of the original. Certain passages of Lu Hsun were distorted only to justify the "bourgeois line" they were driving against the Chairman. What textual changes were made? They deleted all conceivable slurs against themselves, she responded, dismissing the question on that summary note.

V

Chiang Ch'ing's account of Lu Hsun and the politics of the 1930's carried more profound meanings and ironies, personal and public, than she dared to explore in our interview. From an early age she, along with thousands of other young malcontents and idealists had been dazzled by Lu Hsun, a man of letters as adept with ancient ideas as with modern, both Chinese and foreign, but he was never confined by any one academic school. While other scholars of his besieged generation sought to weather political crises in safety, he emerged as supremely engaged, a rebel who refused to be intimidated by a regime that posed as modern while continuing to demand the unquestioning feudal loyalty of the Chinese people. His intellectual eminence and the common plight he symbolized deterred the Nationalist government from arresting or executing him, its usual methods for dealing with lesser dissenters. As Chiang Ch'ing pointed out, the Nationalists "killed" him indirectly by manipulating public opinion — spreading gossip and slander — while they ground down many of his protégés physically and morally.[20]

Hearing Chiang Ch'ing speak of him improvisationally for hours on end brought him to life for me in various ways, not the least of which was his rhetorical style. Conversations about him with most other Communists I met scarcely went beyond dull Marxist sociologese. Of course, Chiang Ch'ing's language was subject to such conventions, though she could rise above them intellectually if she chose. Speaking on her own, she brandished Lu Hsun's hard-edged irony, mocked human folly, and parried inexhaustibly with personal enemies. When she forgot herself and, paradoxically, became herself, she cast provocative statements in a language which coarsely wove literary allusion with the vernacular, all in a vocabulary far richer than most of her political peers. In scope of literary imagination, subtlety of perception, and depth of human compassion, she was not Lu Hsun's equal.

Most discussions I had about Lu Hsun and all those published by the Communist regime were focused upon Lu Hsun's links to the Communist Party and its ideology. The idea that Lu Hsun was a Communist in spirit if not in letter was also keenly important to Chiang Ch'ing personally, as evidenced by the parallels she drew frequently between him and her. Lu Hsun was never a Communist in the technical sense of being a card-carrying member, and she lost her card-carrying status while living in Shanghai, a political disconnection that caused her to be suspected in subsequent years. The heroism of both under such circumstances was underlined implicitly in her account of their comparable persecution not only by the KMT, but also by the literary commissars Chou Yang, Yang Han-sheng, et al., whom Lu Hsun once facetiously dubbed the Four Villains, the black name that has stuck to the present day. Thus, for her, belief in Lu Hsun's connection with the Party and its ideology was of vital importance in demonstrating the continuity of her own political record, which was tided over by a steadfast Communist *spirit* when the letter of Party affiliation was broken.

More than a decade after the Cultural Revolution, ideologues oriented toward Chiang Ch'ing continued to mine Lu Hsun's writings for any statement that could conceivably be construed as damning the Four Villains and supporting Mao's cause. In the reconstruction of the vital but blood-streaked cultural

ambience of the 1930's, Lu Hsun was the one literary figure sufficiently powerful to give Mao Tse-tung an ideological locus in Shanghai at a time when Mao
and his marchers were struggling to survive and gain political respectability in
the hinterlands. Crucial to the reconstruction was Chiang Ch'ing's singling out
of Lu Hsun from among the Shanghai writers and finding him alone fit to
serve posthumously as her champion and as the champion of Mao and their
advocates during the backlash of liberalism in the 1960's.

5.

◇ ◇ ◇

Shanghai Film Afterimages

Wine, music and cinema are man's three
greatest creations. Of these the cinema is
the youngest and most powerful. It can
stimulate minds into daydreaming. Dream
is the free movement of the heart and it
mirrors the sadness of the opressive world.
There is no limit to the cinema's ability to
spread ideas.
— T'ien Han, "Memories of My Film Career"

The cinema fascinated Chiang Ch'ing and always had. She saw it as essential to modern culture. Film and literature were closely related in her mind. In reflecting on her haphazard education, which had fortuitously exposed her to foreign literature, she said during our first conversation at the Great Hall:

"I have tried my hand at novels, plays and poems, but none of them turned out well. The first American writer I became acquainted with was Upton Sinclair, author of *Oil!*, *King Coal*, and *The Jungle*. Sinclair was a reformist. Later I read Jack London and John Steinbeck. But I am too ignorant. However, I have seen numerous movies. Most were from the Roosevelt period, when many films based on literary works were made. Often I skipped meals and went hungry just to be able to save the money to see a film. I greatly admire Greta Garbo's acting. Is she still around?"

Cultivating a private life in New York, I guessed.

"I must put in a good word for her. You Americans have been unfair to Garbo by failing to give her an Academy Award.* I believe this is the fault of

* In 1954, Greta Garbo was given a Special Academy Award "for her unforgettable screen performances."

those in power in the United States and not of the American people. When I was in Yenan a correspondent by the name of Brooks Atkinson used to discuss Garbo with me."

Brooks Atkinson had become well known in America as drama critic of *The New York Times*, I commented.

"No wonder he talked with me at such length about literature and art! Is he still in New York?"

"Yes, though retired from the *Times*."

"If you see him, please tell him that I still remember him. If you see Garbo, tell her I send her my regards. She is a great artist. Greta Garbo is 'Great Garbo'! Her interpretation of nineteenth-century bourgeois democratic works is outstanding. There is a rebellious side to her character. She has an air of dignity; she is not affected; and she does not theatricalize."

Pondering the improbable scenario (R.W. bumps into the legendary Garbo on Fifth Avenue in the small-town New York of Chinese imagination), I commented that in her films, if not also in her life, Garbo projected an air of solitude that set her apart from other people. She strove to be unique.

"Yes, unique," Chiang Ch'ing echoed. "She should be given an Academy Award. I would suggest that Metro-Goldwyn-Mayer make new copies of her *Camille* and *Queen Christina*, show them again, and give her the award. That's only just. She is Swedish. We have copies of these two films."

Intrigued to learn that Garbo's films were still savored in some quarters in China, I remembered that in several speeches Chiang Ch'ing made during the Cultural Revolution she spoke of certain nonproletarian works as being usable for "teaching by negative example." Are the films of Garbo and Chaplin, which once had an enthusiastic Chinese following, now valued positively for themselves or negatively as object lessons on how not to make proletarian films, I asked.

"We can draw something from the actor's skills and the film techniques, but we lack copies." Responding to her implicit wish, I offered to try to arrange to send something to her, though I had little notion of how I would eventually go about doing it.

"Obtaining foreign films has been difficult for us," she admitted. "You have a movie called *The Sound of Music*. We arranged to get one copy from Hong Kong, but the reproduction of the colors was very poor. Then we searched high and low in other countries for a better copy, but still we have not got hold of one. It has not been easy. The film is relatively serious, and it is also antifascist. The director's skill is marvelous." *

---

* After I returned to America I got in touch with the producer and director Robert Wise, who sent Chiang Ch'ing a print of *The Sound of Music*; she sent him a film version of her revolutionary ballet *White-haired Girl* in exchange, but then insisted that I should keep it.

Over the years she had seen an enormous number of films, she said, and her favorites more than once. One particular documentary by the Russian filmmaker Roman Karmen she saw three times.[1]

"I have read the novel *Gone with the Wind* [translated in Chinese as *P'iao*, literally 'whirling,' like the wind] by one of your woman authors," she said. "A film adaptation based on this was called *The Wild and Beautiful Woman*."

"The one that depicted the bourgeois nouveaux riches at the time of the Civil War," Yao Wen-yuan broke in crisply and in his usual jerky style. "The Southern slave owners who upheld the slave system lost out. At that time America was in an upheaval; life was tumultuous. Four years from now will be the two-hundredth anniversary of the United States' Declaration of Independence. These two hundred years of American history are well worth studying. Analysis of America's past and present is useful for understanding the future of America."

"Do you know why I mentioned *Gone with the Wind?*" Chiang Ch'ing inquired. "It is not that it has any great literary merit. Rather, the movie has enabled me to understand the American Civil War in a graphic way.

"I have read some literary works. In my youth I studied some American history, but I don't recall it clearly. I only remember Washington and Lincoln. Washington, at the head of a population of three million, defeated Britain, which had a population of thirty million [actually around ten million in Washington's time]. From our point of view, Washington later committed the crime of killing Indians. Now you are the student of history. I am quite ignorant. Historically, when he was fighting the French he cooperated with the Indians, but after he defeated the British he slaughtered the Indians. Still, Washington was a great man."

Ever since then, the United States government has been laggard in compensating the Indians and supporting their interests, I admitted.

"That is the fault of the monopoly capitalist groups," Chiang Ch'ing affirmed. "The working people would not act like that. The California monopoly groups are latecomers; they coalesced only in the 1930's, considerably later than those in the East. And the white men in the Westerns of the 1930's were savage by nature and terribly cruel toward the Indians."

But the American Westerns made in the 1930's were not documentaries reflecting contemporary actualities, I hastened to add. They were romantic reconstructions of a period that ended about 1900.

"Westerns continue to be produced in America," she declared and ended that conversation.

i

One evening after a late dinner in Canton and a gracious promenade around a hall in her villa, Chiang Ch'ing revealed that she had a treat in store: Garbo's *Queen Christina*. Her face was glowing with anticipation. That Metro-Goldwyn-Mayer film of 1933 was an old favorite of hers. She had ordered it flown down from Peking for the evening's entertainment. Her personal archive of foreign and Chinese films included a nearly complete collection of Garbo. But her single copy of *Camille* was even then in poor condition from having been screened over and over through the years. And she had no copy of *Anna Karenina*, she admitted regretfully.

Her eyes danced as the lights were flicked off one by one, and as we sat in the dark she remarked that no matter how often she saw this film she was entranced by it. Projected onto a portable screen, the film creaked and jerked with age, the actors' movements speeding unnaturally or grinding slowly. The sound track — it was the original one — was practically inaudible. Nor were there Chinese subtitles, a lack that did not daunt Chiang Ch'ing, who knew the screenplay perfectly from beginning to end. In fact, her running Chinese narration murmured into my ear was far clearer than the English dialogue.

The film was fascinating to me, not only because I had never seen it before, but even more because she chose to show it. What was the connection between this European fairy tale and Chiang Ch'ing's extraordinary life? Queen of Sweden in the seventeenth century, Christina is a beautiful and willful young monarch who has rejected matches arranged for her by court elders in favor of a repertoire of lovers of her own choosing. Most recently she has become infatuated with the swashbuckling Spanish ambassador (John Gilbert), who has come to Sweden to seek her hand in marriage to the King of Spain. Fetchingly costumed as a young man, she goes to the inn where the ambassador is expected. Because the inn is full, the two "young men" are assigned to the same room. As the evening wears on she drops her disguise.* They fall into an impassioned love affair which leads to her abdicating the throne for him. But then he dies, leaving Christina bereft of both love and power. The film ends with Garbo standing in classic profile, luminous and serene at the prow of her ship, gazing unflinchingly toward an undetermined future.

The lights were turned up, revealing Chiang Ch'ing's own distinctive but less famed profile — misty-eyed. Weary-eyed myself, I glanced at my watch —

---

* This twist in the plot uncannily fits the cinematic formula for the age-old Chinese knight-errant tales (still flourishing in Hong Kong and Taiwan), in which an unconventional young woman athirst for adventure disguises herself as a young man, shares worldly adventures and soon a bed with her companion, and reveals her femininity at the opportune moment. Since the motif of pretending to be of the other sex is forbidden in current Communist films, Chiang Ch'ing, perhaps like millions of others, may have felt nostalgic for it.

nearly two in the morning — an attention to the hour that did not escape Chiang Ch'ing's notice. Smiling, she blithely announced that this was only the intermission. As soon as the cameras were set up we would see the recent documentary film on archaeological excavations that had been carried out since the Cultural Revolution near the city of Changsha, Hunan province, the environs of Chairman Mao's birthplace. In the meantime we would continue to photograph one another, resuming where we had left off earlier that afternoon: on the moon-viewing platform above the lotus pond in the orchid garden. To create a natural setting indoors she instructed her bodyguard Hsiao Chiao to arrange huge pots of bamboo and powerful indoor lighting. We snapped pictures of each other for perhaps an hour.

Among the wonders of the archaeological documentary was the "pickled princess," her spongy substance brought to light after an embalmment of more than two millennia. Chiang Ch'ing reveled in this film, which she seemed to have guided in production, and commented on the scientific implications without belaboring the film's stern adherence to the new politics of proletarian archaeology.

ii

Chiang Ch'ing worked in films only in 1936 and 1937. With this bit of information, she began her account of a part of her life she preferred to ignore. But those two years must not be seen in isolation from the rest of her life, she cautioned. People love to think that she spent her entire youth striving for fame. Some have claimed that her sole ambition in life was to become a star by the time she was twenty-one. How far from the truth that was! In acting, as in everything, she began at the bottom and worked her way up slowly. By the time she was eighteen she had a steady job as an actress, though her salary was very low. Apart from acting, which was all that outsiders seemed to notice, what she *really* wanted to do in her youth was to work for the Communist Party. Looking at me penetratingly, she said that foreigners have not appreciated how deeply committed to Communism she has been. Nor was the depth and duration of her commitment known to other members of our company before this evening. In saying that she cast an ominous smile upon her entourage; her words were chilling, implying the retribution that was within her power to bring.

She was silent momentarily; her eyes moved intently among the faces of those about her. Then she resumed. For many years she was subjected — and still was — to political persecution from both inside and outside the Party. Throwing her head back and smiling theatrically to dissolve the tension she had created in her audience, she said, "My real specialty has been lifting boulders and stones — there I'm truly a heroine! Of course it is glorious to do any revolutionary work, however lowly or lofty it may be. If done right, one should not brag about it; if done wrong, one should increase one's self-discipline."

She did not seek fame in films, she went on more quickly. But after she established a reputation as an actress, several film companies sought her out and tried to *force* her to sign contracts. Lu Hsun came to her defense. From his august position as a writer, he criticized them for bullying performers so mercilessly. The great film impresarios (who served the KMT directly or indirectly, e.g., through Chou Yang and his Party associates in cultural operations) counterattacked by vilifying him and threatening to *kill her*. Thus, in their Shanghai years, she and Lu Hsun both were subject to the same sort of harassment. And her nerve, like his, was gradually eroded by the constant bombardment. Her voice rose in anguish as she said that all sorts of people and organizations — Nationalists and Communists — had plotted to kill her. Except for the Shanghai newspaper *Ta-kung pao*,[2] all the media — radio, newspapers, and other influential publications — were mobilized against her. The tactics they used were insidious and cunning, though common during the White Terror. They spread the rumor that she was about to be kidnapped. They were, in effect, trying to drive her into committing suicide. As an individual she had no power. Without access to the media she had no way of defending herself against her attackers, among them the very men who controlled the media. When she realized how fully isolated and vulnerable she really was, she lived in terror from day to day. Her health deteriorated and her power to resist disease became dangerously impaired.

Chiang Ch'ing's narration above was delivered with outrage and desperation. Her insinuative remarks and partial information move her present readers, as they did her small audience at the time, to speculate on just what were the historical realities to which she referred and just how she was implicated. In her recapitulation of her role in the film industry of the 1930's she was cautious and evasive because she was building up her personal history with respect to political debates that have vexed the Communist revolution all along, and to personalities who were immensely powerful up to the eve of the Cultural Revolution and who still had followings — writers and artists who were silenced, and some "liquidated." Moreover, her own cinematic involvement in 1936 and 1937 may have been less defiant of Wang Ming's National Defense line (espoused by Chou Yang and his followers) than she would now allow, for the Wang Ming line was the one which dominated the Shanghai underground and urban Communism generally. And should she be unnecessarily harsh now on men who slighted her thirty-five years earlier, as the tables turned in future political struggles, their inheritors — persons given cultural liberalism — could settle comparable scores against her.

We can be certain of her wanting to establish for the record that although she was compelled to maintain a dual identity in the 1930's as a cultural worker in the Communist underground and as a teacher and investigator in reform programs sponsored by the YWCA, she was a *sincere* Communist all along. That is, she was not merely flirting with the left for theatrical advantage, and her commitment to expressing the theme of class struggle in the arts was more ardent than Wang Ming's, and thus closer to the more radical position Lu Hsun came to exemplify. Although she did not detail just how she was "forced" to sign contracts (sexual abuse was not out of the question) and for what films, we can assume that the films she tried to reject generally promoted resistance war without the class struggle element, or neglected politics altogether, and thus were purely commercial. When Lu Hsun came to the defense of actors and actresses who were impressed into unpatriotic, pro-KMT, or "entertainment" filmmaking, Wang Ming's defenders vilified him, and threats were made against her life. Their common enemy (as she reconstructed a fate shared with Lu Hsun) warned that she would be "kidnapped" — seized, forced to sign a contract and to perform as directed — if she did not willingly comply. That threat and the awful prospect of acting against her political principles edged her to the brink of suicide. Had her dissent driven her to kill herself (as did numerous other disgraced Shanghai actresses), her "enemies" would have been only indirectly responsible for her destruction.

In our weighing of her motives we cannot forget that in 1972 she was speaking at a moment of unique advantage: Chiang Kai-shek and his KMT apparatus had been exiled on the island of Taiwan for more than twenty years, and her old enemies on the left — Chou Yang, Hsia Yen, T'ien Han, and Yang Han-sheng — had been publicly disgraced by her six years earlier, and their cultural legacies were destroyed or impounded. Who was there now to confirm or contradict her charges?

Luckily her salary (drawn probably from acting and teaching) was raised, Chiang Ch'ing said when she resumed her narration. But most of that money went to support her "family." Who? "Two comrades and some other friends," she responded noncommittally. Those who knew how little money she had to live on thought certain of her habits strange, especially her penchant for eating in restaurants that catered to the rich. But what they did not know was that when she went to these fine restaurants (her motive for doing so can only be guessed), all she ordered was a portion of steamed bread, which she nibbled very slowly, one quarter at a time. The money she did not use for bare necessities or for the support of her family went to buy books on all sorts of subjects.

She used to spend long hours browsing in bookstores. When the bookdealers got to know her, they learned to trust her. If she wanted a book but had no cash, they just sent the book to her, allowing her to pay later.

At that time in Shanghai money was a nagging problem for most people. For thousands of the hopelessly unemployed, robbery became a way of life. Her pocket was picked a number of times. (She laughed brusquely at the recollection.) When stripped of cash, she had no choice but to go to pawnshops. After her face became known from her work in the theater and in films, dealing with pawnbrokers was acutely embarrassing. Of her worldly possessions only her wristwatch and pen (symbols of the intelligentsia and officialdom in Republican and Communist China) were acceptable pawn. Once, when she set her watch and pen on the counter, the pawnbroker looked at her closely and asked her how much she wanted. "Five yuan," she told him. Without haggle or any comment whatsoever he calmly handed her the five yuan and took possession of the watch and pen. That ease of exchange was rare, showing that he must have recognized who she was and sympathized with her predicament. Future dealings with pawnbrokers were progressively easier. To keep up her credit she always made a point of returning the money within a few days.

To strengthen her argument that poverty finally drove her to sign film contracts, she produced vignettes from her first two years in Shanghai, each illustrating her dire need of money. Often she lacked carfare. She remembered once taking a trolley to a distant part of the city to attend a political meeting. It was pitch-black outside by the time the meeting was over. There was one last trolley, and she had just enough change to pay for a third-class ticket, though she always preferred riding first-class. The only available seats were in the rear, where the jarring motion of the trolley, as it wove erratically through the streets, was intensified. She became more and more nauseated — she was still susceptible to motion sickness, a holdover from childhood. Finally, to keep from vomiting, she got off the train at a point far short of her destination. Now she had no choice but to trudge the whole way home, which was dozens of li away (a li is equivalent roughly to one-third of a mile). Her legs were hugely swollen by the time she got home to her dormitory for women workers.

Another time, when she was visiting the Pei-hsien-chang section of Shanghai, a typhoon blew up and bus service was terminated. All she could find was a rickshaw, but the rickshaw man asked in advance for a fare she could not afford. There was nothing to do but walk all the way home. At one point the wind at her back was so strong that to keep from being swept away she had to grasp a tree. But even large trees were breaking. Branches snapped and flew wildly in all directions. By the time she reached home she was shuddering and running a high fever. As she crawled into her attic room, the small frame house she shared with her worker-students rattled menacingly in the winds.

To round out the dreary picture of her former life, when hard times struck the workers' boarding school where she was teaching, she went hungry like everyone else there. At the same time she belonged to an amateur drama society, which gave three performances a week, always to full houses. Even so, it always lost money and the actors had to dig into their own pockets just to keep the theater alive. She also had to contribute money — "just like a man," she noted with a glint of feminist pride.

So that I should be clear about the kind of person she was, Chiang Ch'ing continued gravely, I must understand that she "never took anything from men." In old China, when a man and a woman went out together, the man always paid. She never did that. When she had no money, she told the man, "This time you pay, but next time I pay." Once she decided on the spur of the moment to see Garbo's *Camille* at a first-class theater. In a Bohemian mood she threw on a mannish overcoat and carried a man's wallet rather than a woman's purse. By the time she arrived at the ticket booth all the best seats were sold; only balcony seats at one yuan each were left. For this price she could see the film from one of the best seats at a second- or third-class theater. She would go in search of one. As she made her way through the streets, she sensed that someone was observing her surreptitiously, then moving in close, but she dared not reveal her suspicion by looking back. In front of the theater she ran into a friend — a man. As they started to buy tickets, she discovered that her wallet was gone — snatched by a pickpocket, who must have been the mysterious person stalking her in the street. Angry and embarrassed, she was afraid that her friend would think that she was only making a gesture of paying without really intending to do so. Besides, she shrank from admitting to him that her money had been stolen, for fear that he would feel sorry for her and try to do something. So she bade him a quick farewell, signaled a rickshaw, and searched for some friends who would lend her money for essentials. Failing to track down anyone she knew, she finally went to a bank and borrowed a small sum at an exorbitant rate. Now she was ashamed to report that she never managed to pay off that loan before she went to Yenan.

Her worsening physical condition depressed her, and recurring fevers made her delirious at times. When she went out during the day she never knew what slander she would find in the newspapers or what gossip she would hear. In those days she often felt as if she were "offering herself to be the captive of the masses." (She did not explain that extraordinary expression of notoriety and vulnerability.) But the masses were so fickle and unpredictable. They could be angry with her, or grasp her hands enthusiastically, or welcome her with flowers.

A friend of hers, a woman correspondent from the newspaper *Ta-kung pao*, knew her precarious state — the haunting fears and repeated threats on her life. The woman encouraged her to make her plight known by reporting it in print. Why should she not fight back? Chiang Ch'ing refused. Soon afterward, however, she ran into a correspondent who had reviled her in another paper. Beaming magnanimously, he extended his hand to shake hers. Enraged, Chiang Ch'ing held her arms tightly to her sides and snarled, "You cursed me in bold type!"

In 1936, as her personal crisis mounted, she wished to escape from Shanghai, especially after the Double Ten celebrations (October 10 was National Day in Republican China). But since she was under contract with a film company, she was not free to leave the city. Around that time some close friends encouraged her to write some articles on matters that distressed her. Knowing her earlier reluctance, they were astonished when she finally decided to do so. Unfortunately, the first article she wrote did not turn out as she intended. At the point in the article where she used the term "Japanese imperialists" the printer altered the character for Japan in such a way that her meaning was perverted. After that, some of her other friends cautioned her against further exposing her radical ideas in print. "You're courting arrest," they warned her. She could only remind them angrily that she had *already been kidnapped* and imprisoned for months just two years ago.

Among the articles she published in Shanghai during these months of crisis was one called "Our Life," which appeared on May 25, 1937, in the leftist journal *Enlightenment*.[3] Though her youthful Marxism may have been naive — she was only twenty-three then — her sense of the actor's dilemma was expressed forthrightly. Her belief in the potential of the modern drama movement was projected in the defensive voice of an actress whose social position, professional competence, and political views were constantly called into question. Thirty years later, she would resume her arguments from the control tower of the Cultural Revolution, but then, in "Our Life," she wrote:

The life of an actor is an unknown quantity in the minds of most people. Often people say enviously, "O, what an agreeable, desirable life!" Or some self-styled aristocrat will contemptuously mock us: "Oh, those are just some dissolute actors." For others, we who take part in the new theater movement are like a grain of sand in the eye, which one wants desperately to get rid of. We are as dangerous as tinder and are attacked from all sides by those who want to destroy us. Imperialism is perhaps the strongest force now; above all [the imperialists] want to preserve their old world and special privileges. Like hunting dogs [a recurring metaphor of Chiang Ch'ing's] they prowl everywhere, ready to spring and destroy . . . the new theater movement. In the International Settlement and the French Concession they wantonly attack our performers, and we know they will strike out voraciously in yet other directions.

Actors and actresses must be strong of body, mind, and spirit, she went on to say. They are not just instruments of entertainment, nor are they playthings. In these critical times actors must become aware of their social responsibilities and act accordingly. They must work as equals with playwrights and directors to deepen their understanding of social problems.

The clear and passionate voice of those years contrasted sharply with her account in our interview of her tormented life as an actress. "Li Yun-ho — now you know how she was created," she observed darkly. She paused, caught hold of herself, and in an instant shifted from despair to determination. After she "awakened" from that nightmare, she said, the image of the red flag of the Communist Party filled her mind. She had to be confident that China would have her own red flag and that the whole world would have its own red flag.

(She was sincere, to be sure, but was she not also echoing the coda of a revolutionary opera?)

iii

The cinema, along with modern drama, got under way just after the turn of the century. Production was centered in Shanghai, though studios sprang up in Hong Kong and other major cities. Challenged by the foreign films flooding the market and stimulated by foreign investment, China's film industry, until about 1925, was transparently imitative of the West: the gamut of Hollywood entertainment and Soviet socialist propaganda. China's new filmmakers, many of them trained abroad, were also affected by the high technological and aesthetic standards set by the Japanese, who were conspicuously more advanced than they were. Employing realistic and naturalistic styles of acting and settings, both alien to Chinese tradition, scores of films explored themes born of urban conflict — development of political consciousness in the working class, education of poor children, emancipation of women and women's rights, and problems of unemployment. [4]

Despite Chinese progress in filmmaking, the preponderant influence was foreign. In 1936, the year Chiang Ch'ing made her film debut, 373 pictures, all but thirty made in Hollywood, had their first runs in Shanghai. The Chinese film studios, which produced just a fraction of the total, nonetheless were dominated by Hollywood substance and style.

Beginning in the 1920's American film technicians trained Chinese counterparts in Shanghai, though before the decade was out most of them were dismissed because of costs. They left behind them spottily trained personnel and outdated Hollywood equipment. Despite these handicaps, which were worsened by lack of capital, several film studios were operating in Shanghai by the late 1920's. Each developed a recognizable character and roster of stars.

From the early 1930's leaders of the left-wing culture movement, above all, men skilled in the modern drama, perceived the unique potential of film as propaganda and began to exploit it. Like the drama, the cinema did not demand literacy on the part of viewers, and in those days films were relatively cheap to produce and distribute. Although there was no formal filmmakers' league in the early 1930's, the interests of radical filmmakers were promoted by some of the leaders of the League of Left-Wing Dramatists. For example, T'ien Han, Hsia Yen, and Yang Han-sheng shaped both the modern political drama and the film simultaneously. After Japan attacked Shanghai on January 28, 1932, Hsia Yen persuaded the CCP of the wisdom of setting up an underground Film Bureau.[5] As cinema was utilized more and more as the purveyor of political statements, film criticism burgeoned and served the causes established by the political left. In July 1932 the CCP established its own cinema journal called *Film Art*, with the goal of promoting "open struggle and objective criticism," that is, ideologically correct film analysis.[6] In February 1933 the Party established in Shanghai the Chinese Film Culture Association as a means of organizing cinematic production in the struggle against imperialism.

Chiang Ch'ing's career was determined as much by forceful men as by politics or art. One mentioned already is the producer and screenwriter Hsia Yen, whose career long paralleled and sometimes intersected Chiang Ch'ing's — and there they crossed swords. Both grew up with the theater — Hsia Yen on the writer's side joined the left-wing drama movement and eventually turned to film. An early Communist revolutionary, Hsia Yen joined a Marxist group in Hangchow and continued his studies in Japan. In 1927 he joined the CCP, and in 1930 and 1931 was among the founders of the leagues of Left-Wing Writers and Left-Wing Dramatists. He began producing avant-garde leftist films the next year, a time when the film industry as a whole was low in morale, suffering financially and politically from the most recent catastrophe of Japanese expansionism in China. In the summer of 1932 he and some other CCP members joined the Star Film Company and made it their business to guide a portion of production away from films with romantic, sexual, and feminist themes, which appealed to the Western-oriented intelligentsia, and to devote that portion to films exploring problems common to the masses of China's population. Hsia Yen was responsible for introducing such Marxian themes as class struggle into the Chinese film.[7]

Ironically, in view of the animosity which in later years would grow to enmity between Hsia Yen and Chiang Ch'ing, at the time when she was involved in the grueling routine of teaching women workers and investigating factory conditions in Shanghai, Hsia Yen was using just those proletarian settings for realistic and naturalistic films of political relevance. His *Outcry of Women*, for example, reflected the harrowing conditions in the textile industry.[8]

Under the pressure of the times, the Star Film Company and other studios produced films exposing the KMT's moral corruption and uncertain prosecution of the Resistance War. Inexorably, such outspokenness cast them into the same antigovernment camp as dissenting journalists, writers, and publishers, and they were punished in similar ways. The Gestapo-like Blue Shirt Society, the Committee to Destroy the Communists, and other security organizations sporadically raided and closed down offending film studios, as they did publishers, bookstores, cultural associations, schools, and universities.[9] Using the old technique of scapegoating, in November 1932 the Blue Shirts dissolved the relatively conservative I Hua Film Studio as a warning to the others against veering either from pure entertainment or political orthodoxy.[10]

The principal leftist members of the defunct studios found refuge in other film companies and resumed work. The government reacted by planting agents and counteragents in the remaining studios in order to crush political independence from within. Agents masquerading as leftist artists altered scripts, cinema programs, and advertisements to promote KMT interests. To muffle public debate over the political implications of films as they were released, film supplements to the daily and weekly papers and independent film journals were censored sporadically or terminated by official fiat.

Nineteen thirty-four was the last year of open opposition between the left-wing filmmakers and the Nationalist government. The next year pressures to forge a united front among rival political groups and to establish National Salvation associations in their stead meant that disputes were to be muted for the sake of common survival. But these National Salvation associations were not without an independent political stance. If they criticized official acts that appeared conciliatory toward the Japanese, they could expect the government to react repressively. More and more now, broad attacks against offending institutions were replaced by insidious persecution of individual dissenters. Most newspapers and journals were controlled by KMT representatives who possessed the power to wage defamatory campaigns against outspoken writers and artists by sensationalizing the "lurid" sides of their private lives and denouncing their political philosophies. In the unevenly liberated society of Shanghai, women were more vulnerable than men to these humiliation campaigns. And women in the arts, especially actresses whose glamorous and romantic auras were not balanced by social prestige, were most easily driven to suicide by the manipulative power of public opinion.

The White Terror launched by the Nationalist government in 1935 forced major transformations in film, as in the other lively arts. In the years preceding, the cinema had flourished as a popular medium of social and political consciousness. Ideological expression was forthright; social evils and revolutionary solutions were portrayed in obvious ways. But the threat of government reprisal after 1935, the year the KMT nominally subscribed to a united front policy, impelled anti-Nationalist filmmakers to create subtler characterizations and to express political themes indirectly. From an artistic standpoint much was gained, though it was lost again in the late 1940's, when the film industry was coopted by the Communist regime and simple construction of character and delivery of message were restored and reasserted absolutely during the Cultural Revolution. As of 1935, though, not only were films more indirect in their delivery of messages, but film producers were forced to use more devious tactics in the recruitment of performers. For security contracts were offered to individual actors rather than to groups as they had been earlier. As Chiang Ch'ing disclosed, she was among those sought out individually by film impresarios, some of whom pressured her to sign contracts which, in retrospect, were politically, and thus personally, damaging.

iv

Chiang Ch'ing's initiation into the cinema occurred at a crucial point in China's modern cultural history. Left-wing filmmakers, driven underground by the government, took with them whatever acting talent they could and tailored names and images to suit new roles. So it was with Chiang Ch'ing, who signed up with the United Photoplay (Lien Hua) Film Company under a cinematic pseudonym. Up to that time, in the political underground and on the stage she was known as Li Yun-ho, or by parts of that name. She emphasized that using the Li preserved her family name. When she was about to sign her first contract, a leading member of the League of Left-Wing Dramatists, a man she admired but would not identify, urged her to take a fresh name, one that would disengage her from the Li surname by which she had become infamous in political circles (the point was not elaborated). Thus she chose her name in film, Lan P'ing. Her reasons were personal. She selected *Lan*, a character whose literal meaning is "blue," because she loves to wear the color blue in any shade — dark, light, or blue-gray. And because she would shortly leave Shanghai for Peip'ing (literally "northern peace" — the name in those days for Peking) she took the *p'ing* character meaning "peace" as the second part of her name. Lan P'ing, as it stood then, meant Blue Peace.

But after she signed the film contract with United Photoplay that same leader in the League of Left-Wing Dramatists decided to change the second character of her name from the *p'ing* meaning "peace" to another more eye-catching character of the same *p'ing* pronunciation but written differently and meaning "apple." He saw that as more effective for films. Thereafter, she retained the "apple-*p'ing*" and was known in films as Lan P'ing — Blue Apple.[11] The man responsible for changing her name was later betrayed by T'ien Han, she added tartly.

Under the White Terror artists were perpetually threatened by the confusion of their "cooperation" with various groups against foreign imperialism with what others could construe as "collaboration" with Chinese representatives, obscure or manifest, of the foreign enemy. Unlike the drama whose performance was always controlled by the actors themselves, a film once made was left to the mercy of editors and censors to do with it what they willed. When I asked her to give some examples, Chiang Ch'ing replied warily that she was not prepared, but would say something.

"In the early 1930's the film studios were relatively close to us because, when a nation is in danger of subjugation, decadent and obscene movies can find no market. The masses demanded democracy and wanted to fight against Japan. American movies were predominant then, and they constituted seventy percent of the films being shown. Tickets were so costly that the working people could not afford them. But in Shanghai some comparatively democratic films were being made, ones depicting the masses to a greater or lesser degree, or suggestive of anti-imperialist themes. But the filmmakers dared not speak out forthrightly. For they knew that if they did so they would be kidnapped right off, as I was once kidnapped and detained for several months by the Kuomintang."

More details than she provided are available in the documentary record. In October 1934 the conservative wing of the Star studio fired Hsia Yen in repudiation of his two-year record of "subversive" filmmaking. Thereupon he joined the left-wing faction of United Photoplay, sustained his ties with the CCP's underground Film Bureau, and resumed his progressive filmmaking.[12] United Photoplay had been founded in 1929 by a coalition of foreign and Chinese financiers, some warlords included, all determined to go beyond the sure-sell formulas, for example, ghosts and knights errant, perennial favorites that are still thriving in pulp literature, on television, and in film cycles in overseas Chinese communities of the 1970's. United Photoplay's earliest productions probed the intellectual and moral concerns of its leading members, who had matured in the liberal and cosmopolitan May Fourth era: revolt against the old family system, "modern" love and marriage, and the conflict between romantic love and social responsibility. Then the wartime tragedies of the early 1930's forced United Photoplay to set aside those sentimental subjects in order to make films with thinly disguised political messages. In pursuit of political immunity they went beyond that by creating a new genre of cinematic allegory. Chiang Ch'ing was recruited to United Photoplay at that juncture.

Speaking from the vantage point of political reckonings made during the

Cultural Revolution, she said: "By the middle 1930's the Four Villains [Chou Yang, Yang Han-sheng, Hsia Yen, and T'ien Han], so named by Lu Hsun, had betrayed the revolution, and no more good movies were produced. At that point I began working with one of the film companies. I was not a brilliant actress, but I stood out rather prominently among the new actresses. I could go down to the grassroots and work as [drama] director among the workers. Of course [proletarian artists] also directed and acted on their own. I also went out to the schools. I did quite a lot of this sort of thing."

Chiang Ch'ing had mentioned stage parts she took, but never film parts, even in response to several direct questions. Besides wanting to disparage films of the late 1930's generally, she had personal motives — some can be guessed. In more than one context she said that she wanted to detract from her movie star image. We can also imagine that she would not want to invite foreigners to track down her old films and make them the occasion for film festivals. For years the rumor has circulated that after marrying Chiang Ch'ing, Mao ordered destroyed all the films in which she played. But that is a spurious notion in view of the historical fact that his regime did not expropriate private film studios and archives until the early 1950's, by which time copies of the vast majority of commercial films had been taken to Hong Kong and other overseas Chinese communities. There is, however, later documentary evidence to show that books published in China after 1950, which cited her as having played certain parts, were banned in the early 1960's, and their authors virulently criticized for a number of offenses having to do with their political stands vis-à-vis the orthodoxy formally established by Mao at the opening of the Cultural Revolution.[13] Possibly the most important motive for her suppressing information on her film career was that the films in which she played were produced during the united front era, when filmmakers were forced to espouse the National Defense line in the spirit of cooperation with the KMT against the foreign enemy, but not all who did so sustained the other leftist theme of proletarian class struggle, which Chiang Ch'ing would champion in later years. Cinematic utilization of the National Defense line was, of course, open to retrospective political interpretation, especially to the discredit of growing ranks of Mao's enemies on other scores.

As China's foremost modern writers, led by the dramatists, began turning out screenplays that promised to make films the most popular of all the media, correspondingly, fresh screen talent was skimmed from the stage. Among the most successful stage-trained film stars were Pai Yang and Chao Tan, sometimes called, respectively, the Garbo and Gable of China. Their names, surely more luminous than Chiang Ch'ing's in those days, she never mentioned. But as she said of herself, she too was drawn into the films on the basis of notoriety achieved in the theater.

Chiang Ch'ing's film career must be viewed in relation to the united front policy in the summer of 1935. The demand for nonpartisanship in the National Salvation associations, which were intended to succeed the left leagues, required all writers and artists to suppress viewpoints that served partisan causes at the expense of the national interest, or which exposed baldly the hypocrisy of the KMT government and the ineffectiveness of its effort to liberate the nation from Japan. Thereafter, critical messages in the cinema could be expressed only through stylistic indirection. Chiang Ch'ing's first picture, *Blood on Wolf Mountain*, demonstrated this indirection through allegory. The original story, "Cold Moon and Wolf's Breath," was written by Shen Fu, a man of working-class background who joined United Photoplay in 1933, when political writers and filmmakers were freer than they would be after 1935. Revised as a screenplay by Shen Fu and the distinguished screenwriter Fei Mu, the film was then directed by Fei Mu and the renowned Chou Ta-ming, with whom Chiang Ch'ing became closely acquainted.

On the surface *Blood on Wolf Mountain* is merely a chilling story of a wolf pack that raids a village, eats a large number of the inhabitants, and throws the rest into a panic. Viewers familiar with the Aesopian language of the decade undoubtedly recognized the wolves as symbols of the Japanese. The villagers differ in their reaction to the aggressors. The heroine, Small Jade, and her father are bent on revenge. Chao Erh, a superstitious teahouse owner, believes that wolves are controlled by mountain spirits and are thus indestructible; the only way to escape them is by casting a spell over them. Lao Chang is without fear — he ventures out alone on wolf hunts. Liu San, like his wife (played by Chiang Ch'ing, alias Lan P'ing), is terrified of wolves (in art as in life).

When Small Jade, her father and the brave Lao Chang go out on a wolf hunt, they are joined by dogcatchers toting a dead wolf to ward off evil spirits. The father, who is unarmed, is consumed by a wolf on the spot. That same night the wolf pack raids the village again and kills the son of Liu San and his wife; their personal disaster provokes the final confrontation. As the wolf pack spills out onto the streets in broad daylight, Small Jade, Lao Chang, and Liu San mobilize the village for the defense. Liu San's wife (Chiang Ch'ing), once cowed by wolves, now courageously joins the ranks of the wolf killers. Carrying torches on high, the villagers sing the "Kill the Wolf Song" as they march to battle:

> *Whether we live or die we go out to*
> *attack the wolves and protect the village.*
> *Our brothers' blood is like an ocean,*
> *our sisters' corpses like frost!*

Though the wolves become ravenous, we
shall not retreat.
We are determined to destroy the wolves
because we cannot be without homes.[14]

Like all films produced under the Nationalist government in the 1930's, *Blood on Wolf Mountain* had to pass several censors before release. Under a KMT regulation, first the screenplay, then the scenario and dialogue, and then the final product had to meet the approval of the Central Board of Film Censors. Next, the foreign-dominated Shanghai Municipal Council tested the film for materials that might offend the Japanese, whose interests they protected. And finally, the Japanese consulate itself was free to censor any film suspected of insulting imperialistic prerogative. Though censors on the Shanghai Municipal Council surmised that the wolves in *Blood on Wolf Mountain* stood for the Japanese, the Japanese consulate, perhaps incredulous of such slander, let the picture pass.[15]

In a volatile political atmosphere the film excited extremes of controversy. Defenders of the civil order, who were tacitly committed to accommodating the Japanese, attacked its transparent allegory. Leftist critics, who deplored KMT collaboration with a foreign enemy, praised its ingenious expression of the resistance theme. Paramount among promoters was a coalition of some thirty radical critics who made up the Art Society, a relatively new and secret CCP organization.* The Art Society's members included various associates of Chiang Ch'ing: her rejected suitor Chang Keng; film impresarios Ch'en Po-chi, Ts'ai Ch'u-sheng, and Li Ssu; and actor and film critic T'ang Na (alias Ma Ch'i-liang) to whom it is rumored that she was once married. (Could they have foreseen how their praise of her acting on the National Defense theme, which expressed the "Wang Ming line" espoused by Chou Yang, would grievously compromise her after she fled to the hinterlands and switched her loyalty to Wang Ming's rival, Mao?)

Spokesmen for Shanghai's rising bourgeoisie were less worried about irritating the Japanese than they were bored by the film's visual austerity. Having become accustomed to cinematic sexuality, in the so-called "soft" movies, they missed being treated to women's eyes "that look as if they are eating ice cream," "voluptuous flesh and big thighs," better bosom exposure, and more enticing makeup.

Though the film was approved officially, showings subsequently were

---

* The Art Society was, moreover, one of numerous formal and informal associations which constituted Shanghai's heady cafe society, a separate stratum of urban culture forcibly dissolved by the triumph of CCP power.

banned in the fall of 1936 by the police of both the KMT and the British International Settlement. The censure provoked the Art Society to make an international appeal: dramatists and filmmakers should be freed from unwarranted political repression.[16]

Few historians writing under the People's Republic have dared to draw attention to Chiang Ch'ing's role in that film. One who did, but did so warily, was Cheng Chi-hua, who not surprisingly became a victim of the Cultural Revolution. His encyclopedic history of the Chinese film included a synopsis of *Blood on Wolf Mountain,* after which he singled out only Lan P'ing's performance for comment. He praised her portrayal of a simple peasant woman whose political awakening was engendered by the brutal experience of losing her child to the wolves. Her performance was as well received by the masses as by the critics, he duly noted.[17]

Wang Lao-wu, the second United Photoplay film in which the former Lan P'ing appeared, dealt more forthrightly with the themes of social exploitation and national resistance. It was set in an urban slum and directed by the famous Ts'ai Ch'u-sheng, also a member of the Art Society. To prepare himself to make a film intended to project authentically the lives of boat dwellers on the Shanghai estuary, he researched that social scene intensively, an artistic pragmatism that has been routinized by the Communist regime. In the film story thus developed from reality, the title character, Wang Lao-wu, is an impoverished bachelor of thirty-five who possesses the "good conscience" of the laboring people, though his political consciousness is not high. He becomes enamored of a saucy seamstress (played by Lan P'ing) who does not return his love. But because he shows her compassion when her father dies, she marries him out of gratitude, shares a typical Shanghai shack with him, and bears four children. As time goes on, the misery of their existence causes him to become deeply depressed and to drink heavily. Japan's attack on Shanghai in January 1932 intensifies his depression and drunkenness, and the family's misfortunes worsen.

The workers' headman (unmistakably the enemy of the laboring people) wants to win over Wang Lao-wu for personal advantage. Secretly he advises him to set a fire among the workers' sheds. Being simple-minded, Wang Lao-wu would ordinarily have been easily inveigled, but this time his instinct is to resist, defy the headman, and denounce him as a traitor before the people. Enraged, the headman retaliates by turning Wang's hovel into a sea of flames from which the wife and children barely escape. Then he manipulates the people's feelings against Wang, making *him* out to be the "traitor who ought to die." Tears stream down the wife's face as she stands before the people and implores them to stop persecuting him; he *wants* to be good, she insists, but he does not know how. By now the fire started by the traitorous headman has alerted enemy aircraft: the village is bombarded, and the Japanese close in upon them from all sides. In the last scene Wang's wife is bent over the corpse of her husband. The people's blood and tears swirl about her as she raises her head defiantly and reviles all foreign enemies and Chinese traitors.[18]

However blatantly melodramatic, the film became a sufficient critical success to win Lan P'ing notoriety as a film personality. By the time it finished shooting in June 1937 Lan P'ing's social appearances and opinions on various matters were being solicited by the press and reported in the newspapers' entertainment sections.[19] Those glittering indulgences of celebrity status were unrelated to the mounting tragedy of national life. Before the film was released Chiang Kai-shek had been captured in Sian in northwest Shensi province (in December 1936) and forced at the price of his life to adopt a staunch national resistance and united front policy. In subsequent months the territory he claimed to control was expected to fall into line. As under any Chinese regime, ancient or modern, Nationalist or Communist, culture was required to conform to government policy. In the cinema world *Wang Lao-wu* became a difficult case. Since its traitorous headman could be construed as standing for the Nationalist government, thereby revealing its hypocritical stand on the resistance issue, the film was impounded; not until April 1938 was it released. By then the entire political picture was reversed. Japan's invasion of Shanghai was a disastrous reality that had forced hundreds of thousands, Chiang Ch'ing among them, into exile.

To make the film inoffensive to the Japanese, KMT censors cut from the original footage the passages in which Wang Lao-wu resisted the Japanese, that is, refused to collaborate with the traitorous headman. Not only was the film's artistic integrity destroyed, but more importantly, the message had been changed to advocacy of acquiescence in Japanese expansionism.[20] All this left Lan P'ing, the revolutionary Chiang Ch'ing, appearing in a film whose cut-and-spliced message was collaborationist.

From Chiang Ch'ing's retrospect of thirty-odd years, her problem then was powerlessness — there was nothing she could do to repair the damage to her reputation. Without power, she and everyone else like her were subject to the incalculable consequences of drastic political change from on high. From that bitter experience she learned one of the most important lessons of her life: the only way to avoid being victimized is to acquire power.

v

Vulnerability to the political instabilities of wartime was but one facet of Chiang Ch'ing's experience in the cinema. Circulation in the world of film people was another. The more closely one examines the intricate skein of writers, artists, musicians, and actors, the more entangled that community appears. Just as national disasters had forced "art for art's sake" out of fashion in the 1930's, so did "film for film's sake" yield to political pressures. That conscientious narrowing of the gap between art and life led some writers to explore general social and political issues through *cinema à clef*. Chiang Ch'ing cautiously drew attention to one such instance, and in so doing she implied parallels between her life and that of the ill-fated star, Yuan Ling-yü.

Besides the screenwriter Hsia Yen, whom Chiang Ch'ing remembered with glancing disparagement,[21] two other prestigious authors, Lu Hsun and T'ien Han, also turned out film scripts for United Photoplay, with which she was under contract. Lu Hsun could do no harm, in her view, but T'ien Han was another case. Because her personal antagonism toward him somewhat prejudiced her view of his past, his brief but effective cinematic career needs additional discussion.

The artistic potential of motion pictures first intrigued T'ien Han in the middle 1920's, when European romanticism and Japanese aestheticism were both in vogue among Chinese intellectuals. "Silver dreams," he called them. "Wine, music and cinema are man's three greatest creations." In 1926 he set up the South China Film Theater, a cinematic variant of the South China Drama Society, the trend-setting drama group he had founded. Upon conversion to Marxism in 1931, he repudiated the idea of "silver dreams" as a capitalist notion.[22] As his politics shifted to the left, he thought more of general audiences and began writing screenplays that projected urban social change. Among the finest of these films was *Three Modern Girls*, which was released by United Photoplay in 1933 and distributed under one of the pseudonyms of the screenwriter, T'ien Han. The star of this political melodrama was Yuan Ling-yü, whom some critics also compared to Garbo (in Chinese eyes Garbo was the celluloid goddess of the West). Yuan Ling-yü was also destined to become a popular cult object to her era.[23]

At the pinnacle of her film career Yuan Ling-yü starred in another sensational film, *The New Woman*, which mirrored contemporary feminism, leftism, and political persecution. Produced by United Photoplay, the film was directed by Ts'ai Ch'u-sheng and Chou Ta-ming (once married to Yuan Ling-yü), two men who might also have selected Chiang Ch'ing for the lead. This silent instance of *cinema à clef* had an eloquent score by Nieh Erh (who five years later in Yenan wrote the lyrics for the *Yellow River Cantata*, which Chiang Ch'ing eventually adapted to the Cultural Revolution).[24] The story was a fictional reconstruction of the life of Ai Hsia, an actress who committed suicide in February 1934. In the film the real Ai Hsia is disguised as a woman writer. Because of the failure of her novel, she can no longer support her small daughter and is plunged into despair. Morbidly depressed, she attempts suicide, but is discovered in the nick of time and rushed to a hospital, barely alive. All efforts to save her fail, and just before she dies she hears through the window a newsboy shouting, "Famous woman writer commits suicide!" The film ends on the proletarian upbeat. A group of women workers who have just read of Ai Hsia's suicide (no illiterates they!) transform their grief into determination, face the future bravely, and march together into the morning sun.[25]

Chiang Ch'ing did not speak of Yuan Ling-yü directly, but from the way she depicted her own career in films, it was unmistakable that Yuan Ling-yü had been her model on the screen and also in real life — up to the point of Chiang Ch'ing's escape from Shanghai. Four years her senior, Yuan Ling-yü was born into the working class in Shanghai, and like Chiang Ch'ing she was raised by a working mother. After beginning her film career with the Star studio, she moved to United Photoplay, where both she and Chiang Ch'ing, still in their twenties, worked in left-wing and avant-garde films. However, Yuan was not only more beautiful in obvious ways and a better actress than Chiang Ch'ing, she was also a spectacular suicide, one who left an indelible mark upon the city's social conscience. Like numerous stars before and after her, she was remembered tragically: the victim of vicious gossip.

The New Woman opened in Shanghai in February 1935, the first anniversary of Ai Hsia's death. Ironically, on March 8, long celebrated in China as International Women's Day, Yuan Ling-yü, the film star who portrayed Ai Hsia's suicide, committed suicide at the age of twenty-five.[26]

In the final months of her life Yuan Ling-yü was publicly scorned for her divorce from the cinematographer Chou Ta-ming and for open affairs with other men. All actresses in the limelight, whether in left-wing films as Yuan and Chiang Ch'ing were or in commercial films, were vulnerable to public criticism, and doubly so if their politics were unorthodox. The more glamorous film stars, on a par perhaps with Clara Bow and Betty Grable, openly consorted with KMT politicians, generals, and business tycoons. However politically naive or reactionary these women may have been, by traditional Chinese standards they were social radicals of the first order. Their pleasure-giving and pleasure-seeking lives flouted the ancient conventions of demure daughters and self-sacrificing wives to which most women subscribed. Universally in old China, and in the countryside in modern times, stringent moral codes and social pressures, which were more onerous for women than for men, combined to drive to suicide those faced or threatened with lost chastity. The dutiful women who carried that moral imperative to their graves were posthumously praised and cited as models for the rest.

Although these one-sided and punitive sexual codes were subscribed to far less among revolutionaries and others with advanced ideas, yellow journalists employed the press and public opinion to humiliate "irregular" women. And in the political world as in the arts there were those whom the KMT government did not mind taunting or destroying. The sequence of publicity, persecution, and suicide became routine.

In Shanghai in the spring of 1935 Yuan Ling-yü was the star suicide whose story leaped from art to life and back to art, gaining in notoriety at each stage. Within weeks of her death, her life was celebrated in *Death of a Film Star*, which was a *succès fou* in the Shanghai theater. In her final recollections of Shanghai Chiang Ch'ing pointed to Lu Hsun's essay, "Gossip Is a Fearful Thing," whose title was taken from Yuan Ling-yü's suicide note. "Read that," Chiang Ch'ing urged, "for in it you will find clues to my own life."

That essay, which cuts to the sadist heart still pounding at the center of modern Chinese life, is about women in the performing arts who are slandered just because they are actresses. Journalists are "lip-smacking gossipmongers" catering to readers who are ravenous to read embellished accounts of the sexual lives of women in the public eye: "If a girl runs away, before it is known whether she has eloped or been seduced, the brilliant writer passes verdict: 'Lonely, she longed for a lover to share her couch.' How do you know? Again, it is very common in poor country districts for a woman to marry several times, but the brilliant writer dashes off a big headline: 'More Concupiscent than Wu Tse-t'ien.' " *

Once a woman is libeled, Lu Hsun pointed out, no matter whether the false statement is followed by apology or correction, the damage has been done: "a helpless woman like Yuan Ling-yü is made to suffer, smeared with mud she cannot wipe clean. Should she fight back? Not owning a newspaper, she cannot. There is no one with whom to argue, to whom to appeal. If we put ourselves in her place, we can see that she was telling the truth when she said that gossip is a fearful thing. And those who thought the newspapers had something to do with her suicide were telling the truth too." [27]

In essence Chiang Ch'ing had said the same of her own predicament after she was libeled "in bold type," her term for the glaring newspaper headlines. If China today were a more liberated society, one in which men and women could disclose with impunity the vagaries of their sexual histories, she would have been more frank about her past. The clues she gave me, combined with the public record and the gossip of expatriates of her generation, give grounds for hypothesis. Her reasons for evasion were personal and political, the two

---

* Empress (self-styled "Emperor") of the Chou dynasty (A.D. 684–705), an interregnum of the T'ang. For centuries popular romances mocked her sexually voracious, tyrannical, and unconventional behavior. In Shanghai in 1939 and Hong Kong in 1963 her legend was made into extravagant films. Kuo Mo-jo's historical romance of her career first appeared in 1960 and was revised in 1963, the end of the culturally liberal era. In 1974 the Communist Party reversed the verdict of history and celebrated her as a "Legalist" heroine, as explained in the Epilogue.

often tangling. In the course of her film career, to which she claimed defensively to have been driven more by dire poverty than by personal ambition, her name was linked to that of the actor and film critic T'ang Na, a leading member of the Communist-sponsored Art Society.[28] Some say she married him, and when she abandoned him grief drove *him* to the brink of suicide. T'ang Na's threat of suicide, which was swiftly sensationalized by the press, pointed a finger at Chiang Ch'ing, making her out to be the guilty partner. Not only did that heighten her status as a celebrity, but it also made her the target of the misogyny and sadism that seem to lie as much at the heart of modern as of traditional society. However unverifiable the Lan P'ing–T'ang Na affair may be now, and however inconsequential that romantic eddy is to the mainstream of her life, the gossip it engendered, combined with political perversion of films in which she played, was the gross public façade she carried to the Communist capital, Yenan. How would she live that down?

PART TWO

◇ ◇ ◇

IN THE
HINTERLANDS

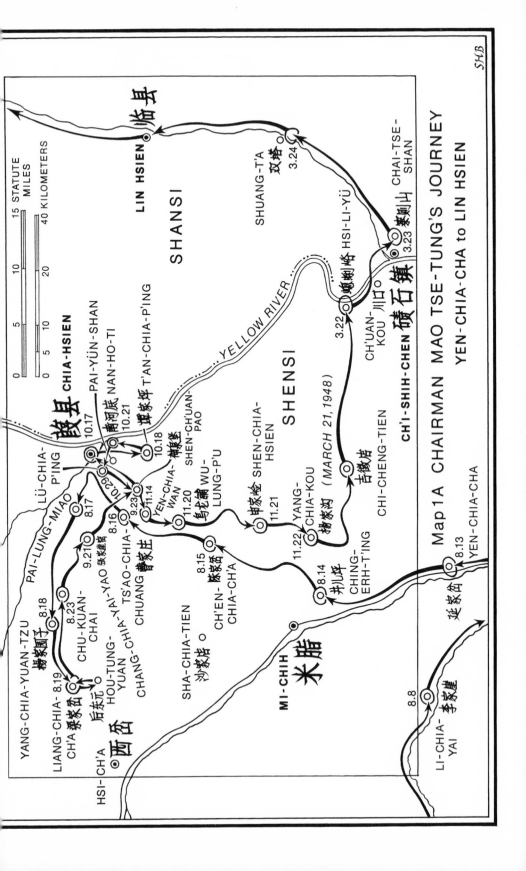

Map 1A CHAIRMAN MAO TSE-TUNG'S JOURNEY
YEN-CHIA-CHA to LIN HSIEN

SHANSI

LIN HSIEN 临县

CHIA-HSIEN 葭县

PAI-YÜN-SHAN

NAN-HO-TI 南河底 10.21

T'AN-CHIA-P'ING 谭家坪 10.18

SHUANG-T'A 双塔
3.24

HSI-LI-YÜ 嘎喇峪

CHAI-TSE-SHAN 寨刺山
3.23

3.22

CH'I-SHIH-CHEN 碛石镇

CH'UAN-KOU 川口
CH'UAN-KOU-CHEN

SHEN-CH'UAN-PAO

SHEN-CHIA-HSIEN 神家涧
11.21

YANG-CHIA-KOU 杨家沟
11.22
(MARCH 21, 1948)

CHI-CHENG-TIEN

CHI-WEI-PU 吉微堡

SHENSI

YELLOW RIVER

LÜ-CHIA-P'ING
PAI-LUNG-MIAO

HSI-CH'A 西岔

YANG-CHIA-YUAN-TZU 杨家园子 8.18

LIANG-CHIA-CH'A 梁家岔 8.19
后圪坨

CHU-KUAN-CHAI 8.23

HOU-TUNG-YAI-YAO 駮烧堡 8.16

CHANG-CHIA-CHUANG TS'AO-CHIA-YUAN 9.21

8.17

10.29 梅塚 10.17

YEN-CHIA-WAN 11.14 9.23

WU-LUNG-P'U 鸟龙舖 11.20

CH'EN-CHIA-CH'A 陈家岔 8.15

SHA-CHIA-TIEN 沙家店 ○

MI-CHIH 米脂

CHING-ERH-T'ING 井儿坪 8.14

YEN-CHIA-CHA 延家岔 8.13

LI-CHIA-YAI 李家崖 8.8

0   5   10   15 STATUTE MILES
0   5   10   20   40 KILOMETERS

SHB

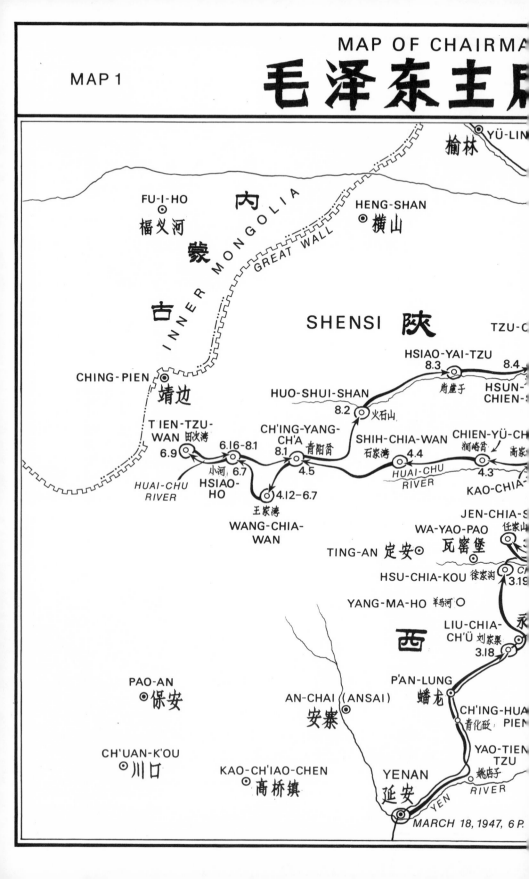

MAP 1

MAP OF CHAIRMA

毛泽东主席

YÜ-LIN
榆林

FU-I-HO
福义河

内

蒙

HENG-SHAN
横山

GREAT WALL

INNER MONGOLIA

古

SHENSI 陕

TZU-C

CHING-PIEN
靖边

HUO-SHUI-SHAN

HSIAO-YAI-TZU
8.3   8.4
肖崖子
HSUN-
CHIEN-

T'IEN-TZU-
WAN 田次湾
6.9

6.16-8.1

CH'ING-YANG-
CH'A
8.1 青阳岔

8.2 火石山

SHIH-CHIA-WAN
石家湾 4.4

CHIEN-YÜ-CH
涧峪岔 高家

小河 6.7

HSIAO-
HO

4.5

HUAI-CHU
RIVER

4.3

KAO-CHIA-

HUAI-CHU
RIVER

4.12-6.7
王家湾

JEN-CHIA-S
任家山

WANG-CHIA-
WAN

TING-AN 定安

WA-YAO-PAO
瓦窑堡

HSU-CHIA-KOU 徐家沟

C
3.19

YANG-MA-HO 羊马河

西

LIU-CHIA-
CH'Ü 刘家渠
3.18

永

PAO-AN
保安

AN-CHAI (ANSAI)
安寨

P'AN-LUNG
蟠龙

CH'UAN-K'OU
川口

KAO-CH'IAO-CHEN
高桥镇

CH'ING-HUA
PIEN
青化砭

YAO-TIEN
TZU
姚店子
RIVER

YENAN
延安

YEN

MARCH 18, 1947, 6 P.

AO TSE-TUNG'S JOURNEY

行动路线图

ANG-CHIA-
H'A 8.19

西岔 HSI-CH'A

10.
17

葭县 CHIA-HSIEN

堆家坪
T'AN-CHIA-
P'ING

10.18

LIN HSIEN ⊙ 临县

For detail map
of Chairman
Mao Tse-Tung's
Journey –
see Map 1 A

SHEN-
CHIA-
HSIEN

申家崄
11.21

SHUANG-T'A

双塔

3.24

MI-CHIH
米脂

(MARCH 21, 1948)

3.22

CHI-CHENG-TIEN

吉镇店

3 23 CHAI-TSE-
SHAN

CH'I-SHIH-
CHEN

YEN-
CHIA-
CHA

YELLOW RIVER

磺石镇 寨则山

8.8 李家崖

-YAI

延家岔 8.13

ANG- 黄家沟

CHIA-KOU

810 绥德

WU-PAO
吴堡

LIU-LIN-CHEN

柳林镇

SUI-TE

'IU-

A-P'ING

3.31

家坪

TSAO-
LIN-KOU

WU-TING RIVER

山

AO-

-HSIEN

崄

3.21

枣林沟

3.28

YELLOW RIVER

SHANSI

RIVER

清涧

CH'ING-CHIEN

SHIH-LOU
⊙
石楼

西

HSIEN

RIVER

YEN-CH'UAN
延川

YUNG-HO
永和
⊙

HSI HSIEN
隰县
⊙

YEN-CH'ANG
⊙ 延长

1:250,000

0   5   10   20   30
╠════╬════╬══════════╬══════════╣ STATUTE MILES
0   10   20   40   60 KILOMETERS

SHB

INNER MONGOLIA

内

SHEN-C

SAN-CH'AO-PAO

神

FU-KU
府谷⊙

三岔堡⊙

WU-CHAI
五寨⊙

SHEN-MU
⊙神木

4.4
K'O-LAN
岢嵐

CHING LE
静⊙

TS'AI-CHIA-YAI
蔡家崖⊙
3.26

兴县
HSING-HSIEN

LAN HSIEN
⊙嵐县

YÜ-LIN
⊙榆林

SHENSI
陕

SHANSI 山

FEN R.

LIN HSIEN
临县⊙

3.24
SHUANG-T'A
⊙双塔

TZU-CHOU
子洲⊙

西

CHAI-TSE-SHAN
(MARCH 23,
1948)

寨则山

LI-SHIH
⊙離石

WEN-SHUI

汾阳
FEN-YANG

MAO TSE-TUNG'S JOURNEY

行动路线图

INNER   MONGOLIA

古

SHUO HSIEN

LING-CH'IU
灵邱

SHA-HO
沙河

FAN-CHIH
繁峙

HUI RIVER

平型关 P'ING-HSING-KUAN

HO-HUI
河会
KUANG-WU
广武

4.7 PA-CH'IANG-CHUANG
坝墙庄

4.6
代县 TAI HSIEN

YANG-LING-CHIEH
杨林街

4.11

武
CHU-WU

HSI-HSIA KUAN
西下关

阜平 FU-P'ING

五台 WU-T'AI
4.12

4.13

CH'Ü-YANG
曲阳

YUAN-P'ING
原平

4.18
花山
HUA-SHAN

城南庄
CH'ENG-NAN-CHUANG

河   北

HSING-T'ANG

HU-TO RIVER

HO PEH
5.27

TA SHA RIVER

HSIN HSIEN
忻县

西柏坡
HSI-PAI-P'O

LING-SHOU
灵寿

行唐

SHANSI

P'ING SHAN
平山

正定 CHENG-TING

MENG HSIEN
孟县

石家庄
SHIH-CHIA-CHUANG

T'AI-YÜAN
太原

SHOU YANG
寿阳

YU T'ZU
榆次

HSI-YAN
昔阳

LIN CH'ENG
临城

0 5 10   20   40   60 STATUTE MILES

0 5 10   20   40   60   80 KILOMETERS

1:500,000

SHB

6.

◇ ◇ ◇

Mao's Way in Yenan

Sometimes by chance
A look or a glance
May one's fortunes advance.
— Proverb quoted in *Dream of the Red
Chamber*, as translated by David Hawkes

Her attention absorbed by the past, Chiang Ch'ing was not easily diverted. Each evening around ten or eleven a slight gentleman moved gingerly to her side to announce that dinner was prepared but she continued to talk as if she had not heard. The message was repeated at intervals until she decided to stop. Then she said, "Wash up if you like and meet me in the dining room."

In that spacious, barely decorated chamber we were seated at a round table with seven aides. The linen was heavy and white, and the porcelain and chopsticks of superior but unostentatious quality in the southern style. Being mistress of the table, as of any situation, was an activity Chiang Ch'ing relished. Mine was to comment upon what she said and to respond to questions, introducing my own topics only as the situation allowed. The others relished the foods, largely in silence, yet they seemed content to be captive to her lively entertainments — these evenings set off by her foreign "straight man."

Since dinner conversation continued the design of her previous narration, though in a lighter vein, I sat down with pen and notebook in hand. Observing this the first night in Canton, Chiang Ch'ing raised her eyebrows and asked teasingly whether I planned to share the meal. Of course, I said, adding that in her presence being deprived of the tools of my trade made me anxious. She laughed and chided me for "working too hard," a common compliment in Communist China. Purposely forgetful, the next evening at table I wielded chopsticks with my left hand and scribbled away with my right, a rudeness Chiang Ch'ing frowned off successfully. I was left envious of our "court recorder," who noted everything that was said, a feat accomplished by his being fed from the chopsticks of the deft female aides flanking him.

Our meals were unusual and handsomely prepared without being vulgarly extravagant.[1] Each consisted of some ten courses on a culinary theme — variations of a flesh or a fowl, or a regional cuisine. Tea was served almost continuously between meals. Only at table did wine and spirits appear, the latter a fiery distillate called *mao-t'ai.* Chiang Ch'ing usually shunned them. When toasts were made she raised her glass to her lips but did not actually take a sip. When she saw that I did, and continued to drink at intervals, she smiled, looked a bit annoyed, and said she did not mind. "All part of my research," I assured her, raising my glass with both hands and beaming at the flushed face of Lao Ch'en, my senior companion from Szechwan. She giggled and announced with bravado, "You and I know how to drink spirits!"

Of herself, Chiang Ch'ing announced dryly that alcohol weakened her nervous system, and she continued to flick her chopsticks over fresh plates of delicacies.

She preferred the mild-flavored dishes, especially the small bowls of gruellike substances served toward the end. These included broths in which were floating exotic seafood and fungi cut to resemble wilted flowers, rice congees sparkling with chopped shrimp and greens, millet porridge with jasmine blossoms on top, and a sweetened puree of walnuts that Chiang Ch'ing recommended as particularly nutritious. Beautiful to behold they were, though out of habit I avoided them in favor of the pungent, hot-and-sour dishes and dipped each morsel into vinegar and pepper jam, a thick sauce of pulverized hot peppers suspended in oil. After our first meal together additional cruets of vinegar and saucers of pepper jam always appeared at my place. Was the Chairman still so fond of Hunan hot peppers, I asked? (Hunan was his native province and the peppers were famous.) "Less so now that he is older," she responded lightly.

i

Chiang Ch'ing had broken off her story at the point where she was about to escape from Shanghai in the gathering storm of renewed Japanese invasion.

Left in suspense, I wondered to myself what she would name as her destination. I recalled a spurious Hong Kong account which claimed that she joined the Central Film Company, an organ of the KMT propaganda ministry, and traveled with it to Chungking and other cities of the interior, making National Defense films along the way, and surfacing a year or two later in Yenan.[2] Seemingly more reliable, the Communist film historian Cheng Chi-hua reported that in 1938 she was working with the Central Film Company in Wuhan, and the next year went to Chungking to film *Boys and Girls of China*, in which she starred with the handsome and versatile Chao Tan.[3]

My silent speculations were dismissed by her declaration that she had left Shanghai after the Marco Polo Bridge Incident of July 1937, the national calamity that cracked the façade of the United Front and started another cycle of Sino-Japanese struggle. Right after exposing her personal predicament in her article, "My Open Letter," which appeared in a Shanghai newspaper, she fled the city in fury and anguish. By the time she had traveled the nine hundred miles to Sian, the war had taken a turn for the worse. On August 13 the Japanese bombed their way into Shanghai and destroyed the unique social and cultural phenomenon that would be remembered as "Shanghai of the 1930's."

In the late 1930's Sian was a poor and sprawling market town of southern Shensi, a relic of the last millennium, when it served as the capital of eleven dynasties. The population had dwindled to about fifty thousand, of whom some five thousand were agents of the KMT, which now controlled the city, mainly through its underground. After the Sian Incident of December 1936, the CCP set up its Eighth Route Army Headquarters there. From 1937 to 1946 that office (restored in the 1970's as a shrine to the rise of communism) served migrant leftists as the point of induction into the mysteries of Party discipline before they were sent on the last stage of their journey: the three hundred mountainous miles north to Yenan. Chiang Ch'ing was one of thousands of young refugees who took to that road. For most of them, the trip was a major turning point in their lives.

"After the December Twelfth [Sian] Incident of 1936, when Chang Hsueh-liang detained Chiang Kai-shek, the situation improved somewhat. But we [the Red Army] were still placed under restrictions. Chiang Kai-shek moved up a force reputedly totaling three hundred thousand men to encircle and attack our base area. It was only after the December Twelfth Incident that I learned that our army had arrived in northern Shensi, and I asked to go there. I did not get to Yenan until the summer [actually, late August] of 1937. By that time it was extremely difficult to get there. I went on one of our army trucks that was being used to transport rice. Then a rainstorm destroyed the road and I had to stop midway and wait for a long time. By that time my money ran out, and I was at a complete loss. Someone got me a horse, but I had no idea how to ride it. Gingerly I climbed onto its back. The horse just kept munching grass, and would not budge. Afraid to admit that I did not know how to ride a horse, I dismounted, snapped off a willow branch, remounted, and whipped the horse on its buttocks. That made him wild and he galloped away madly. I felt as if I were falling to pieces and would be thrown at any minute. Finally the horse exhausted himself and slowed down.

"I arrived in Lo-ch'uan just when the meeting of the Politburo of the Central Committee was in session. I was so shaken up and frightened that I thought I would pass out right in front of them. But I was determined to meet the leading comrades of the Central Committee, all of whom had come out to greet me [usual fanfare for cultural celebrities?]. I said sternly to myself that I could not collapse in front of them and, what is more, that I must stand up very straight. And so I shook hands with all of them. The meeting they were holding was very important." [4]

Skirting the political issues which then occupied the Central Committee, she digressed upon horses, militarism, the ways of men of the north and of beasts to be broken to one's will. Horses were scarce in Yenan, and so were mainly reserved for the leaders. Eventually, her marriage to Mao also entitled her to a horse and compelled her to conquer her fear of them. By forcing herself to ride she gradually worked up to a speed of five kilometers per ten minutes (better than eighteen miles per hour).

"Even now I ride a gentle old horse. I adore riding. Do you?"

I had to admit that I enjoyed the idea of riding more than the experience. A horse, sensing my uneasiness, would have his way with me.

"You must take a fresh horse and break it in yourself," she advised. "When a horse of mine hears me call him 'Ma-erh' [something like 'Horsey'] he neighs back to me. But if I personally haven't broken him in, he may throw me."

Resuming the account of her arrival at the base area, she said that on the last leg of the fifty-mile trek north from Lo-ch'uan to Yenan, she and some others traveling there rode in the back of a truck. As it turned out, her truck was trailing just behind that of Mao Tse-tung, who was returning to Yenan at the close of the Lo-ch'uan meeting. That coincidence she was not aware of at the time, but learned about it later. Her first glimpse of Yenan's ancient wall was unforgettable. On its south gate were inscribed two characters, *an-lan*, "calm the waves," she recalled nostalgically.

Chiang Ch'ing's narrative did not include an account of the recent progress of the Red Army troops, which can be reconstructed independently. Seven months before her arrival in August 1937, the Party moved its headquarters from Pao-an to Yenan, forty-odd miles southeast. Yenan would serve over the next decade as the capital of the Shen-Kan-Ning Border Region (see endpaper map).* The area was bounded by Lo-ch'uan on the south and the Great Wall on the north, with the bend of the Yellow River forming the eastern and western extremities. Chiang Ch'ing had arrived at a breathing space in the rise of communism, almost two years after the termination of the Long March, at once the most harrowing and the most constructive experience in the formation of a Communist identity and ethos. Survivors of its nearly incredible trials of human endurance constituted a generation of revolutionary founders who would always be known among their comrades and the masses as "Long March veterans." That status distinction left her at a permanent disadvantage and prompted her, at another point in our interviews, to expound upon the later Liberation War, in which she did participate.

The objective dimensions of the Long March are generally known, but its human dimensions have been admitted only glancingly to the historical record. The march began in the fall of 1934 with the retreat of the Red Army after a cumulative defeat from five encirclement campaigns mounted by the KMT from December 1930 to October 1934 against the Central Soviet Districts in the Southeast. Only about twenty thousand troops, less than thirty percent of the original participants, survived the marathon of more than six thousand miles, the most westward part of the route looping through Szechwan and Yunnan. The march concluded at Wu-ch'i-chen in northern Shensi in a dizzying spirit of victory. The Party's core then moved some one hundred-eighty miles north to Pao-an, the ruin of a frontier city which was situated in barren hills and famed for sheltering the bandits who toppled the Ming dynasty in the middle of the seventeenth century.

The Central Committee remained at Pao-an through the Sian Incident, Chiang Kai-shek's celebrated arrest. That ploy, which forced Chiang to adopt a United Front against Japan, also enabled the Central Committee to shift strategic operations to Yenan, the massively walled city, now largely ruined, which had served for three millennia as a bastion against invasion from barbarian hordes from the North and continued to flourish until the time of the Moslem and Taiping rebellions of the mid-nineteenth century. The great Northwest famine of 1928–1933 was but the latest episode in that region's history of natural disasters costing millions of lives. Devoid of urban monuments, the "city" of Yenan was actually a natural citadel carved into the loess † cliffs by thousands of human hands over the centuries. Buildings were caves bored

---

* In the spirit of the United Front, the Communists agreed with the Nationalists on September 22, 1937, to change the name of their base in northern Shensi to the Shen-Kan-Ning Border Region, a compound term that referred to the three provinces which by then were partially liberated by the Communists. Among other concessions the Communists agreed to stop confiscation of land, establish democratic rule through universal suffrage, and change the name of the Red Army to the National Revolutionary Army. Events proved that these were mainly paper changes.

† A fine-grained, reddish-brown loam deposited by the winds.

into this hard-packed soil, an insulation that made them unusually warm in winter, cool in summer, and impregnable to bombing. More refined than pueblo dwellings, the caves had arched openings, wood-latticed windows covered with paper, and squared-off interior chambers. The finest caves were equipped with stout black-lacquered doors, in all more civilized than most ordinary Chinese dwellings. Zigzagging footpaths connected one tier of caves to the next along the cliffs flanking the inner city. When the Red Army arrived in Yenan the population was around three thousand; during the next ten years it would peak at one hundred thousand.*

The men of the military who dominated Yenan's revolutionary society were skeptical of neophytes, and especially of women. Success in integration usually depended upon the reputation one brought along, how one managed to characterize one's political past, and the confidence one instilled in Party authorities. Shortly after Chiang Ch'ing arrived she went to see Li Fu-ch'un, deputy director of the Party Organization Committee (and husband of a prominent leader of the women's movement, Ts'ai Ch'ang). In her review of her political history she described the injustices she had suffered at the hands of her political superiors in Shanghai, how for years she had struggled to make contact with the Shanghai underground Party organization and had been barred, despite her claim to have first joined the Party in Tsingtao. Their reasons for discriminating against her were never made clear, she said. These confessions and accusations before Li Fu-ch'un agitated her terribly, yet he remained sympathetic. That was of no consequence, he said soothingly. "From now on everything will be all right."

"All right" was a judgment of political status depending upon the time of one's arrival. The formal establishment of one's relation to the Party prior to arrival determined priority of admission to the Party School and other leading educational units of the Border Region government. After the great wartime influx of students and urban intellectuals, matriculation was highly competitive. Chiang Ch'ing immediately aimed for the highest institute, the Party School. Admission depended on Central Committee action and was limited to persons of proved political rectitude. How well she recalled the sharp pangs of anxiety as she stood before the eminent Party leaders who reviewed her past as an actress and political activist. They considered each detail, whether or not it had anything direct to do with present political issues.

Chang Kuo-t'ao, long an adversary of Mao, was one of the few contemporary leaders to recall Chiang Ch'ing's reception by the Yenan government. At the time he was chairman of the Northern Shensi Border Region government, the

---

* According to my Yenan guides, in the early 1970's the population had dwindled to around fifty thousand. Despite the equities of established Communism, the people were still poor, their skins leathery, and their eyes permanently squinted against the unrelenting sun and winds.

only local regime recognized by the world beyond, he claimed. His memoir confirms her date of arrival from an alternate perspective: in the late summer of 1937 admissions were in the charge of the Public Relations Department. Though nominally under the Secretariat of the Border Region government, it was actually directed by the CCP Central Committee and functioned as a branch organization of its Political Security Bureau. But in fact the Public Relations Department was governed by the will of two men: Mao Tse-tung and Chang Wen-t'ien. Some of the people received by the Public Relations Department, though suspected of being quasi-Communists, were still regarded as friends, among them the "democratic personage" Liang Sou-ming, the left-wing militarist Ho Chi-li, and the woman who became Mao's last wife, Chiang Ch'ing, an *artiste* whose arrival commanded little attention.[5]

Years later, Chiang Ch'ing recalled, when she and Li Fu-ch'un reminisced about their frontier days, he laughed to think of how he had deliberately tried to frighten her during her screening for admission to the prestigious Party School. She made it nonetheless, but that was only the first hurdle. She was also eager to join the Lu Hsun School (later Academy) of Literature and the Arts [6] (whether at the same time or after she attended the Party School was not clear). Past experience in the performing arts was insufficient; political qualifications were paramount. When she went to state her case before Lu Hsun School officials, Ch'en Yun, a Central Committee member who was serving as director of the Organization Department of the CCP, interviewed her. Knowing that he personally controlled the admissions procedure, she took pains to impress him with the sincerity of her desire to study Marxism there; she could not allow him to think that the theater was her sole interest. She told Ch'en Yun that she had packed her trunk and brought it along, so eager she was to move into the school. Her presentation must have convinced him of her willingness to obey any decision made about her by the Organization Department, for he granted her admission straightway. (She laughed now at the earnest way she went about things in those days, but she added hastily that all she was really thinking about then was her desire to study.) Ch'en Yun actually was never a great fan of hers. Not long after he admitted her to the school he went to watch her perform there, and then humiliated her by panning the play in which she appeared.

Taken as a whole, her life in Yenan had begun routinely. In the fall she began a six-month army training program, her first exposure to the military, a matter of record to which she pointed proudly. (She had been striving to appeal to the military since Cultural Revolution days.) Concurrently she underwent her first formal drilling in Marxist-Leninist theory and its Chinese variants, then mainly the Comintern's orthodoxy promoted by Wang Ming at the Party School. Though scarcely older than herself, Wang Ming, whose word was gospel among self-styled Communists in Shanghai, was already the Chinese high priest of Marxism-Leninism, and Mao Tse-tung's only serious ideological rival in Yenan. Her work in the performing arts continued, though she cast aside my questions of which plays and which roles.

She stressed that she did not work long in art and literature. "Of the four years I spent in Shanghai, for two years I worked in the upper strata of cultural circles and the other two were spent at the grassroots level. When I reached Yenan my profession changed. At first I did not want to go to the Lu Hsun Academy of Literature and Arts, but I was obliged by my organization to work there."

I blinked and asked why the reluctance, but did not remind her that in her earlier account to me she had been wholeheartedly for admission.

"I like to do work among the masses. Compared with the arts as such, work among the masses is more important. Mass work is fundamental political work."

Apparently her feelings were ambivalent and the ambivalence came out in the act of recollection. Perhaps she felt that return to the theater work in which the academy came to specialize would restore her image as an actress in foreign "bourgeois dramas" and in National Defense films, both of which were antagonistic to life in Mao Tse-tung's revolutionary base areas. Or was the secretarial work to which she was first assigned, she said, an implicit insult because it was too lowly? Or was the experience of working once again under certain of the academy's new administrators — among them Chou Yang and Chang Keng, who had persecuted her in Shanghai — too painful for her to want to recall? Or did the academy become such an elitist and Wang Ming–oriented institution that she did not want to emphasize to her present company, in an era of aggressive appeal to the masses, that she had been seriously involved in it?

Her feelings aside, she did establish certain facts about the Lu Hsun School, which became the famous Lu Hsun Academy of Literature and the Arts in 1938. In the fall of 1937 she was serving as a secretary (a semiadministrative assignment) at the school. Her primary responsibility was for girl students, whose interests she protected and promoted. Among her charges was Chang Ying, her most trusted aide in our present Canton mission. Another woman comrade named An Lin was there, and others who are still alive. Glancing appreciatively at Chang Ying, she said, "I'm going to show off my seniority by saying that I became her teacher."

ii

Chang Ying merits a brief digression from Chiang Ch'ing's story. Though she held an important post as a propaganda expert in publicizing the People's

Republic abroad, during my visit she served as Chiang Ch'ing's principal aide. In discussing Yenan, Chiang Ch'ing turned to her for additional information or confirmation of a point she had made. Chang was only eight years younger than her patron, but like almost everyone she was light-years inferior in political status. In Chiang Ch'ing's presence she was keenly observant of all that went on and spoke always with cautious economy. But away from Chiang Ch'ing she came into her own as a woman of intellectual vigor, perception, and warmth. In the guesthouse we occupied, or on excursions to monuments or restaurants in Canton, she was responsible both for keeping me entertained and for keeping track of what I said. She also drew out observations and assessments of me from other comrades in our company. All this intelligence was apparently passed on to Chiang Ch'ing during private daytime meetings at the villa. Through the Chang Ying channel Chiang Ch'ing conveyed to me messages she preferred to relay indirectly, among them the wish that I not disrupt her train of thought with questions (conversational reciprocity was not her custom). Chang Ying also delivered documents for me to read, all selected to verify Chiang Ch'ing's reconstruction of events. Through the same channel I conveyed to Chiang Ch'ing a number of questions, among them the confusion in foreign accounts about the time she arrived in Yenan, of which she no doubt was already aware. Chang Ying repudiated the discrepancies adamantly and confirmed Chiang Ch'ing's report of arrival on a direct route from Shanghai via Sian in August 1937.

What were her grounds for certainty? I asked in private conversation.

She arrived not long after Chiang Ch'ing, she said — in November of that same year, not in 1938 or 1939.

She went on to describe her own early days in Yenan and laughed as she did so. She was a mere child, only fifteen. And all she could speak was Cantonese, the dialect of the city where she was born and grew up (though her Mandarin, which we spoke together, was excellent).

What drew her to Yenan?

"I knew I wanted to resist Japan; in fact, that's about all I knew then. When the people in the Northwest first heard me speak they burst out laughing at the strange sound of my dialect. Then when I tried to conform to their Mandarin dialect of the North they mocked my heavy Cantonese accent. To overcome the distortion I got up each morning before everyone else and ran into the hills, where I read aloud scripts of plays in the Mandarin dialect."

"Then you and Chiang Ch'ing were both actresses."

"Not really like Comrade Chiang Ch'ing," she responded shyly. "I could never have made a career in drama because I was not talented enough."

Other elements of Chang Ying's watchful and self-effacing character emerged through seemingly trivial incidents. One evening Chiang Ch'ing stopped speaking and reached for an oblong box that an aide had brought in a few minutes before. From it she withdrew two letter openers, both delicately carved, one of ivory, the other bamboo. "Both are not for you," she remarked in jest. But she had not yet decided which I should have. Turning them over in her hands admiringly, she said that both were beautiful, though the ivory was more precious. "So you should have the ivory one." She handed it to me, then leaned over to present the bamboo one to Chang Ying, who reacted with surprise and embarrassment. Delighted, I thanked her and read the inscription commemorating the archaeological excavations that had been conducted at Changsha since the Cultural Revolution. Those digs into a substantially re-trievable past demonstrated the peoples' scientific achievement and appealed to her dual interests, the arts and history.

A couple of days later Chang Ying came to me privately and gave me the bamboo letter opener, insisting that I keep it. Puzzled, I refused, but she would not yield. So I offered to exchange the ivory one for the bamboo; that too was unacceptable. "I know you love bamboo," she said. How did she know, I won-dered. In roundabout fashion it emerged that she had observed me slipping out of the guesthouse (where we occupied different wings) at daybreak to photo-graph bamboo shoots. Laughing at such an invasion of privacy, I gave in. At our next meeting, Chiang Ch'ing observed with amusement that I had both now. She said she liked the idea of preferring bamboo over ivory, thus spiting conventions of material value.

iii

Now that Chiang Ch'ing was in Yenan, naturally I wondered how she met Mao, how she was swept into his personal domain. The answer came ellip-tically, her romantic imagination flickering behind a public face. Not all that she said was for the public record. While still in Shanghai she had heard rumors about the Red Army's maverick chief Mao Tse-tung and his redoubt-able partner Chu Te. Sporadic news reports and travelers shuttling back and forth between the White and the Red Areas conveyed mixed impressions of Mao, a peasant rebel and people's defender with a modern revolutionary con-sciousness. She had only a faint idea of his appearance and no notion of his personality. Like other recruits to Yenan she was fascinated by differences among the leading comrades and became aware of Mao's aura of aloofness — his Olympian air, as some called it. But during her first few months there, her life was affected by the leaders who exercised direct control over the various po-litical, military, and cultural organizations.

Yet Mao Tse-tung learned about her as Lan P'ing, the actress, not long after she arrived. How could she tell? He sought her out personally and offered her a ticket to a lecture he was to give at the Marxist-Leninist Institute. Startled and awestruck, she declined, then swiftly conquered her shyness, accepted the ticket, and went to watch him perform.

Their liaison evolved in ways not obvious to the community of leaders and hardly apparent to the masses. Her urge for privacy, which stemmed from both the traditional and revolutionary proprieties, would not allow her to deliver to the public record intimate details of a love affair that became a marriage. In moments of ideological purity with me, and so often before her public, she would say that to exhibit individual feelings, romantic imagination, and attractive sexuality in life or literature was to display "bourgeois fallacies" — deviations from the impersonal and asexual "proletarian" ideal. Paradoxically, though, I found her to be a person of intense feelings, extraordinary imagination, and evident femininity. Yet she gave me no reason to believe that she had ever been plagued by any conflict between romantic love and revolutionary determination.

What did Chiang Ch'ing and Mao find in common? On the surface the differences in their personal histories are more striking than the similarities. Was theirs a magnetic attraction of opposites?

Mao was born and reared in Hunan, a province of the southern interior. More than twenty-five hundred years earlier Hunan was the site of the distinctive Ch'u state, and since the Sung dynasty (960–1278) famed for the bandits that lurked in its marshes. Over the last century Hunan spawned numerous Nationalist and Communist revolutionaries.

Chiang Ch'ing, as we have seen, came from the littoral, from Shantung, once the ancient state of Lu, which gave birth to Confucian culture. In the nineteenth century Shantung was torn apart by Taipings and Boxers and by a women's fighting corps called the Red Lanterns (coincidentally the name of Chiang Ch'ing's first revolutionary opera?). Imperialist rivalry for control over peninsular Shantung in the early twentieth century provoked the nationalistic upheavals that awoke her political consciousness.

Born to rich peasants before the fall of the Manchu dynasty, Mao received his education in Confucian classicism. His revolt against his family's commitment to Confucian high culture began by his reading classic novels: *Romance of the Three Kingdoms*, which was about *Realpolitik* among rival kingdoms at the fall of the Han dynasty; *Water Margin*, a story cycle of bandit adventurers; and *Journey to the West*, a fantastic tale of a monk and a monkey, a spoof of social systems.

Born to a culture-poor family in the early years of the Republic, Chiang Ch'ing was exposed only to fundamentalist Confucian values — rigorous self-discipline and deference to superiors. Twenty years younger than Mao, she bypassed earthy historical novels, traditionally more appealing to boys and men, in favor of the modern theater, which was a repository of foreign values and behavior. Yet she was also attracted to traditional culture, particularly as portrayed in the great family romance *Dream of the Red Chamber* and in the pornographic novel of Ming urbanity *Chin P'ing Mei*, works that displayed life among the rich, aristocratic, and powerful.

Although Chiang Ch'ing joined the Party earlier in life than Mao did, she at nineteen and he at twenty-eight, the disparity is misleading, for the Party did not exist before Mao helped to found it, and her rank-and-file membership was discontinuous. An itinerant youth, Mao toyed with several notions of what he would become — soapmaker, teacher, lawyer, businessman. But in his late twenties he pitched all his energies into revolutionary leadership. In contrast, Chiang Ch'ing had devoted herself to one profession for nearly a decade, and until she met Mao when she was twenty-three, she had divided her energies between her career and Party work.

Perhaps the salient contrast between them, one that expresses the major dialectic of the modern era, was his rural and her urban orientation. Mao never lived continuously in a major city until he became head of state in Peking in 1949. From her fifteenth year Chiang Ch'ing lived in the elegant provincial capital of Tsinan, then in the modern ports of Tsingtao and Shanghai, with occasional tours to Peking. Throughout her adult life Shanghai served as her cultural touchstone. There, on the eve of the Cultural Revolution years later, she took a strategic stand against entrenched powers in Peking.

Mao's experience of Shanghai was more fugitive and humble: he was present at the clandestine founding of the CCP in 1921, returned briefly in the winter of 1922, and the next year became head of the Organization Department of the Party and served on the Executive Bureau of the KMT during the first phase of collaboration. He also worked there briefly as a laundryman — that proverbially demeaning job in a city dominated by foreigners. The poverty of his urban experience is revealed in his writings: no single essay is devoted to the political history of Shanghai or to its evolving social or economic structure.

A self-styled revolutionary in marriage as in politics, Mao's first marriage to an illiterate peasant girl, arranged in the traditional way by his parents, was never consummated,[7] a slap in the faces of the old people and their mores. His first genuine marriage was to Yang K'ai-hui, the liberated daughter of his liberal ethics teacher in Changsha. Being a man and thus unconstrained by rules of chastity, Mao was always free to talk about his former mates. Even after two remarriages (his next was to Ho Tzu-chen), he honored Yang K'ai-hui in a classical poem, "The Immortals"[8] (she is "my proud poplar," a play upon her surname, which means poplar):

I lost my proud poplar, and you your willow,
Poplar and willow soar lightly to the heaven of heavens.
Wu Kang, asked what he has to offer,
Presents them respectfully with cassia wine.

The lonely goddess in the moon spreads her ample sleeves
To dance for these faithful souls in the endless sky.
Of a sudden comes word of the tiger's defeat on earth,
And they break into tears of torrential rain.

Comrade Chiang Ch'ing. A new name and a new persona. To divest herself of Li Yun-ho and Lan P'ing and their untoward Shanghai associations, she like thousands of converts took a new name in Communism. Was the name Chiang Ch'ing, as some believed, bestowed by Mao, I asked?

She reacted swiftly, as if I had trespassed in a private realm. The choice was hers. She would explain its meaning, literally "rivers azure." The first character, *chiang*, bears no sign of her family name, Li, with which she wanted to sever connections. *Chiang*, moreover, reflects her love of long and broad rivers like the Yangtze, whose mouth she knew in Shanghai. *Ch'ing* projects her love of lofty mountains and the sea, in Chinese paintings both represented by *ch'ing* or azure, the color of nature, which the Chinese envision as basically blue with a tinge of green. To convey the special blueness of *ch'ing* she quoted the line of T'ang poetry which goes, "Azure comes from the blue but excels blue." [9] That, she said, is how one should read the significance of her name.

The significances are multiple and fascinating. The *ch'ing*-azure of Chiang Ch'ing meant that she should transcend the Lan (blue) P'ing of old. The *chiang* meaning river is powerfully associated with *yin*, the female principle in traditional Chinese thought. In myth and history, women were punished for causing rivers to overflow their banks and flood the land.[10] There was (and still must be) a popular saying "Women are the source of all disaster" — "*Nü shih huo shui.*" The characters making "disaster" are "water disaster" (*huo shui* reversed).

Her clear *yin* association perfectly matched Mao's *yang*. In revolutionary iconography Mao is symbolized by the sun, the cosmic force fundamental to *yang*, the masculine principle. In the graphic arts the sun's symbol, always positive, is dominant, and in propaganda spoken and sung, "Chairman Mao is the reddest red sun of our hearts."

From the early days of their marriage they joked about their disparate backgrounds, Chiang Ch'ing recalled wryly. The Chairman used to tell her that as a child she learned to "believe in deities and read Confucius." From there she went on to learn the "bourgeois stuff," as he put it; that came with indulgence in theater. Only later did she begin to tackle Marxism-Leninism, which was her third stage of learning. But the truth of the matter was that she was opposed to Confucianism from an *early* age. As she matured she learned to support the Communist Party in principle. Even now she had not mastered Marxism-Leninism in theory or practice. Her life was unremitting effort in that direction.

At the time Chiang Ch'ing and Mao joined forces relations between the sexes in the Red Areas were extraordinarily disrupted. Of the Long March participants, only thirty were women, most of them wives of Red Army leaders. Nearly all the married soldiers had had to abandon their wives and children before embarking on the march. Because of distance and warfare, few families were reunited. Where the Red soldiers settled in the Northwest, the ratio of men to women was around eighteen to one. Some of the men formed local liaisons or remarried without bothering to divorce abandoned or lost wives. But the vast majority, too young and too poor to marry, were urged by their commanders not to dissipate their virility on sex or their money on prostitutes. All powers were needed for their first duty, which was to defeat the enemy.

In the areas under Red control, marriage and divorce were to be carried out under the laws of the Chinese Soviet Republic, the original draft having been prepared in 1931, revised in 1934, and revised again in 1939, the year in which Chiang Ch'ing and Mao were married.[11] Its stipulations were untraditional and egalitarian: the Western model of monogamy supplanted Chinese polygamy (affordable mainly by the rich in the past), and freely chosen marriage partners were to supersede those imposed by parents or matchmakers. Simple registration procedures conformed to Russian Soviet prototypes, which were reformulated for China by Wang Ming. But what existed on the revolutionary books did not automatically dictate social realities. Marriage could be as simple as an oral agreement between a man and a woman, its authenticity confirmed by the Party's announcement of the union. The Women's Department also handled some marriage and divorce cases.

Most survivors of the Long March constituted a warrior elite whose opinions, as much as Legalistic innovations, set the standards for everybody in the liberated areas. In the old days they would have been married off at the pleasure of their parents; now, in progressive Yenan circles, where parental authority and Confucian pieties were damned, they were expected to marry according to their own volition, but in line with the Party's interests and certainly not into an exploitative class. As revolutionary idealists they scorned ostentatious romance, flagrant adultery, and all manner of personal indulgence. Their puritanical high-mindedness on behalf of revolution was reinforced by the cultural backwardness of the Northwest. Here, as everywhere in China, divorce was virtually the husband's prerogative. When it was exercised (rarely), the rejected wife was humiliated. From such standards their leaders, even their Chairman, would not be excepted.

Moreover, the independent social behavior of the droves of urban students, artists, and intellectuals who followed upon the army's heels to Yenan clashed with the persisting peasant norms. Men and women both were inheritors of the women's liberation movement that had swept over the young educated classes during the May Fourth era, inspiring the heady Bohemianism of China's modern arts world. Flouting all marriage rites, native or Western — couples drew up their own contracts or dispensed with them altogether — signaled that one belonged to the avant-garde. Or a man and a woman of the cultural "upper strata" could live together with a certain modern conventionality. Gossip about the fluid private lives of movie stars spread from the coastal cities to the interior and would be transmitted abroad.

It reached as far as Chairman Mao. To outward appearance he had broken with his wife, Ho Tzu-chen, the Long March veteran who had mothered his children, and had taken up with a Shanghai refugee — a movie star. She thus had to overcome not only the skepticism harbored by revolutionary chiefs about the political record behind Lan P'ing's glossy image, but also the peasants' instinctive fear of and contempt for the proverbial free-living, free-loving big-city girl.

Lingering controversies aroused by Chiang Ch'ing's liaison with Mao confound the historical record. No one who knew her or Mao personally has dared to discuss various rumors in print. Or was there nothing to explain? Who, for instance, planted the story about a Central Committee action against the marriage, one to the effect that if Mao's peers allowed him to wed this volatile actress, she must be confined to domesticity and kept from meddling in public affairs for twenty years, or even to the end of her days? To some observers her breaking out into cultural revolution not much more than twenty years after the marriage substantiated that piece of hearsay.

Such questions I put to Chang Ying privately, and as I expected, she relayed them to Chiang Ch'ing, who dealt with them in her own fashion late the next evening.

Long after she left Shanghai, she remembered in anguish, she could not rid her mind of the personal enemies she had made there, for many had resurfaced in Yenan. Using all possible devices, including manipulation of public opinion in the Northwest, they had let her know that if she refused to comply with their propositions (which she did not spell out here, though they probably included having been forced to work in politically compromising films), they would *kill* her.*

---

* Since her language was neither conventionally hyperbolic nor profane, implications about the nature of comradeliness among Shanghai Communists are chilling.

Anticipating justice in Yenan, she explained this background of persecution to the highest leaders, members of the Politburo, in order that they should be clear about her past. Then, after she became the wife of the Chairman (recognized in late 1938) * and still found herself alienated from the work she wanted to do, she feared that misconceptions about her personal history were still unresolved. With no one to defend her (apparently not even Mao), she made another special appearance before the Party organization just to impress upon these ostensibly fair-minded men her plight in Shanghai.

"We were clear about your history," they responded.

Their words were meant to be reassuring, but words were not enough. Citing Chang Keng, drama director and a chief of Shanghai's underground Party organization (and her rejected suitor), she asked, "Why did he call me a Trotskyite, leading others to believe this was the case?"

"Chang Keng did not mean it," they replied equivocally.

They said that, Chiang Ch'ing reasoned, only because they were being shielded by Chou Yang.† They claimed that Chang Keng and others "did not know her yet," but that was foolish, for actually Chang Keng knew her quite well. Not until she had lived in Yenan for a while did she come to the full realization that Chang Keng and his company were really "special agents of the enemy" (presumably the KMT, yet one wonders why enemy agents were not exposed in the Red Army camp). She would never forget how difficult they had made her life in Shanghai. Even after she became the Chairman's wife and it was within her power to destroy them, she restrained herself. Take Chang Keng, she said. In Yenan he was allowed to serve as head of the Drama Department of the Lu Hsun Academy, an arrangement she might have blocked, for it was hardly in her own interest. Then after Liberation he was appointed director of the Research Institute of Drama.

Continuing blandishments from the Party organzation could not dispel her suspicion that some of the present leaders opposed her and were responsible for cordoning her off, for not allowing the masses to know her. Above all else she wanted the masses to recognize her for who she was and to welcome her presence in their territory.

With that in mind she made still another appearance at the headquarters of the Party organization and provided further details of political conditions in the Shanghai underground Party apparatus and of how she had been victimized by it. From her position as wife of the Chairman she wanted them to understand

* Doubtless without ceremony, this union may have been formalized simply by the Chairman's making known his most recent living arrangement to his colleagues on the Central Committee. Chiang Ch'ing chose not to discuss the event of the marriage as datable or contractual.

† Who, from his position of strength in Yenan, may not have wanted Politburo members to stress his former promotion, under Wang Ming's auspices, of National Defense literature and arts in Shanghai.

that she would not take revenge against persons who had once thwarted her and continued to bear grudges against her. They should understand that she was willing to work on their behalf. If only they would admit their guilt she would forgive them. She waited. No one confessed.

For years afterwards she suspected that Chou Yang, who had controlled almost single-handedly the Party's cultural affairs since the mid-1930's, was chiefly responsible for her disconnection from the Party in Shanghai, for the unfavorable rumors spread about her, and subsequently for her isolation from the masses in Yenan. But until she was certain she kept silent.

Scanning the impassive faces of her entourage she announced gravely that she was taking this opportunity to clear up once and for all the issue of her discontinuous Party affiliation. For years she had surmised that Chou Yang, T'ien Han, Yang Han-sheng, Chang Keng, and other members of the League of Left-Wing Dramatists were responsible for her misfortunes in Shanghai. Not until she seized the initiative on the eve of the Cultural Revolution did she finally summon the courage to go up to Chou Yang and put it to him bluntly: "Did you know that I was in Shanghai then and what I sought?"

"I knew," he replied cautiously.

"I was trying to make contact with the Communist Party."

He lowered his head, she reported in low, deliberate tones.

iv

Restless, Chiang Ch'ing arose, beckoned me to follow, and motioned her bodyguard to lead the way through the tall doors that opened in to the pitch-black night. Obviously perplexed, Hsiao Chiao reached for his flashlight and plunged ahead into the humid night air and faint moonlight. She followed him and I her. Behind me trailed the interpreters and the young man whose task it was to write down all words that passed between us. He was entirely on his own now because Chiang Ch'ing had deliberately led us out of reach of the indoor microphones.

As she walked along, Chiang Ch'ing spoke briskly and excitedly. But because she did not turn her head around toward us, I could not catch some of her words, and the scribe struggling in the rear obviously caught none. Moreover, we had to pick our way gingerly to avoid being impaled on the glinting bayonets held by young PLA guards hidden in the bamboo thicket lining the narrow pathway. As I glanced over my shoulder, the moonlight and the flashlight's darting beam illuminated the whites of the eyes and the glittering smiles of Chang Ying, Yü Shih-lien, and Ch'en Ming-hsien, also anxious in this mysteriously armed tropical garden.

"There are certain things I want to tell *you, but not the world.*" With these words Chiang Ch'ing opened a torrent of talk to be kept off the record.* She knew of the international gossip about the circumstances of her marriage to Mao, but was not unduly concerned by it. Most was rubbish, malicious rumors possibly started by Wang Ming and his ilk. She was aware of various allegations which had appeared in a biographical sketch of her in the London journal *The China Quarterly*, but that was riddled with errors.[12] Premier Chou was concerned about her welfare. She trusted him, and for that reason he had confidence in her. Both he and his wife Teng Ying-ch'ao knew that she would not want to talk about the welter of controversies which had grown up around her marriage to the Chairman. Nevertheless, she had something to say about it.

By the time the Party arrived in the Central Soviet Districts (she probably meant Yenan in January 1937), Chairman Mao and his third wife Ho Tzu-chen had been separated for over a year. By the time she herself arrived in Yenan straight from Shanghai in the late summer of 1937, Mao and Ho were divorced.[13] Ho had left the Northwest and was already convalescing from illnesses in the Soviet Union. Who initiated the divorce procedure? Ho Tzu-chen — not the Chairman, she said pointedly.[14]

Although she never met Ho, she pieced together elements of her character from comments by various members of the Chairman's family, and occasionally from the Chairman, who was notably reticent about her. Ho Tzu-chen, Chiang Ch'ing was made to realize, was a stubborn woman who "never came to understand the political world of Chairman Mao." Her problems were linked in part to her family background: birth into the landlord-merchant class had accustomed her to fairly high living standards. When cities were taken during the Long March, Ho announced that she wanted to quit the March and settle down there because she was used to living in cities. Spoiled in her youth, she never overcame her scorn of manual labor. She refused to "cut paper" and other simple work for which responsibility was shared.[15]

Those temperamental problems were compounded by misfortune, Chiang Ch'ing continued. During the March Ho was wounded several times in enemy attacks, experiences which destroyed her physical and mental balance.† By the time the Red forces reached the Northwest in late 1935, she was beyond coping with either the political situation, her children, or other personal relations. Naturally, the Chairman found her behavior intolerable. When the Party reached the Central Soviet Districts of the Northwest, Ho abandoned the Chairman, vowing never to settle in Yenan.[16] She returned on her own to

* Throughout I have tried to respect her discrimination between private and public messages. What follows here is what she authorized me to say.

† She, like countless others, seems to have collapsed from nervous disorders, a largely unexplored aspect of China's revolutionary history.

Sian. Chou En-lai and Teng Ying-ch'ao, who were concerned about her relations with the Chairman, tried to persuade her to return to Yenan, but she
refused. With no one to cajole or control her, she took out her frustrations on
her two children by beating them compulsively. Even as adults they showed
the effects of having been battered, Chiang Ch'ing said. Like their mother and
because of her they failed to adjust to the demands of socialist life.

Around 1939 Ho and the two children — the daughter was still tiny — were
sent by the Party to Moscow. There the rough treatment by medical authorities
and by other Russians who tried to control her made her worse. Depressed in
her isolation, she resumed beating her children mercilessly. Eventually she
gave up trying to mother them at all. Others took custody and she was committed to an asylum. In the late 1940's (when Stalin was becoming increasingly
disenchanted with Mao) she was sent back to Shanghai. Aged now, she still
lives there in a mental institution. Periodically she is given shock treatments.

Is there any explanation for her condition? I asked.

Depressive reaction to the harsh circumstances of her life, Chiang Ch'ing
responded quietly.

Unquestionably, there was more to the story of Mao's break with Ho —
loyal wife, fecund mother, Long March veteran — than the sum of Chiang
Ch'ing's publishable statements. Could she have read into Ho's tragic fate
implications for her own?

The destinies of Ho Tzu-chen, Chiang Ch'ing, and other women whom Mao
attracted were linked inexorably to the revolution's most guarded element —
his character and personal power. Contemporary observers have left glimpses.
Like many foreign journalists athirst for political romance, Nym Wales was entranced by the "Yenan mystique." Mao she called "the King Arthur of China
. . . the Chairman of the Yenan Round Table. His men were knights and his
women were truly ladies, with dignity, pride and awareness of establishing the
standards for the rest of China." Although Nym Wales never met Mao's last
wife, Chiang Ch'ing corresponds quite perfectly with her intuitive American
grasp of what Mao appreciated in women. She wrote: "Mao was the type of
man who especially liked women, but not ordinary women. He liked a feminine woman who could make a home for him, and he appreciated beauty, intelligence and wit, as well as loyalty to himself and his ideas. He was not afraid
of independent-minded people and would not have objected to lipstick and
curled hair." [17]

In the revised (1968) edition of *Red Star Over China* Edgar Snow mentioned
Lily Wu (Wu Kuang-wei), an actress who fascinated Mao and uncannily set
the stage for Chiang Ch'ing. In the late 1930's Lily Wu served as the interpreter for the flamboyant Agnes Smedley, a journalist and sometime friend
of the Chinese Communist leaders. A woman of dazzling grace and talent, Lily

Wu was equipped with a mind of her own. While almost all the other women sported short bobs and naked faces, Lily Wu preserved the long curled bob and the habit of wearing lipstick, which she had picked up in Shanghai. In May 1937 Mao dropped in on Agnes Smedley's cave where she, Lily, and Mrs. Snow (Nym Wales) were sharing supper. Like many young political enthusiasts in Yenan, Lily worshiped Mao. As they all drank freely of wine, she enticed Mao to hold her hand.[18]

Ho Tzu-chen found out about that dalliance — whether it was of more consequence than Mrs. Snow observed, one does not know — and brought a formal charge against Lily Wu for having alienated her husband's affections. Mao denied the charge. According to Snow, a divorce was nevertheless granted by a special court established by the Central Committee and both Wu and Ho were banished, the latter, we know, to Russia.[19]

Was the exiled Lily Wu the harbinger of Chiang Ch'ing? Although Chiang Ch'ing did not date specifically the inception of her liaison with Mao, Yang Tzu-lieh, the wife of Mao's rival Chang Kuo-t'ao, has told Ho's side of the story, which generally complements Chiang Ch'ing's. In the very early spring of 1938 Yang arrived from Shanghai at the CCP's Eighth Route Army Headquarters in Sian. There she was assigned to a simple room which was austerely furnished with two wooden beds. On the second bed lay a small, pale, sickly-looking woman who introduced herself as Ho Tzu-chen, the wife of Mao Tse-tung. Yang Tzu-lieh asked her why she was not in Yenan with her husband and comrades. Ho said that she wanted to go to Moscow for a medical cure, and had no desire to go to Yenan. "Tse-tung treats me badly," she explained. "We bicker and have rows. He grabs the bench and I grab the chair! I know we're finished."

Married comrades should not behave that way, Yang Tzu-lieh responded, and offered to visit Mao in Yenan and to persuade him to write her a letter. Ho was despondent.

Later, another comrade, Liu Ch'un-hsien, told Yang Tzu-lieh privately: "Lan P'ing is very pretty and she can act. When she arrived in Yenan old Mao was ecstatic. He applauded her performances so loudly that Ho Tzu-chen became jealous. The two of them often fought about this, with terrible results."

A few days after Yang Tzu-lieh arrived in Yenan she told Mao that she had seen Ho in Sian and had offered to bring her back, but she had refused. "It's all your fault," she told Mao angrily. "You should write to her right away."

Mao just laughed and said nothing. When she saw Mao again several days later, he remarked, "I've written a letter to Ho, but she won't return." Whether or not he had actually written that letter, Yang was not sure. What was certain was that Ho's health was deteriorating, and she had to go to Moscow.

Comrades used to remark how stubborn Ho was — that she had the temper of a Hunanese donkey.[20]

Clearly, Mao had his eye on Lan P'ing as soon as she arrived in Yenan.

v

In all, Chiang Ch'ing spoke little of her own family and ancestry, but a great deal about the members of Mao's family she came to know intimately over the years. One of the reasons may stem from the Chinese tradition that when a girl marries she leaves her own family forever and joins her husband's family. As a consequence her own family fades into the background and her husband's family becomes the center of her life. The pattern of Mao's family life, like that of most of the itinerant revolutionaries, was antitraditional in that husband and wife were the nucleus; the husband's parents, who normally would have been the senior members both in age and authority, had been abandoned and repudiated long before. As late as his seventh decade Mao continued openly to vilify his father. But as a father in his own right Mao took it upon himself to gather as best he could the children of his wives under the wing of his transient household. On that subject, personal and painful, Chiang Ch'ing was voluble.

The tragedies of the Mao family are typical of the generation of the revolutionary founders. By the time the survivors of the Long March reached the Northwest their memories were seared by thousands of personal losses caused by civil war. As the years passed the death toll mounted to the millions, the legacy of vengeance swelling with it. However much individuals suffered, Communist leaders were strategists, not sentimentalists. Blood debts pursued single-handedly could never bring about a fundamental change of historical conditions. Consequently, they made unrelenting efforts to channel the emotion of personal vengeance into the realization of ideological principles.

Paradoxically, revolutionary theater cleaves more closely to popular feeling than does political ideology. Her discussion of Mao Tse-tung's family began while we were watching a performance of *The Red Lantern*, a revolutionary opera set in the Northwest in the late 1940's. Linked to stories of survivors were stinging memories of children, wives, and other relations lost, driven mad, or destroyed by the violence of historical change brought by Mao, his comrades, and his enemies to the twentieth century. During a scene in the opera in which the grandmother recounts the personal tragedies suffered by the Li family (coincidentally the same surname as Chiang Ch'ing's?), Chiang Ch'ing wept as she spoke of the six members of the Chairman's family who "laid down their lives for the Revolution." * They were, in the order and style of her presentation, the Chairman's wife Yang K'ai-hui; his middle brother Mao Tse-t'an, who laid down his life in the Soviet areas; his youngest brother Mao Tse-min, who laid down his life in Sinkiang; his son Mao An-ying, who laid down his life in Korea; his nephew Mao Ch'un-hsiung, who laid down his life during the troops' withdrawal from the Central Plains; and another son who was beaten so severely that his nervous system was destroyed. She added angrily that the KMT maliciously still spreads the rumor that his neurological disorder was "our doing."

In a later conversation Chiang Ch'ing returned to Yang K'ai-hui, nominally the Chairman's second wife, but actually the first with whom the marriage was consummated. Their three sons — Mao An-ying, Mao An-ch'ing, and Mao An-lung — were born early in the marriage.[21] Then the Chairman left her to go into the hills to establish base areas.† Understanding the seriousness of his goals, Yang K'ai-hui gave him all her support, to the extent of courting arrest and being taken hostage by the KMT authorities on account of the Chairman's revolutionary activities. Because she refused to denounce her husband or the Communist Party she was beheaded in Changsha in 1930 by the Hunan warlord Ho Chien, along with Mao's female cousin, Mao Tse-chien.

As for the Chairman's former wife Ho Tzu-chen, Chiang Ch'ing was never clear about all the children born to her; that subject the Chairman did not readily discuss. (Other reports hold that before the Long March, Ho bore one or two children who were given over to peasants, temporarily or permanently.)[22] One son they called Mao-mao, whom the Chairman cherished especially, but that child was lost to them during the war in northern Shensi in the late 1940's (apparently during the evacuation from Yenan).

At some point early in her marriage Chiang Ch'ing took charge of another son of Mao's (apparently Ho Tzu-chen's child). This little boy evidently had been sent to Moscow and later returned to Shanghai (probably in 1944; her time sequence here was uncertain), where he was put in the care of a priest, a man with two wives who turned out to be vicious women. They beat the boy so mercilessly that his sense of balance was permanently impaired. How well Chiang Ch'ing remembered his little body rocking crazily left and right. Even years later he still swerved from side to side, often tripping or pitching suddenly to the ground.

Chiang Ch'ing came to love this child, rearing him as her own son until the early 1950's, when she had to undergo radiotherapy for cancer. Naturally, the intensive medical care made it difficult for her to look after him. "Others" (un-

---

* Meaning that they died either in action or in other defense of the Party.
† Why he did not attempt to protect her by taking her with him Chiang Ch'ing did not explain, nor has Mao.

named) decided that she was no longer able to mother him. Against her plead-
ings "they" tore him away from her, refusing to tell her where he would be
placed. (If custody was Chiang Ch'ing's, could its denial, even after Liberation,
have been beyond the jurisdiction of the father and national leader, Mao?) The
loss was profound, for he was very bright; at the age of three he could sing the
"Internationale" from start to finish. She never found out where his abductors
hid him nor did Mao.

The Chairman never told her much about Ho Tzu-chen, Chiang Ch'ing
said. Most of what she knew she learned from Mao An-ying. Right after the
divorce Mao An-ying, then in his late teens, accompanied Ho Tzu-chen and
her youngest child, a daughter, to the Soviet Union. Upon his return (around
1944) Chiang Ch'ing and An-ying became close friends, for she was only a few
years his senior.[23] The moderate age discrepancy she contrasted to the far
greater one between herself and Ho Tzu-chen's daughter, toward whom she
was explicitly maternal.

From An-ying she learned more about that generation of Mao's family. The
daughter as an infant had been put in the temporary custody of a peasant family. In the Soviet Union, after Ho Tzu-chen was committed to an asylum, the
little girl was sent to board at a state-run kindergarten, where she received a
typically Russian upbringing. Later, when the mother was transferred to a mental institution in Shanghai, the child was given to Chiang Ch'ing to rear as a
stepdaughter. She named her Li Min and brought her up with her own daughter Li Na, who was close in age.

I mentioned to Chiang Ch'ing that some foreign sources have claimed that
she had two daughters of her own and perhaps also a son. She gave birth to but
one child, she replied firmly, and Chairman Mao was the father. In the course
of various conversations she compared her daughter Li Na with me. We were
about the same age, she said, historians by training, and inclined to be overly
intellectual. Li Na had been sent to the countryside — which did her good,
Chiang Ch'ing added with a sparkle in her eye.

The fact that she reared Li Min and Li Na together is reflected in the names
she gave them. She passed on her original surname Li * to both of them and
assigned them given names whose classical meanings are matched in opposition. Their first names derive from the old saying "A gentleman should be cautious in speech but quick in action." Thus Na means "cautious in speech" and
Min means "quick in action." But this contrast of Na and Min did not work
out in reality. Her own child got all "fives" (that is, A's) at school, but then became "stupid" because she studied too hard. Nor was Li Na naturally "cautious

---

* The assignment of the surname Li to Chiang Ch'ing's natural and foster daughters reflects a
progressive trend in China toward sexual symmetry: the matrilinear name is used to counterpoint the
patrilinear norm.

in speech," though she was made more so by political rectification. As for Li Min, she did not grow up to be "quick in action," a point that Chiang Ch'ing did not elaborate.

After Mao Tse-min, the Chairman's youngest brother, died (he was executed by KMT supporters in Sinkiang in 1943),[24] his son Mao Yüan-hsin asked to join Mao Tse-tung's family. Naturally they welcomed him and in time they all became close. Although one would have expected him to call her "aunt," he chose to call her "mother." A gifted child, he grew up to be a typical intellectual and had to be "tempered" along with the rest during the Cultural Revolution.[25]

Her own daughter Li Na was much the same. From childhood she buried herself in history and became a narrow-minded intellectual. When the Socialist Education Campaign got under way in the 1960's, Chiang Ch'ing sent her down to the rural areas, where most people live, for only there could she broaden her grasp of human realities. Thus, Li Na joined hundreds of thousands of city students and intellectuals who trekked to the countryside. She remained there for several years and participated in successive stages of the Socialist Education Movement. When she returned to Peking she married and produced a child. "That makes me a grandmother!" Chiang Ch'ing exclaimed proudly. Her stepdaughter, Li Min, she added, studied natural science, married, and had two children.

vi

Those personal dramas were played to little notice against the panorama of resistance war and civil war. Continual changes in the strategic situation commanded the better part of Mao's attention. Beginning in 1939 KMT troops under the command of Hu Tsung-nan, famed for his defense of Shanghai against the Japanese, formed a blockade around the Communists' Border Regions. This action prevented trade and other communication with the rest of China and the world for five years. The result was rampant inflation within the Border Region: grain prices soared, and cotton and cloth, which were major imports, suddenly were unobtainable. The export of salt, up to then the source of more than ninety percent of the region's exchange earnings, was impossible,[26] as was the import of weapons for the Red Army, now approximately half a million strong. Increasing the tax burden upon the peasants, for centuries the last resort of landlords and warlords, inevitably would have disenchanted them. To avert that negative lesson of history the Communist leaders adopted a radical frontier spirit. A genius at making a virtue of adversity, Mao turned "self-reliance" and "self-sufficiency" into positive slogans. Soldiers were enjoined to take up farming. On the ancient wall encircling Yenan he had inscribed in charcoal:

Self-reliance, Adequate Clothing, and Enough to Eat!

Develop the Economy and Provide for Military Defense!

By Self-sufficiency, We Will Build a Flourishing Border Area in the Northwest!

With a Hoe over One Shoulder and a Rifle over the Other We Will Become Self-sufficient in Production and Protect the Party's Central Committee! [27]

Even now, more than thirty-five years after the Party's arrival, Yenan continues to be a backward area, Chiang Ch'ing acknowledged. But the fault is "ours," she admitted of the leaders — "shortcomings in our work." Their attention in recent years has been deflected by international obligations. The environment of the Northwest has always imposed nearly insurmountable challenges: steep hills, deep valleys, and terraced fields, which make it almost impossible to increase production. Projects to open new lands and to improve those already under cultivation have long been wanting. "Certain elements" among the leaders who have not acted in the public interest are partly responsible for the backwardness.

But when Mao Tse-tung was living in the Northwest (we know from other sources), he initiated some of the most ambitious reclamation projects. In the winter of 1939 he ordered the young commander Wang Chen, with ten thousand troops of the 359th Brigade, to implement a pilot reclamation project in the barren hills and valleys of Nanniwan, a wasteland located thirty-some miles southeast of Yenan. Instructed to raise all food and make all clothing from scratch, they stripped temple bells, urns, and idols from abandoned temples, melted them down, and hammered them into plowshares. [28] Wool was obtained from the flocks they raised. Villages and schools were created by making new cave dwellings. The principle of mutual aid governed the establishment of producers' and consumers' cooperatives, first in agriculture, then in handicrafts and small-scale industry. Though the soldiers set the labor model, eventually all the men, women, and children native to the area were drawn into the production campaign. Even in that wilderness, culture still played its part. Entertained and led by soldiers turned actors, the local people were induced to put on propaganda plays about the fundamental transformation of their lives. [29]

However revolutionary the massive reclamation project carried out under military leadership may have seemed, Mao Tse-tung, a student of history, recognized that it was only a new version of the military colonies that had been imposed intermittently on China's borderlands for more than two thousand years.[30] Periodically the leaders, among them Mao Tse-tung, made visits from Yenan to Nanniwan and occasionally captured their fresh impressions in verse. On one such tour the redoubtable warrior Chu Te wrote "Going to Nanniwan":

> *Last year I first came here,*
> *The whole area was wild grass,*
> *At night there was no campsite,*
> *Even broken crockery was hard to find;*
> *Today we open a new market,*
> *Cave dwellings fill the valley,*
> *We control the rivers and plant excellent crops,*
> *Water inundates the new paddy fields,*
> *The military camp begins construction,*
> *The soldiers fill up on grain,*
> *In the fields cattle and sheep are fat,*
> *Asters become paper beauties.*[31]

Not all impressions of Nanniwan were idyllic. Chiang Ch'ing went there, not as a leader inspecting, but as a leader's new wife working. She arrived in January 1939, around the time of the project's inception,[32] and stayed six months. That tour of duty, she told me, most of the leading comrades and none of the masses knew of. (Were Mao and certain of his comrades testing her, hoping to prove to skeptics and opponents the endurance of a city girl?) After the Japanese attacked the Red armies in their Northwest base in 1939, she said, KMT forces some one hundred thousand strong under the command of Hu Tsung-nan waged "three anti-Communist onslaughts." Not only did the KMT try to wipe out the Communists militarily through their old strategy of encirclement; they also imposed an economic blockade against the delivery of supplies from the surrounding areas to the Eighth Route Army.[33] Just as they were trying to establish a fundamental economic balance in the Shen-Kan-Ning base area, the KMT was doing its utmost to starve them all to death. (In telling this her voice rose with anger.)

When the Chairman saw her group off from Yenan he told them that if they failed to produce all their own food and clothing, they would die in the wilderness. Under that threat they departed, and when they set up camp, Chiang Ch'ing's hand blistered because she had never before performed manual labor. She went on to say that the few women participating in this and other reclamation and production campaigns were treated favorably.[34] During their menstrual periods, for example, they were given a two-day reprieve from regular labor, though they were expected to do laundry and other light domestic tasks. She always refused such routine concessions to women. Some of the women preferred the lighter, conventionally female tasks because they resented being forced to do heavy physical labor like men. In those days they thought that having to do men's work was "second-class."

Since she was suffering from tuberculosis (endemic in the Northwest and other parts of China) in those years, she did not do spinning, which could have been too strenuous. Most of her time was spent knitting (a task conventionally performed by men native to the Northwest as well as by soldiers — all male — of the 359th Brigade). Although she started with no expertise, she managed to turn out ten sweaters while she was there; all were handed over to the collective. Sweaters were essential because the weather was always cold in the mountains, and she wore a thick cotton padded coat the entire six months of her service. As soon as she and her colleagues came down from the mountains to Yenan, they reentered a summer climate. How well she recalled the joy of wearing a single garment again. Thinking back on the Nanniwan experience, she confessed that others worked far better than she did, and added matter-of-factly that there was nothing special about her accomplishments there.[35]

Upon her return to Yang-chia-p'ing and to the cave dwelling and army headquarters she shared with Mao in the gentle hills near Yenan, she resumed the cultural work that was more to her liking, though in those years less instrumental to leadership than she would eventually make it.

7.

◇ ◇ ◇

Yenan's Popular Culture

> History is made by the people, yet the old opera (and all the old literature and art which are divorced from the people) presents the people as though they were dirt, and the stage is dominated by lords and ladies and their pampered sons and daughters. Now you have reversed this reversal of history and restored historical truth, and have opened a new life for the old opera.
> — Mao Tse-tung, after seeing *Driven to Join the Liangshan Rebels*, Yenan, 1944

Ⱨow did Chiang Ch'ing impress others in her Yenan days? Almost no Chinese would dare to print opinions of his leader's wife without authorization to draw up an official profile; so far as we know, such an assignment was never made by Mao Tse-tung. Only after she achieved power during the Cultural Revolution did certain Red Guard factions publish brief and sycophantic summaries of her political history. Candid impressions of Chiang Ch'ing are contained mostly in the reports of foreign visitors, and those visits began in the Yenan years. Most of the visitors were journalists or diplomats, and all, naturally, were eager to talk to the man in power. Several of their accounts show his wife glancingly, living comfortably on the political periphery, or so it seemed. No one foresaw in that pretty woman in her twenties the formidable political figure she would become in her middle years.

Each foreign observer saw in her a reflection of his own culture. Edgar Snow's reports from the Northwest indicate that Mao was never one to press his wife upon visitors. Snow, thus, shows only glimpses of Ho Tzu-chen and

Chiang Ch'ing. Her memory of him was of a biographical opportunity missed. Later, though, he summarized her background in the biographical notes of the 1968 revised edition of *Red Star Over China,* in which some assertions culled from undisclosed sources contradict her present account. He met her briefly in Yenan, a point he gauged to be a few months after her marriage to Mao. In his American eye she was a slender and attractive young woman who "played a good game of bridge and was an excellent cook." [1]

A more spirited portrait comes from the Soviet filmmaker Roman Karmen, a three-time winner of Stalin prizes. In 1938 Stalin dispatched him to China to make a film report of the revolution and the Resistance War. After spending several months roving through KMT-held territory, Karmen arrived in Yenan in mid-May 1939. There he spent a month gathering footage on revolution in action, especially around the Lu Hsun Academy. [2] He first came across Chiang Ch'ing on his way to hold discussions with Mao on May 25. Clearly, she captivated his artist's eye. In our interview she described Karmen as "Stalin's photographer" and spoke of him warmly. He shot her in many situations, but liked her especially on horseback. His photograph* reminds us how rare riding was for a Chinese woman (though Chiang Ch'ing did not mention this) and how, in the Northwest where horses were scarce, to have one was a privilege of the elite. (As she gave this picture to me she said that Karmen had sent it among others back to her in Yenan in 1939. When she had the New China News Agency prepare a copy for me in color, she had decided at the same time to give one to Big Sister Teng — Chou En-lai's wife — as well.)

Karmen's photograph of her, gaily costumed and with her hair plaited, makes her appear more Slavic than Chinese. He wrote:

On our way to see Mao we rode through the city. The newly opened Women's Political University, built for several thousand girls and women who had come to Yenan from all over the country, is situated high on a hill just behind the Lu Hsun Academy and the Anti-Japanese University. We forded the stream twice.

After the second crossing we were overtaken by a horsewoman galloping at full speed. Drawing up even with us, she sharply reined in her horse, and with a wide gesture welcomed us gaily. She was the wife of Mao Tse-tung. Like many thousands of young Chinese men and women, she came to this special region some years earlier to study at the Political University. She had left Shanghai where she had been a famous actress. Now a young Communist, she performed her great and honorable Party work as Mao's personal secretary. She prepares his diary, writes down his speeches, copies articles and takes care of miscellaneous affairs. Just now she is returning from a distant place where she went on 'assignment for Mao. She sits confidently on the small, spirited horse as it prances and chews the bit. Two braids are bound up in ribbons at the back of her head. She is wearing the greatcoat of a captured Japanese officer, and on her bare feet a pair of wooden sandals.

* See the first picture section.

"I will tell Mao that you are coming," she says. Turning her horse abruptly, it charges forth. She waves her right hand behind her, leans slightly forward, and gallops off in a cloud of dust.[3]

Another Soviet journalist, Peter Vladimirov, lived in Yenan from 1942 to 1945, though his controversial diary was not published for some thirty years — after Sino-Soviet hatred had become blatant, and Chiang Ch'ing was obviously in power.* He described her in 1942 as "a thin woman with a lithe figure and dark clever eyes, who looked very fragile next to her husband's stocky figure. . . ." "Extreme purposefulness is her outstanding quality," Vladimirov wrote later that year. "Her mind has the upper hand over her temperament. She drives herself without mercy, and her career is her own concern. She is in a hurry to achieve her ends while she is still young. . . ." The next February he noted that Chiang Ch'ing was not only the personal secretary of the Chairman, but that she had taken charge of all his secret correspondence. Her close friend and confidant was K'ang Sheng, who valued her marriage because it gave access to the Chairman. Vladimirov depicted Mao as being ignorant of Western classics and scorning everything that was not Chinese. He read only antique encyclopedic dictionaries, ancient philosophic treatises, and old novels. Chang Ch'ing was much better read, especially in foreign literature. Dexterously and unobtrusively, Chiang Ch'ing aided her husband in solving the most diverse questions, which had nothing to do with their domestic lives. "She is inquisitive and ambitious, but ably conceals it. She places her own interests above everything else."

When *The New York Times* correspondent Tillman Durdin met Chiang Ch'ing in 1944, he noticed, as others did, how she was overshadowed by the more senior women, especially by the most prominent among them: Ts'ai Ch'ang (wife of Li Fu-ch'un), K'ang K'o-ch'ing (wife of Chu Te), and Teng Ying-ch'ao (wife of Chou En-lai). Not only did they surpass her in status, but also in rapport with the masses, a fact she was painfully aware of. In her, though, Durdin found the qualities of the classic Chinese beauty — "a Chinese painting come to life." She was wearing the same sort of garments as the ordinary people, though the cut and stuff were noticeably superior. Her hair was close-cropped in the Soviet style, which had become fashionable among revolutionary women leaders of the Northwest and was flattering to her (most women were wearing their hair the same way thirty years later). In those days she smoked in the company of foreigners and was a fan of American dance music. One American who danced with her found her English "not impossible."

After Chiang Ch'ing married Mao, Durdin reported, she contracted tubercu-

---

* Peter Vladimirov, *The Vladimirov Diaries, Yenan, China: 1942–1945* (New York, 1975). For the information in this paragraph, see especially pp. 12, 83, 101, 143–144, 155–157, and 293.

losis; its effects were lingering still in 1944. Poor health had not deterred her from continuing to teach dramatic arts at the Lu Hsun Academy, where she also directed a repertory of propaganda plays promoting popular resistance to Japan.[4]

Another perceptive American journalist, Harrison Forman, met Mao and Chiang Ch'ing together in 1944. His comments on her personal history, probably drawn from that meeting, correspond to her report of 1972. He wrote:

Mao Tse-tung met me at the entrance of the little compound fronting a series of a half a dozen ordinary caves where he lives with his family and immediate aides. His comely, youngish wife was with him, the former Lan Ping, well-known Shanghai movie actress, an extremely intelligent woman, a member of the Communist Party since 1933. In 1937 she gave up her movie career and went to Yenan to work in the Lu Hsun Art Academy. Here Mao's interest in the drama brought them together, and they were married quietly in the spring of 1939.

Both were plainly dressed, she in a practical pajama-like outfit belted at her slim waist, he in a rough, homespun suit with baggy, high water pants. I was taken to the "parlor" — one of the caves with a simple brick floor, white-washed walls, and solid, rather lumpy furniture. It was evening, and the only light was furnished by a single candle fixed on an upturned cup. For refreshments I was served with weak tea, cakes and candy made locally, and cigarettes, while youngsters ran in and out during the whole conversation. They would stand and stare at me for a few moments, and then, seizing a piece of candy, race out again. Mao paid no attention to them.[5]

David D. Barrett and John S. Service, both members of the American Observer Group (Dixie Mission) in Yenan in 1944–1945, had similar impressions of Chiang Ch'ing as the attractive wife. Colonel Barrett remembered Mao's introduction of her at a military exhibition — "Colonel Barrett, this is Chiang Ch'ing." Expecting a consumptive, Barrett was surprised to find her looking in fairly good health. She was pleasant, "her manner having all the grace and polish traditionally associated with an actress. She spoke perfect *kuo-yü* [Mandarin], as can almost all other Chinese actresses. I remember her being much better looking and more chic than most of the wives of the Communist leaders." [6]

Service confirmed the general sense that Teng Ying-ch'ao and K'ang K'o-ch'ing were far more visible women leaders than Chiang Ch'ing. Occasionally Chiang Ch'ing attended Saturday night dances, but she was not included in more important functions: official dinners given to welcome the American Observer Group or subsequent visitors to Yenan. Once, on an August evening in 1944, Service shared a supper with Mao and Chiang Ch'ing and their interpreter. Mao directed and dominated the conversation; Chiang Ch'ing participated little if at all. "She was relatively young (in the predominantly middle-aged Yenan society) and relatively attractive (but not a beauty)," Service recalled. Throughout his stay he encountered none of the later gossip about Ho Tzu-chen's degeneration or Chiang Ch'ing's devastation of the former marriage. Among the Chinese in Yenan (if not elsewhere as well) marital relations were treated as private affairs.[7]

When Robert Payne visited Mao in 1945, when Mao was fifty-two, he recalled: "His wife came in, wearing black slacks and a sweater, and she said, 'Nin hao?' in greeting, with a classical Pekingese accent, and suddenly you realized that her long face possessed more beauty and expression than the face of the considerably more famous Mme. Chiang Kai-shek; also, she brought with her the scent of the flowers she had been gathering in the uplands." [8]

So much for impressions of the wife. In Chiang Ch'ing's own recollection of those years constant put-downs by others were offset by her striving toward some sense of equality with Mao. How Chiang Ch'ing chose to remember herself and Mao in those days appears in the pictures in the first picture section. There, beauty and innocence belie emerging actuality: their rising to power over the material and cultural lives of a billion Chinese during the next thirty years. There, too, they give the rare appearance of being two persons on a par.

In the eyes of foreign visitors to Yenan in the middle 1940's Mao Tse-tung was the mercurial centerpiece in a display of revolutionary personalities, a man whom Edgar Snow had introduced to the world in 1938 with the publication of *Red Star Over China*. His and others' projection of the naturalness, idealism, and enthusiasm of this band of self-styled revolutionaries took the chill off abstract Marxism and eased the fears bred of severe Soviet practice.

i

In 1947 the KMT routed the Red troops out of their base areas and bombed Yenan to a rubble. Then, in the early 1950's, after the Communist regime had been firmly established, Yenan was rebuilt as a shrine to the Party, and in its museums were displayed relics of the long march to power. Above all, restored Yenan was meant to kindle the cult of one man's personality: Mao Tse-tung.

For four days in early August 1972, before I met Chiang Ch'ing, I visited Yenan, to see what it evoked of the past. Like the millions of Chinese and trickle of foreigners before me, I was barraged by skilled Red Guards who served as guides at the exhibits in austere buildings in this still barren territory. Having spent so many years reading about the personalities who dominated the frontier days, I was shaken by the disproportion: blown-up images of Mao Tse-tung dwarfed those of Chu Te, Chou En-lai, Lo Jui-ch'ing, and other brilliant strategists. Less surprising, though, was that faces of Liu Shao-ch'i and Lin

Piao, once named as Mao's successors but later discredited, were thoroughly removed from the displays. One blurred image of Chiang Ch'ing, surely to be mistaken by most viewers for a boy soldier, appears behind Chairman Mao, who sits astride his famous white horse.*

From the whitewashed museum I was driven through the glaring sun and fiery red dust of the roadways to the succession of caves where he lived. In those simple dwellings, surely more pristine as shrines than in the working past, Mao Tse-tung came across on a purely intellectual plane. In his second decade of leadership of the Red Army and the Communist Party he was freed of much active involvement in military affairs. In those years he turned to theoretical analysis of the recent past. Youthful guides now calibrated their leader's monumental significance in terms of the number of essays he produced. From their facile phrases I learned that of the one hundred fifty essays which appear in the Chairman's *Selected Works*, one hundred twelve were written during his thirteen years in the Northwest; of those, ninety-two were composed while he lived in the caves of Yenan.

At his caves in Yang-chia-p'ing a humbler side of his character — also to be emulated by the people — was brought to the fore. I was shown at the foot of the hill the victory garden in which he liked to work after writing for hours or days on end. Raising his own vegetables and tobacco kept him in touch with the soil, and his plot is still cultivated. We ate sun-ripened tomatoes — exquisite.

From one suite of caves to the next the same architectural formula was carried out: two rooms, one for sleeping and bathing, the other for writing and eating; and in one instance a third for receiving guests and convening the Central Committee. In the room where the Chairman wrote, attention was drawn to the bare wooden table and to the brush and ink arranged by the empty space where his manuscripts had once lain. A used tin cup (not the original) sat to one side. When the Chairman found the time, he wrote vigorously and incessantly through countless nights, forgetting to eat or sleep.[9] That official characterization — in another culture it would have been philosopher-king — was repeated by guides all over Yenan.

In speaking with my guides I acknowledged that they had told me a great deal about the Chairman's intellectual accomplishments. But did he not have a wife? Was she not Comrade Chiang Ch'ing? How did she occupy herself over the long stretches of time when the Chairman was lost in revolutionary contemplation? Surely their children could not have been running around that small compound. Where were they?

Those simple questions, which a Chinese pilgrim was less likely to have asked, were met by winces and smiles and we-don't-knows (doubtless gen-

* See the first picture section.

uine ignorance among the young). Yet their message was clear. In the official history, which is the only history for the asking in China, Chairman Mao was not to be recalled as a husband or a family man. And Chiang Ch'ing's role, marital or political, was never open to public discussion.

In our interview later her reconstruction of the Yenan years was piecemeal and emotionally tortured. Seen through her eyes Mao Tse-tung emerged fitful, worried, ironic, idealistic, contriving. He was indeed given to long periods of silent speculation and theoretical writing, and to wandering off among the people. Wherever he turned he was threatened by his archrival and their common enemy, Wang Ming. For in the late 1930's, Wang Ming and Mao were still struggling, each with his own formula, to please the revolutionary patriarch, Stalin. Like brothers they competed to impress upon him their separate correctness and brilliance as revolutionary leaders.

On Chiang Ch'ing, Wang Ming had imposed a threat from another direction. While she lived in Shanghai he was absent physically, but still powerful and omniscient, through his remote control of the underground Party operations from his offices in Moscow. In striving to be accepted as a Communist, she had no real choice but to be associated with his policies, later to be denounced as his Right Opportunist line. In addition, she was frustrated by the men who controlled the day-to-day activities of the Shanghai network, among them Chou Yang and Chang Keng. As leaders in Yenan and later in Peking, they would continue to block her access to the masses.

She would not know Wang Ming personally until she came to Yenan and made her own political coup by marrying Mao. Already the two men were seen as charting two roads to revolution: Wang Ming's Russian road, urban-oriented and dependent upon the temporary assistance of the rival Party and the bourgeoisie, and Mao's native way, which was, first, to mobilize the peasants to overthrow the landlords, and then to take the cities. Was Stalin watching? Could he see? Was not Mao's invitation to Stalin's official photographer Karmen to do an exclusive film report on systematic rural revolution a bid for favor? Was not his lissome wife galloping through the red dust an appealing film clip?

To illustrate the ideological differences between Wang Ming and the Chairman, Chiang Ch'ing made a series of black-and-white statements, all of which do not bear repeating here, for the truth surely must lie in between. In her view, land reform and United Front policy were the most controversial issues. While he was still in the Central Soviet Districts, the future Chairman began to lay out blueprints for land reform. On January 23, 1934, he wrote an article stating the need for the masses to undertake land reclamation projects in order to raise agricultural productivity. That summer and autumn he wrestled with the problem of reorganizing manpower and suggested mutual-aid teams as a solution.

She claimed (though documentary evidence is lacking) that before Wang Ming returned from Moscow, he registered formal protests with the Comintern against the land policies Mao Tse-tung was advocating. Then the Resistance War, which threw up the most divisive issues between them, drove Wang Ming to stress forging a united front with the KMT at the expense of class struggle. (She did not mention that Wang Ming was also the fomenter of urban proletarian uprisings, at Wuhan, for example.) In October 1935 the Red Army ended the Long March. However victorious that moment was for the forces led by Chairman Mao, divisions within the ranks of the leaders were not yet reconciled. At the leaders' conference of December 25, 1935, at Wai-yao-pao, Wang Ming's views were relayed from Moscow, where the Seventh Comintern Congress had met in midsummer. Standing upon authority from Moscow, he contradicted Chairman Mao on every major point. As she reported this dispute her face darkened.

But the polemics were less pointed in her own mind than the personal antagonism and Wang Ming's tiresome presence in the community of leading comrades. Wang Ming lost their confidence years ago, she insisted. But as long as it was possible, the Chairman acted magnanimously and came to his rescue at dangerous moments. For example, during the Seventh Party Congress of 1945, which was held near their home at Yang-chia-p'ing, not one delegate would vote for Wang Ming's election to the Central Committee. Only after the Chairman prevailed upon them was he elected.[10] By the time of the Ninth Party Congress in 1969 (when she first joined the Politburo and thus was shaping policy), incontrovertible evidence had been assembled to prove that he was just a "renegade" and a "traitor" (defector from the Party and the nation respectively). Not only was there no chance of his reelection to the Central Committee, but he was expelled from the Party. He then sought refuge in the Soviet Union, where he had spent so much of his youth. Wang Ming is an old man now, she said (he died in March 1974), still clinging stubbornly to his original principles. Since moving back to Moscow he keeps writing letters to editors every two or three days just to vilify their regime. They pay no attention to him.

In a real sense, she reflected, Wang Ming was not a Chinese. By the same token, although Anna Louise Strong was an American, she was more Chinese than Wang Ming.[11]

ii

Resuming the subject of land reform, which she had observed cursorily in the Northwest, she reported that on the first of October 1943 the Chairman drafted an article which he called "Spread the Campaign to Reduce Rent, Increase Production, Support the Government and Cherish the People in the Base Areas." In it he elaborated on the ideas he had first written of in January of 1934, notably the establishment of mutual-aid teams (called labor-exchange teams in northern Shensi), which were to develop into cooperatives to serve the interests of the local masses. They were to be set up with the family as the basic unit. Such organized exchange of labor services, and the use of part-time as well as full-time workers, were imperative during wartime, when farm production, as well as military defense, had to be kept up.

The economic situation of the mid-1940's generally represented the "new democratic economy." The cooperatives were organized as mutual-aid teams and mixed-labor teams, the latter a variant of the mutual-aid team. Whatever the label, all involved full- and part-time work, and whenever possible, living, working, and eating together. Such organizations were considered good so long as they were joined *voluntarily*. Besides these agricultural cooperatives, other collectivization was arranged. For example, cooperatives in production, marketing, and transport were followed by credit cooperatives, transportation cooperatives, and finally cooperatives for handicraft production.

To understand the period of the 1940's, Chiang Ch'ing recommended the Chairman's articles "On New Democracy" (January 1940), "Get Organized!" (November 1943), and "On Coalition Government" (April 1945)[12] for showing how he gave highest priority to the United Front, so long as the independence and the initiative of the Communist Party within it were guaranteed. She also stressed how the issues involved in the United Front illustrated the struggle between the two lines (then the Chairman versus Wang Ming) in all fields — not only the economy, but also politics, the military, and culture.

Brimming with energy when some members of her entourage had begun to yawn and catch themselves from dozing, Chiang Ch'ing arose from her wide wicker chair and strode over to the billiard table set up at the side of the room in which we were talking. Two bodyguards joined her immediately with cues. Her legs swelled if she did not take exercise, she explained as she reached for her cue, bent straight from the waist, and took a level sight. For several moments the only sounds in the room were the sharp click of the balls, spaced by squeals of delight as she gained on her friendly adversaries. As the game continued, she resumed a desultory discussion of problems of the economy of the Northwest. There has always been a struggle between individual economy on the one hand, and an organized economy on the other. Without organization nothing can be accomplished. And organization must include everything: animals, seeds, labor power.

iii

From a historical perspective we can see that had the rules for creating proletarian arts loosely formulated by Mao Tse-tung in a ramshackle auditorium in Yenan been followed literally (were that possible), the Great Proletarian Cultural Revolution of a quarter century later would not have assumed such monumental proportions. This is especially true of what Marxists call the superstructure: education, literature, and the arts. Meager success in creating a total proletarian culture was a structural weakness in the revolutionary edifice from the very beginning. Though neither Mao Tse-tung nor Chiang Ch'ing would ever admit this publicly, he never managed thoroughly to win over to his side major talents in fields alien to his own, most notably in the literary and performing arts. The conflict between totalitarian political authority and creative independence *is* unreconcilable — universally. But in the rhetoric of Mao Tse-tung's regime that insoluble contradiction was grossly oversimplified to supply evidence of the "struggle between the two lines": the correct line of Mao Tse-tung and the incorrect line of his opponent of the hour. In the 1930's and 1940's those lines were represented by Mao and Wang Ming; in the 1960's by Mao and Liu Shao-ch'i.

A long history of public claims that Chairman Mao, the Party, and the people were in solid agreement seems to have calmed seas of uncertainty. But if the ship were secure, why should Mao, "Our Great Helmsman," continue to change his tack ostentatiously every few months or years? To keep the upper hand in Yenan, Mao had to demonstrate to his comrades and the masses that people who disagreed with him intellectually were by the same act disloyal to him personally. Dissenters were singled out in public forms and disgraced as "dogmatists" or Right Opportunists or otherwise as followers of Wang Ming. [13] However, the substance of the charges was not always clear. Many of the dissenters, of course, were simply Marxian writers or artists of an independent stripe.

To marshal enthusiasm for Mao, grueling investigations in "thought reform" sessions got under way in the early 1940's. Overall, thought reform became what was possibly the revolution's most profound and agonizing experience. This was Mao's way of persuading uninformed, skeptical, or dissident persons — intellectuals in the main — of the correctness of his view of the world and his policies. Nor could his reformed subjects simply assent tacitly or keep silence. Successful thought reform was to be demonstrated by their becoming his open advocates, who then went on to proselytize others in their society. To disapproving outsiders, thought reform was "brainwashing."

Mao's method of thought reform has a national background. To bring his revolutionary messages home to the people he used their language and thus spoke of "curing the sickness to save the patient." Such treatment of the mind by reeducation and psychological manipulation set him off from Stalin, who was notorious for physical brutality, for "liquidation" of dissenters and other useless people. While Stalin operated in the tradition of the tsars, Mao tapped roots deep in Chinese history. Like Confucius, who taught that anyone can be educated, Mao has taught that anyone's political beliefs, or "thought," can be reformed. The experience of coming around to Mao's, hence the Party's side, was not unlike religious conversion: one is "persuaded" to abandon lifelong patterns of belief and behavior and to adopt new ones — notably, the belief in the necessity of waging unremitting proletarian class struggle. Liu Shao-ch'i's psychologically astute essays (the most famous, published in 1939, became known as "How to Be a Good Communist") were keys to the conversion process, which was deemed essential to uninterrupted revolution.

Little has been written in China about thought reform, either by journalists or by novelists or by playwrights. And nothing substantial is in the official records.[14] Possibly the agonies of the revolution's trial era are still too immediate — indeed still in process — to allow for detached appraisal. To explore the dynamics of psychological destruction and reconstruction would probably be intolerable for a playwright who was forced at the price of sanity or life to adopt totally different class assignments in the name of revolutionary justice.

From 1942 to 1944 thought reform was the basis of the Rectification Campaign, which was conducted systematically in all political, military, educational, and cultural institutions of the Yenan community and in the Border Region at large.[15] That same method of "purifying class values" would be revived periodically after Liberation.

Rectification of people in the arts was carried out at the Lu Hsun Academy, a revolutionary culture center riddled with personal animosities and intellectual contradictions, most of them too subtle to be explained by the procrustean twin beds of the "two-line struggle." The difference between what the academy's namesake, Lu Hsun, stood for and what actually went on in that exiled artists' colony remains to be studied by future historians. Some of Lu Hsun's most illustrious followers, among them the woman writer Ting Ling and the novelist Hsiao Chün, were assigned to the academy staff. Yet their uncompromising loyalty to his individualistic model and incorruptible artistic standards ultimately destroyed them. When Chou Yang, a cultural commissar whom Lu Hsun despised, arrived in Yenan on the heels of Chiang Ch'ing, his meritorious record in the Shanghai underground Party and cultural front organizations was rewarded by her future husband, who appointed him director of education of the Border Region, and soon afterward president of the Lu Hsun Academy.

Under Chou Yang's administration, the academy established four departments: Literature, Drama, Fine Arts, and Music. There were also a writer's workshop, a research center, and a handcrafts workshop. However, the strongest departments were Drama and Music because the performing arts had the greatest potential for reaching the masses. Who was the chairman of the Drama Department, in which Chiang Ch'ing was instructor? None other than Chang Keng, her superior and her adversary of Shanghai years. In this rural encampment Chang Keng continued to work as he had in Shanghai. He promoted Stanislavsky's "method" acting, a school later repudiated by the Communists because it supposedly encouraged egocentricity and individual autonomy — both anathema to socialist collectivism. He also continued to produce full-length foreign plays, among them Gogol's *Marriage*, a play of bourgeois manners bound to entertain fellow intellectuals, but to bewilder the local folk now guided by the Party to a new pride of proletarian consciousness.[16] On the other hand Chang Keng, Ma K'o, and other seasoned dramatists were pioneers in cultural revolution. It was they who originated a new rural theater starting with patterns of local culture. Thus the *yang-ko*, an ancient folk dance and fertility rite of the Northwest, was made the dance of Liberation, and the local opera was invested with fresh political content. Among the premier productions were *Brothers and Sisters Tame the Wilderness* and *White-haired Girl*, dramas fraught with pathos and highlighting the emerging heroes of contemporary life.[17] Twenty years later Chiang Ch'ing appropriated the latter and reconstructed it as the centerpiece of her new model repertory.

Since buildings and all materials were scarce in Yenan, old structures were salvaged for new purposes. The Lu Hsun Academy was housed in an abandoned Catholic church situated about three miles from the town center. The body of the church was turned into an auditorium, a cacophonous arena for the new synthesis of ancient and modern, native and alien arts. On an ordinary day a solo cellist might be sawing away in one corner, while a small stringed orchestra produced a semblance of foreign tunes in another, and from other quarters might issue strains of a folk singer superimposing topical lyrics upon old melodies.[18]

The quarters once occupied by Christian converts housed revolutionary students of music and drama. Some of them emulated Bohemia by wearing the romantic garb of storybook Russian peasants, which set them off from the military. These students were mostly youngsters recruited from the local populace. After two years of training they were sent to the battlefront to put on impromptu musical and dramatic skits to rouse the spirits of the Red fighters and the local people.

Among the artists, writers, musicians, dramatists, and journalists on the academy's senior staff argumentation was the order of the day. After observing a meeting at which these displaced urban intellectuals held sway, the American journalist Harrison Forman grasped what compelled Mao to attack their "high and mighty airs":

Most of them came from Shanghai which, before the war, was the cultural center of China. But the Westernized, highly sophisticated art and literature of Shanghai were as far from the peasant folklore of hinterland China as James Joyce is from Confucius. Under war conditions, away from Shanghai, the literati resembled fish out of water. It was almost impossible for them not to look down upon the ignorant peasants, the workers and soldiers, who retorted by rejecting them. Without a public, they wrote, painted, and made music for themselves, ignoring the common folk below their cultural and intellectual level. If the peasant failed to appreciate good literature and art, that was his misfortune. Art could not debase itself by talking down to the masses. [19]

Informal get-togethers of the leaders and the led, dubbed "Saturday night barn dances" by some visiting Americans, were held at the Pear Garden, so termed in the Communists' more jocular days when they reveled in comparing themselves to their imperial predecessors, here to the esoteric court theater of the T'ang emperor Ming Huang. In these liberated zones a girl showed personal emancipation by choosing her own dance partner. Nor was Mao beyond reach. Turning to the Chairman she would request respectfully, "Chairman, please dance with me." [20]

Music was either ground out on scratchy records on a battered phonograph or played live. The orchestra combined old Chinese fiddles, foreign violins, mouth organs, a Cantonese zither, a musical saw, and a pedal organ left over from missionaries. The notion of what worked as dance music was even more eclectic. French minuets, Viennese waltzes, "Jingle Bells," and "Yankee Doodle" were played to honor foreign guests, and there was the usual fair share of traditional Chinese folk tunes. To such musical varieties they danced fox trots, waltzes and the sinuous *yang-ko*.

In this state of unsophisticated Communism, the leaders mingled musically with the masses. Western social dancing that entailed body contact had not yet been prohibited. Forman recalled:

On any evening you might see bushy-haired, shirtsleeved Mao Tze-tung, venerated leader of ninety millions under the Communists' protection, having a grand time dancing a fast onestep with a cute coed from Yenta [Yenan University], while a truck driver might be swinging buxom Madame Chu Te. Roly-poly Chu Te himself, commander-in-chief of over half a million Jap-killers, who looks like a fatherly old cowpuncher, was having the time of his life dancing with a bright young thing one-half his size and one-third his age. Battle-scarred generals Lin Piao, Nieh Yung-chien [Jung-chen], Yeh Chien-ying, and a dozen others — for each of whom the Japanese would gladly sacrifice a full division of crack troops — would be seen flitting about like jitterbugging college kids.[21]

The Mao who reveled with the people off the historical record he was preparing was also shifting from one phase of leadership to the next: from youthful revolutionary activist to mature military strategist and political theorist. Though his body was losing the leanness of the Long March, he kept the one romantic symbol that set him off from the rest: a head of long hair.[22] As he moved about the base area in his most cherished role, that of teacher, the Party newspaper *Liberation Daily* pushed him into the first phase of a personality cult that would wax and wane over the years. In the issue of December 14, 1941, his comrade Hsiao San eulogized him as "our brilliant great leader, our teacher and our savior," words which would become standard hyperbole.

As Mao deliberated the principles by which he had gathered a disciplined following within ten years, the central theme of his writing became the adaptation of the ostensibly universal principles of Marx and Lenin to the particularities of the Chinese situation: in essence, the search for a "national form." That search, extended into the realm of culture, spurred the vigorous debates at the Lu Hsun Academy in May 1942. Of those heady encounters the only official record is the Chairman's rambling report he called "Talks at the Yenan Forum on Literature and Art." How much of that was a reflection of the debates and not merely a personal polemic, or an unacknowledged appropriation of views of the late Communist writer Ch'ü Ch'iu-pai, has not yet been determined.

iv

In Chiang Ch'ing's view, the situation in Yenan in the early 1970's was still unsatisfactory, though surely far better than when she and the Chairman were living there. Even then Chou Yang was an incorrigible critic of their performance. Although they strove to establish an egalitarian society in Yenan, he blasphemed their achievement by circulating essays about an invidious "class system" that he fancied prevailed. As he put it, the people were divided into "three grades and nine classes," meaning, of course, that they had not succeeded in escaping from their hierarchical past.

To prove her point Chiang Ch'ing drew from a folder a paperbound volume, slim and untitled, which had been published for limited circulation.[23] Flipping through its pages, she said that these essays first appeared in 1941 and had been reprinted in 1958, during the Anti-Rightist Campaign. "Sheer slander!" she declared. In 1941 Chou Yang, then president of the Lu Hsun Academy, wrote a piece containing such slurs as "every sun has some spots" (already in Yenan Mao's brilliance was being compared to the sun). In March 1942 Wang Shih-wei published a series of essays titled "The Wild Lily," in which he contended that the wild lily, Yenan's most beautiful wild flower, grew from a bulb that tasted bitter.[24] By means of this floral metaphor, he attacked indirectly "bureaucratism" and "corruption" among the leaders — ancient errors they felt they had overcome. At the same time, Ting Ling published an article on International Women's Day that turned out to be a scathing critique of the condition of women under the Communist government of Yenan. "Read those pieces," Chiang Ch'ing said, "and you'll understand why the Chairman had to seize from them the initiative at the Yenan Forum."

Mao's polemic initiatives at the forum and elsewhere sparked tinder from all quarters, Chiang Ch'ing reported angrily. Members of the Central Committee and the Youth League (probably defensive of Wang Ming, as in Shanghai) mounted wall newspapers that repeatedly slandered the Party, the military, and the people. Such censure of the Chairman and those closest to him from within the ranks of responsible comrades set the stage for the Yenan Forum.

In brisk defense of the unremitting simplicity of her own way of life, she said that when she first went to Shanghai she lived in an attic; in Yenan she always lived in caves. She and the Chairman ate the food and wore the clothing of the laboring people. Still she was maligned for assuming the sumptuous style of a "counterrevolutionary!"

During the academy's formative years most of the instructors were rather like Chiang Ch'ing — professional dramatists, writers, and musicians with unshakable self-confidence built from previous experience. Their adjustment to radically changed circumstances came slowly. The dramatist Ma K'o has recalled how literary experts used to lavish hours debating the Greek and Roman classics and the admirable European nineteenth century. Some of the actresses who had been trained in foreign drama (no names mentioned) became so enchanted with the role of Anna Karenina that they worried about nothing so much as the length of the shadow cast by their eyelashes upon the ground.[25]

Chiang Ch'ing's best recollections were of the academy's progressive side. While she was serving as instructor in the Drama Department in the early 1940's,[26] the administrators urged that the spoken drama, at that point the most flexible and promising genre, displace the old opera cycles about defunct subjects: palace life and scholars. Among the new plays she mentioned, all built upon contemporary themes, were *Fire on the Airfield, On the Sungari River,* and *Brothers and Sisters Tame the Wilderness.*[27]

The Chairman made his first appearances at the academy while these plays were under rehearsal. She recalled how much he enjoyed them. Certainly, they aroused his curiosity, for he began to investigate other of the academy's activities. To acquaint himself with problems of modern literature and art, which had not been central to his interests, he engaged members of the staff in wide-ranging discusssions, during which the issues later brought forth at the Yenan Forum were formulated.[28]

These soundings were followed by Mao Tse-tung's well-staged descent upon the academy to open the famous forum in late May 1942, Ma K'o recalled. Word of the Chairman's imminent arrival in a small car spread like lightning. As the spring rain drizzled, people poured out of their caves and carried pads of paper and inkwells to the auditorium. The overflow sat upon the drill ground outside the doors. Presented by Chou Yang, Chairman Mao stood before the people and reviewed the substance of the recent discussions of the arts. He posed what he saw as the central question: Whom should artists serve? Their academy, he joked, was just the "Little Lu I" (Lu I was the academy's nickname), while the liberated regions and the wider struggles of life should be seen as the "Big Lu I." The members of the Little Lu I should not remain cloistered but should go out and propagandize their new culture in the realm of the Big Lu I. The Chairman's keynote speech provoked fierce debate. The controversy continued for several days, during which the fine spring rain turned into thunderstorms.[29]

But who would spell out the ironies that were already apparent and would mount with time? Although Mao Tse-tung set up the Lu Hsun Academy to honor Lu Hsun, the positions that Mao argued there were fundamentally opposed to that writer's. For example, in his pursuit of "national forms" of literature for the masses, Mao implicitly opposed Lu Hsun's position that old or "feudal" forms could not successfully be invested with fresh political content and espoused Chou Yang's contradictory argument that cultural forms familiar to the people were precisely the ones which should be salvaged and supplied with new ideas, namely Communist propaganda and supreme respect for Mao Tse-tung. While thus supporting the ideas of Lu Hsun's former opponent Chou Yang, he attacked Lu Hsun's closest disciples, Ting Ling, Hu Feng, and Wang Shih-wei, who had made the brave pilgrimage to Yenan. Chou Yang, moreover, whom Chiang Ch'ing so despised on personal grounds, remained steadfast as Mao's right-hand man in cultural affairs for more than twenty years after the forum, until Chiang Ch'ing had him removed at the outset of the Cultural Revolution. And at that time, similarly advocating Lu Hsun's model, she absolutely violated his judgment with her grandiose project to invest an old cultural form, the Peking opera, with a new proletarian ethos.

Chiang Ch'ing attended the Yenan Forum of May 1942, she said in one of our interviews. In what capacity? As secretary to the Chairman, a post that by now had superseded her work in teaching and directing theater. Ostensibly about literature and art, the debates at the Yenan Forum actually elucidated various issues drawn from other fields. From the way people argued she could tell whether they were for the Chairman or for his chief rival, Wang Ming, whose claim to orthodoxy originated in Soviet theory, which the Chairman dubbed the Right Opportunist line.[30] Again, she reiterated the point pivotal in her past and China's present: in the cultural sphere Wang Ming's Opportunist line was expressed in the slogan "National Defense Literature," which was pitched against Lu Hsun's slogan formulated in the middle 1930's: "People's Literature for National Revolutionary War." Lu Hsun's slogan, which had a proletarian class character, Mao had adopted and used as the basis of his report to the Yenan Forum. The Chairman mounted his attack at the academy and cast his argument in literary terms. But through the same words he was addressing the far wider audience that had fallen under the spell of Wang Ming, whose antagonism toward the Chairman was splashed all over Yenan and the Border Region.*

She went on to say that at the Party School, where she had studied, and at the Marxist-Leninist Institute *none* of the Chairman's writings was available. The only works on hand were those of the Twenty-eight Bolsheviks, of whom Wang Ming was the chief. The only way the Chairman could break through their "ideological blockade" was to steer clear of other leading comrades and go out to the people and lecture everywhere on ideas directed specifically toward their interests. Only by personal contact with the people could he build up a following.

Returning to the scene of the forum, she said that the sessions were long and rambling. Many people (their names repressed now) held forth in their fields of expertise. The Chairman awaited his turn. He began by making "eloquent criticism" of the reputation of the people (herself among them) responsible for producing *Fire on the Airfield, On the Sungari River,* and *Brothers and Sisters Tame the Wilderness.* The tenor of his remarks was strikingly different from the others'. His judgments were not only about literature and art per se: they were grounded in philosophy and political theory. The drift of the discussion and the conclusions he drew were summed up in his essay "Talks at the Yenan Forum on Literature and Art."[31] That essay she has read numerous times over the years, drawing new insights with each rereading. In it the Chairman posed crucial questions: Should one write on the bright or the dark side? What are the objectives of a given work and what are the results? What should serve as our political and artistic standards? He also warned that those who describe darkness

---

* A revealing contradiction to mainstream historiography, which has held that Wang Ming was basically defeated by this time.

are not necessarily great, and those who extol brightness are not necessarily important.

"Read this often," she urged. (Its complete Chinese text was supplied as part of my "study materials" the next morning.)

Thinking back on the challenges Mao met head-on at a time when they were building their lives together, Chiang Ch'ing remarked ingenuously, "I worshiped Mao." Looking at me quizzically she asked, "Professor Witke, don't you want your students to worship you?"

Surprised by her directness, I said no, adding that I liked them to contend with me and had no desire to be worshiped.

With a quick smile she added that during the Cultural Revolution the Chairman always fought against worship of himself, for that was fraught with grave risks. Moreover, certain people who sought to defeat *her* in the struggles engendered by the Cultural Revolution began to flatter her, then became increasingly extravagant in their praise. For a while she was foolish, and was taken in; then she learned how one must always remain *flexible* in one's revolutionary tactics.

Chiang Ch'ing's quick flashes back and forth from the Yenan Forum to the Cultural Revolution were automatic to her thought because Mao's treatise on the former served as the sole ideological justification for her work in the latter. Neither Mao in his "Talks"nor she in its recapitulation preserved for the record the source of the countervailing views on literature that had provoked the forum in the first place. The failure of Marx, Engels, and Lenin to deal systematically with the problems of cultural revolution accounts in part for Mao's fairly brutal, Stalinist, and pragmatic tack on this subject, so vastly important to the integrity of Communism in China. In mechanistic language obviously designed to send shudders down the backs of "effete" intellectuals, Mao called writers "engineers of the human soul," an epithet Stalin had borrowed from Gorky. Taking off from Lenin, he argued that literature and art are cogs in the revolutionary machine.[32] In Mao's words: "The purpose of our meeting today is precisely to ensure that literature and art fit well into the whole revolutionary machine as a component part, that they operate as powerful weapons for uniting and educating the people and for attacking and destroying the enemy, and that they help the people fight the enemy with one heart and one mind." [33]

If writers were "engineers," the Lu Hsun Academy was a culture factory fraught with unwonted contradictions. As sophisticated in the arts as any succeeding Chinese generation, its staff was admonished to invent cultural forms simple enough to engage the untutored minds of China's "masses of workers, peasants and soldiers," and in the early 1940's that expression was far from being a cliché. New vernacular dramas and reformed local operas were fashioned from the raw materials of their lives. A popular formula featured a clever peasant who assists the Red Army soldier in tripping up the wicked plot of a Japanese marauder. Such simple conventions tailored to the masses were bound to turn off the fine-tuned minds of intellectual engineers, who were accustomed to writing plays with complex and conflicted characters. Faced with that dilemma, which was grounded in the perennial inequality of talent and education, Mao demanded systematic action that was radically compensatory: produce new works endowing the masses with a positive literary life and rectify through thought reform those stubborn intellectuals who fail to comply.

To overthrow the old order, Mao admonished the intellectuals to descend from their ivory towers (the clubbishness of the Lu Hsun Academy not excluded). Like him, they should mingle with the masses. Writers, musicians, and artists long accustomed to working within elite circles should read the wall newspapers put up by the masses, attend folk dramas, and listen to folk music. Only by steeping themselves in common culture would intellectuals and artists, now nominally proletarianized as "culture workers," become the peoples' "loyal spokesmen." He wrote: "Only by speaking for the masses can he [the specialist] educate them and only by being their pupil can he be their teacher. If he regards himself as their master, as an aristocrat who lords it over the lower orders, no matter how talented he may be, he will not be needed by the masses and his work will have no future." [34]

Mao also warned the writers that Lu Hsun's "burning satire and freezing irony," perfected under the "rule of dark forces" when all comrades were denied freedom of speech, were inappropriate under the new regime, which granted democracy and freedom to all *revolutionary* writers and artists: "Here we can shout at the top of our voices and have no need for veiled and roundabout expressions, which are hard for the people to understand. . . . Satire is always necessary. But there are several kinds of satire, each with a different attitude, satire to deal with our enemies, satire to deal with our allies, and satire to deal with our own ranks. . . . What we must abolish is the abuse of satire."

That warning continued to be violated and reasserted, most blatantly throughout the Cultural Revolution, which was one reason why the essay was so terribly important to Chiang Ch'ing.

iv

Among the writers who stood up to Mao at the forum and refused to follow his dictates in the future was the redoubtable and independent Ting Ling. In Chiang Ch'ing's discussion of the background of the Yenan Forum, she pointed to Ting Ling's feminist diatribe, "Thoughts on March Eighth" (International Women's Day), a publicized slap in the face of a society that prided itself on a certain measure of equality between the sexes as well as economic and political equality. That Chiang Ch'ing did not delve into the substance of Ting Ling's critique suggests that the points Ting Ling raised were too sensitive for her to discuss openly. Nor did she say much about the woman behind the complaint. A glance at the life of Ting Ling shows why her insight and candor irritated raw nerves in an imperfect revolutionary society.

Born eight years earlier than Chiang Ch'ing in Mao Tse-tung's province of Hunan, Ting Ling, along with the original core of revolutionary leaders, was educated in the modern schools of the provincial capital of Changsha. There she began her lifelong career as feminist, Bohemian, intellectual dissenter, and political leftist. Those attributes may have disqualified her for life under any government of men who demanded unanimity and conformity — subordination, in effect.

In their student days Chiang Ch'ing and Ting Ling both turned to writing as a way of communicating to an antitraditional and postimperial world. Ting Ling remained with that, becoming China's most spirited woman writer among radical circles of the 1930's. Chiang Ch'ing set aside serious writing for acting, which led to a spotty film career. In the mid-1920's Ting Ling had also flirted with the idea of becoming a movie star, but quit in disgust over the sexual exploitation of women by film impresarios. Both studied at Peking and Shanghai universities, Chiang Ch'ing less formally. Both were members of the League of Left-Wing Writers, and Ting Ling had been a member of the Communist Party since 1931.[35] A far more prominent dissenter, she too was persecuted by the KMT, arrested in 1933, and imprisoned but not released until after the Sian incident of December 1936, when Chiang Kai-shek was compelled to free famous protesters. Both women had complex sexual histories; only Ting Ling, though, dared to expose her personal experience in a modern, candid style of literature. Both enjoyed the friendship of the short story writer Shen Ts'ung-wen, Chiang Ch'ing as his student at Tsingtao University, and Ting Ling as one of a *ménage à trois* shared with her husband, the writer Hu Yeh-pin, who was executed by the KMT in 1931. Both idolized Lu Hsun, Ting Ling from up close and Chiang Ch'ing from afar. Knowing Lu Hsun personally and being a writer herself, Ting Ling must have understood him and what he stood for more profoundly than Chiang Ch'ing did, and her intellectual affinity combined with personal loyalty may have been the reason why she turned sour on the CCP's twisting to its own advantage his original reputation as a rebel against all totalitarianism and latter-day bureaucratism.

With the outbreak of the war both fled to Yenan and joined the staff of the Lu Hsun Academy. Each in her own way became involved with Mao. His close friendship with Ting Ling, which led to long hours of conversation in his cave, was seen as an infatuation by some, who perceived her eventually as the woman rejected.[36] However that may have been, Mao married Chiang Ch'ing, yet sustained an open respect for Ting Ling despite their disagreement during the Yenan Forum. Whatever thought reform she was subjected to did not undermine her independent stance over the next fifteen years. She was vocal during the Hundred Flowers Campaign in 1956–1957 (for the few weeks when everyone was urged to speak freely) and not until the second Anti-Rightist Campaign (1957–1958) was she felled. Rumor has it that she, the most brilliant symbol of feminine independence in a revolutionary situation, was degraded to charwoman for the Writers' Union. There is no record of subsequent rehabilitation, though in the mid-1970's she was still alive.[37]

Chiang Ch'ing had not known Ting Ling in Shanghai, for she was imprisoned almost the entire time Chiang Ch'ing was there. They first crossed paths in Yenan, where Ting Ling enjoyed considerable status and trust as editor of the Party newspaper, *Liberation Daily*. Yet she and her intellectual friends came to offend the leading comrades because they scorned the institution of marriage. Regarding sexual equality as necessary in a proper Communist society, they saw how certain Communist leaders, like Confucian leaders of the past, were still assuming, unconsciously perhaps, that women needed to be controlled.

Ting Ling's "Thoughts on March Eighth," composed after Mao had paired off with Chiang Ch'ing, ridiculed the leaders' general claim to have revolutionized the position of women. Ting Ling showed that despite the struggle for sexual equality that had been waged by modernly educated Chinese since the turn of the century, male chauvinism still reigned supreme. Without naming names, she said that the most disadvantaged were the leaders' wives.

Much attention has been drawn to the condition of women in Yenan, Ting Ling wrote, and it is said that they are more fortunate that women elsewhere in China. But Yenan remains unexceptional. Social pressure still drives women to marriage, and those who resist (such as herself) are condemned. They are urged to bear children, yet mothers find it nearly impossible to have their children looked after, so they are unable to resume the work that the new society demands. Such social conditions force mothers to become classic bourgeoises — "Noras who return home." After a decade of domesticity, women who were progressive when single have retrogressed to "backward wives." In contemporary Yenan "backwardness" or "lack of political purity" has become the most common ground on which husbands sue wives for divorce.

In the old days, Ting Ling continued, a woman was merely to be pitied. But nowadays a woman who has been forced to suffer will turn her resentment into retribution. "That serves you right!" she'll tell a man. Ting Ling openly empathized with the special weaknesses and vulnerabilities of her sex. Overwhelmed by social forces, women fail to "rise above their times," to think theoretically, and to act decisively. Women pursuing equality must tend to their health, use their brains, act responsibly and resolutely, and expect to suffer.

It seems that Ting Ling and Mao were long intrigued by each other's unique powers. Yet Mao's need to stamp out nearly all criticism of Yenan's new society, and hence of himself, finally compelled him to drive this unconventional and irrepressibly talented woman from the community of the revolutionary elect, as he had already exiled scores of associates who had become politically detrimental. Like the women of her political imagination, Ting Ling was made to suffer for rising above her generation, first in Shanghai under the KMT, now in Yenan, and eventually in Peking. Yet as long as she had access to the media, she continued to speak the mind of an independent revolutionary, until the Anti-Rightist Campaign of the late 1950's, when she was silenced — permanently, it seemed.

As a wife plainly overshadowed by her husband, excluded from intellectual circles, and lacking a separate footing in the Communist organization of the women's movement, Chiang Ch'ing was no doubt chagrined by Ting Ling's exposé. Nevertheless Chiang Ch'ing acted on Ting Ling's advice in the long run. After years of floundering about obscurely in Mao's domain, she broke away from the revisionist role of "Nora who returns home" imposed upon her by jealous colleagues. She used her head, composed her own political scripts, and moved out into the world independently. Yet even as a national leader, she would not escape suffering for her defiance of the unequal but seemingly indestructible sexual norms.

8.

◇ ◇ ◇

On the Road to Peking

There is no one here I can speak to
Who can understand me.
My hopes and visions are greater
Than those of the men around me,
But the chance of our survival is too
    narrow.
What good is the heart of a hero
Inside my dress?
                —Ch'iu Chin, "A Letter
                to Lady Tao Ch'iu"

I'm also a soldier," Chiang Ch'ing announced brightly during our interview in Peking, as if to dispel a contrary assumption. "During the Liberation War I served as political instructor in a detachment directly under the Northwest war theater headquarters. I still retain military status."

When she resumed that subject in Canton, her narrative blended personal reminiscence with recent research. To prepare herself for our meeting she had consulted diaries written by and for the Central Committee on the events of each day of the march from Yenan to Peking and carried the whole way in document boxes. These records she supplemented now with hand-drawn maps and tables detailing battles, troop counts, and an overview of the several war theaters. The last few days, which she had spent in making notes covering three and a half decades (1937–1972) were exhausting, she admitted, yet discussing that tumultuous era gave her enormous pleasure. She had mulled over it for years without ever having had the opportunity to express her views in a sustained way. Foreigners must understand that only "we" (the leading comrades) know the history of this period; only "we" can provide the overall outline and fill in the complete picture of what was happening throughout the whole country.

The chance to speak authoritatively on warfare, historically a male prerogative, was uneasily taken, for at moments she acted surprisingly feminine. In the course of the evening's discussion of some seven hours she would suddenly break off her narration of military history and turn with a sparkling smile to blown-up examples of the Chairman's calligraphy adorning the walls, or toy nervously with tiny wreaths of jasmine and orchid blossoms attached to her fan, or adjust the blossoms she had attached to mine.

In advance of the evening's serious discussion she rose and led the way across the hall to another long, high-ceilinged room and motioned me to share an outsized beige sofa with her. Set on a long low table before us were celadon mugs of tea brewed of dried blossoms, their steamy floral aroma perfuming the humid atmosphere, and platters of exotic raw vegetables. Those she described botanically and poetically, never once making a simple aesthetic judgment of their natural beauty or flavor. Translucent slices of the thick stem of the lotus and lotus seeds the size of marbles were arranged symmetrically on plates. Deftly, she pulled back the rose-hued spines of the caltrop fruit, which was crisp and white inside. The most strange, indeed transfixing, were the phoenix eyes; long pods grown on southern trees were burst open, each revealing one large black seed — the pupil in the pod's wide eye. Those dark eyes of the phoenix, the imperial symbol of the female principle in traditional Chinese iconography, stared at us unflinchingly as we detached them with chopsticks and ate them. They were mealy and tasted odd but pleasant.

Arising, Chiang Ch'ing motioned me to follow her across the room where two large tables displayed six maps, each expertly hand-drawn (two are reproduced between pages 142 and 143). They had just been prepared for her in Peking under the guidance of Comrade Wang Tung-hsing (Mao's bodyguard during the civil war). [1] Comrade Wang used to advise the Chairman on military affairs and accompanied him throughout the march in the Northwest. She regarded him as a peerless military historian and disclosed that he was responsible for organizing the military record she was going to present. But with us now was the no less expert Comrade Chang Ch'ing-hua. Exceptionally tall and long-headed, he stood at the other side of the map table. He was intent about his work, but seemed embarrassed by our sudden introduction.

During the northern Shensi campaign, Chiang Ch'ing continued, Comrade Chang Ch'ing-hua was section leader in charge of military operations. Now he was director of the national General Surveying Bureau. His experience of warfare would enable him to speak vividly and concretely about military history, though Chairman Mao's writings provided the thorough analysis of principles. But neither her concrete account nor that of Comrade Chang Ch'ing-hua would be "dry," she promised. As it turned out, Chang handled the sizable maps and charts as she referred to them and respectfully assented to points she made without comment.

"There have been great distortions, even lies and slander," she warned defensively about her own part in the Liberation War. "What kind of Chinese Communist Party member would I be if the enemy did not attack me? To cite one example, during the battles in North Shensi I was continuously doing political work in the army. Yet some have said that I was making shoes. Some others have said that as soon as I saw my first three lice in Yenan, I ran away. Actually, they don't know that I had lice again when I marched with the troops. In those days having lice was revolutionary!

"We're telling you all of this not just for the sake of *your* book," she went on. "Your coming here and your presence now have motivated us to explain this phase of our military history to the entire world." She would focus upon the events of the war in the Northwest, which she had witnessed.

Thus Chiang Ch'ing presented a day-to-day account of what happened, interspersing it with personal anecdotes. In confining her narrative to the Northwest theater, she would of necessity neglect the other theaters, and consequently would not speak of the exploits of generals like P'eng Te-huai, Liu Po-ch'eng, Ch'en I, and Lin Piao. Neither would she describe extensively debates over strategy or abortive efforts at peace negotiations. These we can sum up.

On August 9, 1945, the Soviet Union invaded Manchuria, thereby breaking Japan's thirteen-year hold over China's Northeast quarter, which the Japanese had called Manchukuo. This colonial kingdom was ruled by the puppet Manchurian Emperor P'u-i and an entourage of Confucian scholars. On the same day, the American atomic bomb dropped on Nagasaki put an end to World War II. Japan surrendered on August 14.

For the Nationalists and Communists, who had waged intermittent struggles against Japan for fourteen years, the sudden defeat of the common enemy left them with none to oppose but each other. At the time of Japan's surrender the Nationalist armies enjoyed an almost three-to-one advantage of troops and a five-to-one advantage of arms over the Communists. Their air and naval forces were formidable; the Communists had none. This gross disparity led observers to believe that the nation would soon be restored to order by the Nationalist government that controlled the cities, the financial world, the press and the other media, and also commanded international recognition. At that juncture the United States government, disregarding the anti-Nationalist judgments made by American observer groups in Yenan and elsewhere in China during the previous twelve months, chose to turn over to the Nationalists quantities of war material, which made the Nationalist army the most powerfully equipped military force in Asia. How effectively the material would be used remained to be seen. Which side would win the support of the Chinese people — the endeavor known in the old days as "seizing the mandate" and now, in the new terminology, as "winning over the masses" — also remained to be seen.

The struggle for advantage was swift. As commander-in-chief of the Communist forces, Chu Te ordered all Communist units to take over all towns and communications lines formerly held by the Japanese and their Chinese puppets. The Nationalists countermanded the order, directing that all units remain in position pending formal Nationalist acceptance of Japan's surrender. This was an attempt to "steal the fruits of victory from the people," the Communists protested. As the two antagonists approached a deadlock, Mao Tse-tung accepted Chiang Kai-shek's telegraphed invitation to negotiate in Chungking.

Accordingly, on August 26, Chairman Mao, Vice-Chairman of the Revolutionary Military Council Chou En-lai, General Wang Jo-fei, and United States Ambassador Patrick Hurley flew to Chungking, the Nationalist capital, for the negotiations.* Discussions dragged on for weeks. Finally, on October 10 a provisional agreement was reached whereby a new government would be organized at a Political Consultative Conference, at which all parties would be represented and a constitution drawn up; a joint KMT and CCP committee would see to the nationalization of the armies. In general, the Nationalists would make political concessions in exchange for the Communists' military concessions. Throughout the negotiating period minor military conflicts persisted between the rival forces, and no final agreement had been reached by October 11, when Mao returned to Yenan, or by December, when Ambassador Hurley, having failed as conciliator, was succeeded by the mission headed by General George C. Marshall. Chou En-lai, who since 1944 had spent months negotiating in Chungking, remained there to work out a cease-fire with American and Nationalist representatives and to lay foundations of a postwar government.

By spring of 1946 the mistrust between old foes cut so deep that peaceful settlement of their differences was impossible. Repeatedly in North China and Manchuria truces were violated. In January 1947 General Marshall left China, having failed in his mission to forge a coalition between the Nationalists, whose political skill and popular support were less than the Americans had allowed themselves to believe, and the Communists, whose ideological determination and military goals were more extreme than a mutually acceptable treaty could admit.

---

* Chiang Ch'ing did not accompany Mao on the flight — his first. He had been reelected Chairman of the Politburo and the Central Committee earlier in the year.

In February 1947 the Communist representatives at the year-long Political Consultative Conference were returned by American military aircraft to Yenan. Within a few days of their arrival the Nationalists assaulted and captured the Red capital. And by the middle of the year fratricidal warfare tore the nation apart. The Communists' seven "liberated areas" were transformed into seven theaters of war. [2]

As Chiang Ch'ing resumed her discussion and moved into the Third Revolutionary Civil War Period (the Party's chronology), [3] the scope of her vision alternately narrowed and widened from individual to collective memory. I noticed that she no longer used the personal "I" but shifted to the collective "we." Edgar Snow remarked on a like shift in Mao's autobiographical account of the 1930's, particularly after he told Snow how the Red Army had been formed: "[His] account had begun to pass out of the category of 'personal history,' and to sublimate itself somehow intangibly in the career of a great movement in which, though he retained a dominant role, you could not see him clearly as a personality. It was no longer 'I' but 'we'; no longer Mao Tse-tung, but the Red Army; no longer a subjective impression of the experiences of a single life, but an objective record by a bystander concerned with the mutations of collective human destiny as the material of history." [4] With Chiang Ch'ing, the collective "we" was largely restricted to her exposition of the Liberation War; subsequently, when she was speaking of other struggles, within the Party or within herself, the "I" reappeared.

i

"Why not call this section on the Liberation War of the late 1940's 'Years of Struggles and Battles Waged against Enemies and Old Habits'?" Chiang Ch'ing began. In the entire history of the revolution, she declared, the years of the war in the Northwest, which lasted from March 13, 1947, to June 12, 1949, were the most difficult but the most important for future development. Since she knew those two crucial years from personal experience, eventually, under her guidance, some aspects were transformed into art. The *Yellow River Concerto* and the revolutionary operas *Shachiapang* and *The Red Lantern* * project the significance of that era.

At the time the war began, the Communists were entrenched in their bases in the Northwest, which they had gained control of after the Long March. In the twelve years from 1935 to 1947 the KMT never dared to challenge the boundaries of these Red Areas; instead, they hid cravenly in the O Mei moun-

* Discussed in Chapters 16 and 17.

tains.* Mention of the beautiful O Mei range in Szechwan province reminded her of what she called a wonderful line in the "Lu Shan Ballad" by the T'ang poet Li Po. "I was a madman from the Lu State," she began, and then broke off, saying that she would give me a copy of that poem.

More seriously, she said that when I returned to America and studied this period on my own, I should focus on Chairman Mao's writings on the Resistance War. "On Protracted War," "Strategic Problems During the War of Resistance," "On Guerrilla Warfare," "On New Democracy," and "On Coalition Government" appear in the second and third volumes of Mao's *Selected Works*. All of them she recommended heartily.

Referring to the map that covered the period from August 1945 to June 1946, she showed how it illustrated which areas were in Communist hands at the time of Japan's surrender in August 1945, and which were still in the hands of the enemy (KMT). The end of World War II also brought to a close the Resistance War, which was fought mainly by the Eighth Route Army (commanded by Chu Te) and the New Fourth Army (commanded by Ch'en I). Yet both were directed by Chairman Mao, she insisted.

After the Japanese surrender, the Chinse Communist Party was left at a tremendous military disadvantage vis-à-vis the KMT. In 1945 and 1946 their side had 1.2 or 1.3 million troops and controlled a population of 130 million, while the enemy had 4.3 million troops and controlled a population of over 300 million. Chiang Kai-shek's strength was bolstered by the American imperialists who provided him with planes and warships for transporting his troops. As the Communists gradually gained the upper hand over Chiang Kai-shek, he "graciously" allowed them to appropriate much of the material which the Americans had donated to him. The Communists promptly nicknamed him "Quartermaster of Transportation."

As she continued to recite statistics from battle records, troop counts, gains and losses of men and material, she noticed that I was laboriously taking notes of everything said. "Don't bother," she said jovially. "I'm going to give you these tables."

"That would be excellent reference material," I replied gratefully in Chinese.

Snapping her head around and looking injured, she exclaimed: "Those materials are absolutely true. There is nothing false about them!"

Perplexed by her outrage, I suddenly realized that my faux pas was semantic. "Reference materials" indeed is translated *ts'an-k'ao tze-liao*, but in Chinese

---

* After Nanking fell to the Japanese in December 1937, Chiang Kai-shek moved his capital to Chungking, the provincial capital of Szechwan in the O Mei mountains. Soon he was joined by the military, industrial, and education establishments, which transferred their entire operations there. In 1946, the year after Japan surrendered, the Nationalists returned to their former capital in Nanking.

the term is used to refer to materials of dubious reliability, to be used only judiciously. Laughing, I apologized and explained the contradictions built into the language.

Resuming on an edgy note, she said that in the mid-1940's the American imperialists made a big point of trying to mediate between Chiang Kai-shek and the Red forces. They set up a three-man group, but this was so rigged as to serve only Chiang Kai-shek's cause. Eventually both sides were persuaded to sign the Double Ten Agreement (October 10, 1945), and the Chairman flew back to Yenan.* But no sooner had he deplaned than Chiang Kai-shek resumed civil war.

After the Double Ten Agreement was "scrapped" by Chiang Kai-shek, the Chairman devised the following strategy: the Red forces would keep the initiative by at first appearing to lose it. They would yield small cities and medium-sized towns, which would cause the enemy to break up its troops into garrisons, thereby diffusing its strength and augmenting its vulnerability. Another ploy was to lure small numbers of KMT troops into a "pocket" of Red Army troops, which would then mop up. The Party leadership also decided to confine the fighting to their own base areas because, knowing them best, they could control them most effectively.

To compensate for the disparity in troop strength and material, the Red forces used an active-defense (guerrilla) strategy: they focused their limited forces on the enemy's vulnerable points. Their overall goal was to wipe out the enemy — that is, wipe them out *politically*, not physically, she added hastily. Toward prisoners of war they were open-minded, giving them the choice of converting to their side or going back to the KMT. Those who chose to go back were provided with transport for the return journey. Actually, few chose to return, as she would elaborate later.

"Chairman Mao insisted on staying in that war theater [the Northwest] and from there directing the struggle throughout our country. He commanded two armies, our own and the enemy's. He directed the enemy into places where our army could 'gobble it up.' I personally experienced and witnessed his art of command. That was a crucial period, and it is exceedingly important for you to understand the situation then. At that time the enemy had two fists: one was in East China, in Shantung, where we had retreated to the Chiaotung Peninsula; the other was in the Northwest, directed at northern Shensi. There the enemy had over two hundred thousand troops, though they claimed to have three hundred thousand, pitched against our twenty thousand, just one tenth of

* Chiang Ch'ing confused events here. The "three-man group" — the so-called Committee of Three (General Marshall, Chou En-lai, and the KMT General Chang Ch'un) did not meet until January 1946.

their strength. But we annihilated great numbers of them. At the same time we conducted battles throughout the country."

In a later conversation she qualified her first statement on the withdrawal from Yenan, adding that a blow by the enemy's fist in the Chiaotung Peninsula destroyed her hometown in Chu-ch'eng county. Now she estimated that the enemy's troops were nine times the size of theirs: in 1947 the enemy had 300,000 (on still another occasion she estimated the enemy's troop level at the time of the withdrawal from Yenan at 230,000) and they had 25,000 (also inflated from before).[5] As Chairman Mao put the difference: like the enemy we have legs, but our legs are *longer* than the enemy's legs. With fighting pitched in the nation's interior, the enemy struck out at them like a "blind man" with no sense of where they were, nor of population concentrations. As the war progressed, popular feeling moved increasingly to their side. In most of the areas they marched through they carried out rent reduction and land reform, the political measures that gradually won them mass support.

ii

Chiang Ch'ing remembered the KMT's air attack on Yenan, begun around March 12, 1947, as abruptly terminating an era. The Yenan community, stable for over a decade, was uprooted and dislodged, and her own life was disrupted. The sudden exodus and its vicissitudes forged in her a new strength of character and sharpened her political consciousness, effects similar to those the Long March had on most of her close comrades.

A few days before they withdrew from their base area, she began, the enemy launched the program of strategic bombing. Dispatched by Liu K'an and Tung Chao, each of whom led his own regimental troops in the KMT 29th Army Corps, a force of nearly fifty planes, all American B-24's and P-52's, bombed fields as close as five miles of the center of Yenan. Despite that imposing aircraft and weaponry, none of their people died under fire, she said with a defiant air.

Her expression warming, she recalled how during that emergency she took her small daughter Li Na with her to an air-raid shelter, where the two of them joined others who were singing songs just to keep from feeling afraid. As night fell, the flare from the attacks illuminated the fields, and a few figures began trailing away from the shelters back to their cave homes. When the bombing seemed to be dying down, she joined the others and they all sang military songs as they trudged over the torn-up fields. Eventually, she noted coolly, both the enemy commanders, Liu K'an [6] and Tung Chao, were murdered by their own men.

The air raid, which lasted several days, was what finally forced the decision to withdraw from Yenan. What must be understood, she explained (to offset the obvious impression that they had yielded the capital and thereby lost face), was that the withdrawal was made on their own initiative. At first most of the leading comrades and the troops were unwilling to quit the base they had built with almost no equipment, upon meager soil; they only wanted to retreat to a point just east of the Yellow River. Commander Ho Lung (military historian and Central Committee member since 1945) proposed still another strategy, which the Chairman repudiated. Admittedly, it was not easy for them to make their people want to follow the Chairman's orders. Even after the evacuation from the Inner Mongolian capital Kalgan (October 11, 1946) had been completed, and the withdrawal from Yenan was under way, some "bad elements" in the Party leadership protested the Chairman's decision to hold out in Yenan even for a few days. As they dismantled operations and packed for the journey, she overheard some reluctant comrades who meant well, she knew, remark on how dangerous it was for the Chairman to remain in the beleaguered base area (and by implication themselves). She relayed their anxieties to the Chairman, who snapped back at her: "You're a coward! And if you're going to be a coward, why not join forces with them!"

She stayed with the Chairman, the only woman comrade to remain in Yenan to the bitter end. Someone close, she felt, should stay back to look after him during that dire period.

To show that he was relaxed during his delayed departure, the Chairman spent unusual amounts of time looking after Li Na, then six. He played with her in daylight, when conditions could be seen, but at night several persons were required to guard the child. During those final days in Yenan, Chiang Ch'ing often did political work with Li Na in tow. They went on special missions across rivers and difficult terrain. Unused to such turbulence, Li Na would cry and beg to go back home.

Incidentally, Chiang Ch'ing recalled that, just before they left, Anna Louise Strong asked to join them on the march. Because she seemed old to them (she was fifty-two), they advised her against it and she left China. Still, they did not lose contact with her, for after Liberation she returned.

Troops were called out for March 18. A force of 25,000 men, comprising eight brigades, constituted the First Field Army, which was commanded by P'eng Te-huai. The men were divided into two columns, each column with its commander. Once more she stressed that the withdrawal of the troops was a strategic move deliberately planned and executed by both columns in an orderly fashion.

The air was bitterly cold as troops were arrayed late that afternoon. More than a foot of snow covered the ground, crunchy and slippery underfoot. At dusk, around six, they embarked upon the march, leaving a ghost town behind.*

The Chairman departed by jeep, an advantage not without danger. By the time they reached Liu-chia-ch'ü, a few miles to the north, later that evening, the enemy had sighted the jeep from the air and pounded it with machine-gun fire. Though no one was injured, the roof was perforated. For the rest of the journey soldiers camouflaged it with foliage.

The shells left by that attack showed that the enemy was using three kinds of bullets—all made in America: the armor-piercing type, the explosive type, and the incendiary type. Before long, air fire rained down from all directions, an experience she found less frightening than she had anticipated. Of course they were not foolhardy, she admitted. Most of them ran for shelter.

There were other moments of private panic. When Liu-chia-ch'ü was first attacked, she and the Chairman could not find their daughter Li Na, who they assumed was being well guarded. Naturally they were terrified that she had been lost or killed, as had other children of the Chairman's on the Long March years earlier. After an urgent search they tracked her down at the home of a peasant who had given her shelter. There she was, playing happily, innocent of threatening disaster. For security, Li Na was then sent to join Teng Ying-ch'ao, whose political work kept her apart from her husband Chou En-lai and the Northwest headquarters. Li Na remained in Teng Ying-ch'ao's custody for many months. The two became quite fond of one another, Chiang Ch'ing said, smiling. Li Na still calls Ying-ch'ao "Mama Teng."

The march continued the evening of the next day. Resting by day and moving by night, gradually they picked up momentum. The third day they reached

---

* A member of the Central Guard Corps, Chiang Ch'in-feng, presents a more Mao-centered perspective on the same events. When the air raid broke out on the twelfth, people from all over the Yenan area ran for shelter. At that time the Central Committee was set up at the neighboring community of Yang-chia-ling, while Chairman Mao (and Chiang Ch'ing), who usually lived apart from the Central Committee, were situated at Yang-chia-p'ing. Explosions broke out over both places, some perilously close to the Chairman's hilltop home. Yet the Chairman remained there, bent over his writing desk, absorbed in thought and oblivious to the attack until his comrades Chou En-lai, Jen Pi-shih, and P'eng Te-huai aroused him, telling him to leave ahead of the rest. When attacks were renewed the next day they urged him again to go. Stubbornly, he refused to abandon the people. Strafing and shooting continued for a week, destroying homes and killing children, dogs, and sheep. At dusk on the eighteenth the Red forces withdrew as a group, as Chiang Ch'ing reported.

Chiang Ch'in-feng's eyewitness history corresponds generally to Chiang Ch'ing's account of the stations of the march, the dates, and related events. Of all the Central Committee leaders, he describes Mao and Chou En-lai most positively (Chou looms larger than in Chiang Ch'ing's account). Jen Pi-shih, Lu Ting-i, and P'eng Te-huai also emerge as leaders en route (Chiang Ch'ing scarcely mentioned them — P'eng and Lu fell from favor, in 1959 and 1966 respectively, after Chiang Ch'in-feng's account was published in 1957). He makes no mention of Chiang Ch'ing or of any other woman participant (HCPP, 3: 338–367).

Kao-chia-hsien, some miles to the northeast. There they laid out battle plans, including a battle at Ch'ing-hua-pien. The Chairman made some changes within the Central Committee at this time.

At the time of exodus from Yenan, the Central Committee organization was called the Third Detachment, under which there were four teams. Chiang Ch'ing was appointed political assistant under the Third Detachment, a post she kept throughout most of the march. However, now the Chairman divided the Central Committee into two parts: the Work Committee (also known as the Front Committee) and the Rear Areas Committee. The organization assignments were made by Chou En-lai, who during the Northwest Campaign served as vice-chairman of the Military Commission of the Central Committee.[7] Chairman Mao, Chou En-lai, Jen Pi-shih, and Lu Ting-i were assigned to the Front Committee; so also was Liu Shao-ch'i, she added quickly as an afterthought.* Yeh Chien-ying was responsible for the Rear Areas Committee.

Maneuvering against the enemy situated just beyond the Wu T'ai mountains, Chairman Mao led the troops on a westward course toward the Great Wall. To avoid observation by the enemy, they moved their troops only at night. In fact, they marched almost every night, with a ten-minute break for every hour of the march. The Chairman led one column, while the other column set out separately across the Huai-chu River.

As they plodded along in the dark for hours on end, some teenagers who had just joined their forces were barely able to keep pace. A few collapsed from exhaustion. For them there was little to be done. Her own passage was eased by having a horse. She remembered one boy of fourteen or fifteen who kept clutching the tail of her horse just to keep on track. She too was operating at the brink of exhaustion, terrified that she would fall asleep, tumble off her horse, and be injured. Then what use would she be to her comrades? To keep awake she forced herself to sing revolutionary songs and did not allow herself to sleep before three in the morning. Her general discomfort was exacerbated by the chronic stomach trouble she had suffered from childhood (one of many references to changes in her physiological system). Usually her stomach had abnormally high acidity. But the high altitude of the mountains in which they were marching reversed that condition, causing low acidity and other gastrointestinal disturbances.

On March 31, 1947, they arrived at Ch'iu-chia-p'ing, on the banks of the Huai-chu River. Around that time she was outraged to observe one soldier in their company who was wearing the military cap and badge of the Kuomintang! Furiously she demanded that he take it off. To dramatize her point she removed her own cap, in those days the octagonal cap adorned with the red star,

---

* Liu Shao-ch'i was Mao's first designated successor, who was forced out of power in the mid-1960's. In the late 1940's he marched with Chu Te on a separate course to West Hopeh.

put his KMT cap upon her own head, and glared at him. Other comrades who saw the exchange turned on her angrily. No matter, her point was made. She had demonstrated to the young soldier and to the onlookers that among them lurked some Right Opportunists trying to induce them to decorate their caps with the KMT badge instead of the red star of the Communist Party.[8] One person involved in the dispute was Li Wei-han, in those days president of the Communist Party College. When he saw her wearing the boy's cap, Li shouted, "Take off the Kuomintang insignia!"

"Yes, the Kuomintang and Communist Party are *at war!*" she yelled back. Anyone else still wearing the KMT insignia should take orders from *her* because she was a *political instructor!*

They resumed the march, cleaving close to the mountains until they reached the plains. During the ten-minute break in each hour of the march, they marked time just to fight off the bitter cold. Even her fur coat could not keep her from feeling chilled to the bone. One of their comrades passed around a small bottle of spirits, which warmed them momentarily.

So they continued the pace, one that became habitual: beginning the march at dusk, continuing through the night, camping at dawn and sleeping much of the day (even since Liberation the habit of working the night and sleeping the day continued to be followed by most of this elder generation of leaders, Chiang Ch'ing among them). They were moving on the westward course in early April. On the fifth they arrived at Ch'ing-yang-ch'a. One of the first things they did during their several days of encampment there was to stock up on the "three treasures" needed to sustain the journey — salt, fur, and herbs.

During this phase of the war certain leaders went by pseudonyms designed to cloak their true identity, thereby reducing the enemy's chances of tracking them down. The pseudonyms were carefully chosen. The Chairman decided to call himself Li Te-sheng, "determined to be victorious," and Chou En-lai masqueraded as Hu Pi-sheng, "certain to be victorious."[9] During the encampment at Ch'ing-yang-ch'a the Central Committee changed its name again for security reasons, this time to the Ninth Detachment.[10] It still comprised four teams, and she continued to serve as political instructor with one.

During their short stay at Ch'ing-yang-ch'a the Chairman withdrew alone to his quarters to compose his ideas. On the ninth of April he issued a circular in which he set forth the rationale for the "temporary" (as he called it then) abandonment of Yenan in the larger strategy of defense of the Shen-Kan-Ning Border Region.[11] The attack on Yenan and Shen-Kan-Ning as a whole, he wrote, should not be mistaken as a sign of the KMT's actual power. On the contrary, that assault revealed an acute crisis within the KMT. Thereupon, the Chairman called upon the Party and the army to struggle jointly in the defense of Shen-Kan-Ning.

iii

At Wang-chia-wan, their next station, they remained two months, breaking camp on the seventh of June. A village of some ten families nestled in the side of a mountain in Ching-pien county, Wang-chia-wan was just six miles distant from the enemy during the time of their encampment there. When they arrived, the Central Committee was put up in two adjoining caves. She and the Chairman occupied the inner cave while Chou En-lai, Lu Ting-i, and Jen Pi-shih, who were traveling without their wives, lived together in the outer cave.* When the four men decided to hold a meeting, she was obliged to move out of the cave into a donkey shed. (This recollection of the absurd delighted her.) Sequestered with asses for days on end and with nothing to do, she became infested with lice and fleas, her weight dropped rapidly, and she developed a lump on the back of her neck. What caused that she could not imagine. After the Central Committee meetings were over, the Chairman reclaimed her, examined her complaint, and "enlightened" her, as she put it. Where she had been sleeping he discovered a heap of bedbugs. *Those* were the fellows who had bitten her and caused the swelling, he said. In honor of the bugs, militantly aligned in serried ranks up the walls, they renamed the shed "Bedbug Headquarters." Then the Chairman and she waged an extermination campaign, destroying every last one. (She laughed when she described it.)

During their stay at Wang-chia-wan a bitter struggle arose within the Central Committee. Chiang Ch'ing learned of these tensions and the issues involved only indirectly. The enemy was approaching, but from what direction and in what strength was unclear. Would the Communists be wiped out if they remained at Wang-chia-wan? Would the enemy chase them east across the

---

* Mao's former bodyguard, Yen Ch'ang-ling, gives an account of these cramped living arrangements that generally corresponds to Chiang Ch'ing's, and that is also subtly revealing of her character. When the Central Committee arrived at Wang-chia-wan in April, he recalled, an old peasant, Old Man Wang, lent them his dilapidated three-room cave quarters, which also housed many pickled vegetable vats. Their acrid odor reeked in the courtyard. The Chairman (presumably with Chiang Ch'ing) occupied the inner chamber, while Vice-Chairman Chou and Lu Ting-i shared an earthen *k'ang* in the room near the door. Jen Pi-shih was assigned to a third room no bigger than the *k'ang* on which he slept. Deeply apologetic for his humble quarters, Old Man Wang told his relatives to lend the leaders yet another cave. But Comrade Chiang Ch'ing, then a political assistant in the command headquarters office, told Yen Ch'ang-ling, "Don't move them! He's got a big family — young and old, women and kids. How are you going to squeeze them all into one cave?"

"It's too crowded in this place," Yen protested. "Even a company headquarters usually gets more space than this!"

"But conditions are hard at the moment," she replied. "We're a large organization. Moving into a little village like this, we've already caused the local people enough trouble. The Chairman has instructed us that when we run into difficulties we should think of ways to solve them. He isn't going to like it if we put too much stress on his comfort. Besides, we have to think of what impression this might make on the people." (Yen, *The Great Turning Point*, 58–59.)

Yen's article makes no reference to Comrade Chiang Ch'ing's being the Chairman's wife. She, though, displayed consciousness of the importance of maintaining the right political image.

Yellow River and take Shensi for their own? Less than stalwart, Lu Ting-i wanted to retreat to the other side of the Yellow River and to continue a quick march to the east. Jen Pi-shih went along with that. But the Chairman refused to retreat. He had resolved to maintain a flexible course of evading the enemy within the Northwest territory they knew well and were determined to keep. That policy was thrashed out at the Central Committee meetings, which dragged on and on. The Chairman returned exhausted and angry at her. At first she could not understand what made him so foul-tempered. Later she realized that his anger was not really toward her but toward the men with whom he was quarreling, a response she became used to over the years.

On the whole, though, life at Wang-chia-wan was congenial. The Chairman and she made a point of not isolating themselves; they got out among the people and shared parts of their lives with them. The Chairman befriended some wise old villagers and talked with them late into the evenings, a recollection that prompted her to produce a fragile photograph from a large brown envelope (see the first picture section). This she cherished particularly, she said, because it reminded her of the simplicity of their former lives. (The images, blurred and grainy, led me to mistake Chiang Ch'ing, whose hair was cropped almost to a crew cut, for a slender boy; my confusion brought ripples of laughter.) The Chairman and she were seated with two children and another woman (a servant?) around a rustic wooden table outside their cave dwelling. In those days they were able to live close to the ordinary people.

At Wang-chia-wan they (or "we," as she said) were deeply involved in organizing several battles elsewhere in Shensi province. One was at Yang-ma-ho, a small village to the southeast, roughly equidistant from Wang-chia-wan and Yenan. There they destroyed the KMT's 135th Brigade and reorganized its remnants; over four thousand soldiers under the command of that brigade were captured. At Wang-chia-wan the Chairman wrote "The Concept of Operations for the Northwest War Theater" (April 15, 1947),[12] in which he developed his view of the KMT. Although Chiang Kai-shek's government looked powerful, he observed, inwardly it was weak and defeatable.

Mao's argument had been substantiated by the battle at P'an-lung, due south of Yang-ma-ho, on the fourth of April. During that engagement the Communists had eliminated and absorbed the KMT's 167th Division short of one regiment, and captured 6,700 troops and the division commander himself (Liu Kun-kang). From the enemy's supply depot they took possession of more than twelve thousand bags of flour and over forty thousand uniforms. When the battle was over, the Chairman sent Chou En-lai to the environs of P'an-lung to attend a mass celebration of the victory.

Here Chiang Ch'ing interposed a description of her work as propagandist, or "political instructor," as she put it. In the regions they passed through there were two types of people. One was the pro–Mao Tse-tung group; the rest were the enemy. The pro-Mao group had little land and no American aid. In her capacity as political instructor she lectured to other Red soldiers and to members of the local masses: "We are dialectical materialists. Our goal is to remold world outlook." (She did not elaborate upon whether her listeners, poor and illiterate peasants in the main, grasped the jargon.) When she addressed the peasants, she explained what the Communists were trying to accomplish in China and the world. Chiang Kai-shek's soldiers made so many tactical errors that they actually delivered weapons to the Communists. They were only serving as quartermasters to the Red Army. The KMT soldiers were miserable fighters; one Communist soldier was the equal of ten of them. These remarks and others comparable bolstered confidence in the Red Army and in the people whose support they sought.

When they first came to Wang-chia-wan, the masses were in a terrible panic because the enemy forces had recently swept through, leaving the town and fields in disarray. The Communists won over the people's confidence by proving that although they were soldiers on the march, they were different from the KMT. As they restored order they first arranged for the release and protection of people who had been jailed by the enemy. The KMT had plundered the peasants' grain; now the Red Army helped the peasants gather and store up what food remained. When it was all over, the people were enormously grateful and so attached to the troops that they begged them not to leave. "We have not yet treated you to wheat flour," the Red soldiers replied, meaning that they had not yet done enough on the people's behalf. When the army was about to resume the march, a number of the local people came to the cave houses that the Communists had borrowed from them and asked to join the Red forces. Many did so, even though it meant abandoning their family homes of centuries.

The Communists arrived at Hsiao-ho, a village in northern Shensi, close to Inner Mongolia, on June 7, remaining there overnight. As elsewhere, they moved temporarily into the cave dwellings of the local people. The rain was incessant. That did not daunt the Chairman. He refused to take shelter in the cave given over to the two of them until all the soldiers had been housed.

Almost as soon as they arrived they learned that the enemy was approaching from the east, so the next day they left Hsiao-ho for T'ien-tzu-wan. That dramatic stretch of their journey was well worth describing, she said. Since the enemy might catch sight of them at any time, they kept up an unbroken march through thunder, lightning, and blinding rain. Then their guide lost the way, which forced them to return to an earlier point in the hope that by repeating their steps they would recover the trail. Now within earshot of the enemy, they exercised the utmost caution, communicating only by hand signal.

During this treacherous passage Chiang Ch'ing did not want to burden Chairman Mao and his bodyguards with looking after her. Deliberately she allowed her horse to fall behind the pace of the leaders. Joining other comrades toward the rear, she discovered that she was the only rider among foot soldiers. One anxious comrade told her to dismount because riding through a violent storm was dangerous — the horse could shy or bolt, or slip in the mud and throw her. Seeing how reluctant she was to give up her horse, he reached up and dragged her right off the saddle onto the mucky path. Shocked, she regained her balance, and discovered that at ground level where most soldiers maneuvered there was almost no visibility. To keep track of one another in the dark on the narrow path overgrown with brush, they joined hands, forming so tight a human chain that if one bent forward just a little, his head struck the back of the comrade walking in front of him. They stepped noiselessly to avoid arousing the enemy nearby.

Just before dawn someone in the vanguard led by the Chairman passed word down through the human chain that he was waiting for her to rejoin him behind the upcoming mountain; there they would rest. She responded quickly, slipping ahead of the others. By the time she reached the Chairman her rain-cape, drenched and waterlogged by the storm, weighed heavily on her shoulders. It was not useless, though, and she begged him to wear it (it was the only raincape in the whole army, she said). At first he balked; she insisted. Finally he yielded. Managing to persuade the Chairman to drape that precious rain-cape over his shoulders, however soggy it was by then, was her *personal* victory.

The rain poured down unceasingly, but the march continued. She, among others, was again on the verge of collapsing from exhaustion. A soldier near her in the vanguard with Chairman Mao must have noticed her precarious state. Saying nothing, he removed from his belt a thermos flask filled with spirits and offered it to her. She slipped off the tin cup attached to her own belt and poured some of the liquor into it. Draining that cup revived her, and she then handed on the flask to other comrades.

At daybreak they prepared to rest and scouted about for cave houses to use as temporary dwellings, but almost none could be found. As it turned out, the local population was scant and there was scarcely anything to eat. She must have looked disconsolate, for Chou En-lai came up to her to ask if she were afraid.

"Why should I be afraid?" she answered defensively. "We're two hundred people here.* No one is working alone."

Just after that moment another woman comrade confessed to her privately that she had not endured so harrowing an experience since departing from her mother's womb.

* By "two hundred people" she probably meant only the Central Committee and its guard corps.

June 9 broke misty — the day of their arrival at T'ien-tzu-wan. Scouts were immediately dispatched to ascertain whether the enemy had trailed them there. Apparently not, so they remained a week. The time was not wasted: they devoted it mainly to observing the ways of the local society and economy in preparation for future land reform. Chiang Ch'ing performed various tasks among the people, including combing the long, tangled hair of a sick woman.

The community of T'ien-tzu-wan was based on the households of seven landlords who controlled vast expanses of land. By working with some of the local residents she gained insight into the peculiar conditions of landlord-tenant relations. For example, a hired laborer might be given ninety *mou* of land to work,* but he was helpless because he had no plow or other farm implements with which to turn the land into production. For everyone but the landlords, living conditions were deplorable.

That summer of 1947, when the enemy fought "like a blind man," the Chairman was responsible for entire engagements. First he commanded his own forces and second the enemy's.[13] The "craven nature" of the enemy worked to its disadvantage, certainly on the route they were pursuing. While the Red Army remained in the lowlands and took rest in the caves of village people, the enemy, "cowards at heart," built their camps only on mountain-tops, assuming that there they would be invincible. Ironically, the chill, damp air of the mountains gave them stiff joints, which undermined mobility and morale. That risk was precisely why the Communist leaders had decided against camping at high altitudes. Besides, they preferred to have access to the local people in order to bring them around to their point of view.

As the months passed, the people became sensitive to the ways of the Red Army. They knew, for example, that when they saw Red troops marching with a few horses and a few flashlights Chairman Mao was probably in the contingent. To protect him from enemy agents or hostile parties living among them they refused to utter his name. Instead, they referred to him as "*t'a*" — "him" or "he." Those who were their allies immediately understood. If anyone inquired of them the whereabouts of the Red troops or of Chairman Mao they refused to answer or reacted angrily to the question. They helped keep "our secret," she said sotto voce.†

While strategy called for the Central Committee organizations to remain in the west, she went on, their main force moved eastward in order to deflect the enemy's attention from the course taken by the leaders. Then the Central Guard Corps dispatched a small detachment south to An-chai (Ansai), an area

---

* A *mou* is about one-sixth of an acre.

† The subject of the secrecy of troop movements reminded Chiang Ch'ing that the previous April (1972) she had made an unannounced trip to Canton, but by the first of May the news of her visit was already being bruited about in Hong Kong! Her secret return for our interviews caused her to wonder aloud: "How soon will it be known?"

Chiang Ch'ing knew from an earlier visit to Ho-chia-lun, which was nearby. Another comrade who belonged to that small detachment of the Central Guard Corps was also familiar with the An-chai area and used his knowledge to advantage. Alone on a mission one day, he suddenly came face to face with several KMT soldiers. "Hands up!" he shouted and demanded surrender. His authoritative order confused them. They naturally assumed that there were a lot of people backing him up from the bushes. So they yielded, and all seven were rounded up in one grab. "A fine ruse," Chiang Ch'ing added gleefully.

In those days the village of Huan-hsiang-t'uan harbored a reactionary organization made up of elders and other local leaders. When the village fell under attack by the Japanese or the Kuomintang, instead of inducing the people to fight a resistance war, the leaders' organization actually encouraged people to make a kowtow: to bow deeply or lie prostrate on the ground before the enemy planes looping overhead. Or when food was short, they hoarded all the grains, hiding their stocks in caves instead of distributing them among the people. The landlord Nan Pa-t'ien of the revolutionary ballet *The Red Detachment of Women* is depicted as belonging to a reactionary organization of that type, she pointed out.

On June 16, 1947, they arrived for the second time at Hsiao-ho and remained there approximately one and a half months, until August 1. During that time the First Field Army (under P'eng Te-huai) encountered their most formidable enemy to date, the ferocious cavalry of Ma Pu-fang, chief of the Northwest Moslems and governor of Tsinghai province. He and his brothers and cousins (among them Ma Pu-ch'ing and Ma Hung-kuei) headed a clan that constituted a "landlord bourgeois class"; immensely wealthy and influential, they were called by the nickname San Ma (Three Ma's).[14] They were also chieftains of scores of "reactionary forces." They were distinct politically and culturally from the KMT, and the San Ma were far superior militarily, particularly to the KMT forces under Hu Tsung-nan in the Northwest. Yet the two groups supported each other. The San Ma's political following was not restricted to Moslems, for by the middle 1940's, she asserted boldly without further explanation, most of the Northwest Moslems had shifted to the side of the Red Army in the contest with the KMT.

The economic balance of Ninghsia, a region in the Northwest that had a heavily Moslem population, she found unusual: two-thirds of the people's incomes went for clothing, she was told.* But so far as she could tell, the people native to that region had no *real* clothes. When the local women saw her attired in the simple military dress she customarily wore, their faces lit up in delight, for they had never laid eyes on genuine cloth. Their clothes were mostly sheepskin garments crudely sewn together by strands of wool. At night

* Most peasants at that time would have spent at least that proportion for food.

they slept on coarse felt. Generally, their habits were most unsanitary. After living among them for a few days she became even more infested with lice.

Although these were Han people, rather than national minorities, certain of their customs were strange. She remembered how the local women wore small tufts of hair in front of their ears and pulled the rest back. Unmarried women wore pigtails, while the married ones put up their hair. Only a very few women had dared to cut their hair — the outward sign of becoming revolutionary.

The women of East Kansu, a region just to the west of their present location, were known for their beauty, but those of Hsiao-ho were exquisite. Chiang Ch'ing remembered vividly two sisters, one named Kuei-hua (meaning cassia) and the other Lan-hua (meaning orchid). Their father had not followed the normal practice of the Han people, which was for a woman to marry into her husband's family, but had married into his wife's family. There he served as a hired laborer to his father-in-law, a landlord. When the Red Army carried out land reform at Hsiao-ho, this particular hired laborer was given his father-in-law's excellent piece of land to work. But like so many others in similarly reversed circumstances, he was afraid to accept it and live there as his own master. He would not change his point of view. No matter what they told him about the social transformation justified by land reform, he could not rupture the old relationship with his father-in-law — a landlord toward whom he remained inexorably subordinate.

The experience of doing land reform along the stations of the march sharpened Chiang Ch'ing's awareness of local cultures, especially marriage customs. For example, later she learned of a landlord in Kwangtung province on the southern coast whose situation was just the opposite of the Hsiao-ho landlord's. Because the men of that region were accustomed to migrate overseas, the proportion of women in the population was high and concubinage rife. This particular landlord had several concubines whom he forced to perform all sorts of menial labor to which they were unaccustomed, such as carrying his sedan chair and working in the fields. The resentment bred in them was more powerful than he ever suspected. When land reform was conducted in Mei county, his concubines took final vengeance against him by inciting the whole community to revile him, an open drama which destroyed him. In the end, Chiang Ch'ing said brightly, each concubine was awarded a portion of his land as her very own.

iv

Warfare, costly and painful, was an almost daily reality for two itinerant years. But if the Communists were to recover vast portions of the western Shen-

Kan-Ning Border Region and to win subsequent victories over the rest of the country, they had no alternative. Everywhere they went they worked at building up rapport with the local people, the only way their forces would swell. From July 1946 to June 1947 the Red Army succeeded in eliminating 97.5 divisions of the KMT regular forces and wiped out 1.2 million of the KMT nonregular forces (she spoke here of China as a whole). She hastened to add that when she said "wiped out" she did not necessarily mean destroyed physically.

Contact with KMT soldiers who had surrendered meant working with them, concentrating above all on their ideological transformation. When members of the Red Army met the vanquished enemy face to face they struck up conversations, established confidence, and encouraged them to "recall past sufferings" (their common backgrounds of poverty and exploitation which had driven them to join the KMT Army rather than the Red Army). Sometimes that recovery of personal anguish buried in the remote past made them burst into tears and feel utterly defenseless. Then they begged to join the Red Army. Such a change of allegiance was not easy. For months those who had chosen to come over to the Communist side lived in dread of being seized by the KMT and punished, even executed, for desertion. Aware of these fears, she and her political instructors continued to work closely with the new recruits in the liberation of their home villages and towns. Naturally, many were loath to bring revolution to the places where their families had always lived. As an incentive, the Red Army promised each one of them that he would be awarded land during the land reform movement, which was their only means of taking revenge against their former masters and ultimately against the KMT. Those fresh recruits, she declared without qualification, knew as well as the Communists did that the KMT had impressed them into their army in the first place.

Defectors from the KMT were numerous, but not the Red Army's sole source of new recruits. Others were drawn from the countryside, though such reinforcements were limited because the Shen-Kan-Ning Border Region was thinly populated. They were initiated with one week of political education, which was followed by military training. Most became brave fighters in short order. Under the circumstances, their material expectations were modest. All they wanted in order to signify that they "belonged to us" was a military cap decorated with the red star. The rest of the Red Army uniform was less important. People wore whatever they had. As time passed the burgeoning Communist forces were arrayed in a wild assortment of costumes. (She was obviously delighted by the recollection.)

There has been much false writing about the military history of the Northwest, she continued on a serious note. Some of it came from participants allegedly on their side. A man named Wang Ch'ao-pu, who turned out to be a secret agent of Chiang Kai-shek's, contributed a piece to *The Red Flag Waves*, in which he bragged shamelessly about himself.[15] Another was Yen Ch'ang-ling, whom she knew personally. Since he had no literary ability, he asked a newspaperman to write articles for him. Much of what he told his ghost-writers was false. For example, he maintained that his unit was made up of a force one million strong — a gross exaggeration. As she explained earlier, during the march from Hsiao-ho to T'ien-tzu-wan the enemy occupied the top of the mountain, but Yen Ch'ang-ling claimed that the enemy was situated at the foot and that the Red Army took the mountain route. Moreover, Yen wrote that she was spending her time *making shoes* for the Chairman when what she was actually doing was *political* work! In fact, she was head of one of the detachments under the Central Committee, and Yen knew perfectly well that she was out much of the time doing work among the masses. But when he finally found an opportunity to publish his views years later, he chose not to report that.[16] With few exceptions, the only reliable reports, in her view, were those of Chairman Mao.

When they began the march in the spring it had rained nearly every day, but by late summer the weather was unusually dry. The fields were parched, which made procuring food as difficult for themselves as for the inhabitants. Natural conditions were worsened by the ravages of the enemy, who were "inhuman" toward everything they touched: domestic animals were killed, crops were destroyed, and food grains were seized and hidden from the local populace. The enemy so desolated any place they occupied that "even the sound of dogs and chickens could no longer be heard."

On August 1, 1947, the Red troops set out from Hsiao-ho and marched northwest at a brisk pace — an average of three miles an hour. Ten days later they arrived at Sui-te, once a great commercial center, now decadent and drastically reduced in population. There they were suddenly confronted by a formidable array of enemy forces. Seven divisions quickly began to close in on them from three sides.

Responding swiftly, they marched out of Sui-te, arriving around August 17 at the town of Chia-hsien, which was en route to Pai-lung-miao, a village just west of the Yellow River. During their few anxious hours at Chia-hsien, she remembered happily, she managed to buy some crab apples for the Chairman, who was operating under great tension. The enemy was still pursuing them rapidly from three directions, in its first pincer attack against their First Field Army: one pincer from Wu-pao in the south, another from Yü-lin in the west, and a third from Heng-shan, which was southwest of Yü-lin. The Chairman called an emergency meeting of the leaders to revise strategy. Not being included, she was able to observe some of the Red Army soldiers and noticed signs of uneasiness among them. Gingerly, one young officer from the Code Office came up to them holding a bowl of rice. He wanted to eat that rice on the Yellow River's *east* bank, he said, expressing indirectly his eagerness to retreat over the river to Shansi. "You coward!" she shot back at him.*

Although the enemy forces were only five miles away, they were evidently confused about the Red Army's location. Seizing the advantage, the Chairman ordered their detachment, which was the main force, to charge ahead to Pai-lung-miao. So they did and came to a halt at the broad Yellow River, their destination the opposite shore.† The river, murky and turbulent, was swollen and still rising from the heavy rainfall of the spring. How would they get across? As fast as possible they tore down a temple near the bank and used its parts to build a bridge. They sped across, single file. When the last man reached the opposite shore, they dismantled the bridge to prevent the enemy from crossing after them. With their detachment for the first time realigned on the east bank of the Yellow River, they began a new stage of the Liberation War.

V

The turning point of the Northwest Campaign, Chiang Ch'ing said of this most circuitous passage of the march led by Mao, was the battle of Sha-chia-tien waged at the beginning of the third week of August 1947. Their victory here ended the defensive strategy of the first year of the war and opened the counteroffensive, which would carry them to a brilliant victory by the end of

---

* Yen Ch'ang-ling (*The Great Turning Point*, 92–93) reports that on the rapid march north from Sui-te toward Mi-chih during the second week of August everyone's energies, including the leaders', slackened from lack of food and sleep. Vice-Chairman Chou En-lai collapsed from exhaustion, his nose bleeding. Mao insisted that the stretcher which had been brought for his own use be sent instead to Chou. But when it was offered to Chou he told them to go back and look after the Chairman.

"Just then Comrade Chiang Ch'ing also came up. Only after repeated urgings did Vice-Chairman Chou finally consent to travel on the stretcher."

According to Yen, throughout the march Vice-Chairman Chou was a tireless worker, who personally attended to all matters, large and small. He ate and slept little. Occasionally, to take some of the load of responsibility off the shoulders of the Chairman, he retired later than the Chairman and arose earlier. Although the soles of his shoes had become completely worn through, he would not allow anyone to know of this for fear that they would want to help him. The moment he mounted the stretcher his secret was revealed.

Comrade Chiang Ch'ing observed, "Vice-Chairman Chou, your socks are showing through the soles of your shoes."

"No wonder my feet felt the bumps on the road when I walked!" Chou exclaimed.

† Here I convey her narrative precisely, though this first crossing of the Yellow River is not indicated on the map she provided. Apparently they crossed the river, returned, and resumed their march.

the next year. Their skillful guerrilla strategy against a far more substantial but ill-organized enemy was recaptured in a film called *Sha-chia-tien*, which was made years later.

The momentum of the march picked up on August 18 as they passed through Yang-chia-yuan-tzu on their way to Liang-chia-ch'a. They arrived by dusk the next day. Liang-chia-ch'a, a tiny village that could scarcely contain their troops, now several hundred strong, was situated about seven miles north of Sha-chia-tien where the main forces of both sides were now concentrated. From their station at Liang-chia-ch'a the Chairman commanded the battle of Sha-chia-tien by radiotelephone. Tense and weary, all knew that its outcome would determine whether or not they would be forced to retreat westward again. Since other enemy forces were attacking Yü-lin in the west, the Chairman was reluctant to channel all his strength upon Sha-chia-tien. That dilemma he resolved by calling for a false attack. The ploy worked! Not only did their limited forces eliminate the enemy's main force — Hu Tsung-nan's 126th Division — they also demolished the division's headquarters, wiped out most of the KMT's 126th Brigade, and captured approximately six thousand enemy forces under a brigade commander, who escaped to the south.

Now they turned east again, to Chu-kuan-chai, where they remained for some time and subsisted on string beans; yet their spirits remained high. While they were there the Chairman wrote "The Strategy for the Second Year of the War of Liberation," an essay in which he laid down the basic steps to be taken to win the war. He stipulated that in order to launch a nationwide counteroffensive and prosecute their cause in areas held by the KMT, the Front Committee (that is, the Work Committee of the Central Committee) must transform itself into an Instruction Brigade. Political Commissar Chou En-lai was made commander of the new Instruction Brigade.[17]

A winding march brought them to T'an-chia-p'ing on October 18. There the Chairman and she paid a visit to a paper mill. Rapport with the masses was excellent. Like other villagers elsewhere they protected the Chairman by referring to him as "he" and never speaking his name. Three days later they moved on to Nan-ho-ti, then to Shen-ch'uan-pao. While the Instruction Brigade remained there, the Chairman went elsewhere, and she soon joined him. Together they proceeded through the lanes and streets. The masses came out to greet them and wept with joy. Some said that after seeing Chairman Mao they would face death calmly.

On November 1 they were stationed in the environs of Lü-chia-p'ing. There an accumulation of victories made them feel the tide of history shifting to their side. Buoyed by the change, Chiang Ch'ing temporarily left the main troops on a personal mission. Frightened and excited, she crossed to the east bank of the Yellow River and headed for the ancient city of Shuang-t'a. There she was led to the house where her daughter Li Na, who had been left with Teng Ying-ch'ao soon after the evacuation of Yenan, was hidden. By that time Teng Ying-ch'ao had gone elsewhere in connection with their Rear Area Committee and had left Li Na in the care of others. The child had changed markedly since Chiang Ch'ing had last seen her almost eight months before. Now reunited, the two prepared to leave Shuang-t'a quickly, but just before their departure they climbed the city wall. From the top Chiang Ch'ing caught one last glimpse of Yenan, far to the west, and felt a sudden pang of nostalgia: in that temporary capital she had passed almost a third of her life. Destiny now carried them in another direction.

By the time she and Li Na rejoined their detachment, the Chairman's attention was wholly involved in gaining the upper hand over the military situation. All his time went to policy and proclamations. During the twelve days or so at Shen-ch'uan-pao, he wrote the "Manifesto of the Chinese People's Liberation Army" (dated October 10, 1947), sometimes called the "Double Ten Manifesto" in reference to the date of issuance.[18] He also wrote "On the Reissue of the Three Main Rules of Discipline and the Eight Points for Attention — Instruction of the General Headquarters of the Chinese People's Liberation Army" (October 10, 1947), a reassertion of the Red Army's fundamental ethos.[19] Both documents shaped the character of subsequent political work. The "Double Ten Manifesto" was a call to all people to defeat Chiang Kai-shek and unite the country. She recommended reading those essays in the fourth volume of the Chairman's *Selected Works*. Her own detachment, one among three under the Central Committee, used that occasion to open a campaign to "recall past suffering" (an authorized comparison of the bad past with the good present and better future) and perform the so-called "three checkups" (a routine check on the implementation of the Three Rules of Discipline and the Eight Points for Attention first spelled out by Mao to the Red Army at Ching-kang-shan in 1928).* As political instructor in her detachment her responsibility was to manage the program to recall past suffering. When she recalled her past suffering as a model for others, her inner turmoil stirred by recent events must have come across. All who listened were moved to tears, she said.

Breaking camp on November 11, they reached Wu-lung-p'u within ten days. The masses welcomed them tearfully. They did not stay long, though. On the twenty-second they reached Yang-chia-kou, where they remained far longer than expected — four months — and continued to design the strategy for winning the masses to their side and ending the war. From the twenty-fifth to the

---

* The three Rules of Discipline: (1) Obey orders in all actions; (2) Don't take a single needle or piece of thread from the masses; (3) Turn in everything captured. The Eight Points for Attention: (1) Speak politely; (2) Pay fairly for what you buy; (3) Return everything you borrow; (4) Pay for anything you damage; (5) Don't hit or swear at people; (6) Don't damage crops; (7) Don't take liberties with women; (8) Don't mistreat captives. See SW, 4:155–156.

twenty-eighth of December, the Central Committee held an enlarged meeting of particular moment because the Chairman read aloud "The Present Situation and Our Tasks" (December 25, 1947),[20] an essay she remembered extremely well because he dictated it to her and she took down his words one by one. But the words were all *his*, she hastened to add. *

The purpose of the essay, she said, was to promote throughout the country the idea of a new democracy. Response was swift. Beginning on the twenty-eighth of December all four field armies in the liberated areas launched a new type of army consolidation campaign comparable to the Rectification Movement begun in Yenan in 1942.[21] The new campaign, which began with the "recall of past suffering" and the "three checkups," was preliminary to land reform, which followed immediately. During their four-month stay at Yang-chia-kou the Chairman composed several other articles which also appear in the fourth volume of his *Selected Works*.

Of the maps on the table, Chiang Ch'ing now referred to a situation map covering all of North China showing how the war was fought and the stages by which the enemy forces were eliminated as of July 1947. With a shift of strategy in the spring of 1948, the Communists exercised still more initiative. The Party and army jointly renewed their consolidation campaign begun in December. Counteroffensives (led by Liu Po-ch'eng, Ch'en I, Lin Piao, and other great generals she did not mention) were carried out on several fronts, but their main forces were deployed against the areas still in the military grip of Chiang Kai-shek. In the North the Border Regions liberated by the Communists (during the war against Japan) were combined into new administrative units called Chin-Ch'a-Chi (combining portions of Shansi, Chahar, and Hopeh provinces) and Chin-Chi-Lu-Yü (combining portions of Shansi, Hopeh, Shantung, and Honan provinces). Those political realignments constituted the first step toward the establishment of a people's government of North China.

The momentum of the march of 1948 and of Chiang Ch'ing's present recapitulation picked up with the feeling that the end was near. On March 21 they left Yang-chia-kou for Hsu-pai-kou. Later the same day they arrived at Chicheng-tien. On March 23 they passed through Ch'uan-kou, crossed the Yellow River, and arrived at Chai-tse-shan in Shansi province. Within three days they marched through Shuang-t'a and reached Ts'ai-chia-yai. By April 4 they arrived at the county of K'o-lan where they took possession of some jeeps left by

---

* In 1964 Mao reflected with exceptional impersonality upon that secretarial assistance he once used: " 'The Present Situation and Our Tasks' was dictated by me in 1947. Someone transcribed it and it was revised by me. At that time I had contracted a disease whereby I could not write. Now when I want something written, it is all done by a secretary, not by my hand. . . . But if you never take the initiative and rely on a secretary, it is just like having a secretary assume your responsibility for leadership work" ("Talk at the Hantan Forum on the Four Cleanups Work" [Mar. 28, 1964], in *Miscellany of Mao Tse-tung Thought, 1949–1968*, 2:338).

the enemy. Freshly equipped, they continued to Shen-ch'ih, passed northeast over the Great Wall and then back over it again, reaching Tai-hsien on the sixth and Fan-chih soon after.

In the late spring of 1948 the snow-covered Wu T'ai mountains soared spectacularly eastward before their eyes. Not far to the north lay Inner Mongolia. The air was chill and damp as they mobilized for the ascent on April 11. Laboriously, they made their way, hand in hand, along narrow trails. The fresh-fallen snow was so deep that they had to lift their feet and tilt their bodies back slightly with each step. (Here she demonstrated what the marching was like.) As they gained altitude, the atmospheric pressure dropped. Some of their comrades, herself included, felt light-headed and dizzy. Even the Chairman felt queasy. The point at which they finally crossed the Wu T'ai range was nearly ten thousand feet above sea level. The Chairman and she were delivered by jeep to the summit of the nearest peak. There they got out, regained their equilibrium, and surveyed the breathtaking panorama they commanded momentarily. That same day they reached the Wu T'ai temple, a huge structure roofed in glazed tile — far more magnificent than the temples of Peking she would come to know. She added, with an edge to her voice, that however spectacular the temple was, its head lama was actually a powerful landlord with some such name as Yang Ling-chieh.

Lulled by a recent calm in the fighting, on April 13 they arrived at Ch'eng-nan-chuang in Hopeh province. Suddenly clusters of bombs showered down upon them. Hidden in their ranks, they later discovered, was a traitor who was secretly directing the bombing attack by radio. They continued the march for five disastrous days under air assault. On the fifth day they reached the mountain called Hua Shan in the Tsinling range,* bombs still descending wildly upon them and exploding everywhere, even in areas without people or troop movement. Once the attack subsided, they settled at the foot of the mountain. The Chairman withdrew from the others to write two more articles. [22]

By now the snows banked high against the crags of Hua Shan had begun to thaw, sending down spectacular waterfalls, Chiang Ch'ing recalled. Yet the mountains appeared so steep that they could not imagine how any could be scaled and finally crossed. While the troops aligned themselves single file for the ascent, the Chairman drafted his "Telegram to the Headquarters of the Loyang Front after the Recapture of the City" (April 8, 1948). [23] In this critical document he laid down nine rules of procedure for the liberation of the nation's cities that began to fall into their hands that spring.

On the eighteenth of April, Chou En-lai, who had been away on another mission, arrived at Hsi-pai-p'o, a small community a few miles northwest of the

---

* Centuries earlier viewed by Taoists as the Western Sacred Mountain, one of the Five Sacred Mountains of China.

city of Shih-chia-chuang in Hopeh province. The Chairman did not join him there until the twenty-seventh of May, whereupon they settled into Hsi-pai-p'o for what turned out to be ten months. Then the Chairman moved on to their final destination, the ancient capital of Peking, less than two hundred miles to the northeast. At Hsi-pai-p'o the Chairman continued to write prolifically (on land reform, Party discipline, military strategy, and the KMT).

Even so, he was as active in conducting the war as before. From the Hsi-pai-p'o headquarters he devised the tactics and strategy for three major campaigns at once: the Liao-Shen (Liaohsi-Shenyang); the Huai-Hai (East China and Central Plains); and the P'ing-Chin (Peking-Tientsin). Once again, she insisted that the Chairman commanded the enemy forces as well as their own. Referring to a small packet of notes, she summed up statistics on these campaigns. The Liao-Shen eliminated thirty-three of the enemy's divisions and 472,000 troops; the Huai-Hai eliminated twenty-two army corps and 550,000 troops; and the P'ing-Chin captured the enemy's 39th Army Corps and 520,000 troops.[24] After the last campaign was over (in January 1949), the KMT commanding general, Fu Tso-i, came over to the Communist side.[25]

In 1948, the Central Plains Field Army (Second Field Army), commanded by Liu Po-ch'eng, with Teng Hsiao-p'ing serving as political commissar, employed the strategy of breaking through the enemy's line at midpoint. By the time their forces passed through the Ta Pieh Mountains en route to Wuhan and reached the east side of Nanking, the enemy troops were nearly devastated: "The KMT could hardly parry us at all." At the end of 1948 the enemy was *begging* them to sit down at a peace table. Consequently, a meeting was called for January 21, 1949, but the KMT reactionaries refused to sign the peace agreement offered to them there.[26] In view of the impossibility of the KMT situation — the Communists held all their home places — Chiang Kai-shek tacitly admitted helplessness by withdrawing nominally from the presidency in January 1949 and handing that post over to Li Tsung-jen. Still, the only real authority was held in the jealous palm of Chiang Kai-shek.

Although the leaders realized that the enemy was rapidly losing ground during the final stages of the war, for the sake of the people they continued to promote the slogan "Overthrow Chiang Kai-shek!" To arouse the masses along the line of march they drummed into them incessantly the message that the enemy was *still* formidable; that they must continue to fight on the side of the Red Army until total victory was in their hands.

On March 25, 1949, the Chairman left Hsi-pai-p'o and headed for Peking. Upon arrival at their de facto capital, not official until September 27, 1949, he reviewed the troops that had brought them to their present victory. When he presided over the Second Plenary Session of the Party's Seventh Central Committee in March 1949, he laid out plans for shifting Party work from the villages to the cities, and for the political, economic, and foreign policies to be implemented after the entire country was liberated. These policies were to govern the transition from the stage of the "new democratic" revolution to socialism and China's transformation from an agricultural to an industrial nation.

As for Chiang Ch'ing, she retained her post as political instructor, which also involved heading a debate group (a mobile propaganda unit) up to the time they made their final headquarters at Hsi-pai-p'o. During the organization of the new government in Peking, she was relieved of her duties and promoted to the Party Secretariat. Nodding at Chang Ch'ing-hua across the map table, she said that Hsi-pai-p'o was the point where she parted ways with him.

When the Party first offered a peace agreement to the "KMT reactionaries," they refused to sign, Chiang Ch'ing reiterated. But they had no real alternative because they had no territory to which to return: their former homes were situated in areas now held by the Communist forces. In the last spring of the war 158 KMT divisions (1.54 million regular forces) had been wiped out. Only when the situation seemed to have reached a stalemate, the point at which the enemy had 2.9 million troops and they had 3 million, would Chiang Kai-shek condescend to request the peace negotiations.

During the peace talks in the spring of 1949 the KMT side was represented by Chang Chih-chung.[27] After the talks broke down he too abandoned the KMT and joined their side. That was not so surprising, perhaps, because years earlier, when the Communist Party was still in Yenan, Chang Chih-chung (chief of Chiang Kai-shek's Northwest headquarters as of 1946) once paid them a visit and was obviously fascinated by the transformed structure of their lives. When the Chairman was preparing to make an inspection tour of the Shen-Kan-Ning Border Region, Chang expressed a wish to accompany him. That struck them as odd, but later they appreciated that as early as the middle 1940's Chang "had come to regard their political capital in some sense as his own." (She added that he was no longer alive.)

The peace negotiations continued to April 20, when the Nanking government rejected the proposed agreement. With no recourse but retaliation, on April 21 the Chairman called for "independence and territorial integrity," and ordered the Red Army to march on the Northwest and the South to mop up. Vast numbers of Communist troops then crossed the Yangtse River and marched south. On the twenty-third they liberated Nanking, and a month later, Shanghai. They then proceeded to all other fronts, "sweeping up" the enemy forces wherever they met them.

As for the final reckoning, Chiang Ch'ing reported briskly, the Red Army wiped out 1.9 million regular KMT forces and 980,000 bandits; 1.2 million of the enemy troops came over to their side. Then the whole country was liberated except for Taiwan. On October 1, 1949, Mao Tse-tung was elected Chairman of the People's Republic of China.

Where was Chiang Ch'ing during that monumental celebration? Not at the side of the Chairman. Later she would explain why.

The hour had passed three in the morning. Although Chiang Ch'ing had held forth from early evening almost without interruption, she showed no signs of weariness. The record of the Liberation War she rounded out now on a personal note, which betrayed more acutely than she may have intended the vulnerability of her position among the masculine leaders of those years.

In the final stages of the war, she recalled, the Chairman had sent a crucial telegram to the secretary in charge of the most confidential documents.[28] Even though she was the Chairman's wife (and working for the Party Secretariat), the telegram was not given to her to read, a glaring oversight. Later she reported this to Li T'ao, a veteran of the Long March. Aroused by her disgrace, he went to the leading comrades responsible for the action and told them, "You must respect women comrades!"

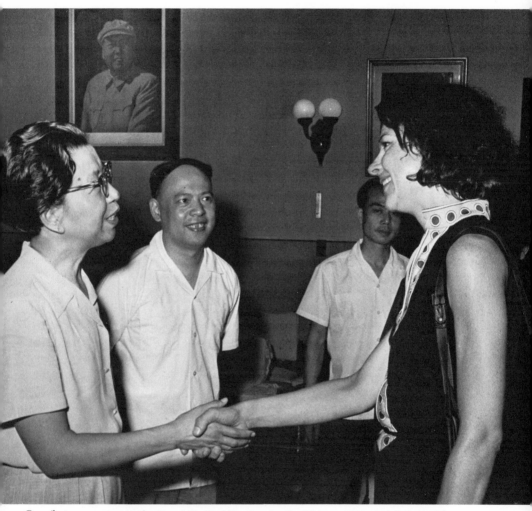

Our first encounter at the Great Hall of the People. To Chiang Ch'ing's left is her ideo-logical and literary defender Yao Wen-yuan.

Chiang Ch'ing, her foreign guest, and Yao Wen-yuan spaced by Shen Jo-yun and Hsu Erh-wei, Chiang Ch'ing's emissaries, interpreters, and our mutual go-betweens.

Chiang Ch'ing holds forth on home gardening (she had cut her thumb) over appetizers at a Peking roast duck dinner in a private dining room at the Great Hall.

This picture and a brief article appeared in the People's Daily *on August 13, 1972. From left to right: Hsu Erh-wei and Shen Jo-yun; Chang Ying, Chiang Ch'ing's chief confidante; Yao Wen-yuan; the foreign guest; Chiang Ch'ing; Ting Hsueh-sung, secretary-general of the Friendship Association, which hosted the journey; my guides Ch'en Minghsien and Yü Shih-lien.*

Chiang Ch'ing posing for the author on a veranda in the orchid park. Responding months after our interviews, Chiang Ch'ing said this picture was her favorite of the many I took.

Chang Ying in her new black skirt (above, left). Assistant and go-between Shen Jo-yun (above, right) and guide Yü Shih-lien (below).

The mirthful raconteur.

"Photograph me at work," Chiang Ch'ing told me as she pressed rare orchid blossom
onto framed paper.

Chiang Ch'ing preparing to shoot the ladies of her entourage against a lotus pond.

Directing her subjects through the lens.

One of several of Chiang Ch'ing's flower studies she gave me, this one shows peonies with water drops sprinkled by her hand.

Chiang Ch'ing as Nora in Ibsen's A Doll's House.

藍
蘋

□ 藍蘋

迢地流注到信眼歡的心圈裏。她說，觀眾都儍心，

此我們想到她遲早會給我們來親人的印象，四

邀請她沒有留下女子們那種嬌弱的憐舊，但却有最美產這樓

上速，她也是有希望的一位，在新人叢中，她有

藍蘋小姐第一次給我們

起識的是舞台上的緹拉，她

那種淒婉的姿態從字際走

來，觀眾的情感從定

由神演出後，我們就肯定了

Chiang Ch'ing just married in her twenty-fifth year. On the reverse of the picture, she dedicates it to me, noting that Roman Karmen (Stalin's photographer in Yenan) took it in color in 1939.

Mao Tse-tung expounding befo
cave around the time of the Y
Forum, 1942.

Père Mao with his two small da
ters, Li Min and Li Na, chatting
a peasant, in 1944.

At Yenan, in March 1945.

Chiang Ch'ing and Mao after nine years of marriage and ten years of life in hilly, sun-drenched Yenan. These pictures were taken in early 1947, before the sudden evacuation under Chiang Kai-shek's bombs of March.

A sense of destiny shows in their faces as exile from Yenan draws near. Their cave dwelling with arched, latticed, and papered windows is in the background.

Mao on his white pony leads the Yenan exodus and the two-year march to Liberation. Behind him, the second rider is boyish-looking Chiang Ch'ing.

30—2 伟大领袖毛主席教导我们说：“我们共产党人好比种子，人民好比土地。我们到了一个地方，就要同那里的人民结合起来，在人民中间生根、开花。”在伟大的抗日战争年代里，毛主席总是和人民群众在一起，和群众同呼吸共命运，和人民群众心连心。毛主席的光辉思想和伟大革命实践，永远鼓舞着我们，教育着我们。（毛主席和贫苦农民在一起） 小13

1 the summer of 1947 Mao, with Chiang Ch'ing seated on his right, shares supper with local peasnts at Hsiao-ho, a station on the march. The Chinese inscription for this photograph reads: "Our reat leader Chairman Mao has taught us: 'We Communists are like seeds, while the people are ke soil. As soon as we arrive at a place we must unite the people, put down roots with the people, nd with them bloom flowers.' During the period of the great war of resistance against Japan, Chairman Mao was always one with the people, sharing a common fate with the masses. Chairan Mao's brilliant thought and great revolutionary line will excite and educate us forever."

In the spring of 1949, Chiang Ch'ing and Mao pore over papers in a cave at one of the last stations of the march, just before she left for Moscow.

PART THREE

◇ ◇ ◇

BEHIND
THE SCENES

9.

◇ ◇ ◇

The Fifties Incognito

> It is not just what we inherit from our fathers and mothers that lives on in us, but all kinds of old dead doctrines and opinions and beliefs. . . . I only pick up the newspaper. It's as if I could see the ghosts slipping between the lines. They must be haunting the whole country.
>
> — Ibsen, *Ghosts*

In conventional accounts by Chinese revolutionaries, 1949, the year of Liberation and of the founding of the People's Republic, is the magical turning point from the bitter past to a sweet future. But October First, a day of official national jubilation, was no red letter day in Chiang Ch'ing's review of her past; in fact, she made no reference to it. Yet we may speculate on how she might have felt.

To be sure, she had moved from the countryside to the capital, from borrowed caves to an appropriated Imperial City, which for seven centuries had housed the emperors of China and their thousands of servants. Yet what unwanted forces of the past and burdens of imperial history were embedded in those monuments? As she moved about the interlocking mazes of palatial compounds — ochre and turquoise, and violet in the Purple Forbidden City — would her simple relation to Mao and their rough-hewn comrades ineluctably be changed? Would she, like imperial consorts and concubines of old, be confined to women's quarters vaguely updated? Or would she, like the irrepressible

Tz'u-hsi, a consort self-propelled to empress dowager, maneuver for years behind the throne and one day sit squarely upon it?

The following chapters show how Chiang Ch'ing's control of some affairs of the Chairman and her moves toward a personal career came about slowly; in the beginning few would notice. In her recollection the decade of the 1950's was a time of political and physical trial, of alternating bouts of disease and recovery, of withdrawal from public affairs and return to them, but of continual work always behind the scenes. Throughout the 1950's she had almost no notice in the press. Her memory of those years displayed a streak of hypochondria — emblematic of China's perennial leisure class, which could afford to cultivate high consciousness of personal pathology.

When well, she strove to gain a foothold in the Party apparatus, but to stand securely at the center she had first to prove herself among the masses and the leaders in the outside world. Toward that goal she took leave of the palace and journeyed to the countryside, where she led the controversial Wu Hsun investigation and participated — against the will of the leaders, her husband sometimes included — in the two great revolutionary movements of the early 1950's: land reform and marriage reform. As it turned out, however, suspicious and jealous comrades obliged her, when away from the capital, to work incognito. The enforced anonymity would bar her from building up a reputation and a personal following among the people.

i

When the Chairman, Chiang Ch'ing, and some leading comrades and their troops descended upon Peking in March 1949 and took possession of its center point, the Imperial City, they appropriated for their own use the western section bounded by the central and southern lakes called Chung-nan-hai (literally, Central and Southern Sea). Each leader, and his wife and children — those who survived the war — were assigned an apartment within this former imperial establishment. Although long stretches of the Imperial City walls had been removed to ease traffic along the great avenues, the leaders' residences were still beyond public view, as were their private lives. Chiang Ch'ing's and Mao's apartments, marked off by intricately carved and colorful pillars in the Ming style, were separate but connected.

Since the founding of the Republic in 1912, the former imperial precinct, which enclosed connected palaces and was called the Purple Forbidden City, had been open to the public. After the fall of the Manchus, it was called the Old Palace. The Communists refurbished its soaring gates, cloud-patterned marble staircases, grandiose compounds, and hundreds of richly adorned chambers as a museum to the imperial past. Except for Chung-nan-hai, it is open daily to the people, to whom, one is told, it belongs.

At midcentury ensconced in quarters unthinkably remote from the peasant hovels borrowed along the march, the leaders faced the perennial challenge to any dynastic founders: how could they keep the people's trust after ceasing to live crudely as the people did? Had not the Communist leaders' most promising predecessors, the Taipings, lost their common touch, and thus their hold over the people, after they allowed themselves to sink into the palatial grandeur of the southern capital, Nanking?

During March of 1949, Chiang Ch'ing recalled, she was so worn out physically by the two years on the march that she wondered how she had managed to hold on during its final stages. As assessments were taken and assignments made, some leading comrades — not instigated by the Chairman, it seemed — resolved that in view of her fragile condition she should be sent to Moscow for a "medical cure." Why, I asked, if she was so desperately ill, should she travel thousands of miles to a foreign capital? Years of strife had destroyed most Chinese hospitals, she replied. In the early 1950's medical facilities everywhere were in terrible disarray. Stalin was consulted and was amenable to the arrangement. Thus, a few days after arriving in Peking she and some nurses and bodyguards were bundled onto a train that crossed northernmost China and plunged into the Soviet Union, the only foreign country she would know. At the Moscow station she was met by an ambulance. The hospital assigned her to a bed for which *the Chinese paid* (her emphasis). A team of Soviet doctors and medical professors submitted her to a complete physical examination, which showed that several ailments were at the root of her persistent fever, enervation, and emaciation. She described herself as "all skin and bones, reduced to forty-two kilos [about ninety-two pounds]." From her sickbed she overheard the doctors and professors, so acutely conscious of status, debate among themselves — at that time she barely understood Russian — which ailment they should treat first.

Her chief doctor, a man she came to know better than the rest, was a professor named Bolshoi. One cause of the fever was tonsillitis; in her case the infection had begun on the right tonsil, then spread to the left. When the doctors announced that they would perform a tonsillectomy first, she rose from her bed and walked unassisted to the operating room. She looked like a "heroic general," the nurses told her (she obviously delighted in repeating their kudos to me). The operation, which lasted only half an hour, was difficult. First they removed the right tonsil, then the left more quickly.

After that ordeal her doctors wanted her to put on some weight. So they arranged for her to travel more than a thousand miles south to Yalta, the resort city on the Black Sea. In that balmy climate she passed one month convalescing in extravagant structures designed for the tsars (and still sought out by pained and pleasure-seeking Soviet bureaucrats). On the return journey to Moscow in late April she was accompanied in her compartment by two Soviet bodyguards and some Russian cooks. Confined to her berth and reduced to amusing herself with the radio, she learned that during the final stages of the Liberation War the *Amethyst*, a British warship, had been struck by Chinese Communist forces. The news thrilled her. And when she learned that the Chairman had declared on that occasion, "The Chinese people have stood up!" she burst into tears.* Her emotional state caused a commotion among the bodyguards and cooks, who scarcely knew what to make of it. The *Amethyst* was a British warship and *the Chinese dared to fire on it!* she impressed upon them.

Upon her return from Yalta, Stalin extended an invitation to her. But their first encounter turned out to be something of an embarrassment. When she and her companions arrived at the Kremlin, Stalin's aides were evidently confused: they had assumed that Chairman Mao was with her and that he was prepared to negotiate. Not until she returned to Peking in the fall of 1949 did the Chairman make his own first journey to the Soviet Union (he arrived in Moscow on December 16 and returned to Peking by March 4, 1950). In that connection she noted that in October 1949 she was made a charter member of the Sino-Soviet Friendship Association (of which Liu Shao-ch'i was chairman).

When the Party leaders arrived in Peking in the spring of 1949, she said, China was half liberated and land reform had begun. For a while they returned to the "rightist line" represented by Liu Shao-ch'i, and began to rely on the support of rich peasants (instead of dispossessing them along with the landlords).[1] That fall, as a result of her stay in the Soviet Union, she felt stronger than in the spring. Their elaborate apartments, staffed more amply than any she had known, she found confining. So she decided to tour the countryside in order to make a firsthand study of land-holding systems at a time when land reform was widely under way. When she first presented her decision to the Chairman, he opposed it. They argued. She went anyway.

As she was making preparations to leave in the fall of 1949, some other women felt compelled to go too, as members of a vanguard from the capital. That is to say, the *wives* of some of the other leaders (a rare instance where she referred to herself as a leader's wife) *followed her* to the countryside.[2] For her

---

* When the PLA was fighting its way across the Yangtze on April 20–21, 1949, the *Amethyst* and three other British warships, along with some KMT warships, fired on the PLA forces, causing 252 Chinese casualties. The PLA returned fire, disabling the *Amethyst*. Mao responded with a communiqué titled "On the Outrages by British Warships — Statement by the Spokesman of the General Headquarters of the Chinese People's Liberation Army" (Apr. 30, 1949, SW, 4: 401–403). Mao's oft-quoted statement about the incident, "The Chinese people have stood up," does not appear in the revised text, which is in SW.

the opportunity to participate in the fundamental class struggle was wonderful. She was not a novice, though. For during the recent Northwest Campaign (since early 1948) she had helped in guiding the overthrow of landlords and land redistribution in accord with the Chairman's draft agrarian laws.

Expecting to join the land reform movement in East China, she took the train to Shanghai, the city she had known most intimately but had not visited for more than twelve years. She was enormously excited at the prospect of seeing it again, though she knew how profoundly its governance and cultural life had been transformed. When her train pulled into the station she found Kao Kang and Jao Shu-shih, the men who controlled the Party's Northeast Bureau and the East China Bureau respectively and thus dominated all the eastern region. Obviously they had been informed of her plans. No sooner had she set foot on the station platform than they made moves to control all her comings and goings in what they considered to be "their territory."

Although she, Mao, and others on their side did not know it then, a few years later they discovered that both Kao Kang and Jao Shu-shih were already "renegades" who had turned against the CCP and joined the enemy.[3] Between them they employed more than three thousand secret agents who infiltrated the eastern cities and countryside, a vast region, still in the early 1950's largely under their *personal* control. Most of her dealings were with Jao Shu-shih. As soon as she got to Shanghai she told him that she wanted to go directly down to rural villages to begin investigations relating to land reform. He tried to dissuade her on the grounds that so many secret agents (as if they were not largely his own) were floating around that her personal safety could not be guaranteed. Such solicitude was pretense, for he was merely trying to cover up his own nefarious activities.

He had her watched incessantly. One day she decided to shop in downtown Shanghai. Before she could get away, Jao Shu-shih insisted upon accompanying her personally to a department store, regardless of her wish to go alone. Thereafter, in East China she was always accompanied by either a director of the Department of Public Security or by Secretary Jao Shu-shih himself. Wherever they went they were surrounded by gun-toting secret agents who made her feel always as if she were on the verge of being kidnapped, a frightening sensation she remembered all too well from her early Shanghai days. Jao Shu-shih and "his company's" peremptory treatment made her realize that conditions in East China had changed only superficially since Liberation.

Jao Shu-shih had made arrangements for her to stay at a hotel called the Victory Mansion. To keep tabs on her he decided to live there too, for the duration of her visit. At first she was given a room with a southern exposure and heat from the central heating system. That winter (of 1950), she remarked, room temperature was of vital concern to her because she was still thin and frail. But Jao Shu-shih must have realized that the location of her room would enable her to make contact with influential comrades at a time when he wanted to keep her cordoned off from other sources of power. Moreover, if she were uncomfortable enough she might leave. He behaved "like a hypocrite," she said. He switched room assignments so that he occupied the best rooms facing south, and she was transferred to a room in a wing of the hotel, with a northern exposure and no central heat. It was freezing cold and sunless. To try to keep warm, she piled on all her clothes and swaddled herself in all the bedding she could find. "See a doctor!" Jao remarked after she finally impressed him with her pain and fever. That was not the solution she wanted, so she held out and drank lots of water to reduce the fever. In the end he capitulated and allowed her to have a heated room.

Since she was not getting anywhere with the East China Bureau, she turned to Ch'en I, the mayor of Shanghai (he had liberated both Shanghai and her home province of Shantung) and told him about her frustrations. He encouraged her to shift tactics and get out and meet people in cultural circles where she had obvious personal and professional affinities. Being too busy to accompany her himself, Ch'en I appointed Vice-Mayor P'an Han-nien as her escort to theaters, films, and other cultural events that abounded in those days. As a companion P'an Han-nien was of dubious value. Not only was he rumored to have been a Wang Ming loyalist in the 1930's, but, like Jao Shu-shih, he was eventually discovered to be a "renegade," she reported irritably. (He was read out of the Party and imprisoned in 1955).

Since Jao Shu-shih was in charge of the East China region, he had to show himself responsible for her, but he was at a loss as to how to keep her innocuously entertained. One day he invited her to attend an enlarged meeting of the East China Party Committee, which he headed, and briefed her in advance. Either to make a woman feel at ease in such a situation (that highly important committee was then all male), or to deflate her, he mentioned that his wife would also attend.[4] At the meeting he arranged to sit directly across from Chiang Ch'ing. During introductions he addressed her mockingly as the "imperial envoy," which infuriated her, but she could say nothing.* His purpose, and that of his cohorts, she surmised, was to humiliate her to the point of driving her away.

Soon she left Shanghai and journeyed some seventy miles west to Wusih, a major industrial city on the Grand Canal in Kiangsu province. There she attended a meeting of the county Party committee, at which she first came up

---

* In Mao Tse-tung's terminology, an "imperial envoy" was one who rushed about, spouting theory about matters with which he had no first-hand experience. Mao's point was that theory and practice should be combined (SW, 3: 13).

against a political trait East China was then famous for: the "internal ranting right wing" (an idiosyncratic term, though apparently meaning infighting among "rightists").

At Wusih she began her work by investigating the historical background of the region as a whole. She learned that the government of the Taipings (whose rebellion raged over South and Central China from 1850 to 1864) decreed that peasants could lease land in perpetuity. By their land allotment system each person was granted somewhat less than one *mou* of land.[5] Such a tiny plot had to be plowed meticulously. Lots of manure (mainly human — "night soil") was required; dog manure could not be overlooked. Because farming on that small scale did not yield enough to live on, the peasants were forced to develop various sideline occupations just to survive. Since tea and silk production had long existed in the Wusih area, most of the peasants grew tea trees or mulberry trees on part of their land and then sold the tea leaves and the silk.

From Wusih she traveled to the surrounding rural areas to survey the tea and silk industries. Both had suffered disastrously from the depredation of the Japanese. In the early 1950's the industries were still disrupted and the peasants were famished. The need for food was so great that a peasant would not accept less than two hundred kilos of rice for fifty kilos of silk cocoons. During their occupation of Kiangsu province (1937–1945) the Japanese had constructed a communications system that entailed chopping down vast numbers of the native mulberry trees, fundamental to the silk industry. Even at present, she said, the Wusih area, and with it China's silk industry as a whole, had not recovered completely from the damage.

The tea industry, on the other hand, had recovered almost entirely. She went on to say that mulberry trees are at their prime after about five years, but tea trees do not reach maturity before ten or twenty years, and sometimes longer. Thus their cultivation is enormously costly of labor.

From Wusih she returned to Shanghai briefly, then went home to Peking. There, the fact that Liu Shao-ch'i was driving for the "rich peasant line" in land reform was impressed emphatically upon her. Already the Chairman was waging struggles against him, though the resolution of their dispute was slow to have an effect on the countryside.[6]

She continued, with considerable annoyance, that her role in land reform had never been presented correctly to the public. For years all sorts of devices were used to distort her public image and those of other leaders. When she was participating in land reform in the Wusih area, she did so incognito. But since photographs of her were taken surreptitiously, perhaps some suspected who she really was. Certainly, it was incorrect for others to have snapped her without authorization. Nevertheless, those photographs, which were unearthed in subsequent investigations,* could serve as material proof of her participation in that stage of agrarian revolution. To illustrate, she slipped out of coarse brown wrapping two such, both yellowed and fragile with age. One showed her threshing and the other, plowing. Although she would not allow either to be published in China, I could publish the second abroad to prove that, contrary to what men like to think, women *can* wield a plow.† There had been other photographs taken unofficially and hence incorrectly at later times, including the Cultural Revolution. No, they were not to be released now.

Then she spoke in her official voice on the changes in the role of women:

"Chinese women played a great part in all the successive revolutionary struggles in China. Not only in the May Fourth Movement [1919] and the December Ninth Movement [1935] as you have noticed, but during the entire period of the War of Resistance against Japanese Aggression [1931–1945] and the War of Liberation [1946–1949] women were of enormous importance as fighters in the militia and as supporters of the front armies. In some villages women carried out most of the work.

"Changes have been tremendous. When I went to another rural district to do a second stint of land reform in 1952, the men were gambling and idling away their time in teahouses and letting the women do all the work. They cursed and beat any woman who came to call them home. But still women were not allowed to plow. So I went and plowed on my own. The area used to be a 'model county' of the Kuomintang. Now women can plow and take part in all sorts of work.

"Don't just look at the progress of today. Although women occupy highly important positions in industry, agriculture, education, and other departments, and there are even women in such critical industries as defense, still there are backward aspects that you should examine."

ii

Turning to the international front, one peripheral to her active interests, Chiang Ch'ing delivered a barrage of accusations about the first episode of "foreign aggression" against their new state — the United States' "invasion" of Korea, a nation on the rim of China's land mass. Comments on her version of events and on the statistics she cited are given in the notes.

On October 1, 1950, she reported, the United States crossed the 38th paral-

* Possibly made by her enemies about her hidden past, or perhaps *her* investigations of those who had snapped her.
† See the second picture section.

lel and pressed toward the Yalu and T'u-men rivers, both within China's borders, and from there launched further attacks. To mobilize the whole nation to the defense, Chairman Mao issued the slogan "Resist U.S. Aggression and Aid Korea." He also wrote "Defend the Country and Our Families," an essay whose title became another popular slogan. On October 19 (officially October 25), the Chinese People's Volunteers crossed the Yalu River to fight on the side of the North Koreans. By June 10, 1951, the Chinese had driven the "United States puppet troops" back to the 38th parallel. And by July 27, 1953, the U.S. imperialists were finally forced to sign an armistice.

The war lasted three years and one month. After the armistice, the Chinese Volunteers, who had fought the U.S. aggressors for two years and nine months in all, stayed on in Korea. According to her figures the enemy had 1.1 million troops, of which 540,000 came from the United States, 520,000 were "Korean puppets" supporting Rhee, and 48,000 were "puppets" coming from other countries.[7] As a result of Chinese aid to North Korea, the enemy was reduced in numbers in four of the five major campaigns. In the fourth campaign, P'eng Te-huai violated orders received from Chairman Mao.[8]

After the war was over and settlements were made, the United States refused to repatriate prisoners of war taken in Korea. They simply shipped them off to Taiwan.[9] The Chinese, on the other hand, made a point of returning American POWs to their own people.

Taiwan's situation has long been troubled. Years before war broke out in Korea the United States declared that Taiwan was Chinese territory. Then see what they did! "Anyway, we'll liberate Taiwan," she said matter-of-factly. She went on to read off some battle scores she had jotted down. On the Chinese side were "brilliant victories" in the Korean War. Of the 1,093,800 casualties, 400,000 were suffered by American troops, and 397,000 by others on the enemy side.[10] The Chinese captured 10,000 aircraft, 560 gunboats, and more than 3,000 tanks.[11] Those figures, she said, illustrate the difference between just and unjust wars. There was justice on the Chinese and North Korean sides. The Chinese Volunteers went to Korea with Chairman Mao's instructions: "Cherish each mountain, tree and blade of grass in Korea." And so they did.

"General Eisenhower was actually quite great," she said more than once, in speaking of the Korean War period. When he ran for President he promised to put an end to the Korean War, and as President he acted on that. His flight to their territory (China and its peripheral nations) they respected. His intent was sincere, though only an armistice was reached.

At the end of the war the Chinese donated all the material used in Korea's defense to the Koreans at no charge and sent numerous Chinese to assist them in national reconstruction. Why so? Because Korea is *attached* to China; naturally the Chinese were grateful for the Koreans' willingness to defend themselves, and thus aided them generously.

Among the Chinese masses, consciousness of the threat of war was deliberately aroused through the press and through films and other performing arts. Even one of the revolutionary operas, *Raid on White Tiger Regiment*, was set in the Korean War period, she pointed out, and it was under revision now.* I should see that upon a return to China.

For another view of the Korean war from China's perspective she arranged for me to see the film documentary *Guerrillas on the Plain* the next morning. It has some shortcomings, she warned, yet is is not boring.†

The death of the Chairman's eldest son, Mao An-ying, in Korea in October 1950 was deeply unsettling to their personal lives. The next January she and the Chairman managed to get away from Peking and move to an easier climate, one in which they could rest, write, and see films. Some of the films, she found, she had to censor (and she moved into her first stage of leading a cultural revolution).

iii

A pawn of film impresarios in the 1930's, soon after Liberation Chiang Ch'ing made a cinematic comeback as the chief censor, whose potential power over the national cinema was unprecedented. In the early 1950's the Chinese film industry and its archives and international connections were still largely in the hands of independent film companies. Despite the national establishment of Chinese Marxism and Mao Tse-tung's avowed commitment (at the Yenan Forum of 1942) to the exclusive promotion of the proletarian arts, filmmakers were still turning out a wide variety of feature films, updating types produced during the war-torn but innovative 1920's and 1930's. The cinema remained one of the most popular urban entertainments until certain Communist leaders took up the challenge of making filmed propaganda "build socialism."

The bid for cinematic loyalty to the Party had begun in the cultural un-

---

* To tone down its extreme anti-Americanism, some aides told me. They were referring to its absolutistic "bad guy" characterization of American G.I.'s, which Chiang Ch'ing apparently saw as tasteless in a period of Sino-American rapprochement.

† The film turned out to be an idealized and stylized view of the Chinese Volunteers in action, not footage of actual persons and events. As is typical of Chinese documentaries, the film did not aspire to re-create historical realities "as they were." The Chinese Volunteers were all "good guys" costumed in uniforms which, even in the thick of acted out but bloodless battles, looked as if they had never been used. Heroes loomed large in the style of Sergei Eisenstein, one of several Russian film artists emulated by avant-garde Chinese cinematographers since the 1930's. Chiang Ch'ing had her own sense of its "shortcomings"; from a Western standpoint its wooden acting and self-serving politics made it hard to believe or enjoy.

derground of Shanghai in the early 1930's. When Japan devastated that city in the summer of 1937, a few bold filmmakers, rudimentary equipment in hand, trekked to Yenan, where they made documentaries (artful and favorable in the Communist style) on the experiment in rural revolution, of which visual evidence in the world outside was still so slight. Other Shanghai talents fled to Hong Kong and churned out war documentaries and patriotic feature films. Concurrently, the KMT operated studios in Peking, Chungking, and Shanghai, as long as those cities remained under their aegis.[12] Then with the surrender of Japan in 1945, Communist filmmakers took over the elaborate Japanese film studios in Changchun, Manchuria. There, for more than a decade, diversionary films innocent of political controversy had been produced by Japanese professionals and their Chinese collaborators. Equipment from Japan, as well as the private studios formerly controlled by the KMT, were inherited by the Communist regime.

Soon after Liberation the Central Committee established under the Propaganda Department the Cinema Department, which set forth an ambitious film production schedule.[13] To succeed in the socialist-realist * fashion set by Moscow, with which China was then on good terms, meant that in the new products the individual styles of Chinese filmmakers, which had been polished over the years, would have to be suppressed. And to be banned were the foreign films, dominantly American, which continued to flood the Chinese market, selling "foreign capitalism and imperialism" (as Chiang Ch'ing chose to put it). Most aggravating to the purist proletarian leaders was the wide popularity of these "wicked" foreign films (which never ceased to captivate the purist proletarian Chiang Ch'ing).[14]

The problem she faced, with little assistance from her comrades, was how to produce films for a largely rural audience in the throes of socialist reorganization. There could be no question in her mind that what had entertained and educated Shanghai urbanites in the 1930's could wreak ideological havoc upon the present constituency, which was no less than all the masses of China, overwhelmingly peasant. The grueling conversion, which included forbidding ancestor worship, local cults, and popular dramas and rechanneling religious impulses toward political ends, left the peasantry extraordinarily susceptible to ideological redirection. So long as bourgeois Chinese and foreign films were widely available, the individualism, sentimentalism, and materialism at the heart of capitalist society would compete with the Party's commitment to the reorganization of labor relations, which was absolutely necessary to the building of socialism.

---

* A term of Soviet origin defined in 1934 by A. Zhdanov, Stalin's literary representative, as, ". . . to know life in order to depict it truthfully in works of art, to depict it not scholastically, not lifelessly, not just as 'objective reality,' but to depict real life in its revolutionary development" (Gleb Struve, *Soviet Russian Literature*, 1917–50 Norman, Okla., 1951, 245).

Chiang Ch'ing's appointment to the directorship of the Cinema Department quickened her determination to use film and the arts generally to reshape the people's sense of the past at a historical turning point and to set forth new mores for the contemporary era. The end of the Manchu dynasty was less than a half century away, and its demise still provided a rich vein of historical anecdote. Moreover, judgments about that dynasty's decline and fall served to test present political orientation. Stories set on the verge of the Manchus' fall drew upon diverse materials: the fanatical Boxer Uprising; the mercurial Empress Dowager Tz'u Hsi, popularly remembered as China's most recent example of a "bad female ruler"; sycophantic eunuchs and wayward princes; foreign imperialists whose Eight-Power Invasion of the Forbidden City nearly toppled the dynasty; the infamous courtesan Sai Chin-hua, whom some saw as prostituting herself for patriotism. In Chiang Ch'ing's view, among the most seditious films about that era was the Hong Kong made–*The Inside Story of the Ch'ing Court,* which was based upon Yao Hsin-nung's popular drama called *Malice of Empire.* The argument sparked by the film was whether the Empress Dowager's quelling of the Boxer Uprising was "patriotic" because it preserved the nation against foreign takeover or counterrevolutionary because it suppressed the Boxers' "proletarian" class struggle against the ruling feudal class.

The Inside Story of the Ch'ing Court disturbed Chiang Ch'ing from her first viewing. After Liu Shao-ch'i saw it, she said, he praised it, calling it "patriotic." Chairman Mao contradicted him, alleging that it was "traitorous." It was *correct* for the Eight Powers to invade China at that late point in the history of the Manchu dynasty, Liu and his supporters argued. The Chairman would not yield.* The script editors of the film were extremely cunning in finding ways to embed political slurs in the text, she said, without specifying those she took the hardest.

Chiang Ch'ing did not go into the background of the film or the plot (perhaps because she assumed that I and everyone knew it). However, it merits our review because re-creations of the past have been read proverbially by China's rulers as *romans à clef.* Those which flattered the rulers were praised; those which insulted them were condemned, and the authors were sometimes executed. An extravagant and glamorous film, *The Inside Story of the Ch'ing Court* has as its principal character the Empress Dowager Tz'u Hsi, who was neither loved by the people nor praised by later historians. She and her dazzling court are attempting to sustain the splendors of imperial living in the face of increas-

---

* In a wider ideological context the argument should be seen as a dramatization of the ongoing "two-line struggle," here waged between Mao and Liu, and applied ex post facto to a pre-Communist event. The basic contention was whether all historical experience, and hence the art that represents it, should be judged in terms of class struggle (Mao's thesis) or in terms of patriotic national defense (the opposition's thesis).

ing internal rebellion, foreign invasion, and rising Chinese nationalism. Yao Hsin-nung's exacting modern portrait shows Tz'u Hsi adoring exotic flowers, the theater (her extravagant open stage still stands on the imperial palace grounds), and the technical novelty of photography. But in human relations she is a termagant. The young Emperor is well-meaning but cowed by the Dowager, and the chief eunuch, Li Lien-ying, is a vicious sycophant. Eventually the Manchu princes break the imperial ranks by conniving with the xenophobic Boxers. At the peak of the crisis the Dowager strives to save herself by throwing in her lot with the rebels. Later she reverses herself and sides with the oppressors.

Dramatic action arises from tensions between the women at the top: the Empress Dowager and the Emperor's consort, Lady Chen. The Dowager recognizes that Lady Chen, not the Emperor (whom she can manage handily), poses the real threat to her autonomy. Thus she must prevent Lady Chen from gaining ascendancy over the Emperor. The play demonstrates a historical axiom that revolutionary leaders may have preferred *not* to replay before their people: that the power of succession rests in the hands of women.

In 1949 the Chinese Press Association of Hong Kong, whose constituency has always loved sensuous extravaganzas and mockeries of the imperial past, named this the best film of the year. Although the Communist government banned the original stage play in the early years of the People's Republic, the film version was shown to wildly enthusiastic audiences — until Chiang Ch'ing scotched it.

But film censorship alone could not disenchant the story or end the controversy among the leaders. In 1954 an operatic version titled *Emperor Kuang-hsu and the Pearl Concubine* was produced in the Shaohsing style, which uses an all-woman cast. Over the next three years Shanghai, Nanking, and Hangchow adapted the opera to their local styles. During Liu Shao-ch'i's ascendancy, in 1957 the original stage play was reintroduced in Peking and put on an official list of "exemplary plays," indicating that the play was thought of not merely as good, but also as a model to be followed.

During Mao's Anti-Rightist Campaign of 1957–1958, however, Yao's notorious *chef d'œuvre* was attacked in all adaptations and banned from public performance. In 1962 an opera version made a brief comeback, but was squelched once more the next year. At the height of the Cultural Revolution in 1967, Yao Wen-yuan savaged the film and publicly chagrined Chou Yang and others long responsible for saving it. Ch'i Pen-yü,[15] a member of the Cultural Revolution Group headed by Chiang Ch'ing, denounced both the film and Liu Shao-ch'i for supporting it. In May of 1967 Mao Tse-tung delivered the *coup de grace* (or tried to) when he ordered that this irrepressible film be shown once again nationwide, this time as a "negative example." Thereafter, each showing was accompanied by heavy propaganda belaboring all the film's vicious political features.

The long dispute over Inside Story was important not only in itself, Chiang Ch'ing said when she resumed her account, but also because it was linked to larger issues of cultural policy. Right after Liberation the importation of Hong Kong films was prohibited, but it was not long before the Ministry of Culture ignored that ruling and allowed Hong Kong film companies to resume dumping on the Chinese market "extremely corrupt films, starring cowboys in jeans and their ilk." The fundamental flaw of Inside Story, Chiang Ch'ing argued in a routine Marxian fashion, was that it was produced by a capitalist film company (K'un-lun of Hong Kong). The powers in China who had acquired the film rights were "naive" to think that the film was all right long as the content was not flagrantly reactionary.

In recalling her first actions against the film, she said that as soon as she saw it she called a meeting of cultural administrators, writers, and historians at her home so that they could determine collectively whether the film should continue to be shown to the people, at what peril no one (at the meeting) seemed to know, or be banned immediately. Lu Ting-i, her boss in his capacity as chief of the Party's Propaganda Department, presided. Among the guests were two historians she scarcely knew. In their view, however flawed this film by K'un-lun of Hong Kong, it should be shown in China simply because it was "patriotic": it dealt positively with "national defense." She responded to their far-fetched justification with cold silence. Their refusal to consider the film's dire class implications infuriated her. But at that point she did not feel that her position was strong enough to oppose them outright. Lu Ting-i mumbled some truculent words, then pronounced that it was indeed "patriotic." She shot back that it was "traitorous!" Someone else at the meeting told her to stand up and denounce Lu, Liu, and all its defenders. So she did, repeating loudly, "It's traitorous!"

Before the meeting was over she instructed the two historians to write a critique of the film. Later she got in touch with them to find out what they had written. They responded evasively, saying that she should have someone search for their critique at the home of the Party historian, Hu Ch'iao-mu, a man trusted by the Chairman and herself. As it turned out, their critique, which was not worth much, had been hidden in the home of an enemy of Hu Ch'iao-mu's. Having failed to recruit professional historians to her cause, she simply took the matter into her own hands and banned the film.

In 1950 and 1951, years of prolific film production and numerous film festivals,[16] she continued to see films and denounce many. One of the most vexing was Sons and Daughters of China and Korea, cast in the contemporary context of the Korean War. After she exposed its errors (she would not rehash them now) in the name of the Cinema Department, those associated with the production of the film "failed to escape." One of the filmmakers turned out to be a "counterrevolutionary," the other a "Party renegade"; and the company that produced the film had previously been owned by "traitors." She searched out Vice-Minister of Culture Chou Yang, and found him at the Shanghai film studio in question. She pointed out that a film on so timely a theme as the Korean War was bound to have a political impact upon their relations with the "brotherly country" of Korea, whose cause they were supporting. The impact must not be adverse. Make it revolutionary or ban it, she said.

"Hypocritically, he nodded in assent," she said, "and went on about his business." Chiang Ch'ing returned home, still uncertain of what he would do. Not long afterward she telephoned him again at the studio and asked him to revise the film. In time he yielded and carried out some revisions at enormous expense. Ch'en Po-ta and Hu Ch'iao-mu, who had been in touch with Chou Yang, called her long distance to tell her that *Sons and Daughters of China and Korea* had indeed been revised. Why not look at it, they said. Fed up with the cumbersome politics of the revision in tandem with them, she had no desire to witness their results.

In her discussion of film censorship of the early 1950's, Ting Ling's name came up once again. By then Ting Ling, winner in 1952 of the Stalin Prize for her novel on land reform, *Sun Shines Over the Sangkan River*, was in the limelight. She was serving on several committees of cultural administration and as editor of the *Literary Gazette*, China's most prestigious literary journal and one that then enjoyed remarkable political autonomy in the light of what was to come. Chiang Ch'ing's remarks about Ting had nothing to do with Ting's art as art or with her literary leadership, but simply and finally wrote her off as a political infidel. (Such typecasting makes one wonder whether Ting Ling and others similarly scorned by those in power will ever return to lay their case before the people and the state.)

Years ago, Chiang Ch'ing said, it was assumed by the Chairman and his supporters that Chou Yang and Ting Ling belonged to separate factions. When Ting Ling "went astray" in the late 1950's she simply "gave herself over to the enemy" (supposedly the KMT and its literary representatives). Some suspected that she was actually a "secret agent" (of the KMT) but they had no proof. When she was a protégée of Lu Hsun's in the 1930's, he obviously had no inkling that she was a renegade. At least Hu Feng, Hsiao Chün, and other writers with whom Ting Ling associated had taken the trouble to "assume revolutionary disguises." Their clubbishness went back to the time of the Yenan Forum (1942), when Ting Ling, Hu Feng, Hsiao Chün, and their followers "divorced themselves from the masses." It was clear then to the Party leaders and it was still obvious a decade later that those writers were indulging in "sectarianism." Eventually, they became total sectarians.

In the early 1950's Ting Ling was in the habit of writing "on commission." * When Ting Ling perceived that Chiang Ch'ing was at odds with Chou Yang — and perhaps also to ingratiate herself with the wife of the Chairman (Chiang Ch'ing surmised) — she approached Chiang Ch'ing and offered to compose some articles critical of Chou Yang and his erroneous positions on film censorship. Such profound disputes could not be settled by Ting Ling's pen alone, Chiang Ch'ing told Ting Ling at the time. Chiang Ch'ing added in our interview that simply "hitting her and others like her over the head" (relentless direct attack) would not have worked either!

iv

In 1951 and 1952, the Chairman was too preoccupied with other affairs to see and evaluate many movies, Chiang Ch'ing said, and she was too involved in her own work to follow closely what he was doing or to go out with him. Film criticism was only tangential to her "real work," which she characterized as using "persuasion" to make the landlords and the bourgeoisie aware of what needed to be accomplished during the land reform period. No matter what her recommendations, "no one listened" to her then, she remarked sardonically.

Nevertheless, in those years she made two trips to the rural areas, each time incognito.[17] Though recognized as Chiang Ch'ing by a few leading comrades, to the local masses she was Li Chin—her original name. In different ways both excursions were involved with problems of land reform. The first, which lasted eight months, was an investigation into the historical background of the notorious nineteenth-century beggar-turned-educator, Wu Hsun; the second was a three-month tour of duty in land reform.

When the film *The Story of Wu Hsun* was first released (in December 1950), Chiang Ch'ing began, it was shown all over the country.[18] Disturbed by its implications, she made a preliminary report on its background and wrote an article summing up her findings. Once that was published, "the enemy was disarmed," she said ominously, and the film was immediately withdrawn from circulation. Thereafter it would be seen only selectively, never again by the masses. That article, however, was just the beginning of a grueling investigation.

* For pay, perhaps as a ghost-writer. Since the 1940's the top Chinese leaders have hired able writers to publish their views in persuasive ideological rhetoric. For years Ch'en Po-ta and Yao Wen-yuan (among others) both wrote in their own names and under pseudonyms and drafted articles for Mao and Chiang Ch'ing respectively.

On the surface the Wu Hsun legend, which Chiang Ch'ing did not spell out in detail, appears to be a straightforward Confucian success story. Wu Hsun made the astounding though not impossible social leap from the impoverished masses to the ruling class. How he did it has invited more than a century of historical analysis by leading thinkers.[19] Chiang Ch'ing was first to authorize a Marxian critique.

Although Chiang Ch'ing's involvement in the Wu Hsun affair had not been made public before her telling me now, Wu Hsun's legend was a matter of general knowledge in China. Briefly told, Wu Hsun, born in 1838, was the youngest of seven children of a poor family in Wu-chang village, T'ang-i county, Shantung province. His parents died young, forcing him to survive by begging. Instead of consuming what he gathered, he saved as much as possible. He regarded his strings of cash as capital, which he deposited with landlords and usurers for interest. Eventually, he too went into land speculation. By his fiftieth year he realized his lifelong ambition, an emulation of his social superiors of the Manchu dynasty: in his own name he established a school offering a free education to sons of the poor. His first school was set up in the town of Liu-lin, close to his native village, a second in K'uan-t'ao county in 1889, and a third the year he died in the town of Lin-ch'ing — all three in Shantung province.[20]

Reactions to Wu Hsun's unusual case had been diverse. Members of the old ruling class were flattered by a poor man's aspiration to model himself after them — landlords and gentry. Reformists lauded his promotion of education for the poor, a policy having both Confucian and democratic implications. The Communists responded slowly, until Chiang Ch'ing took a stand. Continued veneration of Wu Hsun's model, she argued, was dangerous because his actions discredited present national imperatives: overthrow the landlord class, bury Confucian scholars, and put down the reformist (tantamount to revisionist, from a Communist perspective; *vide* Liu Shao-ch'i) tenet that education dissolves class contradictions and leads to social and political success. In her view Wu Hsun defected from the proletarians, collaborated with the Confucians, and practiced some capitalism along the way.

Chiang Ch'ing's interest in Wu Hsun was aroused by the film version, the most modern manifestation of his legend. When Chou Yang and Hsia Yen presided over the completion of the film, one that was begun by the China Motion Picture Company before Liberation (and directed by Sun Yü, trained in America), she objected to the way they went about it. At that time no one took seriously what she said. Although she lacked the power to stand in the way of their producing the film as they chose, at least she could see that someone was commissioned to write a critical article that would discuss its reformist implications. Accordingly, she made an appointment with Vice-Minister of Culture Chou Yang and proposed that to him. He scoffed at the idea and told her, "I can put up with a little reformism."

"Then go ahead with your reformism!" she shouted at him, slammed the door in his face, and returned to her apartments.

Left to her own devices, she prepared her case. First, she gathered all the materials she could find on Wu Hsun's background, then drafted a position paper. In those days, she said, some "leading senior comrades" (she named no names) were still praising Wu Hsun.[21] She was the only one turning out letters and articles that took account of opposing views as she formulated her own. Her papers assembled, she presented them to the Chairman. He disapproved of her action, an argument ensued, and she walked out on him. For the next few days she stayed in her own apartments. Her long absence he must have found strange, for he finally tracked her down to her study, where she was half-concealed by stacks of books and writing materials. "So you're still up to this," he remarked drily.

Whatever he said could not deflect her from her course. Shortly afterward she invited Ch'en Po-ta and Hu Ch'iao-mu, both trusted ideologues, to drop by her apartments to discuss the Wu Hsun case. She alerted them to the film's ideological dangers, especially its softening of the image of the landlord class and excessive praise of education as a ladder to social success. Such points could not fail to make an impression on innumerable viewers.

Chou Yang soon caught wind of what she was up to, the people she was seeing, and the writing she had commissioned. He began to create difficulties, forcing her to decide whether to continue to pursue the matter in Peking or leave and work elsewhere.

Thus in the late spring of 1951 she made preparations to get to the root of the Wu Hsun legend by going down to western Shantung, where he had flourished. Since he and she had both been born in the same part of the province, she would have no difficulty with the dialect — an asset to the undertaking. Because Mao had objected to her going, and being recognized for such work, she traveled as Comrade Li Chin. After all this time, no one would remember her childhood name, and she would enjoy greater freedom of movement. She was the first leading comrade to go out and do original investigative work there, she said proudly.

When Chou Yang was informed of her project, which she knew he scorned, he sent along his secretary (and writer on cultural politics) Chung Tien-fei on the pretense that he would serve as her assistant. The *People's Daily* was also mobilized to send along the journalist Yuan Shui-p'o, who would be responsible for filing reports of their investigation with the Peking bureau. At the beginning of the investigation she generally trusted Chung and Yuan. But soon she realized that Chung was just a "rightist" dispatched to disrupt her project.

The three of them with their aides took the train to western Shantung. In T'ang-i county they transferred to a jeep. The sudden exposure to an alien climate made them all catch colds, with endless rounds of dripping eyes and noses. Her own sore throat she dosed with penicillin pills (here she went off on another of her dissertations on self-medication). Colds they could put up with, but it was intolerable that these men who were supposed to be assisting her in the investigation were most unwilling to listen to her. Only through dogged persistence on her part did they come around.

At the T'ang-i county seat they were met by Tuan Chun-ch'ing, the secretary of the local Party committee, who was a widely reputed advocate of Wu Hsun's example. Since he had no idea who she was, they fell immediately into an argument over the model Wu Hsun upheld to the people. Continued veneration of such a man would ultimately destroy their Party and the nation, she tried to convince him. Through persuasion Secretary Tuan eventually accepted her point of view, agreed to cooperate, and began by giving her information.

A powerful local landlord was responsible for promoting the Wu Hsun cult over the last two decades, Secretary Tuan told her, and put her in touch with agents, "lackeys," and soldiers linked to the landlord's underground defense system. When she learned how the landlord's son was also involved, she asked Tuan to conduct a special investigation of him, its results to be turned over to her. The old landlord himself had even more troops than Huang Shih-jen, the notorious landlord of the revolutionary ballet *White-haired Girl* (which she later produced during the Cultural Revolution). Once she grasped the dynamics of his vast operation, she knew that others like him had to be lurking in the area and elsewhere, and that all of them jealously protected the ancient privileges of their class.

While her work got under way, two other investigation groups suddenly appeared, one from Hopeh province and the other from P'ingyuan province.* She was not sure who commissioned them. Yuan Shui-p'o and others supposed to be assisting her were adverse to pooling information with these other groups, which they saw as rivals. But Chiang Ch'ing was against monopolizing information. She was willing to share her findings with the others; she also wanted to use the "broad masses" of the area for gathering intelligence on the landlord class. That was arranged. As the momentum of her team increased, the Hopeh and P'ingyuan teams lost interest and drifted elsewhere.

Throughout their work they practiced the rigorous empiricism of Chairman Mao's instructions on scientific investigation, she said. While still in Peking she had prepared herself by studying gazetteers and histories of the Shantung

---

* Created mainly from parts of Honan and Shantung provinces in 1949; dissolved in 1952, when previous provincial borders were restored.

area; after she got to Shantung she continued her research, which she supplemented by interviews with many local residents. Names, ages, occupations, and recollections of Wu Hsun were meticulously recorded. Gradually the historical background of Wu Hsun's life took shape.

After a couple of days at Lin-ch'ing, where Chiang Ch'ing had sent him, Yuan Shui-p'o telephoned to say that he had discovered nothing new about Wu Hsun's links to the landlord class. Disappointed, she urged him to double his efforts, then shortly joined him at Lin-ch'ing and took over. In the guise of Li Chin — her subterfuge held up perfectly — she lectured the members of the town and county Party committees as persuasively as she could on the evil potential of "the spirit of Wu Hsun." Moved and possibly terrified by her words, they turned their talents over to her project and vowed to join her in getting to the root of the original historical situation.

She instructed Chung Tien-fei and Yuan Shui-p'o to stay on at Lin-ch'ing, and withdrew to nearby Kuan county, where for several weeks she pursued other angles of the Wu Hsun story.

The investigation wore on through the summer into the early fall. That long stretch of time without some of the amenities to which she had grown accustomed taxed her health, precarious under any circumstances. Periodically she had dizzy spells, but still she never flagged in her determination to carry on.

One day Yuan Shui-p'o telephoned her from Lin-ch'ing to say that he had come across a book of land titles bearing Wu Hsun's name as owner. Thrilled to find material proof that Wu Hsun was a landlord, she told Yuan to bring the book immediately to Kuan county. They photographed it and sent one copy to the historian Kuo Mo-jo, who had been following their investigation from Peking. [22]

As Chiang Ch'ing reconstructed the conditions under which Wu Hsun lived, she sensed what she called his profound sadness and disenchantment, subjective states not conveyed by the laudatory earlier accounts. In emulation of his social superiors he indulged in women and acquired several mistresses, one of whom was still alive at the time of their investigation and willing to be interviewed.

In an effort to understand the motives for his behavior, they tried to pinpoint not only his class origins but also his class associations in later life. Though born poor, he grew up to be no more than a "loyal lackey of the landlord class." They also strove to see him in the context of his time. For example, he established the first of his schools in Liu-lin township in 1888. Liu-lin was among the most flourishing towns in China by then. But what the pious local legends about his philanthropic career concealed was that at the time of widespread disturbance in the mid-nineteenth century, several thousand peasants in the area rose up in rebellion, an event not in the least reflected by his retrogressive career. One native of Liu-lin, the bandit general Sung Ching-shih, emerged as a formidable leader of other peasant uprisings.[23] The Black Flag troops had also been active there.* The Taiping leader Li K'ai-fang once passed through with his followers, but the Taipings refused to support indigenous peasant uprisings in western Shantung — they only praised the landlord class(!). Nor did Wu Hsun take part in any peasant revolt. Later biographies always characterized him in the most obsequious terms, actually a far cry from his original reputation. Some of the old peasants they interviewed remembered him by his nickname, Wu Tou-mou, given him because of his repugnant appearance — his lips dripped with saliva, a symbol of his greed.

In Chiang Ch'ing's judgment Wu Hsun's most profound error was to concentrate all his energies upon formal education. If there were just a few schools around, everything would be fine, he thought. Yet her own investigation of the records of the Liu-lin schools showed that although his school was cost-free, it was not open to the poorest people. A few children of the middle peasants could be admitted, but those of poor peasants and hired laborers were excluded. Consequently, only the sons of the middle peasants were able to master basic reading and writing, and thereby alter the conditions of their lives. Those actualities were passed over by apologists for the ruling class. After Wu Hsun died the top official in Liu-lin, acting in self-interest, honored him by changing the name of the school he found to the Wu Hsun Middle School and erected other flamboyant monuments in his name.

Over the eight months of the investigation in Shantung she prepared a series of reports, then presented them to the Chairman for review. Each of her articles he revised. She added that some of the literature on Wu Hsun was, in fact, written entirely by the Chairman.[24]

While the investigations were going on, the *People's Daily* published their reports day by day. To keep the reports flowing, interviews of old people whose memories went back into the late nineteenth century were conducted at a brisk pace. Members of her team dealt with them individually and also called frequent meetings of the masses. Drawing out the aged was not always easy. By 1951 survivors of Wu Hsun's schools were all over seventy; a few had even passed the century mark. Some of the oldest, whose minds were untouched by the revolution, were actually skeptical of their interrogators' motives. They accused Chiang Ch'ing and her comrades of pursuing the question of "reformism" (which arose in a Confucian and socially hierarchic context) only because they belonged to a "higher class," and so looked down upon them. (She was amused by having once been mistaken for a reformist.) After the group's reports

---

* Commanded by the former Taiping soldier Liu Yung-fu, who led Chinese irregulars against French forces seeking to establish a protectorate in Indochina in the 1870's and 1880's; most active in Yunnan.

came out and were widely circulated, she continued more seriously, some oldsters who had never wavered in their loyalty to Wu Hsun were humiliated. So were the present leaders who had eulogized his example. Even Vice-Minister of Culture Chou Yang, who had objected so intensely to her dismantling the legend in the first place, was driven, in the Chinese Communist jargon, to make public self-criticism. [25]

v

After wrapping up the Wu Hsun case in early September of 1951, Chiang Ch'ing returned to Peking. Restless, she decided to go back to the rural areas to take part a second time in the land-reform movement, then at its peak. Impressed by her recent accomplishments, this time the Chairman supported her decision. Some others, however, continued to oppose her having direct contact with the masses. Chou Yang, still vice-minister of culture, fomented among Party chiefs a "big struggle" over whether she should be allowed to go. In the end she won out and joined a group that included some leaders, among them the economist and Politburo member Li Hsien-nien. They traveled by train to Wuhan, a large industrial center on the Yangtze River. When the train pulled into the Wuhan station, Chiang Ch'ing was suddenly ordered to get off with her bodyguards, leaving the others to continue the journey deep into the countryside. Such discrimination infuriated her, but she could do nothing about it. Li Hsien-nien, whom she regarded as a supporter, stayed at Wuchang, the nearby city on the south side of the Yangtze.

Her sincere intention to do land reform in the normal way was frustrated at every turn. The composition of her work team — all bodyguards besides her — was highly peculiar.* In accordance with instructions from above, her team was not allowed to move beyond the environs of Wuhan, nor was she permitted to live among the peasants or even to get close to them — unless she forced an exception. Moreover, persons who did not want her true identity known to the people compelled her to work incognito again, as Li Chin.

As soon as her contingent of bodyguards was installed in a rural township near the city of Wuhan, the Central South Party Committee sent its own security agent. This additional bodyguard was a tough-looking woman who carried a pistol and shadowed all Chiang Ch'ing's movements, an arrangement that hampered the work severely. Once when Chiang Ch'ing decided to pay a visit to the home of a peasant, no sooner had she sat down than the woman body-

---

* A normally composed work team would have been balanced politically, socially, and geographically, and might possibly have included intellectuals, students, government personnel, local officials, and experienced officials from other areas.

guard pronounced stonily, "That peasant is sick!" Chiang Ch'ing saw that this was just a ploy to get her out of there, and responded by kicking out the bodyguard and continuing the interview privately.

Another time she tried to have some dealings with a woman cowherd who recently had been drawn into the local militia. As soon as they started talking the woman bodyguard stood squarely between them. Chiang Ch'ing faced her furiously and said, "As a bodyguard, are you subordinate to my work or superior to my work? You divorce me from the masses!"

The woman's tactics were quite wonderful, Chiang Ch'ing continued. She could only assume that Chou Yang, so intensely opposed to the whole venture, had put the woman up to these tricks. The woman used to tell Chiang Ch'ing that she should eat better food. Actually *she* wanted to eat better food and expected Chiang Ch'ing to order it for both of them. What the woman liked best was "greasy food" that Chiang Ch'ing would not have served at her table. To keep the meal situation from getting out of hand, she set a modest quota of dishes to be served. That incensed the bodyguard, who then arranged for her husband to prepare and send her special foods for the duration of her service.

Throughout their involvement, the woman bodyguard never learned the true identity of Comrade Li Chin. Only Chiang Ch'ing's own bodyguards, who had come down with her from Peking, knew who she really was, and that was kept secret. Nor did the chairman of the county peasant association, a man she dealt with frequently, know who she was. Though close to Wuhan city, the area was remote culturally and the population was scant. More than two years after Liberation, outlaws, bandits, and "hooligan factions" still lurked in its broad, watery marshes. Though hard to believe now, under KMT rule the area was designated a "model county" to commend its progressiveness. But in reality the region was intensely backward and the masses stubbornly resisted mobilization for land reform. When her work team of bodyguards began to pursue members of the oppressor classes, they discovered that they did not possess the legal right of arrest. To detain someone, they first had to sue him through legal channels, which was cumbersome. Throughout their service her team adhered to the policy of "touching" (apparently destroying) only those landlords known to be murderers.

Chairman Mao and the Central Committee had determined that in the prosecution of land reform the work teams should concentrate on the "three big mountains" (feudalism, bureaucratic capitalism, and imperialism), advice they followed. In the countryside their main enemy was the feudal landlord class, but they punished only those known to be the worst killers and criminals; the rest were given a way out. The poor and lower-middle peasants, who constituted the main force, had allies among the middle peasants, a group which was also spared. As for the rich peasants, they were allowed to retain the portions of land they had worked by their own labor, but those they had gained by exploiting others were seized.[26] To verify those points, Chiang Ch'ing searched among the papers on her lap, and drew out one fragile copy of the Agrarian Reform Law, which has been passed on June 30, 1950, and now skimmed through it, reading aloud.

The first step in land reform was to identify the chief of the "local tyrants," who was usually also the head of the landlord organization. As a rule, there were besides him many smaller landlords, and their land holdings could be widely scattered. Chiang Ch'ing's work team decided to channel its offensive at somewhere between 8 and 20 percent of the most tyrannical landlords. Among the "local tyrants" so identified by her team was one nicknamed by the local people "Pockmarked Chin." The landlords' organized power was exercised through an underworld of security agents. Although these men were supposed to be "secret security agents," the armbands they wore in different colors gave them away, making them the easy prey of muggers and murderers — and now of land reformers.

Working from the outer circles of the community, her team gradually converged upon the most powerfully exploitative and brought them to justice. All procedures were carried out according to the Agrarian Reform Law. Mao and the Central Committee had limited the right to execute offenders to the provincial government organization (she did not clarify this point). The People's Court determined the punishment in accordance with the kind of crime perpetrated by the tyrants upon the local peasants. The sight of the masses rising up in anger was extraordinary. Chiang Ch'ing marveled to recall it. If the people's enthusiasm went wild, her work team would have to intervene to protect the local tyrants from being beaten to death on the spot. Often they had to call on the local militia to help quell mob violence against those brought forward and charged as oppressors. Once when a trial got out of hand, she and other members of her team were attacked physically as they struggled to act as a buffer between the tyrants and the unleashed masses who threatened to tear them all to pieces.

As soon as the masses were brought under control, the team seized the tyrant and dragged him before the People's Court, which condemned him to death. If their work was done well, the spectacle of execution made the people ecstatic. The brilliant and bitter drama of the land-reform cycle — naming the tyrant, arousing the masses, setting the sentence, and witnessing the execution — she would never forget.[27]

Throughout these convulsive episodes, she continued more calmly, the local people were never quite certain of who she and the other members of her team actually were. Because they were well equipped, a few apparently surmised that they were in some degree "official." Still, her personal role mystified them.

Since she had taken a camera and used it often, some peasants guessed that she was a professional photographer. From that they speculated that if a photographer was there, the others must be county officials. To understand the peasant mind, Chiang Ch'ing explained, one must realize that in their limited experience of the world the county official was the very highest they would ever know. Thus the status they recognized in the county officials whom they imagined were present heightened respect for her as well.

In the total scheme of land reform, identification and execution of the local tyrants was the first stage; land redistribution was the next. In Chiang Ch'ing's experience both stages took ten to twelve days altogether. When land redistribution was begun, the work team was responsible for making class designations: identification of landlords, rich peasants, and middle peasants. That labeling determined the details of redistribution. Since each area had a different social complexion, application of the Agrarian Reform Law varied accordingly. While she was working in the Wuhan area she heard reports of another area where both district and county representatives of the government wrongly identified rich peasants as landlords and middle peasants as rich peasants. While that distortion of class analysis doubtless was well intended by the comrades in charge, it had the negative effect of widening the social target. In her area she was most conscientious about limiting needless violence. After her preliminary investigation was complete, she called the local officials together and asked what rules of procedure they had set for themselves. They said they were classifying from 16 to 20 percent of the local population as landlords and rich peasants. Numerically that target was too wide, she told them, and they argued endlessly about that.

But their craftiest device for augmenting the amount of land to be distributed was to persuade even the middle peasants to turn over land for redistribution. Yet the land belonging to those in the middle peasant category was typically too meager to matter. Since she was getting nowhere by arguing on her own authority, she telephoned the provincial Party committee. Deliberately, she asked some local officials to stand beside her to overhear the ensuing conversation. Such irresponsible widening of the social target disrupted Party policy, she announced over the telephone. The erroneous policy of tearing away land from middle peasants must be stopped!

Aggravations were endless. That November of 1951 a cold wave struck Central China. Although she always wore fur coats and a heavy jacket, she shuddered from the cold and her lips turned blue. Regularly informed of her situation, Chairman Mao sent down the greatcoat she had left in Peking. But she dared not wear it because its distinctive cut and quality might have let people know who she really was.

Li Hsien-nien was also informed that the bitter cold was keeping her from sleeping more than two or three hours a night, and that she had developed a cough which had turned into bronchitis. He told her to come to Wuchang to see a doctor. She went, but the medicine prescribed had little effect. Soon after she returned to her rural post, Li Hsien-nien sent down a load of charcoal which her bodyguards burned each night, all night long. She was grateful for the charcoal, but her relentless cough was not cured. To carry out her work she had to walk several exhausting hours each day, mostly over rough terrain. Naturally, the local people were used to the harsh winter climate. Some of the peasants who observed her energies flagging taunted her: "Who do you think you are?"

She was chagrined, and kept up a perpetual struggle on two fronts, "outwardly against the landlords and inwardly against myself."

Fighting against her own weaker nature, she with her team pushed through the land redistribution stage. After class origins were ascertained, land and movable property were redistributed. Some landlords who knew what was in store for them panicked and resorted to absurd ploys. To save their wardrobes they dressed themselves up in dozens of suits or long gowns. Such ludicrous sights they were, too padded to move! Not only the landlords', but everyone's thinking was slow to change. She remembered one hired laborer who owned no clothes at all. When he was given a quilt and a gown, he dared not accept them because he was still cowed psychologically by the landlord to whom they had once belonged. Of course, peasants could also be greedy — they did not know any better. Not only clothing, but also surplus beds, bedding, and furniture had to be distributed. When these goods were first set out, the poor peasants and hired laborers, who had never owned such things, grabbed everything for themselves.

"Why take a big quilt if you don't need it?" she challenged some hired laborers. To them she had to explain the obvious: since most were bachelors (that is, too poor to marry), they had less need of household items than poor peasant families, many of whom had never owned a bed. Part of her task was to teach them "broadness of mind," by which she meant equity and cooperation.

Land distribution engendered other problems. Some peasants balked at accepting swampy paddy fields or plots of land that were susceptible to flooding and contingent perils. So she had to convince them that "moist" land would bring them better crops. Other disputes arose when widely scattered fields were assigned to a single household, and still others, when unequally fertile fields were distributed.

Curious dilemmas arose when they tried to assign houses to cowherds. These nomads had never lived in houses before, and scarcely knew what to do with them. Even political activists could be stubborn when it came to accepting things. None was willing to take anything out of the home of another: not until each was newly awakened politically did he dare appropriate anything. The distribution of draft animals, buffaloes, and farm implements, all of which were desperately needed but in short supply, was invariably problematic. Her area had only one or two buffaloes to go around.

During the distribution stage of land reform she brushed up on socialist theory, reminding herself that in principle and practice the fundamental task was to *get organized*. Hence the next stage — establishment of a new local government on a democratic basis.

Knowing that the peasants were nearly beside themselves with excitement over the drastic changes that had been made and were full of utopian hopes, she dared not attend (because of fear of mobs?) the final land-reform meeting of the community as a whole. When it came time for her work team to depart, the peasants thronged all around them, beating gongs and drums. Among the people who came to see them off was a widow who, in the course of land reform, had broken the convention of retirement and had become a political activist. She came up to Chiang Ch'ing, tears of appreciation streaming down her face, and Chiang Ch'ing cried too. From a later report of elections conducted in that town the next day, Chiang Ch'ing learned that the woman had been elected to the peasant association, and that upon acceptance of her new post, confessed to the masses that she had once belonged to the secret society (of the traditional underworld) called I Kuan Tao. In all their days of working together, the woman had never told her that, Chiang Ch'ing remarked incredulously (possibly suspecting that the woman was continuing to serve in this traditional underground operation).

Land reform behind them, her work team returned to Wuhan, the provincial capital of Hupeh, to make a "summing up" of work accomplished. Justice in land reform was not always carried out; deviations expressed the varying political orientations of the officials in charge. Those leaning too far to the left identified too many landlords and condemned them, while those too far to the right named too few, with the result that many landlords got off scot-free. How to identify and treat middle peasants plagued almost all the land-reform teams. During the final deliberations at Wuhan, representatives from other districts asked Chiang Ch'ing and her team which side they leaned toward (easy on middle peasants). When they went to Wuchang for further meetings, both the secretary and the chairman of the local Party committee reported that the masses with whom they had worked were convinced that their slogan, "Don't touch middle peasant interests," had been truly implemented.

Next they stopped at Hankow, one of the Wuhan triple cities on the Yangtze, where Teng Tzu-hui was in charge of rural affairs. Although Lin Piao was nominally responsible for the government of the Central South Region, she saw nothing of him there. During the land reform movement he did absolutely no work at all! [28]

After the Ninth Party Congress (in 1969, at which Chiang Ch'ing and Yeh Ch'ün, the wife of Lin Piao, were the only women appointed to the Politburo), Yeh Ch'ün decided to "kick up a row," as Chiang Ch'ing put it. Yeh Ch'ün claimed that during the land-reform movement *she* had gone down to work at the grassroots, which was *totally untrue.* She said, moreover, that in the areas where Chiang Ch'ing had gone down to do land reform, nothing had changed at all! When Yeh Ch'ün said all this, Chiang Ch'ing managed to restrain her anger, but right afterward she submitted formally (to the Politburo) a criticism of Yeh Ch'ün's false allegations.

Admittedly, the area in the environs of Wuhan, where she had undertaken land reform, was most resistant to change. Again, she mentioned how preposterous it was for the KMT to call it a model county; by Communist standards it was exceedingly backward. Old customs and reactionary politics were largely unshaken. Even after Liberation numerous KMT members still infiltrated the area, and their persecution of women and young people was unconscionable. Almost everyone gambled. Bandits roamed everywhere, murdering at random. Even the workers were recalcitrant. One worker she knew broke his own legs just to avoid doing labor.

While she was living in that "model county," a rumor that a tiger was on the loose caused tremendous anxiety.* But people had been so cowed by authority that no one dared to report the matter officially. So she took it upon herself to make the village rounds, telling all the people to arm themselves with sticks and get organized. Then, as she lay on her bed one moonlit night, a roar pierced the sky. Her bodyguard sprang to his feet and paced about anxiously. "You've nothing to worry about," she remarked to calm him, though she admitted now that his rifle could not have held off a tiger.

Around that time a district head was almost eaten up by a tiger. In making his rounds one day he took a shortcut along a narrow path in heavy undergrowth. Suddenly a tiger roared ferociously from nearby. "My hair stood on end," he reported later, for like her bodyguard he knew that the weapon he was carrying, a pistol, could not have saved him. Luckily, he was walking through the brush. What tigers fear most and attack compulsively are people they meet on an open road. She always chose her paths wisely. "And you can see that I wasn't eaten up by a tiger!"

* Hupeh is not famous for tigers.

vi

Doing land reform drew Chiang Ch'ing into another major piece of social legislation of the early years of the PRC, the Marriage Reform Law. Passed in May 1950, its prime goal, she said, was to protect women. Yet it was most onerous to enforce. In every region people of all ages, even the young, who were its prime beneficiaries, resisted it, often to the point of physical violence.

One bloody event, which occurred in a community where she was working, was etched sharply in her memory. Some villagers discovered the body of a man floating in a pond, his arms bound behind him. Retrieved, the bloated body was scarcely recognizable. Evidently, he had not simply drowned, but had been beaten and thrown into the water. Soon stories about how ghosts had killed him were circulating among the frightened villagers.

Intrigued by the mystery, Chiang Ch'ing decided to gather all possible information on the case. Through a series of investigations, she learned about a woman villager who had been on poor terms with her husband. "Dirty Head," she called him. After the Marriage Law was passed, she asked Dirty Head for a divorce. He would hear nothing of it. With no apparent alternative, she and her lover took justice into their own hands. They seized the husband and beat him to death. His body was the one hauled out of the pond, and she and her lover, perhaps to deflect attention from themselves, fabricated the ghost stories about him.

Armed with that much information, Chiang Ch'ing and her work team arranged to meet the woman and interview her. The lover was present. Asked about the fate of her husband, the woman admitted insouciantly that she and her lover had destroyed him. Encouraged by the work team, she spoke freely of her situation, and the details they sought — the class background of the three principals — began to emerge: the woman and her husband were poor members of the working class, and her lover was a hired laborer. All three were very young. She had two small children, one still nursing. Her husband, formerly a soldier, was discharged after Liberation. The loss of his pay left them grindingly poor.

Now a confessed murderess, the young woman was put on trial. During the proceedings she "acted like a child, as if she had done nothing wrong at all," Chiang Ch'ing reported disapprovingly. So the wife and her lover were sentenced to death.

Their story was typical of tragedies erupting all over the country, Chiang Ch'ing went on. The roots lay in the old marriage system. If one party was dissatisfied and pulled away from the relationship, the other very likely would refuse to yield or to move along with the new order. Where law enforcement was negligent, suicide or murder commonly occurred.

As the case wound up, Chiang Ch'ing visited the district head and admonished him for not having shown proper concern for the lives of the people under his jurisdiction. In this instance, she explained to him, he had failed to *propagate* the new Marriage Law. He protested lamely about how hard it was to enforce the law. "No one shows concern for women," he admitted.

As for public opinion, all the local people wanted was to have the couple shot! The people who used public opinion to prevent the divorce of the incompatible couple were also to blame. Old people were the most reluctant to accept the Marriage Law and the right of divorce it guaranteed.

Later the provincial government was persuaded to suspend the death sentence imposed upon the woman and her lover and to substitute a period of hard physical labor in their own community. Summing up, she said that the point to grasp was that none of the people ostensibly responsible for this woman were willing to watch over her.

In that same community there was another woman, a widow with several children. The widow, she learned, was stricken with malaria and acute pneumonia. Thinking that she might help, Chiang Ch'ing wanted to see her. But her aides and bodyguards tried to stop her because they feared that she would become infected. She ignored them and went ahead. She found the woman's eyes lusterless and her breathing almost imperceptible. In that deathly silence, the only sounds were the wails of the children in the courtyard. Chiang Ch'ing gave the woman some Western medicine, which was all she had. The woman took it for two or three days, regained her strength, and returned to society a new person. For the first time in her life the woman took her community's political situation into account and became an activist. Being a widow, she was given the task of overseeing and, if need be, disciplining the murderess who had been given the suspended death sentence.

As for the marriage problem in general, Chiang Ch'ing said, custom dies hard in the rural areas. Even after the enactment of the Marriage Law, in many regions marriages were arranged by parents and matchmakers as they had been for centuries. The ritual was antiquated and the expenses could be crippling. A man might be obliged to give a bicycle, watch, radio, or some other equipment to the bride or to her family. The bride, who was always given a new wardrobe, attired herself gorgeously for the wedding ride in a sedan chair. Numerous guests were feasted. Socialist society cannot endure such waste, she declared indignantly.

Nor was land reform a panacea for women. Although the Agrarian Reform Law assigned land to women and men equally, that did not mean that the law was automatically carried out. Because women were unused to exercising their rights, they allowed themselves to be given smaller portions of land or inferior land. Most of them took what they got without complaint. Despite the government's upholding the principle of equal pay for equal work, women in the rural areas have long been paid unequally because men use every conceivable trick to assure themselves of the superior jobs and the wages that go with them. Typically, the men monopolize farm implements and refuse to share them with women who are deserving. Rigorous political education is needed to convince the rural people that women should also be allowed to plow. Material inequities have always been greater in the countryside than in the cities where the rule of equal pay for equal work has been more readily accepted.

Chiang Ch'ing once again warned that ideals and reality must not be confused. Women in China still have a long way to go.

10.

◇ ◇ ◇

Peking and Moscow

They are hidden and suffer; that is all they
do;
A bandage hides the place where each is
living,
His knowledge of the world restricted to
The treatment that the instruments are
giving.
— W. H. Auden, "Surgical Ward"

Chiang Ch'ing reconstructed the 1950's, years when she was shunted
back and forth from Peking to Moscow, in alternately personal and global
terms. From her shifting vantage point she perceived political trends in sharp
detail: disagreements over medical science that affected reports prepared by Soviet doctors and so her future; sensationalized dissent in the Soviet Union that
could challenge China's revolutionary orthodoxy; mounting personal conflicts
between the Chinese men she knew best and their Soviet counterparts who
behaved abominably at banquets and treacherouly on their own; and the final
desecration of eternal friendship with the Soviet's sulking withdrawal of much-
needed technical talent and industrial equipment.

Such upheavals intensified her personal anxieties. Witnessing rivalries between vastly ambitious men, irreconcilable ideological disputes, and unpredictable power conflicts, she would inevitably have speculated about her own future. Might not the cunning Soviets keep Mao's wife as hostage? Was there not
a dread parallel with Ho Tzu-chen, who spent years as a mental patient in the

Soviet Union only to be returned to a Chinese asylum? Might she be discarded for another Chinese wife? The possibilities were endless and unthinkable.

In the 1950's her identity was mainly a mystery to the Chinese people and foreign observers. Few knew that as she moved back and forth between China and the Soviet Union the question of her political as well as physical survival always hung in the balance. In the early 1950's in Peking she was stripped of all high office and left to play court politics mainly through Mao, the pivot of the world she knew through the windows of Chung-nan-hai. During episodes of forced exile in Moscow she led the life of an invalid — high-ranking but estranged from Soviet centers of power, society, and culture.

In contrast to the years before when she was casting about on her own in the countryside, or the years after when she was drumming up a cultural revolution, the middle 1950's Chiang Ch'ing summed up mainly in terms of Mao's signal policy statements on foreign and domestic affairs. Not surprisingly, only the dimmest sense of the consequences of his and others' actions upon the masses, now some six hundred million strong, emerged. All along absorption in the state of her health rivaled attention to the state of the nation.

i

Chiang Ch'ing resumed her tale with the winter of 1951. Returning from Central China to Peking, she found the leaders deeply involved in promoting the Three Antis Movement (against corruption, waste, and bureaucratism) to improve the work style of the nation's growing corps of official personnel. With land and marriage reform behind her, she resumed the life of the capital where her recent work was recognized by her assignment to new posts. The most important was chief of the Secretariat of the General Office of the Party's Central Committee. But this administrative work, more grueling and pressured than she had expected, aggravated her illnesses. She began running a high fever again and an old pain in her liver flared up.

Yang Shang-k'un, director of the General Office of the Central Committee, and some others she knew to be ill-disposed toward her involvement in the exercise of power, recommended that in view of her failing health she should resign from her post as chief of the Secretariat and live instead in quiet retirement. She raised the question of these "recommendations" (from her tone of voice, obviously unwelcome) with Chairman Mao, who, as it turned out, concurred with the others' judgment. But through his mediation the leaders were given to understand that she should continue to work "on her own." Thus, near the close of 1951 she relinquished not only the position as chief but also her directorship of the Cinema Department of the Propaganda Department and her membership in the Sino-Soviet Friendship Association.* From that point on she would serve in one capacity only: as Chairman Mao's secretary. But even that job was taken from her when certain leaders decided in the name of the Party that she should go to Moscow for another medical cure. Anguished at the thought of leaving home again, she managed to delay departure until the winter of 1952. By then Chinese medical services were so disrupted by the Three Antis Movement's routing out of corruption and bureaucratism from the staffs of city hospitals that she had little choice but to be sent abroad for more sophisticated treatment.

Memory of her arrival in Moscow was shaped by recollection of her pathological calamities. Because of the severe pain in her liver, the Soviet doctors put her directly into surgery and explored the liver, but failed to relieve the fluid accumulated in the gall bladder. Under surgery specimens were withdrawn for diagnosis. Treatments were administered and she was sent south once again to Yalta where she languished (with no present recall of that luxurious setting or society). To reduce the constant fever she was given massive penicillin dosages, twenty million units each, the size and frequency of which only made her feel worse. The absolute lack of power and authority over her personal condition she deplored, but her protests were to no avail.

During the tedious Yalta winter she became increasingly homesick, but the doctors would not allow her to return to China. She assumed that they wanted to keep her there only because they were ashamed not to have cured her. Finally they sent her back to Moscow where she was installed in a fairly ordinary hospital. Later, fortunately, she was transferred to the grandiose Palace Hospital within the Kremlin itself. That, she added, was reserved for senior officials of their regime.†

* The extreme of political disengagement, for that membership was pro forma among prominent comrades — not an active political assignment.
On the subject of the Soviet Union, Chiang Ch'ing digressed, in the early 1950's when Sino-Soviet friendship and cultural exchange were dominant themes, the tallest building in Peking was the Sino-Soviet-Friendship Hall, which included a theater. Despite its name, the hall was built *entirely* with Chinese money. After breaking relations with the Soviet Union, the Chinese changed the name of the building to the Peking Exhibition Hall, and so it remains.
† On the staff of the Palace Hospital was one exceptionally capable woman doctor who assumed responsibility for her case. Among her experiments for the treatment of gall bladder and related liver disease was injection into the gall bladder of a preparation that made it possible for fluid to be extracted (an uncommon procedure in the West). In Chiang Ch'ing's case the fluid was black, about to turn to stones — a condition usually found in a man who was fat and forty, her doctor told her. Although she was around forty then, she was *not* fat, Chiang Ch'ing reported with laughter and indignation. Other tests, including one for tuberculosis (negative, and important to her because in the 1940's she, like millions of her countrymen, had suffered from TB), were conducted to determine the cause of her chronic fever. In reaction to the testing the esophageal plexus — she continued in her self-styled analysis — the gateway organ between the esophagus and the stomach, began to bleed from "portal tensions." Gradually the treatments she received at the Palace Hospital took effect, and her bile began to test colorless and clear.

The day before Stalin died (March 5, 1953), she heard news of his recent stroke over the radio at the suburban sanitarium to which she had been transferred. The other patients, mostly high-ranking officials anxious about the impact his death would have upon the structure of the leadership, and hence on their own careers, remained glued to their radios. The solemn announcement of his death threw everyone, inmates and staff, into a great emotional upheaval for days. During that crisis her two Russian bodyguards and the doctors and nurses assigned to her case showered her with political advice. The death of their leader was so momentous that Chairman Mao should join other world leaders in coming to Moscow to attend the funeral. That was none of *her* business, she told them; a decision of such gravity would be made by the Chinese Central Committee.

On the day of Stalin's funeral, Moscow's temperature fell below zero. The Chairman had not come, though he sent a message.* Still under intensive care, she kept vigil with the other patients at the sanitarium. From her window she watched the funeral procession wending its way to Red Square. The crowds lining the roadway were wildly upset, which astonished her. They acted "fanatical" as they jammed and crushed against each other. One of Stalin's failures, she remarked, sharing a judgment of the Chairman's, was not to have prepared the masses mentally for the day he died.

Among the world leaders who came to pay their last respects were Klement Gottwald, who led the February Seventh Revolution in Czechoslovakia, and the Polish leader Boleslaw Bierut. Both Gottwald and Bierut were in good health before they came to Moscow for Stalin's funeral, but died from exposure to the subzero weather. So did Palmiro Togliatti, chief of the Italian Communist Party, and William Z. Foster, chairman of the American Communist Party, she said, delivering a fantastic set of errors,† but clearly implying that Mao had escaped the mortal contagion of Stalin's last rites.

Although her second visit to the Soviet Union lasted nearly a year, from the winter of 1952 through the fall of 1953, it was almost impossible for her to learn anything about that country because all Chinese were cut off from the Soviet masses.‡ Cultural events were out of the question, and she had no other

---

* Personally delivered by Premier Chou En-lai, who led a delegation and served conspicuously as the only non-Soviet pallbearer. His dramatic appearance at Stalin's funeral ushered in a new era of Sino-Soviet brotherhood that peaked with Khrushchev's visit of September 1954, so Franz Schurmann has maintained (*The Logic of World Power*, New York, 1974, 247).

† Gottwald died on March 14, 1953, but the rest survived: Bierut to March 12, 1956, Foster to September 1, 1961, and Togliatti to August 21, 1964.

‡ Actually, the thousands of Chinese students, scientists, technicians, and others in the Soviet Union through the amicable decade that ended in the fall of 1960 enjoyed considerable cultural access. Although they normally lived together, they could buy tickets to the Bolshoi and other theaters and purchase from a wider selection of books and newspapers than they had at home.

entertainments. Her reading materials were restricted to documents delivered by China's diplomatic courier, and human contacts were confined primarily to Russian doctors, nurses, and bodyguards. These she judged to have been mostly "good people," although they seemed to be obsessed by money. One Russian nurse told her that the prominent writer and editor Konstantin Simonov was a "millionaire" [1] from royalties as well as from his salary as a government minister, and his wife adorned herself with fabulous jewels. That nurse also wore jewels, Chiang Ch'ing noted, and when asked about it, responded that jewelry should be judged not as having political meaning, but only as being a matter of habit. Someone had written letters to the Soviet magazine *Krokodil* to expose the gross materialism of the Simonov family, the nurse had learned. But that matter was both so sensitive and so widespread that *Krokodil* dared not publish the letters.

The importance of money among her few human contacts there was disconcerting. The government personnel she and her aides dealt with demanded gifts and tips as part of their regular service. Evidently consumer goods were in short supply. But, she said, the leaders were to blame because they offered no *ideological* incentives to deter people from "grasping."

Although relations between China and the Soviet Union were still amicable in 1953, she had already begun to feel an undercurrent of hostility. Since open contacts between Chinese and Russians were "officially frowned upon," she made a point of keeping to herself when she found the strength to venture out onto the streets. One day she was surprised to hear China's national anthem being played nearby. A Russian pedestrian, who could have had no idea who she really was, walked up to her in a friendly way and asked her to convey his greetings to Chairman Mao and other leading comrades of her country. No sooner had he uttered those words than a security agent grabbed him and dragged him off.

In its cultural ways, Chiang Ch'ing continued, the Soviet Union of the early 1950's was more pro-American and pro-European than most Chinese leaders then realized. People still seemed to be under the spell of the "aristocrats" who preferred speaking French to Russian, ostentatiously cultivated European habits, and were most conscious of personal appearance. The elaborate hospitals and sanitariums where she lived catered to such aristocrats, many of whom had become powerful officials of the new regime. With little better to do, some criticized her for looking too plain or for failing to keep up with the latest fashions.

Even the ordinary people were far more conscious of style and color than the people of China. One day when she was gazing down onto the streets from her hospital window, she noticed a woman wearing a bright green hat, which did not match her other clothes, and a number of men also sporting green hats.

Others were outfitted in all-green costumes. She remarked on this pervasive color to some other inmates of the hospital. "Don't you know that green is this year's color?" one replied archly. Women of all sorts were wearing cosmetics, which was repugnant to her because it was not revolutionary. But she would never comment on that, she added.

Eventually some other patients noticed that she was not attired in the standard hospital gown; hers was of a slightly different cut and color, actually the same shade of green she had observed on people in the street. So she told them that the gown she wore was custom-made on the personal orders of Stalin. It had come to his attention that the gowns regularly issued by the hospital were too big for her, since she was far slighter than the average Russian. Those he specially ordered for her were made up in his favorite shade of green. Not only did the others envy the deep green, but they also envied her slimness, she said with a smile.

She was still languishing in the Soviet Union when the Chairman introduced to the Politburo on the fifteenth of June, 1953, the "general line for the transitional period" (the First Five-Year Plan in the transition to socialism), which she heard about through diplomatic correspondence. Yet she was not allowed to return to China until the late fall. After almost an entire year, the famed Soviet doctors had not really cured her. In Peking she was still plagued by such acute abdominal pains that she could not walk, and as her Chinese doctors discovered (and the Soviet experts had overlooked), her white blood cell count was abnormally high. New tests showed that the gall bladder, liver, and kidneys were still diseased.

As Chiang Ch'ing ran on about these and other aspects of her medical history,* she checked out details with one or both of the doctors seated in the back of the room. They agreed with her, though sometimes they elaborated upon her descriptions. Her liver was enlarged by two fingers' breadth beneath the rib cage, she went on, a condition relieved partially by drawing off excess abdominal fluids. The inflammation of the liver ducts was reduced by a special diet. Her formidable medical history taught her that certain pathological condi-

* That high consciousness of illness can be class-linked was observed by Mao Tse-tung, who managed to keep the upper hand and relative silence on his many ailments. At a "Talk on Health Services" on January 24, 1964, he said: "China's health service emulates that of the Soviet Union, and I cannot completely accept what health doctors say. . . . I only follow half of what the doctor says and expect him to follow me in the other half. If we abide by everything the doctor says sicknesses will multiply and life will be impossible. I have never before heard of so much high blood pressure and liver infections. If a person doesn't exercise but only eats well, dresses well, lives comfortably, and drives wherever he goes, he will be beset with a lot of illnesses. Excessive attention to food, clothing, housing, and means of transportation are the four underlying causes of illness among high-level cadres" (*Miscellany of Mao Tse-tung Thought, 1949–1968*, 2: 325).

tions incurable by medicine can be cured by diet. With pleasure and authority she delivered more homespun advice.

ii

The period from the winter of 1953 through 1958 was the most difficult of her life, she reflected, for she was bedridden most of the time. Periods of acute illness alternated with gradual improvement. Of her two other medical journeys to the Soviet Union during that five-year span she spoke later.

In the winter of 1953 her "office" was her bedroom at Chung-nan-hai, her desk a reclining bed protected by a quilt against the winter chill. Here she accomplished more in the next few months than in the entire previous year. She read widely, focusing upon "the main political struggle between ourselves and the class enemy"; that is to say, "between the socialists and the bourgeoisie." From the incoming mail, new books, and her own library, she selected materials for the Chairman to read and pointed out to him what she considered to be the salient issues. While he sat at her bedside she read newspapers and telegrams to him and kept him generally abreast of events. She also prepared reports of her own and investigated problems with which she was still only vaguely familiar.

She was still bedridden in February 1954 when certain regional disturbances which for some time had been under secret investigation broke out into the open. At the Fourth Plenary Session of the Party's Seventh Central Committee, held from the sixth to the tenth of February, 1954, Kao Kang and Jao Shu-shih (who had dominated the Northeast and East China Bureaus respectively since Liberation) were formally exposed as constituting an anti-Party clique. During the Plenary Session a resolution was passed to strengthen the unity of the Party. Only recently, Chiang Ch'ing added, she and Mao discovered that Lin Piao formerly belonged to the Kao–Jao clique. Although Lin was not exposed at that time, they now had *proof* of his connection.

That same February the writer Hu Feng published a petition of over 300,000 characters against the Communist Party. Its appearance triggered a "frenzied attack" from all quarters against the Party. Letters from Ah Lung, Lu Ling, and Shu Wu, members of Hu Feng's "counterrevolutionary clique," launched fierce ideological battles. Each diatribe she devoured as soon as it came out, but lingering illness kept her from reading all the Chairman's commentaries on them. In the months following, the Chairman worked up his commentaries into essays that served as the ammunition in the counterattack he launched in May and June of 1955.

Although Chiang Ch'ing did not delve into the substance of Hu Feng's complaint, it deserves brief comment, for the issues were at the heart of the perennial conflict between writers and rulers in the People's Republic. Born in Hupeh in 1903, Hu Feng's thirst for modernity carried him to Japan in the late 1920's and early 1930's. As of 1934 he worked with the League of Left-Wing Writers in Shanghai where he joined Lu Hsun's circle. Apparently never a Communist Party member, he was nevertheless a self-proclaimed Marxist who took the unorthodox view that the artist's "subjective struggling spirit" was more valuable to the creative process than centrally programmed formulas for expressing "class struggle." Hu's conflict with Mao dated from the Yenan Forum of 1942, where he spoke up for the group of Shanghai writers (Ting Ling, Hsiao Chün, the poet Ai Ch'ing, et al.) who insisted upon a measure of intellectual independence from Party-determined orthodoxy in culture. In the early 1950's he sustained close contacts with influential people in Shanghai publishing circles. Then in July 1954 (perhaps the occasion Chiang Ch'ing described as the spring of 1954), a period of calm in the Party's relation to the intellectual community, he submitted a long report to the Central Committee in which he blamed China's present intellectual sterility on dogmatic leadership and on "scholastic Marxism," by which he meant that only the Party's chosen few explicated Marxian theory. Certainly, he was not opposed to the Party's reform of a few wayward individuals; he only deplored brutal repression of all creative spirits.

The implications of the case laid by Hu Feng before the nation were more profound than the Party dared acknowledge in its rebuttal. The problems he raised would smolder, flaring again in future years. Was the Party dealing with the superstructure (books and ideas) the same way it dealt with the management of the economic base (land and labor)? Would gifted writers, even those ardent socialists of the old regime, be treated like rich landlords — labeled "class enemies" and mowed down? Was Mao's rule so totalistic as to deny writers the right to plow fields of the mind and cultivate ideas as they saw fit? Or should fields of literature, like fields of soil, be chopped up and parceled out to workers, peasants, and soldiers to till on their own, producing (if ideas grew at all) from the ground up?

Beginning in January 1955, the condemnation of Hu Feng, China's symbol of artistic integrity who had counterparts in the Soviet Union, and East Europe, was absolute and unmitigated.* Major writers who had come into their own before Liberation, among them Pa Chin, Lao She, Ai Ch'ing, and Kuo Mo-jo, were marshaled by the Party to turn against their erstwhile col-

---

* Hsiao Mu of Shanghai's Revolutionary Committee represented Hu Feng to me in the conventional Party clichés. In his words, "Hu Feng was crafty. For years he pretended to respect Chairman Mao's 'Yenan Talks,' but that respect was false worship. In fact, he finally came out and slandered the Chairman's ideas. He just wrapped his whip in rubber and used that to beat the CCP."

league Hu Feng by publishing letters and essays defaming him in the *People's Daily*. Yet "counterrevolutionary," the charge laid against him, did indeed seem excessive in the absence of evidence that he had attacked Marxism in principle or that he sought to subvert the regime. His publicized self-criticism of May 1955, which had been solicited by the Party, was then rejected. The next month a collection of private correspondence between Hu Feng and friends was seized and published, along with the official criticisms, in the *People's Daily* and elsewhere. The ensuing purge of intellectuals who had displayed a similar independence of mind has been called a "reign of terror." [2]

Chiang Ch'ing's reference to these humiliating trials of men of letters — persons she idolized in her youth — was ideologically orthodox, devoid of humanitarian or philosophical sensibility. Although she did not express it directly, the fundamental issue concerning her and Mao was preservation of power. What she said was that these literary challenges to the Chairman's guidance in the arts coincided with the stubbornness of the Soviet-siding warlords Kao Kang and Jao Shu-shih and worsening relations with the Soviet Union.

That falling-out with the Soviets she grasped less in terms of policymaking, from which she was excluded in 1954 and 1955, than of abuse of protocol and cantankerousness among men on top. When well enough to be about, she carefully observed the Russian chiefs shuttling back and forth for advantage and great occasion, visitations that became increasingly unfriendly and fruitless.

Khrushchev (who never received her in his country) visited China three times, she said. The purpose of the first visit, which lasted from September 29 to October 2, 1954, was to celebrate the fifth anniversary of the founding of the Chinese People's Republic. The second, from July 30 to August 3, 1958, met no special occasion that she could recall. The ostensible point of the last visit, from September 30 to October 4, 1959, was the celebration of the tenth anniversary of the Chinese People's Republic. But his presence there was unfortunate.

Her only brush with him was in 1954, since sickness kept her from seeing him on the second and third trips. She remembered standing among the leaders on the rostrum of the Gate of Heavenly Peace to review the parades, demonstrations, and fireworks that marked the state's fifth anniversary. Chou En-lai, always alert to proprieties, made a move to introduce Chiang Ch'ing to Khrushchev. Seeing what was about to happen, Chairman Mao stood up, walked over to Chiang Ch'ing (almost never did they appear publicly side by side), and brusquely escorted her away, leading her down one of the two alleys that ran along the sides of the rostrum.* There the two of them enjoyed the fireworks together, out of the public view. The memory she cherished.

---

* The mockery of that play of leaders before the Chinese masses was not missed by Khrushchev, who later revealed: "I remember that when I came back from China in 1954 I told my comrades,

And the gesture was significant, she explained. The Chairman's decision not to have her introduced showed that as early as 1954 he despised Khrushchev, who had been crude toward them. They knew that behind their backs he ridiculed them, calling them the "patriotic Party" and the "children's Party." In September 1959 Khrushchev went to the United States, where he visited the United Nations. At a formal session he removed his shoe and made a vulgar scene. Then he came to China and flaunted similar behavior. At a banquet they gave for him he denounced them as "cocks fond of fighting," and indulged in other unseemly conduct by which they best remember him.

While she continued her slow convalescence in the fall of 1954, major changes occurred within their own leadership. At the First National People's Congress of the People's Republic of China on September 15, 1954, Chairman Mao made the opening speech in which he spoke of the Party as the core and main force of the state, and Marxism-Leninism as the theoretical basis. On that occasion he was elected Chairman of the People's Republic (and the PRC's first constitution was adopted).

Five years after the adoption of the Agrarian Reform Law of 1950, the Chairman returned to the overwhelming problems of the countryside, sensing that the time was ripe to impose a new organizational model, the cooperative. That summer he initiated the process of persuading the rural people to shift from semisocialist to fully socialist cooperatives, where each member's share was determined solely by his own labor. To arouse mass enthusiasm for another arduous change, he had first to teach the local leaders how the transformation could be brought about. On July 31, 1955, he addressed a meeting of secretaries of provincial, prefectural, and municipal Party committees on the manifold problems of setting up such cooperatives. The opposition he encountered there, which he dubbed Right Opportunism, was led by Liu Shao-ch'i. The Chairman's defiance of Liu and his followers on that occasion would have far-reaching consequences.*

'Conflict with China is inevitable.' I came to this conclusion on the basis of various remarks Mao had made. During my visit to Peking, the atmosphere was typically Oriental. Everyone was unbelievably courteous and ingratiating, but I saw through their hypocrisy. After I had arrived, Mao and I embraced each other warmly and kissed each other on both cheeks. We used to lie around a swimming pool in Peking, chatting like the best of friends about all kinds of things. But it was all too sickeningly sweet. The atmosphere was nauseating. In addition, some of the things Mao said put me on my guard. I was never exactly sure that I understood what he meant. I thought at the time that it must have been because of some special traits in the Chinese character and the Chinese way of thinking" (Nikita S. Khrushchev, *Khrushchev Remembers*, Boston, 1970, 466).

* In Mao's words, "A new upsurge in the socialist mass movement is imminent throughout the countryside. But some of our comrades are tottering along like a woman with bound feet and constantly complaining, 'You're going too fast.' Excessive criticism, inappropriate complaints, endless anxiety, and the erection of countless taboos — they believe this is the proper way to guide the socialist mass movement in the rural areas. . . .

"The high tide of socialist transformation in the countryside, the high tide of cooperation, has already reached some places and will soon sweep over the whole country. It is a vast socialist revolu-

To get the people on his side for the cooperative movement, in September 1955 * Mao arranged for the preparation of a book he called *Socialist Upsurge in China's Countryside.*[3] He wrote the preface and the notes to well over one hundred of the articles in the original three-volume edition. The articles themselves were solicited from people all over the country who were engaged in successive stages of the cooperative movement, which was gathering momentum. At an enlarged meeting of the Sixth Plenary Session of the Seventh Central Committee held from October 4 to 11, 1955, the Chairman distributed copies of articles already submitted to representatives from provincial, municipal, and regional Party committees, requested comment, and asked that more articles be contributed.

As they came in, the Chairman rewrote the preface in late December and gave it final form. The book's lead article, "The Party Secretary Takes the Lead and All the Party Members Help Run the Co-op," is one he liked particularly, she said. In the preface he commended the Wang Kuo-fan cooperative, originally a "Paupers" Co-op of Tsun-hua county, Hopeh, for the frugality demonstrated in its organization and production techniques over a three-year period.

Socialist Upsurge in China's Countryside appeared at a crucial point for the national leadership and for economic planning, and should be recognized as evidence of the "struggle between the two lines." What provoked the Chairman to compile such a book? The conspiratorial activities of Kao Kang and Jao Shu-shih, whose clique had been exposed in February 1954, Chiang Ch'ing explained. Yet Kao and Jao did not stand alone. Supporting them were the Soviet revisionists; they were, in fact, collaborators. Some worked at the front, others secretly behind the lines. Kao Kang's ambition was to become chairman of the Council of Ministers — a "Soviet-style institution."[4]

On January 25, 1956, at a meeting of the Supreme State Conference of the State Council, the Chairman presented the fourteen-point program for national agricultural production for the years 1956 and 1957. On April 5, 1956, the *People's Daily* carried his editorial "On the Historical Experience of the Dictatorship of the Proletariat," and on December 29, 1956, it carried another editorial under the same title — both well known, she said.† At an enlarged meeting of the Politburo, between the twenty-fifth and the twenty-eighth of April, 1958,

tionary movement involving a rural population of more than 500 million, and it has great and worldwide significance. . ." (*On the Question of Agricultural Cooperation*, Peking, 1956, 1).

* That same month Chiang Ch'ing wrote an article titled "Do the People Get Enough to Eat from Grain Ration?" published in *Shih-shih shou-ts'e* [Current events] 17 (Sept. 10, 1955); ECMM 19 (Dec. 19, 1955): 23–25. Her article promotes grain rationing in the urban areas where there was evident resistance to the radical transformation of the organization of rural production. Her detailed analysis, helped by figures, shows how the grain ration should be based on individual needs — age, sex, body type, energy expenditure, etc.

† This two-part editorial, which appeared as a pamphlet in English (Peking, 1956), was a reaction to Khrushchev's disclosure in February of Stalin's "crimes" and repudiation of his "cult of the individual," and a reflection on problems of leadership and the revolution's future. By implication

Chairman Mao spoke "On the Ten Great Relationships" * fundamental to China's governance.

In 1956 cultural affairs, which Peking wanted to control alone, suddenly assumed global dimensions. Would news of anti-Party challengers by intellectuals of East Europe undermine the CCP's supremacy in China? To blunt the danger the Chairman called a meeting of the Supreme State Conference of the State Council (on May 2, 1956) and issued the directive, "Let a Hundred Flowers Bloom, Let a Hundred Schools of Thought Contend" (a bid for open expression, including freedom to criticize the Party). At the national Eighth Party Congress held from the fifteenth to the twentieth of September in Peking his opening speech signaled that the "Hundred Flowers" directive should begin a movement.† Thereupon, she said, "the class enemies at home began to chime in with the Soviet revisionists." The Polish and Hungarian incidents of 1956 had inspired class enemies at home to expound all sorts of Western fallacies and counterrevolutionary opinions.[5] Evidence abounded in essays, novels, and other literary works rapidly published during the year of the Hundred Flowers Campaign. Among the most pernicious pieces were Ch'in Ch'ao-yang's essay "Realism, The Broad Way" and Wang Meng's story "A Young Newcomer in the Organization Department." [6] In the winter of 1956 Chung Tien-fei's article "Gongs and Drums in the Film Industry" (pointing out the socialist cinema's lack of box office value) was published under his pseudonym Chu Chu-chu, stirring up angry rebuttal.[7] Then in February 1957 the renowned sociologist Fei Hsiao-t'ung released his essay "The Early Spring of the Intellectuals." [8]

These and other sinister pieces were spewed out in the "all-around frenzied attack against the Party in March of 1957." Assaults by intellectuals flared on posters all over the cities. The Chairman summarily responded with his deliv-

---

Mao was defending himself against a successor who would devastate his own record and the popular cult — the streak of old-fashioned idolatry — that protected it.

* Circulated among the leaders though never officially published, this is a dialectical analysis of ten fundamental social dichotomies, such as the urban-rural, industrial-agricultural, central-regional. While stressing the need for maintaining balance between opposing elements, Mao now leaned toward agrarianism, decentralization, and local initiative — thus correcting what he saw as the errors of his First Five-Year Plan, which followed the Soviet model of political centralization, bureaucratism, and industrial emphasis. The text appears in Stuart Schram, ed., *Chairman Mao Talks to the People: Talks and Letters, 1956–1971* (New York, 1974), 61–83.

† At the end of the month Lu Ting-i, chief of the Propaganda Department, controller of publications, and an authority on literature and the arts, transformed Mao's bid for public discussion into a national campaign. Lu Ting-i publicly followed Mao in acknowledging that both science and the arts were stagnating in China and that new initiatives must be taken — without forgetting, of course, that literature, art, and scientific thought inexorably are weapons of class struggle. Chou Yang, second in command in the Ministry of Culture, facilitated implementing the exposure and subsequent purge of critics among literary talents and other professionals. But the past survives at the mercy of the present: Chiang Ch'ing overlooked the support of Lu and Chou. Her personal animosity toward them and her suspicion of their other ideological commitments led to their downfall during the Cultural Revolution a decade later.

ery to the Supreme State Conference of the State Council of "On the Correct Handling of Contradictions among the People," a speech published as an essay of the same title on June 18, 1957. Its purpose was to sharpen class analysis and to prepare for the rectification of those intellectuals who in recent months had flaunted bourgeois resistance to socialism and proletarian dictatorship.

On March 12, 1957, the Chairman spoke at the National Propaganda Conference. What he said there was later published in pamphlet form. Then, after the bourgeois rightists launched their treacherous attacks on the Party, the Rectification (Anti-Rightist) Campaign against them was formally announced by the Party's Central Committee on April 27, 1957. In May the Chairman issued the directive, "Things Are Changing." The subject of future "socialist education" was introduced in a speech of the eighth of June. That day and on the tenth, the *People's Daily* published the Chairman's editorials under the title "What Is This For?" Those editorials, beginning the counterattack against the rightists, were followed by another essay by the Chairman called "Things are Picking Up," which spread the counterattack all over the country.

The Rectification Campaign should also be seen in the international context, she continued, with evident agitation. Its causes lay not in China alone but also in the Polish and Hungarian incidents that had shaken the socialist world the year before. The relation between the Rectification Campaign and the Polish and Hungarian incidents * was explained to thousands by Premier Chou's report of June 26 at the fourth session of the National People's Congress. There he refuted the shameless fallacies of some foreign socialist parties that had been implicated in the rebellion by intellectuals against Party authority. This report was followed by the Chairman's treatment of the major offending parties *within* China. On July 1, 1957, he published an article in the *People's Daily* called "The Bourgeois Orientation of *Wen-hui-pao* [Literary Gazette] Should Be Criticized!" †

After the worst was over Chiang Ch'ing and the Chairman went to Nanking to convene meetings, but the midsummer heat was so devastating that they stayed only a short time, then moved north to Tsingtao. Its weather was also

---

* Mao explained bluntly on January 18, 1961, "After the events in Hungary in 1956, by means of free expression of opinion we got to the bottom of things and purged several hundred thousand rightists; we also did a purge of the collectives in the countryside, but we did not anticipate the landlord restoration," "Speech at the Ninth Plenum of the Eighth CCP Central Committee," *Miscellany of Mao Tse-tung Thought*, 2: 243).

† Dissatisfied by the *Literary Gazette*'s self-criticism in June, Mao expressed himself in the mixed metaphors of the Hundred Flowers Campaign. Its purpose, he explained, was "to let the evil spirits and demons of all kinds 'contend freely' and let the poisonous weeds gain a luxuriant growth so that the people will be startled at such things in the world and will take action to wipe out these low scamps. . . . We told the enemy beforehand: demons can be wiped out only when they are let out of the cage and poisonous weeds can be got rid of only when they are let come out of the soil. Do peasants not weed several times a year?" (SCMP 1957 [July 11, 1957]: 20).

terrible. Everyone, including her, caught cold. Worried about her health, the Chairman insisted that she return to Peking, as she did.

Before he left Tsingtao the Chairman summed up the situation as of the summer of 1957, presented a rationale for the Anti-Rightist Campaign, and drew up a strategy for transforming it into a national movement. What she called a "socialist education campaign" was formulated on the eighth of August by the Central Committee. Five days later the campaign, along with the Rectification Campaign, was launched throughout the nation.

Mass reaction was swift. The people, determined to assert themselves, pasted up huge posters on walls where they worked or walked. The presss was dominated by debates over the significance of what the Chairman had said. As the arguments that had first flared in the city spread to the countryside, "the revolutionary situation was excellent."

By the end of 1957 the Chairman for the first time had gained the upper hand over the nation's literary life. But that did not include films, which continued to be produced in the spirit of the 1930's, even though those historical conditions were remote and better forgotten. Among the films she found most aggravating (though the people loved them) were Hsia Yen's *The Lin Family Shop* (1959) and Ko Ling's *Nightless City* (1958).* Not until the Cultural Revolution, however, would she manage to settle final accounts against their makers. She deplored those films because "politically they sought to weaken the dictatorship of the proletariat by praising the class enemy, economically they sought to establish capitalist enterprise, and agriculturally they strove to undermine the collectives by restoring the individual economy."

---

* *The Lin Family Shop* was based on a short story written in 1932 by Mao Tun (Shen Yen-ping), a leftist author unconstrained by Communist Party orthodoxy in the arts. His story, which centers on Japan's surprise attack on Shanghai of January 28, 1932, is about Lin, a shop owner whose patriotic instincts are stronger than his wish to subscribe to a theory of class struggle. For translating that story into film Hsia Yen was charged with exhibiting capitalist class and counterrevolutionary sympathies and failing to "reflect the lives of workers, peasants, and soldiers." Speaking in his own defense (and perhaps also for a generation of autonomous leftist writers and filmmakers, now suppressed), Hsia Yen declared that the films celebrating workers, peasants, and soldiers were poor artistically and lacked psychological insight, sophisticated plot, and believable characterization; they had no climax or suspense. Formal diatribes against *The Lin Family Shop* were not published until the peak of the Cultural Revolution, in JMJP, May 29, 1965; June 9, 1965; and June 13, 1965.

Nightless City was originally a play by Ko Ling (Kao Chi-ling), also a scriptwriter and critic since the early 1930's. Set in a Shanghai textile factory and covering a twenty-year period, his film was vilified during the Cultural Revolution for featuring a "capitalist hero" and the principle of "national salvation through industry," aspects that allegedly linked the film with the condemned Liu Shao-ch'i and his revisionist associates (Leyda, *Dianying*, 342).

iii

While everyone's attention was riveted upon the pursuit of dissidents, Chiang Ch'ing suffered another physical relapse, this one wholly incapacitating. Her fever ran high and constant. Her weight dropped rapidly, leaving her shockingly thin. All her doctors were summoned to examine her. The gynecologist diagnosed cervical cancer.

In 1955, she recalled, she had been sent back to the Soviet Union for a medical checkup that proved ineffectual, for in those years Soviet doctors did not believe in "cell theory." [9] Consequently, the Soviet doctors rejected the diagnoses made by the Chinese before she went. Not until 1956 did her Chinese doctors notice that deformed cells were about to break through the membrane of the cervix. In their judgment two methods of treatment were possible, surgery or radiation therapy. Since her previous surgery for liver disease had caused abdominal adhesions that were still painful, she could not tolerate further surgical intervention. That left only radiation therapy, which was carried out by using both radium implants and cobalt 60. The radium treatments she found too agonizing, and the cobalt 60, which was stronger, intolerable. Since she could not endure their treatment, her doctors were at a loss to save her. So they recommended that she return to Moscow and let the Russian doctors take over once again. Although she was desperately ill, she knew, she could not accept the idea of being away from China again, not knowing what would happen in her absence. Fiercely she protested their decision. But others who knew nothing about medicine intervened and pressured her to leave immediately. For the first time Chairman Mao and the Central Committee arranged for a woman gynecologist to accompany her abroad. Defenseless against their collective resolve, she capitulated and made a fourth Russian journey.

She remembered arriving in Moscow, completely enervated, running a constant fever. She knew that she had a dread disease and that prospects for recovery were dim. When her condition was evaluated upon admission to the hospital, the Soviet doctors said they could not accept her because her white blood cell count was down to three thousand, a side effect of radiation therapy, leaving her resistance to infection perilously low. Frantic, she, her gynecologist, and their aides told the doctors that so long as they had sickbeds in their hospital they were *obliged* to admit her. They yielded, and for the first time allowed her to keep the Chinese medical expert at ·her side. To neutralize the cervical cancer they "overdosed" her with cobalt 60, she charged. She lost her senses and was certain that her bone marrow was damaged. Next they gave her blood transfusions, but each transfusion drove her fever still higher, whereupon the whole program of treatment was called to a halt.

Having reached a standstill, the Soviet doctors decided that the fresh air of

Moscow's suburbs would be more salubrious than the inner city. So they sent her off to a suburban sanitarium, one where they obviously would no longer be responsible for her.

That winter was bitterly cold and the treatment violent. The sanitarium's medical personnel tried to "cure" her by plunging her into air twenty degrees below zero. Instantly, beads of perspiration sprang from all the pores of her body, and her eyesight went awry: all images were blurred and distorted. Her legs were so wobbly that she could not stand unsupported. To "temper herself" she tried to exercise, however feebly. But willpower alone could not arrest extreme physical degeneration. In her recollections the nightmarish winter changed to spring and spring to summer. After giving her desultory attention for a long time, her doctors solemnly announced that she was suffering from "rickets." With a sudden burst of laughter she recalled that in northern Shensi in the 1930's and 1940's many comrades suffered from what they called "rickets," a condition they thought was caused by lack of iodine and calcium. But at this time the real motive for diagnosing rickets was to find an excuse to get her off their hands and return her to the city hospital.

The city doctors now released upon her their most powerful weapons against cancer. First one, then a second and a third round of cobalt treatment. The massive dosages so weakened her system that she needed a constant oxygen supply. During the fourth episode under an oxygen mask she fell into a coma. How vividly she recalled the fitful returns to consciousness, the terrifying sensations of breath being stifled, the imminence of death.

As soon as she could muster up the energy, she issued two demands: first, quit the cobalt treatment, and second, send her home. Demanding was one thing, but getting action was another. The medical profession in the Soviet Union was strictly ranked, which meant that getting a doctor or medical professor to assume responsibility for a case on his own authority without the sanction of his superiors was nearly impossible. She had lapsed into another coma before a medical professor could be found to take charge of her case at that point. As she regained consciousness under an oxygen mask, dizzy and drenched with perspiration, she told them that she was desperate to go home, but no one listened to her. Too weak to eat, she continued to lose ground. The city doctors, chagrined by their manifest ineffectiveness, ordered her back to the suburban sanitarium beyond their jurisdiction.*

Throughout those months Chairman Mao knew that more than anything

---

* The medical profession in the Soviet Union was already a subject of public scandal. Fear of "murderers in white coats" who held the fate of Soviet leaders under their scalpels was widespread. On January 13, 1953, *Pravda* circulated stories of "miserable spies and assassins masquerading as professors of medicine." And Stalin's death has been reconstructed in terms of a "doctors' plot." Of such politico-medical vulnerabilities Chiang Ch'ing, who could have been so easily used in a power play by any Soviet leader, surely was not unaware.

she wanted to come home, she said passionately. Yet he was also apprised of the details of the medical report prepared by the Soviet doctors. When Premier Chou was sent to Moscow to negotiate with the government,[10] he came to see her at the hospital. It was he who conveyed the Chairman's instruction that she remain in Moscow until she was clearly on the way to recovery. While the Premier was in the hospital he spoke with the medical personnel and studied the reports on her case in order to determine for himself just what her situation was. When the picture of the diagnosis and the treatment began to emerge, he grew furious at the Soviet doctors for what they were doing and not doing. Of course the Premier was there mainly to negotiate with Khrushchev, Chiang Ch'ing reasoned. Those drawn-out and tedious discussions distorted his general outlook.

Still she was overjoyed to see the Premier because she was trying as best she could on her own to keep up with the political situation at home and abroad. There was much he could tell her. But in his view there was only one kind of medicine — diversion. One day he brought along to her bedside Mrs. Borodin* and Ch-eng Yen-ch'iu, the famous traditional opera singer (and specialist in female roles) who insisted upon visiting her.[11] Some others joined them and stayed for quite a while, though the Premier was not always there because he was dealing with Khrushchev. To amuse her, Ch'eng Yen-ch'iu concocted pantomimes showing that members of their Party organization in China followed one of the two styles of performance. Either they followed the orthodox school of Mei Lan-fang (1893–1961, a still more famous specialist in female roles in traditional opera) or they followed his, the Ch'eng Yen-ch'iu, style, which was innovative (within the tradition of female impersonation).

They exchanged jokes about people and politics they knew intimately deep into the evening until the others got hungry. They left to dine elsewhere because the hospital had not provided her with food suitable for guests. Still later that evening Premier Chou with other companions arrived raging against Khrushchev for his obduracy in negotiation. Khrushchev was impervious to persuasion, he despaired. How embarrassed she was because she had nothing to offer them either. Ordinary Russian fare, the coarse bread, fish, and eggs dispensed to her room, was inadequate for entertaining, she thought. The Premier did not care, and did his best to amuse her. Actually, he had brought along a letter from his wife, Teng Ying-ch'ao, but, Chiang Ch'ing remembered, he forgot to give it to her. Unwittingly, he took it with him all the way to India, and then back to China before he remembered it.

As for Ch'eng Yen-ch'iu, an innovative actor whom she might have used in

---

* The widow of Mikhail Borodin, a Comintern representative who accepted Sun Yat-sen's invitation to vist China in 1923, and remained as political adviser to the Central Executive Committee of the KMT from 1923 to 1927. In 1951 he died in prison in the Soviet Union.

later years, she said that she had long tried to get the Premier and the Chairman to protect him against their common enemies. When he was first attacked (in the late 1950's), the Premier tried to protect him in various ways, but ultimately failed. In 1958 Ch'eng was "persecuted to death" by the Four Villains. Why should they persecute him? Because his acting style was *new*, while that of his rival, Mei Lan-fang, was *orthodox*.

The longer she remained in the Soviet Union, the more she deteriorated, she said. To correct her blood count she was given additional platelets through transfusion. Before the struggle against cancer began, her blood count was quite good, at 240,000, which was its present level. But in the course of radiation therapy it dropped to 70,000. After the transfusions she felt strangely cold, then numb, and discovered that she could not move half her body, a semiparalysis that terrified her Soviet doctors. Her skull felt about to burst — the pain was excruciating. Fever flared. She begged repeatedly to return to China. Finally they let her go. On the return flight subcutaneous bleeding broke out all over her body.

iv

With the detachment acquired by time, she made some glancing remarks about foreign affairs. China was not a rich nation, she began, yet it gave its limited funds to the support of oppressed nations and oppressed peoples. The Chairman often told his countrymen that they must teach the youth who will eventually lead the country two things: "Don't act like munitions merchants," and "Don't force repayment." The leaders still followed those precepts. They should support the oppressed nation and people of North Vietnam, they believed, because they were fighting *at the front*. If the North Vietnamese did not fight, then the enemy would attack the Chinese. It was the same in Korea.

Khrushchev's behavior was quite something, she declared in a voice full of revulsion. In September of 1955 Adenauer of West Germany visited the Soviet Union. Khrushchev told him then that the biggest question on the international scene was the "yellow peril," as he called the Chinese, and asked the West Germans to help him *deal with China*. In the course of the *Chinese* revolution, she continued, the Soviets did not give them much help. During the Korean War, Stalin lent them three hundred million American dollars at considerable interest. After Khrushchev came to power and was imperiled by the Polish and Hungarian incidents of 1956, the Chinese flew to his aid. They also supplied him with numerous essays and documents on the historical experience of proletarian nations.

272 ◇ Behind the Scenes

Khrushchev's visit to China in the fall of 1959, ostensibly to celebrate National Day on the first of October, was tedious and painful. On that occasion Khrushchev announced he would withdraw all his experts from China and pressed the Chinese to pay all their debts. His statement came as a shock, for the late 1950's were most difficult for them in all areas of endeavor. Still, Khrushchev expected them to kowtow before him! He could not understand that after the Soviets withdrew their experts (some thirteen hundred in July 1960) the Chinese would stand up and tighten their belts. Moreover, as the Soviets pulled. out their men and apparatus, they did not exchange goods at an equal value. They told the Chinese they wanted to set up a long-range broadcast station in China. Had they won that argument they would have been able to control China's *entire* communications system. They also offered to establish a joint fleet that would have enabled them to dominate all of China's waters, coastal and inland. As a matter of fact, the Chairman agreed to the last proposal, but *only* on the condition that the Chinese *pay* for such a system. Chairman Mao told Khrushchev, "This is a matter of principle: otherwise you'll take everything away." *

Khrushchev was a "big fool," she said. "We will go to the mountains," the Chairman once remarked to him philosophically in response to their disaffection. Stupidly, Khrushchev failed to understand what he meant. Nor was Khrushchev above waging "guerrilla warfare" against his enemy.†

While the Soviets still had access to China, they plundered many rare and precious minerals, among them titanium. That she discovered during her first trip to Hainan Island off China's southern coast to carry out investigations relating to her cultural work.‡ There she interviewed two former fighters of the Japanese war period and took photographs to clarify the record of military maneuvers carried out under the Japanese occupation of 1939. The tropical island turned out to be far more lush and beautiful than she could have imagined. The Sung dynasty poet Su Tung-p'o also found it extraordinary. He and other romantics after him called it "the end of the world" (*shih-mo*).

---

* Compare this account with Khrushchev's recollection: "This was our last trip to China. It was in 1959. Our discussions were friendly but without concrete results. Among the things discussed was the subject of the radio station. I said, 'Comrade Mao Tse-tung, we will give you the money to build the station. It doesn't matter to us to whom the station belongs, as long as we can use it to keep in radio contact with our submarines. We would even be willing to give the station to you, but we'd like to have it built as soon as possible. Our fleet is now operating in the Pacific Ocean, and our main base is in Vladivostok. Comrade Mao Tse-tung, couldn't we come to some sort of agreement so that our submarines might have a base in your country for refueling, repairs, shore leaves, and so on?'

" 'For the last time, *no*, and I don't want to hear anything more about it' " (*Khrushchev Remembers*, 472). The joint-fleet deal was never made.

† She meant surreptitiously stirring up trouble on Chinese soil, or conspiring with Mao's detractors, as he had presumably with Kao Kang and Jao Shu-shih, and would with P'eng Te-huai.

‡ This was in 1964, to gather background information for the model revolutionary ballet *The Red Detachment of Women*, which is set on Hainan Island.

One day when she was walking around some barely inhabited parts of the island photographing scenery she tumbled into a heap of gray, floury material. Embarrassed, she stood up, dusted herself off, and asked her guides to identify the strange substance. "Titanium," they replied. That was obviously a valuable mineral, so she questioned them. Not long ago, some islanders told her, a group of Russians came there declaring to lay claim to the titanium. How did the islanders respond? They stood their ground, refusing absolutely to yield to Soviet demands.* Pursuing the matter further, Chiang Ch'ing discovered that Hainan Island has extensive titanium resources.

Brezhnev she was less interested in. His ideas were also shot through with "fallacies," she remarked brusquely. His "Doctrine of Limited Sovereignty," which could also be called "Social Imperialism," meant only the right to ride roughshod over others. The Soviets assumed that they constitute the patriotic party, while all others are merely children's parties. Was this Marxism? Could this theory be found in the words of Marx and Lenin? Brezhnev was the "biggest clown in the world!" Consequently, the Chinese did not promise the Russians any assistance. Chairman Mao told his people to assist others who assist them. Both the United States government and the revisionist Soviet government served the interests of the munitions industries in their countries. Without warfare, how could the munitions industries make profits?

That aspect of international relations reminded her of a movie she once saw about the Sino-Indian boundary war (of October 1962). The story concerned an Indian soldier who saved some money for return to his home in India after the war was over. Somehow the money is lost in the thick of battle, and he bursts into tears. A Chinese soldier finds the money and returns it to him. The Indian is ecstatic.

Now Khrushchev, she continued, was the one to blame for the inception of the Sino-Indian boundary war. It was he who prodded the Indians to take the initiative against the Chinese in order to expand their territory. The Chinese won't fight back, he told the Indians. How wrong he was! When Lieutenant-General Kaul of the Indian Army knew that he was about to be captured by them, he disguised himself as an ordinary soldier and fled. There was no question that if the Chinese had persisted in that war they could have fought *all the way to New Delhi*. But they chose to do otherwise. They withdrew

* In his memoirs Khrushchev recalled a material interest in Hainan that may have been related to the one to which Chiang Ch'ing was referring: "Then one day we were sitting around at Stalin's, trying to figure out some way to meet the demands of our rubber industry without having to buy crude rubber from the capitalists. I suggested getting Mao to let us set up a rubber plantation in China in exchange for credit loans and technical assistance. We went Mao a cable proposing this plan. The Chinese replied that if we would give them credit, they would let us use the island of Hainan for our plantation. We drew up an agreement between us, but it turned out that the area we were given on Hainan was too small for a decent rubber plantation, and the idea was dropped" (*Khrushchev Remembers*, 463).

their troops and sent back to India the soldiers they had captured and the equipment over which they had taken temporary custody. However, the Chinese knew they could easily have fought all the way to New Delhi, she repeated. In the course of the Sino-Indian war it became clear to them that although India was a newly independent country, its people were oppressed. The people of India fought the Chinese forces *only* because they were compelled by their leaders to do so. Like her father, Nehru, Mrs. Gandhi practiced Big Nation Chauvinism. [12]

Troubles with the Soviets were continual, as demonstrated by the battle over Chenpao Island (March 2, 1969), Chiang Ch'ing went on. That was superbly commanded by Sun Yü-kuo, a young man in his twenties who "really knew how to fight." His valor was rewarded by his being made a delegate to the Ninth Party Congress (April 1969).

To illustrate how Chairman Mao practiced democracy with respect to the Soviet revisionists, Chiang Ch'ing said that when the Soviets vilify the Chinese, their cursings are published in the Chinese press. But the Soviets never publish any Chinese criticism of them. When President Nixon visited the Soviet Union (May 22–29, 1972), the Chinese said nothing against his move. They kept their silence even though, at that very moment, the American government was conducting severe bombing raids over Vietnam. Of course they recognized that Nixon was "an old hand at opposing Communism." Yet he was also the first American president to come to China. It was he who took the first step in forging a Sino-American friendship. Yet he was criticized on this and other issues by his fellow Americans! she commented, half in irony, half in dismay.*

Nixon was capable of changing his mind quite radically, they observed. China, which he used to regard as "expansionist," he later saw as "introverted." They needed to keep alert to all changing phases of his foreign policy. If Chairman Mao were not sensitive to precipitant shifts in Nixon's ways, how could he ever have invited Nixon to come to China as a traveler, as a tourist, or in any capacity he chose?

On the subject of Nixon she drew a clear line between ideological commitment — hatred of American imperialism — and political propriety — respect for Nixon as a national leader at a time of détente. In response to some disparaging remarks I had made on American foreign policy in Indochina she snapped back, "If President Nixon had not come to China, you would not have come either."

The focus of her life was mainly in the realm of public affairs, and inevitably that realm impinged upon their private lives. They always lived simply, Chiang Ch'ing said of Mao and herself. Most of their time was given over to reading,

* Her standards obviously were set in China where no one criticized Chairman Mao openly.

study of current events, writing, and occasional involvement in the world outside. Rarely did she and the Chairman go out together. Almost never did they
dine out for their own pleasure. Since they made their home in Peking, they
went to restaurants (a pleasure of her younger days) only a few times. The
Chairman was not very careful about what he ate, she admitted with a wry
smile. He ate quickly, and was usually full by the time the last course arrived.
What happened was that he forgot that there would be a last course, and by the
time it arrived he had no interest in it. That habit of his reminded her of Wang
An-shih, the prime minister of the Sung dynasty, who was known always to
consume the dishes positioned closest to him without taking notice of other
dishes arrayed on the table. When his wife told the cook that he always favored
those dishes placed near him, the cook thought it was the dish he liked, not
just its proximity.[13] When she mentioned this to the Chairman, he chuckled
and said to her, "That's all you know about history, and you tease me about it!"

11.

◇ ◇ ◇

Redreaming the Red Chamber

Pages full of idle words
Penned with hot and bitter tears:
All men call the author fool;
None his secret message hears.
— *Dream of the Red Chamber*

The *Dream of the Red Chamber*, a classic eighteenth-century Chinese novel, is scarcely known to most Westerners. Generations of Chinese have read it five, ten, or twenty times and make its interpretation both a literary hobby and a process of intellectual maturation. Chiang Ch'ing's comments on *Dream of the Red Chamber* display her command of the novel and also preface her intimate involvement with radical reassessments of literature and art during the Cultural Revolution.

Other dynastic founders might have "burned the book and buried the scholars" associated with a novel depicting so graphically an unwanted past. The Communist leaders chose instead to live with it, but to make it their own in vital ways. Reasons can be found in political strategy. For instance, reinterpretation of a work of fiction so indelibly part of the old tradition is less destructive than a drastic excision and less likely to provoke protest by the people. Uncannily, the novel is also self-correcting: its dreamlike narrative suggests disbelief in, disillusion with, and discredit of the social system it describes. Moreover, the Chairman and his Party were confident of their pedagogy. They assumed that the people could be taught to be critical of earlier interpretations and to read the novel, or to discuss it publicly at least, from a Marxian perspective.

To appreciate Chiang Ch'ing's evaluation of *Dream of the Red Chamber*, a cursory outline of its plot and identification of its chief characters will help Western readers. All the people in the book are linked to one or the other of the two main branches of the aristocratic Chia clan, one of which lives at the mansion Ningkuofu and the other at Jungkuofu, also a great house.*

Jungkuofu is headed by Chia She, a son of the dowager matriarch of the family, and Ningkuofu is nominally headed by Chia Chen, who attained that position when his father abandoned the household to become a monk. Chia Cheng, nephew of Chia Chen and another son of the matriarch, is attached to the Jungkuofu family. Chia Chen's son, Chia Lien, is married to Phoenix (Wang Hsi-fen), an able and influential woman who nevertheless sickens and dies during the course of the novel. Her activities are revealed as being responsible for the eventual raiding of and confiscation of the Chia property by imperial guards.

Chia Cheng's son by his wife, Wang Fu-jen, is Pao-yü, the hero of the story. Pao-yü is expected to study hard and prepare for the civil service examinations to become a high official. But Pao-yü, aesthetic and sentimental, prefers the company of his girl cousins and maidservants. One of the cousins with whom he has played since childhood and whom he adores is Black Jade, enchanting, neurasthenic granddaughter of the matriarch.[1] Another beautiful cousin, Precious Hairpin, moves into the Jungkuofu. It is she whom Pao-yü should marry. When the marriage takes place, Black Jade dies of a broken heart on the wedding night. But Pao-yü is so ill-suited to the real world that the marriage brings no joy to Precious Hairpin. Eventually Pao-yü manages to sit for the civil service examination, but soon he renounces the world and becomes a monk, leaving Precious Hairpin with a child.

So brief a summary inevitably stresses the love element, which is only part of the story. Rich with characters, each one highly individualized, the novel has long fascinated readers because it displays both the splendor and squalor of the private lives of a vanished elite. These idle rich of the eighteenth century exhibit all the social, cultural, and political enticements that the Communist leaders, advocates of plain peasant style, have tried to make their people abjure: religious myth and symbolism; great mansions inhabited by the glamorous rich, with only glimpses of the poor; courage and corruption in official life; the natural aggrandizement of great families at the expense of the state; sexual dalliance and unabashed sexual deviance.

Beyond the social panorama the novel makes skillful use of metaphysical

---

* Ostensibly the two families live in the north, in Peking. But cognoscenti recognize that the true location is Nanking.

contrasts: outer splendor and inner decay, sensuality and suffering, fiction and fact, reality and illusion, the waking world and the dream world. Elaborately sustained metaphors bring these contrasting realms together.

i

"I have read *Dream of the Red Chamber* five times," Mao Tse-tung remarked in 1964, "but I haven't been influenced by it because I regard it as history." [2] After reciting long passages about fairies, jade, and palaces, Chiang Ch'ing warned me, "Don't read the novel as if it were just a story, but see it as a book of history which demonstrates class struggle."

Just as with the historically based films *Inside Story of the Ch'ing Court* and *The Story of Wu Hsun*, Chiang Ch'ing presented herself as the one who first alerted the leaders and the nation to iniquities in the current literary criticism of the *Dream of the Red Chamber*. Yet her motive for spending several of our hours together on this collection of story, poetry, myth, and history was not strictly censorial. In her telling, the two aspects of her personality again emerged clearly. On public duty she was the literary watchdog who had alerted her master to dangers at the gate. But in her private person she was an ebullient lover of the tale.

Chiang Ch'ing blithely took upon herself to articulate the issues of the novel's authorship and meaning, complex problems that demand true expertise.* Although some of the details she cited and her judgments about the novel's political questions were flawed by overenthusiasm or perhaps by fatigue, she was demonstrably up on the new criticism and doubtless the source of much of it. Several interpretations she expressed in a monologue of several hours became part of the official line published within a year of our interview. [3]

The legend enveloping the novel begins with the mystery of its origins and speculations on how its final form was achieved. Was there one author or several? How authentic are the manuscripts that survive? To what extent is the novel a fair reflection of historical conditions and personalities? Such questions will be debated endlessly, perhaps never answered finally.

The author of the first eight chapters is generally believed to be Ts'ao Hsueh-ch'in (1715?–1763), the scion of an affluent and influential family that managed the imperial brocade factory at Nanking during the reign of K'ang-hsi, the second Manchu emperor. K'ang-hsi carried the dynasty to its heights of grandeur, then to the brink of decline. Likewise the Ts'ao family lost both its

---

* For pinpointing some of Chiang Ch'ing's errors I am grateful to Professor Chao Kang, one of the world's true experts on *Dream* lore.

fortune and the imperial favor. The Chia family of the novel represents the real Ts'ao family. Before the novel opens the Chias are awarded two dukedoms by the Emperor, and during the course of the novel they are linked to the court by the most beautiful of their daughters, who has been appointed imperial consort. In the sequel their fortunes decline.[4]

The Marxian attack upon *Dream of the Red Chamber* came within five years of the founding of the new political order. This novel, along with the rest of the literary, theatrical, and cinematic heritage, was continuously available to readers during the PRC's early years. Not until Chiang Ch'ing returned from her second trip to the Soviet Union were the novel and its modern interpreters put on trial before the nation. There had been circumstantial warnings. After the death of Stalin in 1953, suppression of nonproletarian literature in the Soviet Union abated somewhat, an easing of control that gave way to the Thaw. But a threatening aftermath — the emboldening of Chinese dissidents — could not be overlooked. Was Hu Feng's brusque defiance of Party-determined orthodoxy an early swell in a great wave of self-assertion by men of education and conscience? Not only in the literary world centered in Shanghai, but also in the capital, the quashing of independence became imperative. In the deep winter of 1953 Kao Kang and Jao Shu-shih, seasoned comrades who had enjoyed extraordinary regional autonomy over the years, challenged Mao's personal supremacy over the state structure and personal determination of priorities in national development. The public disgrace of Kao and Jao in the spring of 1954 was also an omen.

ii

Since she did not read foreign languages, Chiang Ch'ing began, her access to foreign literature was limited. But judging by what she had read in translation, no other books of the eighteenth or nineteenth centuries of any culture could compare with *Dream of the Red Chamber* in subtle analysis of human relations.

Of foreign authors she admired especially Mark Twain, a "progressive" who deliberately exposed inequitable social conditions. Even so, she went on, his major characters all belong to the petty bourgeoisie, for all strive to clamber up the social ladder. So does the hero of Dickens's *Great Expectations*. And so does Julien, the hero of Stendhal's *The Red and the Black*, who aspires to military office; his father-in-law wants to buy a title for him, and provides him with a wristwatch and other bourgeois symbols. However repugnant this petty-bourgeois theme of social climbing, it did not spoil her admiration of Stendhal.

The Red and the Black is "immortal" and will always enjoy a high position in world literature because it reflects the political and economic situation of Europe in the early nineteenth century. Not only does it depict the struggles between church and state, but also the internecine quarreling within these establishments. Like the old-time critics of *Dream of the Red Chamber*, certain French revisionist critics degraded the historical significance of *The Red and the Black* by considering it primarily a love story. As for Stendhal, he actually was an "incorrigible reactionary." Born and brought up in a small town, he eventually traveled all over Europe in the service of the "dynasty." Yet that aspect of his life heightens the book's value as a mirror of the contemporary political scene.

Another great novel she had long admired was *Chin P'ing Mei* (translated as *The Golden Lotus*), which dates from the Ming dynasty and is set in a Shantung town not so different from vital commercial centers she knew as a child. Its descriptions of sexual relations are so explicit that for centuries most people were not allowed to read the original, unexpurgated edition. In spite of convention, she refused to read the bowdlerized version, she reported primly. She could not tolerate literary adulteration in any form (!).

"I am a semi-expert on *Dream of the Red Chamber*," said Chiang Ch'ing of the novel she first read for political truths in the early 1950's. The background of the continuing debate over the novel is worth reviewing because it sets in relief certain stubborn personalities with whom the leaders have had to deal for years.[5] All that began in 1954 when she was recuperating at home, leafing through some journals, and happened to notice an article about the novel in the September issue of *Literature, History and Philosophy*, a publication of Shantung University. The authors, Li Hsi-fan and Lan Ling, two demonstrably talented students whom no one had heard of, had taken to task the judgments, recently published, of Professor Yü P'ing-po, whose career was built upon a widely recognized "bourgeois" appreciation of the novel.[6] Immediately she handed the article over to the Chairman, who agreed that the piece had promise and should reach a wide audience. He asked her to instruct the *People's Daily* to reprint Li Hsi-fan's article (throughout her discussion Chiang Ch'ing emphasized Li Hsi-fan over Lan Ling); the editors complied.

Meanwhile, she began an investigation of her own. She learned that Li Hsi-fan had first submitted his article to the *Literary Gazette* (the major literary journal published in Shanghai and edited by Hu Feng, Ting Ling, et al.), which rejected it. Next he sent it to the *People's Daily*, which had also refused it. Not until she had asked the editors in the name of the Chairman would they agree to reprint it. The reason why the *People's Daily* had refused to carry it the first time around was attributed to the power of certain prominent persons and the literary doctrines they still venerated. It was "no secret" that Yü P'ing-po and Hu Shih belonged to the same clique.* Li Hsi-fan's article struck both men at their "most vulnerable spot" (literary expression of bourgeois politics). Their authority, however, which had been established in the 1920's, was still so pervasive that the new scholarship, which Li's article exemplified, would have never reached national circulation without her personal intervention.

She was still convalescing from illness when she made a special trip to the Peking offices of the *People's Daily* to promote Li's article and arrange for its publication. Next she appeared at a meeting of the Propaganda Department of the Central Committee, where she handed the article to Chou Yang and Hu Ch'iao-mu, who were in charge. They scanned it and remarked with contemptuous irony, "That's written by such *small* people. How can such small people dare to criticize another *small* person — Yü P'ing-po?" Chiang Ch'ing was furious but did not reveal then that the *People's Daily* had already agreed to publish the piece.

On her instigation, on October 16, 1954, the Chairman sent a communiqué to the Politburo and other government offices about "The Question of the Study of *Dream of the Red Chamber*" and called a meeting to review all sides of the question. Chiang Ch'ing, who attended, remembered well what he said. He spoke theoretically on the mistakes of the "great bourgeois oppression of small people" and on the "bourgeois oppression of newly emerging people." The implications for the novel were not difficult to grasp. Even though Yü P'ing-po and Hu Shih belonged to the same clique of idealistic "bourgeois oppressors," the leaders of the Propaganda Department and the Ministry of Culture — Chou Yang and Lu Ting-i — were known to have long admired the collaborative study of the novel that Hu Shih and Yü P'ing-po had made. To repudiate them now would cause present leaders to lose face.

When Hu Shih and Yü P'ing-po were working on this book in the 1920's, they "monopolized" the rare sixteen- and eighty-chapter editions, with the result that "the masses no longer had access to them." But now the original copies of those two rare editions are kept in the public trust; all other copies are photographic. The original copy of the eighty-chapter edition is preserved in the Peking Library. Once she borrowed it and asked that a copy be made for her. When certain "bourgeois authorities" discovered her request, they denounced her. Why? Because they wanted to monopolize the original editions for their own purposes.

* Educated at Cornell and Columbia, Hu Shih was China's most prominent liberal publicist of the Republican era. In the early 1920s he and his student Yü P'ing-po employed rigorous empiricism and other modern methods to discredit traditional dogmas about the provenance and the historical and literary significance of *Dream of the Red Chamber*. In particular they tried to validate Ts'ao Hsueh-ch'in's claim that the novel was essentially autobiographical and not a veiled attack upon the ruling Manchu household. Hu Shih's "bourgeois liberalism, humanism, and reformism" were vilified by the Communists from the time he departed for Taiwan, leaving behind Yü P'ing-po, a professor at Peking University, to take the heat.

The value of subsequent criticism has been uneven. One contemporary critic named Chou Ju-ch'ang wrote a book called *The New Verification of "Dream of the Red Chamber."* [7] Although his point of view was close to that of Hu Shih's group, his one advantage was to have used the archives of the Ch'ing court. Despite flaws in his method of verification, the book is still worth reading. When Chou Ju-ch'ang was attacked during the Cultural Revolution she tried to protect him (she added quickly that until now she had never admitted that to anyone).

Although *Dream of the Red Chamber* was written in the form of a novel, she said, it is as vivid as history. Its social panorama is encyclopedic. Of the novel's three to four hundred characters, the author chose to focus upon some twenty lives. The twenty he favored were the masters, and the rest were slaves, who subsisted on garbage produced in the mansions where the masters lived. [8]

The eighty-chapter edition is uniquely valuable because it includes numerous marginal notes made by the author, Ts'ao Hsueh-ch'in. Those second thoughts on the novel are important historically. Since Ts'ao wrote from the point of view of the first half of the eighteenth century, his judgments were reactionary, to be sure. But present-day readers must realize that his ideas were quite progressive for his own time.

All literary works must be discussed in terms of the historical background of the period in which they were written, she went on. Ts'ao wrote *Dream* when he was in his twenties and revised it over a period of ten years. After studying his annotations in various editions she recognized, as had others before her, that Ts'ao had prepared a sequel or a second half of the book. Since he died without children to inherit his works, the sequel fell into the hands of some people who pretended to "borrow" it, but actually never returned it. Thus, the original was lost to posterity. Ts'ao's notes show that the sequel evolved tragically: the family falls from official favor, their property is confiscated, and those who had once lived in grandeur become beggars.

After the original sequel was lost, other authors worked out their own. The last forty chapters of the complete 120-chapter edition as it now stands have been attributed to Kao E, yet he refrained from signing his name to them (allowing others to believe that it was Ts'ao's original). It is in this part that Pao-yu qualifies as a *chü-jen* (passes the civil service examination at the provincial level), abandons his home and child, and becomes a monk. *

Ts'ao Hsueh-ch'in did not seek to change society, she said, returning to strict Marxist judgments, but only to patch it up. To be sure, he was dissatisfied with the bureaucratic system, yet he would not have gone so far as to advocate overthrowing the dynasty that supported it. He was merely trying to mend mat-

---

* Kao E, by comparison, did far better in his own life, for he passed the *chin-shih* (the civil service examination usually preliminary to high bureaucratic appointment, awarded at the capital).

ters as they stood. Even within those limitations, *Dream of the Red Chamber* was the swan song of the feudal aristocracy.[9] Yet Ts'ao said conventionally, "The novel is words without truths." *

iii

The novel's setting, characters, and language are freighted with meanings that are often misunderstood, she continued. The characters of the two houses, Ningkuofu and Jungkuofu, are opposed in many aspects. Ningkuofu is the east and Jungkuofu is the west. They function like political parties: Jungkuofu is patriarchal and Ningkuofu is matriarchal. Both the patriarchal and matriarchal families fight to possess Pao-yü, but in the end both lose. The first five chapters, she asserted, have long been misunderstood, but Chairman Mao has clarified them, saying that they should be perceived in terms of class struggle and from the perspective of those who suffered and died.

Hundreds of characters are tied together by complex familial and servile relationships. Most devotees identify with the young master Pao-yü; the beautiful Black Jade; Precious Hairpin, his cousin and destined wife. All the main characters are introduced in the first five chapters, and the structure and main themes of the story are suggested by the "Song of Hao and Liao" in the first chapter. She chanted lightly:

> *Men all know that salvation should be won,*
> *But with ambition won't have done, have done,*
> *Where are the famous ones of days gone by?*
> *In grassy graves they lie now, every one.*[10]

She could not recite the whole of it, she apologized.

Throughout the novel the author's choice of words and names is highly symbolic. In Taoist allusion he says that the true story is hidden and that a false story is used instead: in a dream sequence Pao-yü meets another Pao-yü surnamed *chen*, or "true," while the real Pao-yü is surnamed *chia*, or "false." This interplay between *chen* and *chia* continues in names and words used throughout the novel.

She quoted from the commentary to the "Song of Hao and Liao," pointing out that this passage and the one which follows often vary from edition to edition.

---

* He also wrote paradoxically: "Truth becomes fiction when the fiction's true. / Real becomes not-real when the unreal's real."

Mean hovels and abandoned halls
Where courtiers once paid daily calls:
Bleak haunts where weeds and willows scarcely thrive
Were once with mirth and revelry alive.
While cobwebs shroud the mansion's gilded beams,
The cottage casement with choice muslin gleams. [11]

———

Would you of perfumed elegance recite?
Even as you speak, the raven locks turn white.
Who yesterday her lord's bones laid in clay,
On silken bridal-bed shall lie today.

Discussing the novel's mythical, supernatural, and dreamlike qualities, Chiang Ch'ing recounted one of the episodes embedded in a chapter. An old lady, Liu Lao-lao, enters Ta-kuan-yuan, the palatial garden at Jungkuofu where her affluent relations live. The garden's design reflects the plan of heaven, which the author calls the "dreamland of great emptiness." The story illustrates the correspondence between the garden and heaven, and the possibility of escape from reality to unreality. Originally there was grass (conceived as feminine) in heaven, and Pao-yü was once a god in heaven. The god took pity on the grass and watered it every day (conventional sexual symbolism in Chinese letters). The grass responded, saying that when she became a person in the world she would repay the god with her tears.

Chiang Ch'ing explicated the significance of many lines and longer passages. "White bones," for instance, she said referred to Precious Hairpin (although Precious Hairpin is alive throughout both the present version and Ts'ao's original, she probably meant Black Jade, the heroine who dies). "Coffers with gold and silver filled" means that someone grand becomes a beggar whom everyone despises — this must mean Pao-yü. It is less clear to whom the following lines refer: "One at some other's short life gives a sigh./ Not knowing that he too goes home to die!" But the lines "The judge whose hat is too small for his head / Wears in the end a convict's cangue instead" refer to Precious Hairpin's brother Hsueh P'an, who received a good education but narrowly escaped becoming a robber.

Chiang Ch'ing paused with the fifth chapter, and began to quote passages from the famous episode in which the Fairy of Disenchantment provides Pao-yü with an illustrated volume of twelve songs, each of which describes allusively one of the twelve maidens of Chinling who are characters in the novel. This episode, Chiang Ch'ing said, takes place in heaven, here called the Land of Illusion, where there are two books, one orthodox and the other supplementary. The supplementary book belongs to the Ch'ing-wen tradition, and

Ch'ing-wen (Bright Design) is the name of Pao-yü's most attractive but ill-starred maid, who dies a tragic death.

From memory, Chiang Ch'ing quoted the following lines with an emotional intensity that implied personal meaning:

> *Seldom the moon shines in a cloudless sky,*
> *And days of brightness all too soon pass by.*
> *A noble and aspiring mind*
> *In a base-born frame confined,*
> *Your charm and wit did only hatred gain,*
> *And in the end you were by slanderers slain,*
> *Your gentle lord's solicitude in vain.* [12]

A painting preceding the following poem shows two withered trees hung with a jade belt. Below them a heap of snow is pierced by a gold hairpin.

> *One was a pattern of female virtue,*
> *One a wit who made other wits seem slow.*
> *The jade belt in the greenwood hangs,*
> *The gold pin is buried beneath the snow.* [13]

The "jade belt in the greenwood" plays with the meaning of Black Jade, as does "the gold pin buried beneath the snow" with the name of Precious Hairpin. The jade and gold symbolism runs throughout the novel. Pao-yü is also exemplified by jade, and the saying that a good marriage is not made between gold and jade is epitomized by the unsatisfactory marriage between Precious Hairpin — gold — and Pao-yü — jade.

The girls of the Ningkuofu household, Chiang Ch'ing continued, each exquisite in her own way, were destined to tragedy. For example, Chin Ko-ching, daughter-in-law of Chia Chen, head of Ningkuofu, is seduced by Chia Chen and hangs herself. Why did she do that? Because she knew that Chia Chen's wife, Wang Fu-jen, and two of her maids had witnessed the illicit sexual act. The two maids were so traumatized that one committed suicide and the other fled to a nunnery. The point of this sequence of sexual encounters, escapes, and suicides is to show that when mutually susceptible members of the master class and the serving class live together in a large, unwieldy household, no good will come of it. It is often said that the bad things always happened at Ningkuofu, but actually most of the bad things were happening at Jungkuofu!

A telling description of the families (the Chia, and the equally great Shih, Wang, and Hsueh families) who control the social world is given in the fourth chapter:

Shout hip hurrah
For the Nanking Chia!
They weigh their gold out
By the jar.
The Ah-fang Palace
Scrapes the sky.
But it could not house
The Nanking Shih.
The King of the Ocean
Goes along,
When he's short of gold beds,
To the Nanking Wang.
The Nanking Hsueh
So rich are they
To count their money
Would take all day . . . [14]

iv

Chiang Ch'ing's monologue on the novel was accented by dramatic gestures.
The heat of late evening was ferocious. Once, without pause in her narrative,
she picked up a white terrycloth towel from the table beside her chair and tied
it tightly around her head to form a tricorne. For several moments she patted it
here and there to absorb perspiration, untied it, flipped it out, and shook her
hair free again.

At other moments, while she talked or presided at the dinner table, she
quickly pulled her green and white plastic comb through her hair. "I like it
short because it's cool," she commented brightly but defensively (leading me to
wonder whether she might have thought back to the pageboy or the corkscrew
curls she sported in her more glamorous Shanghai days).

Ebullient at the table, she recited from memory long passages of verse, in-
terspersed with personal commentary over her maids' delivery of delicacies.
Quite carried away, she once lifted the large white linen napkin from her lap,
tied the two corners around her neck and fixed the other two under her plate,
thus erecting a sling between her chin and the table. Without a bib, she
remarked in laughter, her clothes got as messy as a child's!

Hours of concentration upon the elegantly articulated and turned-out world
of *Dream of the Red Chamber* seemed to heighten her feminine consciousness of the present. Once she signaled over her shoulder to her bodyguard, who
promptly delivered a large oblong box of undecorated cardboard. Laughing like

a girl, she lifted the cover and pulled out, as if by magic, one long, pleated black skirt after another.

"I like skirts," * she announced as she handed out one each to her female attendants (myself excluded). "And they're comfortable in summer."

Never having seen such obviously foreign garments worn in revolutionary China, I asked her where they came from.

"From the Friendship Store!"

No matter to her that the official line on the Friendship Stores was that they were reserved exclusively for foreign consumers. Judging from the heavy corsetings and stodgy styles, Chinese designers had a vanished species in mind: the buxom Soviet matrons of the 1950's.

The next day when Chang Ying, Chiang Ch'ing's two interpreters, and my two companions gathered for our interview, each wore her new black skirt, which left exposed white calves and ankles formerly hidden from the sun. Out of the customary trousers, they sat awkwardly, self-consciously, scooping the pleats rippling around their laps from one direction to another, not knowing quite how to arrest their motion.

v

When Li Na was small, Chiang Ch'ing said of her daughter, she gave her *Dream of the Red Chamber* and taught her how to read it correctly: from the viewpoint of the class struggle that animated all their lives. The Chairman had also taught their children members of the Communist Party generally not to focus upon the obvious — the love story. They must ferret out the theme of class struggle, bearing in mind the fact that more than twenty of the characters die as a result of it. Hundreds of others are sustained by things given to them by the rich. So long as serving maids enjoy their masters' favor, they can afford to be truculent. But once they fall from favor they die.

From his idealist stance, Yü P'ing-po concocted imaginary and arbitrary explanations of events and relations among characters in the novel. For his analysis of the chapter called "An Evening Party Held in Celebration of Pao-yü's Birthday" Yü prepared an illustration that purported to show which characters sat where. But that was just a figment of his imagination. Then he argued ridiculously that the two major female characters, Black Jade and Precious

---

* Chiang Ch'ing's liking for dresses, which she regularly wore during our Canton interviews, first caught the eye of foreign journalists in June 1973. She appeared in the company of David Bruce, the American chief liaison officer, at the Peking sports stadium wearing a dress reaching to mid-calf. Not until the early spring of 1975 did a selection of dresses, conservatively styled, appear on the Peking market (*New York Times*, March 3, 1975, 20). Dresses, along with long hair, curled hair, makeup, high heels and all other outward signs of Western femininity had been banned during the Cultural Revolution; persons who persisted in wearing them were publicly criticized.

Hairpin, were two sides of one person. How could Yü have known that! He was being completely *subjective!*

A careful reading shows that although Precious Hairpin and Black Jade are both aristocrats, Precious Hairpin is at the zenith of that class while Black Jade is merely an orphan living in the home of Precious Hairpin. Under those circumstances Precious Hairpin inevitably tries to persecute Black Jade. But Black Jade is naive; she tries to resist, but gives up because she cannot bear causing pain to others.

The author praises Precious Hairpin for her beauty — her white skin, red lips, eyes like two apricots, face like a plate. Of course this would be ugly by contemporary standards, Chiang Ch'ing added hastily. His detailed description of Black Jade is quite the opposite, indeed critical. Never explicitly praising her beauty, he speaks of her long black eyebrows and her eyes slanted like those of a phoenix. She pants when she walks, "like resting a hand on a breeze." Difference in the characters of the two girls are brought out in the descriptions of their rooms, revealed through the eyes of the old woman, Liu Lao-lao. Black Jade's room looks like a boy's because it is filled with books. In her time that was not natural.

Precious Hairpin exhibits some intellectual ambition, for once she attempts to pass a court examination.* But Black Jade is the one who was brought up and educated like a boy. In economic terms one woman is high and the other low. Black Jade is low because she is a proletarian with no property. Of course her ideas are aristocratic, but that must be understood in terms of her times. By contrast, Precious Hairpin comes from a merchant family linked by blood† to the imperial family. Despite those fundamental differences, Yü P'ing-po persisted in the argument that the two women were just two sides of one person.

All the characters Ts'ao Hsueh-ch'in features belonged to the aristocratic class. Yet two of the most prominent, Pao-yü and Black Jade, are *rebels* against that class. Though Ts'ao presents them as such, he also criticizes them for their antagonistic stance: Pao-yü behaves poorly and Black Jade displeases others. But he always praises Precious Hairpin lavishly. She is gracious, has lots of money, and uses it to buy people over. In this respect she is able to act like a sort of "secret agent." Nevertheless, Pao-yü in his limited fashion is a genuine rebel. Perversely, he declares that all books *except* the Four Books (*Analects, Great Learning, Doctrine of the Mean,* and *Mencius* — the core classics) are true.‡ Bored by the classical heritage, he refuses to leave his home to study serious books and the art of government in the outside world. This is just one of many ways in which he resists officialdom. He says that the lure of fame is

---

* Possibly she was sent to court for a screening for future appointment as maid or concubine.
† Not demonstrated in the novel.
‡ This is precisely the opposite of received Confucian wisdom.

the only motive civil officials have for seeking to advise the Emperor. Indeed, some ambitious officials go so far as to commit suicide before the eyes of the Emperor just in order to make a big name for themselves. Pao-yü perceives that the generals of his era paid no genuine heed to the security of the Emperor, and that the only reason guardsmen, soldiers, and others went to war was to gain fame and its rewards.

Unlike Precious Hairpin, Black Jade has no money to speak of. All she receives is a modest monthly allowance from her grandmother. Nor does she monopolize that. Once she took her allowance and some other personal effects and distributed them among people she thought needed them.* Had Black Jade and Pao-yü survived to present times, Chiang Ch'ing postulated wryly, they would have been called Big Rightists! But that is beside the point. For if one appreciates them in their historical context it is evident that both are resolute in their opposition to feudalism. Even in their romantic and sexual love Black Jade and Pao-yü behave as rebels against the feudal aristocratic class. That was wonderful!

"My understanding of the first five chapters may not be entirely correct. I am only a semi-expert on *Dream of the Red Chamber*," she stressed. The novel should be analyzed by the method of dialectical materialism. All the issues it raises stem from the basic question of how to accept the cultural inheritance. Hu Shih and Yü P'ing-po considered the novel as a *roman à clef* — a biography of living persons. But would it not be better to regard it as a novel with the character of biography? Does it not make sweeping generalizations about Chinese society? Does it not exemplify critical realism with supplemental romanticism? Or is it merely vulgar literature that describes such trifling matters as love affairs of living persons and other stories about them? Should we recognize that Pao-yü and Black Jade act as rebels? Are Black Jade and Precious Hairpin *really* two sides of the same character? If so, can we relate the issue of two-sided character to the philosophic point that an argument has two sides in contradiction, that "one divides into two?"

What she prefers to think, she said, is that Black Jade is a rebel against the feudal class, whereas Precious Hairpin supports the feudal class. That difference ultimately causes the death of Black Jade. Hu Shih and Yü P'ing-po's debate was conducted outside the Chinese Communist Party. However, since 1960 their point of view has been taken up as an issue *within* the Chinese Communist Party (by implication triggering more debates over the literary heritage).

In 1962 or 1963 when she was undertaking various cultural projects in Shanghai, she dealt with the director of the Propaganda Department of the East

---

* Actually only Precious Hairpin distributes money and objects to people, possibly to buy their affection. Chiang Ch'ing's inclination was to pay most compliments to her "rebel," Black Jade.

China Party Committee (Hsia Cheng-nung), a man whom they assumed then to be a "good comrade," though later they found out that he could not be trusted. One day while the two of them were talking about the novel's historical background, he told her that a garden by the name of Ta-kuan-yuan (as in the novel) had been discovered in Peking.* Well, she told him, if that's true they should change the title *Dream of the Red Chamber* to *The Travelogue of Ts'ao Hsueh-ch'in!* He did not get what she meant by that, she reported sarcastically.

Ts'ao's novel made so powerful an assault on the ruling class that officials were compelled to ban it and put it in the category of "forbidden books" for the dynasty's duration. But that censorship only made it all the more delectable to the general public. People were so eager to own the original uncensored version that they would pay several ounces of silver to have it copied. Being copied by hand so often over the years inevitably caused variations among the several extant editions. Still, the cutting edge of the original has not dulled with time. During the Tao-kuang period (1821–1851) and at the time of the Opium War (1839–1840) a certain high official considered *Dream of the Red Chamber* a drug that could be exported to stupefy foreign peoples just as opium had been imported by the British imperialists to stupefy the Chinese people.

vi

The eighteenth-century gardens, poems, and coveys of female company so alive now in our imagination had subtle reverberations in Chiang Ch'ing's southern style of life. Although she did not have *Dream of the Red Chamber*'s famous garden, Ta-kuan-yuan, at her disposal, for the duration of her Canton retreat she had reserved for her pleasure something comparable: an orchid park stretching between her villa and the Pearl River. Thus, at the end of the surprise morning meeting at which she plunged into the volatile issues of the Cultural Revolution, she suggested a change of scene. Why not rendezvous at the orchid park later that afternoon?

We arrived separately at Chiang Ch'ing's lush secret garden. Chang Ying led my guides and me along winding paths, pointing out the most exotic of the hundreds of varieties of orchids along the way. At a gentle pace we passed through moongates, traversed gardens skillfully landscaped "naturalistically," bypassed rustic tea pavilions, and crossed arched bridges over artificial streams and ponds. Only long-gowned scholars and crouching boy servants were missing from the idyllic setting. In the hazy distance arose a moonviewing pavilion. Chiang Ch'ing, dressed in luminous silk, was seated on its veranda overlooking a lotus pond.

---

* By expert consensus, as noted before, the novel was actually set in Nanking.

As we approached her, she greeted us gaily from her wide wicker chair and continued her "work," as she explained. From a basket she lifted rare specimens of orchid plants and laid them upon blotting paper stretched on light wooden frames built by her bodyguard. She mounted the specimen on one frame, covered that with a second, and bound the two together with a cord pulled tightly around the four corners. "You may photograph me at work," she allowed as she kept up her brisk pace, laughing and chatting in accompaniment. So I did. Despite the strong sun of the late afternoon, her bodyguard cast powerful artificial lighting upon her figure. Suddenly, she admonished herself for appearing so frivolous, walked to the balustrade, and affected a neutral expression of officiality against the lotus pond's lush background.

"Now it's my turn," she said as she descended upon her elaborate Swiss photographic system set up at another section of the veranda. Maneuvering her twin-lens reflex upon a tripod, she shrouded her head and camera with a worn square of sky-blue velvet, shot pictures at a brisk clip, and made muffled calls for changes of arrangement. She handed the large negative frames, one by one, to her bodyguard, who, she explained, would oversee their development. Continually she motioned other members of her entourage into range of the viewfinder.*

Aromatic mugs of tea brewed of fresh orchid blossoms drew us back under the eaves of the pavilion. There we watched birds in fanciful cages, received rare blossoms from the gardens, and chatted idly. Soon Chiang Ch'ing initiated a stroll around the veranda; goldfish in rainbow colors darted in waters beneath.

Some glimmer of the fish reminded her of horses, of the challenges of winning them over and riding high. Her conversation then shifted from horses to humans and the arts of currying favor and gaining loyalty. And myself? I queried mischievously as we leaned on the balustrade. Our laughter mingled an instant. She changed the subject to the evening.

"Change before dinner, and why not wear something brighter? Why did you choose to wear black when you knew I would photograph in color naturally?"

I explained to her that my companions Yü and Ch'en had recommended this somber costume.

"You should never listen to others," she declared. "You should always make your own decisions. Wear what you like and feel happiest in."

When we reunited in the early evening she was still attired in an ecru silk dress. I wore a red and white polka-dot blouse and white flared pants; that seemed to please her. Some hours later, around midnight, she turned again to her cameras reestablished indoors now. To simulate a natural environment she ordered Hsiao Chiao to carry in huge potted palms to form a backdrop, this also illuminated artificially. On the verge of shooting again, she reached to smooth

* See the first picture section.

my naturally wavy but normally disheveled hair. "It's rebellious without being revolutionary," I confessed. She laughed, and lowered her hand to allow me to pull a brush through it.

When she was out from under her sky-blue headcloth I reached for my Nikon once again. "Color?" she asked. No, black and white happened to be in the camera at that moment. She preferred color, she reminded me. I was aware of that, I said, but added that black and white film picks up more subtle details of appearance and nuances of character. She said nothing, but hid her normally lively expression once again behind a straight mask. Peering through the viewfinder, I recognized how much more plausible and engaging she appeared when she was not looking toward posterity.

Later, when I reflected upon her intense study of *Dream of the Red Chamber* and her compulsive need to share it with me, I realized how in her own mind truth and fiction, history and literature, past and present had blurred. Such synthesis was at the heart of the propaganda by which she lived.

PART FOUR

◇ ◇ ◇

CULTURAL REVOLUTION

12.

◇ ◇ ◇

Setting the Stage

> If people bring so much courage to this
> world the world has to kill them to break
> them, so of course it kills them. The world
> breaks everyone and afterward many are
> strong at the broken places.
> —Ernest Hemingway, *A Farewell to Arms*

I want to maintain my political youth forever," was one of Chiang Ch'ing's first remarks to me. Smiling confidently, she spoke not only for herself, but also for an aging corps of revolutionary leaders. A few, Mao most visibly, were determined to preserve the mental agility and physical energy needed to guide the nation on the radical political course undertaken a half-century earlier. Nor could they allow the youth-heavy population (nearly half a billion under thirty) to lapse into premature political middle age, or through neglect to restore the old order.

She went on with her easy balancing of personal and public interests, "I suffer from ailments, yet I keep on with my work and the struggle."

"Comrade Chiang Ch'ing battles against illness as staunchly as she fights politically," Yao Wen-yuan added with his customary revolutionary courtliness.

"Do you know who Comrade Yao Wen-yuan is and what he has done?" she queried as she introduced one of her most loyal and voluble followers in the recent crusade, a true warrior of the pen.* "Long before the Great Cultural

* "Polemicist laureate," as Gordon Bennet notes aptly in "Mrs. Mao's Literary Ghost," *Far Eastern Economic Review*, 62 (Oct. 24, 1968): 197.

Revolution he was one of our Party's literary critics. Then in the initial and middle periods of the Great Cultural Revolution, particularly in the initial period, he organized the writing of articles criticizing the reactionary line in art and literature. Of course, first of all Chairman Mao Tse-tung gave me his approval and then I went to Shanghai where Comrade K'o Ch'ing-shih [late mayor and Party secretary of Shanghai] supported me. However, most of the articles were written by Comrade Yao Wen-yuan."

"The work was done under the leadership of Chairman Mao and was organized by Comrade Chiang Ch'ing," Yao Wen-yuan pointed out. "It was quite a hard struggle at that time. That's why Chairman Mao said that Peking was then watertight and impenetrable."

"For nineteen days [November 10–29, 1965] Peking newspapers refused to carry Comrade Yao Wen-yuan's article 'On the New Historical Drama *Hai Jui Dismissed from Office*,' " Chiang Ch'ing continued. "On the tenth of November it had appeared in Shanghai's *Literary Gazette*. At Chairman Mao's suggestion it was next published in pamphlet form, but still it was not allowed to be circulated in Peking for two or three days. That was how imperious those people were! It took seven months to complete his article, which underwent numerous revisions. And the writing of it had to be kept secret. Then the manuscript was delivered to Peking where I went over it three times, and this had to be done secretly too. Does this surprise you?"

Actually, that story had circulated among China Watchers for some time.* But the formidable Yao Wen-yuan, present only at my first meeting with Chiang Ch'ing at the Great Hall of the People in Peking, had long intrigued me. As early as 1955 Yao joined the attack against self-determined socialist writer Hu Feng. Two years later Yao joined the Anti-Rightist Movement following the Hundred Flowers Campaign. His laudatory *Lu Hsun, The Giant of China's Cultural Revolution* (1962), developed new and vital themes. Three years later he collaborated with Chiang Ch'ing and Mao on the devastating Hai Jui essay, which undermined the Peking Party Committee's control of that city and its cultural offerings. That yeoman service was rewarded by his appointments as editor of Shanghai's *Literary Gazette* and its major newspaper *Liberation Daily*, and as director of the Propaganda Department of Shanghai's Party Committee. Thus through Yao Wen-yuan's new dominance of publications in Shanghai, Mao and Chiang Ch'ing, who had temporarily lost such control over Peking, mounted an ideological offensive against both the municipal and the national government at the capital.

Yao Wen-yuan's battering ram against Peking's propaganda citadel was his

---

* Also the rumor that Yao was Chiang Ch'ing's son-in-law, which I did not attempt to verify because we had just met and history had taught me that such questions were fatal intrusions upon the personal life that the Chinese leaders guard closely from the masses.

critique of *Hai Jui Dismissed from Office*, the play written by that city's Vice-Mayor Wu Han. The political debacle it provoked was grounded in an axiom of Chinese history: the drama, as well as the novel, poetry, and written history, are mirrors that either flatter or disfigure the images of the ruling class. Wu Han possessed all the political, historical, and cultural keys to the kingdom. He was a powerful urban and Party administrator (and close associate of Mao's rival, Liu Shao-ch'i), and was also famed as a liberal historian of the Ming dynasty and as an author of historical dramas in the modern style. In his drama Hai Jui, an upright Ming official whose first concern was the people, takes issue with the emperor's land policy and is punished "unjustly" for his candor. The drama's allusions to recent politics were all too clear. Poor harvests combined with poor planning during the Great Leap Forward had caused painful setbacks among the people. The "upright official" P'eng Te-huai had pinned responsibility upon "Emperor" Mao Tse-tung for the disasters. Through historical analogy the drama called for "a redress of grievances": retrenchment and return of some collectivized land to individual farming. The Chairman's loyalists grasped one overall message: restoration.

Continuing with her introduction to the crisis of the 1960's, Chiang Ch'ing said, "The prelude of the Great Cultural Revolution started with Chairman Mao's call issued at the Tenth Plenary Session of the Eighth Central Committee of the Communist Party of China in 1962. From 1962 to 1966 such events as the Peking Opera Festival and the article on *Hai Jui Dismissed from Office* constituted the buildup."

That the Cultural Revolution had a literary genesis was just one of several hypotheses held by foreign observers of Chinese politics, I responded. Generational tensions and struggle over succession were also recognized as causes. There seemed to have been civil war.

"There's some truth in that," Chiang Ch'ing acknowledged. "Chairman Mao told Edgar Snow that it was an all-round civil war."

"An all-round civil war!" Yao Wen-yuan echoed and continued briskly. "It was a struggle for leadership between the proletariat and the bourgeoisie in a state under the dictatorship of the proletariat." *

"It can't be said that there was already all-round civil war in the period from 1962 to the middle of 1966," Chiang Ch'ing qualified. "The all-round civil war did not start until the masses rose up in 1966. That year I went to Peking University several times and could hardly get out of it. Some clamored that they wanted to hang me and some others said they would fry me. I replied that I was terribly busy, but would invite them to hang me and fry me when I found the time.

* Not until the Constitution of 1975 did China declare itself formally to be in the stage of the dictatorship of the proletariat.

"The investigations started much earlier — in 1961," she said. "By 1963 we took action and attacked.[1] In 1964 I made a speech on the reform of the Peking Opera. But they deliberately created mistakes in it, so I could not have it published then.[2] At that time great power was in their hands,* and my words did not carry any weight, because the masses had not yet risen up."

In the early stages of the Cultural Revolution, Chiang Ch'ing continued, the Chairman spoke on the Four Greats: placards, debates, airing of views, and reasoning things out. Those Four Greats governed the conduct of the Cultural Revolution. While the May Sixteenth Circular drafted by her and presented at the Tenth Plenum of the Eighth Central Committee in September 1962 belonged to the prelude of the Cultural Revolution, the real beginning was marked by mass mobilization.† First Chairman Mao wrote what he called "My placard." Then he went forth to receive the masses at the Gate of Heavenly Peace. Earliest to arrive were the students, workers, and peasants. On successive occasions he received (at his grandstand at the Gate of Heavenly Peace) some thirteen million youths who called themselves Red Guards — actually more than that all told, she added. When soldiers joined forces with the people, civil war broke out everywhere. Thereafter, equilibrium and disequilibrium alternated: first the seizure of power by one group, then the reestablishment of political power by another. That pattern kept repeating.

In the course of the Cultural Revolution Liu Shao-ch'i was the "first to assert himself." He was followed by Lin Piao, who fomented *the most serious* struggle in the history of the revolution, she said. His challenge to the leadership and life of Chairman Mao they now call the "tenth struggle between the two lines." She listed, staccato, the names associated with the struggles: first, Ch'en Tu-hsiu; second, Chü Ch'iu-pai; third, Li Li-san; fourth, Lo Chang-lung; fifth, Wang Ming; sixth, Chang Kuo-t'ao; seventh, Kao Kang and Jao Shu-shih; eighth, P'eng Te-huai; ninth, Liu Shao-ch'i; tenth, Lin Piao.

"I'm not especially brilliant, but I've gone through practical struggle," she said, adding that her "revolutionary dual tactics" are less skillful than the "double-dealing tactics used by the counterrevolutionaries." Often she was clumsy. After Liu Shao-ch'i and his followers made their self-criticisms and admitted their mistakes, she called upon them to unite with her group. But they continued to engage in wild designs against her people! Still, "when the Liu Shao-ch'i renegades and the Lin Piao counterrevolutionaries exposed themselves, it was a great victory for us."

* Chief of State Liu Shao-ch'i, Peking's mayor P'eng Chen, Chou Yang, then chief of the Cultural Ministry, and their followers. Chiang Ch'ing's rise to power was predicated upon their fall.
† See Chapter 13.

i

The brisk preview of the Cultural Revolution, which cast her into the national limelight, yielded later to a more careful reconstruction of that upheaval. Her discussion highlighted three successive historical trends. During the first, the Great Leap Forward, Mao rushed headlong toward a materially egalitarian society to be attained within the third decade of the People's Republic. Defiant of the Soviet model, which plodded along the road of socialism, allowing "capitalist" indulgences along the way, the Mao depicted by Chiang Ch'ing waged a one-man campaign over the countryside to promote the ideal of the people's commune and to validate the radical organizational changes demanded by a massive push toward communism. But in the late 1950's, Mao neglected the superstructure — the need for concomitant changes in education, literature, and the performing arts.

Mao's failure to enforce his will for immediate communization on an unwieldy nation of peasants still ignorant of the political advantage of their "poverty and blankness" was impossible to mask, though intolerable to see reflected in the judgment of others. Inevitably, famine and disorder brought China to the verge of a classic rebellion. The danger of loss of the popular "mandate" caused a move toward retrenchment in 1960–1961: limited "concessions" to private plots, rural markets, personal property, and compensation for goods seized by the state in the zeal for immediate communization. In her recapitulation of these gambles with national destiny Chiang Ch'ing focused almost exclusively upon Mao. Dutifully, she cited his provocative, mediating, and sometimes waffling directives. Liu Shao-ch'i and Secretary General of the Party Teng Hsiao-p'ing, who quietly commanded the retrenchment, were officially disgraced by the time of her narration, and so were scarcely mentioned. Still, they continued to have immense but muffled followings.

With the shift to the Socialist Education Campaign that opened in the fall of 1962, Mao, with the assistance of the PLA and its chief Lin Piao, struggled to edge ahead of Liu Shao-ch'i in charting a Chinese path to socialism. In heroic rhetoric, Mao was "Our Great Helmsman." Such swings in the revolutionary movement Chiang Ch'ing observed mainly from her stations of convalescence. Not until the early 1960's did she turn to the theater, a didactic cultural medium that had been spotlighted by the Socialist Education Campaign.

She had brought her narration of domestic events in the late 1950's up to the Rectification Campaign against dissidents in 1957 and 1958. At that point, she said, Chairman Mao shifted his attention from that small but yeasty portion of the urban population to the rural outreaches, where revolutionary momentum had slackened. On February 19, 1958, he laid down his challenge in the "Ten Points of Working Methods Regarding the Party." [3] Next, he began an inspection tour of the countryside, spending March and April in Szechwan province. At the city of Chengtu he addressed an important meeting where the general line for the transition to socialism, first introduced to the Politburo five years earlier, was formally adopted. On the first of June 1958 "On the Introduction of Cooperatives" appeared in the Party journal *Red Flag*. *

To promote rapid collectivization of farming, in August 1958 the Politburo held three meetings in the city of Chengchow in Honan, Central China, to deal with "excessive requisition of properties" (excessive taxes in kind) and other sorts of "blind demands from above." It also issued decrees against the persistent notion of the individual economy and individual farming; that is, against all forms of farming that were not collectivized. To get his point across, Chairman Mao challenged bluntly, "Do you believe in Marxism or not? Do you believe in the law of value or not?"

Continuing his personal campaign in the countryside, from August 4 to 13 he made inspection tours of villages and cities in Honan, Hopeh, and Shantung provinces, and of the city of Tientsin just southeast of Peking. At each stop he called meetings of local officials and promoted the *commune* as a model all should strive for. The idea was stressed, and in some places adopted with enthusiasm. From November 28 to December 10, 1958, the Eighth Central Committee held its Sixth Plenary Session at Wuchang, where several resolutions on the problems of communism were passed. Around this time Mao elaborated his earlier warning against fear in "Imperialists and All Reactionaries Are Paper Tigers." [4] The same Plenary Session adopted Chairman Mao's decision against being "President of the State," she announced calmly of a decision open to other interpretation. [5]

From historical retrospect we can see how the Politburo meetings of July and August 1959 that climaxed in a shake-up among the leaders presented perhaps unforeseen opportunities for the political career of Chiang Ch'ing. These meetings, like many among the top leaders, were held in ethereal Lu Shan, a mountain resort on the west bank of Lake Poyang in Kiansi province. The historical moment was tense. Filiation with the Soviet Union, on which the Chinese had so depended ideologically and materially, was about to be severed. The Great Leap Forward had brought famine and suffering, which to the traditional mind spelled a decline in the dynastic cycle. However Mao's "scalp may have stiffened" from humiliation and stress, he was not about to yield political

* That editorial included his famous metaphorical redemption of mass poverty: "Apart from their other characteristics, China's six hundred million people have two remarkable peculiarities; they are, first of all, poor, and secondly, 'blank.' That may seem like a bad thing, but it is really a good thing. Poor people want change, want to do things, want revolution. A clean sheet of paper has no blotches, and so the newest and most beautiful pictures can be painted on it" (translated in PR, June 10, 1958).

supremacy to rivals, to accept judgments of literary men of conscience, or to open himself to popular revenge.

Nevertheless, cautious realignments were made at the top. Mao stepped down as chief of state, ostensibly to devote the better part of his talent to revolutionary philosophy. Although Liu Shao-ch'i had been committed to the primacy of agriculture and had enthusiastically promoted Mao's Great Leap Forward, the community of leading comrades held Mao, rather than Liu, personally responsible for recent setbacks. At the Lu Shan meeting where Liu replaced Mao as head of state, lingering tensions between these two men and their respective followers emerged with increasing clarity. As always, Mao distanced himself from present dangers by a sense of history. He reconstructed the immediate conflict between dominant personalities in ideological terms, as if it were a class confrontation:

The struggle that has arisen at Lu Shan is a class struggle. It is the continuation of the life-or-death struggle between the two great antagonists of the bourgeoisie and the proletariat in the process of the socialist revolution during the past decade. In China and in our party, it appears that such a struggle will continue for at least another twenty years, and possibly even for half a century. In short, classes must be completely eliminated before the struggle will cease. With the cessation of old social struggle, new social struggle will arise. In short, in accordance with materialist dialectics, contradiction and struggle are perpetual; otherwise, there would be no world . . . intraparty struggle has merely reflected the class struggle in society.[6]

In a sizzling summer these men and their contentions were remote from Chiang Ch'ing, who was convalescing in the villa reserved for the Chairman and herself at Pei-tai-ho, a seaside resort east of Peking. She recalled how her pleasure in the temperate coastal waters and breezes was suddenly shattered by a note from the Chairman. It included a draft of his reply to P'eng Te-huai, the minister of national defense, who had just submitted his "undoing," a so-called Ten-Thousand Word Letter that repudiated the Chairman's vigorously enforced general line for the transition to socialism. P'eng handed over his letter on the fourteenth of July — the same day, she recalled from reports, that resolutions were passed against the "crimes" of Huang K'o-ch'eng,[7] and issues relating to the Three Red Banners (the general line, the communes, and the Great Leap Forward) were considered. Since she could not comment reasonably upon the Chairman's draft before seeing P'eng's original letter,[8] she telephoned the Chairman to tell him that she was preparing to fly immediately to Lu Shan to learn more about the issues behind the confrontation.

"The struggle's too acute," he shot back and said "no" to her coming. She went anyway and to his dismay sat in on the meetings. The clash of men and ideas, more violent than she had seen in years, aggravated her illness. That worried the Chairman, for as soon as the meeting was over he took her to their retreat in Hangchow where they rested together and planned their next moves.

For official history the high point of the Lu Shan meeting was P'eng Te-huai's rude challenge. But that was, indeed, tangential to personal history — a husband's and wife's private passion for aesthetic life. As usual Chiang Ch'ing had taken along her camera, and in her free time photographed what pleased her eye. Her most successful picture, she thought, was a mountainscape of the marvelously gnarled Cave of the Gods, the site of an ancient Taoist shrine. To centuries of travelers that epitomized the famous Lu Shan resort.

Two years later, on September 9, 1961, Chiang Ch'ing, Mao's muse, inspired him to compose a quatrain that he copied onto the reverse of her photo of Lu Shan and dedicated to Li Chin, the childhood name she used to sign her art photography. During our interview Chiang Ch'ing gave me an enlarged print of her cherished Lu Shan photograph with Mao's poem, copied in her own hand, on the reverse (see the second picture section). His sense of the place and of the woman who captured it is unabashly romantic:

> At bluegreen twilight I see the rough pines
> serene under the rioting clouds.
> The cave of the gods was born in heaven,
> a vast wind-ray beauty on the dangerous peak. [9]

In 1961 who would have known that the Chairman's lyric dedicated to Comrade Li Chin would become part of the language of the Cultural Revolution they now were planning?

They were still in Hangchow on August 15, Chiang Ch'ing continued her tale, when the Chairman wrote "Empiricism or Marxism," an essay in which he advised all the leaders and other responsible comrades to read a certain small dictionary of philosophy then in its third edition. [10] At the same time he recommended a textbook on political economy. [11]

Hangchow was lovely as always, but in late summer intensely humid and hot, the temperature rising to around 106 degrees. Even with air conditioning, the temperature could not be forced below 86. Enervated by the ovenlike atmosphere, she left the Chairman there and moved on to their residence in Shanghai. To regain her strength she forced herself into a regimen of physical activity, which included tending their garden, a work she usually enjoyed. But now even watering for irrigation and observing the flutter of leaves caused her to perspire profusely (in her mid-forties were menopausal symptoms coinciding with a political change of life?). She fainted, revived, and fainted again. Thinking that she was suffering from low blood sugar, she gorged herself with sweets, which caused "the position of her stomach to drop" with sensations of nausea. She could digest nothing, and for days on end imagined that she was about to vomit.

To get her mind off her physical ailments, her doctor recommended that she go to see some shows. So she did, and in the later summer of 1959 turned anew to the cultural world. What she found shocked her. Attending the Shanghai theater resounding with ancient and bourgeois plays was like perusing an archaeological dig and suddenly coming across a heap of antiques, long buried, crazily arranged. The problems she foresaw in "making the superstructure fit the base" were staggering.

To prime herself for the projects ahead she underwent a series of acupuncture treatments and a still more rigorous program of physical exercise. Each day she did fifteen minutes of *t'ai-chi-ch'uan* (sinuous exercises based on mimes of animals and flowers), twenty minutes of table tennis, one or two rounds of billiards, and a bout of swimming. "One hundred and fifty meters of swimming with four rest intervals, was it not?" she tossed the question to Hsiao Chiao, her bodyguard, evidently, for more than thirteen years. He nodded agreeably. Three years of that rehabilitation program carried her to the end of 1962, by which time she considered herself fully recovered and able to devote herself entirely to cultural work.*

By then the Chairman had spent years writing prolifically to establish his viewpoint among the people. Should he continue to communicate only through pamphlets, occasional books, and the daily press, or seek some more permanent form? It was Stalin, actually, she said, who first suggested to Mao Tse-tung that he publish his *Selected Works*. The project took several years.

In 1960 Stalin had been dead for seven years, his reputation was vilified by Khrushchev, and Sino-Soviet relations had deteriorated. Responding to that dire situation, in March 1960 the Chairman wrote the Anshan Constitution.†

---

* Speaking of swimming, she digressed, she knew that I liked to swim and so had arranged an opportunity. Because the masses would become too excited if they caught sight of her swimming, she would not join me this time, but would upon some later visit to China.

Thus an Olympic-sized pool in a recreation park near the Pearl River was, upon her instructions, closed to the masses, the water changed, and four national champion swimmers, all strapping females, dispatched to accompany me. "So you won't drown!" my companions responded, to my dismay. An hour's swim in a vast tepid pool surrounded by colorful splashes of tropical flowers was splendid. The discussion with experts of undulation patterns in the butterfly stroke was delightful. But after a second morning of such indulgence I declined still another. Not only had they changed the water before I arrived, I learned, but also after I left!

† The Constitution of the Anshan Iron and Steel Company (*Anshan kang-ling*) laid down the law for governing socialist enterprises in a style diametrically opposed to the Constitution of the Magnitogorsk Iron and Steel Combine, which stressed first production, then the authority of specialists, material incentives, profits in command, and other Soviet and "capitalist" techniques (later attributed to Liu Shao-ch'i). Mao's Anshan Constitution stressed politics in command, dominance

In July the Soviet Union unilaterally withdrew all its experts from China and scrapped contracts previously negotiated between the two countries. The Chairman was shaken by this setback, she admitted, but took it in stride. Abandonment by the Soviets forced him to take fresh account of national resources (still, as always, mainly land and labor) and to go to the people with a renewed call for economic "self-reliance." * The sudden policy shift came in August when agriculture was given priority in national economic development.

At the Ninth Plenum of the Eighth Central Committee, which was held from January 13 to 18, 1961, Chairman Mao took into account the disequilibrium in the current situation (natural disasters and the mismanaged Great Leap Forward) when he spoke of "adjusting, consolidating, enriching, and improving the national economy." [12] In February and March the Central Committee convened at Canton where the Chairman helped prepare the draft of the "Sixty Rules for the People's Commune," [13] a document designed to codify organized principles already in practice. The rationale of the people's commune, as she explained, was to consolidate collective ownership at three levels — the team, the brigade, and the commune. However, implementation of the commune would not rule out small plots to be retained by peasants for growing vegetables or raising pigs and such things for their personal consumption. That modified version was applied over subsequent months.

While they promoted the commune in most parts of the country, the leaders also defended their economic work, which was being obliquely attacked by journalists and dramatists. These onslaughts provoked the calling of a working conference of the Central Committee in January and February of 1962. There the Chairman addressed an enlarged meeting attended by several thousand. His message, she said, was of utmost importance.†

By the spring of 1962 she had convinced the Chairman (as she had argued for years) of the compelling need to gain the upper hand ideologically by vigorously promoting proletarian supremacy in the arts. For the first time he assigned her the task of drafting a policy statement to be adopted by the highest council of state, the Central Committee (of which she was not yet a member). The document she drew up was known as the May Sixteenth Circular [14] and should be seen as belonging to the prelude of the Cultural Revolution, she emphasized. On August 6, 1962, when the Chairman presided over the Central Committee at Pei-tai-ho resort in Hopeh province, he introduced the directive "Class: Situation and Contradiction," an elaboration upon the problem of na-

of Party leadership, mass movement, cadre participation in productive labor and worker participation in management, discard of outmoded regulations, and close cooperation among cadres, workers, and technicians. Those principles were aggressively applied by Mao's side when the Cultural Revolution reached the industrial sector.

* *Tzu-li keng-sheng*, a slogan first promoted under the KMT blockade of Yenan.

† "Talk at an Enlarged Work Conference" (Jan. 30, 1962), in Stuart Schram, ed., *Chairman Mao Talks to the People*, 158–187.

tional and international class struggle and promotion of proletarian ideology nationwide. The message from Pei-tai-ho would be remembered later as the "spirit of the Tenth Plenum." It too belonged to the prelude of the Cultural Revolution, particularly in the performing arts. But, she repeated, the real beginning was marked by *mass mobilization*, which was not aroused until the summer of 1966.

Presently the struggle with Liu Shao-ch'i intensified. She noticed this in the tack taken by the Chairman at the crucial Tenth Plenum of the Eighth Central Committee held in Peking from September 24 to September 27, 1972.[15] Presiding there, the Chairman laid down the "basic line of the Party in the Socialist stage," a message of "great historical significance" that was designed to counteract Liu Shao-ch'i's foreign policy of conciliation toward imperialism, revisionism, and reaction. In domestic affairs Liu advocated a free market economy: private plots, free enterprises responsible for their own production, and quotas fixed for each household (rather than for the teams).*

When the Central Committee met at Hangchow on May 20, 1963, Chiang Ch'ing made a point of being there as an auditor. On that occasion the Chairman formulated resolutions on several questions regarding the countryside.[16] These discussions later became the original Ten Point Document, which stressed the power of ideas over material force.[17] Four months later, in September 1963, Liu Shao-ch'i published his so-called Later Ten Point Document, which was "leftist in form but rightist in essence." Ostensibly a complement to the Chairman's Ten Point Document, Liu's document was actually written to refute it, she charged.

ii

The Cultural Revolution was a "political course not given in the classroom," Mao once quipped. In the early 1960's Chiang Ch'ing was both taking that course and giving it. In the past when her mentor Mao sensed that he was losing ground in the perpetual power struggle, he quit his headquarters, disregarded normal Party channels, and went out on his own to make contact with his only real constituency, the masses. The wisdom of his actions came from the long span of Chinese history, from recognition that the masses and only the masses offer ultimate validation for government. Those able to confront the masses confidently and constructively merit, in traditional metaphor, the Mandate of Heaven, and thus prove their mettle as leaders. That political lesson so forcefully demonstrated by Mao was not lost on Chiang Ch'ing.

* A distortion of Liu's foreign and domestic principles in order to show his "contradiction" of Mao's new ideological goals.

Physically rehabilitated in the early 1960's (and presumably cured of cancer), she was more determined than ever not to be forgotten by the revolutionary movement. She began to publish in youth and women's journals under her own name, which few recognized in those days.[18] More importantly, she resumed traveling on her own, reporting to the center on what she saw, and auditing some Central Committee meetings by virtue of her special relation to Mao. Those steps were only preliminary to her storming of the barriers raised around wives in high places. After two decades of isolation could she restore contact with the ordinary people and persuade them to accept her as a leader?

She began her return to the people through the Socialist Education Campaign, when the "spirit of the Tenth Plenum" was brought to bear upon the masses through highly publicized festivals of education and the arts. The People's Liberation Army headed by Lin Piao lent not only physical but also moral force to the cause. Both the Spring Forum on Education and the PLA's Third Literature and Arts Festival promoted the slogan "Learn from the PLA." The story of the young soldier Lei Feng, whose accidental death elevated him to martyrdom, figured as a popular model in most of the media.

The slogan hastened the coming of the Cultural Revolution. The Socialist Education Campaign demanded renewed determination to meld civilian with military interests, and also a narrowing of the gap between urban and rural peoples and privileged and underprivileged classes generally. At the Spring Festival Symposium Mao laid down the law: "It is necessary to drive all singers, poets, playwrights, and writers from the cities to the countryside. They should be sent group by group and stage by stage to the countryside and factories, and must not be permitted to live indefinitely in offices, otherwise they cannot put out good things. Those who have not gone to the grassroots level should not be fed and only those who have gone there should be fed." [19]

Concurrently but less visibly Chiang Ch'ing started her own crusade against all theater evocative of a useless past. In Marxian language she denounced "ghost plays" (animated by superstition and folk religion) and plays about feudal society and the bourgeoisie as superstructural elements not fitting with China's emerging socialist base. Among the most intolerable "feudal" dramas were of course Wu Han's play about Hai Jui, which appeared in 1961, Meng Ch'ao's *Li Hui-hsiang*, and T'ien Han's *Hsieh Yao-huan* of the same year (a great one for all the liberal arts). *Hsieh Yao-huan*'s arousal of ire at the top revealed abiding political anxieties, perhaps in Chiang Ch'ing more than anyone. Its parallels with *Inside Story of the Ch'ing Court*, which she had censored ten years earlier, were striking. Both featured female rulers: *Inside Story* the Empress Dowager Tz'u Hsi, and *Hsieh Yao-huan* the Empress Wu of the eighth century. T'ien Han's title character, however, as female president of the Board of Rites and confidante and loyal counsel of Empress Wu, was a fictional creation, for the historical Empress Wu officially had been served only by men. In his new play T'ien Han, whose dramatic skill with ancient as well as modern female characters was by now well established, showed both the Empress and her female counsel resisting powerful families and aristocrats out of "consideration" for the people who suffered injustice in the management of land. From a Marxian viewpoint such a characterization was untenable. Since the Empress and her counsel belonged to the feudal ruling class, they could not have been the least sympathetic toward their class enemy, the peasantry, whom they oppressed, if only by class definition. Like *The Story of Wu Hsun*, which came out during the land reform movement, *Hsieh Yao-huan* (and a spate of modernly styled "feudal" and "ghost" plays, among them *Wu Tse-t'ien* and *The Fragrant Silk Handkerchief*) appeared during the accelerated rural transformation of communization and the Great Leap Forward, a time when all ideological and moral forces were needed for support. Such dramas as these were accused of arousing nostalgia for the past, of weakening the class struggle by softening the images of old imperial and landlord classes, and of promoting at least a moral restoration of feudalism at a time when the leaders were trying to quicken spirits in the pursuit of socialism. T'ien Han and Wu Han were charged with using their "loyal counsels" Hsieh Yao-huan and Hai Jui as vehicles for personal and public complaints. Both dramatic figures, and hence the authors behind them, claimed to "speak for the people," a privilege the leaders of proletarian dictatorship intended to monopolize, but did not fully exercise until they seized cultural authority in 1966.[20]

Among the few leaders who then supported Chiang Ch'ing's determination to purge the national theater of all religious masques, "demons and monsters," and gaudy and glamorous types from a politically outmoded past was her friend Shanghai Mayor K'o Ch'ing-shih. In January 1963 he called upon his city's diverse and influential communities of performing artists to abandon old repertories, adopt the class struggle spirit of the Tenth Plenum, and stage new dramas with heroes drawn from the ranks of workers, peasants, and soldiers — the people who had led socialist construction over the last thirteen years.

Soon Chairman Mao, prevailed upon by his wife, uttered the brilliant aphorism that became part of the jargon of the coming years. All plays portraying "ghosts" or "emperors and princes, generals and ministers, gifted scholars and beauties" should be banned. To drive home his point he accused the Ministry of Culture, since Liberation dominated by Chou Yang, Hsia Yen, Lin Mo-han, and their coterié,* of being a "ministry of emperors and princes, generals and ministers, gifted scholars and beauties. . . ."[21]

---

* Although the Ministry of Culture was formally headed by the distinguished writer Mao Tun (Shen Yen-ping) from 1949 to 1965, neither Mao Tse-tung nor Chiang Ch'ing held him chiefly responsible for obstructionist cultural policies during these years.

In December he spoke more ominously: "The 'dead' still dominate in many departments. . . . The social and economic base has changed, but the arts as part of the superstructure which serves this base still remain a serious problem. Hence we should proceed with investigation and study and attend to this matter in earnest. . . . Isn't it absurd that many Communists are enthusiastic about promoting feudal and capitalist art but not socialist art?" [22]

Liu Shao-ch'i, allegedly the protector of these maligned ministers, responded defensively, " 'Emperors and princes, generals and ministers' must still be portrayed but they should be portrayed less often. . . . Speaking in terms of art, the level of music, novel, poetry, and opera of the capitalist era — what we call the new democratic era — is not as high as that of the feudal era. The novels and plays of today are in most cases also not so good as those of the feudal era. Therefore, plays about 'emperors and princes, generals and ministers, gifted scholars and beauties' should be performed." [23]

Chiang Ch'ing's investigation of the performing arts put her in touch with eminent political figures who were previously remote from her, and few would she respect. Prominent among them was T'ao Chu, strong man of the south,[24] no less interested than she in employing cultural control to widen his sphere of political influence. While she was struggling for the power to reform the Peking opera of the north, T'ao Chu was exercising his formidable powers to bring the *Yueh* opera indigenous to Canton up to date politically.

Sketching his record, she said that on October 11, 1961, T'ao Chu spoke on the subject of intellectuals in Canton where he was first secretary of the CCP's Central South Bureau; much of what he said then was pejorative (hence commendable), she recalled, though his personal commitments were not yet clear. The following spring a series of convocations on the arts was held nationwide. T'ao Chu attended the one on March 5, 1962, to foster the creation of new modern dramas and operas. He also attended the Conference of Art and Literature Circles for the Promotion of Creative Writing; on May 23, he took part in another important literary meeting. The actual motives for T'ao Chu's appearances at the March and May meetings where he was highly visible have only recently begun to be understood, she said. Before May 1963 little was known about his cultural policies; even in 1965 his values and intentions were not well understood. Her assistant in the early stages of the Cultural Revolution, Yao Wen-yuan, was among the first to examine T'ao Chu's works carefully. Yao wrote about two of T'ao's books, she said, one of which was *On the Style of the Pure Press*. Astutely he demonstrated that T'ao Chu actually supported the Four Villains who opposed her and Chairman Mao in cultural affairs. After the publication of Yao's rebuttal "they" (she and Mao) discovered that Lin Piao was T'ao Chu's boss behind the scenes, she added in a flash of historical revisionism. Even in the early 1960's Lin Piao and Liu Shao-ch'i were "on good terms," a disclosure not made until recently.

Chiang Ch'ing did not assume a conspicuous role in the huge convocations until the Festival of Peking Opera on Contemporary Themes held in June and July 1964 at the Great Hall of the People. Like its precursors, this was no simple revel of pure culture. Authorized by the Ministry of Culture on the instigation of the Central Committee, the festival offered the opportunity to show off new theater, hereafter to be instructed by advice from the central propaganda organs on how to promote proletarian politics from the stage. The arranger of speakers, Premier Chou En-lai, took into account Chiang Ch'ing's recent investigations of opera companies all over the country by inviting her to write an article on the problem of revolution in Peking opera. She could present that viva voce at the festival, he said.

The festival was unprecedented in Chinese history, both for the number of companies and people it involved, and more importantly for its resolve to bring the performing arts, far more the expressions of local culture than of national consensus, in line with the proletarian politics of the center. Thirty-seven new operas were performed by twenty-eight opera companies from nineteen provinces, cities, and autonomous regions. Thirty-three of the operas dealt with the current revolution; the rest described revolutionary struggles that antedated the Communists. Propaganda Chief Lu Ting-i — no friend of Chiang Ch'ing — was the keynote speaker. Mao Tse-tung, who seemed to have thrown himself entirely behind the extravaganza, Liu Shao-ch'i, whose objections to it were unconcealed, and Chou En-lai, who withheld opinion, made their appearances. So did Mayor P'eng Chen, who was later quoted for calling the revolutionary operas "still at the stage of wearing trousers with a slit at the seat and sucking the fingers." [25] "The breeze of reform would stop blowing only if capitalism were restored and modern revisionists got into power," he noted elliptically in a report of festival proceedings. [26]

Comrade Chiang Ch'ing, whose face and voice were still unknown to most of the people, delivered her maiden speech. But its publication, she pointed out in our interview, was delayed for three years; the others'speeches were published immediately. Not until May 1967 did hers appear in the Party journal, *Red Flag*. Why? Because her "enemies" (men opposing her assumption of authority in the arts) tampered with her original text and then refused to grant it official validation. Not until they were immobilized could her ideas be published.

In that article (from which she did not quote in our interview, though parts had been read to me earlier by her aides), she railed against anachronisms in art and political life and demanded the creation of the proper superstructure "to protect the socialist economic base." The political motive for her presentation of "shocking" statistics was transparent. But those same figures also underscored the theater's broad command of popular imagination and public opinion. According to her rough estimate,

there were 3,000 theatrical companies in the country [not including amateur troupes and unlicensed companies]. Of these, around 90 are professional modern drama companies, 80-odd are cultural troupes, and the rest, over 2800, are companies staging various kinds of operas and balladry. Our operatic stage is occupied by emperors, princes, generals, minsters, scholars and beauties, and on top of these, ghosts and monsters. As for those 90 modern drama companies, they don't necessarily all depict the workers, peasants, and soldiers either. They too lay stress on staging full-length plays, foreign plays, and plays on ancient themes. . . . There are well over 600 million workers, peasants, and soldiers in our country, whereas there is only a handful of landlords, rich peasants, counterrevolutionaries, bad elements, Rightists, and bourgeois elements. Shall we serve this handful, or the 600 million?

That simple Marxian argument, which pivoted upon an idea of absolute class service, would be repeated over and over again in coming years. So also her appeal to a new proletarian class conscience, first presented at the Opera Festival, would become catechismal:

The grain we eat is grown by the peasants, the clothes we wear and the houses we live in are all made by the workers, and the People's Liberation Army stands guard at the fronts of national defense for us and yet we do not portray them on stage. May I ask which class stand you artists do take? And where is the artists' "conscience" you always talk about? [27]

In opera they must "foster some pacesetters." Among those pacesetters still at an experimental stage were *The Red Lantern*, *Spark among the Reeds* (later called *Shachiapang*), *Raid on White Tiger Regiment*, and *Raiding the Bandits' Stronghold* (which became *Taking Tiger Mountain by Strategy*). All were on the way to achieving the status of "model opera." Among the leaders who saw these operas and recommended changes were the Chairman, of course, proletarian drama buff K'o Ch'ing-shih, and K'ang Sheng, a fellow townsman and security chief, of whom she spoke often with caution, warmth, and jest — "He wanted my favorite tree peony photos but I wouldn't let him have them.

More sharply remembered were her enemies,* the cultural commisars

* One who was often named during the Cultural Revolution, though scarcely mentioned by Chiang Ch'ing during our interview when he was undergoing "rectification," was Teng Hsiao-p'ing, formerly secretary general under Liu Shao-ch'i, and after ten years of disgrace restored temporarily in 1975 as vice-premier acting in lieu of ailing Chou En-lai. At a meeting of the Secretariat of the Central Committee held during the Peking Opera Festival Teng cast aspersions on Chiang Ch'ing's self-made political character: "Some people try to gain publicity for themselves just by criticizing and repudiating others. They step on the shoulders of others just in order to mount the stage. . . . Because of the [opera reform] movement many people no longer dare to write articles. Nowadays the New China News Agency receives only two articles a day. Only soldiers and warfare are featured in the plays" (CB 842 [Dec. 8, 1967]: 14).

who, she was convinced, had thwarted her political career for thirty years. During the weeks of the festival she made a point of going over to talk with the Four Villains — Chou Yang, Yang Han-sheng, T'ien Han, and Hsia Yen — and also with Chang Keng, who *still* was producing bourgeois drama. Even then, as she had been in Yenan, she was loath to take revenge against them. She approached them goodnaturedly (so she recalled) and encouraged them to go and *make revolution for a change*. They stood there dumbly. Still, she restrained herself because the situation was precarious. That summer she and the Chairman suspected, though they lacked conclusive proof, that these men were "turncoats, Trotskyites, or special agents of the Kuomintang." [28]

To test the goodwill of T'ien Han (whose acquaintance she had first made as a frightened young girl cut off from the Party branch in Shanghai), she invited him and his wife to dine with her. They accepted. She used that occasion to ask T'ien Han to adapt the script of *The Red Detachment of Women*, now a modern drama, to Peking opera form. He agreed. But what he produced some weeks later was far *worse* than the original, she recalled hotly.

After the Peking Opera Festival, considered by Chiang Ch'ing an overall success, Liu Shao-ch'i and his wife Wang Kuang-mei, apparently piqued by Chiang Ch'ing's success, campaigned all over the country throughout August and September. Ostensibly they were promoting the Four Cleanups Movement, she said angrily, but actually they were working to undermine Chairman Mao's proletarian revolutionary line.

The Premier observed all these developments closely. In the work report prepared for the first session of the Third National People's Congress, which was held on December 21, 1964, he addressed himself to cultural trends of the year and explained how the history of mankind is one of continuous development from the realm of necessity to the realm of freedom. That day, Chiang Ch'ing added incidentally of a significant political achievement, she first served in the National People's Congress as representative from Shantung, her native province.

As she gained a foothold in political establishments, others countered her moves, she was convinced. That same December the crimes of the once-renowned military leader Lo Jui-ch'ing were exposed. The case broke in Shanghai where he was repudiated for his "bourgeois military line." Lin Piao shared such views, she added. Even *before* the lines of Cultural Revolution began to be drawn in 1965, the Chairman was a foe of Lin Piao. Contradictions between them were already evident.

During Lo Jui-ch'ing's denunciation it emerged that his long involvement in public security had extended to espionage within her organization (aides and entourage) earlier that year. In fact, Lo Jui-ch'ing turned out to be the one who had requested that the *People's Liberation Army Daily* expose her personal initiative in the early Cultural Revolution, a fact she had been trying to keep secret. When she learned this, she immediately telephoned him and "struggled against him." Lo Jui-ch'ing's view, naive to be sure, was that anything the army did was fine. "Is the PLA living in a vacuum?" she asked him. He had no answer.

As usual the PLA was producing its own plays, musicals, and films. One film in particular, purportedly a historical recreation of the Long March, struck her as having a "reformist" motive. She arranged for the Chairman to see it. He called it "sectarian" (self-serving), for it did not project the way in which all the front armies joined forces in the military effort. Instead, it focused solely upon the role of the First Front Army (commanded by Lin Piao), showing it to be made up of the staunchest fighters. (The roles of the Third and Fourth Front Armies were glossed over.) To overcome the film's flaws of "sectarianism" and "mountain-strongholdism" the Chairman recommended specific improvements, but "Lin Piao and his company" thwarted all attempts to revise *their* film.

By the spring of 1966 conflict flared in all fields, Chiang Ch'ing continued. That February (while Mao visited Hangchow and Hunan) she was directing a Forum on Work in Literature and Art in the Armed Forces in Shanghai when the February Outline was "dished up" by the Group of Five in Charge of the Cultural Revolution.[29] This peculiar group was headed by Peking Mayor P'eng Chen, a man who already had opposed her updating of opera. Indeed, *their* program, she recognized, was a calculated rebuttal of *her* program to bring socialism to the arts. Presented as mere "academic" discussion without necessary political import, the February Outline promoted such fatuous slogans as "everyone is equal before the truth" and other outdated notions. This sort of "counterrevolutionary revisionism" was cropping up everywhere. In philosophy some began to struggle against the principle "one divides into two" (essential to dialectical thought, according to Mao).[30] The economist Sun Yeh-fang, who was even more extreme than Y. Liberman of the Soviet Union, advocated "profits in command" and "other revisionist price and profit theories." Among historians the "theory of concessions" was gaining ascendancy. That theory held that the victory of peasant uprisings in the past was not the result of strenuous efforts on the part of the peasants themselves, but rather the effect of concessions made by the emperors to the people. She added that implicit reference was made to T'ang T'ai-tsung (A.D. 627–650), second emperor of the T'ang dynasty.

While the Central Committee met in Hangchow on April 16, 1966, the Peking Municipal Party Committee, dominated by the same men who controlled the Group of Five in Charge of the Cultural Revolution, was persuaded to make gestures of "rectification" toward some intellectuals who had offended the Party leaders. With elaborate formality they organized a series of articles nominally critical of Wu Han's newspaper column, "Three Family Village" (written jointly with the journalists Teng T'o and Liao Mo-sha and already recognized for satirically using historical anecdote to criticize the foibles of Mao and his supporters). But actually the Peking Party Committee was only protecting this seditious column, she said. And their falsely critical reviews were circulated nationwide. Even T'ao Chu * published them in his region's newspaper, *Canton Daily*. During the Hangchow meeting certain aspects of the role of P'eng Chen, then chairman of the Peking Party Committee, were disclosed. The urban organization he ran was "a watertight place" impenetrable to outsiders, she said.

One of P'eng Chen's men now put under pressure was Liao Mo-sha, the journalist she knew all too well when he was young and struggling to survive in Shanghai in the 1930's. He was now disgraced not only for co-authoring "Three Family Village," but also for having maligned Lu Hsun (whose reputation was being reconstructed as his erstwhile rival Chou Yang's fell) — expecially Lu's "fringed writing" (*hui-pien wen-hsueh*). She added the term, hinting that Liao was pro-Kuomintang. Why speak of "fringed writing"? Lu Hsun had taken over the term from Kuomintang usage; indeed he used it as the title of one of his volumes. The term "fringed writing" came from the Kuomintang practice of having in its newspapers so-called "open heavenly windows" [31] (*k'ai-t'ien ch'uang*), or blank spaces, where a censored article, one by Lu Hsun or another dissident, might have appeared. Such were the ways of Chiang Kai-shek's fascism.

Her antagonism toward P'eng Chen also antedated the Cultural Revolution. How well she remembered paying a visit to his Municipal Party Committee meeting and asking his permission to give a Peking opera troupe revolutionary scripts and scores. The committee would hear nothing of it. Sometime later in 1965 when Li Tsung-jen (in the late 1940's acting president of the Republic) visited Peking, Chairman Mao gave a dinner in his honor, preceded by a reception to which she was also invited. Forewarned that P'eng Chen would also be present at the reception, she attended the banquet only. During the dinner, however, she summonded the courage to go up to P'eng Chen and invite him to leave the banquet hall and join her in an inside chamber. Alone there with him, she explained her keen interest in bringing socialism to the arts and cited the precedent of Chang Ch'un-ch'iao, Party chief in Shanghai, who had organized (under her impetus) the reform of the ballet *White-haired Girl* and other revolutionary pieces. With an opera score in hand she again asked P'eng Chen to give her a Peking opera troupe to reform on her own. Angrily he

---

* By 1966 elevated to the directorship of the Propaganda Department, and fourth among the CCP leaders, ranking after Mao, Lin Piao, and Chou En-lai.

snatched the score, refused her request, and told her to take a "strong position." She reported that exchange to the Chairman, who was furious.

It was plain to both of them and to others who shared their goals that without high rank she could accomplish nothing. In the short run she could continue to work behind the scenes on the unmasking of seditious literature and the reconstruction of salvageable works. But that was not the long-term solution.

13.

◇ ◇ ◇

Learn to Swim by Swimming

> When we learn to swim, we do not learn to
> swim first and then go into the water. We
> learn to swim by swimming. . . . When
> we make revolution it is also not a matter of
> learning first and then doing, but of learn-
> ing in the course of doing, or rather, of
> doing and then learning. Doing is itself
> learning.
> — Editorial, *People's Daily*
> (August 17, 1966)

Rulers of imperial China lived in lavish palaces walled off from their
subjects, dressed magnificently, dined sumptuously, and surrounded themselves with courtiers. They governed by edicts cast in elegant literary language
and transmitted through a vastly stratified bureaucracy of scholarly gentlemen,
no "gentle-women" among them.

Meeting the people head on in plain style has become the hallmark of the
twentieth century's revolutionary governors. But only rarely has that direct
confrontation been initiated by women at the pinnacle of the power structure.
Such sexual imbalance Chiang Ch'ing began to correct when she regularly left
her comfortable enclosure, Chung-nan-hai, and mobilized trusted comrades to
shatter the social order by turning the streets where once she demonstrated
against other leaders into arenas of loosely governed political action. Thus, she
became the first woman since Liberation to summon the masses, address them
on topics of her choice, order her speeches published, and mark some for export in translation.

Those simple facts of sexual assertion were never commended by the official

Communist press. Yet they should be noted by history like the revolutionary thought she espoused. Is it possible that other leaders thought that the consciousness of the people was not yet revolutionized enough to be willing to accept a woman arriving *as a woman* at the summit of power?

Since the middle of the twentieth century, improved food production and distribution, better health care, and curtailment of warfare doubled China's population from four hundred to nearly eight hundred million. At the onset of the Cultural Revolution the majority of the population was under thirty. Consequently, leaders had to address themselves to the needs of a restless, idealistic, and sometimes cynical constituency. Although China appeared from the outside to be hermetically sealed from the rest of the world, its younger generation was not wholly immune to the infection of the revolution of rising expectations. Throughout the early 1960's foreign literature, films, and touring companies from abroad were widely available to the urban population. From the strictly pragmatic viewpoint of some leaders, such diversions were distractions from the fundamental task of "building socialism." Unification of the people's energies required control of their minds, and especially of their cultural interests. Mao and Chiang Ch'ing above all recognized that all sources of bourgeois ideology — domestic or foreign — had to be cut off and youth's perennial gift for moral commitment and rash action had to be marshaled to the best advantage.

Revolutionary continuity beyond the founders' era required a linking of generations by bonds of ideology. Who should bring that about? By the middle 1960's Mao Tse-tung already seemed a mythical figure, an image that obscured his very real talent for manipulating men, women, the masses, and ideas. To cynical China Watchers the Chairman appeared to be not only drifting into seniority, but also sinking into senility. But it was hard to accept that hasty conclusion after his well-advertised swim in the Yangtze in July 1966. Surrounded by masses of vigorous young swimmers, how better symbolically could he dissolve differences between generations?

Symbols would not suffice. With death haunting every founding leader, Chiang Ch'ing, at least a decade younger than they generally were, became more conscious than ever of mortality and of imminent crises that would determine the course of history. What were her chances of survival among comrades acquired only since Yenan? How well would she fare in a succession struggle waged by men who never drew her completely into their inner circle of power? How much did she need Mao?

The Cultural Revolution, prompted by a succession struggle not only of men and women but of generations, was possibly the most massive ideological and social upheaval in Chinese history. How it came about is unanswerable in simple terms, though the question has generated inexhaustible speculation outside China. Was it merely or mainly a power struggle or a policy debate? Did Mao and Liu Shao-ch'i clearly and unswervingly represent alternate policy lines, one socialist and the other revisionist, respectively good and bad by Mao's dominant standard?

Some answers come from Chiang Ch'ing's course over three years, traced in this and the following chapter. Naturally, her rhetoric was always in the terms of Chairman Mao and the laboring people he supported. Her burden, though, was double. Not only was she fighting for Mao and his ideas, but also for herself, a woman defying the masculine dominance of history as she strove to gain a separate trust from the masses and become a leading comrade in her own right.

In the background of Chiang Ch'ing's personal drama stood the two men whose personal and ideological antagonism has been captured by Franz Schurmann:

> The great protagonists in the struggle emerging dramatically during the Cultural Revolution were Mao Tse-tung and Liu Shao-ch'i. Mao and Liu are depicted in Manichaean form as the personifications of good and evil, like characters in classical Peking operatic drama. Outsiders need not play a part in that drama and take one or the other side. The historical fact is that Mao won and Liu lost, and no one can quarrel with that. Each represented a deep-rooted current in China, and each played a major and necessary role in the Cultural Revolution. Mao was the organizer, as he showed in all of his reflective writings. . . . One of the most popular portrayals of Mao during the Cultural Revolution showed him in scholar's gown with an umbrella walking on a high mountain ridge surrounded by distant peaks.* Even during the period 1962–1966 when Liu was officially considered Mao's successor, he was always portrayed in the wooden, impersonal style common to Russian publications in Stalin's day. . . . Mao argued constantly that "one be divided into two," while Liu argued that all efforts should be made to keep divisiveness to a minimum: let the struggle be fought out within the closed walls of the party.[1]

About the horrendously complex events that constitute the "story" of the Cultural Revolution Chiang Ch'ing was intermittently enlightening, for good reason. She did not think like a general historian seeking, obviously in vain, to reweave the total fabric of an era. Her choice of focus also showed me that she wanted to detract from her widely reflected "radical" or "Ultra-Left" image acquired from haphazard foreign journalism. I asked for photographs of her from the mid-1960's; she offered none. Perhaps hardest for foreigners to understand is that she considered her "real work" to be the revolution of the nation's theater. There proletarian values could be embodied in dramatic figures, erected as political models for all the people.

---

* This youthful portrait in oils, painted in both Western style and substance, was promoted by Chiang Ch'ing during the Cultural Revolution.

The documentary record, consequently, is the main source for this and the following chapter. In them, Chiang Ch'ing's tone shifts from personal reminiscence to public rhetoric, becoming especially shrill when she is at her most revolutionary: hectoring the masses.

i

In 1965 China was ruled by a triumvirate. Symbolically, if not entirely effectively, Mao headed the Party. Though rudely challenged of late, Liu Shao-ch'i and the men loyal to him held sway over the Party and the capital city. Lin Piao, the hero of the Long March and the Liberation War, commanded the army. In her bid for national leadership Chiang Ch'ing needed to attach herself to one or more of these three; to stand alone as the mistress of a fourth estate of culture was precarious. Exclusive reliance on Mao showed nepotism. Liu Shao-ch'i, too obviously his rival, was on the way out. That left Lin Piao, whose credibility at that time could not have been so poor as revisionist politics of the next decade and her slanderous account of him to me indicated.

In February 1966 Chiang Ch'ing and Lin Piao struck a fair exchange. She offered him whatever fortune redounded from association with the Chairman's wife, versed in "culture," for a position in the top echelon of the army's command structure. After a quarter century of marriage to the revolution's supreme commander, she was still as unknown to his military following of millions as to the masses at large. How could Lin Piao, the symbol of masculine culture, present the long-neglected ex-actress wife of Chairman Mao as the comrade best suited to be their supreme adviser on cultural affairs, their "pacesetter" in the performing arts?

Formally "entrusted" by Lin Piao, Chiang Ch'ing convened the Forum on Work in Literature and Art in the Armed Forces in Shanghai, where her cultural leadership would be untrammeled by the resentful overlords of Peking. "Comrade Chiang Ch'ing talked with me yesterday," Lin Piao briefed his men nervously before her arrival at the forum. "She is very sharp politically on questions of literature and art, and she really knows art. She has many opinions which are valuable. You should pay good attention to them and see that they are applied ideologically and organizationally. From now on, all the army's documents concerning literature and art should be sent to her."

Chiang Ch'ing arrived on schedule, sporting the men's-style military fatigues that would remain her regular costume throughout the Cultural Revolution years. Facing a sea of soldiers, she began apologetically, in a manner reminiscent of the self-abnegating woman of Chinese tradition. Ill health had hampered her work of recent years and she had not studied Chairman Mao's thoughts assiduously enough. To be sure, she was the one who drafted the report for the Tenth Plenum that set the base line for cultural renovation, but the Chairman revised it three times before it went to press. That report, she reminded them, stressed the need to provoke class struggle throughout the country, foster proletarian ideology, and liquidate bourgeois ideology. The last she nicknamed the Black Line of the 1930's, which included such literary sins as "truthful writing," "the broad path of realism," "the deepening of realism," "middle characters," and "opposition to the smell of gunpowder." "Besides those bourgeois fallacies, literary critics of the Russian bourgeoisie — Belinsky, Chernyshevsky and Dobrolyubov, and Stanislavsky of the theater — must be condemned."

Bowing to the historic role of her new constituency, Chiang Ch'ing resolved to celebrate the army's revolutionary achievements; to create works of literature and art about the three great military campaigns of Liaohsi-Shenyang, Huai-Hai, and Peking-Tientsin; and to do that "while the comrades who led and directed them [notably Lin Piao] are still alive." Hereafter, the monopoly over literary and art criticism should be wrested from the so-called "critics . . . , those wrong in orientation and deficient in militancy," and be put in the hands of the masses. "We must reform our style of writing, promote the composition of short, popular articles, turn literary and art criticism into daggers and hand grenades, and handle those skillfully in close combat. . . . We oppose the use of terminology and jargon to frighten people. Only in this way we can disarm the self-appointed literary and art critics." [2]

Thus Chiang Ch'ing goaded the soldiers on to extraordinary battles: a new order of class warfare against the mystique of men of letters and the legacy of ancient and foreign culture they were brought up to hold in awe. Now plain soldiers, narrowly literate, were ordered to take up pen, paint, baton, and camera, revel in their own exploits, and master the propaganda of their own past.

During the four months after her military appointment Chiang Ch'ing continued to be active on other fronts in Shanghai, she recalled. Much of her time was spent behind the scenes with dramatists, actors, and choreographers whose political consciousness, individually and collectively, she was struggling to transform. All the while she followed the daily reports circulated among the chief leaders, watching for changes in the tide of political events across the nation. Also estranged from the Peking political situation, the Chairman spent several weeks eluding other leaders and the press by making an inspection tour of the countryside. Then in early summer he joined her in Shanghai, where they quietly collaborated in preparing the next moves.

For several years now both had been uneasy about the nation's young people, knowing that they could follow their leaders loyally or repudiate them with equal ardor. Early in 1965 Mao told Edgar Snow that he distrusted educated young people because they "had never fought a war and never seen an imperialist or known capitalism in power." Thus in the future they could "negate the revolution." [3] Beginning in late May of 1966, Chiang Ch'ing recalled, she spent a month or more analyzing trends on leading campuses, focusing particularly upon news dispatches out of Nanking University, Chiaotung University in Sian, and Peking University.

By early summer her potential to act was stronger than ever before. In February she had been appointed cultural adviser to the army. In May the Chairman, then in Hangchow with the Central Committee, was finally moved to discredit the Group of Five in Charge of the Cultural Revolution, authors of the February Outline that deviously repudiated the proletarian line represented by the Chairman and herself. In its stead the Chairman, with the authority of the Central Committee, convened the Drafters of Documents of the Cultural Revolution Group, a second team of leaders judiciously selected for combined talents and loyalty to Mao. The group was headed by Ch'en Po-ta, a man long experienced in voicing the Chairman's policies. Chiang Ch'ing and Shanghai's ebullient Chang Ch'un-ch'iao were made deputy leaders. Their trusted comrades Yao Wen-yuan and K'ang Sheng (the only member carried over from the Group of Five) were also included. [4]

She was still in Shanghai when the Chairman assigned her the task of drawing up a second May Sixteenth Circular, this one a point-by-point refutation of the arguments of the February Outline, which had been in circulation among Party committees at many levels for three months now. She sent the draft to the Chairman, who revised it several times, with the result that much of it was written by him alone, she said.

Although Chiang Ch'ing did not delve deeply into the contents of this May Sixteenth Circular during our conversation, it deserves separate notice because it set forth her side's offensive of the spring of 1966. Cast in bold, antagonistic language, the circular accused the authors of the February Outline (specifically P'eng Chen; K'ang Sheng was spared) of resisting the Chairman's call at the Tenth Plenum of 1962 for socialist cultural revolution. The outline revealed the bourgeois rightist orientation of "scholar-tyrants" who used muddled language to mute class struggle, raised academic and theoretical questions apart from political questions, and promoted the fallacy that "everyone is equal before the truth." The circular's sixth point, a demand for destruction, was crucial: "Chairman Mao often says that there is no construction without destruction. Destruction means criticism and repudiation, it means revolution. It involves reasoning things out, which is construction. Put destruction first and in the process you have construction." That dossiers (typically unfavorable personal histories) were being built up on members of the left to be used against them in an ensuing rectification campaign was also observed. The May Sixteenth Circular was not made public until May 17, 1967, in the *People's Daily*, and in the *Peking Review* two days later, a year's delay showing how long it took for Mao's side to regain command of the press and public opinion.

At an enlarged meeting of the Central Committee held on May 18, 1966, at Hangchow, Lin Piao delivered his "notorious counterrevolutionary speech," * which provoked another enlarged meeting in Hangchow at the end of the month. She attended and recalled the highly charged atmosphere, for Liu Shao-ch'i (backer of P'eng Chen and the just-repudiated February Outline) was present. Lines were drawn. Right after it was over she returned to her cultural work in Shanghai, and Chairman Mao withdrew to prepare his counterattack.

Within days the struggles among the men of the Central Committee spilled over to the university campuses and entered the public domain. On May 25 a poster, made by the female philosophy instructor Nieh Yuan-tzu and her friends, was mounted against the conservative administration of Peking University president Lu P'ing (long supported by P'eng Chen). Rejoicing in this spontaneous defiance, Chairman Mao telephoned K'ang Sheng and told him to circulate the poster nationally. On the first of June, Mao composed his own poster, which he called "China's First Big Marxist-Leninist Poster," and published it. That was the green light for widespread student revolt.

Suddenly all the campuses were torn by factional strife, murder, suicide, and general violence. Prestigious Peking University was as always the bellwether. At the time of the May Fourth Movement of 1919, the December Ninth Movement of 1935, and again during the Hundred Flowers Campaign of 1957, Peking University had produced idealist and articulate young people who set fire to student revolt and kindled leftist political consciousness on other campuses and in society at large, especially the cities. Would that process be repeated?

Peking University puzzled her. Was the student uprising — the bloody June Eighteenth Incident — counterrevolutionary (against Mao) or revolutionary, and so to be promoted as a positive trend on the part of the younger generation? As she recalled later before the public, the situation as it appeared from reports was highly "abnormal." "I was astonished to recognize that some young people of irreproachable family background [peasant and proletarian], whose posters and other writings showed that they wanted to make revolution, had come to be branded counterrevolutionaries, a charge which drove many out of their minds and some to suicide." [5] In our interview she wondered again why so many young people of "good class origin" should want to commit suicide. What had gone wrong?

At the height of the student protest in June, "work teams" were sent to Peking University to quell what were interpreted as counterrevolutionary riots. On

---

* Of great personal candor and historical consciousness, discussed in Chapter 15.

July 18, Chiang Ch'ing remembered, Chairman Mao returned from Shanghai to Peking, and she followed two days later. A mass rally was being held at the Gate of Heavenly Peace, perhaps on the issue of Vietnam; she could not recall for sure. To know the temper of the students she decided to visit Peking University and read their posters for herself. When she told Liu Shao-ch'i of her plans he "pulled a long face." Quickly, she got in touch with Ch'en Po-ta, K'ang Sheng, and other members of the Cultural Revolution Group, sounded them out on the situation at Peking University, and reported their views to the Chairman. At the campus she was met by Nieh Yuan-tzu, maker of the first inflammatory poster. Together they roamed about the Ming-style buildings, scanned the posters plastered on the walls, and stopped to talk with students and teachers, all stunned, naturally, by Comrade Chiang Ch'ing's surprise visit. Only after hours of interrogation did she realize that the rebel students and teachers recently suppressed by the work teams were *not* counterrevolutionaries, as originally reported, but revolutionaries responding to the first flourish of posters of late May. In early June the Chairman had ordered that the work teams should not be sent there in haste. Those orders were obviously countermanded, she declared, for the student uprising should not have been suppressed.

Flanked by Ch'en Po-ta and other Cultural Revolution leaders, Chiang Ch'ing put in several more urgent appearances before Peking University groups. Sensitive to the fear and awe their physical presence might instill in their listeners, the leaders humbly called themselves "students" seeking to learn from their "teachers," the masses. "One must make better use of one's ears, eyes, and brain to hear what the masses have to say," declaimed Ch'en Po-ta. "Only a pupil of the masses can become a teacher of the masses," the elderly K'ang Sheng relayed the words of Chairman Mao. Chiang Ch-ing rejoined, "We're just service personnel of the revolutionaries."

Relying on powers of persuasion, they worked swiftly to convince students and staff that the work teams were not authorized by Chairman Mao, but were sent by P'eng Chen to assist President Lu P'ing in maintaining order on the campus. On July 26 the Cultural Revolution Group ordered the dissolution of the work teams, and the satisfaction of Maoist demands for less administrative bureaucracy, more flexible teaching, shorter degree periods, and an admissions policy based upon the students' demonstrated proletarian class orientation rather than upon past academic record or the parents' political rank.[6] All were long-range educational goals of the Cultural Revolution.

ii

August and September 1966 were months of tremendous social unrest, especially among the young whom the leaders bade to rise to revolutionary succession. In the turmoil, most of the middle schools, colleges, and universities were closed. Some thirteen million youngsters who were invited by the Central Committee to abandon parental and pedagogical authorities made their way from communities throughout the nation, by foot, bicycle, bus, truck, and train to Peking. There they were received "personally" en masse by the supreme patriarch, Chairman Mao.

Chiang Ch'ing spent the long hot summer of 1966 breaking out of her past character. Her team of Cultural Revolution leaders, all men accustomed to exchanging views behind closed doors and propounding policy through journals, now served as the liaison between the Chairman and the transient masses — more millions witnessed their leaders' live presence than ever before in Chinese history. After years of being cloistered and disguised by other names, she plunged among the people and hustled support for the Chairman's cause. On August 6 she spoke to a group of Red Guards at Peking's splendid T'ien-ch'iao Theater, one of several cultural centers she claimed as her special arena.

"Chairman Mao sends you his kindest regards," she opened disarmingly. She had made some mistakes, she admitted then, and would often in future. "But we revolutionaries are not afraid of making mistakes!" She was there to present the formula for revolutionary action, one to be applied relentlessly over the coming months. First, drag out the "capitalist roaders" in the Party; second, get rid of the "four olds" — old ideology, culture, custom, and habits; third, carry out the process of struggle-criticism-transformation (*tou-p'i-kai*). Or, rendered plainly, "We have a big enemy to deal with, and we must sweep away all monsters and demons.* I'm sure you'll do a good job."

How should the young, going about exterminating "monsters" and "capitalist roaders," treat their parents? Her answer survived as a slogan:

> *When parents are revolutionaries,*
> *their children should succeed them.*
> *When parents are reactionaries,*
> *their children should rebel.* 7

On August 16, just two days before Mao received a million political pilgrims, Chiang Ch'ing, with Cultural Revolution Group members Ch'en Po-ta, Li Hsueh-fang, Yao Wen-yuan, K'ang Sheng, and Chang Ch'un-ch'iao, ar-

---

* Folkloric sobriquets for dark forces in the world.

rived at the Peking Workers' Stadium to take charge of a massive rally of "revolutionary students and teachers." Clad alike in plain military fatigues, her party stood in the rain under a steely sky, an atmosphere reflecting the turbulence of revolutionary transformation. Chiang Ch'ing again opened proceedings with her electric phrase, "I have been asked by Chairman Mao to send you his regards!"

"Today we are in a raging storm and are not flowers in a hothouse," Yao Wen-yuan fulminated. All must steel themselves for "stormy class struggle." He intoned the hymn of the Cultural Revolution, by then recognized by all as a paean to Chairman Mao: "Sailing the seas depends on the helmsman . . ."

The major task was to quicken the revolution by drawing a firm line between enemies and friends (a perpetual dialectical action fundamental to class warfare). This was to be done in accordance with the Sixteen-Point Directive and the communiqué of the Central Committee adopted under the direction of Chairman Mao on August 8. Those procedural rules authorized the Cultural Revolution Group to "discover" the leftists and develop their potential as revolutionary leaders. Thus the leftists should join forces in exposing the reactionaries, rightists, and counterrevolutionary revisionists, criticizing their crimes against the Party, and isolating them absolutely.[8]

K'ang Sheng, broadly cultured controller of the secret police, briskly built up rapport with the students; his masterful style Chiang Ch'ing learned to emulate. "Do you want to study the Communiqué and the Sixteen-Point Directive?" he asked. "Yes!" they shouted back. "Do you want to study them again and again?" "Yes!" "Do you want to get well acquainted with them?" "Yes!" "Do you want to grasp them?" "Yes!" "Do you want to apply them?" "Yes!" "Do you want to make use of them in the great cultural revolution of your school?" "Yes! Yes!" they thundered repeatedly. K'ang, as Chiang Ch'ing would on later occasions, drew special attention to Point Four of the Sixteen-Point Directive, *self-reliance* in revolution (soon misconstrued as a license for anarchism). Individuals must depend on themselves to carry on revolutions, and the masses must liberate themselves. Students must have faith in and rely on the masses. Again, he demanded audience response.[9] Thus, using oratorical techniques that would be termed religious in another culture, K'ang Sheng, Chiang Ch'ing, and others of Mao's most trusted disciples drummed into the hearts and minds of the masses the revolutionary rhythms which would reach a fevered beat by mid-August.

"Chairman Mao received a million people. . . ."[10] So opened the worshipful report of the first grand-scale rally of Red Guards at the square before the imperial palace. From the rostrum above the Gate of Heavenly Peace, the leaders gazed down upon the masses below. There, as in similar performances over the months to come. Marshal Lin Piao, appointed vice-chairman, thus designated successor the week before, stood next to Chairman Mao, with Chiang Ch'ing nearby. That precarious juxtaposition, and the extraordinary day as a whole, Chiang Ch'ing chose not to recall in our interview; yet she was, in fact and in appearance to the masses, rarely closer to the top.

"Chairman Mao arrived at the Gate of Heavenly Peace which was covered by a vast sea of people and a forest of red flags," the official report lumbered on. "Turning towards Chairman Mao, people raised their hands overhead and jumped up, cheered and clapped. Many clapped until their hands became sore, many shed tears of joy. . . . The crescendo of cheers roared up to the sky." Representatives of the masses proclaimed:

A great proletarian cultural revolution without parallel in history is being carried out in our country under the leadership of our great leader Chairman Mao. This is a revolution of world significance. We will smash the old world to smithereens, create a new world and carry the great proletarian cultural revolution through to the end.

Sailing the seas depends on the helmsman, the growth of everything depends on the sun, and making revolution depends on Mao Tse-tung's thought. . . . Chairman Mao is the reddest sun of our hearts. . . .[11]

By November 1966 Chiang Ch'ing had appeared in the motorcades, on the rostrum, and on the podium at seven of the eight major Red Guard rallies. As a speaker she became more confident and relaxed, blending personal revelation with public declamation. Her speech of the twenty-eighth of that month to a rally of literary and art workers she regarded as a major philosophic statement.[12] After her long series of illnesses, she said, she was suddenly confronted with the fact of historical incongruities. A socialist nation persisted in producing (and relishing) ghost plays or plays about emperors, officials, generals, scholars, and gorgeous women and in seeking entertainment in famous foreign dramas. If the superstructure was not forced to correspond to the socialist economic base, such drama would inevitably "wreck" it.

In hyperbole intended to shock an educated Chinese audience grown accustomed to the pleasures of imported culture, she warned:

Imperialism is moribund capitalism, parasitic and rotten. Modern revisionism is a product of imperialist policies and a variant of capitalism. They cannot produce any works that are good. Capitalism has a history of several centuries; but it has only a pitiful number of "classics." They [capitalist writers] have created some works modeled after the "classics," but these are stereotyped and no longer appeal to the people, and are therefore completely on the decline. On the other hand, there are some things that really flood the market, such as rock-and-roll, jazz, strip tease, impressionism, symbolism, abstractionism, Fauvism, modernism — there's no end to them. . . . In a word, there is decadence and obscenity to poison and corrupt the minds of the people.

Having spent the whole summer making speeches and keeping abreast of the revolutionary situation, she had neglected her earlier cultural work; for that she apologized and vowed to make up her deficiencies. Now she took to task those members of the Peking First Opera Company who had not yet proved their revolutionary mettle by criticizing openly individual members of the freshly dismantled Peking Municipal Party Committee, which for years had protected this prize company from her proletarian blandishments. To prove their present loyalty to her and Chairman Mao they must draw a firm line between enemies and friends, and must permit young and daring members of their company *to follow her* in making revolution in the performing arts. Those senior company members who had resisted her guidance should "repent genuinely and make a fresh start." But use reasoning, not violence, she insisted once more. "Don't hit others and beat them. Struggle by force can only touch the skin and flesh, while struggle by reasoning things out can touch them to their very souls." [13]

November 28 marked the transfer of the Peking First Opera Company from relative artistic independence and traditional integrity protected by the former Peking Municipal Committee [14] to submission to the authority of the Cultural Revolution Group, of which she was deputy leader, and of the People's Liberation Army, of which she was cultural adviser. In the style of the Paris Commune, she said, company members should elect cultural revolutionary committees from within their own ranks. Moreover, *all other* major groups of performing artists in Peking must be incorporated into the ranks of the PLA and follow its dictates. (It was as if the Pentagon suddenly took over the Metropolitan Opera Company and all other performing arts groups in New York City, and stipulated that their subsequent work be directed personally by a close female relative of the President.)

What inspired Chiang Ch'ing to change the world of the 1960's was the specter of the 1930's, which haunted her and, she thought, cast a spell over the nation. The reminder that deplorable labor conditions still persisted in Shanghai impelled her to demand abolition of short-term and contract labor arrangements. [15] But concern for labor injustices was tangential to her fascination with the political role of culture. By the mid-1960's, Chiang Ch'ing and Mao, for separate reasons, shared a sense of being opposed by alternative political, economic, and cultural systems, which they ascribed summarily to the rivalry and dominance of Liu Shao-ch'i. Both she and Mao knew that to regain command required the creation of favorable public opinion, which meant first winning the upper hand ideologically. To make the cultural realm her province, she condemned the cosmopolitanism of the 1930's. In her terms Liu's enjoyment of cultural diversity, of "bourgeois liberalization," meant that he preached a "literature and art of the whole people" and "seeing life in the country from a caravan," whereas the Chairman taught that literature and art should serve "proletarian dictatorship" and that writers and artists should "go deep among the workers, peasants, and soldiers into the heat of class struggle." Liu's "counterrevolutionary revisionist" principles were displayed in not only the films of Hsia Yen, Chen Huang-mei, and Ts'ai Ch'u-sheng, but also the film histories by Cheng Chi-hua and Hsia Yen, which commended the virtues of Shanghai's culture of the 1930's and sought to sustain and develop them in the 1960's.[16]

The most comprehensive and devastating critique of the cinema cult of the 1930's appeared in the Peking newspaper *Enlightenment Daily* on March 12, 1966.[17] The author of this extraordinarily long article, "On the Reactionary Thought of the Play *Sai Chin-hua*, Dissecting and Analyzing a So-called 'Famous Play' of the 1930's," was editor-in-chief Mu Hsin, who would become a member of Chiang Ch'ing's Cultural Revolution Group. The views he expressed might as well have been Chiang Ch'ing's. There was no figure in modern Chinese history she despised more than the courtesan Sai Chin-hua. Nor was there a modern writer and cinematographer that she resented more than Hsia Yen, who wrote the highly successful (by public, not by Chiang Ch'ing's standards) play about Sai Chin-hua, first produced by the Nineteen Forties Society in 1936.

Even in the 1930's, Mu Hsin wrote, Hsia Yen "swam against the current of his times." Although in the early 1950's Hsia had been persuaded to denounce the film about Wu Hsun that Chiang Ch'ing had first condemned, in the 1960's he was still defending his play about Sai, calling for a "reopening of her case." He "fawned upon foreigners"; his heroine Sai was a "secondary foreign devil" because of her liaison with a German; he tolerated the Japanese and foreign culture in the 1930's, and espoused left-wing liberal arts (by implication, foreign) in the 1960's. In his play he ridiculed the Boxers, who should have been commended as revolutionary, and showed ordinary Chinese people to be prostitutes, opium smokers, jugglers, women with bound feet. Such negative characterizations bared his "national inferiority complex." By insulting his countrymen, he made Western civilization look far too good.

These accusations in the spring of 1966 commenced a settling of scores throughout the rest of the year. As millions of youths came from all over the country to Peking in the summer, Chiang Ch'ing and her Cultural Revolution Group "dragged out ringleader Chou Yang" and his "Black Gang" that included Hsia Yen and T'ien Han. Destruction of their good names and works of thirty years was designed to "dig up the old roots of the Black Line on bourgeois literature and art of the 1930's" and to expose the "capitulationist character" of their old slogan, "national defense literature," which covered a multitude of pro-Kuomintang sins. The black banner of "national defense" dramas, movies, and music must be torn down. Red Guards were ordered to "rip off the masks" of the "songs of national defense of the 1930's" to see what they really were. T'ien Han, for example, was accused of wanting people "to forget old scores." His song "Public Hatred" was charged with slandering the revolutionary masses, who, like "pitiably clumsy cows," waged struggles under Party leadership.[18]

Violence mounted in the fall. Although a circular of November 20, 1966, prohibited popular initiative in arrests, torture, and trials,[19] the order was scarcely heeded. Public enemies named from the Gate of Heavenly Peace in early autumn were brought to trial in December, among them Peking Mayor P'eng Chen, Hsia Yen, T'ien Han, Propaganda Chief Lu Ting-i, and Director of the General Office of the State Council Yang Shang-k'un (who had shunted Chiang Ch'ing off to Moscow fourteen years earlier). On December 12 they were delivered by military escort to the Workers Stadium where 10,000 Red Guards awaited them. Much as prominent offenders in "feudal" days had been publicly executed as a warning to all, the present victims wore heavy wooden placards around their necks. The placards bore their names in huge black characters, over which bold X's were slashed.* They were tried and condemned, with the leaders standing on high.[20]

iii

"Chairman Mao sends you his best regards!" Chiang Ch'ing again announced buoyantly. The day was December 19 and the occasion the reception of some 100,000 PLA soldiers ordered to Peking to ride herd, in comradely fashion, on the millions of youngsters camping out, each for a week or more, in the capital city. "You must all want to know how Chairman Mao is," Chiang Ch'ing cried. "Let me tell you, he's in robust health!"

So opened still another political extravaganza, this one designed to foster a new spirit of camaraderie among diverse social groupings: youths decorated with red Mao books, armbands, and badges, the unwieldy masses, and now the soldiers, set off from the rest by their drab green garb. Chief of the Cultural Revolution Group Ch'en Po-ta pulled out all rhetorical stops to inflate military morale, for the soldiers' aggressive loyalty was essential to the implementation of Cultural Revolution policy.

"There has never been an army like yours in the history of the world," Ch'en declared. "With an army such as yours armed with Mao Tse-tung's thought we are invincible. All enemies, be they imperialists, revisionists, or monsters and demons, can be smashed to smithereens in your hands. Led by Chairman Mao

* See the second picture section.

and Comrade Lin Piao, you have truly understood how to serve the people.
. . . As pupils we hope to march forward with you our teacher."

Their challenge, they were told, was to carry the revolution beyond their
ranks, to form groups of "revolutionary rebels," analogous to the student corps
of Red Guards active in industrial and mining centers, and wherever possible
on communes.

By the end of the year Premier Chou En-lai was fully allied with the Cultural Revolutionaries (though as a supreme strategist he was also flexible —
prepared to retreat). Now he stood unswervingly as the ideal revolutionary who
would not compromise his principles to ease his personal life. For five months
masses of youngsters of the postwar generation had been riding, sleeping,
and eating around the country at government expense. Were they now spinning off into anarchism beyond anyone's control? Restore the fundamentalist
spirit of the Long March, Chou urged them. Instead of riding to Peking to receive instructions from Chairman Mao, walk! The young people thundered,
"Long live the Long March spirit! Long live the Great Proletarian Cultural
Revolution!"

The young, unexpectedly liberated from home and school, seemed to turn
over their hearts and minds to new masters, the Cultural Revolutionaries. Fired
by the enthusiasm of these radical spokesmen, among them one tough and
winsome woman who defied all conventions, they smashed the symbols of the
old order and realigned themselves under the aegis of the People's Liberation
Army, designated to lead them in the service of the people as a whole.

Thus the historical dialectic, moved by a more massive human energy than
ever before, shifted from an incipient revisionist order to a new revolutionary
disorder. All over the country fighting broke out among rival student groups,
between rebellious youths and soldiers commissioned to restore order, and between students and workers, resulting in drastic losses of production. Both the
prime mover of the Cultural Revolution and the prime beneficiary of a new
stability, Mao Tse-tung had no choice but to try to contain the headlong rush
toward anarchism he had loosed upon the world.

From the time the student movement accelerated in August 1966, its leaders
rejoiced in Mao's apt slogan of 1939, "To rebel is justified!" But when generational rebellion became a way of life, Mao qualified his earlier statement to
read, "It is right to rebel against reactionaries" — an adjustment Chiang
Ch'ing affirmed in her own speeches later on.[21] But the students, whipped into
an enthusiasm natural to their age, stuck by the original slogan for another two
years.[22]

To dramatize this moment, certain high points in the world's revolutionary
history were invoked. History-poor Chinese youth were reminded of the Paris

Commune of 1871 (in Point Nine of the Sixteen-Point Directive) as an expression of revolutionary purity and corporate self-determination.[23] Chiang Ch'ing, who had long held romantic notions of French culture derived from novels and films, avidly promoted the model of the Paris Commune through December 1966, when she finally heeded the Chairman's call for restraint. But her group's leader, Ch'en Po-ta, continued calling for another Paris Commune well into January. To radicals that meant "seize power," though not necessarily under the guidance of the Cultural Revolution Group. So an ominous "January Storm" broke over the country, becoming a January Revolution.

Attempts were made to seize power in the city of Harbin and the provinces of Heilungkiang, Shansi, Anhwei, and Kiangsi. But only in Shanghai, now a city of ten million, did the Paris symbol become momentary reality. Chang Ch'un-ch'iao and Yao Wen-yuan, members of the Cultural Revolution Group stationed in that city, facilitated the reception of radical student leaders from Peking and extended total control over the *People's Liberation Army Daily* and the *Literary Gazette*, and all radio and television stations. Through their command of the media they turned the tide of public opinion against the Shanghai Municipal Committee by denouncing its "economism" * and revisionism and directing the proletariat to "seize power." Consequently, all normal urban activities ground to a halt. Factory production, transport, communications, water supplies, and electricity were scarcely available. Railway service north of Shanghai was cut off.[24] Presiding over apparent chaos, Chang Ch'un-ch'iao and Yao Wen-yuan called the Shanghai Commune into existence on February 5; Chang was named head. Birth of the new government was celebrated by more than a million demonstrators streaming through the city streets and holding aloft colorful posters and red flags.

Shanghai's expression of revolutionary autonomy amounted to urban secession, and that brought on the wrath of Mao Tse-tung and Lin Piao, whose effective lead of the Party and the army depended upon the uneasy combination of local stability and perpetual responsiveness to changes of revolutionary authority. In late February Chang and Yao were summoned to Peking where the Chairman reportedly denounced their anarchistic behavior as a form of "reactionary politics." To neutralize the Shanghai Commune before its extreme model could dangerously sway the nation, the Shanghai Municipal Revolutionary Committee was created. This first institutional expression of a new order was to be governed by a new three-way alliance, whereby members of the "revolutionary masses" would be combined with two more stable and senior components: loyal members of the PLA and loyal Party officials.

During these difficult months other revolutionary committees were es-

---

* "Economism" meant offering workers economic and material incentives; in other words, appealing to short-term individual interests rather than to longer-term collective and national goals.

tablished to replace former governments of cities and provinces. Because of the increasing importance of the military during these transitions, Chiang Ch'ing's military status was enhanced in mid-January when she became adviser to a second Cultural Revolution Group, this one within the PLA. Her frequent addresses to regional groups during the tumultuous period show her wrestling with the dilemma of revolutionary leadership: how can ideological aggression against revisionism be sustained without stimulating physical aggression, which might sever lines of communication between the leaders and the led? More to the point, how could the violence that was no more than political enthusiasm in action be curbed without breaking off the revolutionary momentum needed to prevent society from sinking back into the status quo ante where poor people and women were excluded from responsibility for public affairs?

As always, Chiang Ch'ing had little choice but to accept Chairman Mao's criticism and follow his change of mind. On December 22, 1966, she had addressed a rally of teenagers from Peking Middle Schools. "Your [political] level is high," she commended. "I want to learn from you. I have not done much. What sort of person is a Chinese Communist Party member? A CCP member is one who does not fear criticism!" She told these youths in effect to keep their heads together and unite with the majority who were not yet aroused to violence. "If you want to unite, you must be dictatorial toward the minority who persist in violent behavior." [25]

On January 10, Chiang Ch'ing, speaking at the small west chamber of the Great Hall of the People, continued the routine practice of the Cultural Revolution: political condemnation combined with personality assassination. Although the political careers of Liu Shao-ch'i and Teng Hsiao-p'ing, the prime leaders of the "bourgeois" line, had been suspended the summer before, their influence was still too much alive in the minds and habits of others, she argued. Liu's wife, Wang Kuang-mei, was reviled for following her husband's line. Their revisionist notion of economism was still practiced in Peking, Shanghai, and elsewhere. "Drawing the line between the enemy and ourselves," she issued further judgments on revolutionary rivals, without offering much by way of justification. Her language (destined to rattle foreign ears) was plausible to an audience long accustomed to such verbal violence. Ch'en I (the respected foreign affairs leader) was a "good comrade," she countered recent charges to the contrary. He may have said some wrong things and written some "erroneous poems," but he was not "double-faced"; his excellent record with the New Fourth Army and early opposition to the Wang Ming line could not be forgotten. Li Fu-ch'un (economic administrator, member of the Politburo, and long a personal friend of hers) had been incautious, she alleged without specification. Li Hsien-nien (financial specialist and member of the Central Committee) and Hsieh Fu-chih (in the 1960's public security leader and vice-premier of the State Council), though once subordinates of Teng Hsiao-p'ing, were also "good men."

T'ao Chu (strong man of the south, Politburo member, and propaganda chief since 1966) was another case. He belonged to the "two-faced" group, she explained. At a rally held during the Cultural Revolution he had the temerity to take a photograph of the leaders, cut off the head of Ch'en I, and paste it upon the body of Teng Hsiao-p'ing (who had ridiculed her reformist efforts in the arts).[26]

Thus the open invitation to rebellion of 1966 gave way little by little to an urgent but poorly heeded demand for restraint early in the new year. Revolution should neither be linked necessarily to violence nor denied in its absence, Chiang Ch'ing counseled a group of young rebels in Peking. Revolution in the sense of perpetual self-criticism and criticism of others (her personal formula expressed repeatedly in our interview) should become a way of life. Leftist factions should join forces with other revolutionary groups. The young people who had admitted their tendencies toward anarchism and ultra-democracy should be corrected. Besides struggling against the class enemy, such students should apply the dialectical principle, "one divides into two," to their own thought. Every mind had a "dark side and a bright side. . . . Be self-critical and admit your faults."

Get out of Peking, a city still infiltrated by P'eng Chen's counterrevolutionary schemes, she urged. Go down to the factories or the counties around Peking — one need not go far. To be a true revolutionary you suppress private interests and take into account the needs of the entire country. But first anarchistic behavior must cease and power unjustly seized be returned.[27]

iv

During the weeks that Shanghai was establishing its Commune, Chiang Ch'ing remained in Peking. On January 22 she addressed a gathering of Red Guards, "fellow warriors" as she called them, hoping they would struggle nonviolently. Her subject was the situation at Tsinghua University, where months of political divisiveness had led to public trials and condemnations, open warfare, and loss of life. The personalities involved she did not delve into substantially; her reasons were political, though not the usual sort. Her protagonist was another woman at the political center, Wang Kuang-mei, wife of her husband's archrival, Liu Shao-ch'i.

Chiang Ch'ing and Wang Kuang-mei were both loyal wives and absolute devotees of their husbands' causes. While Chiang Ch'ing had taken her husband's case to Peking University, the center of liberal arts with which Mao was once associated, Wang Kuang-mei had also gone on her husband's behalf to Tsinghua University, the nucleus of scientific and technical studies in which Liu was especially interested. Such parallels combined with the presumption that only one man can be on top have prompted observers to believe that the women were bitter personal, if not also ideological, enemies. In China, moreover, it has long been assumed that jealousy is a woman's "liveliest nerve." To deflect from that impression, perhaps, and to cover possible evidence of her having been instrumental in Wang Kuang-mei's fate, Chiang Ch'ing was notably reserved about her in our interview.[28] Nor could she have failed to foresee other possible parallels: if Mao were overthrown she would be also, or if he died she would be at the mercy of those tempted to exterminate his family and political line.

Who was Wang Kuang-mei? Although I interviewed other women leaders, Wang, a revolutionary loser, was out of bounds. The dossier built up on her during the Cultural Revolution became diabolical, disconnected from any reality. Some facts still can be sifted from the dustbin of historical prejudice. These are important, for Wang's tragedy demonstrates the universal risk taken by women who marry men of high political authority and then pursue power in their own right.

Wang Kuang-mei was a woman of striking intellect, social talent, and political fidelity to her husband (she was his fifth or sixth wife). Born in America, Wang returned to China, attended the Catholic Fu Jen and Yenching universities, and served as interpreter for the Communists in Yenan in 1946, where she became acquainted with some American mediators. In the early 1960's, when Chiang Ch'ing as yet had no national profile, Wang Kuang-mei became highly visible as a political wife. In 1963 she accompanied Chief of State Liu Shao-ch'i to Djakarta, and in the spring of 1966 to Afghanistan, Pakistan, and Burma. As diplomatic occasion demanded, she temporarily eschewed proletarian plain style for fashion (some said Chiang Ch'ing warned her against pearls), and yielded now and then to the chance to dance socially. In China she and her husband jointly entertained visiting heads of state, though among socialist leaders acting as a couple was not the norm. Nor was she neglectful of internal politics. Like Chiang Ch'ing more than a decade earlier, in 1963 she journeyed incognito to the Hopeh countryside where she spent several months wiping out local corruption on behalf of the Four Cleanups Campaign.[29] But when Mao's Cultural Revolution was at full tilt, all the sins of Liu Shao-ch'i were heaped upon her, including the charge of having invoked his supreme authority in the countryside instead of Mao's.

Just before Chiang Ch'ing descended upon Peking University, Wang Kuang-mei in June 1966 arrived at Tsinghua, also on behalf of the Central Committee (of which neither woman was then a member).* Although Wang claimed to represent Chairman Mao and the Party, the contingent she led, a "work team" of some five hundred officials drawn from all parts of the country, had actually been authorized by Liu (according to later Red Guard reports) in order to quell leftist disorder on that campus. Instead of allowing students to write big placards she restricted them to small, discreet ones, labeled disaffected students "sinister gangs," and moved to dissolve them. When Liu was discredited in August, her work team was expelled from the university. Thousands of radical students and teachers took over immediately and traveled all over the country to support Mao's cause. In December they returned to Tsinghua and established the United Ching-kang-shan Regiment to commemorate the place where Mao first organized workers and peasants. At a rally of more than ten thousand on December 25 the reputation of Liu Shao-ch'i was shouted down and the campus was festooned with huge, garish placards. Persistent rebelliousness turned into springtime civil war. Despite Mao's orders to the contrary, students would not stop waging the war of ideas through physical violence.

And despite Chou En-lai's counsel, on April 10, 1967, K'uai Ta-fu, the student leader of the United Ching-kang-shan Regiment, once praised by Chiang Ch'ing as a "rebel hero," organized a rally of more than three hundred thousand people. The entire campus and the special kangaroo court were decorated with anti-Liu posters. Wang Kuang-mei, wife of Mao's close comrade of forty years, was led in person before the masses. Now a gross caricature of her "bourgeois" diplomatic days, she was costumed in a tight evening gown, spike-heeled shoes, an English aristocrat's straw hat, and a necklace of gilded Ping-Pong balls decorated with skulls. Although we are told that under socialism China has evolved beyond folk religion, that belief in witches and the power of exorcism has been discarded, the present masses chanted at her, "Down with ox devils and snake gods!" [30]

Liu Shao-ch'i was dispensed with in more gentlemanly fashion. He was vilified mainly behind his back, and the conventional charges that flowed ad nauseum became ritualized over the years. But his wife, a woman who excited the sexually distorted imagination of the people, stll alive with scapegoats and witches, was made to take the heat.

* Most of the following information about Wang Kuang-mei was relayed to me by Tsinghua professors in interviews in July 1972.

Chiang Ch'ing turning the soil incognito outside of Wusih in 1951. Is the on-looking peasant, a woman, stunned by Chiang Ch'ing's pointed demonstration that "women can guide the plow"?

...ng Ch'ing again works the land — here at the ...l Tachai Brigade, Shansi province, on Sep-...er 15, 1975.

Chiang Ch'ing's photograph of Lu Shan. On the reverse is Mao's poem prompted by the picture and dedicated to the artist. Her landscape's composition conforms to high tradition — close to the style of the twelfth-century painter of the Sung dynasty Ma Yuan.

庐山仙人洞

录

毛主席为李进同志题所摄庐山仙人洞

暮色苍茫看劲松，乱云飞渡仍从容。天生一个仙人洞，无限风光在险峰。

赠

维特克夫人

江青
一九七二年八月十二日

In a bold, cursive hand Chiang Ch'ing has copied on the reverse of the Lu Shan picture her husband's quatrain "Chairman Mao's 'Fairy Cave of Lu Shan' for Comrade Li Chin," her original name also used for her art. It is dedicated to me as "Madame Wei-t'e-k'e." Chiang Ch'ing's signature and the date, August 12, 1972, appear at the lower left.

Chiang Ch'ing's photograph of Coal Hill, which she called by the less familiar name, Gorgeous Prospect Hill, and cherished for its command of Peking's cityscape. Coal Hill is one of five tumuli erected some six centuries ago from soil dug from the moats surrounding the imperial palace. Emperors since the Mongol dynasty have stocked the surrounding park with fruit trees and wild animals. The last Ming emperor hanged himself from a locust tree on Coal Hill's eastern slope in 1644.

An opening scene in the revolutionary ballet The Red Detachment of Women. *The slave girl Wu Ch'ing-hua is chained to a post, awaiting the whip.*

The ultimate in balletic class struggle: Wu Ch'ing-hua takes final vengeance against her landlord-oppressor.

Liberated girl soldier from The Red Detachment *settles scores with the landlord's lackey.*

In The Red Detachment of Women, *the "Bermudas" are decorous simulations of military garb (opposite).*

Intermission at the revolutionary opera The Red Lantern. *In this vestibule reserved for the leaders, the sofa's slipcovers are topped with lace.*

During the performance of The Red Lantern. *From left to right: Chang Ying, Yao Wen-yuan, the author, Chiang Ch'ing, Hsu Erh-wei, Yü Shih-lien, and Ting Hsueh-sung.*

Backstage after the performance of The Red Lantern, *the author greets revolutionary ingenue "T'ieh-mei" in her artfully patched costume. The male lead, Ch'ien Hao-liang, familiar to Chinese audiences as Hao-liang, and Chiang Ch'ing clasp hands behind (above, left). The author meets Ch'ien Hao-liang. To his left is "Granny Li" and Chiang Ch'ing, their creator, is to the right (above, right).*

"The Revolutionary Red Lantern Illuminates the Stage" — a Disneyesque confection of Chiang Ch'ing surrounded by her creations in opera and ballet.

Chiang Ch'ing and Mao, who had been absent from public view since mid-May, prepare for the Cultural Revolution at the Tenth Plenum, September 1962.

Culture commissar Chou Yang (top left), filmmaker Hsia Yen (top right), and dramatist T'ien Han (bottom left), who outranked and plagued Chiang Ch'ing from the 1930's, were arrested by her in 1966. So was Yang Shang-k'un (bottom right), formerly head of the General Office of the Central Committee. All four are shown with their names inscribed but crossed out on placards hung from their necks as Red Guards forcibly march them before the masses.

我们的文学艺术都是人民
大众的，首先是为工农兵的，
为工农兵而创作，为工农兵所
利用的。

毛泽东

Chiang Ch'ing as cover comrade of the Red Guard pamphlet New Peking University,
March 30, 1967.

*Observing the masses parading from the Gate of Heavenly Peace, April 26, 1967. Chou
En-lai and Chiang Ch'ing are at the left. Others in the front row include K'ang Sheng,
Chang Ch'un-ch'iao, Wang Li, and Yao Wen-yuan.*

During the Cultural Revolution Chiang Ch'ing with players who followed her from the People's Liberation Army.

President Nixon, interpreter Nancy T'ang, and Chiang Ch'ing at a performance of the revolutionary ballet The Red Detachment of Women, *February 22, 1972.*

Overseeing a reception for Chinese diplomats in May 1974. From left to right: Yeh Chien-ying, deputy chairman of the Military Affairs Commission; Wang Hung-wen, Chiang Ch'ing's handsome right-hand man in Shanghai, also on the Politburo; Yao Wen-yuan, stiffly behind Chiang Ch'ing; Chou En-lai.

With Imelda Marcos at Tientsin, September 24, 1974.

Under her original name, Li Chin, Chiang Ch'ing's portrait of Mao in the early 1960's appeared in Chinese Literature *(no. 4) in the spring of 1976, prefacing a collection of his poems.*

Standing before the remains of Chairman Mao on September 13, 1976, at the Great Hall of the People, from the left, Hua Kuo-feng, Wang Hung-wen, Yeh Chien-ying, Chang, Ch'un-ch'iao, Chiang Ch'ing, Yao Wen'yuan and Li Hsien-nien.

Chiang Ch'ing, her head crowned in a Confucian-style hat, poses in a frame labeled "official portrait." She wears the badge of Party Chairman, but "revisionism lies in her heart." "How does it look?" she asks Chang Ch'un-ch'iao, tagged "premier" (her punning question can also be read as "What sort of model?"). Yao Wen-yuan and Wang Hung-wen acclaim her from the left.

On the black flag upheld by a pen are the characters "chi-ting," referring to principles "laid down," words Chiang Ch'ing allegedly forged in order to make herself Mao's successor. Her official portrait, including a Western-style crown, sticks out of her handbag. The badge "student" — her special relation to Mao — adorns her breast. Beneath her foreign skirt, from left to right, are Wang Hung-wen; Chang Ch'un-ch'iao carrying a stack of hats, meaning "labels" to pin on people; and Yao Wen-yuan, wearing the banner of a "genuine Marxist-Leninist."

g Ch'ing appears as a smoking
t with lipstick, rouge, and crim-
ngernails. Wang Hung-wen, at-
as a high military officer, offers
golden crown, each point tipped
a skull. Her official tunic, deco-
with a snake in its heart, hangs
en behind. Chang Ch'un-ch'iao,
dy hatchet in his belt, paints an
al portrait" of Chiang Ch'ing in
costume. Salivating Yao Wen-
writes a "manifesto for opening
untry" — that is, national be-
. A stack of hats bearing deroga-
abels used by the Gang of Four
s to the left.

like Chiang Ch'ing is set aflight
Yao Wen-yuan and Chang
-ch'iao. Her broom reads,
nterrevolutionary revisionist line
arts." Yao Wen-yuan's belt car-
hatchet labeled "literary critic."
g Ch'un-ch'iao has the horn of
aganda" slung over his shoulder.
Hung-wen poses as the "helicop-
because he rose to power so fast.
four have trampled over the
red Flowers Garden (meaning
al freedom), where books, records
Canton opera, movie reels, and
al scores are heaped. Vultures fly
ead.

A Canton poster of November 1976. Chiang Ch'ing offers Party and state secrets to a Western figure in exchange for an imperial crown. The four characters on the lower right read, "National betrayal in pursuit of glory."

14.

◇ ◇ ◇

Against the Current

The four seas are tempestuous as clouds
  and waters show their wrath;
The five continents are shaken as gales
  and thunder rage.
Pests should be stamped out
So that we may become invincible.
—Mao Tse-tung, "Reply to Kuo Mo-jo,"
  January 9, 1963

In November 1966 Chiang Ch'ing had warned that the leaders of the Cultural Revolution would not be content with shallow rectification of political offenses. Because the roots of the enemy had gone deep, retributive justice was in order. "We must take into account not only the fifty days and the seventeen years but also the 1930's." [1] The "fifty days" was the period from early June through mid-July when the Chairman was forced out of the "watertight kingdom" of Peking where Liu Shao-ch'i, Teng Hsiao-p'ing, and others held sway, defending their interests through the work teams dispatched to the universities and other arenas of conflict. Then the Chairman swam in the Yangtze, regained his capital with a great splash, and summoned millions of Red Guards to his defense. The "seventeen years" covered the history of the People's Republic, years when she, as well as the Chairman at times, had not commanded the full power she saw as their due. And the 1930's was the heyday of left-wing cosmopolitanism in which she first struggled to come into her own as a Communist and an actress, but was put down.

After Chiang Ch'ing had acquired the power to arrest personal enemies, especially Chou Yang, Hsia Yen, and T'ien Han, the most eminent administrators, Liu Shao-ch'i, Teng Hsiao-p'ing, and T'ao Chu, were also seized. On August 5, 1967, a rally of one million was held at the square of the Gate of Heavenly Peace. Now sequestered at Chung-nan-hai, these once-revered leaders heard the live broadcast of the mass rally and response. Along the roadway leading from the compound their effigies swung from trees. Within days insulting caricatures of them were distributed to all parts of the country.[2]

In most cases the wives and children went down with the fallen leaders, as they had with miscreants and criminals in the old days. But the Liu family were different, even progressive. Although the wife sank with the husband, the children rose up in ideological rebellion against their parents, in the name of Chairman Mao and *his* generation of young revolutionary successors.

Verdicts mounted with the new year. Incriminating dossiers were compiled against other revolutionary patriarchs, some for nearly fifty years subject to no public comment except high praise. Prominent among them was Chu Te, long the occupant of an honorary seat on the Politburo. "Facts" lifted from an early biography that traced his maverick progression from opium addict, womanizer, and warlord to founder of the Red Army were used to defame him. Now his young accusers argued that the army was established exclusively and thereafter led personally by Chairman Mao, never (contrary to demonstrable fact) conjointly with Chu. Chu's apartments at Chung-nan-hai were ransacked, and his wife, K'ang K'o-ch'ing, a slave girl turned Red warrior, was paraded ignobly through the streets.[3]

Another victim of the new left was Foreign Minister Ch'en I, long feared and admired for his independence of mind, devastating wit, disgust with narrow-minded propaganda, voracious love of the arts, and savoir faire with diplomats. Attacks were mounted against him late in 1966 and again the next spring, culminating in April with a Red Guard invasion of the Foreign Ministry. Files were ransacked, personnel were disgraced, and the normal conduct of foreign relations was suspended for several months. Also Ch'en's wife, Chang Ch'ien, equally adept in military and theatrical arts, was forced to suffer for her husband's alleged misdeeds.

The man for all seasons, Chou En-lai, that spring shouldered Ch'en I's responsibility for foreign affairs. Concurrently he kept in touch with Chairman Mao and the Party center, Lin Piao and his Military Affairs Commission, and Chiang Ch'ing and her Cultural Revolution team, with whom he appeared in a tight program of seminars and mass meetings. As he juggled those roles, often to the brink of exhaustion, dossiers were compiled against him and Chiang Ch'ing as well. By whom? The Ultra-Left,* Chiang Ch'ing would eventually explain.

* Persons anarchistic or opposed to her from the left.

One old militarist, T'an Chen-lin, who had served Mao since his early days, finally spoke up for the senior cohort so suddenly threatened. From the viewpoint of the Cultural Revolution Group that Chiang Ch'ing maneuvered, this February Countercurrent was an intrusion from the right into the achievements of *her* group. T'an's offense earned his arrest and the extravagant charge of having sought to rehabilitate Liu Shao-ch'i and Teng Hsiao-p'ing and to mount a "capitalist restoration."

Meanwhile the Cultural Revolutionaries pushed ahead with their goal of establishing a balanced and flexible mechanism for governing a new order of "purified class ranks." To widen their spheres of influence, they communicated the stringent standards of the students, who were naturally quick to learn, act, and forget, to the peasants and workers who adapted more slowly, but once changed, were more manageable under a new order.

Throughout these months of civil warfare Chiang Ch'ing continued to focus on the superstructure — communication of Mao-centered ideology through the media. In addition to the revolutionary opera and ballet, where she was making real gains, she struggled to control the cinema, which, she was convinced, was potentially the most powerful means of shaping public opinion. But her immediate and also ultimate goal was the creation of a model revolutionary personality for the nation. To that end she spent her days teaching the arts of subjugating the Ego and acquiring habits of self-criticism and criticism of others. Mao had established a collateral ideal: serve the people.

i

With the dismantling of the propaganda and cultural establishments in late 1966 the media fell into the hands of the Cultural Revolutionaries. Newspapers and journals were discontinued by the dozen; the few spared were forced to toe a strict Maoist line. Book publishers who finally began in the late 1950's to regain the intellectual momentum lost in the late 1930's were stopped short. All except approved experimental theater, most notably Chiang Ch'ing's model works, was banned. Film studios were closed down, and screenwriters, producers, directors, and actors humiliated and swept from sight. All feature and documentary films, save for those few newly approved by the Central Committee, were banned from theaters, and years of writing by film critics and historians were crudely discredited by the press.[4] Along with the innovative proletarian literature and fine arts of the 1930's, the film cult of that decade was publicly exorcised by the high priests of the Cultural Revolution Group.

But in film as everywhere, destruction had to be followed by construction. Where could decent human talent be found? The most mature filmmakers were those men who animated the Shanghai underground of the 1930's. Working under the Kuomintang's inefficiently authoritarian regime, they were able to be their own masters in the radical arts. Paradoxically, when the Communist Party, fought for by the most ardent leftists, came to power, film production was monitored by a censorship far more stringent than the Kuomintang's.

Chiang Ch'ing's recollections, like her actions, continued to entwine ideological and personal motives. The once-vulnerable Lan P'ing, now the powerful Chiang Ch'ing, finally had turned against Hsia Yen, her old boss in Shanghai's cinematic underworld. He and her other three "Villains" were immobilized, apparently under house arrest.

On the first day of February 1967 Chiang Ch'ing called together representatives of two demobilized film studios to register complaints. "Hsia Yen and Ch'en Huang-mei and their company [all purged filmmakers] have nothing to do but languish in bed all day," she declared.

"Drag them out and struggle against them," Ch'i Pen-yü (a political essayist on Mao's side) shouted to her band of young radicals who had already dragged out and abused other film personalities.

The "rogues," she charged, had prepared a newsreel of the Chairman reviewing the Red Guards, but had cunningly filmed the spectacle so as to cast favorable light upon Liu Shao-ch'i. All shots of Liu, Teng Hsiao-p'ing, and T'ao Chu (her rival cultural authority now linked to the enemy side) must be cut from the film. A documentary showing Liu Shao-ch'i and his wife, Wang Kuang-mei, on their infamous mission to Indonesia in 1963, one they also had planned to show, only propagandized "bourgeois court life."

"The Chairman hates being filmed," she reminded the filmmakers. "He was already like that when I got to know him in Yenan. Now all aspiring 'revolutionary' cameramen want to take shots of the Chairman. [Apart from ceremonial events] the Chairman will not allow them to photograph him while he is at work. Representatives of the bourgeoisie, on the other hand, will fight tooth and nail just to get a single shot. Liu Shao-ch'i was quite peculiar. He used to make a point of standing right next to the Chairman and to act as if he were speaking to him. . . . He would never make a point of standing back." [5]

Sabotage of film production was rife, she acknowledged. Cameras and photographic supplies were seized, state-owned autos were taken from film personnel, and homes were confiscated, not all deeds that were authorized by the center. With the resumption of film production under the Cultural Revolution Group, leftist representatives, routinely equated by her with the masses, must unite with "proletarian elements" in the film industry and struggle jointly against the class enemy. She commanded colorfully, "Demons and monsters must not be allowed to rise. You must keep a sharp watch on landlords, rich peasants, counterrevolutionaries, bad characters, and rightists. *Only the left is allowed to rebel. The right is not allowed to rise!"* *

Though "allowed to rebel," the left, with its weakness for anarchism and internal bickering, must not allow itself to be manipulated by the right and divided into factions. The right would turn the people into tigers, she warned, and would provoke them to strike out wildly at each other. How the rightists would relish that spectacle!

Ch'i Pen-yü echoed, "When the masses fight among themselves, the Black Gang applauds at the ringside."

Chiang Ch'ing concluded her remarks on a cherished subject, the problem of the Ego. That subjective aspect of revolutionary transformation was always (and most emphatically in our interview) at the forefront of her consciousness, and seemingly was her sense of the heart of the Cultural Revolution. Making revolution, she said in effect, was simultaneously an introverted and extroverted experience, a personal and public affair. Conflicts were not only external — between the enemy and ourselves — or internal — among ourselves, as Chairman Mao had argued. They must be waged also *within* oneself — *against* the so-called Ego. She read from a *People's Daily* editorial of the day before:

> We are prosecuting two revolutions simultaneously, one revolution to reform the objective world and another to reform the subjective world. We are also waging simultaneously two struggles to seize power, one to seize power from the power holders who take the capitalist road, and the other to seize power from the Ego in our heads. Only when power is thoroughly seized from the Ego in the mind will it be possible to insure a complete victory in the struggle to seize power from the power holders who take the capitalist road.
>
> The seizure of power in the mind is a painful process. But the struggle must be waged, and the courage to draw blood with a bayonet is demanded. The best way to wage this struggle is to throw oneself into the torrent of the Great Proletarian Cultural Revolution in factories and rural villages and to unite oneself with workers and peasants. . . . Only that way can intellectuals overcome their weaknesses and become revolutionaries. [6]

How should they bring about the grand alliance of workers, peasants, and intellectuals? her listeners asked.

"Don't ask me for instructions. We're all comrades!"

"Comrade Chiang Ch'ing, please convey our regards to Chairman Mao."

* My emphasis.

ii

On April 12, two days after Wang Kuang-mei had been seized in her home at Chung-nan-hai and devastated by trial at Tsinghua University, Chiang Ch'ing spoke before the Military Affairs Commission of the Central Committee.[7] Her tone suggested that she may have been chastened by the moral destruction of an august wife and leader. Her select audience headed by Lin Piao, the Chairman's successor, were men steeled in the military and now seeking the greatest political advantage from the present turmoil. Before them she stood as the paragon of modesty and reason, displaying absolutely no trace of the demagoguery she had learned to exhibit before the masses.

She identified herself as an ordinary Communist Party member, Chairman Mao's secretary over many years, and since last year secretary of the Standing Committee of the Politburo. Indeed, the entire Cultural Revolution Group was nothing more (or less!) than a secretarial team for that Standing Committee, the most authoritative body in the land. Their work she likened to that of sentries and staff officers. They made suggestions and provided references for Chairman Mao, Vice-Chairman Lin, Premier Chou, and other members of the committee.

She characterized her special relation to the Chairman as that of a sort of "roving sentry" in the fields of culture and education. She scanned newspapers and journals, picked out noteworthy materials good and bad, and presented them to Chairman Mao for his perusal.

The Chairman was strict with her and a severe teacher, she continued. Of course he did not guide her by the hand as he did some others. Still, he was exceptionally strict with her. She was very ignorant, she admitted. Indeed, some comrades present must know more about the Chairman than she did.

We live together, but he is the silent type; he does not talk much. When he does talk it is usually about politics, economics, culture, the international scene, domestic affairs — whatever comes to mind. Sometimes he talks about the "little broadcasts" from society [popular pro-or-con rumor] but not very much. . . . The knowledge gained from such little broadcasts from society strikes me as being not very useful and a waste of energy.

In learning she was no match for other comrades. Her learning was insufficient and lacking especially in systemization. "If I have any virtue it is that when I undertake to study something I stick with it and get it done."

To illustrate the Chairman's teaching that leaders should not live off their capital but should perform new services for the people, she repeated one of his favorite historical anecdotes.* The Chairman, she said, explained that the story

---

* A story about the Queen Dowager of the fifth century B.C. state of Chao, it is a subtle tale of nepotism and political intrigue among female leaders at a time of disunity.

was about redistribution of property and power within the landlord class at a point of transition from serfdom to the feudal system. Such land redistribution must go on uninterruptedly.

As for themselves, she said, they represented not the exploiting class but the working class. But if they failed to raise their children strictly, they would regress and some day attempt to stage a capitalist restoration.

Comrades at the present meeting possessed far greater power than figures in ancient history. Comrade Ch'en Po-ta often said that he was just a common man. She was even less significant, she said. "However, power should not be used lightly. Now that people have given us high positions, good pay, and great authority, if we fail to make new contributions could the people want us for long?" Consequently, she told the men in control, the People's Liberation Army must perform new services.

She reminded her listeners of the dominant role of culture and education in molding the consciousness of the people. There they had made mistakes over the last seventeen years. Persons of dubious ideological character and competence were put in charge of cultural and educational affairs. Their influence, combined with that of the "several million bourgeois intellectuals" inherited by their regime, caused them to be overwhelmed with things bourgeois and feudal. "Any class, whether proletarian or bourgeois, which wants to seize political power, must first exert influence over public opinion. In the past I did not pay enough attention to that point," she admitted. Leaders of the military should seize that control now.

Children should not be treated as "private property," she counseled. They should rather be considered as the "wealth of the people, the descendants of the people." One who monopolized his own children as treasures from heaven inevitably would ignore the children of others, especially the children of the working classes, regarding them as worthless.

Take our child [Li Na], for example. When she was in primary school she told me one day that her teacher mentioned to her a book titled *Tun-tun ti ching-ho*. What a terrible teacher! I told her that was wrong; that should be translated *Ching-ching ti tun ho* [*And Quiet Flows the Don*, by Mikhail Sholokhov]. Do you want me to read it? I asked her. "Yes, Mama." In reading it, I told her, she should regard it as Soviet historical material, or as the history of Soviet wars. Yet it is not a good book because a traitor and a counter-revolutionary are its heroes. "How can you say that, Mama? Everybody says it's good."

The reason she criticized me was that the book was not yet allowed to be criticized. I told her not to say anything about our exchange. I had read the book and that was my personal opinion only, I explained. . . .

I think parents should treat their children as equals. They should not treat them in the feudal way by regarding themselves as lords of the household. One should follow the example of Chairman Mao who is utterly democratic at home. Our children are allowed to talk back to their father; sometimes we even make them talk back on purpose!

. . . But most of the time they don't because they respect their parents. It is good for them to argue. Let them rebel a little. . . . What good does it do for them to say "Yes Papa, yes Mama" all the time?

Three days later, a red-letter day for the Cultural Revolutionaries, Chiang Ch'ing was back out among the people. Joined by Hsieh Fu-chih, the public security leader who had weathered two years of political storms and had just been appointed vice-premier, she led the celebration of the founding of the Peking Revolutionary Committee of which Hsieh was chairman.

"The situation is excellent," she announced of the capital's new political order. It consisted of a three-way alliance of workers, peasants, and soldiers, and a three-in-one combination of army, officials, and masses — the two tripartite models of government to be followed in administrative, educational, and production units throughout the country. Generalizing from Peking where power, they believed, had been wrested from the hands of an incipient capitalist class, she warned in her public hyperbole: "The handful of top Party persons in authority taking the capitalist road, agents of a capitalist restoration, and behind-the-scenes bosses of the counterrevolutionary revisionist clique of the city of Peking" had been overthrown. Still, the two-line struggle between socialism and revisionism must go on and should be carried out by the unremitting process of struggle-criticism-transformation. Since there never would be a permanent balance in the political situation, unity, self-criticism, and unity must continue to offset one another indefinitely. But "violence must be avoided at all costs." [8]

iii

In the course of the Cultural Revolution Chairman Mao allowed himself, for the sake of governmental stability, to become the object of a personality cult more intense than any in imperial times when the throne, as much as the man who occupied it, was the habitual object of veneration. Not only the Chairman but also other leaders on his side, especially Lin Piao, condoned that Stalin-like flourish of personal idolatry.

No other leader was praised to the skies during the 1960's or allowed to publish his political essays and speeches in a separate volume. The one exception was Chiang Ch'ing. In the spring of 1967 she too began to be something of a cult object thunderously praised by the masses. Was that mainly by virtue of her relation to Mao or on the strength of her separate power as a leader? Was a matriarchal orientation appearing? Was the patriarchal past of five thousand years about to be subverted?

Her veneration as a leader of men and women was revolutionary in sexual-cum-political history, though never thus indicated at the time. Paradoxically, the romantic youths and some elders enchanted by her commended her conservative virtues over her radical departures. They praised her not as a leader, but as a follower; not as a rebel, but as a loyalist; not as a teacher, but as a student.

In an article (whose title transferred Mao's epithet for Lu Hsun to Chiang Ch'ing), "Salute to Comrade Chiang Ch'ing, the Great Standard-bearer of the Cultural Revolution," the Red Guard editors wrote:

Thirty-five years have elapsed since she [Chiang Ch'ing] first participated in the revolution at the time of the "September 18" [1931] Incident. What a heart-stirring thirty-five years! In thirty-five years she has done much for the Party, yet she has never appeared in public.* When the Hu Tsung-nan bandit clique was frantically launching its attack, Comrade Chiang Ch'ing kept Chairman Mao's company and was in the last group to leave Yenan. During the most critical period she closely followed Chairman Mao in marching and fighting in the south and north, routing the several million troops of the Chiang [Kai-skek] family. Since national Liberation Comrade Chiang Ch'ing has served all along as Chairman Mao's secretary and has followed his thought. . . ." 9

That judgment, they felt, had been authorized six years earlier by Chairman Mao himself in his poem on the reverse of her photograph of Lu Shan:

At *bluegreen twilight I see the rough pines
serene under the rioting clouds.
The cave of the gods was born in heaven,
a vast wind-ray beauty on the dangerous peak.*

The following Red Guard commentary was echoed by adulatory young people in months to come:

Forceful, magnificent, and inspiring, [Chairman Mao's poem] reveals the grand ambitions of a proletarian revolutionary and, in our view, presents the most comprehensive, most perfect, most impressive, and most graphic portrait of Comrade Chaing Ch'ing. Today, in rereading the powerful lines of the poem, one is filled with unbounded emotion and infinite admiration for Comrade Chiang Ch'ing.

In May 1967, the twenty-fifth anniversary of Mao's "Talks at the Yenan Forum," several radical student journals featured Chiang Ch'ing as their cover comrade. She was always portrayed severely in military fatigues, holding the Red Book in her right hand, illuminated by radiations from the sun of Mao's face, and with miniature masses filling the background. Such revolutionary

---

* As far as they knew she had assumed no public role until the Cultural Revolution. Such a history of feminine modesty was admirable in their conventional minds.

iconography was accompanied by prolix and predictable editorials. *New Peking University* praised her for being Mao's "best student," thus a model of loyalty to the Chairman and his proletarian line in culture and for "distinguishing between love and hatred" in class attitudes.[10] Among the welter of details disclosed was her piquant habit of giving away copies of the Chairman's *Selected Works* autographed by her. Nothing, however, was said either of her special boost through marriage to Mao or of the feminist struggles she had waged silently over the years.

Not only the young, but also some aged were moved to sing her praises. The venerable writer Kuo Mo-jo eulogized her at the twenty-fifth anniversary celebration over which Chiang Ch'ing, only a mute observer at the Yenan Forum, now presided.

Dear Comrade Chiang Ch'ing, you are the fine example for us to follow,
You are good at creatively studying and applying the invincible thought of Mao Tse-
tung.
Fearlessly, you charge forward on the literary and art front,
Thus, the heroic images of the workers, peasants, and soldiers now dominate the Chi-
nese stage;
And we must do the same for the stage the world over!
China's yesterday is the today of many Afro-Asian countries,
And China's today will be their tomorrow.
We will fight for the complete emancipation of the oppressed nations and peoples,
We will fly the great red banner of Mao Tse-tung's thought over all the Afro-Asian
countries,
And over the six continents and the four seas.[11]

Such encomia, however, were secondary to the dire political realities that commanded Chiang Ch'ing's serious attention that summer. The various popular forces strategically mustered the year before had gained separate momenta and opened threats of civil war. Composed mainly of peasants and workers, the People's Liberation Army was needed to stabilize the emerging order. Yet it also posed a perpetual challenge because its forces stationed all over the country were responsive to regional command structures. Unless it was actively on the side of the Cultural Revolutionaries, the army or parts of it could as well go against them.

In February 1966, Lin Piao had appointed Chiang Ch'ing the army's adviser on cultural affairs, a high rank reinforced the next January when she was named adviser to a Cultural Revolution Group newly constituted within the army. Both appointments were designed to sharpen her public image, defend the political leadership of the Cultural Revolution Group at large, bolster the army as a propaganda machine, and strengthen Mao's hand.

However, the army was no less subject to petty-bourgeois conservatism and self-interest than any other huge organization. Nor was Lin Piao necessarily capable of or willing to make it respond to sharp jerks in the Cultural Revolution line. The Wuhan Mutiny of July 1967, occurring in the industrial center of China, was among the most worrisome clashes of regional and central interests.[12] Although the details are in dispute, what seems to have happened was that members of a conservative mass organization called the Million Heroes and members of a Wuhan workers' group fell into a murderous confrontation on a bridge over the Yangtze. The local military commander, Ch'en Ts'ai-tao, known for his moderation, threw his support behind the Million Heroes. This move apparently embarrassed Marshal Lin Piao and compelled the Chairman to dispatch Premier Chou En-lai, Wang Li (deputy editor-in-chief of *Red Flag*), and Hsieh Fu-chih to admonish Commander Ch'en and restore order. When the Million Heroes backed by Ch'en's military force took over the city, mutiny against the Maoists flared. Chou En-lai escaped through a ruse, leaving Wang Li and Hsieh Fu-chih to be kidnapped, disgraced, and tortured. After his release, Wang Li returned to Peking and was accorded a hero's welcome. Chou En-lai, Ch'en Po-ta, Chiang Ch'ing, and K'ang Sheng greeted him at the airport, arrayed the nation's pro-Mao leaders along the rostrum above the Gate of Heavenly Peace, and summoned "a million" masses to demonstrate in the Chairman's name along the broad avenues below.

Incensed by military disobedience in a major industrial center, Chiang Ch'ing suddenly changed her tune. Although she had insisted upon verbal over physical violence throughout the strife-torn summer, after the Wuhan Mutiny she issued the tough slogan, "Offend by reasoning and defend by force." She warned Peking youths never to allow themselves to be so bullied as the Chairman's emissaries had been. "Take up arms and defend yourselves!" she commanded.[13] Her radical reversal was reflected by the center. In short order various trusted Red Guard and revolutionary rebel (mainly worker) units in Peking and in the provinces were equipped with arms to protect them against retaliation from other conservative wings of the PLA.[14]

The mutiny and its aftermath forced the Cultural Revolution leaders to face a series of agonizing decisions. How wise was it to let chanting, parading young people seize arms from the military and take the initiative in civil war? To what extent could armed students be trusted? How faithfully did the Cultural Revolution Group Chiang Ch'ing dominated implement Mao's thinking on the advantages and risks of distributing arms to thousands, perhaps millions, of amateur defenders of his political ideals? Not surprisingly, armed youths were hard to control. In the late summer of 1967 youthful anarchism and retaliation by local communities appeared in reports nationwide. Abetted by the general suspension of schools, hordes of students turned vigilantes assailed all forms of authority, including several new and approved revolutionary committees. Rocked by the chaos, the Cultural Revolution Group issued a barrage of directives, some favoring violence, others against it. The line between verbal and physical violence was far more easily drawn ideologically than in reality.

When Mao Tse-tung returned to Peking from an inspection tour of the provinces in September 1967, he must suddenly have prevailed upon Chou En-lai, Chiang Ch'ing, and her Cultural Revolution Group for restraint. For Chiang Ch'ing, who had careened back and forth between advocacy of verbal violence and approval of armed struggle, now espoused the verbal.

September 1967, she explained to me in our interview as she had to her former constituencies, was a turning point in the Cultural Revolution.[15] On the fifth, the day of the circular that prohibited further seizure of arms, Chiang Ch'ing delivered a major speech before representatives sent from Anhwei province. Although never published officially, it was printed and circulated among the masses,[16] and upon her request read to me in Peking by her aides.

"My old friend K'ang Sheng dragged me here," she protested jovially. Although "not prepared," she reviewed in detail recent changes in the revolutionary situation, which had seen more violence than she cared to recapitulate to her listeners. Defending herself against the charge that she had advocated physical violence, she advised all to emulate her in following Chairman Mao's order that verbal rather than physical struggle be practiced. "Learn from Camrade Chiang Ch'ing! Respect Comrade Chiang Ch'ing!" they shouted back. To which she responded, "Learn from our comrades! Respect our comrades!"

Just a year earlier, she told the Anhwei group, "a handful of top capitalist roaders in the Party were in control." Now they were "paralyzed" and were being removed from control by the gradual establishment of revolutionary committees province by province, city by city. The top capitalist roaders, she maintained, were *more notorious than Trotsky!* Such counterrevolutionary doubledealers and capitalist roaders as Liu Shao-ch'i had been removed *without* resorting to force. But if the enemy resorted to force, she warned, her side would strike back and *she would strike back personally.* It was far better, however, to rely upon verbal struggle: don't use machine guns unless absolutely necessary.

Their present goals were threefold: first, to maintain Chairman Mao as head of the Party's Central Committee (did others have candidates?); second, to allow the PLA to defend the Cultural Revolution (don't counterattack the PLA); and third, to establish revolutionary committees through the Great Alliance, which meant the three-way alliance, struggle-criticism-transformation, and revolutionary mass criticism (verbal over armed struggle, an end to open fighting).

The Ultra-Left was another sort of enemy, she continued; there were also rightist enemies who undermined the integrity of the Party's Central Committee. She mentioned the May Sixteenth Clique of Peking, a "counterrevolutionary conspiratorial clique," that manifested *both* deviations. Counterrevolutionaries had *seized* her May Sixteenth Circular of 1966 and circulated it in the clique's name. The membership of the clique was small and fairly young. Only a minority were bourgeois reactionaries; the majority were young people who were taken in, "hoodwinked by the bourgeois reactionary leaders," as she put it. Although vast numbers of youths had been tempered by the Cultural Revolution, being young made their ideology unsteady, thus subject to manipulation by "bad people" pulling strings behind the scenes. The political color of the clique was deceptive. Its outward appearance was Ultra-Left, and its chief enemy was Chou En-lai. It compiled a dossier not only against him, but against other leaders as well (herself included), and circulated, on the basis of unofficial personal histories, groundless rumors against them. Consequently, the Cultural Revolution leaders must maintain vigilance and educate the masses against the proliferation of such conspiratorial groups.

Society was rife with "secret agents," she warned. The Central Committee's archives showed how "bad elements have wormed their way into the Party." Though hidden for decades, these individuals and cliques had been cleared out. Still, self-serving factionalism and "mountain strongholdism," a kind of anarchism, must be avoided. The main task was to seize upon a common ground and leave behind minor differences (another warning against fighting back at the Chairman's military force — the PLA).

This year young people's revolutionary service backfired when they dragged out only a small handful within the army (at Wuhan and several other places). "You must not fall into the trap set by the enemy," she cautioned. As soon as the Wuhan rebels finished there, they began roaming around other parts of the country; without local investigation they would make still more mistakes in correctly identifying and rectifying the Chairman's enemies.

In the annual spiraling of the Cultural Revolution the student upsurge of the summer of 1966 gave way to the clash of vigilantes and the military in 1967, and that to the renewed engagement of the working class in the summer of 1968, an expansion of the revolutionary movement secured at incalculable costs to production. On September 14, 1967, Chiang Ch'ing spoke to newly formed propaganda teams of workers and soldiers on their progressive inheritance of the revolutionary movement. In the aftermath of a violent summer and of titanic clashes within the central elite, her tone was restrained and her appeal to unity over conflict. Chairman Mao, she said, should be credited for launching on July 27 a struggle-criticism-transformation campaign in the superstructure on behalf of the working class. Students who persisted in armed struggle divorced themselves from the masses, and hence from the working class, whose turn it was to assume leading positions in the educational, governmental, and cultural superstructure.

How easy it was to make revolution against others, but hard to make revolution against oneself, Chiang Ch'ing challenged, returning once again to the theme of struggle within the Ego. Everyone had a seamy side and a bright side (an admission of internal conflict that did not carry over into her model operas and ballets). If you didn't get rid of your seamy side — petty bourgeois and bourgeois attitudes, one day you would find yourself lagging behind. What was the "seamy side"? Small-group mentality, individualism, departmentalism, anarchism, and unwillingness to listen to anybody.

Her speech to the Anhwei delegation, she remarked in our interview, was designed to "stop the evil wind." What did she mean by that? In the fall of 1967 she could not yet break ranks with other members of the Cultural Revolution Group, she responded with the simplicity of hindsight. By then most of her comrades in that group [17] were not restraining themselves to propaganda. They had resorted to force, and their example naturally was emulated. Chief among those undermining her appeal to avoid unnecessary bloodshed was the head of the Cultural Revolution Group, Ch'en Po-ta, whose maneuverings behind the scenes had untoward repercussions.

Incidents of violence triggered by the Ultra-Left were mentioned to the public at a rally of September seventeenth. Chou En-lai, who frequently appeared with her group in those weeks, was principal speaker. Ch'en Po-ta (whose Ultra-Leftism she suspected) and K'ang Sheng were also present. The advocate of moderation, the Premier denounced gun-toting activists as "petty bourgeois anarchists" persisting in civil war. To her audience Chiang Ch'ing disclosed that the day before more than thirty people "acting like robbers" had ransacked the office of the Party journal (and her group's organ) *Red Flag*, while ten people from Kansu province had forced their way into Chung-nan-hai and burst in upon Chairman Mao's headquarters at Huai-jen Hall, where they were seized. [18]

The forced entry into Chung-nan-hai reminded Chiang Ch'ing of an incident she mentioned with profound annoyance in our interview. While she was meeting with some Anhwei representatives, she recalled, the Chairman was on an inspection tour of the countryside. In his absence their adversaries ordered a contingent of people to surround their home at Chung-nan-hai, so that it was inaccessible. One member of the Party's Central Committee (she named him inaudibly) audaciously fired off to the Chairman a telegram designed to deflect his attention from actual dangers facing them in Peking. What a traitor he was! she seethed, then muttered how his life had been made miserable by an oppressive marriage. When she and the Chairman discussed that telegram he remarked on how much it smacked of Wang Ming's influence. He would learn from Sun Yat-sen, the Chairman resolved. He was referring, Chiang Ch'ing commented enigmatically, to the fact that there was a sizable age difference between him and Sun Yat-sen (twenty-seven years).

In our conversation she also disparaged other nihilistic acts by the Chinese people. The burning of the British chargé d'affaires office * was an instance of physical brutality by the Ultra-Left instigated by the May Sixteenth Clique, and was entirely wrong, she said. So was the seizure of foreign ships during the Cultural Revolution unjustifiable.[19]

In November 1967 Chiang Ch'ing, now a full-fledged leader of the nation, returned to the cultural world. She was full of apologies for having neglected the transformation of music, drama, and film during the massive upheavals of the last two years. In accordance with her instructions from Mao, the three-way alliances and three-way combinations applied in other units must now be extended to the cultural groups still eluding their command. "The enemy is cunning; he has many companies of actors. After you dispose of one company he will turn up in yet another," she warned in the language of guerrilla warfare. For that reason exhaustive investigations should be carried out in cultural circles. Those who demanded to join the army (a haven from full-time cultural warfare?) must be patient. Vice-Chairman Lin Piao and the Military Affairs Commission have made arrangements. But fixation upon the army caused people to forget other things.

Ch'en Po-ta commended her speech about the eight model works (of music, opera, and ballet) and her aspirations to convert all models to film, the only medium that could easily propagandize the whole country. A taped version of her speech should be distributed to cultural units nationwide, Ch'en said. On November 13 an edited version was adopted as a document of the Central Committee.[20]

In the language of traditional Chinese thought, by the end of 1967 the historical process had moved by degrees from a stage of chaos to a stage of harmony. In the language of the Cultural Revolution, the political way was shifting from the revisionist road of Liu Shao-ch'i to progress along the proletarian road of Mao Tse-tung. And in the language of Chiang Ch'ing, as of November 27, "the situation was excellent: proletarian politics were taking command." That day in Peking she addressed a forum of workers, representatives of a vastly important new constituency of the Cultural Revolution — industrial labor. Loss in factory production caused by armed struggle had been overcome now, she told them. Study classes in the works of Mao Tse-tung were well under

---

* Preceded by kicking, spitting on, and sexually abusing British officials of both sexes by Chinese youths of both sexes. Their xenophobic behavior seemed to recapitulate the Boxers' more express and virulent program to purge China of all foreign influence, with the Empress Dowager's tacit permission, at the turn of the twentieth century.

way. Although the students were first to arise, their revolutionary élan had been transmitted to the poor and lower-middle peasants (since land reform the conventional label for the vast majority of the peasants) and the workers. Hereafter, Red Guard students should not interfere in factory affairs. Students who violated those orders and disrupted factory labor must be routed out. Anarchism was a bourgeois ideology that corrupted proletarian revolutionaries, she asserted once again. Everyone must join in the struggle against it.

People have said, she reported with amusement, that Party members past the age of thirty were conservative. But Chairman Mao was over seventy! Which proved that age alone is not the main cause of conservatism. "I myself am still young politically," she announced brightly. "Working with such comrades as you makes me feel young politically." [21]

iv

Conscious of dangerous swerves in the revolutionary movement and of the need to propel the spiral higher and prevent it from slipping back, the Cultural Revolution leaders set up a spate of meetings in March 1968. The evening of March 11 the Premier, Chiang Ch'ing, Lin Piao's wife Yeh Ch'ün, and others met with a group of Peking college students, among them a representative from the Petroleum College of Ta-ch'ing Oilfield (site of China's major resource, the undeveloped basis of its future national industry). Four years earlier Mao had declared this area a model of self-sufficiency, saying, "In industry learn from Ta-ch'ing." Nevertheless, the present leaders charged it with failing to meet new political standards. Their vaunted Petroleum College had refused to denounce the February Countercurrent of the year before, thereby tacitly condoning the old guard formerly supported by Liu Shao-ch'i (more closely identified than Mao with primacy of industrial development). Ta-ch'ing was now accused of having mounted petroleum and agricultural exhibits that honored Liu but neglected Mao.* Chiang Ch'ing deplored their setting up private radio stations, tapping telephones, and operating listening devices — all illegal counterrevolutionary actions. Those responsible she compared to "white-livered devils" who had been conservatives all long. [22]

What is the great Cultural Revolution? K'ang Sheng quizzed a delegation from Anhwei province that met in Peking on March 18. "The Great Cultural

---

* During the vilification of Chiang Ch'ing eight years later, Hua Kuo-feng's new regime accused her of having attempted, in the spring of 1975 to ban *The Pioneers*, a feature film based on the Ta-ch'ing Oilfield and produced at Kirin's Chang-ch'un studio without her direction. Her antagonism was explained as an attack on Mao and Premier Chou En-lai and as evidence of her ambition to monopolize the arts in order to "usurp Party leadership and seize state power." These and other dubious charges appear in PR 47 (Nov. 19, 1976): 14–16.

Revolution is a proletarian political revolution as well as a continuation of the civil war and a continuation of class struggle between the Kuomintang and the Communist Party," he asserted.

That is what Chairman Mao said, added Chiang Ch'ing.

By then some eighteen provinces and cities had established revolutionary committees. Chekiang perhaps would be next in line. This province of thirty-one million people surrounded China's most complex city, Shanghai, which had submitted to government by revolutionary committee the year before. Under conditions of unresolved civil warfare, Premier Chou, Ch'en Po-ta, Yeh Ch'ün, K'ang Sheng, and Chiang Ch'ing emphasized to Chekiang delegates to the capital how their province was on the front line of national defense against Taiwan, where the forces of Chiang Kai-shek and the American imperialist were installed, and thereby served as a constant reminder that the civil war had not ended. Moreover, Chiang Ch'ing and the others were firmly convinced that Chiang Kai-shek, the United States, and the Japanese government had planted scores of secret agents there. The security specialist K'ang Sheng charged that Liu Shao-ch'i's wife, Wang Kuang-mei, tried and condemned the year before, was no less than a secret agent for the Americans, the Japanese, and the Kuomintang. Wang, Chiang Ch'ing added hotly, was a "strategic intelligence agent."

The specter of secret agents always haunted Chiang Ch'ing. Not only did she, Premier Chou, and the others believe that KMT and foreign agents infiltrated Chekiang, but also that P'eng Chen and other "top capitalist roaders in the Party" planted agents, some of whom, according to Premier Chou, "persecuted" Chiang Ch'ing during her rest cures at her private retreat in Hangchow.

"They fixed listening devices in the residences of the Chairman and Vice-Chairman Lin and tapped phones, behaving like secret agents," Chiang Ch'ing declared. Moreover, the culture of Chekiang was intensely feudal. The Shaohsing opera in which women in their sixties took men's parts still was performed.

K'ang Sheng remarked sardonically on the scads of monks and nuns rampant there, and said that those nuns ought to get married. Tens of thousands of such idlers strolled the streets each day, Chiang Ch'ing cut in.[23]

Three days later Chiang Ch'ing, Chou En-lai, and K'ang Sheng met with representatives from Kiangsu, another strategically situated province stretching along the coast north of Shanghai. Once more they warned against the "reversal of the verdict," the restoration of the old guard under Liu Shao-ch'i and P'eng Chen. That was "the enemy who would not quit the stage of history of its own accord," K'ang Sheng quoted Chiang Ch'ing as saying. Two forms of rightism threatened the tenacity of the revolutionary movement. Those who were left in form but right in essence plagued the movement during the latter half of 1967. The offenders (Wang Li, Kuan Feng, et al.) were placed, in a devious move by Liu and Teng, on Chiang Ch'ing's Cultural Revolution Group. Once discovered, "we dragged them out and hung them up," she said. Then there were obvious rightists who refused to repudiate the February Countercurrent, thereby seeking to restore Liu, Teng, and others to power. [24]

By the end of March fighting flared again on the campuses of Peking and Tsinghua Universities, and sporadically on the streets of towns and cities all over the nation. Execution of Chairman Mao's instruction to consolidate the new order through revolutionary committees had forced unwanted waves of reaction from the Ultra-Left. One such clash had occurred in January in Hunan province where preparations for the establishment of a revolutionary committee were resisted by an Ultra-Left group that called itself Sheng-wu-lien; it was possibly inspired by some "May Sixteenth" deviators from Chiang Ch'ing's Cultural Revolution Group. Sheng-wu-lien's manifesto recapitulated certain Ultra-Left arguments set forth at the time of the January Revolution and the Shanghai Commune the year before: denunciation of Chou En-lai as leader of a "Red capitalist class," and a determination to carry the revolution through the field armies, to smash all the old state machinery, and to establish in lieu of a Hunan provincial revolutionary committee a Hunan People's Commune. [25]

Thus the Ultra-Left, which had threatened both the new order of revolutionary committees and the integrity of the army, now pointed a dagger at the heart of the revolutionary body politic, Chiang Ch'ing's Cultural Revolution Group. From confusing reports of March 8 emerges an incident in which the commander of the Peking Field Garrison, Fu Ch'ung-pi, mounted an attack against the group's offices and prepared to make arrests. The rebels were seized, and in retaliation for their mutiny Vice-Minister of Defense Yang Ch'eng-wu and another high officer were captured on the orders of Chiang Ch'ing. Personally and politically the incident was shattering, inasmuch as the PLA was assumed to have lent military force to the Cultural Revolution Group, and embarrassing to Lin Piao, for Yang Ch'eng-wu was considered his protégé, and Chiang Ch'ing had now disgraced Yang directly and Lin by implication.

On March 27 Chiang Ch'ing summoned a rally of a hundred thousand and reported that incident of armed threat against herself, her followers, and their regime in their inner sanctum of power. Vigorously in command, she delivered a blow-by-blow account of challenges from the right and victories on the left to the shrill counterpoint of Yeh Ch'ün (Lin Piao's wife, who stepped forth to lead Chiang Ch'ing's mass chorus that spring) and Hsieh Fu-chih, who demanded of all, "Learn from Comrade Chiang Ch'ing. Salute Comrade Chiang Ch'ing. Vow to defend Comrade Chiang Ch'ing to death!" Reveling in the thunderous response, Chiang Ch'ing jocularly reminded her audience that not long ago students threatened to "fry her in oil and strangle her."

After the ritual condemnation of fallen chiefs, Chiang Ch'ing made a stunning new announcement: arrest of Vice-Minister of Defense Yang Ch'eng-wu on grounds of having schemed to seize the air force for counter-revolutionary purposes (premonitory of Lin Piao's airborne conspiracy three years later). And T'an Chen-lin (whom she used to defend, she chastised herself), leader of the February Countercurrent of the year before, she denounced as a renegade. Now they possessed certain proof that he and his followers wanted to "turn back the wheels of history and bring about a capitalist restoration." [26]

Three days later Chiang Ch'ing, the Premier, and other key leaders met at the Great Hall of the People where she formally deplored the disorders of the spring, especially the explosion of "renegades and rotten eggs" in Hunan, the Chairman's province. Most despicable was the Sheng-wu-lien, the motley group of Hunan extremists whose left-wing perversions had been under attack since late January. Sheng-wu-lien was charged with the same faults as the February Countercurrent. In passing, Chiang Ch'ing commended the numbers of women pathbreakers who emerged during the Cultural Revolution and said that more should be encouraged. [27]

Among the crucial encounters with regional representatives in the spring of 1968 was one with the preparatory group for the Szechwan Provincial Revolutionary Committee, which met on the fifteenth of March. With Chiang Ch'ing were the Premier, K'ang Sheng, Yao Wen-yuan, Wang Tung-hsing, and Yeh Ch'ün.

"Szechwan has always gotten into trouble before the rest of the country and is last to be restored to order," Premier Chou opened with an old adage, but one, he said humorously, he did not want to perpetuate.

"You are guests from far away," Chiang Ch'ing welcomed these representatives with Confucian courtesy. A population of seventy million and abundant natural resources made Szechwan province the size of a huge European country, she exclaimed, and wondered with a sense of history whether it might not once again be turned into an independent kingdom.

"Is that not true, Comrade Li Ta-chang?" she turned to a man she may not have seen for thirty-five years. He was reluctant to step forth. This long-esteemed secretary of the Southwest Regional Bureau had been criticized, though not severely. Chou En-lai — who had not seen him since their underground days in 1932, as they realized mutually — assured him that his written "self-examination" need not be long. He must come out boldly against the Szechwan leader Li Ching-ch'üan, who was accused of being in the same revisionist camp as Liu Shao-ch'i, Teng Hsiao-p'ing, and Yang Shang-k'un.

It was Li Ta-chang who had proposed her to the Party when she joined (in 1933), said Chiang Ch'ing, proud to announce the length of her Party membership. He was how old now? "Sixty-eight," he responded. "Then let us help each other and preserve our political youth," she cheered him.

Reports of disturbances and warfare in Szechwan had been showered upon the leaders for at least a year. By now they added up to some six or seven volumes, not all of which the Premier had studied, he said. What especially troubled him, K'ang Sheng, and Chiang Ch'ing was the Kuomintang legacy. The ancient city of Chungking, which the KMT had seized as their capital after the Japanese chased them into the interior in 1937, Chiang Ch'ing now called a "den" full of the dregs of their regime, of the old society, and of plain traitors. Its present public security, procuracy, and law courts were deplorable. "Counterrevolutionary" listening devices were installed everywhere. During Li Ching-ch'üan's ruthless suppression of counterrevolutionaries in February nearly one hundred thousand people were arrested and untold numbers killed. Szechwan, moreover, was equipped with the country's most up-to-date weapons, including double-barreled antiaircraft guns. Factionalism was rife and people ignored ideological precepts issued from the center.

"Today we have bombarded you and tomorrow you may bombard us," she continued in mock combat. Yang Shang-k'un, against whom she bore personal grudges of a quarter of a century was a despotic landlord. Nor was his family any good. His wife should be "struggled against" as well as the wives of all other "bad men." However, some women comrades have done good work, she allowed, and warned present Szechwan representatives against being so "feuda-listic." "Why not recruit some women generals!" 28

May 16, 1968 was destined to be a bittersweet anniversary in Chiang Ch'ing's personal and public history. She passed that day on a tour of inspection of Shaohsing, Chekiang province, the birthplace of Lu Hsun. The memory of that man she admired, juxtaposed with the feudal and bourgeois remnants surviving in the local culture, was distressing. She found the Chekiang Institute of Fine Arts, originally patronized by Lu Hsun in days when it was studded with struggling young proletarian artists, to be a hotbed of reactionary painters poor in skill and pursuing relentlessly the Black Line of the 1930's. The theater was still dominated by aging actresses performing ancient operas and ghost plays, most despicably dramas about "insane women, drunkards and vampires and other things at sixes and sevens." The opera *Looking for Mother in a Nunnery*, also special to Shaohsing, was intolerably bourgeois. Local music was profoundly depressing. 29

Over the following year Chiang Ch'ing entered the wider historical stage as a protagonist supported by the Party, the military, and the performing arts, a vast revolutionary arena too often slighted by outside observers. At the Ninth Party Congress of April 1969, the first to be convened in thirteen years, formal notice of Chiang Ch'ing's rise to top leadership was posted. The men purged as revisionists and turncoats in the intervening years, among them Liu Shao-ch'i, Teng Hsiao-p'ing, P'eng Chen, and T'ao Chu, had been stripped of office and arrested. The dominant themes of the Cultural Revolution era — combat individualism and repudiate revisionism, cherish the army and support the people, struggle-criticism-transformation — were adopted as national policy. Along with her staunchest supporters during the Cultural Revolution, among them Hsieh Fu-chih, Yao Wen-yuan, and Chang Ch'un-ch'iao, Chiang Ch'ing was promoted to the Politburo. One other woman, the second in Party history, was comparably rewarded (for lesser labors); she was Yeh Ch'ün, wife of Lin Piao, officially designated successor to Chairman Mao.

All this was for the public record and disclosed nothing about the anxieties Chiang Ch'ing claimed later to have harbored about the cunning successor and his ambitious wife. Those resentments would fester until the summer of 1972 when Chiang Ch'ing, speaking for her husband's regime, broke open Lin Piao's case and painstakingly taught its bitter lessons to the people.

15.

◇ ◇ ◇

Lin Piao the Overreacher

Icarus, you fly into the air,
With melting wax
Fall into the sea.
May heat and wax
Revive you so that you
May teach this lesson.
Let the foreteller beware—
The imposter falls
Flying beyond the stars.
— Alciato, *Emblemata*

On May 18, 1966, Lin Piao delivered to the Politburo one of the most extraordinary addresses in Chinese history.[1] His fixation upon coups d'etat, illustrated by a string of bloody examples drawn from world history, alarmed Chairman Mao, who was never unaware of his vulnerability as a lifetime leader. Lin Piao's raw analysis of power struggles also unnerved Chiang Ch'ing, who was no less vulnerable physically and politically to his brutal manipulation of history and his willingness to adopt ruthless precedent. On that day (and we must assume on other less famous occasions) Lin Piao dissected murderous politics at the top and prefigured his own soaring to the title, successor, and his own disastrous fall.

As arresting as the substance of Lin Piao's discourse was its timing. Three months earlier P'eng Chen and others loyal to Liu Shao-ch'i had circulated the February Outline, which ostensibly acquiesed in Mao's demand for Cultural Revolution but actually resisted it. They hoped to contain power over cultural affairs within the offices of Propaganda and Culture, where authority over the media, education, and the arts had resided for the last sixteen years. Incited by

Chiang Ch'ing, Mao had supplanted Liu's loyalists with the newer Cultural Revolution Group composed of Mao's apparent loyalists, and this group was commissioned to pilot the revolt of the masses on his behalf. That same February Chiang Ch'ing was named cultural adviser to the army, an assignment that closely involved her with Lin Piao, backed up her aggressive cultural projects with potential military force, and made possible realization of Mao Tse-tung's long-term demand that Red soldiers sustain both military and civilian roles. Only that way could he defend his ideas with the word as well as with the sword. On May 16 the Politburo adopted Chiang Ch'ing's and Mao Tse-tung's circular calling for proletarian class struggle in all cultural fields. Two days later Lin Piao went before the same group of leaders to lecture on the nature of coups d'etat.

Working from notes that strung out in sensational detail power struggles from the ancient Chou dynasty to the recent past, Lin Piao led up to the February challenge by the Four Family Inn — his sobriquet for Liu Shao-ch'i's leading team. They were political theorist P'eng Chen; Lo Jui-ch'ing, who had controlled the military; Lu Ting-i, who was commander-in-chief of the cultural and ideological warfront; and Yang Shang-k'un, who managed personnel and intelligence operations.

As a rhetorician, Lin Piao was far less inhibited than his peers by revolutionary optimism or the Marxian jargon used in mass propaganda. "Political power is an instrument by which one class oppresses another," he declared. "It is alike with revolution and counterrevolution. As I see it, political power is the power to oppress others." Chairman Mao, he reported admiringly, had militated against counterrevolution by planting observers in radio broadcasting stations, the armed forces, and public security systems. "We ought to learn from such methods of Chairman Mao."

There are two prerequisites for a coup d'etat, he went on. One is control over propaganda organs — newspapers, broadcasting stations, literature, cinema, and publications. The other is control over the armed forces. Only when civilian and military power are coordinated can a counterrevolutionary coup be brought off. More succinctly, "seizure of political power depends upon gun barrels and inkwells."

That spring of 1966 Lin Piao and Chiang Ch'ing possessed between them the gun barrels and the inkwells, both symbols with long historical significance. In the traditional language of Chinese governance Lin Piao commanded *wu*, the realm of military affairs, and Chiang Ch'ing, acting on Mao's authority, sought a comparable command over *wen*, the realm of culture. Regardless of personal ambitions, each always operated in the name of Chairman Mao and strove generally to apply his teachings. In peacetime, *wen* — morality, history, literature, and the administrative arts — was the dominant governing mode.

Thus, after the Resistance and Liberation Wars, and the upheaval of establishing the PRC, the Chinese Communist government returned to the primacy of *wen*. Under Chinese communism *wen* can be loosely equated with propaganda, a no less comprehensive and not necessarily pejorative concept. The question of leadership was always one of who sustained dominant control over propaganda organs. By the spring of 1966 Lin Piao had been persuaded of Chiang Ch'ing's argument that over the last sixteen years authority over propaganda had slipped out of Mao Tse-tung's control into the hands of his rivals, who were conniving to do him in.

To the public Lin Piao was a tough realist on all subjects except for the one he chose to make sacrosanct: Chairman Mao. Lin Piao extolled him as a "genius" and claimed that his thought was "everlasting truth." Was he, like millions of others, simply fanatic about The Leader? Or had Mao instructed him, a man of impeccable military and civilian reputation, to inspire the worship of, and, in effect, deification of Mao by the masses? Or did Lin Piao's lofty language conceal subtle calculations — possible seizure of power? [2]

Mao was uneasy. Chiang Ch'ing had observed that at emergency meetings of the Politburo held in Hangchow soon after Lin Piao's diatribe. The malaise aroused in the Chairman was evident in their correspondence of the next few weeks, while he was traveling and she was working on cultural affairs in Shanghai. His reply to her letter of June 29 was philosophic and introspective. He was determined to "know himself" and to have Chiang Ch'ing know herself also. [3] Quoting Lu Hsun, he said that both should dissect their own motives more carefully than they dissect those of others (Chiang Ch'ing's frequent refrain in conversation). Weaving through his thoughts was wariness about "our friend," their intimate term for Lin Piao. He warned,

Things always go toward the opposite side. The higher a thing is blown up, the more seriously it is hurt at the fall. . . . I suggest that you should also pay attention to this problem and should not become dizzy with success. You should remind yourself often of your weak points, shortcomings, and mistakes. On this I have talked with you numerous times, and I did so last April in Shanghai.

Reflecting on the perils of his own position, and the paradox of personality cultism, he wrote,

I have always felt that when tigers are absent from the mountain, the monkey there professes himself a king. I have become such a king. But that does not mean eclecticism. In my mind there is some air of the tiger which is primary, and also some air of the monkey which is secondary. Once I quoted Li Ku's letter to Huang Ch'iung of the Han Dynasty, saying, "A tall thing is easy to break; a white thing is easy to stain. The white snow in spring can hardly find its match; a high reputation is difficult to live up to." The last two lines refer to me precisely.

In a revolutionary era that would begin to call itself a "dictatorship of the proletariat," Mao knew the risks of restoring to the people one dynastic element — the monarch — that he felt they needed but could not admit wanting. He was aware of how kingmaker Lin Piao had "blown up" his reputation, and of late, Chiang Ch'ing's, and how both could be destroyed in a fall. But whatever suspicions Mao may have harbored about Lin Piao's personal motives were not sufficient to warrant an immediate purge. He could not then have taken seriously Lin Piao's elaborate analysis of coups d'etat as a revelation of personal strategy. Nor is the inception of Chiang Ch'ing's distrust of Lin Piao easily pinpointed. In our interviews, however, which took place when Lin Piao's heretofore superb reputation was being officially destroyed, she dated his flagrant disloyalty at mid-1966. It was he, she claimed, who enticed Ch'en Po-ta to pervert members of the May Sixteenth Group, which had formed in the late summer of 1966 into what she called the "May Sixteenth Clique." The clique, which splintered from the group with which she had been associated, moved to the Ultra-Left, by promoting physical struggle, including military violence, over the verbal struggle she preferred (her aberration in the late summer of 1967 notwithstanding).

Despite Chiang Ch'ing's retrospective charges, out of the miasma of events and coalescing and dissolving of factions, Lin Piao's star continued to rise. At the Ninth Party Congress of April 1969 his role as "successor" was formalized. That April over half the people newly admitted to the Politburo came from the military. On the same occasion the official transliteration of the Chairman's name was changed to "Mao Tsetung," a stylistic simplification intended to set him linguistically and ideologically on a par with the European patriarchs Karl Marx and V. I. Lenin. Over the next sixteen months the Chairman was rarely photographed without his apparent alter ego, Lin Piao.

These displays of amity persisted until the Second Plenum of the Ninth Central Committee at Lu Shan in September 1970. That meeting was ostensibly called to consider revisions of the Party constitution. But as a secret report divulged two years later, it became the scene of an attempted "seizure of power" by Lin's group from Mao's.[4] Publicly, Lin Piao was still praising "Mao Tsetung Thought" to the skies; in the realm of *Realpolitik* he had won the backing of the majority of the Politburo, his wife and Ch'en Po-ta included.[5] Mao's secret report shows that Lin Piao had wanted to restore (and presumably to occupy) the position of head of state, which had been suspended with the dismissal of its last occupant, Liu Shao-ch'i. Mao had said in 1958 that he did not want this post for himself, by which he meant that it must not exist. Had Lin Piao won the renewal of that argument twelve years later and became head of state, he would have outranked Chou En-lai. Moreover, the army, which he commanded, might have dominated the Party, the primary locus of Mao's, Chou's, and Chiang Ch'ing's interests.

A dialectician and believer in historical recurrence, Mao could hardly have been surprised by Lin Piao's challenge. In the periodicity of power showdowns that Mao himself had described, the timing of that struggle was predictable. P'eng Te-huai in 1959 and Liu Shao-ch'i in 1965 had challenged Mao at Lu Shan. Now at the predicted five- to six-year interval, Lin Piao — in the same Lu Shan setting — initiated the "tenth struggle between the two lines."

When in human history has the role of designated successor to the founder of a dynasty been absolutely securable? With the chance to replace the Great Helmsman a heartbeat — or a dagger — away, Lin Piao knew that he was vulnerable to rivals who might try to destroy him politically or physically; that Liu Shao-ch'i's loss of the mandate demonstrated that Mao was not above changing his mind; and that Mao, a man fourteen years his senior but generally healthy (Lin Piao was chronically ill, and on sick leave in the early 1950's), might, Lin hazarded, live "over one hundred years." [6]

To manage the interval to the mutual satisfaction of himself and Mao, Lin Piao addressed himself to historical principles without neglecting old-time religion. Mao Tse-tung, he knew, always acted on the fundamental paradox of revolutionary rule: that he must belong simultaneously to the communities of the leaders and the led. It was easy in the days when he was guiding bands of disaffected commoners. Success caused his constituency to swell, and correspondingly, the ranks of leaders. To remain *primus inter pares* among close comrades and secret rivals, Mao was compelled to stand head and shoulders above them, thus elevating his image still further above the masses. In that process of singularization without severing himself from communication with the people, Mao moved not only within the tradition of rule by emperor, but also according to the example of Stalin, a socialist nation builder and personality cult object whom he admired — more, certainly, than Stalin admired him. To elicit comparable worship in China required political engineering. That task was assumed with Mao's permission, if not active encouragement in the first stages, by Lin Piao.

The cult's ideological substance was the popular digest dubbed by foreigners the Little Red Book or the Bible of Maoism. Its genesis went back to 1960 when Lin Piao, appointed defense minister the year before, presented to the Military Affairs Commission a set of propositions that came to be known as the Four Firsts: the priority of men over weapons, of political work over other work, of ideological work over routine political work, and of living ideology over ideas derived from books. Revised by Mao and titled "On Strengthening Political and Ideological Work in the Army," that document, adopted by the

Central Committee in December, foreshadowed the anthropomorphism of the Cultural Revolution. Part of it reappeared as the first paragraph of the Foreword to the *Quotations of Chairman Mao* of August 1, 1965, ostensibly edited by the General Political Department of the PLA, and frequently reissued down to the end of 1966.

In 1962, the year Chiang Ch'ing saw as the prelude of the Cultural Revolution, a new cooperation between the army and the Party was in evidence. Lin Piao had arranged for quotations from Chairman Mao to appear regularly boxed and in bold type in *Liberation Army Daily*. In December 1963 Mao responded by launching the campaign, Learn from the PLA. The next year Lin Piao began bringing out pithy passages from Mao's longer writings and brief essays in a pocket edition designed to be toted in soldiers' packs. By 1966 the students, and soon the masses, followed suit by holding aloft their red-covered pocket books of the *Quotations* during political demonstrations at the capital. As the pace of the Cultural Revolution quickened, quotations from the *Quotations* cropped up ubiquitously: at the start of all periodicals, at the beginning and end if not also the middle of every cultural performance, in huge characters plastered on the sides of buildings, and on billboards on the roadways. Nor were children's toys neglected: full Mao slogans were printed, one to a wooden block, the orders of the words never to be scrambled. For several years after the demise of promoter Lin Piao in the fall of 1971, the Chairman's image and utterances would be scarcely less omnipresent.

At the height of the personality cult in 1970, Mao Tse-tung displayed to Edgar Snow his consciousness of living in history. How hard it was for people to overcome a three-thousand-year tradition of emperor worship, he remarked. The so-called Four Greats thrust upon him — Great Teacher, Great Supreme Commander, Great Leader, and Great Helmsman — were a nuisance. In the long run all he cared to retain was the title "teacher," which was what he began with in Changsha. "Sometimes I wonder whether those who shout Mao the loudest and wave the most banners are not — as some say — waving the Red Flag in order to defeat the Red Flag." [7]

Mao's speculation of 1970 became Chiang Ch'ing's passionate conviction two years later. She denounced Lin Piao as the secret chief of the Ultra-Leftists — persons who instigated violent subversion of the Chairman's and her struggle against revisionism during the Cultural Revolution. Not all she divulged to me (in fits of resentment and revenge against a man who wronged her) was for the record, she said. Nor would all the evidence she released to me become part of the official case against Lin Piao, which, quite possibly under her aegis, was in the process of being assembled.

i

Anyone who worked in ways that were out of the ordinary inevitably would make some mistakes, Chiang Ch'ing said, resuming her narration. A member of the Communist Party should always strive to do his work correctly. If he erred in the pursuit of the extraordinary goals he set himself, but allowed his mistakes to be corrected, he was all right. "Certainly, if I have made mistakes I will make a self-criticism and correct my mistakes," she announced. "To do so is not a bad thing; actually, it's a good thing."

Chiang Ch'ing recalled with amusement and bravado how nearly she missed being a casualty of the battles of the 1960's. After she was named to the Cultural Revolution Group, which replaced the Group of Five headed by P'eng Chen, some representatives of the repudiated group burst into one of the new group's first meetings. Wielding arms, obviously they intended to assassinate them all. They started shooting, but bungled and were taken into custody.

In the formal determination of who were the "genuine enemies" and who were the "temporary offenders" in that clash, she said without naming names, she and her comrades decided that those who had attempted the lives of members of the Cultural Revolution Group but had no "serious" ideological problems would be released in due course. Some others who had made ideological mistakes in the past were "stabilized," meaning that with their coming over to Mao's side their political positions and good names were restored. The leaders held no lasting grudges against such "tempered officials," she said. Their "correct" attitudes at present were the result of the pounding they suffered during the Cultural Revolution. Such individuals (circumstantial comments indicated that she had Teng Hsiao-p'ing foremost in mind) who were "tempered" through the arduous process of struggle-criticism-transformation could become more valuable to the people than before.

However, justice was not always dispensed evenhandedly by persons who held power, she admitted. Prominent among those who were punished unfairly were Teng Hsiao-p'ing, T'ao Chu, and Ch'en Po-ta.* All three had failed to meet or adhere to the revolutionary standards that she, Chairman Mao, and their supporters had struggled to maintain against heavy odds during the Cultural Revolution. When the power to render justice was wrested from the hands of Chairman Mao and those closest to him, such comrades were wrongly attacked from both the right and the Ultra-Left.

Grievous losses resulted from the failure of certain veteran revolutionaries,

---

* At the time of their denunciations Teng Hsiao-p'ing was general secretary of the Central Committee and a supporter of Liu Shao-ch'i; T'ao Chu was a regional leader in the south and Chiang Ch'ing's rival in the revolution of the performing arts; and Ch'en Po-ta, a Maoist ideologue and member of Chiang Ch'ing's Cultural Revolution Group, was, she charged, coopted by Lin Piao's Ultra-Left.

among them Teng Hsiao-p'ing and the old general Yeh Chien-ying, to keep up with the swerving course of the revolutionary movement. And some comrades on her side clearly did wrong. Perceiving their errors, the enemy ferreted them out and subjected them to public criticism. Both the Chairman and the Premier tried to protect those unfairly attacked. Despite their efforts, some fell under the impact of the Cultural Revolution. Such loss of human dignity — and sometimes life — must be assessed from the perspective "one divides into two."

On the one hand, the Cultural Revolution was good for those who were criticized. But on the other, it was evident that the process of self-transformation (ideological rectification) would not be finished quickly. Such was true of Teng Hsiao-p'ing and Yeh Chien-ying. In time all their work and prestige would be restored — so she predicted in the summer of 1972.

Although she was reluctant to name many who were unjustly attacked, she spoke compassionately of the old warrior Hsu Hsiang-ch'ien, then vice-chairman of the Military Affairs Commission of the Central Committee. When his life was threatened in 1966, the Chairman invited him and others similarly imperiled to move into their home at Chung-nan-hai and to remain there until the situation was brought under control.

All sorts of losses — of life, property, and farm production — resulted from the Cultural Revolution, she said. But the most severe setbacks were in industry, where recovery still was incomplete (in the summer of 1972). In numerous factories ideological struggle broke out into open warfare, which was disastrous in view of the nation's need to continue production. Battles also flared on rural communes, though losses there were less devastating. Throughout tumultuous months the leaders forced themselves to be discriminating in their judgments of such disorders and to perceive them as manifesting the principle "one divides into two" They knew that the battles were not good of themselves because they engendered loss of life and property. But at the same time they clarified contradictions between classes and promoted ideological and cultural transformations that were beneficial in the long run. In retrospect, the most important "victory" of the Cultural Revolution was the initiation of change in people's attitudes.

Lu Hsun's widow, Hsu Kuang-p'ing, was also unjustifiably persecuted during the Cultural Revolution, and it killed her.

Why was Hsu Kuang-p'ing attacked? I asked Chiang Ch'ing.

Aftereffects of the literary struggle between Chou Yang and Lu Hsun during the middle 1930's, she responded. "I learned about that [Hsu Kuang-p'ing's predicament] only after someone sent me a letter exposing it. Then Lu Hsun's wife wrote to me herself, and I went to see her. It was not long after our encounter that she, like her husband, died from persecution [on March 3,

1968]. News of her death grieved me deeply. The persecution occurred while we were preoccupied with other problems. If she hadn't been abused by May Sixteenth elements [the Ultra-Left — in Chiang Ch'ing's account governed by Lin Piao, not by Chou Yang, who had been immobilized two years earlier], she might have lived longer.

"Soon after that Comrades Chou En-lai, K'ang Sheng, and I went to see her son, a technician with the government broadcasting station. He told about how she had been persecuted right up to the time of her death."

Political prudence prevented Chiang Ch'ing from saying whether Hsu Kuang-p'ing's persecution was political, physical, or psychological, or something else. What is clear is that Chiang Ch'ing empathized with Hsu — and for good reason. On the surface, honoring the widow was a way of honoring the memory of her husband, whom Mao and she appropriated for their cause. But on the less obvious, feminist side, these two women, along with numerous others less famous, potentially shared the fate of wives who become casualties of political battles commanded mainly by husbands. Both women — unusually talented, politically ardent — came to maturity in the thick of Shanghai's political warfare of the 1930's. Both married famous men, and finally outlived them. However Hsu, the more conventional, lived out her life in accordance with the legend of her husband as it was forged by the cultural politicians of the PRC.[8] Outsiders are left wondering whether she ever resisted the Party's suppression of the bulk of his writings, its relentless persecution of his finest protégés (Ting Ling, Hu Feng, Hsiao Chün, et al.), and Chiang Ch'ing's exploitation of his general fame and a few pieces of his writings in her vendetta against their mutual enemy, Chou Yang.

Might Hsu Kuang-p'ing's yielding to others' determination of history and her failure to pursue a separate career have been a negative example? Chiang Ch'ing was no less loyal to her husband and what he stood for. What set her off. from Hsu was that from her early twenties Chiang Ch'ing harbored high ambitions for herself and a stubborn conviction of her power to change history. In the early 1950's she began the delicate but grueling process of establishing work and constituencies separate from her husband's. But after Mao died, she, like Hsu, was forced to grapple with his inheritors and their self-serving manipulation of his legend.

ii

During our meeting in Peking Chiang Ch'ing opened the most recent chapter in the history of Chinese court politics of the Communist era: "The Chinese Communist Party has gone through ten major struggles between the two lines.

The tenth has been the most serious. The man involved was Lin Piao. He not only wanted to assassinate Chairman Mao and drew up many plots to do so, but he also intended to kill all the comrades of the Politburo. His men drew up a sketch map of our residences and were going to attack and bomb them and finish us off all at once. The struggle was very fierce. These people were so insidious, cruel, and brutal that they even dared to attempt to assassinate Chairman Mao!"

More pointedly, she said that during the time Lin Piao's men secretly controlled their residence he arranged for toxic substances to be added gradually to the meals consumed by Chairman Mao and her. They became ill, though mystified about the cause. Her sickness developed neurologically, affecting her brain and memory, during most of 1969. Only recently had she recovered.

"He had his backing in Soviet revisionism," Yao Wen-yuan interjected. "When he failed, he fled toward the Soviet Union together with his wife and son. He was utterly disconcerted, fled in panic, and flung himself over to the enemy. Betraying Party and nation, he courted his own destruction — his plane crashed in Mongolia."

Chiang Ch'ing went on, "Comrades like the Premier, K'ang Sheng, Chang Ch'un-ch'iao, Yao Wen-yuan, and myself were on the side of Chairman Mao. They [Lin Piao's Ultra-Left] set fires everywhere, and we acted like a fire brigade, fighting to protect our veteran comrades. Lin Piao's goal was to overthrow all the veteran comrades, put himself in power, and have the Soviet revisionists immediately send in their troops. However, just as Chairman Mao said to Minister Schuman, Chairman Mao applied a drop of alcohol* and Lin Piao was finished."

The propaganda movement against Lin Piao, which got under way in the summer of 1972, was one of many lessons to be learned by people of all ages as a result of the Cultural Revolution, Chiang Ch'ing explained. The Chairman had told them it was to sharpen people's perceptions generally. People must learn to discriminate among leftists, rightists, and those vacillating in the middle in order to be able to draw class lines under any circumstance. Above all, the movement demonstrated that Lin Piao *never equaled* the People's Liberation Army, as he was wont to claim. The PLA was created by Mao Tse-tung "and some others." All along it was led and personally commanded by Chairman Mao.[9]

Lin Piao's treachery began long ago, she said, without explaining why it took her and the Chairman so long to counteract it. After Lin Piao was appointed minister of defense in 1959, he announced, "One sentence of Chairman Mao is the equal of ten thousand sentences." Disliking such hyperbole, the Chairman later replied: "On sentence equals one sentence, and there is one

---

* I.e., eradicated Lin Piao's good name from the historical record.

matter [refusal to reestablish the state chairmanship] on which I have spoken six sentences which have come to nothing, not even half a sentence." [10]

There was no end to Lin Piao's appropriation of the words of others. Take the phrase he harped on, "Sailing the seas depends on the helmsman. . . ." Lin Piao used to claim that those were *his* words, but in fact he had only plagiarized them from the popular song, written by someone else. She told the other leaders that Lin Piao's exploitation of that highly important line about the Chairman made the Chairman look immodest.

As for the Chairman's book, *Quotations of Chairman Mao,* Lin Piao contributed nothing to it, though he claimed otherwise, she charged. As Ch'en Po-ta pointed out to them, the original preface (dated August 1, 1965) was signed by the General Political Department of the army and edited by persons other than Lin Piao. When Lin Piao got hold of the preface all he did was to change the beginning and the end. Yet he signed it, giving the false impression that the entire revised preface (dated December 16, 1966) was composed by him.

She had read two editions of selections from the Chairman's writings, she said. The first, which was simply titled *Supreme Instructions* (*Tsui-kao chih-shih*) was published jointly by the army and the Politburo in 1968 and 1969. She wondered just what "supreme instructions" meant. Only one title and one name, the Chairman's, were linked to it. Being cited as the sole author of "supreme instructions" made the Chairman appear to be a most immodest man. So whose writing really was this? To speak of "supreme" instructions, she reasoned, implied that somewhere someone was also delivering "subsupreme" instructions. But no one would admit to her or anyone that his were the subsupreme. Some associates (of hers, apparently) finally managed to block that first edition.

The men controlling the publishing houses (that is, PLA publications directed by Lin Piao and his supporters) always kept the Chairman and those on his side in the dark about their schedules. With no advance notice to the Chairman, the Premier, or herself, they issued several editions of the Chairman's works on their own authority. Once, when Chiang Ch'ing heard rumor of still another pamphlet, she told Chou En-lai to get her a copy. What he delivered to her was titled *Long Live Mao Tse-tung Thought.* That turned out to be no mere "pamphlet"; it was actually quite a thick book. After she and the Chairman perused it, and passed it on to others for opinions, they realized that two-thirds of it was Lin Piao's thought. Only one-third was the thought of Mao Tse-tung.* By the time they got their copies almost everyone else had

---

* The "thick book" was probably *Mao Tse-tung ssu-hsiang wan-shui,* a two-volume work totaling 996 pages, issued in 1967 and 1969 with no specific publishing information; later it was available in Chinese in four volumes. I have used the JPRS translation, *Miscellany of Mao Tse-tung Thought, 1949–1968,* in this volume. Chiang Ch'ing's saying that "two-thirds of it was Lin Piao's thought" probably meant that Lin Piao had selected and edited some two-thirds of the remarks

one, for they cost only sixty cents (an American quarter). Hers, she noted ironically, she kept in the parlor of her home at Chung-nan-hai. Soon she discovered that this was only one of several editions of the same book which proved to her that the purpose of issuing corrupt books was to *overthrow Mao Tse-tung*!

Lin Piao was a traitor to the nation, Chiang Ch'ing continued angrily. For a long time no one realized that he was a big "embezzler" of their material and spiritual wealth. Early on some perceived the flaw in his excessive enthusiasm: he was opposing the red flag by waving it. Soon they realized that the flag he waved was red on one side only; a black skull and crossbones were emblazoned on the reverse. Over the years he built up a reputation as an extravagant man who entertained lavishly and distributed gifts among friends. What he did in fact was to take what he wanted from state properties and disburse them at will (Confucian zeal to "become an official and get rich" topped by Soviet-style materialism). In various parts of the country he had built himself huge mansions to which he invited entire families whom he entertained royally.

In the spring of 1967 some members of Lin Piao's clique seized a factory in Szechwan and for no reason at all "fired ten thousand shots" (a conventional exaggeration) into the air, a vulgar military show to no purpose.

Fighting had its good points, she assured me. But since the tapering off of the Cultural Revolution, open warfare eased. A good thing, she added cheerily.

However, during the Cultural Revolution fighting broke out in many places remote from Peking. She recalled an incident related to an armed uprising in southeast Shansi. Late one evening (in the summer of 1967) she was reading documents at their headquarters in the Great Hall when Premier Chou burst into the room and tried to bustle her away. "Go home and get some sleep," he pressed her. No sooner had he spoken than a band of soldiers, maps in hand, broke into the Great Hall and descended upon the headquarters. Leading them was the old soldier and political commissar Cheng Wei-san, already a member of the Lin Piao clique, she would eventually learn. Cheng had been authorized (presumably by Lin Piao) to carry out a mopping-up campaign against rebels in southeast Shansi. Both Yang Ch'eng-wu, acting chief of the General Staff, and a deputy chief of the General Staff were on hand while artillery, armored cars, and equipment for digging trenches and tunnels were requisitioned and assembled. As she watched in astonishment, one of the General Staff officers said to her provocatively, "Comrade Chiang Ch'ing, you know how to fight!" What he was driving at, she surmised, was that she should be joining that expedition. She let him know that after living at the side of Chairman Mao for years, she had learned that arms should never be used recklessly.

ascribed to Mao. The book is the most comprehensive collection of speeches and writings attributed to Mao since the official Peking publication of his *Selected Works*.

Very late that night the Premier reached her by telephone at home. She should steer clear of military confrontations, he told her. She should continue to concentrate upon making propaganda among the masses. But she had to force him to understand that when tensions mounted, shooting could break out as easily among the masses as among men of the military.

Lin Piao's conspiracy also involved members of her family. He was not above trying to use her children against her. Though amusing to her now, it was hardly so at the time when, during the Cultural Revolution, Lin Piao plotted to kidnap her daughter Li Na, for what vicious purpose she could only imagine. Obviously, he did not know her well. The trap he set caught the wrong woman! Another time, when Li Na was working for *Liberation Army Daily* (as chief editor pro tem) during a crisis period, some members of Lin Piao's "anti-Party clique" wrongly accused her of "seizing power." *

During a difficult period of the Cultural Revolution she made her step-daughter Li Min a leader of the Science and Technology Commission (responsible for nuclear development) of the National Defense Ministry in Peking. The commission's chief was then Nieh Jung-chen, who was concurrently serving as vice-minister of defense. At this time Li Min also belonged to a mass organization called "September 16," headquartered in Peking. A certain air force general took Li Min aside and told her maliciously that some mistakes made by Chiang Ch'ing had been reported to that commission, and that Li Min, by association, was also held responsible.

Some time later, in 1971, Chiang Ch'ing went to visit Li Min at Tsingtao where once again Li Min had been falsely charged on account of her step-mother. There had been confusion over Chiang Ch'ing's judgment of the commission's chief, Nieh Jung-chen. Contrary to reports that she had attacked him, she actually had said that he should be *protected* from unjust criticism.[11] Those were but a few threads in a seemingly endless network of rumor and false allegations from which she, the children, and others close to them so often had to extricate themselves.

Despite the risks, both daughters followed their parents in making revolution. Moreover, they were spirited, independent, and critical. Li Na, Chiang Ch'ing added humorously, often accused her of being partial to boys and neglecting girls; for that matter, Li Min said the same thing.

---

* Li Na had apparently been assigned by her mother to that crucial post, which had vast potential power over military and civilian affairs. At the time that Li Na was serving as chief editor (late August 1967), *Liberation Army Daily* had temporarily displaced *People's Daily* as the Central Committee's major publication.

iii

It was never Chairman Mao's principle to distort the past by repressing the historical record, Chiang Ch'ing insisted. Lin Piao was just the opposite. An Ultra-Leftist, he repressed photographs, films, and other media in accordance with his own ambitions. Even the Americans were taken in by that. When Ch'iao Kuan-hua was welcomed to the United Nations (in mid-November 1971), American television broadcasters displayed shots of Chairman Mao and Lin Piao (presumably dead in September 1971) together. In the next clip "superspy Lin" stood alone. That video-journalism proved to the Chinese leaders that political research conducted by the American government is far-reaching (though perhaps less official and less diabolical than she surmised). Even President Nixon was afraid of the intelligence working against him! No one was immune, she added ominously.

Of all the rightists and leftists operating in the 1960's Lin Piao was the most cunning. His plot to seize control of the Party, the state, and the military included many vicious devices. One was to use the publishing industry to turn the Chairman into a god or an idol that one day could be smashed. Another was to create chaos. During the Cultural Revolution Chairman Mao often said privately to the leading comrades and declared openly to Edgar Snow that everyone should "cool down." On several occasions he turned to the Premier and asked him to help cool down the fiery struggle raging all over their country.

Once when she withdrew from the chaos of Peking to rest in Shanghai, she found that city completely under the thrall of Lin Piao's clique. Quotations from Chairman Mao were plastered ostentatiously all over the city walls. One preposterous sight, a gigantic photograph of the Chairman with one of his quotations printed in mammoth characters above his head, enraged her. Such vulgar displays made Mao Tse-tung look like an "immodest man." When she registered her complaint with Chang Ch'un-ch'iao, who was responsible for Shanghai's government, he warned her that if the Chairman's portrait and quotations were taken away, Lin Piao's image and attitudes would loom all the more prominently. Still she insisted that he get rid of that blown-up picture and permit only discreet displays of quotations from Chairman Mao hereafter.

Since the remains of earlier historical eras were so easily exploited by ambitious men, not all sites and relics should be preserved, Chiang Ch'ing said. The world had *too many people* for everything to be kept. Thus the Chinese leaders began to get rid of some monuments to the past. One huge arch was removed from the front of the Summer Palace and three others from the center of the city. The three arches that used to stand before the Gate of Heavenly Peace and obscured it looked like "three curious little caves." I might have thought them venerable, she commented wryly, because my country is built upon only two hundred years of history. Because China had a long past such arches and gates were of no historical significance. Moreover, they caused traffic accidents, which provoked her to call for their demolition. When Ch'en Po-ta and Yang Tzu-chen countermanded her order, she lectured them generally and told them to climb Coal Hill just north of the imperial palace and from the summit observe how the Peking Hotel, the tallest building in the city, disfigured the capital's profile.*

Regardless of what she said about aesthetic and practical considerations, Ch'en, Yang, and others were adamantly opposed to architectural change — especially the removal of the arches. Finally, in 1971, she won the argument. The arches were removed to T'ao-yüan-t'ing, a park near the old Temple of Agriculture in Peking. That act of preservation did *not* enhance the arches' meager historical significance, she added pointedly.

However, ancient monuments and objects that have been unearthed and have genuine historical value must be preserved, she said. She mentioned the diggings of the last decade at the archaeological sites near the city of Changsha in Hunan province. The treasures dug up there, some from as early as the Shang dynasty, belong not only to the Chinese people, but to the people of the whole world.† Handling such objects was always fraught with peril. Some Chinese archaeologists and their students who were allowed to work at liberty with these ancient objects grew to identify with them too closely, and consequently their revolutionary ardor slackened. The risk was perpetual, she said, but emphasized that the leaders never neglected or destroyed anything of genuine importance.

Returning to Lin Piao and the men who served him, she recalled an unnerving visit in 1970 to the Azure Cloud Temple at the Sun Yat-sen Park in Peking. She was accompanied by Wang Li (in 1967 accused of belonging to the May Sixteenth Clique) because Wu Te (acting mayor of Peking after P'eng Chen's dismissal), whom she admired and thus had made responsible for cultural affairs, had some other business. Wang Li was such a fool, she remembered with disgust, and that day he behaved most immodestly. He was not the only one, though, for in 1970 people's attitudes generally were poor.

When they reached the park Wang Li told her that he wanted to show her some Buddhas. She reminded him that the point of her visit was to locate certain exotic plants specially grown there and to take specimens for her own garden. But he insisted upon Buddhas. So she yielded and followed him to the

---

* In 1973 more stories were added, making the Peking Hotel the capital's first middling skyscraper.

† A selection of those post–Cultural Revolution finds went on international tour in 1973, opening in Paris.

Azure Cloud Temple. Being nearsighted (almost always wearing glasses) she did not immediately pick out all the details of this somber setting. He first showed her some sacrificial equipment and food offerings to the Buddha. Then they came upon Sun Yat-sen's famous hat and other relics, mainly clothing, buried there. Finally, deep in the temple she was stopped short by a small portrait bust of Chairman Mao. That must just have been put there! she thought.

She was infuriated. Although it was acceptable to put remnants of Sun Yat-sen's life alongside the Buddha, no one had the right to place images of Chairman Mao or things relating to him in a religious shrine. She scanned the temple more carefully. Five or six centuries old, it contained statues of some five hundred *lohan* — Buddhist saints. She immediately ordered military personnel to clear away all items pertaining to the Chairman and to restore the temple's original order. Addressing Wang Li, she reminded him that numerous foreign guests and working-class people visited the park and it was indecent for them to be subjected to such a perversion of the Chairman's image in a religious setting. Her fury created quite a scene (she recalled with an embarrassed laugh). But she did not care. She thought that the people should recognize her for who she was. She had made the point that Wang Li's arrangement was absolutely inadmissible. To dramatize it she bought up all the foodstuffs set out as offerings to the gods and idols and distributed them among the bystanders. "Eat!" she told them.

On another day, in 1971, while touring the Summer Palace, she decided to ascend its tallest structure, the White Cloud Palace, to take in the full panorama of the lake, pavilions, and parks. As she approached the building she was stunned to find inscribed upon its walls huge characters saying, "Read Chairman Mao's book; listen to his instructions." Each machine-made character was over six feet tall and designed in Lin Piao's calligraphic style. By having these characters plastered on famous walls in his own outlandish style, Lin Piao was pretending that these were *his* own words. But in fact that phrase had first been uttered by Lei Feng (the young military martyr made the subject of a national campaign in the early 1960's).

Long before she discovered this evidence on her own, Chairman Mao pointed out to Edgar Snow the error of inflating his words and his image. He told Snow that such things should never be imposed on foreign friends, a rule understood among their leaders. But Lin Piao chose to ignore it. When she first witnessed the grossly enlarged words at the Summer Palace, she dared only to remind those in her company that "the Chairman's power is literary and his calligraphy is art." But on the twelfth of September (the day Lin Piao's getaway plane allegedly crashed over Outer Mongolia) Li Tso-p'eng (Politburo member since 1969 and thought to be on Lin Piao's side) was dispatched to the Summer

Palace to strip from its walls Lin Piao's machine-made characters. The Chairman always opposed Big Nation Chauvinism, she added brusquely, in apparent reference to Lin Piao's self-vaunting.

Lin Piao's maneuverings against Chairman Mao, herself, and their defenders gained in frequency and intensity in 1971. Chairman Mao continually advised the Premier on how to deal with such clashes, but Mao's ideas were not easily carried out. During the peak of the crisis she flew to the side of the Premier several times to help "cool things down." Constant threats, divisiveness among the people, and conspiratorial actions made it almost impossible for them to work — even at their home at Chung-nan-hai, which had also become infiltrated by the enemy. Nor could they sleep or eat there safely. Just to survive, the Chairman and their defenders quietly evacuated Chung-nan-hai and established themselves at the Chinhai Hotel. That was inconvenient, so they moved on to the Great Hall of the People. Its superb facilities made temporary governing there fairly easy. Since the Chairman had been driven from his home, throughout the crisis period he was forced to receive all visitors at the Great Hall of the People.* The leaders' search for a haven against Lin Piao's conspiracy to overthrow Chairman Mao had not been revealed to outsiders before this moment, she added.

iv

The victorious leaders, Chiang Ch'ing continued, credited Lin Piao with teaching by negative example how to educate successive generations in the conscientious study of Marxism, Leninism, and the thought of Mao Tse-tung. Without unremitting study, the people would be repeatedly "taken in by swindlers like Lin Piao."

To counteract the revisionism still lingering among the people, a rectification movement was begun. On September 13, 1971, the day after Lin Piao crashed, the Chairman's office initiated an arduous movement to repudiate Lin's leadership and to rectify his work style that others had emulated. The next year a movement to repudiate Ch'en Po-ta (criticized for Ultra-Leftism in 1967) was launched. The decisions of the Chairman, Chiang Ch'ing, and their defenders were conveyed first to the ranks of Party members, then to the masses at large. Their ultimate goal was the repudiation of the entire anti-Party clique of leaders and their followers. The masses were thus encouraged to renew their studies of Marxism-Leninism and the thought of Mao Tse-tung.

* Judging from news dispatches, the Chairman did not receive any foreign guests at Chung-nan-hai from January 1970 through 1971. After Lin Piao's demise, the first foreigner to be greeted there was President Nixon in February 1972.

Over the last year or so, said Chiang Ch'ing, those systems of thought found their proper place among the people, and the thinking of the masses appeared to be "well armed." A certain amount of "ostentatious study" was required in order to discredit persons belonging to Lin Piao's group. When the people were armed with Marxism-Leninism and the thought of Mao Tse-tung, they would criticize their situations, sum up their experiences for one another, and persist in the struggle. Not just younger comrades, but also older ones must study political theory daily. "That includes me," she said, smiling.

Since so many people had resumed serious political study, the present revolutionary situation was "excellent." The "big chaos" passed and the "initial stage of good order" was reached (her terminology for stages of historical progress). Because China is so large, there would be still more chaos. So they must devote themselves to managing problems of future development.

Three tasks lay before them. The first, which was noted by some foreign correspondents, was to promote the process of struggle-criticism-transformation (away from revisionism and toward socialism) in all factories and other units of production. Political rectification should not be allowed to interfere with increasing production; and the latter, she remarked pointedly, is easier. In medical science, however, struggle-criticism-transformation had not yet begun. The second and third tasks, Chairman Mao told the whole Party and the nation, were that China should never become a superpower, and that it should never use nuclear weapons.

Will there be an eleventh "struggle between the two lines"? I asked Chiang Ch'ing.

"Inevitably," she replied. The leaders did not advocate the view that class struggle would fade away. Agents of the bourgeoisie still infiltrated their country and they were surrounded by capitalist nations.

In July 1966 Chairman Mao wrote her a letter that contained "brilliant predictions," she remarked of the correspondence spirited from China by agents and discussed earlier in this chapter. In it he set forth their task, which was to overthrow rightists within the Party and throughout the country. Of course, it would be impossible to overthrow *all* of them, she added. After seven or eight years there would be another movement "to eliminate demons and monsters." Then there would be still more "cleanups." The Chairman made it clear that any Communist rightist who attempted a coup in China would be short-lived. Any action that offended ninety-five percent of the population was doomed to fail. What he wrote in 1966 was not wishful thinking. His predictions were borne out. The Cultural Revolution did indeed serve merely as the rehearsal.

Lin Piao's final exposure of himself proved that the Chairman's letter contained brilliant predictions (a remark she often repeated). Of course the exposure came only at the end of prolonged and widespread disorder. In Peking alone destruction was costly. Certain institutions, such as Peking University and Tsinghua University, where political and academic commitments were tightly entwined, were especially vulnerable and collapsed immediately. Their demise demonstrated that in the institutions where the rightists were most arrogant, their failures would appear the most ignominious. Moreover, reaction from the left would be all the more swift and decisive. The collapse of those eminent universities, which for decades had supported noted professors and talented students, but also had cut them off from current realities, should be seen as belonging to the nationwide rehearsal for struggles beyond the horizon. Eventually everyone would learn his lesson. The rules for approaching the struggle must be drawn from the words of Chairman Mao: "Although the road is tortuous, the prospect is bright."

Last year (1971) was the fiftieth anniversary of the CCP, she said. The leaders recognized that the struggle between the two lines erupted on an average of once every five years. The struggle against Wang Ming was the longest — always an open confrontation. But the struggle against "Lin Piao's dictatorship," though subterranean for years, erupted for only two and a half days at the Lu Shan meeting of September 23–26, 1970.

What fruits of revolution have been reaped so far? The leaders were concentrating on strengthening the "backbones of the revolution," who should be the middle-aged and the old as well as the young. So long as those who had committed errors admitted them and adopted Chairman Mao's revolutionary line, they would be forgiven by the people. Take the case of Teng Hsiao-p'ing. He made mistakes, but afterward admitted the error of his ways. Once "rectified," he and others like him become "treasures of the people."

Early in 1972 some younger leaders held an enlarged working conference of the Central Committee, which she attended. Afterward, she sat in on another meeting of military personnel. The mental outlook of both groups appeared entirely new to her. Criticism of Lin Piao, rectification of persons who had fallen under his sway, and renewed study of the thought of Marx, Lenin, and Chairman Mao were providing the ideological mechanism of the new movement. People *were* learning a new language and a new thought. Moreover, they had a *continual need to be criticized*. The majority of the people were not ossified; they could change their views.

Such popular power to transform world outlook was volubly demonstrated at another gathering she attended. This was comprised of workers, peasants, and soldiers, including a fair share of women and members of national minorities. Some women activists spoke astonishingly well, especially one from Tibet. Mongolians also made useful contributions. In the course of the meeting the young spoke first. They were followed by some veteran revolutionaries who spoke at greater length, referring often to thick packets of notes they had brought with them. In the end some members of the Party's Central Committee came forward and performed well. Meetings such as these have convinced the leaders that the movement to repudiate Lin Piao and his values was deepening.

Setting aside Chiang Ch'ing's reconstruction of the Lin Piao affair, which was understandably subjective and self-serving, observers should not overlook the comparability of Lin Piao's and Chiang Ch'ing's goals with respect to present political authority and the power of succession. Although he operated mainly in the military sphere and she in the civilian, they became rivals in the pursuit of supreme leadership. Each began by presenting himself to the masses, explicitly or implicitly, as the Chairman's "best student." Each, on the strength of that claim, sought, from the early 1960's, to become the dominant implementer of his ideas — a role that would be vital should the Chairman die. Lin Piao rose to ideological prominence during the Socialist Education Campaign; Chiang Ch'ing soared during the subsequent Cultural Revolution. Lin Piao's method was the skillful editing of Mao in the Little Red Book. Chiang Ch'ing went still further in the art of propaganda by turning the nation's performing arts into a vehicle for Mao's ideas. Her dogged pursuit of supreme cultural control, with Lin Piao's brief assistance in 1966, is the subject of the following chapters.

PART FIVE

◇ ◇ ◇

MISTRESS OF THE ARTS

16.

◇ ◇ ◇

Theater of Revolution

History is made by the people. Yet the old opera stage presents the people as though they were dirt. The stage is dominated by lords and ladies and their pampered sons and daughters. Now you righted this reversal of history and restored historical truth, thus opening up a new life for the old opera.
— Mao Tse-tung, letter to the
Yenan Peking Opera Theater, 1944

. . . All this is sustained by a music unfamiliar to me, which mingles the Western scale with the meowings and shoutings of the old Chinese opera. . . . Of the revolution, there remains nothing but museums — and operas.
— Andre Malraux, *Anti-memoirs*

When President Nixon visited China in the early spring of 1972, Chiang Ch'ing invited him to a performance of the revolutionary ballet *The Red Detachment of Women*. He seemed to enjoy it and asked her to name the playwrights, composers, and directors of this and other current Chinese "musicals." They were "created by the masses," she told him. That explanation was not easy for him to accept, she smiled at me, and added that one could not have expected him to grasp the magnitude of her personal responsibility for the creation of a new model theater for the nation.

She admitted with anguish as she thought back on the early 1960's, that after years of shunning the stage, to present herself suddenly in dance, drama, and music circles and to partake of their work made her terribly vulnerable to criticism. When she quickly came to exercise personal authority over the arts, people refused to cooperate, and some conspired against her. But their hostility could not deter her from plunging ahead.

Viewing her from the cultural distance, we may wonder how aware Chiang Ch'ing was of the fundamental revolutionary nature of her actions. Defended by few, she rushed against the tides not only of Chinese but also of world history. On the premise that drama shapes consciousness, she sought supreme authority over the performing arts, and ultimately over the national culture. Her overall goal was control of — or better, "revolutionization of" — people's minds. She felt that she needed such command over popular consciousness, including recognition by the masses, as the basis of her personal power and authority, and as a means of stabilizing the positions of her loyal followers. Becoming directress of the national drama was a usurpation of men's historical prerogative "to play the role of presentor, to define the presentable." [1]

The greatest problem for both revolutionary leaders and historians is neither the decay of empire nor the cataclysm of political revolution, but the process by which ideas become social attitudes. In China the drama, known best to foreigners as "opera," is the medium. Luigi Barzini has observed of the Italians that opera is their dominant national metaphor. The same could be said of the Chinese, no less so in their revolutionary state, where consciousness of the relation between politics and the arts has been heightened by Marxian thought. Both peoples re-create the past melodramatically, thrive on historical pageantry, and persist in the worship of patriarchs. The difference lies in the degree of tolerance of traditional culture. The Italians have preserved the medieval church in a modern state and continue to support traditional opera's accompaniment to contemporary life. But the Chinese, in their revolutionary enthusiasm, have overthrown not only the political structures of "feudalism," but also the religious and social institutions that went with it. To establish a new, totalistic proletarian culture, China's leaders have destroyed nearly all ancient and modern, rural and urban rivals. Tea shops, coffeehouses, independent local theaters, private restaurants, and free markets have been closed down. Storytellers, fortune-tellers, and itinerant musicians, actors, and acrobats have been swept from the streets. Religious festivals, extravagant weddings and funerals, and the great holiday celebrations of the old calendar have been exterminated from the environment — as if they were a plague from a dead civilization.

Leaders in power since the Cultural Revolution have permitted no operatic re-creations of that banished past. Because the love of music, drama, and public performance has survived, indeed thrived, under improved economic and liberated social conditions, Chiang Ch'ing and her followers designed a model repertory of shows built upon the structures and symbolism of the socialist present. In what might have become a cultural wasteland, the "newborn things" of a projected proletarian civilization have found a chance to grow. People flock to the opera on stage and in moving pictures, sing arias in the alleys and on the farms, and perform favorite passages at the drop of a foreign visitor. Even the children — with no specialized youth culture of Disney, Sesame Street, or rock bands proliferated through television and capitalist marketing — ease spontaneously into the swing of revolutionary song.

As elsewhere, ideology in China gains force through passion. Revolutionary commitment is displayed not by words alone but through action. The Chinese used to say of cultural, hence moral and political affairs, "Good has good effects; evil has evil effects; stimulate people to be good." The classical theater used to propound Confucianism, and the far more raucous theater of the commoners promoted popular religion, often casting aspersions on the Confucianism of the master class.[2] Nowadays the revolutionary theater aspires to teach people to know evil and do good. In the workshop of revolution Chiang Ch'ing's special assignment was to cast ideas as social levers built into the performing arts. Her revolutionary dramas are stocked with physically glamorous and morally (read, politically) good characters of both sexes belonging to successive generations. Through the dark hypnotism of the theater, their styles and values are transmitted consciously and unconsciously by mimesis into people's daily lives.

Since the Cultural Revolution, the model works, which include ballet, symphony, and sculpture as well as the formal drama, have become a grandiose exercise in history, myth, and national policy. What Mircea Eliade has observed of traditional societies applies to China's revolutionary society as it struggles to establish traditions for the future. "All the important acts of life," he wrote, "were revealed *ab origine* by gods and heroes. Men only repeat these exemplary and paradigmatic gestures ad infinitum."[3] In China today all the "gods and heroes" who star in the model theater were born of the history of the Chinese Communist Party. No one drama is set earlier than the 1920's, when the revolutionary movement began. In none, though, is an historical individual, such as Mao Tse-tung, Liu Shao-ch'i, or Lin Piao, realistically portrayed. Only abstracted and generalized figures, who are said to be "typical" of the masses, stock the stage. The heroes all epitomize the well-glossed virtues of the proletarian class, and the villains caricature the vices of the KMT or the foreign enemy. Unlike the sea-faring mythology born of the Mediterranean or the southern seas, the myths that have coalesced about the founding of the Chinese Communist Party are landbound, with aquatic reference coming mainly from rivers.

The Chinese leaders are less concerned that art imitate life than that people imitate art. Consequently, their economics of the theater, unlike that in most parts of the world, is not measured commercially — what makes money — but politically — what makes people behave well. Theater tickets are cheap. An opera ticket costs about a dime in United States currency, an acrobatic show about eight cents, and the ballet and films about six cents. Children can get in anywhere for about a penny. Those Chinese who bothered to ask about prices in American theaters were horrified: "The capitalist class *does* control and consume culture!" Knowing the staggering differences in cost, Chiang Ch'ing remarked that when certain of the model works were to go on tour in America, the price of tickets must be kept artificially low — "to encourage attendance by the masses."

i

"If you want to write about the arts," Chiang Ch'ing remarked to me, "first you must 'grasp' the correct political, economic, and social analysis of Chinese society. Then you'll understand how the arts function within the superstructure."

"Superstructure," the Marxian term she used so frequently, is roughly equivalent to our widest concept of culture: art, literature, education, science, and ideas and values generally. Communist theoreticians have held that the superstructure must complement the economic base; if history moves on the correct course, the superstructure keeps pace with changes in the base. The problem of coordination of changes in the superstructure and in the base, and the question of the side on which historical initiative lay were debated in the early 1960's. Unresolved arguments were thrashed out during the Cultural Revolution. Then Mao's defenders, Chiang Ch'ing in the lead, argued that China's superstructure, most notably in education and the arts, had failed to keep up with economic changes. Should that lag be allowed to persist, the socialist economic base inevitably would be "wrecked," thereby making possible a "capitalist restoration."

By the mid-1960's revolutionary theater had a long proletarian and Communist tradition. In 1931, in the original Central Soviet Districts in Kiangsi, the Party established a theater at its Red Army Academy. The next year a Gorky Theater Arts School was founded, and Soviet influence continued to flow in through Chinese translations of Russian proletarian writers, and through the brisk three-way traffic of young Chinese Communist leaders who shuttled back and forth among Shanghai, the Chinese soviets, and Moscow. From 1933 onward news of Stalin's promotion of "socialist realist" drama was transmitted to China's propaganda-conscious leaders. Under Moscow's influence a Chinese Blue Blouse Regiment and the "living newspaper" style of impromptu theater became a regular means of projecting political ideology from mobile stages.

Chiang Ch'ing's theatrical life in Shanghai in the mid-1930's highlights other more sophisticated modes of revolutionary drama. But in the cities governed by the Nationalists, such leftist "superstructural" innovation arrived without the support of a socialist economic base.

After Liberation, educational and cultural institutions, along with land and industry, were nationalized by stages. Progress was slow. Just as some joint state and private shops were tolerated in the economic base up to the eve of the Cultural Revolution, so certain superstructural phenomena, including privately owned and managed drama companies, survived to that time.[4] Certainly, signal efforts had been made to nationalize the theater. In June 1950 Chou Yang summoned over forty leading opera performers to the first meeting of the Opera Reform Bureau. Soon an Opera Research Institute headed by Chang Keng (one of Chiang Ch'ing's rejected suitors) was established under the Ministry of Culture to promote cooperation between the new commissars and scattered communities of actors, singers, acrobats, and musicians — the motley performers of local opera who had known nothing of government regulation. In 1952, a Peking People's Art Theater was set up to transform the modern drama, which had developed from a bourgeois Sino-foreign matrix, into a new theater to promote the goals of socialist society. There the tactics of populist theater, which had been used to raise political consciousness since the early twentieth century, were implemented systematically. To spread Communist ideology and to narrow the class breach between professional artists and working people, troupe members typically were divided into four teams that were dispatched to perform among workers and peasants on a rotating basis. The same format was aggressively and broadly used during the Cultural Revolution.

Social projects in class leveling failed to uproot ancient cultural traditions or to exclude modern imports from abroad. Well into the 1960's thousands of local opera companies continued to flourish, some independently and others with state support. Among the urban cognoscenti, especially those searching for new and unconventional solutions to their lives, enthusiasm for the plays of Ibsen, O'Neill, Shaw, Chekhov, and Ts'ao Yü (their most illustrious Chinese imitator) did not wane. Russian dramatists and their Chinese apprentices taught Stanislavsky's method acting up to the Cultural Revolution, the point at which all demonstrations of soul searching, "domestic exile," and "internal emigration" were finished by the intervention of the state.

In the early 1950's, when cultural control from the center was barely effective, ancient and modern, feudal and bourgeois styles began to blend, producing new theatrical phenomena. The career of Mei Lan-fang, an extraordinary actor who specialized in elegant feminine roles in the opera (only after Liberation were actresses regularly used on the Chinese stage), demonstrated the cultural initiatives still available to individual performers. In the beginning of the century he had experimented with Peking opera in modern dress, but abandoned it.[5] By midcentury his reputation as a female impersonator was international. After the Communists came to power he continued to add modern glamour to his ancient style, issued his memoirs in English, made records and films of his performances, and flaunted his friendships with Hollywood personalities.[6] From midcentury on playwrights produced new dramas that made greater use of dialogue and realistic settings than did the traditional opera. T'ien Han's play about Empress Wu Tse-t'ien, Hsia Yen's about Sai Chin-hua, and Wu Han's cycle about the sterling Ming dynasty official Hai Jui were but a sampling of the new wave of historical romances based upon tantalizing passages of feudal and imperial history — with memories of that past now tortured by love and hate.

Since actresses generally were morally suspect, or appreciated only as entertainment, did not Chiang Ch'ing, whose ultimate goal was a revered masculine type of political power, have every reason in her world to avoid restoring her theatrical image in the public mind? Moreover, in China, as almost everywhere, "culture" was never a predominantly feminine sphere of responsibility. For centuries, men had dominated the theater as playwrights, directors, and musicians, and until recently had monopolized the stage.

There is no simpler explanation (though inadequate psychologically) than the ideological one for her single-minded pursuit of ultimate authority over the performing arts and more generally over the national culture. In our interview she recalled how in 1962 she was shaken as never before by "ideological struggles reflecting struggles at the economic base." At the Tenth Plenum (1962) of the Eighth Central Committee, the question was raised whether she should be allowed to take the initiative in organizing commentaries and criticism of the leaders of the Peking Municipal Party Committee (who also controlled the nation's cultural policy). In the ensuing arguments she was supported by the Chairman, Chou En-lai, K'ang Sheng, and K'o Ch'ing-shih, a valued ally inasmuch as he was chief of the East China Party Committee. After five years of battles with the old cultural guard, which she finally routed from office, she had convinced younger opinion-makers that her authority in the arts was justifiably paramount. Loyal Red Guard journals published biographical profiles that traced and praised each step of her rise to cultural power.[7] In these broadsides her revolutionary model plays were commended for "making the superstructure really conform to the economic base," for being a "precious asset of the world proletariat," and for becoming "shining pearls of proletarian literature and art . . . sparkling with the thought of Mao Tse-tung . . . a splendid product of Comrade Chiang Ch'ing's personal participation in the practice of struggle and art." [8]

Chiang Ch'ing's course also followed the imperial tradition of patronage of the arts in general and the theater in particular. The T'ang dynasty emperor Ming Huang established at his court a circle of actors he called the Pear Garden; similar patronage of theater was cultivated by his successors. The final Manchu ruler, Empress Dowager Tz'u Hsi * so adored theatrics that she had built for herself at the Summer Palace an elevated and open stage in the ornate Ming style. Performed there were romances of star-crossed lovers, edifying stories of filial piety, and religious masques drawing upon Buddhist lore. The Empress Dowager was not content to be merely an observer. Occasionally she and her protégé, the young Emperor T'ung-chih, costumed themselves fantastically and assumed parts far less august than their own.

China's present rulers have no more time for idylls. Determined to transform the character of the masses whose cultural patterns were set in imperial times, they cannot afford (at least publicly) to be absorbed in personal entertainments, their libraries, art collections, and film archives. Their overwhelming concern is what to choose for the nation to read, hear, and watch.

In cultural revolution as in industrial modernization the Communist leaders could not exclude elements from the West. Since the late nineteenth century — decades before the introduction of Marxism — tensions had been felt between the ideological superstructure and the economic base. "Chinese learning for substance and Western learning for function," [9] exhorted the late Manchu dynasty reformer Chang Chih-tung, who feared that China would be culturally contaminated by the introduction of the Western industrial and weapons technology needed for the nation's survival against threats of foreign imperialism. In the early 1920's Hu Shih, the liberal promoter of vernacular literature, American style, and gradual reform, warned against the tendency toward "wholesale Westernization." [10] The same problems of balancing foreign and Chinese values were encountered by the Communist leaders. In the earthy metaphor of Chairman Mao, "Weed through the old to bring forth the new, and make things foreign serve things Chinese." That formula was utilized by Chiang Ch'ing as a means of justifying critical assimilation of the national heritage and the infusion of new foreign ideas into genres long familiar to the people. But *critical* assimilation meant getting rid of superstructural weeds.

"How can we critically assimilate ghosts, gods, and religion?" Chiang Ch'ing challenged a huge contingent of dramatists at the Great Hall in November 1966. "That's impossible because we are atheists and Communists. We don't believe in ghosts and gods." Such superstitions were used by the landlord class

---

* Although Tz'u Hsi's name occurs in this book, Chiang Ch'ing never uttered it in her recollections of the Manchu era. Surely her reasons were political: not to draw attention to this most infamous and unpopular female ruler of modern times.

to exploit the people. "To sweep away all the remnants of the system of exploitation of old ideas, culture, customs, and habits of all exploiting classes is the fundamental challenge of our Great Proletarian Cultural Revolution." [11]

Through the end of the Manchu dynasty the old guard was convinced that its system of government, depth of history, and richness of literature and fine arts were superior to those of the "barbarians" — men of the West. While a Marxian historical perspective has compelled China's present leaders to repudiate the "feudal" government and the literary tradition of the past, the ancient material culture — the bronzes, pottery, porcelain, architecture, and public monuments — have become a new source of national pride. They are celebrated not as the genius of artists and experts, but as the "creations of the masses."

In their struggle to produce a literary culture for the revolutionary era, various Party leaders, including Mao and Chiang Ch'ing, have admitted feelings of inadequacy, even failure. The century-old love-hate attitude toward the West remains unabated. It is not that nothing has been achieved since the founding of the Communist Party in 1921. Had China's political environment of the 1930's and after been more receptive, Lu Hsun might have become China's Solzhenitsyn, T'ien Han its Arthur Miller, and Hsia Yen its Federico Fellini. Each, moreover, was only the center of a promising creative circle. Their tragic flaw, it seems, was genius linked to individualism and the courage to defend the combination. Lu Hsun died in 1936. The other two survived to be felled during the Cultural Revolution, paradoxically the same movement that launched Lu Hsun's heroic reputation not only as a revolutionary "standard-bearer" but also as a "Communist," although he never wrote under a regime staffed by card-carrying Communist bureaucrats. In 1956 Mao commented on this cultural dilemma:

> We must acknowledge that in respect of modern culture the standards of the West are higher than ours. We have fallen behind. Is this the case in respect of art? In art we have our strengths and also our weaknesses. We must be good at absorbing the good things from foreign countries in order to make good our own shortcomings. If we stick to our old ways and do not study foreign literature, do not introduce it into China; if we do not know how to listen to foreign music or how to play it, this is not good. We must not be like the Empress Dowager Tz'u Hsi who blindly rejected all foreign things. Blindly rejecting foreign things is like blindly worshipping them. Both are incorrect and harmful. [12]

ii

No history-conscious Chinese can forget Confucius' observation that music tempers men's souls. From earliest Chinese history music was made to accompany state rites. During the Western Chou dynasty (1100–771 Bȷ.C.) archery ceremonies were accompanied by orchestras that included lyres, flutes, drums, and bells. Imperial orchestras in the Han dynasty progressively added more instruments. After four centuries of disunion, the Sui and the T'ang dynasties, which followed from the sixth through the tenth centuries, were both preeminently concerned with the consolidation of empire and the enrichment of culture, including the adaptation of some foreign traits. Emperors of both dynasties established highly articulated music departments that sought to amalgamate music from Central Asia and that of national minorities with the dominant Han tradition. [13] A thousand years later the People's Republic, as concerned as any past dynasty with political consolidation after disunion, underwrote fresh research into the music of the minorities, or "folk" music, as it might be called. This would be synthesized with elements of the classical Han tradition and of the West — all ideally purged of overtones of feudalism, imperialism, and capitalism.

At the same time Empress Dowager Tz'u Hsi was "blindly rejecting foreign things," the imaginative reformer Liang Ch'i-ch'ao was admiring foreign music, which he found much more powerful than China's. Among the reasons Liang cited for China's feeble military spirit, which was never more evident than during the challenge of foreign imperialism during the late nineteenth century, was the "lethargic" quality of Chinese music. Like the Athenians who taught the Spartans how to use martial songs to spur soldiers on to victory, he argued, the Chinese should devise ways to stimulate the daring and aggressiveness of their people. [14]

The desire to strengthen state music through selective borrowing from foreign sources and from China's past was never more intense than on the eve of the Cultural Revolution. An overriding goal of that national upheaval was to orchestrate anew the revolutionary will of the people so that they would engage collectively in ambitious tasks of "socialist construction." When Chiang Ch'ing undertook that epic challenge in the 1960's, the problems she faced were still those of cultural balance and synthesis. In the pursuit of *cultural* self-strengthening, how much foreignness could China tolerate? What cultural advantages could alien races and nations offer to China's emerging proletarian class?

Since the mid-nineteenth century the challenge of the West seemed to encompass cultural as well as industrial and military standards. In the wake of China's humiliation in the Opium War of 1839–1840 and the conclusion of a system of "unequal treaties," a few brave reformers launched a movement in the 1860's to install industrial foundations and promote national defense. Given China's basically agrarian, nonindustrial tradition, their unprecedented pursuit of energy and power over nonhuman nature has been aptly termed by historian Benjamin Schwartz as Faustian-Promethean.[15] The same spirit of dynamism and aggression was consciously adopted as a general operational principle by the Chinese Communist Party. Land reform and industrialization continued it in the material, hence socioeconomic order, and the monumental upheavals of the mid-1960's raised it to the cultural order.

Music became central to the celebration of the Cultural Revolution. From the West were borrowed a range of instruments and wealth of symphonic music that were as appropriate to China's present historical moment as the techniques of industrial and military civilization had been the century before. Foreign violins, violas, base viols, clarinets, horns, and the grand piano orchestrated in the manner of Tchaikovsky, Liszt, Rachmaninoff, Beethoven, and Smetana could yield unprecedented sonority, volume, and instrumental color. In the music of the Chinese stage, the Faustian-Promethean spirit projected proletarian class aspirations, militance, wealth, and power.

The Chinese used to scorn their own musical heritage, Chiang Ch'ing said to me when she discussed the Cultural Revolution's musical foundations. Whenever they heard a piece of Western music, they assumed unthinkingly that it was superior to their own. Nor did it ever seriously occur to them that new music could be *composed*. After decades of exposure to Western music, some finally awoke to the fact that it was a function of foreign capitalism. Still, she said, easing her straitlaced Marxism, there was much to be learned from it. Generations of Chinese musicians who had devoted themselves to the mastery of foreign instruments and musical scores did not feel humiliated by that experience. Their enthusiasm for foreign music had made China abound in musicians. Pianists were legion, some quite skilled and versatile. Their joke was that "China has more Liszts than Liszt."

She had not listened extensively to Western music, she continued. Nor could she read music fluently until she began teaching herself in the early 1960's. But for years she was confident that the Chinese could improve their own musical culture on the basis of foreign accomplishments.

"With hammer in hand," she announced as she raised a fist, "I set out to attack all the old conventions." Her offensive triggered volleys of arguments in musical circles. People used to believe that a symphony could have only four movements; others said eight. Some wanted all musical scores to be symphonic. Others preferred to hold the line at solo instrumentation, or sought to make the human voice dominant.

Her own musical background was uneven. As a girl at the drama school in Tsinan, she had learned to play several instruments, including the piano, which she studied for three months. Although her teacher liked her as a person, she recalled, at the keyboard he was a strict disciplinarian who struck her wrist with sticks in order to regulate her style. She hated that, and so never really got beyond scales and basic exercises. In the briefing before President Nixon arrived in the spring of 1972 she was told that he played the piano exceptionally well. So she did not dare tell him that she had once dabbled. "You're the first foreigner to whom I've admitted playing that instrument," she said, laughing.

For some years, most often since 1964, she visited various music conservatories, spent long hours listening to recitals, and observed up close how foreign instruments are constructed and played.[16] After watching clarinets, oboes, flutes, and other instruments performing in solo, chamber, and symphonic arrangements, she began to appreciate the versatility of these instruments and their potential for blending with other groups — Chinese instruments included. Those forays into esoteric musical circles were not easy, she admitted. She was painfully aware of the disdain with which distinguished musicians regarded her because she lacked a serious musical background. But they dared not disparage her express purpose — to bring revolution to the music world.

As she educated herself musically, she worked at arousing the musicians' interest and eliciting their commitment to turn music into a revolutionary medium. Their nominal consent was offered freely, but that was meaningless, she found. Li Te-lun (Shanghai-trained, his Communist career begun in Yenan), the conductor of the Central Philharmonic Orchestra, and his prize pianist, Yin Ch'eng-chung (then in his twenties, trained at the Leningrad Conservatory), each sent her a letter saying that by all means he wanted to make revolutionary music. But such letters were pointless until their authors got out and did something. Knowing the kind of Western music they adored and would be most unwilling to forgo for any reason made her want desperately to strike out at them, shattering the foreign conventions they followed so slavishly. To achieve her goal she worked with them continually until they gradually began to grasp the innovative syntheses she was after.

Though skilled with instruments, Li Te-lun, Yin Ch'eng-chung, and their colleagues knew next to nothing about musical composition. In the creation of revolutionary music, she instructed them, it was imperative that both Chinese and foreign conventions be broken down. As she waged that campaign singlehandedly, she would appear unannounced at rehearsals of the Central Philharmonic Orchestra. After she rendered her judgments conductor Li Te-lun would shriek back at her, "You're attacking me with a big hammer!" The recollection delighted her. But he was honest and good-natured because he knew that her grueling criticism did him good. For many years, she added, both Li Te-lun and Yin Ch'eng-chung had flaunted foreign musical conventions, with political insouciance.

Li Te-lun thus learned to cooperate, and in time presented her with new works by "master composers," who had been recruited from among his co-workers. Their offerings included draft versions of the *Yellow River Piano Concerto* and the *Shachiapang Symphony* (based on the libretto of the revolutionary opera *Shachiapang*), the two major pieces of music to be produced during the Cultural Revolution. As originally presented, both were marred by foreign influence. Yet under her direction each was revised to the point of being counted among the model works — though they were still imperfect, she admitted. Arrangement of them as symphonies was enormously difficult because she had to struggle not only with the fundamental conceptualization of the musical scores, but also with the expert composers who had been commissioned to work out the details, and finally with the performers themselves. When she undertook reconstruction of the *Yellow River Piano Concerto*, composers and performers alike were incredibly stubborn about learning how to do things correctly. At first the singers she recruited refused to repudiate earlier professional loyalties by joining the Chinese Association of Music (which she underwrote). So she had to "hit them with a hammer," she repeated, until they came around.

The *Yellow River Piano Concerto* took off from an earlier composition, the *Yellow River Cantata*, which was written as a chorale by Hsien Hsing-hai in Yenan.[17] She had a hand in it because she was working at the Lu Hsun Academy at the time he composed it. In later years she discovered that the *Cantata* included certain "unhealthy" passages. Those had been eliminated from the present work — which had other flaws, she hastened to add. Personal experience inspired her conception of how the music should be redeveloped. Crossing the Yellow River several times and exploring its upper reaches during the Liberation War in the Northwest had given her a vivid sense of the river's form and movement. She had also participated in battles waged near its banks. To prepare Yin Ch'eng-chung to compose his solo piano part, she sent him out to retrace the march led by Chairman Mao. Thus he was able to recapture musically the original spirit of the struggles waged by the elder generation of revolutionaries in the Northwest.

Under her guidance the glaring foreign tonality of the original *Yellow River Cantata* was reduced. At each stage of the transformation she and her assistant solicited opinions from the masses, and adjusted the music accordingly. The same routine solicitation of popular reaction was carried out during the composition of the *Shachiapang Symphony* and the Peking opera version of *The Red Lantern* with piano accompaniment.[18] Both were altered repeatedly to achieve the desired effect upon the masses.

iii

As Thomas Jefferson observed in the eighteenth century, "the present belongs to the living" is an assertion made by every revolutionary generation of people newly sensitive to the fate of their fellow men. Mao Tse-tung's similar assertion of the present, "serve the people," was made at the funeral of a friend in Yenan. Picked up by slogan-happy Party leaders, "serve the people" was put to millions of purposes in education, scientific research, public health, and military and official behavior. In the 1960's Chiang Ch'ing turned the slogan into the sole standard of creation in the performing arts.

To conceive and produce a model revolutionary theater Chiang Ch'ing would have no real help from Mao, whose literary talent flourished in essays and verse. By the time she began to play an active part in public affairs in the 1960's, he had long been accustomed to defer to her greater knowledge of theater, though not without occasional digs at points where she seemed to be arrested at a bourgeois stage of cultural consciousness.

Chiang Ch'ing's production of proletarian symphonies and theater followed the centuries-old tradition of revising classic forms in the light of contemporary interests. As meter is necessary to give tension to poetry, classical operatic form was necessary to give tension to revolutionized theater. The people of China — the prime audience of the new proletarian arts — were accommodated by the preservation of certain structures from the classical and popular drama. Tunes, tempi, singing styles, acrobatics, and exaggerated social typologies were salvaged to give familiar shape to unfamiliar goals. Although such Western innovations as the proscenium stage, realistic backdrops and props, and an enlarged orchestra removed from the stage to the pit may have appeared strange at first, that Sino-foreign liaison was less offensive to popular expectations than unadulterated spoken drama — dialogue devoid of song and acrobatics — would have been.

The slogan "destruction must precede construction" was applied to the performing arts, as well as to numerous other institutions, during the Cultural Revolution. Verbal rather than physical struggle was the drama's style. Out of the havoc wrought by Chiang Ch'ing and her defenders who banned all available entertainments — music, drama, and film to begin with — a select corpus of model works known as the *yang-pan hsi* was born. The evolving use of *yang pan*, meaning "mold" or "model," had political significance. During the late 1950's *yang-pan* referred to "demonstration fields" — model farms constructed for general emulation during the Great Leap Forward.[19] Thus the term *yang-pan hsi*, "model *theater*," extended the metaphor from the base to the superstructure. The message was that styles of public entertainment, no less than agriculture, should fit a mold but change with the demands of revolutionary leaders and their times.

By the time the Cultural Revolution began winding down in 1968, a total of eight *yang-pan hsi* had been produced: four operas (*The Red Lantern, Shachiapang, Taking Tiger Mountain by Strategy, Raid on White Tiger Regiment*); two ballets (*The Red Detachment of Women* and *White-haired Girl*); the *Yellow River Piano Concerto*; and a series of sculptural tableaux done in sinified socialist realism, *The Rent Collection Courtyard*. The appearance of each was a national event lavishly reviewed on the first page of the news, with philosophical exegesis in the Party journal *Red Flag*. The eight "revolutionary classics" would expand gradually to admit some graphic arts, most prominently the portrait in oils — Western in style and substance — of a blue-gowned and boyish Mao Tse-tung going to investigate labor conditions at the An-yuan mines in the early 1920's. [20]

In the years when cultural destruction far outpaced construction, Chiang Ch'ing was often defensive of the limitations of her new model repertory. If new operas continued to be thrown together as they had been in the recent past, she remarked in a talk of November 1967, "people would strike us down." It would be better for the eight model works to monopolize the stage for the present, for they had cleared away the emperors, generals, and bourgeoisie; the ballet and symphony also had been reformed. "Although they still have shortcomings and areas which need further adjustment," she said, "at least they have caused a sensation and shocked the world!" [21]

Chiang Ch'ing and her corps of expert assistants were clearly the leaders of radical cultural change: they felt compelled to destroy lingering faith in the bourgeois notion of individual genius and to foster in its stead the proletarian ideal of mass creation. This ideal was derived from the Leninist notion of democratic centralism, which was applied to all phases of political life during the mid-1960's. In her address "On the Revolution in Peking Opera" (1964), Chiang Ch'ing commended Shanghai's Mayor K'o Ch'ing-shih for employing the "three-way combination of leadership, playwrights, and masses. The leadership sets the theme; playwrights go out to experience the actualities they are to re-create in writing; opinions are solicited widely at each stage of construction and in rehearsal." In our interview eight years later she was tougher: "All theatrical works must be submitted to the masses for their opinions. Their good opinions are acted upon, their erroneous ones rejected, and those which cannot be put into effect immediately are set aside temporarily. We call that democratic centralism on a broad scale."

If that was democratic centralism, what was to be done with the modern drama? I asked her.

During the Cultural Revolution, Chiang Ch'ing responded edgily, she tried to revise some modern dramas but failed to get necessary cooperation. The writers, producers, and actors who were the "backbones" of the theater world learned their values and styles in the 1930's and 1940's when the political climate was far different. Among them were some nominal Communists who actually were traitors to the Party and secret agents of the KMT. Although these notables of the theater lived in cave dwellings like everyone else while the Party was stationed in Yenan, as soon as they regained their beloved cities, they resumed their plush bourgeois lives. Such luxurious homes and furnishings made it impossible for them to want to cater to a widening constituency of workers, peasants, and soldiers. What energy she expended trying to reform their attitudes! she exclaimed. How futile in the long run.

Despite the incorrigible life-styles of certain playwrights left unnamed, was it possible for others to rewrite modern dramas, Chinese or foreign, for present purposes?

That depended on the nature of the play, the willingness of the playwright to make the required changes, and the adaptability of the players themselves to the new roles. By now, she said, most playwrights had ceased to bask in the splendor of their mansions (though not all were wealthy). Along with the leaders and other intellectuals, they too had gone out to mingle with the common people to whom they would have to address their work hereafter. But the overriding problem in the creation of modern drama was one of *leadership*: of knowing how to exert the right pressures at the right times. The leaders would support the revival and revision of spoken dramas, she said confidently, "once their prospects were good."

Her efforts to produce *model* spoken dramas began in the early 1960's, the time of the Socialist Education Campaign (and of the ascendancy of Lin Piao and the military generally), when she had hoped to redeem several new plays that had been solicited on military themes. One was about the young military hero Lei Feng (whose martyrdom began to be celebrated in 1963). Another was on the Long March of 1934–1935, and a third was titled *Letters from the South* (a political melodrama about U.S. imperialism in Vietnam). In their original forms these dramas were worthless because the leaders had failed to recruit playwrights who had practical experience of military life. The actors in the early presentations were equally innocent of military experience, and strutted upon the stage, flaunting urban airs totally unrelated to the simple ways of soldiers and the Red Army. How divorced their art was from politics!

The transposition of a story from one genre to another, from the novel to spoken drama, opera, or film, though not necessarily in that order, had been practiced for centuries, she emphasized. At present she found opera and film to be the most desirable media. Because the operatic form was familiar to the people, radical changes of content were acceptable. But film was cheaper in the long run because it could be easily distributed to China's vast and scattered populations.

Inevitably, the administration of changes from one genre to another touched off battles of will. She mentioned a work first called *The Great Wall*, and later retitled *On the South China Sea*; written first as a spoken drama, it was later converted into an opera. During the Cultural Revolution the playwright agreed to submit the script to her for consideration. She made changes in it which he accepted. But when she presented the revised script to the director he began protesting in a "reactionary" way. Although he ostentatiously invited *her* to direct *him*, when she explained to him how to improve the acting, he paid no attention to her. Such stubbornness, she said, proved to her that he was a counterrevolutionary.

Actually, she continued more calmly, the abortive efforts to salvage spoken dramas were the fault of the leadership. The leaders were compelled to realize that the people who had always controlled the dramas — writers, directors, and actors — were totally creatures of theater. Being screened off from "practical experience" made them oblivious to the structure and motivation of ordinary peoples' lives. Then some theater people were plain lazy, refusing to undertake any new tasks.* Younger people were generally easier to remold. The leaders were increasingly conscious, however, of the need to encourage the older, experienced playwrights, directors, and actors not to lose heart in the turmoil, but to keep up their work in accordance with new conditions.

In the early 1960's no one supported her efforts to bring the drama up to date. Of all the leaders she knew, only K'o Ch'ing-shih agreed to go along with her. After failing to revise a play called *A New Generation* on her own, she handed the script over to K'o Ch'ing-shih and told him to use his mayoral office to have a Shanghai troupe produce it in revised form. But in that Shanghai version the contrasts of characterization never jelled; that is, the politically advanced characters never rose dramatically above the bad characters. Other problems came up about the design of realistic stage sets — a breaking away from the tradition of the bare stage. Moreover, she observed, as they strove to teach experienced actors to portray proletarian characters, to leave behind their more sophisticated repertory, they continued to draw the absurdly high salaries

---

* Vice-Minister of Propaganda Chang Ying interjected that one of the newest revolutionary operas, *Ode to Dragon River*, started out as a spoken drama, then was changed to Peking opera on a socialist theme. She compared China's recent situation in the performing arts to that in the Soviet Union, where veterans of the October Revolution continued to monopolize the stage for years after the war was over. By the time the proletarian revolution could be portrayed in theater, the actors who had begun their careers during the period of the war against the tsars were aged, fat, and incapable of undertaking new roles. Then in the Stalin era cultural authority was monopolized by revisionists, who continued to dominate drama circles, as they did in China up to the last decade. Although the old dramatists could be encouraged to carry on after remolding their ideology, Chang Ying continued, casting her eye for approval to Chiang Ch'ing, they would always be hamstrung by lack of experience in political struggles waged beyond the walls of their academies.

of the past. When the leaders drew attention to that injustice, the actors panicked. They thought they would lose their jobs, which was most unlikely. But
even after 1968, when actors along with other professionals and government
personnel were sent to May Seventh cadre schools* for political reeducation in
rural settings, they continued to draw the same inflated salaries. Premier
Chou never approved of that, she remarked.

People often scolded her for throwing herself into the reform of spoken
dramas that seemed to be beyond repair. She cited the one-act play *The Man
Leading the Troops*, produced by the People's Liberation Army. When it was
first performed, some associates of hers telephoned her and urged her to go and
see it. She went, accompanied by the literary critic and vice-director of the
PLA Culture Bureau Ch'en Ya-ting. She found the play's characters offensive
because their politics were ambiguous (neither absolutely good nor bad). During
the intermission she asked Ch'en Ya-ting whether the soldiers portrayed on
stage were to be construed as "individual" or "universal" types. Was the male
lead, whose character annoyed her, "typical" of China's military?

Although *The Man Leading the Troops* had problems as a play, she thought
that it might be salvageable as a film. For after almost all filmmaking had
ground to a halt during the Cultural Revolution, she was desperately in need of
film scripts to be used for her new productions. She explained her plan to
Premier Chou, who promptly invited her to make a speech about the conversion of the play to film at the forthcoming film festival (probably of 1965). That
news took the Chairman by surprise, and he put an end to her action. For he
too had seen the play, and now disparaged it as "liberal." He was certain that
even a revised film version would mislead the people. What he perceived more
keenly than the rest, Chiang Ch'ing explained, was that its portrayal of military
life was skewed — not "typical." That incident, she said, proved once again
that drama reform ultimately is the responsibility of the leaders. From the
perspective of the leaders the fundamental question remains: will writers in-
tegrate themselves with the workers, peasants, and soldiers? [22]

A few spoken dramas about military life have achieved sufficient realism to
be converted to opera, feature film, or historical "documentary" (in China's
cinematic language imaginative reconstruction of historical events rather than
newsreels or original film). She cited as a good example *Fighting on the Plain*,
a play about guerrilla war which included realistic scenes of tunnel warfare
against the Japanese. That she appreciated especially because she too had
crawled through such tunnels dug by the masses and preserved for future neces-

---

* Exurban camps where bureaucrats and intellectuals were sent for several months or years to
practice self-reliance, by raising their food, building their houses and furnishings, and confining
their reading and discussion to the Marxian classics and the works of Mao. Most foreigners who
have visited China since the late 1960's will remember the inmates' cheerful smiles and musical
performances.

sity. But *Guerrillas on the Plain,* a play on a similar theme (the film of which I saw), failed to attain such realism.

I asked her about the possibility of reintroducing foreign dramas into contemporary China.

There seemed to be no point in it, she replied. Foreign dramas were, of course, once popular in the 1930's, years when eagerness to produce exceeded the literature available in translation. Consequently, a number of the plays were adaptations of foreign films. The Japanese film *Babies' Murder* and an Irish one called something like *Lock Up Your Suitcase* went from screen to stage as spoken dramas; she played the lead in each. However, the most successful shows, among them Ibsen's *Nora* (*A Doll's House*), Ostrovsky's *Grazia,* and Gogol's *The Inspector General,* were produced from the original scripts. Their own dramatic interpretations were superb, far better than straightforward presentation by Europeans could have been.

Recently attempts were made to transpose the story cycles from traditional Chinese novels (for centuries the source of plots for traditional opera) into revolutionary theater. Some "bourgeois playwrights" turned parts of *Romance of the Three Kingdoms* into contemporary opera. But the script, musical score, and stage directions were revised so continually over the years that the final result bore scant resemblance to the original. That was undesirable from the leaders' viewpoint.

Original pieces of literature and music should be altered and transformed to revolutionary theater only under the authorization of the leaders, and then with the utmost care. There was always the danger of striking an effect opposite to that intended. When she and other members of the Lu Hsun Academy of Literature and the Arts first set about composing revolutionary music in the wilderness of Yenan, they had no resources, no musical heritage from which to draw. Nor was there much foreign music on hand. So they turned to the local music. They gathered up ancient folk tunes, played them on their own instruments, and wrote fresh, political lyrics. But that was risky because the associations in people's minds were not always known. Some people she was working with had taken over tunes that turned out to have obscene lyrics. Even so, they went right ahead, just changing the words. But she knew that the listeners' minds could not be so quickly cleansed of the lewd associations. She herself had never been involved in the adaptation of such obscenities, she remarked primly.

Returning to the subject of spoken drama, a genre derived from the West, she said that plays considered for revision fell into three categories. First were those that were nakedly counterrevolutionary, thus hopeless. The second category had good motives, but so crudely presented as not to make revision worthwhile. The third also had good motives, but expressed them in such subtle ways (especially without morally identifying makeup, music, and costume) that most people would miss the point. This category was the most difficult to salvage.

An example of the first type was a play by the woman dramatist Lan Kuang, who once belonged to the Children's Art Theater of Shanghai ("linked to the Trotskyites," Chiang Ch'ing added disparagingly). When Chiang Ch'ing was combing through Shanghai's cultural world for dramas to revise, Lan Kuang's *The Last Act* was recommended to her. The play was set in the 1930's, when the KMT suppressed all political demonstrations and revolutionary literary and art workers were forced to operate behind the lines. Both that era and the cultural underground Chiang Ch'ing remembered painfully. But this play, she recognized when she first saw it, was dangerously misleading, being a "parable about secret agents of the enemy." Nowadays, a play eulogizing enemy agents who threaten the state cannot be presented to the people (who must be shown only clear-cut defenders of the CCP). Right after seeing Lan Kuang's play she reported to Shanghai Mayor K'o Ch'ing-shih that it was terrible. He closed it immediately.

Ying Shen-chen's recent novel, *Youth in the Flames of Battle*, presented similar problems. It was about several CCP traitors working in the former White Areas controlled by the KMT. To meet the current political standard, Ying Shen-chen was compelled to revise his novel several times. It was adapted to film, and later he recast it as an opera in the Shaohsing style, where actresses take all parts. But women who portray men "ruin their appearance," she protested. And in this Shaohsing version even the Japanese imperialists were played by Chinese women. That so disgusted her that she walked out right in the middle. Finally, during the Cultural Revolution, Ying Shen-chen was persuaded to admit how reactionary it was to have written a Shaohsing-style opera "in our times."

Azalea Mountain (set during a memorable event in the rise of communism, the Autumn Harvest Uprising of the late 1920's) originated in Shanghai as a spoken drama, and began to be revised under others' guidance. Eventually some self-appointed "revolutionaries" tried to convert the play to Peking opera — her preferred medium. But their version failed, she thought, because it had "no real proletarian style." The "proletarian heroes" they concocted were indistinguishable from old beggars!

The Cultural Revolution showed the leaders that although most plays could be redeemed, not all playwrights could. Their country was vast, and surely they were not in want of talent. No longer could anyone (least of all seasoned writers and artists) monopolize anything, not even the cultural realm. The Central Committee's present responsibility in drama reform was to serve as a "processing plant." The *Yellow River Piano Concerto* exemplified music that could be "created by committee" — by the Central Committee, or at least by its concerned representatives.

If it was so. hard to bring the spoken drama up to present revolutionary standards, how about the traditional opera, which for centuries enjoyed the broadest popular appeal? She began with remarks about the esoteric and elitist aspects of some varieties of old opera.

When she was growing up in Shantung, she said, the *K'un-ch'ü* (a Confucian connoisseur's opera originated in Soochow) was widely performed, though poorly attended. In the *K'un-ch'ü* theaters only the first few rows were occupied, mainly by professors and other intellectuals who had to pore continuously over their libretti just to know what was going on. Likewise, in the Peking theaters (though the opera there was less arcane, and often was grounded in popular history) devotees sat in the first few rows, leaving the rest vacant.

Shanghai used to offer other local varieties. Among these were the *T'ien-ching*, which combined traits of Tientsin and Peking ôpera, and *Ching-k'un*, a style mixing several local strains. There, too, attendance was poor. To prevent these companies from going bankrupt after Liberation, the state provided each with a subsidy of some two to three hundred yuan per year. But even when tickets were freely distributed, few people wanted to go. Had she been issued a free ticket, she too would have refused to go, she declared flatly, obviously wanting to affirm the worthlessness and unpopularity of the national theater she had destroyed. Although most *K'un-ch'ü* operas were reactionary, if not also counterrevolutionary, still some of their aspects were useful to the present. A few old *K'un-ch'ü* melodies were retrieved and used in new productions.

The model operas she authorized interwove several local types. They reflected the Shanghai opera (already in the 1930's exhibiting some gloss and glamour imitative of Hollywood cinema), and the Huai opera, which also developed in Shanghai. Others, to be produced over the coming years, would incorporate the Shantung style of Peking opera, the Kweichow, and the Inner Mongolian.

In the early 1960's, when she began to investigate all varieties of opera, she remembered dropping in on a performance of Peking opera. The audience was scant as usual and plainly visible from the stage (lights were not dimmed in the old theater). When the renowned actor Ma Ch'ang-li * caught sight of her he suddenly forgot his lines and just stood there dumbly, she recalled with mock astonishment. By then the quality of performances had so fallen off that it was no wonder that people did not bother to go.

Neither Chinese youth nor "foreign friends" enjoyed going any more, she maintained.[23] Of course there was her daughter Li Na, who used to be an opera

---

* Evidently salvaged, for by 1968 he was playing a lead in her revolutionized opera *Sha-chiapang.*

buff. Being well educated, she could appreciate the arcane language and subtle symbolism of the traditional opera. Most people, however, could not make sense of it all — the women's "water sleeves," the flowing beards, and other historical details (analogous to the Elizabethan theater, commedia dell'arte, and of course the grand opera patronized by Western cultural elites).

Creation of a thoroughly new art without benefit of past precedent was almost impossible, she said; it required meticulous and unrelenting labor. The Chinese have encountered the same problems in extracting modern from ancient art as did the Europeans who wanted to break away from the "court art," but found themselves still continuing to depend on it. In China's retrieval of traditional melodies, the leaders operated from the axiom that words and music are inseparable: from ancient times all poetry was ballad style — meant to be sung. For that reason the revolutionary ballet *The Red Detachment of Women* incorporates tunes from classical operas. And the revolutionary opera *Ode to Dragon River* gives prominence to traditional instruments.

Chiang Ch'ing hazarded that foreigners might regard the constant revision of old works for new purposes as peculiar. But the Chinese knew that they were not the world's only people to do that. Historians must understand that these innovative operas, with elements drawn from various cultural traditions, were grounded in actual history — the history of the Communist Party of China. To prepare herself to construct model works she also read numerous books on military history. "With such goals in mind," she declared spiritedly, "I and the ordinary people [*lao tai hsing*] girded ourselves to go out and wage war all over again!"

iv

By the middle 1960's the cinema had suffered the same devastations as the modern drama and opera. And by 1967, all films — Chiang Ch'ing did not choose to censor or revise any — were withdrawn from public screening. Music and drama can survive apart from oral tradition as literature, without need of performance. But films, like painting and sculpture, are art objects complete in themselves. Were these simply destroyed or locked up for the future? No answer was forthcoming.

After her success with the Peking Opera Festival of 1964, Chiang Ch'ing began to lay plans for a film festival the next year. As before, her goal was to give national exposure to faults in the current cinema and to set forth new guidelines. From the beginning her efforts were obstructed by culture commissar Chou Yang and his cinematic phalanx. And by 1966, as reported in *Red Flag*, Chiang Ch'ing "passed the death sentence on the capitalist rule of cinema circles." "Creative monologues" were condemned as "nihilism and decadence." The "bourgeois system of centering on the director" was abolished and replaced by the "Party system of democratic centralism."[24] Throughout the fiery debate, by then dominated mainly by Mao's defenders, no Party or Red Guard publication dared to mention, for good or for ill, that Chiang Ch'ing, the new mistress of the film arts, was once a movie star.

Film actors and actresses, along with producers and directors, had been immobilized or destroyed by her. In this profoundly demoralized cultural environment, how would she pick up the pieces, trust technicians, and assemble the loyal talent needed to start cameras grinding again?

Producing good films was even more onerous than reforming opera, said Chiang Ch'ing. The art of the film is multifaceted and technically complex, and her own background was not in production. Her attempts to control the industry were blocked by enemies on most fronts. To illustrate, the city of Paoting in Hopeh province had a film processing plant where valuable negatives of work she had authorized were stored. During the Cultural Revolution she tried to maintain control of that plant and its archives. But the enemy (Lin Piao and his cohort) so detested her projects that they conspired to destroy her archive with hand grenades. Had they succeeded, all her new work in film would have been lost. She tried but failed to stop their continuing sabotage, then told Chou En-lai to intervene. He did, but failed to terminate their disruptions.

Just to be troublesome, "Lin Piao and his company" egged on some film technicians to alter the movie film she was having developed so that the color turned out reddish and unnatural. Their subversion of film processing quickly escalated into open warfare among the people of Paoting prefecture.

Once she invited three photographers and directors to join her at the Summer Palace where they would spend the day photographing. The subject she chose as a common test of skills was her protégé (and international table-tennis champion) Chuang Tse-tung, who was matched with some other players. When they got together again some days later to compare results, they discovered that in the film used by the others the red and green tints were off. But her film, developed in her private facilities, turned out to be quite natural. This was, she was certain, additional evidence of malicious interference at the film developing plant.

"Well, Comrade Chiang Ch'ing, have you managed to turn out any new films yet?" Lin Piao and his operators used to say, grinning at her as she worked furiously. They knew she was failing, and their sort of needling was what she least needed.

Subtle sabotage of her film projects still persisted, she said, and was premonitory of struggles lying ahead.

Other countries made great strides in filmmaking, and there was much the Chinese could learn from them, Chiang Ch'ing remarked more than once. Were there time, we should see several of her favorite films together. She mentioned the Mexican film *Cold Heart*. Although the film's content was reactionary in that it prettified colonialism, its technical solutions to problems of light and color were marvelous. However, the leading comrades never saw an original print. Their three copies were synchronized with Chinese sound tracks. One copy was deposited with the Central Committee, a second in Shanghai, and the third under a special arrangement in Peking (possibly in her personal film archive).

When she came to make her own films, her overriding problem was locating talent. She had to persuade people to risk their careers, if not also their lives, in following her new lead in revolution. Actors were "strong-minded" and not easily won over, she admitted. Take the actor T'ung Hsiang-ling, currently playing the part of the hero in the revolutionary opera *Taking Tiger Mountain by Strategy*. (His older sister, T'ung Chih-ling, also acted in Peking opera, Chiang Ch'ing digressed. In her personal life she used to be quite notorious — a "complicated story." The brother also had his own youthful reputation for disruption.) She first noticed T'ung Hsiang-ling when she was searching through Peking and Shanghai for acting talent. Few persons she saw possessed the necessary combination of youth, good looks, and talent for singing, acting, and dancing. Hsiang-ling was known for his voice, but she was not sure he could dance. To test him, she cast him in a minor role in *The Red Lantern* at an early stage of its reconstruction as a revolutionary opera. His sister was then cast as Granny Li, and her performance was most arresting — but she had gone there to study Hsiang-ling, she said, apologizing for further digression.

In Hsiang-ling she liked what she saw. After the show was over she sought him out backstage. Was he an amateur or a professional actor? she quizzed him.* Caught by surprise, all he managed to blurt out was that he was a fan of Peking opera and that he could do somersaults (essential to operatic acrobatics). That awkward encounter, funny to her now, convinced her that he had promise.

To size him up more exactingly, she asked Chang Ch'un-ch'iao, a Shanghai-based comrade and close friend, to reach Hsiang-ling and sound him out. Through Chang she learned that he was versatile in both singing and dancing. Most important, he was willing to cut other professional and political ties and

---

* A question not of dramatic skill, but of whether he had another primary occupation. The Chinese Communists have continued the tradition of amateur acting, for centuries a cultural attribute of the educated people. The new regime values amateur acting as an easy means of getting peasants, workers, students and others to learn political principles by acting them out in skits that accompany daily work. These are familiar to all foreign travelers.

work with her exclusively.* Delighted, she awarded him the part of Yang Tzu-jung, hero of the model opera *Taking Tiger Mountain by Strategy*, which she was then deeply involved in revising.

As soon as "bad elements" of the May Sixteenth Clique discovered that the esteemed T'ung Hsiang-ling had switched over to her side, they plotted to "seize" him — take him in their custody — just to prevent him from working with her. Put on the defensive, she sternly informed these elements that T'ung Hsiang-ling, an actor formerly loyal to his own "T'ung style" of opera, had changed loyalty, and was totally committed to her in making revolution. *No one should touch her actor*, she warned.

Undaunted, the May Sixteenth elements persisted in making life difficult for T'ung Hsiang-ling. Their strategy was to invite him to Peking on the understanding that they would do special favors for him there. No matter what could be said about his sister, who, being an actress, was easily seduced by one thing or another, Hsiang-ling was of a different sort — a man of stronger character. Eventually he and the opera troupe with which he was working accepted the invitation to go to Peking. There they would be treated to some film showings and engage in filmmaking that *she* intended to control. But once the actors got to Peking her enemies denied them the amenities normally provided for actors. Their housing and food were abysmal, she was told.

As soon as she returned to Peking, she reported that injustice to Vice-Premier Hsieh Fu-chih (also responsible for public security). Together, they went to the film studio where the troupe was quartered, inspected dormitories, and arranged for improved housing and food and buses for transportation. She personally made sure that the actors would receive the hot meals without which their voices would deteriorate.

When it came time to shoot the film version of *Tiger Mountain*, her enemies suddenly cut off power from their sound stages and terminated the hot meal program. She was furious, and decided then to put her project directly under military control. At her request, Ti Fu-ts'ao of the State Council immediately signed over Army 8341 (Mao's special guard stationed in Peking) to protect her people.

Unassisted by the seasoned screenwriters, producers, directors, and stars who now were mostly in disgrace, Chiang Ch'ing admitted that she really had no choice but to select actors from among the opera and ballet whom she could trust and educate in the art of filmmaking. The problems were staggering. They were used to performing with the boldness and exaggeration necessary for opera but overwrought for film. The "revisionism" to which they had been subjected in the past taught them "awful things," she declared without going into details.

* Both the master-apprentice relationship and monarchic patronage were traditional in Chinese theater.

And having grown up since Liberation, their opportunity to learn technique from foreign films certainly was limited. When her actors first stepped before the searing lights and cameras, they were visibly uneasy, and she had to keep cheering them on. "You should not fear failure," she said; "the Party organization will support you." To improve their cinematic skills as quickly as possible, she selected from her personal archive some foreign films and had them screened at their studio. As they watched they should ask themselves, she said, "Where can we learn and where can we avoid mistakes?"

T'ung Hsiang-ling was one of the first major performers to follow her in making revolution. Others came along quickly. Among them were Liu Ch'ing-t'ang, the superb male ballet dancer to whom she gave the major role in *Red Detachment of Women*, Ch'ien Hao-liang, star of *The Red Landern*, and T'an Yuan-shou, preeminent in *Shachiapang*. When the famous Ma Ch'ang-li came over to her side, she awarded him with a chief negative role — the Japanese gendarme in *Shachiapang*. All along, though, she was aware how their becoming loyal exclusively to her made them vulnerable, especially to Lin Piao's May Sixteenth Clique, which continued to persecute them relentlessly. She managed to reach Liu Ch'ing-t'ang, Ch'ien Hao-liang, and T'an Yuan-shou in time and to protect them from brutality. But they caught the elderly Ma Ch'ang-li and trounced him.

Through these and other actors whose careers she would redesign, Chiang Ch'ing continued to experiment with film. Others joined her in various phases of production. Those with evident literary talent — Ch'ien Hao-liang, Liu Ch'ing-t'ang, and Yu Hüi-yung * — she persuaded to assist her in the composition of film scripts, a task new to them all. But their naiveté as screenwriters, the actors' poor skills before the camera, and the enemies' invidious obstructionism resulted in her failing to turn out even one good feature film during the Cultural Revolution.

Impatient for quick results, she turned to television, the medium in which she intended to project her works to the widest possible audience. She began by carefully analyzing all the program schedules of the nation's television. Then she submitted a list of criticisms to the men in charge. Her judgments, she said, compelled the administrators, along with technical personnel and performers, to come out and make self-criticisms on points she had raised. She then commended them heartily and invited them to join forces with her in bringing revolution to national TV. It was not long before they were convinced of the correctness of broadcasting and televising her model theater and initiat-

---

* Composer, leading figure in international cultural exchanges, and a follower of Chiang Ch'ing's opera reform since 1967. At the Fourth National People's Congress of January 1975, he was appointed minister of culture, the post vacated by Chou Yang nine years earlier. In October 1976 he allegedly was arrested along with Chiang Ch'ing.

ing other revolutionary programs under her direction. Seeing the first TV production of *Shachiapang* and subsequently other model works was enormously exciting to her. To share her pleasure, she summoned a large contingent of filmmakers and Peking opera performers to the Great Hall for a demonstration of how to *learn from television*. Their celebration proved to the world that she had broken through still another blockade — that erected by recalcitrant TV bosses. "I smashed their monopoly!" she exclaimed gleefully.

As for film, after three abortive attempts over three years, she and her assistants finally came up with a passable version of the opera *Taking Tiger Mountain by Strategy*. Each film version was shot in Peking, though throughout that time most of the performers and staff members continued to maintain their homes in Shanghai, where their opera troupe first formed. The actors became so engrossed in the Peking project that they repeatedly declined her permission to visit their families in Shanghai, she recalled with gratification. They insisted upon sticking by her in Peking until she was satisfied with a finished film.

Even now, Chiang Ch'ing admitted frustratedly, films are wanting. The technique of matching colors is poor and projection of actors' images lacks skill. The stage appearance of her actors was still far superior to that on the screen.

To understand the profound human transformations of the 1960's, I must realize, she said, that these performers, along with others less celebrated who chose to follow her lead in the drama, grew up in the old society. They were not advanced ideologically when she met them. What mattered was that they grasped her message and followed her during years of widespread disorder and violence. The great risks they took quickened their ideological remolding. And since the situation calmed down, they remained loyal to her and to her teaching.

To show how these revolutionary changes came about, she arranged for me to speak with Ch'ien Hao-liang, T'ung Hsiang-ling, and other leading actors and dancers who would, she said, tell their side of the story.

17.

◇ ◇ ◇

Heroics in Song and Dance

If you don't go into the tiger's lair, how can
you get the cub?
— Chiang Ch'ing, quoting an old
Chinese saying to the performers of
The Red Lantern

Of all the purposes of revolutionary theater, entertainment is the least important. Demonstration of ideology in action, of the rise of the working class, and of the triumph of Communist Party leadership is dominant. Reenactment of high points in revolutionary history is featured. Good and bad models for the people are presented throughout. Also necessary to the founders' era to which Chiang Ch'ing saw herself as belonging was the transformation of a simplified official history into a mythology of national origins, and the creation of a new pantheon of culture heroes and heroines. These were introduced to the people through the revolutionary opera and ballet. A less obvious but also important purpose was to show the priority of biological survival during wartime over the more subtle but lasting challenge of psychological survival, namely, the individual's preservation of sanity and self-respect in a constant state of revolution. And as fundamental to the theater as to the life it described was the Aeschylean theme of revenge, an emotional substratum ignored by the political theory of Marx, Lenin, and Mao.

The Marxian materialist view of history underlying the new drama depicts the past not as a series of arbitrary accidents, but as a coherent structure leading to an end, thus eliminating both the fascination and the terror of uncertainty. Such a redemptive view of history denies the reality of personal tragedy, a concept alien to Chinese culture. In the new theater as in political life, those who die for the cause are resurrected as martyrs to be celebrated with each performance or in political movements that are imposed periodically upon the masses.

The role play that has long been fundamental to Chinese social life has enhanced the theater's potential as a political instrument. In the traditional extended family system, each member existed with many affinities or roles, each labeled with a kinship name. Under the revolutionary regime familial roles have been supplemented, if not superseded, by numerous political roles: memberships in associations of youth, women, peasants, and workers, in the Party, on revolutionary committees, and so forth. Social relations are thus described and conducted more between roles, which can be regulated, than between individuals, who are less controllable from afar.

The new potential for social control from the center has been augmented by the stage, where dramatic roles are designed as political archetypes. Banished is the old hierarchy that was represented by lavishly costumed aristocrats. In their stead is a roster of working-class characters, who are turned out in glamorized proletarian dress. Chief among their enemies are the aristocrats, mainly the landlords of the past, and foreign invaders, predominantly the Japanese. Although the class character of revolutionary life and theater has changed radically, respect for exemplary individuals in actuality and in art is sustained. Moreover, the didacticism of traditional opera has been carried over to the modern stage. Chiang Ch'ing's proletarian archetypes in the drama serve as models of behavior for all the people.

As real life was made to imitate political art, actors, no less than audiences, were swept up in the rigorous political dialectic of art and life. An actress who performed T'ieh-mei, the leading female role in *The Red Lantern*, was induced to write for *Red Flag*:

> The process of playing a heroic character is also one of learning from that heroic character. To play a heroic character well on stage, one must at the same time learn from the heroic character off that stage. . . . To propagandize the thought of Mao Tsetung on the stage . . . I simply shorten the distance between myself and the proletarian heroic character in the play.[1]

Thus actors, who were the dregs of the old society, were made official spokesmen for the new. Theatrical performers in the old days were mostly illiterate, degraded to the ranks of vaudeville performers and members of traveling circuses, though there were always a few great artists who attracted wealth and

won social acclaim. After Liberation, theaters, along with other private enterprises, were taken over gradually by the state. Actors were provided with
shelter, salaries, and stages on which to perform. But the price of such social
security was agreement (often disregarded) to make exclusive use of scripts that
were generally condoned, and eventually provided, by the Central Committee.
In contrast to the old days when actors were free to improvise upon generally
remembered scores, "liberated" actors were enjoined to follow unerringly the
detailed scripts set by the Party.

Chiang Ch'ing's past involvement with the theater bore only a remote relation to the role she assumed during the Cultural Revolution. By then she had
long left the ranks of actors, and the society she helped to rule maintained no
public record of her acting career. Political and artistic talent linked to her
special relation to the Chairman made her, for a time, the prima donna on the
stage of history, and a de facto culture commissar who was responsible for
creating parts to be emulated by the masses. The actors who followed her were
cast not only onto the revolutionary stage but also into revolutionary history.
Up through the middle 1970's gigantically blown-up photographs of her pantheon of culture heroes and heroines, new stars of the superstructure, were
mounted high on walls all over the cities and countryside. Their gaudy faces
were the only ones to appear besides the stern portraits of communism's founding fathers — Marx, Engels, Lenin, Stalin, and Mao.

Revolutionary heroics have demanded monumental literary restraint, including denial of much of the best of China's ancient and modern literary heritage.
Eradicated almost entirely from the present stage is social satire, the literary
device of which Chiang Ch'ing's idol, Lu Hsun, was past master. Party leaders
have had compelling reasons for restricting the satirical mode, allowing it to be
deployed only against obvious class enemies — tyrannical landlords, KMT
rulers, and Japanese imperialists. Up to recent times the two main objects of
the satirist's pen were the poor and the powerful. But the present regime has
protected both from mockery and vilification. The poor, equatable with the
masses, are to be glorified, and the powerful, namely the leaders, are to be
praised. Chiang Ch'ing's revolution of theater has freed the poor from serving
as comic relief and protected the powerful from exposure of their tragic flaws.

As Chiang Ch'ing raised revolutionary standards over the new political order,
she was conscious of the need to stimulate heroism both in the people and their
leaders. Heroism elicited from the masses would be rewarded from on high.
And she seemed to relish popular recognition of her own heroic traits. Speaking of the drama in 1966, she said, "We should not confine ourselves to actual
persons and events. Nor should we portray a hero only after he is dead. In fact,
there are many more living heroes than dead ones." [2] The next year revolutionary students at New Peking University extolled her as a "proletarian

heroine," Chairman Mao's "best student," who made the "beams of the red lantern" flash out in all directions.[3]

Yet the very force of mimesis, which made vast audiences manipulatable from the stage, and hence from the Central Committee, long frustrated Mao Tse-tung. A democratic centralist, he knew that in effective governance central control must always be balanced by local initiative. At a 1957 conference of Party secretaries he chided,

> Every province needs one or two Marxes or Lu Hsuns. You ought to write articles. All of you who are below sixty should write.
>
> Every province should train theorists. We are training actors and actresses and painters but not theorists. This is a deficiency in the system. You rely upon the central government, but the central government has never prohibited you from doing anything on your own.[4]

How much initiative would Chiang Ch'ing's followers dare to assume when they discussed her with me on their own territory?

i

Over dinner at the Great Hall Chiang Ch'ing called her revolutionary opera *The Red Lantern* a "tragedy," showing how members of three generations of one family from the 1920's up to the time of the Japanese War "heroically sacrificed themselves" in the struggle against Japanese aggression. It also featured "the Eighth Route Army led by our Party," underground work in the White areas, armed struggle, and Eighth Route Army soldiers rescuing ordinary people working for the Party outside the army's base area.

After dinner we were swept off to the T'ien-ch'iao theater where a full house (miraculously supplied) had been kept waiting more than an hour in sweltering heat. Suffused with the drama of her occasion, Chiang Ch'ing swept into the theater; the hush of astonishment broke into thunderous applause. Skillfully spotlighted from above, her figure appeared electrified. She smiled brilliantly, raised her arms, and clapped in response to the audience.

As the theater darkened, Chiang Ch'ing, who was seated to my left, chattered sotto voce about crises in the opera's trial productions during the Cultural Revolution. To avoid retaliation from her enemies, she stationed her actors a safe distance from Peking, and remained there with them. Premier Chou telephoned her almost every day to keep her abreast of activities in the capital. Through open rehearsals to which the public was invited and continual revisions and polishings, *The Red Lantern* gradually gained in appeal. What the people loved best were the dramatic poses carried over from the old opera.

Sometimes they became so overly excited that she and her aides had to calm them down. Her major collaborator, Ch'ien Hao-liang (called by her and known to the public simply as Hao-liang), kept a log of their progress and dispatched regular reports to the other leading comrades in Peking. Although the Premier once had doubts about her project, he came to see a late version and announced that he liked it. Gradually, they gained the confidence that sustained them.

The curtain rose. The three leading characters were archetypal representatives of their generations, which spanned the history of the CCP before Liberation. Li Yü-ho (played by Hao-liang), a switchman on a railroad controlled by the Japanese, is the paradigmatic proletarian hero of the second generation. His adoptive mother, Granny Li, symbolizes the first generation, and his seventeen-year-old adopted daughter, T'ieh-mei, orphaned during the railway strike of 1923, stands appealingly for the youngest generation.

While Japan occupies North China, Li Yü-ho is entrusted with a secret code to be delivered to the Communist guerrillas in the mountains. Another underground Communist who is tortured by Hatoyama, chief of the Japanese military police, betrays Li Yü-ho. He is then put under surveillance, threatened, and bribed, but refuses to give in. His stubborn courage maddens Hatoyama, who seizes and tortures all three members of the family and executes Li Yü-ho and Granny Li for refusing to yield the code. The surviving daughter, T'ieh-mei, "turns grief into strength" and vows to take revenge on behalf of the Party. Aided by neighbors, she escapes by outwitting police spies. Clutching her only possession, the red lantern that was used by her martyred father and remains the symbol of unended revolution, she completes his mission of delivering the secret code to the guerrillas in the mountains. Such vindication of his martyrdom establishes her as the revolutionary successor.

As we watched the fifth scene in which Granny Li sings movingly an aria recapitulating the history of martyrdoms of the Li family (the same as Chiang Ch'ing's original surname), tears welled in Chiang Ch'ing's eyes and coursed down her cheeks. Daubing her face with a simple white handkerchief, she named the six members of Chairman Mao's family who had "laid down their lives for the Revolution. Every time I see these operas I shed tears. In his poem 'Shao-shan Revisited,' Chairman Mao wrote, 'Bitter sacrifice strengthens bold resolve / Which dares to make sun and moon shine in new skies.' " If I want to study the history of the Chinese Communist Party, she continued less emotionally, I should concentrate upon Chairman Mao's prose and poetry, which provide a clear outline.

Between acts she handed her program to interpreter Hsu Erh-wei, seated behind us, and asked her to write out the English translation of the play's title, *Hung teng chi*. In bold capital letters Hsu penciled the English title and returned the program to Chiang Ch'ing, who delightedly copied each letter. "How should that be pronounced?" she asked Hsu. Her eyes followed Hsu's lip movements as she articulated "The . . . Red . . . Lantern."

Turning to me she asked, "What's the point of 'The'?"

"Nothing, really," Hsu interjected.

"Then it's an empty word!" Chiang Ch'ing concluded, referring to certain particles in the classical Chinese language. (On another occasion she admitted to me that she did not easily read this esoteric style.)

Speaking of the highly charged scene where Li Yü-ho visits his imprisoned mother, she explained, "Since he has just gotten out of prison, logically his clothing and hair should be disheveled. But because he is on the verge of becoming a martyr, we have made him appear clean and tidy, white and pure, for he must present a dignified image. We don't go in for naturalism."

In the old opera, she continued, gongs and drums fettered the actors literally and figuratively. Although these instruments were eliminated from the new opera, their brisk rhythms are sustained by Western percussion instruments, most emphatically the piano (introduced to Chinese opera by *The Red Lantern*).[5]

After the final curtain she led the way backstage to congratulate the perspiring players, who were enthralled by her presence. Introducing Ch'ien Hao-liang, the glamorized railway switchman, she said, "He came to political consciousness earlier than the rest and followed me on in revolutionizing Peking opera." Of T'ieh-mei, played by the vivacious young Liu Ch'ang-yü, she remarked humorously that her father used to be an official with the KMT in Peking, but she grew up and decided on her own to follow Comrade Chiang Ch'ing in making revolution. Yuan Shui-hai, who portrayed Hatoyama, had a considerable international reputation in Asia. Some Japanese leaders had remarked to her that in China's revolutionary operas the best actors get to be the villains!

ii

A few days later I traveled to the outskirts of Peking to visit the academy of the China Peking Opera Troupe, which had produced *The Red Lantern*. The formidable Hao-liang, surely among the most strikingly handsome and physically robust men I met in China, was in charge. Large deep-set eyes and a long slender nose made him look vaguely Caucasian. His shirt and trousers were well cut in fine fabrics. Those combined with an expensive watch and Italianate leather sandals projected a certain prosperity that is rarely exhibited in contemporary China.

Other troupe members were also handsome though not "theatrical," as they might have been in old China or in the West. Decorously seated on long sofas, they gently stirred the oppressive August air with large black fans, all matching, but none bearing the quotations from the Chairman so prevalent elsewhere. After conversation about the history of the theater we proceeded to the huge airy studio where arias were sung, and dance and acrobatics were demonstrated to piano accompaniment. After a spate of photographs, we returned to the parlor where we consumed gigantic grapes, peaches, and pears grown by members of the academy, proving that despite their artistic skills and social prominence, they were "not divorced from the soil," but were also able in agricultural production.*

"After Liberation the revolutionary left began to support the cultural interests of the ordinary people," Hao-liang began formally. "But when they carried the revolution to the Peking opera the Four Villains [Chou Yang, Hsia Yen, Yang Han-sheng, and T'ien Han] panicked and obstructed historical progress. From the control tower at the Ministry of Culture, the Four Villains repeatedly ignored the Central Committee's instructions that they transform the opera in accordance with Comrade Chiang Ch'ing's requests. When she and others undertook a revolution in Peking opera, the Ministry of Culture denied them publicity and few knew what was going on. Thus, in the early 1960's the people felt disenchanted because the theater offered no encouragement for the new social roles they were assuming in their daily lives. In no one instance did the opera incite their will to commit their lives to revolution. Because luxurious palace life displayed on stage was remote from daily experience, popular interest in theater fell off sharply. Only a few middle-aged and old people continued to attend."

In the traditional opera actresses portrayed aristocratic women who were oppressed by the former class system, Hao-liang continued. On the rare occasions when working women were portrayed on stage "they were made to look vulgar, just the reverse of their present heroic stances." The change from negative to positive characterization of working-class people was extraordinarily difficult. Besides radical shifts of acting technique, profound interior changes of thought and values within the actresses themselves were required.

To improve their acting skills, all troupe members made annual treks to the countryside where they "gathered raw materials" for works in progress and "broadened their world view." In contrast to actors of the old school who never soiled their delicate hands, members of this troupe regularly tilled the soil in their spare time.

---

* Mao Tse-tung's demand for general participation in manual labor was renewed during the Cultural Revolution, and exhibited notably by writers and artists, as well as scientists, bureaucrats, and professors, who normally would not have had the least inclination for farming.

Elements in the Peking opera can be traced back to the T'ang and Southern Sung dynasties (covering the seventh through the thirteenth century), Hao-liang went on. Their evolution culminated in the cosmopolitan capital style of the Manchus. But the original Peking opera was created by folk artists rather than scholar-aristocrats. When the conquering Manchus first recognized how the opera flourished among the ordinary people, they called for command performances at the palace. Under their imperial patronage the "people's opera" gradually was refined into the "court style," at which point the historical development of Peking opera stopped (though it remained China's most highly sophisticated opera style, which some honored as the "national drama").

"Inevitably, in the operas patronized by the imperial establishment peasant uprisings were always quelled. But the mere fact that peasants were known to rise up demonstrates to *us* that the peasants were *acting against exploitation.* What they sought was equality. Their motive was explicit in the story cycle that became the novel called *Shui-hu chuan* [*All Men Are Brothers* in Pearl Buck's translation]. Other Sung operas depicted Chinese patriots fighting against foreign invaders."

Would old operas on historical themes be produced again in the near future? I asked.

"That depends on the development of the situation," Hao-liang responded cautiously. "In no way can old operas reflect contemporary life. While the Black Gang and the 'capitalist roaders' were conniving to deny Comrade Chiang Ch'ing the right to create her own operas, she had no time to experiment in reviving old operas in modern form. The guideline is Chairman Mao's 'Let a hundred flowers bloom,' and 'Weed through the old to bring forth the new.' The opportunity to extend these principles to traditional opera certainly will arise."

"There is no easy sailing in revolution," Hao-liang continued in political cliché. "All along there has been the struggle between Chairman Mao's correct line and Liu Shao-ch'i's counterrevolutionary revisionist line. In the Peking opera the struggle was the sharpest of all. More than thirty years ago Chairman Mao presented the correct line in his address to the Yenan Forum. His overall point was that art should serve the people. Among the operas produced in Yenan in accordance with his instructions were *Driven to Liang Shan* and *Three Battles Against Chu-chia Village.* Why don't we perform these now? We simply don't have time."

I asked about the fate of the writers and artists who had spent their lives producing the modern dramas that Chiang Ch'ing had banned summarily during the Cultural Revolution.

Most were sent down to the countryside for programs of struggle-criticism-transformation, he responded and changed the subject.[6] The point to grasp was that the modern dramas of the 1930's spread poison in the 1950's. Dumas' *Camille* and romances about Yang Kuei-fei (the voluptuous imperial concubine of the eighth century) were dangerous distractions from contemporary life. "After China committed itself to the cause of the proletariat, theater had a long way to go to catch up, and the going has not been easy." Hao-liang was smiling intensely, his face perspiring, as he spoke.

He went on. In 1963 Comrade Chiang Ch'ing began dropping in at their academy. She lectured to them, explaining how in recent times the Peking opera had become rigid, refusing to yield to historical forces. If this "feudal fortress," this "most die-hard" of the traditional arts could be restructured to suit living people, all the other arts (literature, music, and fine arts) would yield. "And she was right!" Hao-liang declared.

"Do you want to make revolution?" she challenged them, he recalled. "If you decide to change and to devote yourselves to revolution, how would you project *attractive* images of workers, peasants, and soldiers?"

In 1963 they had no inkling of the signal role to be played either by the opera or by Comrade Chiang Ch'ing in the genesis of the Great Proletarian Cultural Revolution. In fact, they had not the foggiest notion of what "cultural revolution" meant. That a change in the arts could engender nationwide class struggle was unthinkable. (The idea that the superstructure could lead the base was the most radical tenet of Chiang Ch'ing's Marxism.) Their cultural revolution came about only because Chiang Ch'ing managed to persuade them that they had been "hoodwinked" by class enemies and "victimized" by the old opera. "To act revolutionary you first must be revolutionary," she insisted.

Hao-liang laughed explosively to recall one of his first jolts of political consciousness. In 1963 he was playing the role of vice-marshal of the army. "To advance myself in rank I had to murder my superior, the marshal, with a poison arrow. After one of her unannounced appearances at our performance, Comrade Chiang Ch'ing flew backstage seething with rage. 'Although your acting skill is formidable, I could not bring myself to clap for you because you played the part of a selfish egotistical character who got ahead only by destroying others.' Turning to the whole group she set the basic question: 'What you eat is grown by the peasants; the clothes you wear are made by the workers; the frontiers are defended by the PLA; if you do not defend the workers, peasants, and soldiers, where do your consciences lie?' "

In the preparation of new scripts, Chiang Ch'ing did not do the actual writing, but commissioned professional writers to prepare them according to her specifications. That became her usual pattern. The original story for *The Red Lantern* was found among the local operas in some twelve versions, none of which was suited to the Peking opera style. She also provided them with a play called *People in the PLA Helped in a Flood Disaster in Peking*, and the script for *The Red Detachment of Women*. Because of interference from "capitalist roaders," *The Red Lantern* took an entire year to produce. Another company was given the script for *The Red Detachment of Women*, which they turned into a ballet. After seemingly endless revisions, *The Red Lantern* was finally designated a "model opera." "Yet its personal cost was high: the blood of Comrade Chiang Ch'ing and the staunch support of Chairman Mao and Premier Chou. We are deeply indebted," Hao-liang added piously.

At the outset certain "capitalist roaders" in their troupe only pretended to concur in rendering *The Red Lantern* in revolutionary style. Their insincerity was exposed only when it came time to reconstruct Hao-liang's part, the railway switchman, in a positive way. He knew that Comrade Chiang Ch'ing had wanted to divest Li Yü-ho of his weak characteristics — sentimentalism and a penchant for liquor. But the opposition did not want him to be admirable, preferring to give equal attention to the representatives of the three generations.[7] They claimed that would add up to a balanced presentation of the working class. Actually, they sought to strengthen the role of the daughter, T'ieh-mei, thereby highlighting her as a symbol of the younger generation. But he and Chiang Ch'ing insisted upon a sharp delineation of the generation that *fathered* the successors (namely Chiang Ch'ing's generation) because that demonstrated the principle of revolutionary succession.

The bureaucrats who resented Chiang Ch'ing's direct and regular contact with them retaliated by trying to "uglify" Li Yü-ho's working-class image. They gave him a hunchback and forced him to wear a wretched costume and a scraggly beard. "That's naturalism for you," they said. "Old switchmen always look that way."

He was forced to portray this dismal character up to the eve of the Cultural Revolution. With the dismantling of the old Ministry of Culture,[8] their troupe was put through marathon struggle-criticism-transformation sessions, which were excruciating. Only then did they really begin to know Chiang Ch'ing.

After she took to attending all rehearsals, there was scarcely any aspect of production which she did not alter — the text, the use of voice, costumes, staging, the overall structure. Sometimes she was accompanied by Yao Wen-yuan, whose observations they found quite astute. In those days Comrade Yao Wen-yuan spent most of his time in Shanghai where, in addition to other writing projects, he supervised the revision of the opera *Taking Tiger Mountain by Strategy*. When Comrade Chiang Ch'ing worked in Shanghai she was protected by Comrades Chang Ch'un-ch'iao, K'o Ch'ing-shih, and Yao Wen-yuan. In Peking she had the continual backing of Chairman Mao, Premier Chou, and Comrade K'ang Sheng. Throughout their grueling revisions and rehearsals, the actors could never forget that those three leaders backed her up.

Thus they redesigned their show to achieve a first in Chinese theater: to present working-class characters who were strong, attractive, and clever. To exemplify changes, he cited scene 3 of the present version, which is set at a gruel stall in a junk market. When a truckload of Japanese military police arrives, Li Yü-ho immediately hides his CCP code in his lunch box and douses it with a famous foul-smelling gruel that throws the gendarmes off his political scent. However, years before, "capitalist roaders" cut out that scene, saying that it was silly and revolting. Once she gained power, Chiang Ch'ing restored it in order to show Li Yü-ho's cunning and the cooperation of workers at the junk market.

"Comrade Chiang Ch'ing went through everything with a fine-tooth comb," Hao-liang recalled wearily. In the original version of scene 5, Li Yü-ho, who is terrified that T'ieh-mei may disappear under the Japanese occupation, takes her into hiding just to protect her. The personal and individualistic implications of that scene offended Chiang Ch'ing, who changed the script to make the father put the revolution's interests first.

She was always attentive to body movement. "When you sit, sit well. When you stand, stand well," she used to tell them. "Each movement must be sculpted." When she choreographed the scene called "Struggle on the Execution Ground" she mounted the stage, demonstrated the steps, and then drew diagrams for them to follow.

"The new opera was not mere happenstance," Chiang Ch'ing insisted, "but a work of art." Costume designers should "improve upon reality but not go overboard in idealism." By that she meant that the "plain realism" of old work clothes on proletarian heroes would fail artistically, and new work clothes would show no signs of hardship. The art of patching was most bitterly disputed in the costuming of *The Red Lantern*.

The costume designers she inherited had been trained to embroider silks and satins for the aristocracy, or smart suits and dresses for the bourgeoisie. When they first costumed the poor they just tacked sloppy patches onto the belly of the jackets, which revealed that they had no idea how working people used their bodies. Chiang Ch'ing told them to patch up the elbows, knees, and collars — the places that thinned and snagged the fastest. The shapes of the patches should be neat and pleasing to the eye. As important to image-making was color-combination, she said. Working-class people could wear only certain shades — mostly modest and dark. But the young heroine T'ieh-mei was allowed to wear a stunning red jacket in the folk style and an attractive hairpin that Chiang Ch'ing selected for her.

Chiang Ch'ing also supervised the composition of the entire musical score. She personally wrote the music and lyrics for scene 8, "Struggle on the Execution Ground," which preserved the rhythm and tonality of the old Peking opera. As T'ieh-mei witnesses the execution of her foster father and Granny Li, she sings the *wa-wa tiao*, the classical song form for a person who has reached maturity.

The opera must illustrate Chairman Mao's military principles, Chiang Ch'ing told them as she demonstrated *wu-shu*, the martial art featured in the final scene. The dance must show the surprise skirmishes and other tactics of guerrilla warfare that finally defeat the enemy. The opera ends on upbeat themes: rising armed struggle and the expansion of the military base areas.

"You see how willingly we became her instruments," Hao-liang concluded with a magnificent smile.

Among the "willing instruments" was the vivacious actress Liu Ch'ang-yü, who admitted to being very young and malleable when she first made contact with Comrade Chiang Ch'ing. Her delivery in our interview was a perfect balance of responsiveness and resolve. Her rhetoric was stocked with the self-criticisms ritualized by the advantaged youths who had been tempered by the proletarian standards imposed during the Cultural Revolution.

Liu Ch'ang-yü explained that formerly, in scene 9 when she learns of the deaths of her foster father and Granny Li, she wailed in the style of a grieving woman of the old opera. Chiang Ch'ing deplored that method, saying that she should be overwhelmed not only by grief, but also by anger. Both emotions should change immediately to power, her voice projecting fury and resolve.

Though painful to hear, Comrade Chiang Ch'ing's criticism showed Liu what was wrong with her ideology: she had failed to grasp the emotional dynamics of the working class. "Where does your conscience lie?" Chiang Ch'ing challenged her repeatedly. "To perform revolution you first must be a revolutionary." Likewise, Chairman Mao had told them, "To be a teacher, you first must be a student." In the production of this opera, Liu Ch'ang-yü said, Comrade Hao-liang was her teacher. He had sent her down to live with the workers, peasants, and soldiers. There she remained until she had learned to depict their images enthusiastically and to demonstrate to all that she had gone over to the proletarian side.

iii

Our first night at the opera Chiang Ch'ing leaned over my lap, elbowed Yao Wen-yuan, and told him to arrange a Shanghai performance of *Taking Tiger Mountain by Strategy* for me and to set up interviews with the performers the next day. Its orchestral music was the best in all her model works, she assured me.

More than a week later in Shanghai I was treated to that swift-paced, visually spectacular opera. The interviews were conducted on the top floor of the Ching-chiao Hotel, where I was staying. The man in charge was T'ung Hsiang-ling, Chiang Ch'ing's loyal actor who had played the hero Yang Tzu-jung for more than a decade. He introduced musical director Hsia Fei-yun, a slight man who spoke gingerly about the opera's orchestration, which had evolved from the *Yellow River Piano Concerto*. Though produced by Chiang Ch'ing during the Cultural Revolution, the *Concerto*'s lyrics describing the un-folding of the Resistance War had been written by Nieh Erh (producer of popu-lar tunes and cinema scores in Shanghai, of the 1930's). Ordinarily the lyrics are not sung, he noted, but are projected in huge characters onto screens set to the right and left of the stage (the same is true of opera lyrics, even when sung). The *Concerto* was the first to set Party messages to folk tunes rendered on the piano with a Western-style orchestra. Its successful combination of the *p'i-pa* (an instrument like the lute or guitar), the pentatonic scale, and Western har-monies emboldened their troupe to attempt a similar synthesis in the music for *Tiger Mountain*.

Chiang Ch'ing's idea was to combine Chinese percussion and Western har-monies — the best of each tradition, she thought.* So she added to the Chinese percussion section and introduced foreign stringed instruments: four first vio-lins, three second violins, two violas, one cello, and one bass. The wind sec-tion was enlarged by an oboe, a clarinet, two trumpets, two French horns, and another large horn. Western timpani were also added. The former group of eight instruments — four percussion and four strings regulated by the drum — used to sit to the side of the stage. Now this group was enlarged to thirty, plus a conductor, and all were moved off stage. Never before had Chinese opera musicians experienced such musical volume and flexibility.

Comrade Chiang Ch'ing was not easy to please, Hsia Fei-yun went on. When they submitted trial scores, she criticized them for "continuing to com-pose in the thrall of tradition." She told them to avoid the shrillness of the clas-sical style because it drowned out the actors' voices. So that the audience would give primary attention to her new proletarian characters, musicians should con-sider the relation between the orchestra and the singers as between guest and host. The orchestra-guest should not overpower the singer-host. The orchestra should accompany the human voice, but not obliterate it.[9]

The story of *Taking Tiger Mountain by Strategy* is set in Manchuria in the winter of 1946, the opening of the Liberation War. In contrast to *The Red Lan-tern*, which depicts trials in the Party underground, *Tiger Mountain* shows the PLA contesting with the "mountain strongholdism" of bandits. A pursuit-de-

---

* Decades before, some operatic troupes in Hong Kong and other overseas Chinese communities had added saxophones and violins to the orchestra. Sequined costumes were embellished with tiny electric light bulbs. Occasionally an actor affected a crooner style in a classical aria.

tachment unit of the PLA moves deep into the pine-ridged mountains to mobilize local people against the bandit forces commanded by Vulture, self-appointed king of Tiger Mountain who has both KMT and American backing. Yang Tzu-jung, the dashing symbol of the PLA, leads a scout platoon to assess the possibility of taking Tiger Mountain by strategy (by implication, Lin Piao's guerrilla style) rather than by direct assault (Liu Shao-ch'i's conventional warfare).

On his way up the mountain Yang Tzu-jung asks about the suffering of the local people (raising consciousness of oppression), and accepts assistance from hunter Ch'ang and his daughter, clever and winsome Ch'ang Pao, who vow blood vengeance against Vulture's bandits, destroyers of their family members. Disguised as a bandit who is glamorized by a white fur-lined coat, a tiger-skin vest, and a red fox hat, Yang Tzu-jung wins entry to the bandits' lair, tricks Vulture into trusting him, and lays the groundwork for the arrival of the pursuit-detachment unit. At the Hundred Chickens Feast at Tiger Hall, Yang cajoles the bandits into a drunken orgy. Undone, they are wiped out by the PLA forces, whose arrival on skis over the mountain slopes is one of the high points of realism in China's contemporary theater.

Like other contemporary Chinese operas, this one allegorizes ideological struggle through historical allusion. After Japan's defeat in August 1945 and the Soviet Union's withdrawal from Manchuria, Lin Piao, who commanded the PLA forces, displaced P'eng Chen, at the time secretary of the East China Bureau, as strong man in the Northeast. During the Cultural Revolution, when Lin Piao's credit was high, the opera was said to commend Lin Piao's prosecution of "people's war" over P'eng Chen's "opposition to the smell of gunpowder." [10] Thus Yang Tzu-jung's character has dual significance: on one level it is "a concentrated representation of the countless heroes in real life"; [11] on the other, it is representative of Lin Piao's career.*

After the fall of Lin Piao in 1971, however, it became possible to read the opera as premonitory of Lin's plot to overthrow Mao. Yang Tzu-jung's strategic seizure of the bandits' stronghold and the murder of Vulture, king of the mountain, could symbolize Lin Piao's attempt to kill Mao and seize Party and state power. In his July 8, 1966, letter to Chiang Ch'ing, Mao confessed, "I have always felt that when tigers are absent from the mountain, the monkey there professes himself a king."

Like Ch'ien Hao-liang, T'ung Hsiang-ling won theatrical stardom and political prominence by following Chiang Ch'ing's lead throughout the Cultural Revolution and its aftermath. Stripped of stage makeup in our interview, T'ung's features were sculpted sharply on a flat-planed face. Though he was in

---

* Yang's assumed name in the bandits' lair is Hu Piao, which, in the opera's Cultural Revolution version, uses the character "Piao" of Lin Piao's name.

his mid-forties, his taut body was electric with controlled energy. His smile was challenging and slightly wicked — a welcome relief in this straight-faced society.

"The modern opera that became known as *Taking Tiger Mountain by Strategy* was first produced in 1958 by the Peking Opera Troupe of Shanghai," T'ung began and charged ahead impatiently. "At that time Liu Shao-ch'i's revisionist line commanded the arts. Although the present Yang Tzu-jung is a proletarian hero, before the Cultural Revolution he was indistinguishable from the bandits. All wore the same crazy sort of costumes; in fact, the bandit chief Vulture now wears the beaten-up hat that once belonged to the former Yang Tzu-jung. His lines used to be shot through with 'black language' [of the underworld], and he danced to 'yellow music' [imitation of popular Western songs], waving a pipe in his hand. The directors forced him to violate his proletarian dignity by 'bending over eighty degrees' in submission to Vulture. In the raucous scenes in the bandits' lair Vulture was positioned at stage center, proudly surrounded by his men, while Yang Tzu-jung, then played by a man much older and less vigorous than myself, stood meekly in the corner of the stage."

After Chiang Ch'ing saw this so-called modern opera in 1963, T'ung Hsiang-ling continued, she came backstage and called it "mostly rubbish." Revision began the next year, under her lead. She cleansed Yang Tzu-jung of his unsavory aspects, transforming him into an admirable symbol of the proletariat. Vulture and his gang were relegated to peripheral positions on the stage.

The actors over whom she had taken charge had no idea of the enormous implications of the changes she had wrought until the Peking Opera Festival of June 1964, to which every province except Taiwan sent a delegation. After Chiang Ch'ing's production was deemed representative of Chairman Mao's military thought as developed in the Northeast, Liu Shao-ch'i's lackeys rose up and vowed to turn Yang Tzu-jung into a totally vicious bandit. Lin Mo-han, then vice-minister of culture and vice-head of the Propaganda Department, was vehement.[12] He ordered the playwright Lin Han-piao (a pen name) to recast the opera in accordance with the Liu Shao-ch'i line.

Liu Shao-ch'i's men soon twisted their frontal assault against the modern Peking opera into an "academic attack" (as in the February Outline of 1966) not only against modernization, which could be contained, but also against revolutionization, which went beyond their control. Cunningly, they deflected attention away from the ideological substance of the opera by criticizing merely its "artistic form." Since the story required Yang to be disguised as a bandit, for artistic effect, they said, he should appear *worse* than a real bandit. That suggestion confounded the questions of class and ideology at the forefront of Chiang Ch'ing's interests.

During the prelude to the Cultural Revolution Comrade Chiang Ch'ing often dropped in on Shanghai Mayor K'o Ch'ing-shih and regaled him with the philosophic premises she held as basic to opera reform. She argued for the mutually supportive relation between practice and cognition (the old Chinese philosphic debate over the relation between thought and action). Practice leads to cognition, she said, and cognition to further practice. She also emphasized how, in the construction of heroic characters, the music, lyrics, dialogue, dance, costuming, and stage directions all must relate to the theory of the "three stresses." First, stress positive figures; second, among the positive figures stress the heroes; and third, among the heroes stress the main heroes. That theory was eventually applied to all her model works.[13]

The heavy burden of state affairs during the height of the Cultural Revolution allowed Chiang Ch'ing to visit Shanghai only for limited periods. T'ung Hsiang-ling's troupe sent regular progress reports — tapes and records of their performances — to her in Peking. She told them later that she played these over and over again during her meals and weighed each detail. Because her overriding concern was to convey messages, she was most alert to elocution, insisting that they lay stress upon key words. She cited the word "hate," which should be hurled powerfully and dramatically against the enemy.

"You must reverse the reversed history of mankind," she quoted Chairman Mao. By that she meant that people, and people alone, are the motive force in history. They could not be buffoons or toy soldiers. To illustrate her points she recommended the Chairman's essay "On Coalition Government."

However, critical theory was the lesser side of Chiang Ch'ing's interest in the arts, T'ung observed. Her guidance was mainly of a practical nature, and that was unbounded. "She even managed to rejuvenate my acting style!" T'ung laughed to recall. He used to specialize in "old fellows." Whenever he mounted the stage, no matter for what part, automatically he hunched over and doddered about. Comrade Chiang Ch'ing despised that. "Whenever she caught me in that posture, she ran her fingers up my spine and said, 'Stand correctly! Your Yang Tzu-jung is no better than Chu-ko Liang.* Subdue the antique style! Stand tall and sing powerfully!' " Moreover, his costume should be changed from an old silk gown to a dashing fur-lined coat. When Yang Tzu-jung gestures with two fingers, meaning to plunge a dagger into Vulture's heart, she told him to project three fingers — that was more threatening.

Nor could she be awed by musical conventions. In the rules of the old opera two distinct singing styles, one delicate (*erh-huang*) and the other forceful (*hsi-*

---

* A heroic strategist in the ancient story cycle *Romance of the Three Kingdoms*. The failure of Chu-ko Liang, unrivaled for seventeen centuries, to match the high ideal set by Yang Tzu-jung, who aspires to make "the red flag unfurl on five continents," is argued in JMJP (Nov. 7, 1969): 3.

p'i) could neither be exchanged between characters nor be used in the same passage. To express intense feelings in a mild manner Chiang Ch'ing combined qualities of both styles in one aria. Feelings should be subtly articulated, she told them. Only under special conditions, such as vowing to bury the bandit Vulture or to support the Communist Party against all odds, could the forceful style be used alone.

To prove that artistic style must express social substance, she smashed the classical convention that falling tones be used to round off words at the end of musical phrases. Resolve to act was best expressed by rising tones, she taught them.

T'ung's favorite passage in his opera was the fifth scene, where he matures as a revolutionary hero with "the morning sun in his mind." This was projected through a dance that Chiang Ch'ing personally designed. In the original version Yang merely climbed the mountain on foot. Then in 1965 Chiang Ch'ing told him to ride up on horseback instead, to enhance his heroic image. In the old opera, the horse, whose presence was only mimed, was always represented as a gentle beast. To ride, an actor was symbolically hoisted up and set straight down upon its back. Instead of the delicate pantomime of old, Chiang Ch'ing wanted lively action and thus combined modern choreography with traditional acrobatics. As an experienced rider (which T'ung was not), she demonstrated the use of gesture and symbol to show mounting an imaginary steed and galloping heroically, all the while struggling with and against the animal's physical mass and power.

T'ung Hsiang-ling bounded from the table and re-created the interplay between Chiang Ch'ing's demonstration and his imitation. She had told him: "To mount a powerful horse in pantomime step quickly and leap into the air, doing a split. When the horse collapses at the sight of a tiger, show that by doing a split flat on the ground. At the end, don't simply slide off his back — that looks weak. To dismount impressively, spring over his head."

After seeing the opera's 1969 film version, she said that the horse dance still displeased her. At her own stables in Peking she experimented with all possible mounts and dismounts. When she returned to Shanghai, she told him, "Artistry requires exaggeration. To mount a huge but imaginary horse lift your leg as high as you can. Instead of dismounting by springing over the horse's head, sit sideways, lift one leg, then the other, and jump off. But don't land flat-footed! Point your toes and land on your toes. That looks majestic."

At the next moment in the script Yang Tzu-jung cocks his pistol and shoots the tiger through the head. The bandit chief asks him whether he killed it. "It got in the way of my bullet," Yang coolly replies.

Comrade Chiang Ch'ing was very keen on appearance, T'ung went on. She taught them tricks of costuming to accent certain features and to play others down. "Observing that I am fairly short but committed to a heroic role, she advised me to wear short-proportioned clothes and to raise my belt high on my torso. That made my legs look longer and me taller from the stage."

Her concern for them as individuals, T'ung said, was far greater than might be expected from political leaders. Playing Yang Tzu-jung in the old days, he carried his pistol in front on his belt. "Carry it to the side," she told him. Why? She explained: "Wearing a pistol in front for a long time can cause internal damage to a man's pelvic area."

The Central Committee was regularly briefed on the opera's revision; so was Chairman Mao. Early in July 1967, he came to Shanghai to review their performance. His only criticisms were literary. One line in scene 5 was changed to read, "and usher in spring to change the world of men" (more stress on revolutionary optimism). He also told them to exchange the classical expression for officers' uniforms in scene 9 for the modern one. After two years Chiang Ch'ing was still tutoring T'ung on the enunciation of the word "spring" so as to project its "social and political content" most powerfully.

T'ung Hsiang-ling introduced Ch'i Shu-fa, a shy and girlish-looking actress in her late twenties who portrays Ch'ang Pao, the hunter's daughter. Dressed in plain overblouse and trousers, she scarcely resembled sprightly Ch'ang Pao of the crimson jacket and the thick black plait whipping behind her in quick, decisive movements. Now, as on stage, her voice was plaintive, earnest, and high-pitched.

Ch'i Shu-fa presented herself cautiously in the terms of an ideal artist of the Cultural Revolution. She said she deplored personal fame, refused to portray the "bloodsucking class" of emperors, ministers, and beauties, and condemned the "art for art's sake" attitude of the bourgeoisie. Comrade Chiang Ch'ing had taught her that she would have to overcome her natural diffidence and become militant. Like Lu Hsun, she should cultivate the spirit of the ox: only bovine stubbornness would enable actors to smash the hardened conventions of Peking opera.

Through the example of Ch'ang Pao's character Comrade Chiang Ch'ing began a revolution in the portrayal of women on stage. All gestures signifying the feudal class were to be abolished. Lifting her hand in the air, fingers curved delicately, Ch'i Shu-fa demonstrated the "orchid fingers" of the old opera. How silly and effete that looked, she said, as she clenched her fist with the militant air she had acquired.

In the old opera, as in the old society, women were never supposed to show their teeth. When they smiled, they covered their mouths with their hands, their "water sleeves" shrouding their bodies. Now everyone smiles openly. Little girls used to be forced to bind their feet; they grew up crippled, with "three-inch lilies." If actresses did not have the ideal peg feet, or if actors por-

trayed women, they mimicked them by wearing little stilts or hobbling gro-
tesquely about the stage. "Nowadays women don't mind feet of any size, and
we enjoy a natural stride. When we used to cry, we shielded our eyes." Originally, when Ch'i Shu-fa sang the passage telling how her mother was murdered
by bandits, she burst into tears, sat down, and covered her face with her hands.
That was not proletarian crying, said Chiang Ch'ing. She pulled herself erect,
faced an imaginary audience, and showed the tears rolling down. "Working-
class people don't sit down or bury their heads when they cry," Chiang Ch'ing
said. "They cry standing."

Yet she should not linger over sorrow, insisted Chiang Ch'ing. "Focus upon
transforming sorrow into hatred, hatred into indignation, and indignation into
determination to fight!" If her interpretation of Ch'ang Pao evinced the slightest
self-pity, Chiang Ch'ing would frown at her, saying, "Project only class hatred,
class indignation, and class determination to fight. Though day and night you
long for the sun to rise, you must fight to the bitter end. You must show determination *to wipe out all the wolves*. We educate the people to keep their chins
up and never to forget that beauty is less important than will and power."

Ch'i Shu-fa had been trained to sing pure falsetto, the style of aristocratic
women and fairies. When Comrade Chiang Ch'ing became her coach in 1964,
she taught her to combine falsetto with a natural voice in the low and middle
ranges of the scale; pure falsetto should be used only in the high range. Only so
bold and resonant a voice could threaten vengeance.

Singing must never convey self-gratification, Chiang Ch'ing told her repeatedly. "You're singing for the workers, peasants, and soldiers." Nor should performers ever flaunt individual skills that detract from mutual efforts. "Personal
conceit has no place on the revolutionary stage," she said.

In an earlier version of *Tiger Mountain*, the scene where the PLA soldiers ski
to T'ung's rescue was performed as pure acrobatics. Such "extreme manner-
ism" Chiang Ch'ing disliked because the workers, peasants, and soldiers could
not understand it. To engage the masses she added realistic backdrops, a mobile stage, illusory screens, and dynamic lighting. But the "reactionaries," who
were desperate to preserve stark symbolism on a bare stage, fought each innovation. She fought back and charged ahead, combining ancient and modern
dance styles and costuming her men in white wool capes that whirled spectacularly in the wind, conveying the illusion of swooping over slopes. Chiang
Ch'ing explained to the troupe how this "collective image" of soldiers on skis
"showed how lives were risked for the revolutionary cause."

As for her role, Ch'i Shu-fa said, until the ninth scene she was just a simple-
minded hunter's daughter — without even the spark of a "spontaneous revolutionary." What transformed her into a woman warrior, a full-fledged *conscious*
proletarian heroine determined to fight for the liberation of mankind, was the

experience of watching the militia practice and singing to the military bugle. When she eulogizes the proletariat, Chiang Ch'ing told her, the music's tempo should slow down and her voice should sound firm but calm. But when she vows to kill all the wolves she should step up the tempo and sing in high excitement.

"Settling blood accounts" is among the most profound but least celebrated themes of Chinese revolutionary theater and the politics it epitomizes. The relation between Chiang Ch'ing's personal history and emotional life and her model theater has never publicly been explained. Ch'ang Pao's catalog of woes called "Asking about Bitterness" may recapture Chiang Ch'ing's grief at the loss of family members — though not only hers, of course — and her wish to speak freely and dress like a girl. Revenge is personal as well as general. Ch'ang Pao sings,

> *Vulture killed my grandma and carried off my mum and dad;*
> *Uncle Ta-shan in Chiapi Valley took me in,*
> *My dad escaped and came back,*
> *But my mum threw herself off a cliff and died.*
> *Oh, dear mum!*
> *In the mountains we hide;*
> *Afraid I'd fall into those devils' hands,*
> *Dad dressed me as a boy and said I was mute.*
> *We hunted in the mountains during the day,*
> *At night we thought of grandma and mum;*
> *We looked at the stars and the moon*
> *And longed for the time*
> *When the sun would shine over these mountains,*
> *When I would be able to speak out freely,*
> *When I could dress like a girl again,*
> *When we could collect our debt of blood.*
> *If I only had wings I'd take my gun*
> *And fly to the summit and kill all those wolves!*

"Oh Dad," she cries, flinging herself into her father's arms. Yang Tzu-jung responds furiously:

> *Pao's tales of the bandits' crimes*
> *Brimming with blood and tears,*
> *Rouse me to the utmost rage.*
> *Oppressed people everywhere have blood accounts*
> *To settle with their oppressors.*

They want vengeance,
An eye for an eye and blood for blood!

iv

After opera, ballet is the most important mode of revolutionary theater. A national tradition, the Peking opera reenacts historical episodes from the viewpoint of the ruling class. Now the emperors, ministers, and generals who stood far above the masses of old have been displaced by representatives of the Party and the PLA claiming to speak for the proletariat as a whole. Since men still dominate without monopolizing the new ruling class of "proletarian dictators," the opera continues to be primarily a man's art. Women play strong secondary roles, especially in their emerging capacity as "revolutionary successors." The ballet, which in all respects is less attached to Chinese history, remains more lyric in style and mythic in content. Since ballet has been always dominated by women, their contemporary revolt against oppression is more dramatically projected by dance than by the Chinese opera.

China's revolt against the purity and "tyranny" of classical ballet lagged at least a half century behind the West's. In 1909 Sergei Diaghilev shocked Paris with his Ballet Russe. Soon Martha Graham rebelled against ballet's cult of prettiness with the artful barbarism of her modern dance. Agnes De Mille's smart refurbishing of country dances for Broadway musicals began a process of enriching current dance styles by regional variety. These exercises in modernism, populism, cosmopolitanism, and sometimes commercialism, were paralleled by those of the Soviet Union's Moiseyev, Mexico's Folklorico, and Israel's Inbal. China's revolutionary adaptation of ballet technique and use of the dance of its minorities are the most recent.

Years before Liberation Shanghai offered to the rich and the foreign Greek eurythmics, a choice of master-centered schools of ballet, Hollywood-style team dancing, ballroom and taxi dancing, and frequent cultural exchanges. By the eve of the Cultural Revolution, everything but the classical ballet had been banned. Although Chiang Ch'ing enjoyed the ballet as dance movement, she deplored it as a vehicle of unwanted foreign culture. Dancers prancing in pink tutus and pretending to be dying swans revolted her. Her call for rebellion against the tyranny of ballet classicism provoked recrimination from enemies on the right and the left who resolved either to keep ballet classical but segregated from revolutionary life, or to ban it entirely, but certainly not to try to salvage it politically. Some followers of Liu Shao-ch'i reportedly threatened to break the legs of ballerinas who pretended to dance to China's revolution.

Political power backed by Mao Tse-tung enabled Chiang Ch'ing to salvage the ballet in accordance with his formula for moderating innovation: "Make the old serve the new and things foreign serve things Chinese." Chinese opera lent acrobatics, song, exaggerated facial expressions, and frozen stares. Local culture contributed rhythmic music, dance patterns, and colorful costumes. Yet the basic footwork, pirouettes, and arabesques were drawn straight from the classical ballet. The orchestration wavered between intimations of nineteenth-century program music and the theme-song style of movie music that had been quietly absorbed for decades from foreign cinema.

Revolution of ballet, Chiang Ch'ing told me, meant that she and her assistants "struggled against the bondage of Russian classicism that enslaved Chinese dancers for decades." Stalin was responsible for conserving the "bourgeois classics featuring the contest between good and evil." Succeeding Soviet leaders persisted in the same absurd "policy" of making an animal — a black swan, actually — the central figure of *Swan Lake!*

By contrast, *The Red Detachment of Women* (premiered in October 1964) was based on historical actualities. Set on Hainan Island off the coast of South China, the ballet shows political resistance by people of the Li nationality. All the minorities in old China were oppressed — "treated just like animals," she said.

I had seen this bold and brassy ballet in Peking before Chiang Ch'ing and I first met. The reasons for its location in Hainan's hot tropics were as much political as aesthetic, it seemed. Nearly the size of Taiwan, Hainan is extremely rich in natural resources. Moreover, it had not been liberated by the Communists until April 1950, after the Nationalists had failed to win American backing for their claim.* *The Red Detachment's* insular environment balances that of *White-haired Girl*, which is set against the severe mountainscape of the northwest interior.

Like the opera, the ballet follows the Marxist-Leninist and Maoist thought that is based on the law of the excluded middle. Positive characters are either heroic at the outset or become so through Liberation. Negative ones have no choice but to be destroyed so that victors may arise. Between the positive and negative characters are negligible or no "middle characters," to use the Chinese term. In the old and new opera and the new ballet positive and negative characters are identified by conventional makeup design and body movement. A good character enters the stage proudly and ceremoniously, arm raised and palm out, displaying his "good face" directly to the audience. But a bad character enters hunched over with an irregular gait, his ashen or blackened face avoiding the audience.

* Could President Nixon have missed this element of cultural politics underscoring the Shanghai Communiqué, and its implication for reintegrating the province of Taiwan with the mainland of China?

The Red Detachment of Women opens in a dungeon where the beautiful slave girl Wu Ch'ing-hua (clearly a positive character) has been bound to a post by Nan Pa-t'ien, the symbol of wicked landlords in the old South. To the accompaniment of anguished song she twists herself free, wreaking violence upon male guards along her escape route. A boy messenger from the Red Army finds her and guides her to its Red Detachment, which is led by handsome Hung Ch'ang-ch'ing, the Party representative who induces her to seek refuge in the Women's Detachment. Driven by Wu Ch'ing-hua's vengeance, the whole detachment rises up against the grand manor of Nan Pa-t'ien. Wu Ch'ing-hua murders him. The liberation of the village is celebrated by a buoyant ethnic ballet of the Li people. At the end Wu Ch'ing-hua pledges to model herself after the heroic Hung Ch'ang-ch'ing, and to live by Mao's motto: "Political power grows out of the barrel of a gun."

Chiang Ch'ing explained to me how, when she undertook this ballet in the early 1960's, there was absolutely no precedent for using ballet to show military history, and almost no one would support her intent to establish it.* To prepare herself, in late 1963 she traveled alone to Hainan Island where she followed the activities of that region's formidable military installation. From there she went to Shanghai to take personal control over the ballet company. The situation was perilous, for some powerful figures in the cultural world were already scheming to sabotage her rendering of a model revolutionary ballet, one she had hoped to inaugurate in the fall of 1964. In search of approval from among the leaders, she invited Premier Chou to attend a rehearsal of an early version, which he did. The weak spots that he pointed out they changed. To educate her dancers in the ways of the military, she decided to send them down to live with a PLA unit for some months. As soon as she had released her order, Chou Yang announced from his high office in the Ministry of Culture that he was sending the very company she was working with to Hong Kong to perform *Swan Lake!* She was outraged but helpless. Ordinarily Shanghai Mayor K'o Ch'ing-shih would have supported her stand against Chou Yang, but K'o had just fallen ill. So she turned to Premier Chou and "delivered a barrage of opinion" against a "certain person" who was undercutting her fledgling ballet. She assumed that he knew whom she meant, then asked him to name the person in question. He couldn't imagine, he said. But soon tensions in the cul-

---

* However, in February 1961 Mao Tse-tung wrote on the back of a photograph the following poem called "Militia Women":
Early rays of sun illumine the parade grounds
and these handsome girls heroic in the wind,
   with rifles five feet long.
Daughters of China with a marvelous will,
you prefer hardy uniforms to colorful silk.
(Translated by Willis Barnstone in collaboration with Ko Ching-po, *The Poems of Mao Tse-tung*, New York, 1972, 99.)

tural world were so blatant that no one could profess ignorance of Chou Yang's obstruction of her reform of the ballet (reportedly maligning *The Red Detachment* as an "infant in swaddling bands sucking its thumb" and an "ugly daughter-in-law"). [14]

Despite Chou Yang's contemptuous opposition, she continued the revisions and finally accompanied the ballet on tour in the major cities. Back in Peking, she went with Premier Chou to another performance, which had been much revised. His calling it "real revolution" gratified her. After the final curtain she and the Premier went backstage to congratulate the dancers and musicians who had remained loyal to her throughout the battles of creation.

She was still worried about how this Sino-Western dance synthesis would strike the masses. While the National People's Congress was in session in the winter of 1964, she invited some delegates, among them workers from the industrial center of Wuhan, to a performance. During the show she overheard one worker remark that in the old days he couldn't make head or tail of the ballet. Now he got it!, he said. How she relieved she felt.

To demonstrate fully to the delegates the contrast between the classical and the revolutionary ballet, she told her Shanghai troupe first to perform *The Red Detachment*, and second their old standby, *Swan Lake*. During the latter some workers protested loudly, and a few asked permission to leave. "We're convinced that *The Red Detachment of Women* is much better," they assured her and the other leaders (though Chiang Ch'ing never expressed to me that under the circumstances workers might not have dared to say otherwise). The leading male dancer, Liu Ch'ing-t'ang, who reported to her regularly on audience reaction, corroborated her sense that it was generally positive.

Two days before I met Chiang Ch'ing, I interviewed at the Peking Hotel members of the Shanghai troupe that had performed *The Red Detachment* and nothing else since 1964. Chiang Ch'ing's loyal Liu Ch'ing-t'ang was chief spokesman. I was told that in the early 1950's the study of ballet in China was monopolized by Russian instructors and their private students, and that national and folk dance was controlled by a professional Chinese elite. In 1954 the Party established in Peking a dance school whose goal was to train a corps of native-born ballet and national dance teachers, who would draw students not only from the upper classes in the cities, but eventually from the rural poor as well. Still, in the middle 1950's ballet devotees aspired only to master "famous foreign ballets." They started with small sections, such as the dance of the Little Swans from *Swan Lake* and passages from *Giselle* and Byron's *Sea Pirates*, then slowly worked up these and other foreign ballets in their entirety.

The Soviet Union's "one-sided withdrawal" of all its experts from China in 1960 jolted the ballet world, leaving half-trained teachers and students to survive on their own. Yet that forced self-reliance also stimulated diversification, and in the long run made possible the present "revolutionary ballet."

Right after the Soviets withdrew, a group of teachers from the original Peking Dance Institute split off and set up a branch in Shanghai. As late as 1962 and 1963 both troupes were totally involved in producing "foreign bourgeois classics." Laughing incredulously, one ballerina remarked that Victor Hugo's *Hunchback of Notre Dame* and Aleksander Pushkin's *Spring of Tears* were once their best shows.

When Comrade Chiang Ch'ing first appeared at the Peking Dance Institute in 1963, she made no pretence of knowing anything about ballet. Her mission was purely political. Yet they knew that over the preceding two years she had gathered strong followings in the symphony and opera. *Shachiapang* had already been revised as a model opera, symphony, and film. Foreign classical ballet was the next stage from which she was determined to wipe out all feudal class remnants and reframe technique and content.

In the early 1960's a film titled *The Red Detachment of Women* had been made from a spoken drama on the same theme. Although the film was flawed, Chiang Ch'ing told the dancers, she was confident of her power to turn it into a revolutionary ballet. Thus she made her trip to Hainan Island in late 1963. Besides investigating the military, she carefully studied the topography, climate, trees, flowers and overall color, and the indigenous culture of the Li people. She also interviewed people on the history of the Women's Detachment (formed in 1930–1931). She returned to Peking (despite Chou Yang's obstructionism), brimming with confidence, and closed the academy, which meant that all current productions were suddenly terminated. From among their members she singled out the few whom she trusted and reconstituted them separately as the Creation Group. (Having won Chou En-lai's support) she sent this group, which included writers, musicians, choreographers, stage designers, and principal performers, to Hainan in order to cull "raw materials" from the local culture.

These northerners who made up the Creation Group were nearly devastated by the tropical climate. And not surprisingly, their intrusion offended the local people. Disputes within the Creation Group over the politics of dance interpretation flared into open warfare, which was an embarrassment, especially since their troupe was attached to the PLA unit responsible for Hainan's defense. Attempting to draw art from the experience of living in military barracks taught them above all that "political power grows out of the barrel of a gun."

In their pursuit of historical authenticity, the dancers interviewed some aged ladies who had fought in the original Red Detachment. These ladies described how the woman who is represented pseudonymously as Wu Ch'ing-hua in the present ballet had been abused by the landlord family for whom she was once a maidservant and came to maturity only after escaping. One woman whose experience was similar said that she had made five or six attempts before she finally escaped her tyrannical landlord and found haven with the PLA.

Some people — especially foreigners — mistakenly think that this ballet is mainly about women, Liu Ch'ing-t'ang commented. Actually, the central figure is the hero (Hung Ch'ang-ch'ing, whom he portrayed) — not the woman Wu Ch'ing-hua!

Unquestionably, the Cultural Revolution had destroyed the classical ballet. But since 1963 their troupe had been authorized to perform only one work, *The Red Detachment*. Were other new and revolutionary ballets in the offing? I asked.

Ode to I Mountain, first put on trial performance in 1971, was still being revised, Liu Ch'ing-t'ang responded. Eventually, this would be included in the model repertory and be made into a movie. (It premiered in Peking in 1973.) Set on the Shantung peninsula, the site of two revolutionary base areas during the Liberation War, the purpose of *Ode to I Mountain* was to demonstrate Mao Tse-tung's unique combination of guerrilla war and people's war — "the fish and water relation of the army and the people." To prepare itself, the troupe traveled to Shantung where the dancers fostered their own fish and water relation with the local people. The opera troupe at I Mountain invited them to use their stage to present trial passages from the new ballet. The Shantung players, obviously flattered by the Peking dancers' attempts to represent their lives, responded by making an impromptu operatic interpretation of the same historical theme. The ballet troupe's first full performance of *Ode* attracted more than forty thousand people, many from great distances. Children climbed trees to get a bird's-eye view of the stage. Liu Ch'ing-t'ang assessed the ballet's strong and weak points in terms of audience response: noisy reception meant that the passage was good, and a pall of silence that they need to strive harder for social and regional authenticity.

Another male ballet dancer commented piously that the experience of performing classical ballet years earlier was always "very cold. Only a few old patrons bothered to attend. Knowing that the masses were uninterested left us feeling chill. We are grateful to Comrade Chiang Ch'ing for having brought warmth and enthusiasm to our work."

v

When Chou En-lai and Edgar Snow were visiting a cave town north of Yenan in 1936, a crazed woman suddenly appeared stark naked at the edge of a bluff. Seeing them, she cursed viciously and fled. Snow learned later that personal trauma — a pestilence had destroyed her entire family — had left her demented.[15]

In times of brooding violence and sporadic revolt, stories of women who became maddened by intolerable circumstances were common. Sparked by reality, such stories were transformed into modern mythology. One of the most famous evolved from rumors about a white-haired girl. As it moved from opera to film to ballet, her story traced the Communist Party's changing attitudes toward the human body, sexuality, illegitimate childbirth, romantic love, and potential for political redemption.

In the original folk opera, *White-haired Girl,* which was produced at the Lu Hsun Academy in 1944, [16] the heroine, Hsi-erh, is the daughter of an old tenant farmer who cannot pay his rent. To retaliate, the landlord and his lackeys seize the daughter, which so devastates the father that he commits suicide. Hsi-erh is forced into servitude in the landlord's household, where he rapes her and the women persecute her. When she becomes pregnant, he tries to murder her, but she escapes to the hills where she bears a son who dies of starvation. Lack of salt and sunlight cause her hair to whiten prematurely (according to local lore). Some villagers who catch sight of her wraithlike figure stealing food from temple offerings mistake her for a fairy or a ghost. In the Yenan opera version, which was authorized by Chou Yang,[17] Chang Keng, and others, Hsi-erh flees from a "feudal" society, to be redeemed in the end by representatives of the Eighth Route Army (Mao's Red Army) and the Communist Party.

In this primitive local opera Hsi-erh, her father Yang Pai-lao, and the landlord Huang Shih-jen are archetypal characters and their names are bitterly symbolic. Hsi-erh means "joy," Yang Pai-lao, "toiling in vain," and Huang Shih-jen, "charity of the world." They are joined by the young and handsome Ta-ch'un ("great spring"), Hsi-erh's former fiancé, who recognizes through her ghastly and bedraggled appearance the girl she once was. Their sentimental reunion is capped by her joining the Eighth Route Army. When the opera was performed in Yenan the sight of the landlord so enraged the peasants that they rose up shouting *"Sha! sha!* [kill! kill!]."

In the early days the opera was said to show that "the old society turns people into ghosts and the new society turns ghosts into people" (during the Cultural Revolution that moral was denounced for revealing superstition and lacking class character). Persistently popular, in 1950 the story of the white-haired girl was made into a "naturalistic" film starring T'ien Hua, a peasant girl trained by the Eighth Route Army players. In 1951, the film, which had been exported to several countries, was awarded a second-class Stalin Prize.[18] Although set during the war of resistance against Japan, no Japanese ever appeared in the stage or film version. Still, the inheritors of Japan's imperialistic generation were so fascinated by this ghastly but romantic story that a classical ballet was built upon it in Japan. Peking welcomed its performance in 1957, and again in the early 1960's.[19] At that point Chiang Ch'ing brought about her own updating of the story, making it a "proletarian ballet" to be stripped of its earlier romanticism and naturalism and to be suffused with class struggle ideology. In separate interviews she and her balletic loyalists explained how, in the revolutionized ballet, episodes of rape, childbirth, and child death were eliminated to achieve newly positive images, an overall "brightness." The sexual attraction of Hsi-erh and Ta-ch'un was played down, and the roles of the Eighth Route Army and Chairman Mao played up bombastically in the finale.

A ballet so intimately linked to China's revolutionary history has struck foreigners in various ways. In 1973, the year Chiang Ch'ing sent me the most recent film version of *White-haired Girl* in exchange for a print of *The Sound of Music*, *The New York Times* music critic Harold Schonberg reported of the live ballet he had seen in Shanghai:

To Western eyes the ballet is anything but revolutionary. It is a naive, innocent propaganda fairy tale, primarily stemming from Russian ballet, saturated with the dance vocabulary of the West. Once in a while, Chinese elements are introduced — native instruments, the pentatonic scale, and even a few microtones. But these too somehow sound Russian. . . . Most Western listeners would classify the score of *The White Haired Girl* as movie music. Certainly all the clichés are there.[20]

vi

Late one August afternoon I met with the troupe that had produced this provocative ballet at their attractive European-style academy in the outskirts of Shanghai. Lin Yang-yang, another of Chiang Ch'ing's cultural loyalists, was in command. Both ballet master and political commissar for his troupe, he had a swift wit and a knack with a foreigner. In 1960, he began their political story, their "younger brother" team of dancers broke off from the "elder brother," the dance institute in Peking. Over the last decade his troupe had managed to open the ballet, which once catered to rich girls who could afford foreign dance masters, to the people at large. Students now were trained entirely by Chinese dance instructors.

Comrade Chiang Ch'ing above all was responsible for starting the cultural warfare that transformed the ballet from a "bourgeois classical art" to a "sinified popular art." Her chief opponent was Liu Shao-ch'i, defender of the "sacred fields of the landlords and the bourgeoisie." Liu Shao-ch'i, along with Lin Mo-han, vice-chairman of the former Propaganda Department, and Ch'en Pei-hsien, secretary of Shanghai's Municipal Party Committee, used to say how absurd it was to think that a foreign dance, the ballet, could be divorced from foreign social and political realities and be used to represent contemporary Chinese realities. These three and others collaborated to manipulate members of their troupe to resist Chiang Ch'ing's carefully wrought revisions.

For example, she wanted to stress the hero Ta-ch'un's revolutionary initiative by showing him organizing the struggle against the local despots and Japanese imperialism. But the revisionists insisted that Ta-ch'un first attend to affairs of the heart by pursuing the heroine Hsi-erh, which meant putting love ahead of revolution. In the scene in the mountain cave where Ta-ch'un comes face to face with Hsi-erh after many years, the revisionists wanted him to display a sewing kit he once gave her as a sign that he knew who she was. They encouraged him to dance erotically and to swoom from an attack of love. The ballet was to end with a duet showing the pair settling down to a pastoral life. If there were group dancing, it could celebrate only production and nothing more political (or extravagantly Mao-centered). Chiang Ch'ing fought against that "peaceful finale" because, she said, it propagated the theory of the dying out of class struggle. Although the landlord Huang Shih-jen and the village despots were overthrown by the end of the ballet, she reminded the dancers that in the late 1930's most of their country, along with the rest of the world, still awaited Liberation. Thus Hsi-erh and Ta-ch'un should set aside romance and pitch into the unfinished work of revolution.

Of himself, Lin Yang-yang said, "Born and brought up in the new society, I lacked genuine feelings for the laboring people. So, too, these dancers [listening dutifully and demonstrating to the young master's snap of the finger] were once hamstrung by ignorance of the real world. To break away from the academy's elitism, they were sent on a rotating basis down to industrial and rural settings to learn how to convey through dance the complaints of plain people. Most of these dancers and musicians suffered from a 'generation gap.' Grown up since Liberation, they have known only material comforts and national security. The meaning of poverty, exile, and threatened extinction had to be learned."

Musicians with the ballet explained the transition from the original North Shensi folk opera to the present symphonic arrangement, which was heavily Western. Comrade Chiang Ch'ing had taught them to direct the newly synthesized power of the music toward revenge, which was the fundamental theme of the story. She also reversed the relation between the musicians and the dancers. She said that in classical ballet the music is primary and the dance is its expression. But in revolutionary ballet the dance is the main feature; from that the heroic images of the leading characters must loom large. When their troupe embarked upon a tour of North Korea and Japan in April 1972, she and Premier Chou came to see them off. She reminded the dancers that their skill was often wanting; they should tighten their fifth positions and make straighter extensions. Hsi-erh should raise her legs still higher on the pirouette. The musicians should be conscientious about playing softly because the loudness of old Chinese music grates hard on foreign ears. She insisted (as she had to her opera musicians): "Music should serve as the guest, not the host."

Continuing comparisons, Lin Yang-yang said that the true classical ballet never featured the human voice in solo or in chorus. But Chinese audiences brought up on the opera said that a stage without song felt "naked" (foreign-style bare thighs topped by net skirts also appear too naked, others explained). Thus the revolutionary ballet has added a solo voice and chorus that swell emotionally in dramatic passages so that the audience will be moved as the leaders intend. For example, in the first scene where the father Yang Pai-lao is killed by the landlord, Hsi-erh's song (by an offstage singer in operatic style) highlights her grief and indignation.

Western instruments have been added for volume, but Chinese instruments express the theme songs keyed to characters (as in *Peter and the Wolf*) and render moments of high musical drama. When Hsi-erh accepts a gift of yarn from her father, when she rises up against oppression, or when she recalls her own past suffering, the *pan-hu*, a wind instrument, projects her turbulent emotional state. The *san-hsien*, a three-stringed instrument, ominously announces the landlord Huang Shih-jen. A range of percussion instruments give vibrancy to Ta-ch'un's heroic image. Bamboo flutes evoke the pastoral scenes.

The ballerina Mao Kuei-fang danced Hsi-erh in the first part of the stage and film versions; another dancer always relieved her in the arduous passages in the mountains. A self-possessed but unpretentious prima, she was most likely the idol of tens of millions of girls of her generation who were warned incessantly by their leaders against pursuing stardom. She had the typical look of Chinese dancers whose bodies, no matter how arduously trained, would never turn hard or sinewy. Her hair, unusual in its length, was plaited and wound around the crown. Despite her preeminence in China's cultural world, neither she nor any other ballerina tempered by the fires of the Cultural Revolution had soared in skill to the ethereal ranks of Fonteyn or Plisetskaya.

Signaled to begin, she said that when she first danced the passage where she receives a piece of red yarn from her father, her nonchalance offended the peasants recruited to judge their trial ballet. Only after she had been sent down to live with poor peasants could she feel and portray the profound pleasure afforded by one small piece of red yarn. In the scene where she crosses a mountain stream on point, she used to strive for exquisite pantomime. "If you've suffered a lot you can't be delicate!" the peasants protested, whereupon her technique and choreography were made bolder.

In the adaptation of foreign ballet, toe dancing along with the basic steps has been preserved, but with modifications. The Chinese arabesque is intentionally less romantic. Comrade Chiang Ch'ing was adamant against excessive use of "orchid fingers" (thumb and third finger forming a circle) and delicately up-turned palms, Mao Kuei-fang reported. To show resolution and indignation, they had to make fists. "Orchid fingers" could be used only selectively, such as in the scene where exiled Hsi-erh gingerly feels her way out of the mountain's dark caves into the clearing and uses her palm to scoop drinking water from the stream. At her birthday celebration Hsi-erh is allowed to stand on point in a sustained élevée while Ta-ch'un reveals his identity by taking off his mask.

Overall, Chiang Ch'ing took far greater pleasure in teaching violent move-ments showing hatred of the landlord class and determination to seek revenge.

The revolutionary ballet limits solos and duets because of their individ-ualistic and romantic suggestions, Lin Yang-yang said. In the classical ballet male soloists project the aura of personal nobility and exhibit skills that out-shine the performances of others in their companies. Their tenderness toward ballerinas actually shows condescension toward women. In the revolutionary ballet revenge is the only justification for a male solo. For example, when the landlord tears Hsi-erh away from her father, her fiancé Ta-ch'un performs a spectacular solo of pirouettes and splits to incite his class brothers to join in re-taliation against the tyrannical landlord.

The ballerina of classical ballet is often the center of attention, making the principal male dancer secondary to her. The Chinese have found that rela-tionship puzzling, Lin said. Their new ballet strives for a parity between male and female principals, though romantic yearnings, once relished by China's revisionists, have been toned down.

In *White-haired Girl*'s original Yenan opera, the landlord's entire family was cast in an evil light. During the Cultural Revolution that was changed so that only the matriarch, the mother of the landlord, is vicious, and the other women of the household are victims of her tyranny. The eldest woman servant extends great sympathy to Hsi-erh in her plight. Not only is the matriarch the single evil woman in the present ballet, but also the single negative female character left on the model stage. This repellant female is preserved only because today's youth no longer are victimized by the old family system and mothers-in-law. This ballet presents their only (!) chance to see what vicious women once were like.

A most important strengthening of proletarian character came with Chiang Ch'ing's transformation of the image of the father, Yang Pai-lao, from defeatism to dignity. When the father of the former version was threatened with the loss of his daughter, he cringed before the landlord and committed suicide by taking poison. She taught him to stand up defiantly against the landlord, flail out at him with his shoulder pole (once a shameful, now a proud symbol of labor), and die fighting.

And Hsi-erh was transformed from being merely a wronged woman to one militant and vengeful who defends herself against the landlord with the huge candlesticks that adorn his household. Other elements of the old story — the landlord's rape of Hsi-erh, her retreat to the mountains to give birth, and the infant's death by starvation — are eliminated from the present version because they are too "naturalistic."

To accentuate feelings of hatred and revenge, steps from the Chinese national dances used in opera are incorporated in the ballet. When prolonged exile and deprivation gradually drain Hsi-erh's hair of its natural color, causing it to become gray, then white, she dances with bold movements (not unlike those in the West's modern ballet). Male dancers have spurned the "duck foot" (turned-out) position of classical ballet in favor of the straight walk of the military march. Ta-ch'un's solo dance to encourage his peasant companions to take vengeance against the landlord Huang Shih-jen combines pirouettes from the ballet with splits from the opera. And both male and female dancers affect frozen, dramatic poses of the old opera. In the first opera version, the peasants fought with swords and spears. Now they dance with rifles — even hand grenades — because they are modern.

vii

"Madame Witke," Chiang Ch'ing said to me privately, "on several occasions you remarked that art and literature are 'advanced' in our country [remarks spurred by their obvious striving toward socialism and communism]. Yet we feel that the artistic level of our work is not commensurate with the high prestige we now enjoy."

She cited the present version of *White-haired Girl*, the outcome of years of piecemeal revision. She and her supporters had intended further improvements, but their efforts were sabotaged by the Lin Piao clique, whose manipulations behind the scenes went undiscovered until it was almost too late. Some of Lin's followers who were made responsible for the revision of *White-haired Girl* exaggerated the romantic elements. They allowed Hsi-erh to retreat to the mountains, remaining there seemingly endlessly, with the result that she divorced herself from class struggle. Since Lin Piao's demise, Chiang Ch'ing was still striving to reduce the sexual attraction between Ta-ch'un and Hsi-erh. This final adjustment, she felt, would further enhance the ballet's popular appeal.

Yet all these model works are flawed, she admitted. Besides providing

China's masses with images of their own revolution, the only thing to be said for the new repertory is that no other nation's music and theater combines alien traditions so boldly. The full range of their revolutionary works the world has yet to see.

18.

◇ ◇ ◇

Decompression

Reach the ninth heaven high to embrace
   the moon.
Or the five oceans deep to capture a turtle;
   either is possible.

     . . .

Under this heaven nothing is difficult,
If only there is the will to ascend.
   — Mao Tse-tung, "Ching-kang-shan
     Revisited"

Could I not stay longer — some weeks or months? Chiang Ch'ing and her aides pressed me after she had been talking for several days about her past. In this exclusive proletarian realm where her will was uncontested, my departure was the one initiative I wanted to keep. No, I said, for I was under contract to teach history at Stanford University and had other professional and personal obligations. She knew I cherished my daughter, but in China children belong to the state, as she had reminded me more than once. But if I was determined to leave quickly, she would continue selectively, telescoping complex experiences. I agreed then to remain in China two more days during which I submitted in writing, at her request, a set of questions — some points of clarification and other summary judgments. Near the end of the last evening she responded.

All along I had been impressed with the fluidity and seeming informality of leadership at the top. Chiang Ch'ing's work in the arts, for example, seemed now, in the early 1970's, to be conducted without the benefit of formal authority over cultural affairs. Nor had she bothered to describe other high political appointments she had won in recent years, ones that set her in a special class in the annals of Chinese history. Her nonchalance about status, hers and others, was the opposite of foreigners' swift seizure upon the labels of leadership in order to make portentous judgments.

i

"I belong to the Chinese Communist Party," she responded to my question of what posts she held. "I am a delegate to the National People's Congress. I am a member of the Politburo of the Central Committee of the Chinese Communist Party. I hold no other formal posts."

Her daily work was of a routine nature, she said. She analyzed internal and external trends, then passed on policy recommendations to the Central Committee and to Chairman Mao. All major policy issues discussed by the Politburo were reported to Chairman Mao. Premier Chou was in charge of "routine work."

"Besides that I study. The Chairman has set the task of studying Marxism-Leninism, and I set myself the task of studying the thought of Mao Tse-tung." His articles "On Contradiction" and "On Practice" are most useful. Often she rereads his essay on the Yenan Forum. She also reads deeply in his essays on warfare. "Anyone can see that my work is always related to warfare," she smiled.

What most intrigued me about China was the immense control exercised by the leaders who inspired and regulated "proletarian consciousness," the myth that drove the people on to formidable tasks of transforming themselves spiritually and their country materially. Almost all intellectual modernity and cultural variety, except for what served Mao's concept of Marxism, had been barred from China, or admitted for the exclusive enjoyment of the leaders away from public view. Her responses to questions about this were surprisingly frank.

On the question of public performances in China by foreign artists of works not necessarily of a socialist character, she said that such decisions would be made on the basis of the foreign work's ideological content. A variety of cultural exchanges with other countries were conducted up to the time of the Cultural Revolution. But since the Cultural Revolution (during which she also had seized control over international cultural exchange) only two troupes, both personally remolded by her, had been sent abroad.

There are two categories for the presentation of cultural works: public and private. The exchanges just mentioned were for public showing. Works regarded as "unhealthy for the people" are restricted to private showing among the leading comrades who consider them for "reference," which means that they learn from them mainly as "negative examples." In that connection they imported a number of fascist films from Japan for private showing among the leaders. They know that the left-wing elements in Japan rarely see such films because of the high price of admission, she said. Other foreign works are acquired in order to study them as art. The aesthetic dimension can also be used for "reference."

In the foreseeable future cultural exchanges with foreign countries must be restricted. The Foreign Ministry will handle exchanges with countries with which they have formal diplomatic relations. Where there are no diplomatic relations, the exchange will be handled by the Friendship Association. In either case works to be exchanged must be progressive in content and meet the approval of the State Council.

"Many foreign friends would enjoy our works," she said confidently. "But because your country, the United States, forcibly occupies Taiwan, we have no diplomatic relations. So our exchanges must be made through the Friendship Association." Some of their works would be welcome in America, she ventured. Americans would not be made uncomfortable by seeing *Taking Tiger Mountain by Strategy* or some other revolutionary operas. All such works have historical importance and some have bearing upon Sino-American relations.

Again she praised General Eisenhower for going to Korea to sign the armistice two decades earlier. The Koreans, she said, have learned to handle their problems on their own and do not welcome interference from other countries, a policy the United States also seems to approve. Several films have been sent by (North) Korea. The Chinese have also welcomed progressive works from Albania and Yugoslavia, she added. But the Soviet Union keeps silent.

During our conversations she had reminisced several times nostalgically about the movies of Greta Garbo, Charlie Chaplin, and other Hollywood stars. Could they be taken from their archives and presented now to the people as stellar negative examples?

"Those bourgeois democratic films are to be reserved for private showing," she declared flatly. If the people could view them they would criticize them bitterly on political grounds. Such public exposure and attack would be most unfair to Garbo because she is not Chinese. The same was true for Chaplin, almost all of whose films she saw in the 1930s. *Modern Times* she recognized as a diatribe against dictatorship. Others of his films seemed to be pitched against Stalin and, most powerfully, against Hitler, which makes them "progressive" in her judgment and that of her comrades. What must be understood is that those films were created in an earlier era when foreign filmmakers were friendly toward China. Thus, it would be most unfair to criticize the stars under the current political situation, which is totally different. Still, it is all right to screen these films "among ourselves" (the leaders), who decide on their strong and weak points. But those private showings cannot be publicized.

I had observed no separate children's culture in China, and surely nothing special for adolescents. Would children continue to be made to perform, and thus conform to the standards of, revolutionary operas created by and for adults, or would another cultural order be created expressly for them?

"We have not taken enough initiative," Chiang Ch'ing responded officiously on the leaders' behalf. "But much has been done already by the masses on their own initiative." (What that was remained a mystery.)

Their goal of raising artistic standards but only on the basis of popularization had been set for them by Chairman Mao at the Yenan Forum. In art and literature they must always be serious, careful, and diligent. The enemy cannot be dealt with in a gross manner. He cannot be criticized crudely. He must be depicted negatively, but only after careful reasoning and analysis.

As international relations advance and cultural exchanges keep pace, great contradictions will emerge, she predicted. But the contradictions (meaning the shock of showing foreign and bourgeois culture in their country) will appear mainly on their side. The real question in her mind was whether the Chinese would be able to produce art for revolutionary people of the entire world. To achieve that both artistic standards and ideological content must be kept high. But under no circumstances should they preach to others. In exposing their works abroad, she repeated several times, they know they run the risk of failing to live up to the prestige they already enjoy.

"I'm never satisfied with my work because it's never perfect" was a statement she made often. "I always try to find faults with it. We must never slacken in our pursuit of artistic and ideological perfection. Nor can we allow ourselves to become conceited."

What in her estimation were the greatest achievements and greatest failures over the last twenty-three years?

Above all, the Chinese people have *stood up*. No longer can they be called "the poor man of Europe, the sick man of Asia." No longer are they subject to imperialism. Some nagging problems remain to be solved. The United States imperialists still "forcibly occupy Taiwan." Some areas along the northern borders are still occupied by foreign powers (the Soviet Union), and India still occupies some of their western territories, causing intermittent skirmishes there.

Chairman Mao laid down the following principles. One is that they must preserve independence and sovereignty. Foreign interference in their sovereign territory has made Taiwan a problem for them, but one which they and Taiwan should solve between themselves. Even President Nixon finally recognized that Taiwan belongs to China. He signed a statement (the Shanghai Communiqué) to that effect. Looking at me sharply, she said, "Do you realize that the position your country maintains in Taiwan is tantamount to our occupying your Long Island?" The very analogy I had drawn to my students, I remarked, triggering a volley of laughter. Now the Chinese (PRC) have independence and sovereignty "in small part," she went on. Before long they will have "the whole part."

Economically they must be self-reliant. But that does not mean that the Chairman does not want international trade and exchanges of various sorts. Are they advanced? she asked rhetorically. They are the only country in the world that has neither internal nor external debts. This is the main side of the argument.

As for shortcomings, their economic development has been uneven, reflecting the law that evenness and balance are only temporary. Some economic fields and branches of science have been neglected.

Ideologically, they have a relatively mature Marxist-Leninist Party, which is the main side of this argument. But on the other side, they have not studied Marxism-Leninism well enough. As a result, many good comrades are vulnerable to "political swindlers still dwelling among them." (Was the art of political survival, then, mainly one of ideological expertise?)

We talked about the problem of women. Feudalistic and prearranged marriages still can be found in the countryside, she said. And in the rural areas women are not always paid equally for equal work. Despite these shortcomings, in the area of political leadership they have made great strides. "Now in *essence* Chinese women hold more leading posts than in any other country. I mean in *essence*, not just nominally." (Possession of more essential than nominal roles was surely true in her case.) Although in capitalist countries women hold leading posts, their power is only *nominal.* That differs from China where women are not simply decorative additions to the political scene. They have advanced beyond the West with respect to political leadership; still, in other (unspecified) areas the position of Chinese women is backward. Only through unremitting political and ideological work can that be changed. The combination of advancement and backwardness in the changing role of women demonstrates the "unity of opposites." The position of women must be perceived from such a developmental perspective.

The fear of political reprisal that inhibits writers and publishers from producing anything has spread to all cultural fields, film included, she admitted of a subject few Chinese leaders would dare discuss at all. She cited T'ao Chu's "manipulations." A gnawing fear of criticism must have driven him to cut off the casts of characters shown at the beginning of certain unsavory films for which he knew he was responsible. When she learned he had done that, she ordered an investigation of his total involvement in the cinema, for the leaders did not want him or anyone to seize (from Mao and his coterie) the initiative in repressing public knowledge of the past.

She was dissatisfied with their working personnel (tiers and teams of officials nationwide) in several cultural fields. But their poor performance she always recognized as the result of insufficient political work on the part of the leaders themselves (continuing the Confucian tradition of leaders establishing models and setting standards for the people).

Publications in their nation are intolerably wanting, she admitted (apparently in response to my earlier observations that their recent Party-authorized histories grossly simplified the past, that even these were scarcely available in bookstores, and that faculties and students were barred from university libraries). She personally had criticized publishers for their reluctance to produce, she said. Premier Chou had also taken them to task. But the leaders know that publishers are terrified they will suffer for political mistakes (the fear of reprisal for publishing heterodoxy was unabated from imperial times).

The books she had decided I needed for my historical research were not yet available, she said. But she would persist in tracking down some books by Fan Wen-lan, a historian whom she trusted, and other works of modern history. She had dispatched some comrades to check out titles in secondhand bookstores. But, she remarked in amazement, even when Chairman Mao and Comrade Chiang Ch'ing authorize the old-book dealers to sell certain items, they still are reluctant to yield. (Sensing the depths of the people's fear, could she be surprised?) "Thus even I must spend time preparing what you need!" If she could not find what she wanted in the bookshops, she would give me her own copies, for she felt personally responsible for my study of history. Often she urges those around her to read some history and learn what they can from it.

Did I own a set of the *Twenty-four Dynastic Histories?* I did not, and explained that it was rare for an individual scholar in America to possess this mammoth collection. She challenged: how can you expect to be an historian when you don't own the tools of your trade?

Hardly arguable. But in America, I said, research libraries collect these basic works just to spare individual scholars the burden of private ownership. She looked puzzled for a moment and declared that she would provide me with my own set. She knew, she said, that I suspected not only renegades but also good Communists tampered with the written record of the past, or were afraid to confront the totality of history. Presenting the complete histories of the dynasties should dissolve that suspicion. She could not be certain how long it would take her now to track down a complete set. If her assistants failed, she would give me the set from her private library. I must appreciate her integrity, that of the Chairman and other leaders.

Since the Chairman and she could not manage to spend all the money they have earned from royalties (!), she remarked later upon the delivery of tall stacks of books in traditional binding, they purchased for me a complete set of the *Twenty-four Dynastic Histories*. She led the way to the table where we leafed through them. The edition was that of the tenth year of Kuang Hsu (1884). As soon as she located the *Draft History of the Ch'ing*, which, joined to the *Twenty-four Dynastic Histories*, would constitute the complete official record of the past, she would send it to me in America (as she did, not long after my return). To be sure, those histories are feudalistic, she said, but they must be read. It is imperative for all people — Chinese and foreigners — to study the past. Although these collections might be available in America, there they would be expensive. For that reason Premier Chou had purchased a set for the U.S. State Department. Although pertaining to the distant past, they are full of relevance for the present. Take, for example, the *History of the Later Han*, which includes the famous letter from Li Ku to Huang Ch'iung that Mao quoted to her in 1966.

Although she had taken the position that Chairman Mao and the people who work closely with him respect history and "never distort the past," I found precious little evidence of historical work in process. In her judgment what was the future of the study of the past?

In their country, she responded in her official tone, academic studies are conducted not only in the universities, but also in academies of science and by the masses. The archaeological excavations at Changsha demonstrated scientific work carried out by the masses. No matter who does the work, however high or low his status or educational background, it must always be undertaken from a proletarian standpoint. That rule applies to all intellectual pursuits — not only history, but also the classics, literature and art, and the opera, of course.

ii

As dawn approached Chiang Ch'ing summoned other gifts. Two men hauled in a huge wooden crate that they opened under her orders and commentary. On the top and sides were numerous tiny packets of dried and pulverized lotus stock (used medicinally since the T'ang Dynasty). Buried at the bottom, in wads of shredded wrapping paper, was a large clay pot, lidded and thinly glazed. The lotus stock, whose alkaloids were not to be ingested alone, she commented, resuming her medical pronouncements, should be brewed with water in the pot. So that I might survive political trials as well as she had (the result of knowing her, she implied), she carefully demonstrated how to empty one packet of the lotus preparation into 300 ccs of water and boil that continuously until it was reduced to 100 ccs. Drink immediately, she said, and urination will be enhanced.

Next to arrive was a complex seawater solution to be heated in the bamboo provided and sloshed through the mouth. "Good for the gums," she said. And last some dried white lilies whose curative powers she did not bother to explain. Foolishly, I speculated aloud about the border and the bafflement of foreign customs officials taking account of these mysterious potions from the heart of China.

"Then you should not take them!" Chiang Ch'ing responded with alarm (prompted by profound distaste for being subject to agents and investigation and for premature publicity). Sadly, she motioned them away, and returned to an easy subject, the state of her health. An imbalance in her blood count had been corrected by two years of acupuncture, which increased both the platelets and white blood cell count to normal. Besides sleeping pills she took no other medicine. Fluids and exercise are the best medicines, she reiterated.

It was four in the morning of August thirty-first when an aide whispered to me that Comrade Chiang Ch'ing had drawn her story to a close. Though I had anticipated it, the remark was jolting. I was about to be expelled from her private enclosure, its air heavy with jasmine, sandalwood, and judgments suspended.

Was I satisfied with her report? she asked.

Certainly I was, but at that moment also profoundly humbled, and feeling the sharp tug of home and the distance it would leave between us. Although I probably appeared to her to have been lost in the process of note-taking, I said, I had come to appreciate her not only as a unique revolutionary leader, but also as a teacher — *lao-shih*, literally, "old master scholar," a classical term laden with feudalism. What she had taught me, which was more than either of us could have sensed then, I would try to share abroad.

"You're the professor, no, I mean associate professor," she returned the flattery. She felt modest, she said, and uneasy about making final statements. As I turned to leave she announced once again that the American government's "forcible occupation" of Taiwan was the sole issue precluding full diplomatic relations.

Indeed! Now I would do a book on the history of the revolution mainly from her viewpoint, I replied. Her personal history largely as she presented it would be included.

My parting words met with an awkward silence whose rationale I quickly perceived — the perennial contradictions between self and society, individual and mass, the leaders and the led, private and public history, Chiang Ch'ing and Mao. Could there be any authority on the past apart from Chairman

Mao's? Could there be any biography besides his and a few others drawn from the frontier days in the 1930's? Was not her determination to commission her own story the most severe test of her independence as a leading comrade?

"Writing's your area of expertise," she broke the silence. "Mine is revolutionary leadership!"

On that we shook hands. I turned and left.

iii

In the minds of my Chinese companions (if not also in my own while among them) their ordered nation of millions of mutual observers and oral reporters was totally protective as long as one yielded to and moved with its hidden currents and overt systems. As far as I could tell, their knowledge of what lay beyond China was limited to Marxian mechanics — a bourgeois-imperialist grotesque — and of course that was frightening.

In the later stages of our Canton meetings Chiang Ch'ing's aides and mine had begun to show anxiety over what might befall my notes, photos, documents, and indeed myself once I crossed the Chinese border. Speaking on behalf of Chiang Ch'ing and other leading comrades, protocol representative T'ang Lung-ping warned that reporters, agents, or spies might have caught wind of our secret meetings. They could possibly seize me in Hong Kong and exploit my materials, distorting them for their own purposes. For safety, should I not leave everything with them and have it sent to me upon my return home?

Terrified at being separated, even temporarily, from the documents that would be my only means of carrying out my mission, I responded firmly, "No."

In the course of our next meeting Chiang Ch'ing casually resumed that issue. When Edgar Snow first interviewed Chairman Mao, she said, he left his notes temporarily in Chinese custody. Such notes as ours might contain errors or opaque passages which could be used disadvantageously by ignorant or hostile people.

Laughingly, I assured her that I was tough, ready to defend myself, and used to the world beyond. Our sense of risk was obviously not the same. And from the beginning our only common ground was trust.

Shen Jo-yun dropped by as I was packing up in the guest house the next day. She brought up the security issue of the day before and spoke with rules drawn from guerrilla warfare. I should dissimulate, she said, and arm myself in advance with remarks to throw off voracious Hong Kong reporters from the scent of my recent trail. Already protection had begun. The name "Comrade Chiang Ch'ing" had been dropped from our language, for the magical lady behind it, like the fox fairy of Chinese legend, had vanished. Only the prickly feeling of recent exposure to beauty and terror remained.

Shen, our companions, and I, more relaxed than we had been for days, rode in noisy cars through the vibrant and disordered street life of Canton. Our formal parting at the railway station precluded communications of mutual confidence and the rush of emotion. A young Yunnanese woman, who belonged to the Canton branch of the Friendship Association, was assigned to accompany me on the Canton–Hong Kong Express. When I sensed from a rambling conversation that she knew my mission, I shared with her wilted orchids from Chiang Ch'ing. As I glanced about at the few fellow travelers in the railway car, I suddenly recognized the faces of men who, without my realizing it until now, had shadowed my public movements for weeks.

At the border town of Shumchun I was delivered to the sleek and seasoned Mr. Lai of my arrival. A PRC agent who operated internationally, he said that he was several times the escort of Edgar Snow and "other foreign friends." Chinese customs waved us past. We crossed Lowu Bridge separately, by a ruse. A waiting limousine whisked us off to the quiet hotel in which I had first stayed. Muscular PRC agents clad in drab blue were stationed outside my room, at the elevator, and behind each massive pillar in the dining room. Our glances rarely crossed.

The next day my movements along avenues and alleys of Hong Kong, a setting so familiar but newly offensive in the unrepentant haggle and hassle of capitalism and colonialism, were guarded down to the moment of my delivery to TWA. My seat, Chiang Ch'ing had told me in advance, was secured by Premier Chou, who had bumped another passenger from a booked flight in order to delay my departure, as she had requested.

19.

◇ ◇ ◇

Eleventh Hour

Who controls the past controls the future;
who controls the present controls the past.
— George Orwell, 1984

Reflecting on her years as a young wife and uncelebrated comrade in Yenan, Chiang Ch'ing observed that sex is engaging in the first rounds, but what sustains interest in the long run is power.

Without her realizing it, perhaps, that candid judgment epitomized the formula of her extraordinary life: how the tortuous course of her girlhood led to marriage to a supreme leader, and how that marital constraint was finally eased by pursuing power in her own right. The status of leading comrade — attained by no other woman of her times — was won by a succession of personal struggles: teaching the Chairman not only to love her as a woman, but also to respect her as a political figure not to be monopolized by any one man; gaining a separate respect from his colleagues who resented her sometimes thwarting direct access to their common leader; making personal contact with the masses from whom rulers of any stripe could be so easily cut off; and not merely cleaving to revolutionary standards established by her elders, but creating standards of her own that would eventually change the nation's history.

Chiang Ch'ing's prediction of some future trends during our interviews was borne out by subsequent events. Numerous comrades who had "received a pounding" during the Cultural Revolution were rehabilitated. Teng Hsiao-p'ing, once a powerful Liu Shao-ch'i supporter, resurfaced in April 1973 as the prime though short-lived example of that redemptive trend. The model theater born of the fires of the Cultural Revolution survived, beginning gradually and fitfully, to project its stylized mythology of Communist history and a revolutionized present to the provincial stage. Cultural exchange continued to be risked, with the "sharper contradictions" occurring on the Chinese side, which meant that the leaders would continue to exercise the utmost caution against cultural contamination by "foreign things."

As disease and death eroded the founders' ranks, Chiang Ch'ing's interest expanded beyond the cultural arena to other internal and foreign affairs. Faced each day more rudely with the mortality of men, and of revolutionary ideas, the aging leaders exploited the record of the past with more blatant self-interest than ever. How would they as individuals, the Party they fostered, and the people whose lives they had transformed fare in the ultimate reckoning: the compilations of official histories?

i

From outside China Chiang Ch'ing remained a woman of mystery whose image flashed in and out of the public eye. Her individual will (or that of any other leader, save for Mao's under his own signature) was hardly discernible, though from her self-revelations emerge consistency of interest and patterns of operation.

Unlike Chairman Mao, whose political strategy combined with patriarchal mystique earned him the right to be perennially excused from ongoing routines of banquets, parades, and airport ceremonials, Chiang Ch'ing was obliged to appear at numerous state affairs. Her occasional absences, which typically stimulated foreign press reports of her disfavor or "fall," might have been due to prerogative, pique, political pressure, or poor health. Whatever the explanation, for several years she continued to maneuver behind the scenes and behind pseudonyms in the Party press. There is no reason to believe that she did not sustain an authority shared by few over the realm of ideology and culture.

China's national culture was never more popular and participatory than in the wake of the Cultural Revolution. At the same time, the performing arts, which include sports as well as stage and screen, were never more grandly guided by state organs. Never in the history of the world has the orchestration of ideas, images, and mass behavior been more forcefully arranged.

Fundamental to all great civilizations — Mayan, Greek, Roman, American — are public games, ranging from contests between lions and Christians to wrestling matches. Not until the middle twentieth century did the Chinese come to that realization, but then with a keen acumen.

Juvenal once quipped that the inhabitants of imperial Rome could be interested only in bread and circuses. In the year 2000 the people of Peking may be moved only by the prospect of "noodles and public games." Peking's Circus Maximus is the Workers' Stadium. From the time of ancient Rome, and of the ancient China that has survived to the near present, the rules against playing for death have changed. Displays of brutality toward criminals and toward wayward members of the masses — so feared and deplored by Chiang Ch'ing from childhood — have been banned from public scenes. The violence, murder, and ruthless competition that were legitimized in controlled spaces in most ancient and modern cultures have been ruled out of China's public games. In the revolutionized opera and ballet, the expression of violence is deliberately mock, even playful. Both theaters incorporate the *wu-shu*, martial arts, which have always been pure mimesis. Likewise, the sports arenas allow only simulated aggression. No man-to-man combat such as boxing or wrestling is officially fostered. The cockfights and cricket combats of the old days are proscribed. Individual sports and the dominance of men have given way to mass sports and the recruitment of women — including all-girl basketball teams. "Ping-Pong diplomacy" was not without its political points. However, "friendship first, competition second" remained the slogan the Chinese played by at home and on foreign soil.

Following the Cultural Revolution, the Party-sanctioned repertory of spectator sports proliferated, and Chiang Ch'ing occasionally presided at openings, often dramatically costumed in a Western dress that set her off from her pants-clad countrywomen. Seated conspicuously with her guests, who were diplomats from important nations, she emanated what I found so extraordinary about her: a regality expressed by perfect posture, facial animation, and exquisite timing.

These public appearances before the masses, and before television cameras that sometimes projected her to the world, were tangential to her real work: the continuing creation of a national drama that controlled the imagery and ideals of contemporary life. As the Cultural Revolution wound down in 1969 and 1970, her group, which had piloted that massive upheaval since 1966, was quietly disbanded. In 1971, a new Ministry of Culture was established under the State Council. Its director, Wu Te, was a man of whom Chiang Ch'ing spoke admiringly in our interviews. His concurrent service as mayor of Peking and chief of the Peking Municipal Party Committee, a combination of posts previously held by the disgraced P'eng Chen, indicated the centrality of Wu Te's new assignment.

Nineteen seventy-four, the tenth anniversary of the Peking Opera Festival at which Chiang Ch'ing made her political debut, opened with paeans to the model revolutionary theater, by now established as the leading cultural institution. Ch'u Lan (literally "First Wave"), a pseudonymous Party spokesman who promoted Chiang Ch'ing's cultural work,* proclaimed, "Revolutionary model theatrical works have directly created revolutionary public opinion for the Great Proletarian Cultural Revolution. They are a powerful ideological weapon for consolidating the dictatorship of the proletariat and preventing capitalist restoration." [1]

From this tenth anniversary to her fall, Chiang Ch'ing's personal sponsorship of the model theater was less in evidence. This was in keeping with the general denial of ideological or creative authorities other than Mao, and with the increasing appearance in Party journals of pseudonymous authors, each of whom appeared to serve the interests of one or several leaders. In typical hyperbole defiant of cultural translation, the new theater was termed "vivid historical scrolls . . . dazzling galleries displaying the heroic images of the proletariat." The latest addition to the repertory, *Azalea Mountain*, was lauded for showing Chairman Mao's line of military build-up in the 1920's and for denigrating the Right Opportunist line of Ch'en Tu-hsiu (a CCP founder) and the disgraceful political performance of Lin Piao (the first historical drama constructed to condemn Lin).

No one, Chinese or foreign, could fail to notice the slimness of the new repertory, expanded since the Cultural Revolution by one or two works only. This contrast to the richness and diversity of China's theatrical tradition begged explanation, which came defensively. Attacks upon the "scarcity" of cultural offerings are "an evil wind fanned by class enemies, an argument reflecting class struggle in literature and art," pronounced *Red Flag*, and added that the real issue is quality versus quantity. Rich reactionaries can afford to produce great quantities, but China's leaders have resolved never to envy the abundance of their stuff. Reactionary works must be shunned, scathingly criticized, and "dumped on to the garbage heap of history." [2] Quality in the arts was described metaphorically as "A waterdrop reflecting the sunlight." [3]

Still, in the name of dramatic virtue, "stinking weeds" could proliferate upon the stage. In 1973 local troupes had been encouraged nationwide to create socialist dramas that might win approval from the center and finally be canonized as a model theater. In that spirit Shansi province produced *Three Visits to Peach Mountain*, on the surface simply another opera. But its underlying messages aroused storms of indignation from Peking.

This overwrought reaction to alleged political implications in a local drama

---

* Quite possibly the writer who called himself Ch'u Lan was commissioned by Chiang Ch'ing to write exclusively on her behalf.

points up the necessity of deviousness in a society where criticism of leaders and their programs cannot be conducted openly by governing bodies or by the press. China's historic repression of criticism of its rulers is long-standing: punishments were harshest during autocratic phases of the empire. Although polemic attacks were prohibited, imaginative literature, particularly the historical drama, could be fashioned as a vehicle for dissent. The imperial tradition of punishing intellectual and political dissent was sustained by Mao Tse-tung's regime. In the early 1960's, Wu Han's cycle of plays about the righteous sixteenth-century official Hai Jui was noticed by Mao Tse-tung's defenders as an assault upon his dismissal of P'eng Te-huai, the famous general who criticized Mao's Great Leap Forward of the late 1950's. Although *Three Visits to Peach Mountain* was properly responsive to the Cultural Revolution's requirement that the drama exclusively highlight the history of the CCP's rise, its authors chose to set the opera at the time of the Great Leap Forward, a most inglorious moment in Mao's political history. To compound meanings, the events to which it referred obliquely were shown to occur in 1964, the eve of the Cultural Revolution, when Chiang Ch'ing was rising and Liu Shao-ch'i and his wife Wang Kuang-mei were about to be ruined.

Early in 1974 Ch'u Lan condemned this Shansi opera as a "counterrevolutionary" attempt to "reverse the verdict" against the bourgeois reactionary line. Through cunning allusion it glorified the policies implemented by Liu Shao-ch'i and Wang Kuang-mei in Hopeh province during the Socialist Education Campaign. Horses symbolized the rival masculine leaders and their policies. The "sick horse with brain illness," which was driven until it collapsed and died from exhaustion, represented Mao Tse-tung's Great Leap Forward. A huge red horse called Lao Liu (Good Old Liu), an allusion to the splendid horse Wang Kuang-mei personally donated to the Peach Garden Brigade in 1964, was heroic. The leading female character, Ch'iang Lan, was a composite of Wang Kuang-mei's allegedly negative attitudes: subscription to the doctrines of Confucius and Mencius and acceptance of the dying out of class struggle. The opera as a whole was charged with peddling the "theory of no conflict" and that of "people in the middle," in other words, with repudiating the class struggle ethos and the politically antithetical characters prevailing in Chiang Ch'ing's model works.[4]

Acceptable examples of post–Cultural Revolution theater were scant. Among these was *Half a Basket of Peanuts*, a playlet from Chekiang province, which was rewarded by being made into a color film shown all over the country, accompanied by ecstatic reviews. After numerous revisions this short drama about a student who used spare time to pick up peanuts left in the fields after a bumper harvest was still imperfect, acknowledged Party spokesmen. Nevertheless, the arguments of poor and lower-middle peasants showed how "philosophy had been liberated from the philosopher's lecture hall and textbooks were turned into sharp weapons in the hands of the masses." Its persuasive depiction of the two-line struggle (communism versus capitalism) in the countryside demonstrated how the universality of contradiction could be embodied in the particular, proving that "the big can be seen through the small." [5]

To preserve the illusion of Mao Tse-tung's singular authority in the arts as everywhere, and of consensual administration under his guidance, Chiang Ch'ing's personal role in these censorship campaigns was shielded from the public. Exposure of her initiative (displayed so unequivocally in our interviews) would have shown her authority as not only complementing the Chairman's, but possibly competing with it as well. Inexorably, evidence of personal ambition, an old-time misogynistic accusation against women of worldly interest, would heighten her vulnerability during future crises.

Less perilous ways of honoring debts were available. In July 1974, the tenth anniversary of the Peking Opera Festival, Chiang Ch'ing was extolled as an "expounder of Mao Tse-tung Thought,"[6] an honor previously reserved for Chou En-lai and Lin Piao. Throughout thousands of years of feudalism and hundreds of years of the bourgeoisie, Ch'u Lan claimed, in a vulgar Marxian mode, only a few works were handed down. By the time imperialism was reached, capitalism was declining, and "the stage became the platform of the modernist school, Fauvism, teddy-boy dance, striptease and other degenerate rubbish. . . . The works were numerous and varied but share the common characteristic of poisoning or lulling the minds of the people." [7]

Promoters of the model theater, the mysterious Ch'u Lan conspicuous among them, put China in the vanguard of world history — in the throes of creating a proletarian culture to supplant all feudal, imperialistic, and bourgeois culture. Echoing the current campaign against ancient philosophers, Ch'u Lan argued that the ethics of the old opera sprang from the "fanatical" doctrines of Confucius and Mencius: ruler over subject, father over son, husband over wife; the "five constant virtues" (benevolence, righteousness, propriety, wisdom, sincerity); the woman's "three degrees of dependence" (father before marriage, husband after marriage, son after decease of husband) and "four moral obligations" (good character, good manners, good appearance, good handiwork); "loyalty, filial piety, chastity, and righteousness," and loyalty, forebearance, benevolence, and love.

"We are not only good at destroying the old world but also at building a new one," proclaimed Ch'u Lan of China's "quality" achievement in culture. After ten years of effort "the proletariat" had produced seventeen model revolutionary stage productions. The basis of the new repertory was of course the eight model works conceived and produced by Chiang Ch'ing during the Cultural Revolution. Now those were supplemented by nine others: selections from *The Red*

Lantern, The Yellow River Piano Concerto, the modern revolutionary Peking operas *Song of Dragon River, The Red Detachment of Women* (originally a model revolutionary ballet), *Fighting on the Plains* (originally a film), and *Azalea Mountain;* the model revolutionary dance dramas, *Ode to I Mountain* and *Children of the Grasslands* (conceived in Yenan); and the revolutionary symphony created for *Taking Tiger Mountain by Strategy.* Creation was slow indeed, for at least five of the new works were portions of earlier ones or spinoffs from them.

Looking ahead to 1984 (with what irony?) Ch'u Lan resolved, "The next ten to twenty years, 'on swift mount, raising the whip, never leaving the saddle,' we shall redouble our effort and continue to compose new chapters for the history of proletarian literature and art." [8]

By the fall of 1975 the reconstructed Ministry of Culture was sanctioning events authorized by Chiang Ch'ing alone in the years when the name of her corporate authority was the Cultural Revolution Group of the Central Committee. Under the ministry's auspices another handful of films and dramas was released. All were straightforward celebrations of contemporary political actions, including the training of barefoot doctors and the production of torpedo boats and ocean vessels. Now more than ever actors and actresses, society's new heroic order, dominated National Day, October 10. Local communities nationwide performed balladry, storytelling, dialogues, and spoken dramas, genres mainly outlawed during the Cultural Revolution. The next March five literary and art journals that had been suspended a decade earlier reappeared on Peking newsstands. Though the genres and formats were familiar, their content was uniformly updated to celebrate proletarian supremacy cum late Maoism.

A most striking contribution to revolutionary history on stage was a ten-act play titled *The Long March,* produced by the General Political Department of the PLA. This was not only the first major spoken drama (free of song and dance) to appear under high auspices since the Cultural Revolution, but also the first acceptable rendition of this most memorable passage in CCP history. The plot was strictly political: a description of "the great victory of Chairman Mao's revolutionary line over Wang Ming's opportunist line and over Chang Kuo-t'ao's line of Right Deviationist Flightism and Splittism." [9] The earlier problem of representing the Chairman on stage was resolved by making his ideas omnipresent, leaving his body to the audience's imagination. (Was not that the very style of Mao's governing since his ideological renaissance in the mid-1960's?)

ii

Chiang Ch'ing had explained in our interview how cultural exchange maintains foreign relations in the superstructural sphere. And she knew that cultural exchanges were much riskier than the usual trade material. For the Chinese exposed their aggressively proletarian, morally naive, and artistically mixed culture to foreign judgment, if not ridicule, while imported "bourgeois" culture might stimulate a dangerous thirst for variety in China's guarded proletarian realm. In the minds of modernly educated Chinese people and the old connoisseurs were fresh memories of China's annual release of hundreds of films, plays, and books of considerable quality by any standard. Through the early 1960's they had also known the freedom to attend performances of ancient and foreign drama, music, and foreign films. Those relaxed policies ended abruptly at the onset of the Cultural Revolution. In the early 1970's could the slightest easing be chanced without piquing hunger for more cosmopolitan fare?

Two fascinating cases of foreign exchange central to Chiang Ch'ing's interests were Michelangelo Antonioni's film report of China and the Philadelphia Orchestra's visit to Peking. The official accounts of both events demonstrated perennial contradictions between China's flair for hospitality and quest for cultural purity, neither less ardent than in the imperial past.

In the spring of 1972 the Italian director Antonioni visited China as a state guest commissioned to make a film documentary for Chinese television, in recent years developing as a prime propaganda medium. He was ostensibly invited by television and radio authorities (media Chiang Ch'ing claimed to have controlled since the Cultural Revolution). His visit had its precedents in the 1930's, when other distinguished foreign filmmakers came to China, among them Eisenstein and Karmen of the Soviet Union and Joris Ivens of the Netherlands (filming again in China in the summer of 1972). Antonioni's film report demonstrated the truism that a subject always takes shape in the eye — or in this case the camera — of the beholder. The flaw of this four-hour film by the director of *Red Desert* and other languid exercises in cinematic naturalism was that it was unerringly Antonioni-esque, and thus a travesty of proletarian China. His unglossed presentation of daily realities contradicted the Party's projection of ideal images and governed motion. Antonioni's film — relaxed, unpretentious, listless, angry, and dreamy — was a stream of impressions available to any pedestrian on China's byways or in public places.

After the film was shown privately among the Chinese leaders and Antonioni had released substantial portions of it to foreign television (it was shown in January 1973 in America), a *People's Daily* commentator denounced it as a "downright fraud" designed to "slander and smear China." Neglecting Chinese-built oceangoing vessels in the Shanghai harbor, the film displayed only foreign freighters and little Chinese junks. The footage of Lin county, Shantung, the proud site of the Red Flag Canal, which was scarcely noticed, showed "a boring succession of shots of fragmented plots, lonely old people, exhausted draught animals and dilapidated houses." During a scene of people doing Taichi shadowboxing Antonioni claimed (falsely) that the leaders wanted to abolish that ancient tradition. Among his "grotesque" subjects were people sitting in teahouses, women with bound feet, people picking their noses and going to the toilet. These people are nostalgic for the past, Antonioni implied; actually they "deeply hate the 'past' when demons and monsters swept in a swirling dance for hundreds of years. . . . But the wheel of history cannot be turned back. Anyone who attempts to do so will be smashed by the wheel of history!" Photographing the Yangtze River Bridge at Nanking (symbol of industrial China), he "intentionally" showed it from bad angles, making it appear crooked and tottering. A shot of trousers hanging to dry below the bridge was an added mockery. Although he did not shoot a single scene from China's revolutionary theater, he ridiculed an aria, "Raise Your Head, Expand Your Chest," sung by the heroine of the revolutionary drama *Song of Dragon River*, by using it as background music for the sight of a swine shaking its head.[10]

Dismayed by Peking's panning, Antonioni responded calmly, "They just did not understand what my documentary meant. They were just incapable of viewing the enormous stage that is their country and fathoming what a score of actors and eight hundred million extras were saying in the most colossal and mysterious of dramas." [11]

In September 1973, a season of warming Sino-American relations, the Philadelphia Orchestra was invited to perform in Peking and Shanghai, though no moves were made to deliver Chinese music to America on an equal footing. The extremes of diplomacy and disenchantment occasioned by this visit epitomized China's paradoxical attitude toward delegates from the outer world: hospitality laced with endless toasts to "friendship" with foreigners on Chinese territory was followed by revulsion toward foreign culture right after the bearers left.

The official report of the visit of the Philadelphia Orchestra played up the fact that the orchestra hailed from the home of American independence and that it arrived under the baton of Eugene Ormandy, a man commendably advanced in age (seventy-three) and experience (in China's storybook vision of the West his snow-white hair made him look the part perfectly). In keeping with the general policy Chiang Ch'ing had described in our interviews, the four performances in Peking and two in Shanghai were arranged for the leaders, not the masses. The exclusive audience was composed of the chief American representatives in Peking and high Chinese officials of government and culture. Conspicuous among the Chinese were Li Te-lun, long the conductor of the Central Philharmonic Orchestra, and the stars of the revolutionary opera and ballet — all ardent followers of Chiang Ch'ing, the most prominent hostess.

The Philadelphia's selections were conservative, programmatic, and colorful. Among them were Beethoven's Fifth Symphony (appreciated for its martial "victory" theme), Brahms's First Symphony, Dvořak's *New World* Symphony, and Samuel Barber's Adagio for Strings. Chiang Ch'ing reportedly made a special request for Beethoven's Sixth, the *Pastorale*. Told that the score had not been brought along and that (unlike Chinese orchestras) they could not improvise, she simply dispatched a plane to Shanghai to fetch from archives the one copy that made it possible to play the *Pastorale* at the next Peking performance. The Party's official review lauded the *Pastorale*'s clear musical colorations, babbling brooks, bird songs, village dances, thunderstorms, and final absolution in sun-drenched fields. Could Beethoven's aural impressions of the Viennese countryside in the nineteenth century have awakened romantic socialist notions of China's countryside in the twentieth century?

As parting tokens the Americans played the *March of the Workers and Peasants* and Chiang Ch'ing's masterwork, the *Yellow River Piano Concerto*, with her protégé Yin Ch'eng-chung at the keyboard. Unaccompanied by Peking's Philharmonic, which kept silent during the visit, Yin also played his version of a typical American tune — "Home on the Range."

At the close of the third Peking concert Chiang Ch'ing presented Mr. Ormandy with a set of books from her private collection, saying that these were a century old and the only such set in existence. At the back of one volume were several pages of Chinese musical notation that Mr. Ormandy would be unable to decipher, she pointed out, adding that when she was a girl she and her friends always referred to Western musical notation as the "beansprout" style. "Having been separated several decades from the beansprouts," she remarked philosophically, "we have become coarser grain." [12]

Those musical hours were whiled away in the courteous realm of international diplomacy. The friendly facade vanished as soon as the guests were gone. The old pull of sinocentrism stiffened by a new proletarian righteousness impelled the leaders to redefine their antagonism toward foreigners and wage a class attack against their "bourgeois" music. Possibly the leaders' overt enthusiasm for Ormandy's offerings lulled anxious Chinese musicians trained earlier in foreign classicism into expecting that the recent severe prohibitions against listening to, playing, or teaching foreign music would be relaxed. This was mistaken.

Among socialist forefathers, the precedent for such cultural high-handedness was slight. Moscow's Proletcult of the early years of the revolution was never so absolute in its exclusions. Marx, we know, adored Shakespeare and Balzac, and Lenin loved Pushkin, Chernyshevsky, and Beethoven. But in the spring of 1974 Peking's leaders linked classical music to the rise of capitalism and impressionist and modern music to its decline — an explicit repudiation of the recently professed (by whom?) notion that music has no class nature. The sage Confucius, whose philosophy was disinterred the year before in order to be attacked, was accused of using music to elicit benevolent and harmonious feelings, thereby denying contradictions and class struggle. The Chorale in Beethoven's Ninth Symphony, which includes the lyrics "All mankind shall be as brothers," and "love to countless millions swelling, wafts one kiss to all the world," was charged by Ch'u Lan in another article with spreading "bourgeois humanitarian" ideas. The works of the "bourgeois impressionist" composer Debussy were "rife with decadent *fin de siècle* moods of despondency." [13]

Summed up bluntly, "The current tendency to idolize the foreign and revive the ancient in the realm of music is aimed in essence at negating the Great Proletarian Cultural Revolution, attempting to reverse the wheel of history, and reviving the practices of the sinister revisionist line in literature and art. This tendency stems ideologically from the theory of human nature." *

Certain people (unnamed) were accused by Ch'u Lan of blindly worshiping foreign bourgeois works and lowering their guard against cultural infiltration by imperialism and social imperialism. Not everything "foreign" was to be forsworn. But a class viewpoint must be used to analyze traditional Western music. People who "fawn on foreign things to the marrow of their bones" must be stopped. Assimilate critically, following the slogan "Make the past serve the present and foreign things serve China."

Chiang Ch'ing's musical hospitality seems to have backfired. Had she ordered Ch'u Lan's seething disavowal? Or had an enemy ordered it against her?

The New York Times music critic Harold Schonberg, who had accompanied the Philadelphia Orchestra to China, reported as candidly for the other side. Invited to play the august *Yellow River Piano Concerto*, the Americans nicknamed it the "yellow fever." The whirlwind virtuoso Yin Ch'eng-chung, despite his old-fashioned training in the capitals of communism, was neglectful of Mr. Ormandy's baton. The musical score was at best "movie music. It is a rehash of Rachmaninoff, Khachaturian, late Romanticism, bastardized Chinese music and Warner Brothers climaxes." [14]

So much for "making foreign things serve China."

---

* In his speech to the Yenan Forum Mao had said, ". . . there is only human nature in the concrete, no human nature in the abstract. In class society there is only human nature of a class character; there is no human nature above classes" (SW, 3: 90).

iii

The overwhelming question, one never far from Chiang Ch'ing's consciousness, was of her place in history. Had she served primarily as consort of a founder of a new order? Or was she a leader in her own right whose tenure in power would not expire with Mao's death? Or had she performed both roles with shifting emphases? The nature of her daily activities of the 1970's and her implication in philosophic debates raging in the press provide clues.

In the course of the Cultural Revolution Chiang Ch'ing had been promoted to the Politburo and had earned the title "national leader," yet her impact continued to be mainly among the leaders and among her own followers. Rarely was she visible or accessible to the world at large. On occasion she greeted foreign visitors, among them President Nixon,[15] Prime Minister Edward Heath of Britain, Archbishop Makarios of Cyprus, and a series of African dignitaries, but she did not grant them substantial interviews or expound upon national priorities, foreign affairs, or trade relations. Express authority in those vital areas continued to be monopolized by Chairman Mao, Premier Chou, First Vice-Premier Teng Hsiao-p'ing, and Foreign Minister Ch'iao Kuan-hua.

But as wife of the chief ("First Lady" be spared) Chiang Ch'ing played the major host to certain foreign counterparts on missions to China. Most dazzling was Imelda Marcos, wife of the president of the Philippines, stragetically positioned Asian nation with which China had tenuous relations. Imelda Marcos, a former beauty queen recognized internationally for her flawless appearance, concern with humanitarian affairs outside her own country, and zest for power, was received by Chiang Ch'ing in September 1974. Señora Marcos, who later admitted that she first feared that Chiang Ch'ing would live up to her reputation as a "radical ideologue," found her to be "soft-spoken, very feminine." Their common ground was "oriental womanhood," she said, and curiously equated that with being "open-minded."[16] In this post–Watergate era she reported Chiang Ch'ing's saying, "Nixon is a brave man," and crediting him for having initiated détente. "His virtues surely outdid whatever his liabilities were."[17]

Chiang Ch'ing entertained Señora Marcos in royal proletarian style by escorting her to the opera, to advanced factories, and to a very special hamlet in the outskirts of Tientsin called Hsiao-chin-chuang. Following the historical precedent for establishing progressive model communities,[18] Chiang Ch'ing had recently transformed this hamlet of nearly six hundred peasants, who constituted a production brigade, into a tiny utopia of proletarian culture. She showed her guest the simple room and bed she occupied while tutoring her peasant subjects in the continual production of proletarian poetry, fiction, song, dance, and opera. Among her goals was to make the social and political roles of the local women equal to men's.[19]

If the revolutionary ardor of these ordinary people turned actors in the daily drama of the present was sustained and broadened, they would become the makers of a new national history, one where "millions of heroes" exercised their "dictatorship of the proletariat." The Cultural Revolution had tried to demonstrate that the question of revolutionary succession was as pertinent at the mass level as at the top. Still, the well-propagandized model of Hsiao-chin-chuang could not belie the fact that the power to "create public opinion" about it or any other issue remained the preserve of the leading comrades. Otherwise how could the socialist dynasts who had accompanied Mao secure their place in history and hand down a clear pattern of governance?

Often she urged her comrades to study history, Chiang Ch'ing remarked several times during our interviews. But that must be done correctly, only under the guidance of the leading comrades. By the end of the third quarter of the twentieth century the writing of history had been removed from the domain of China's professional historians, most of whom previously worked with official sanction, and was made the exclusive privilege of the leaders. Their views were usually delivered in one of three ways: by Mao Tse-tung directly, or under the pseudonym of an important leader or group of leaders, or in the name of a newly discovered member of the masses whose work surely was ghost-guided from the top.

Why dynasties decline or fall after the founder dies is a question that obsessed Mao and drove him and leading contemporaries to study history in order to master the art of surviving periodic downturns of the historical cycle. During the 1970's the Party continued to recover the history of China, whose written record was the most abundant of all ancient civilizations, through Marxian dialectic.[20] The perspective was long, yet the motives were immediate. Lin Piao's crimes against the leaders and the people were "explained" by linking him to "retrogressive" Confucianism, while the Party was aligned with "progressive" Legalism, now recognized as a historical antecedent of communism.

Both Chinese Legalism and communism sought nearly absolute power for the ruler, and in each the ruler assumed the role of father, who treated the masses like children. They shared belief in the state as the sole determinant of right and wrong (to the exclusion of other secular, religious, or personal standards of morality). Social control was implemented through a strict system of rewards (fame and ease) and punishments (shame and pain), and through the institution of mutual espionage. Both systems promoted agriculture and the military, hence peasants and soldiers, over commerce and the merchant class.

During the vigorous campaign against him, Lin Piao was linked with Confucius, the fifth-century B.C. sage lionized by later dynasties and remembered as Legalism's chief adversary. Now he was attacked as the straw man of opposition to Mao's régime. The connection was hard to believe. For throughout Lin Piao's lifetime, which included some thirty-five years of Party-sponsored esteem, he had no reputation for teaching Confucian precepts (among them hierarchialism over egalitarianism and harmony over struggle) or of practicing them in his daily life. On the contrary, he was the archsymbol of armed struggle, an expert in guerrilla warfare, and a hero of the Liberation War. Chiang Ch'ing's attack on him in our interviews said nothing of his Confucianism, nor did any of the secret Party documents released soon afterward by the Party center. The Confucian connection was forged no earlier than 1973, two years after he allegedly attempted to murder his colleagues. In January he was accused not as an Ultra-Leftist (as Chiang Ch'ing called him), but as a rightist.[21] Thus his reported demise in Outer Mongolia was only the beginning. What remained was the onerous process of defacing his hallowed image in the minds of over eight hundred million people. There was recent precedent. When Mao's only other heir apparent, Liu Shao-ch'i, was disgraced six years earlier, hatred of the Soviet Union was so high that merely to call him "China's Khrushchev" damned him. Lin Piao had blundered later, when the leaders had begun to glance backward in order to surge forward in political time. Consequently, the authors of his purge linked him to Confucius.

Such high-handed manipulation of men and ideas, past and present, was quickly transformed into a broad popular movement to condemn Lin Piao, Confucius, and the "restorationist" values ascribed to each at his extreme of the historical continuum. Language shattering both idols, one feudal and presumably superseded, the other revolutionary and presumably unassailable, became ritualized in daily life. The formula was reportedly Mao's, and Chou En-lai was the public initiator.[22] Chiang Ch'ing appears to have been not only the major beneficiary, but also the manager of public opinion. Documents seized by Taiwan agents in China indicate that she led the distribution to key military units nationwide, all previously under Lin Piao's command, of evidence against him and arguments for compelling all who were once loyal to him to save themselves politically by denouncing him.[23] It has also been conjectured that Chiang Ch'ing was the person in charge of the Office of Criticism of Confucius and Lin Piao.

For long months, Lin Piao was reviled, along with Confucius and the philosopher Mencius. Among other accusations was that of male chauvinism. Though only Confucius and Mencius left literary evidence of this, all three were charged with opposing women's rise to power.[24]

As the posthumous persecution wore on, Chiang Ch'ing's reputation soared in the fall of 1974 and into the next spring, and so did those of empresses. Who could forget that throughout Chinese history becoming the imperial consort was the fastest feminine means for upward social mobility?

iv

In contemporary China signs of a changing verdict on women's right to political power have been subtle but pointed. Both material and literary remains of the past have been ransacked for present political interests. All Chinese museums feature calculated political exhibits. Visitors to the ancient northwest city of Sian have been guided routinely to the museum constructed around the site of Pan-p'o village, said to date back six thousand years to the Neolithic era. Discovered in 1953, it was excavated five years later and given renewed attention after the Cultural Revolution. The "primitive communist" society it displayed through material remains is described as matriarchal. Women controlled agriculture, which was fundamental to the economy, and men controlled hunting, which was peripheral. Children were raised by the mother and took her name, as indicated etymologically by the character *hsing*, whose two elements signify woman and birth. Despite China's patrilinear history, the word *hsing* is still used for "surname." Surviving as myth in revolutionary culture,[25] such matriarchal prehistory counterbalances, symbolically at least, "Confucian" history's exclusion of women from the conduct of ancestral rites in the home, from participating in public affairs, and from command over the state cult. If respect for matriarchy was to be revived, were not political reversals in the offing?

In his youth Mao Tse-tung idolized history's most colorful rebels and bandits, but in his old age he studied establishments, taking as his model the first Ch'in emperor, Shih Huang-ti, who lived in the third century B.C. and was China's most genuine Legalist ruler. For more than two millennia Confucian convention regarded him as a tyrant. That judgment was reversed in 1974, when numerous erudite and polemic studies of Ch'in Shih Huang-ti appeared under the pseudonym of Lo Ssu-ting (probably a ghost historian for Mao). Although Confucian wisdom held that this Legalist emperor, called the Unifier because he put an end to warlordism, was overly severe, Lo Ssu-ting argued that he had not been severe enough. Because he failed to exterminate all his reactionary enemies (only 460 Confucian scholars were buried alive), they finally rose up against him, undermined the rule of his successor, and ushered in the epic contests that were resolved by the founding of the Han dynasty. Though born a peasant, the Han founder Liu Pang came to represent the interests of the landlord past. But he also inherited Ch'in Shih Huang-ti's Legalist line, Lo Ssu-ting carefully pointed out.[26]

The Communist Party's piecemeal efforts to come to terms with the historical past, especially with the experience of Legalism, was not unreasonable. Like the Ch'in government, which mobilized its masses to construct great public works, most memorably the Great Wall, the Party has organized its masses for other defense works, including underground tunnels, and to rebed the great rivers, build bridges, and dredge canals. Both regimes condemned ghosts, magic, and spirits, and both disdained excessive "book learning." Stoping at nothing to control thought and the intelligentsia, Mao honored the Legalist precedent for "burning books and burying scholars." By reappraising Ch'in Shih Huang-ti through essays and archaeological digs [27] Mao implicitly raised the question of whether his own regime would be as short-lived as that of Ch'in Shih Huang-ti (fifteen years) or more enduring.

"The leaders never suppress or distort history," Chiang Ch'ing claimed during our conversations. Yet it was plain to see that they used it to political advantage. And she was equally compelled to attend to her place in history by making strategic reference to the past. During the same years that Ch'in Shih Huang-ti's negative image was being reversed, Confucian contempt for female rulers was being challenged. New Party-inspired scholarship showed that from the Early through the Later Han dynasties (206 B.C. to A.D. 220) at least six dowager empresses had attended court and had controlled some aspects of government. A few continued to rule after the emperor came of age, thus rendering him a figurehead.[28] In revolutionary revisionist accounts of the transition from the Ch'in dynasty to the Han, a commoner who became the Empress Lü was depicted admiringly as the vital connection. A guerrilla organizer in her youth, she fought at the side of the bandit Liu Pang against the Confucianists. After Liu Pang became emperor they married, and after her husband and son died, she became empress. During the eight years of her reign she staged a Legalist comeback against Confucian opposition.[29] Using her example, present historians expressed resolve to upgrade generally the record of women as actors in history.[30]

"When Wu Tse-t'ien became Empress, who would dare say 'men are superior and women are inferior'?" Lu Hsun once challenged.[31] For over twelve centuries the "usurper" Wu Tse-t'ien served the public as a fascinating subject of official and unofficial history, of tireless gossip, and eventually of modern dramas and film extravaganzas. Not until 1974 was her character vigorously praised by the rulers and her reign mined for Legalist precedent.

Born to a modest landlord family, Wu Tse-t'ien at age fourteen entered the palace of T'ai Tsung, second emperor of the T'ang dynasty, as a low-ranking concubine who soared to first place. He died and she retreated to a nunnery, remaining there until his son, Emperor Kao Tsung, recalled her. In recognition of her literary skills, he invited her to serve as a court official. Less than a year later he divorced his queen and married Wu Tse-t'ien. This action outraged his Confucian advisers, who favored the first wife, daughter of a famous aristocratic family, and despised Wu Tse-t'ien, who was of humbler origin. Calling her a "jealous" woman, they compared her to the most infamous concubines of popular legend. Infatuation with her would precipitate "national subjugation." "If Wu Tse-t'ien were made queen, the T'ang dynasty would perish," they predicted with classic Confucian misogyny.

Despite the dire forecasts, Wu Tse-t'ien eschewed the luxuries of palace life and employed Legalist methods to assist the emperor in rationalizing state affairs. During Kao Tsung's lifetime she was named Sage Queen. Throughout her nearly half-century of power, reactionaries attacked her relentlessly for being "tyrannical and frivolous" and for "meting out punishment according to whim." But in the eyes of her Communist (and Legalist-leaning) admirers, "she ruled the world with the handle of reward and punishment." To reform the government she favored plebeian landlords over the big landlords and the old aristocracy. She advanced new talent on the basis of merit proved through written examinations and contests in the martial arts. Land equalization among the peasants was included among her reforms. Her promotion of the less powerful and her introduction of Legalism into political, economic, ideological, and cultural life served to sharpen contradictions between the reactionary and the progressive classes.

After Kao Tsung died, the Sage Queen refused to retire. Die-hard Confucianists allied forces against her; she responded by raising 300,000 troops to march south against their rebel stronghold, which was crushed within fifty days. In the year 684 she ascended the throne as the self-styled Holy Empress, founder of the Chou dynasty, an interregnum in the T'ang. Of that extraordinary act of succession, a Party spokesman remarked, "The fact that a woman dared to ascend the throne was itself a forceful criticism of the doctrines of Confucius and Mencius."

The Communist authorities also counted among Wu Tse-t'ien's Legalist reforms her having raised the status of women (though the original Legalists were not known to be feminists). She initiated an examination system for women and permitted those who passed to enter the palace in groups of three and five to attend state banquets. Although this concession did not affect the conditions of rural or working women or otherwise alter the feudal system, "the appearance of women at state banquets was itself a forceful negation of the teaching that 'distinction between men and women is one of the big regulations of the state.' " For the first time in history women were appointed to the fourth and fifth ranks of the civil service. However, by the end of her second decade of rule the Holy Empress had yielded to luxury and to the wiles of the Buddhists who had long supported her against the Confucianists. Her Chou dynasty fell and the power of the Confucianists gradually was restored. The pertinence of such anecdotes about a spouse become ruler would be tested — after Mao.

V

"Better get your photos of water buffalo now because in five years they will be obsolete," a Chinese commented to an American visitor in the late fall of 1975.[32] Although farming was still the foundation of China's revolutionary state, during the 1970's increased energies were devoted to mechanizing agriculture and to stepping up industrialization, its progress having been slowed during the Cultural Revolution. In January 1975 Premier Chou arose for the last time from his sickbed to address the Fourth National People's Congress. There he announced the goals of "an independent and relatively comprehensive industrial and economic system by 1980," and "a powerful modern socialist society by the end of the century."

In the fall of 1975, when news of Chiang Ch'ing's model repertory was less featured than before, she turned to agriculture, where she had not been involved directly since land reform days, and then only obscurely. Since the Cultural Revolution the Tachai Brigade, located in arid Shansi province, was acclaimed nationally as the model of self-reliant and productive agriculture against all natural odds. In mid-September, at the opening of the much-publicized conference for the study of Tachai's agriculture, Teng Hsiao-p'ing and Chiang Ch'ing (unaccustomed to and perhaps uncomfortable at appearing on the same turf) addressed some thirty-seven hundred delegates. They spoke of the need to "strengthen the material foundations of the proletarian dictatorship" by sending no less than four million workers to new lands to develop irrigated cultivation.[33] Chiang Ch'ing rolled up her sleeves and joined Tachai's famous peasant leader Ch'en Yung-kuei, two years earlier elevated to the Politburo, in digging a canal under the gaze of Teng Hsiao-p'ing. Such breaking of the soil was consonant with the seasonal ritual of rulers ancient and modern.

Foreign affairs, which had been always managed by a handful of senior comrades trusted by the Chairman, seemed to have been beyond Chiang Ch'ing's (and most other women's) sphere of authority. The spring of 1975 showed signs of change. In March she delivered a rambling, provocative speech that considered the profound dilemmas of China's dealing with the outside world.[34] In foreign affairs she was an "outsider" who must "start from scratch," she began.

Only if we follow Chairman Mao's correct line shall we dare to struggle without fear of encirclement or threats . . . upholding the revolutionary principles amid great world disorder.

The ultimate aim of Marxism-Leninism and Mao Tse-tung Thought is the realization of Communism in the world. . . . For the present political period we propose, "States must be independent, nations must be liberated, and people must revolt."

Our foreign policy must concentrate on black friends, small friends, poor friends. They will be grateful to us. We may have no white friends, great friends, rich friends; but we are not isolated. It was on the insistence of the voices of the small friends that in the end we entered the United Nations, and, in consequence, have had the great powers come to our gates.

She went on to speak of Nixon's arrival at their gates (perhaps their greatest diplomatic coup in modern history) and more critically of Henry Kissinger, United States secretary of state. During his talks with the Chinese, he revealed that the United States intended to "abandon" the Asian area of the Pacific (was this clear to his countrymen?), a scheme the Chinese perceive as "one divides into two." She continued:

We believe that Kissinger cannot rid himself of his small bourgeois politician's mental categories. His fundamental ideas are limited by class interests. He is unable to understand all the contradictions arising from the complex international situation. Kissinger is like every other reactionary class politician in history. He is only an adventurer and a defeatist. . . . The United States must return to the real world. It cannot go on interfering with other countries' sovereignty and interests. Kissinger spoke of the balance of power, which shows that he recognizes the existence of contradictions but does not seek to resolve them under new conditions, in struggle. On the contrary, he wants to avoid antagonism. His is an ostrich policy.

Knowing how to control the behavior of Chinese nationals abroad and to shield them from corruption by foreign values was no less a problem for the Communists than it was for the Confucians, admitted Chiang Ch'ing. It was risky to dispatch high-level foreign missions during episodes of ideological purification at home, most recently the campaign to criticize Confucius and Lin Piao. Certainly, men on foreign service could not be expected to behave exactly like people at home. "You cannot paste up a poster against your ambassador or against the [Chinese] foreign minister in the middle of New York or Paris!"

"Abroad one is not under the orders of the prince," she quoted an ancient proverb, in order to cast it aside. Foreign service officers abroad should not slip away from the Party's unified leadership, particularly not in the present age of quick communications, cables, telephones, and air travel. Some embassies, consulates, and trade offices cabled and phoned every other day, but talked only about business, devoting no attention to political affairs (meaning ideological calisthenics within the mission). Their intoxication with work outstripped even that of the bourgeois diplomats and monopoly capitalists. Some embassies in eastern and central Africa had done no political study for half a year and had not sent a single report about study or on the current campaign. "Chairman Mao has told them, 'Ask for more instructions. Report more often. Don't be afraid of inconveniences. If necessary, return to Peking more often.' "

The Party center must keep a "firm grip" on all Chinese embassies, she continued Legalistically, and mutual responsibility must be enforced. Chinese serving abroad must never appear factional; they must show perfect unity to the outside world. Nor should one assume that an ambassador performing united front work by attending capitalist banquets exposes himself to bourgeois corruption. "Since contact must be made with people of all sorts, revolutionary vigilance must always be high."

As a stateswoman she had come a long way.

vi

Near the end of 1975 a series of deaths quickened the pace of revolutionary succession. In December Chiang Ch'ing's old comrade, security chief K'ang Sheng died. Eight days into the new year Chou En-lai, her subtle champion over the years, succumbed to cancer. Teng Hsiao-p'ing, who had been resurrected after a decade of obloquy to conduct domestic and foreign affairs on behalf of the dying Premier, presided over a week of funeral ceremonies. Proudly projected by Chinese satellite to the world, the ceremonies offered rare and intimate glimpses of the survivors as they quietly realigned themselves in the hierarchy. Chou En-lai's widow, Teng Ying-ch'ao, her grieving face ashen and puffy, embraced and kissed the old and a few young leading comrades as they stepped up to pay final respects. Chiang Ch'ing's face was somber as she strode up in battle array. She and Teng grasped each other momentarily, at arm's distance.

Holding sway over the Premier's funeral turned out to be Teng Hsiao-p'ing's final political act under Mao's regime. That spring saw heightened celebration of Chiang Ch'ing's cultural standard, which the more pragmatic and less culturally oriented Teng Hsiao-p'ing had so shamelessly disparaged. In the March 1976 issue of *Red Flag* Chiang Ch'ing's pseudonymous spokesman, Ch'u Lan, argued, "Agreement or disagreement with the revolutionary model theater is the central point in the struggle of the two classes and the two lines in literature and art." [35] The second national campaign against the "unrepentant capitalist roader" Teng Hsiao-p'ing was well under way.

This time, though, the masses took a separate stand. At the time of the traditional Ch'ing Ming festival to honor the dead, which in 1976 fell on April 5, nearly one hundred thousand people gathered at the square in front of the Gate of Heavenly Peace. A demonstration in honor of the memory of Chou En-lai became an episode of physical violence, verbal slander, cars set aflame, and more than a thousand arrests. In its press the Party center pronounced these unscheduled demonstrations "counterrevolutionary": against Chairman Mao and the leading comrades of the Central Committee. Some wreaths laid to honor Chou had borne slogans opposing women rulers, including Indira Gandhi and Empress Dowager Tz'u Hsi. But most stinging was the poem barbed with topical references to ancient history: "We spill our blood in memory of the hero [Chou En-lai?]; raising our brows, we unsheathe our swords. China is no longer the China of yore, and the people are no longer wrapped in sheer ignorance; gone for good is Ch'in Shih Huang-ti's feudal society. We believe in Marxism-Leninism, to hell with those scholars who emasculate Marxism-Leninism." [36]

"They [the protest poets] accuse the proletarian dictatorship of being the feudalism of Ch'in Shih Huang-ti," an editorial in *People's Daily* countered on April 20. The real question was one of judging whether Ch'in Shih Huang-ti was a good or evil ruler. The protesters were acting on the old schoolboy cliché that Ch'in Shih Huang-ti was a "tyrant." Had they forgotten — or rejected — Mao Tse-tung's revolutionary admiration for the founding Ch'in emperor precisely because he had had no qualms about demolishing aged patriarchs and their antique morals?

The Chinese have long thought that dynastic decadence and imminent change of rule are signaled by natural disasters.* In April 1976 a huge meteor, the largest ever recovered and preserved by man, fell on Kirin province. In July and August three earthquakes shook North China. Great sections of Peking were devastated, and the nearby industrial city of Tangshan was largely ruined. As the earth shook spasmodically for weeks, millions of people abandoned their homes and camped in the streets. Foreign seismologists estimated that some 665,000 persons had died and over 775,000 had been injured, which made it the second largest earthquake in history.

As remarkable as the human loss and metaphysical implications of these natural disasters was the cheerful treatment accorded by China's press. No dead were mourned and the number of casualties was never published. Like revolutionary art, revolutionary reportage stressed the bright side, urging people to

---

* During Yao Wen-yuan's purge for collusion to seize power, he was charged with having ordered the following nineteenth-century poem incorporated in an article: "When the earth turns, it augurs the emergence of a new land; / When the heavens whirl, it gives rise to an everlasting new heavenly dynasty." (PR 48 [Nov. 26, 1976]: 17.)

"turn grief into strength." Chiang Ch'ing's model village, Hsiao-chin-chuang, located near the hard-hit city of Tientsin, kept its revolutionary song-and-dance routine going full tilt throughout the quakes.[37] Newspapers ordered the rest of the nation to follow its model.

Despite the revolutionary romanticism, the relief work organized by Vice-Chairman Hua Kuo-feng was superb. "Resist the earthquake and overcome disaster" was the slogan of the day. A *People's Daily* editorial of August 1 was titled "Man Can Be Victorious Over Heaven." (Was that not a shake of the fist at old-time fatalism?)

During the tension of the July earthquakes Chu Te, co-founder with Mao of the Red Army, expired in his ninetieth year. Mao Tse-tung himself had not been seen by the masses since May Day 1971, though over the last quarter century the media had made him the most familiar ruler in Chinese history. On September 9 he died.

Memorial services went on for eight days. In the televised ceremonies, which were shorter than those for Chou En-lai, Chiang Ch'ing appeared drawn, her head bound in a black scarf. She had inscribed on her wreath, "Your student and comrade-in-arms, Chiang Ch'ing." [38] (The last leader to style himself Mao's student was Lin Piao.) In contrast to Teng Ying-ch'ao at Chou En-lai's funeral, Chiang Ch'ing did not play the widow — her sense of a separate leadership was long-standing. On September 18 the entire nation stood in silent tribute for three minutes, while planes, ships, and factories were still. Behind the scenes, rivals for the mantle disputed over what to do with Mao's remains. Soon it was announced that the Chairman's body would be enshrined in a crystal sarcophagus around which a mausoleum would be raised.

The person who emerged as China's new strong man was tall and burly Hua Kuo-feng, who became visible in highest Party circles after Teng Hsiao-p'ing's downfall. Little was known about this simple-mannered Shansi native. After 1955 he had built his career in Mao's Hunan province and after 1971 had served under Chou En-lai in Peking. Less than a month after Mao died, Hua accomplished what no one had predicted: he became Party Chairman, at the same time retaining his positions as Premier, head of the Military Affairs Commission, Hunan Party secretary, and minister of public security. Although he displayed neither the personal doctrine and new jargon usual in a traditional ruler, nor the sophistication or worldliness of a modern national leader, he had proved one thing: he was a master politician if of unknown stripe.

By the middle of October Hua had won control over the press. From that followed the power to impose upon the public an account of his accession to the Chairmanship on October 7. He lost no time in immobilizing rivals (forestalling a coup — or countercoup?). On October 16, the national media made an announcement more stunning than the death of Mao Tse-tung: the arrest of the "Gang of Four." These persons, who had been Mao's closest disciples, were Wang Hung-wen, Yao Wen-yuan, Chiang Ch'ing, and Chang Ch'un-ch'iao. Chiang Ch'ing was depicted as the ringleader.

When she was arrested on October 6, she must have been appalled at her change of state. Her own Party had condemned her as a "counterrevolutionary," when thirty-some years earlier the KMT had locked her up as a "Communist revolutionary." But then hardly anyone knew her face.

On October 16 masses of people surged through the streets of Shanghai, much as they had during the Cultural Revolution, when the present victims held sway. From the twenty-first through the twenty-fourth millions paraded through Peking's broad avenues, to the accompaniment of official broadcasts, fireworks, cymbals, and drums. Mao Tse-tung's famous guard, Army 8341, maintained order over the marchers as they chanted against this "anti-Party clique" in brutal jargon passed down from above.*

Hua's sudden rise to supreme power grew out of the unsettled situation that had prevailed since the Cultural Revolution. Observation of legal procedure had been almost nil. Major decisions had been made by fiat, often with no clear indication of the agency. For example, in the spring of 1976 the appointment of Hua both as vice-chairman of the Party and as Premier had been made by the "Party center," which could mean the Central Committee, but could also have meant Mao, or the group of leaders who monopolize power.

Was Hua a self-made Party Chairman? Was he elected by his comrades of the Central Committee after Mao died? Or had Mao actually designated him successor before he died? How did he, of all men, acquire the power and authority to arrest the seemingly inviolable Chiang Ch'ing?

What actually happened may never be known. Set forth to the Chinese public were judiciously selected parts of Mao Tse-tung's notes and conversations, to be accepted as the authoritative account of his handing over "the mandate of heaven" in his dying days. On October 25, the day after Hua was proclaimed Party Chairman before a million people, *People's Daily*, *Red Flag*, and *Liberation Army Daily* printed the official, however fragile and questionable, justification, to be reinforced with other "quotations" in the following weeks and months. On April 30, 1976 (though the context may only have been his taking charge of the current campaign against Teng Hsiao-p'ing), Mao Tse-tung had written to him in his own handwriting: "With you in charge, I'm at ease."

The vilification of Hua's obvious competitors for Mao's position came

---

* Only a month earlier this same Army 8341 had announced to *People's Daily* that Chairman Mao had sent them to see Chiang Ch'ing's model theater (CNA 1060 [Nov. 13, 1976]: 3).

quickly. The first feature was a "history" of Mao's presumed displeasure with Chiang Ch'ing and her circle. Concurrently wall posters and other media defamed them with fantastic illustrations of their "towering crimes."

On the day Hua Kuo-feng became Chairman the following account of his predecessor's words against the Gang of Four was published. On July 17, 1974, Chairman Mao had warned: "You'd better be careful; don't let yourselves become a small faction of four." On December 24, "Don't form factions. Those who do so will fall." In November and December of that year, as preparations were being made for convening the Fourth National People's Congress, he said, "Chiang Ch'ing has wild ambitions. She wants Wang Hung-wen to be chairman of the Standing Committee of the National People's Congress and herself to be chairman of the Party Central Committee." * At a Politbureau meeting of May 3, 1975, the Chairman reiterated the "three do's and three don'ts": "Practice Marxism-Leninism and not revisionism; unite and don't split; be open and aboveboard, and don't intrigue anymore; why do you keep doing it?" He threatened, "If this is not settled in the first half of this year, it should be settled in the second half; if not this year, then next year; if not next year, then the year after." [39]

Once control of the media was wrested from Mao's most strident defenders, the abusive language Chiang Ch'ing had used against her enemies over the years was hurled back at her. The verbal weapons borrowed from Lu Hsun backfired. "Ruthlessly beat the dog in the water," her enemies repeated as they vowed to fight the Gang of Four to the finish. Their claims to have been the standard-bearers of the much-exploited Lu Hsun were mocked.

When had Chiang Ch'ing's long-harbored doubts that the Chinese were a "civilized people" been more justified? And when had success in Mao's monumental struggle to revolutionize consciousness been less in evidence? Posters disgorged a vile residue from the past.† Some demanded "Cut Chiang Ch'ing into 10,000 pieces" — an ancient Chinese torture. Others called for Yao Wen-yuan to be "deep-fried," or portrayed him with his head pierced by a pen — a reference to Lu Hsun's using his pen like a dagger. Still others showed the four with their tongues lolling out and blood spraying from their mouths. [40]

As unrestrained by reason and reality were radio reports and articles accusing Chiang Ch'ing of crimes linked conventionally to her sex and the bourgeoisie. She was called promiscuous and a prostitute (without evidence, though many of her male comrades — openly and with political impunity — had their share

---

* On December 20, 1974, I had sent Chiang Ch'ing a long letter, inviting her to clarify certain points in her report of 1972, and from her position as a national leader to comment on subsequent Chinese and foreign developments. For the first time no answer was forthcoming. In January Ho Li-liang and Huang Hua, who had been in Peking, increased their pressure upon me to write Chairman Mao's history rather than hers, as noted in the Prologue.

† See the second picture section.

of wives and lovers). She had nagged Mao (who was praised for ragging her). She kept up a poker game for several hours when summoned to Mao's bedside four days before he died. A Hunan provincial broadcast quoted her admission that she had wanted to become another Empress Lü or Wu Tse-t'ien, but allowed that although her class was more progressive than theirs, she was less able, for they won over confederates (which of China's bureaucrats and generals could she count on?). Her habit of borrowing from libraries books on ancient history as well as those on empresses proved her ambition to become an empress in her own right (who blamed Mao for attempting to secure his rule by reading and referring to history?). As Mao lay dying, someone allegedly heard her say, "The man must abdicate and let the woman take over. A woman too can be the monarch. Even under communism, there can still be an empress." [41]

To prove that Hua had saved the nation from a self-made empress, the new Party authorities continued to quote Mao advantageously: "Chairman Mao, before he died, in all seriousness told Comrade Hua Kuo-feng the story of Liu Pang, who, just before his death, perceived that Empress Lü and others in her clan were conspiring to betray the nation and usurp power. Comrade Hua Kuo-feng kept Chairman Mao's words in mind and lived up to his earnest expectations." [42] Chiang Ch'ing was reported disapprovingly to have masterminded the refurbishing of empresses' images over the last two years, and to have characterized Empress Lü as a Legalist. [43] A poster showed her poring over books about Wu Tse-t'ien, the empress whom popular legend held to be not only ambitious but also promiscuous. [44]

Was this sudden onrush of filth deserved by Comrade Chiang Ch'ing? What did it mean to say that she was a "capitalist roader" and a "typical representative of the bourgeoisie inside the Party"? Or was this merely the start of another exercise in political invective of the sort thrown at Mao Tse-tung's comrades who had fallen earlier, most memorably Liu Shao-ch'i, Lin Piao, and Teng Hsiao-p'ing?

After Chiang Ch'ing's arrest, illustrations of her unproletarian behavior were legion in the press. Tachai Brigade reported of a visit by her in September 1976: "This anti-Party woman who bragged that she was 'the standard-bearer of the revolution in literature and art' came to Tachai with everything bar the kitchen sink, including a truckload of motion picture reels, and spent every night enjoying imported obscene films. Going up a hill only several hundred meters away, she rode a horse for a while and then changed to a limousine with dozens of people in attendance. She wanted her picture taken everywhere she went, which cost some 3,000 yuan." The only reason she appeared at the conference to study Tachai's agriculture the year before was to extend her personal control over it. [45]

How would groups and individuals who had been intimately connected with her over the years manage her demise? There was the example of Hsiao-chin-chuang, her personal stronghold in the countryside. She was still powerful on Army Day, August 1, 1976, when the press had advised the military to follow Hsiao-chin-chuang's experience by setting up political night schools, reading rooms, and propaganda teams. Prominent among the imitators was Fang-hua-lien, the army troop Chiang Ch'ing had showered with letters and other personal favors.[46] A week after Hua's accession to power, the peasants of Hsiao-chin-chuang expressed their allegiance to him in the most stereotypic terms.[47] Not until the end of November did they succeed in turning against their fallen mistress Chiang Ch'ing. This "rotten egg," as they called her, had claimed egoistically that Hsiao-chin-chuang "belonged" to her and the Party center. On frequent trips there she flaunted the airs of an empress. At nightfall, she had all the livestock penned up so that their noise would not disturb her slumber.[48]

Similar reports of Chiang Ch'ing's imperious demands for absolute quiet while she slept (usually through the morning hours) issued from the Summer Palace, where planes had been prohibited from landing at the nearby airport, and from Hainan Island, where cars nearly a mile away were forced to turn off their engines. When she resided at her Canton villa (where we had met) river traffic had to be blocked off and shipbuilding suspended. All the leaves of trees lining the roadway leading to the Canton orchid garden were dusted in advance of her coming.[49]

Less ludicrous than the bad class implications of her neurasthenia were malicious renderings of her personal history. Our interviews had led me to believe that the one thing she feared the most was investigation of her acting career in the 1930's. A prominent article exposed "counterrevolutionary" evidence of her involvement in plays and films (*Sai Chin-hua* and *Blood on Wolf Mountain* were cited) built upon the national defense theme associated with Wang Ming and relatively sympathetic to the KMT.[50]

Other charges having less to do with idiosyncrasies of manner and vagaries of personal history would be more serious in the long run, for they were integral to Mao Tse-tung's ethos and the nation's history. She and her supporters were said to have abused principles and persecuted the people. The Gang of Four had tampered with Mao Tse-tung's thought and had muddled people's thinking concerning the relationships between knowledge and practice, matter and consciousness, the leaders and the masses, the relations of production and the productive forces, the superstructure and the economic base, politics and vocational work, revolution and production, democracy and centralism, and freedom and discipline. In simpler language, "They confused right and wrong theories and damaged both revolution and production. Waving the banner of

Marxism-Leninism, they sabotaged Chairman Mao's revolutionary line and policies and pushed an ultra-right counterrevolutionary revisionist line." [51]

Feelings of perpetual persecution and of the hopelessness of doing anything right were voiced, under guidance from the top, by the people of Tachai: "This bunch of scoundrels let metaphysics spread unchecked and put idealism in vogue, causing people to be always in the wrong, no matter what work they did and how they worked. They made you suffer in one way or another because it was all wrong to do something or not to do anything, so that nothing could be achieved. They hated to the marrow all those who went all out for building socialism." [52]

The day of Hua Kuo-feng's ascendancy Peking Mayor Wu Te reported of the Gang of Four to the millions thronging the square at the Gate of Heavenly Peace: "They worshiped things foreign, fawned on foreigners, and maintained illicit foreign relations, engaging in flagrant activities of capitulationism and national betrayal." [53] The statement was repeated in the press, with more specific charges about Chiang Ch'ing's having been a "traitor." According to editorials, broadcasts, and rumor, in 1972 or 1973 Mao had become infuriated at Chiang Ch'ing on account of the interviews she had granted me without first having obtained either his permission or that of the Central Committee (though certainly she had Chou En-lai's sanction and Wang Tung-hsing's assistance). Allegedly, he blamed her for betraying Party and state secrets and for trying to build a cult of her own personality. Some time after that Mao was said to have stopped living with her. That was followed by his reputed warnings in July 1974 against her forming a faction of four. [54]

Early in October 1976 Hua Kuo-feng reportedly told a meeting of the Politburo how the interviews had provoked the Chairman's wrath and had adversely affected his health beginning in the fall of 1975, [55] when descriptions of the Chairman's outrage first appeared internationally. According to accounts, Chiang Ch'ing was so demanding that Mao dropped her the following note: "I am already eighty years old. Even so you bother me by saying various things. Why don't you have sympathy? I envy Chou En-lai and his wife [married, amicably, it seemed, for fifty years]."

When Hua forced her to return some of Mao's documents she was charged with having taken—and altered—shortly after he died,* she allegedly tele-

---

* The role of Wang Tung-hsing in this matter was crucial. Besides heading Mao's guard, Army 8341, which had also protected Chiang Ch'ing until Wang joined in turning against her, he directed the Central Committee's general office, where many of Mao's papers were kept. Shortly after Mao died, Chiang Ch'ing allegedly went to that office and prevailed upon a secretary to yield certain documents to her. He complied but reported the incident to Wang Tung-hsing, who told Hua. When Hua persuaded her to return them, he said that two had been tampered with and counted this as evidence of her planning to take over the government (*The Washington Post*, October 29, 1976).

phoned him, shouting, "You want to throw me out when Chairman Mao's remains have not yet turned cold! Is this the way to show your gratitude for the kindness rendered to you by Chairman Mao, who promoted you?" He replied, "I will never forget Chairman Mao's kindness. . . . As to throwing you out, I have no such intention. You live peacefully in your own house, and no one will dare to drive you out." [56]

On December 7 *People's Daily* printed in a special box on the front page a previously undisclosed quotation by the late Chairman. Dated March 21, 1974, it read: "It's better not to see each other. You have not carried out what I've been telling you for many years; what's the good of seeing each other any more. You have books by Marx and Lenin and you have my books; you stubbornly refused to study them." [57]

Who could tell whether Hua Kuo-feng and his men were writing history or rewriting it?

Inevitably, the purge of four senior officials who had enjoyed a far longer association with Mao than had Hua was merely the beginning. Behaving in a Stalinesque manner by making mass arrests and meting out harsh punishments might have provoked a resistance movement or a civil war; thus Hua proceeded cautiously. Among the hundreds who had known Chiang Ch'ing personally and the untold numbers who had built careers upon her works, a reign of inner terror had begun. Who now would speak for the clusters of superstructural stars who had pledged loyalty to her, and who had believed sincerely that she represented, as the official press had confirmed, the wish of Chairman Mao?

Around the time Chiang Ch'ing was taken into custody, a few of her major followers were arrested. Among them were Yü Hui-yung, minister of culture; Chuang Tse-tung, table tennis champion and chairman of the Committee for Physical Education and Sports; Chih Ch'ün, chairman of Tsinghua's revolutionary committee; Hsieh Ch'ing-i, the female vice-chairman of the revolutionary committee of Tsinghua University. By the end of November Ch'iao Kuan-hua, the urbane foreign minister who had vociferously promoted Mao Tse-tung's China at the United Nations and elsewhere since 1971, was dismissed and replaced by Huang Hua. Both Ch'iao Kuan-hua and his wife, Chang Han-chih, also a diplomat, were publicly accused of having had "opportunist" relations with Chiang Ch'ing.*

To preserve order within a cultural world so thoroughly dominated by the losers, the successors did not immediately criticize and ban Chiang Ch'ing's model repertory. To temporize, it was said to have been prepared "under the

Such reports, whose validity remains to be established, should be compared with Chiang Ch'ing's frequent statements to me about the Chairman's matchless calligraphy (who *could* forge it?) and the criminality of distorting his words or using them to wrong purposes.

* Also reported under arrest was Mao Yüan-hsin, Chairman Mao's favorite nephew, then deputy commissar of the Shenyang Military Region. Nothing was said about the fate of Li Na and Li Min.

direct care of Chairman Mao" [58] (details of his responsibility were not provided). Naturally Chiang Ch'ing's involvement (not detailed either) was denounced summarily. Soon the China Peking Opera Troupe, which had created *The Red Lantern*, duly slandered the Gang of Four: "Their crimes are so multitudinous that they should die a thousand deaths. . . . They took possession of literature and theater and created evil public opinion. They were the evil lords of literature and the theater." [59]

As Chiang Ch'ing must have realized, the high-handedness with which she exercised film censorship on and off over a quarter century had engendered widespread resentment. Few would dare to express it until a succeeding authority had made them safe by condemning her. After eight nonproductive years (including movie versions of operas and ballets), a few stiff and didactic films were released in 1974. Among the best promoted nationally and abroad was *Breaking with Old Ideas*, about the implementation of Cultural Revolution principles. Theatrical variations on Chiang Ch'ing's established themes had begun to appear locally. But after half a century of revolutionary progress, China's cultural fare was still paltry. The resolve to encourage individual initiative in cultural innovation could not be made so long as Chiang Ch'ing was at large. Within days of her arrest films produced before the Cultural Revolution and banned in its course were shown to a select public and that was taken as a sign of change. Of course, the nation's extremely conservative program of radical arts had been monitored in the name of Mao. Soon after he died, though, Chiang Ch'ing and her team exclusively were blamed for a "fascist dictatorship over literary and art circles." [60] Would China, like Russia after the death of Stalin, experience a Thaw?

The years of Lin Piao's demise, Chou En-lai's death, and Mao's slow deterioration were Chiang Ch'ing's eleventh hour. How could she manage to pull herself through the impending succession crisis? Hua Kuo-feng outmaneuvered her when Mao died, and by the end of the year sent her to political damnation. On December 25, 1976, he labeled the Gang of Four as "ultra-rightists" and "counterrevolutionary revisionists," who for years had pretended to be leftists and revolutionaries. Their challenge to the Party he implied was the eleventh struggle between the two lines. The central task he set for the country in 1977 was "to deepen the great mass movement to expose and criticize the Gang of Four." [61]

vii

China may be unique in the world in the extent to which historical allusion and the art of indirection reveal meanings in the colossal drama of the nation's

478 ◇ Eleventh Hour

political life. How could any public not perceive attacks on the nation's female lead, a woman of imperious character, vaunting ambitions, and the highest connections, as anything but an indirect assault on the dynastic founder, who used to fancy himself another Ch'in Shih Huang-ti? In the weeks after his death his successors had insinuated into the historical record a destructive element in Chiang Ch'ing's and Mao's relationship. Was there not contrary evidence that could slip through the iron cage of opinion imposed by the new regime?

In Mao's letter to Chiang Ch'ing of July 1966 he had speculated that after his death anti-Communist rightists might use some of his words to gain power; yet their power would not last long because the leftists would perform a "nationwide exercise."

Ten years later Mao sent Chiang Ch'ing another message in the form of a poem. She circulated it among her supporters while he was still alive, as if it were his last testament.[62]

"You have been wronged," he told her. "Today we are separating into two worlds. May each keep his peace. These few words may be my last message to you. Human life is limited, but revolution knows no bounds. In the struggle of the past ten years I have tried to reach the peak of revolution, but I was not successful. But you could reach the top. If you fail, you will plunge into a fathomless abyss. Your body will shatter. Your bones will break."

Terms
Personalities
Abbreviations
Chapter Notes
Index

Terms

CCP
Chinese Communist Party.

Chung-nan-hai
Since 1949 the leaders' residence within the precinct of the old imperial palace in Peking.

Cultural Revolution
Mao's mounting of a nationwide attack against rivals and revisionism, which crested during 1966–1968. In general a promotion of class struggle in all fields, giving priority to cultural and ideological transformation.

Cultural Revolution Group
Formed in May 1966 to supplant the first such group of February under P'eng Chen. Headed by Ch'en Po-ta with Chiang Ch'ing as deputy leader, this pilot group's other most active members included K'ang Sheng, Chang Ch'un-ch'iao, and Yao Wen-yuan.

December Ninth Movement
Nationwide student movement of 1935, sparked at Peking University, against Kuomintang acquiescence in Japanese imperialism.

Democratic Centralism
Developed by Lenin, this concept is the PRC's basic organizational and dialectical principle: expression of popular views is "democratic," while obedience to national authority shows "centralism"; the ideas of the masses are sent upward, while general policy set by the leaders is transmitted downward.

Four Villains
Borrowed from Lu Hsun, Chiang Ch'ing's sobriquet for Yang Han-sheng, Chou Yang, Hsia Yen, and T'ien Han.

Gang of Four
Hua Kuo-feng's sobriquet for Wang Hung-wen, Chang Ch'un-ch'iao, Chiang Ch'ing, and Yao Wen-yuan, whom he purged in October 1976.

Great Leap Forward
Mao's programmed acceleration of agricultural and industrial development through mass mobilization, including formation of the communes, from 1958 to 1960, in actuality an economic setback.

Hundred Flowers Campaign
Brief era of relative cultural freedom in 1957, followed by a rectification campaign against nonconformist intellectuals.

KMT
The Kuomintang, the ruling party of the Nationalist government led by Chiang Kai-shek until his death in 1975.

Left leagues
Urban organizations of artists and professionals centered in Shanghai, most serving also as Communist front organizations in the early 1930's.

Liberation
The founding of the People's Republic of China in 1949, and, generally, the previous Communist takeover of areas controlled by the KMT and warlords.

Long March
Yearlong trek starting in October 1934 of the Red forces from Kiangsi in the southeast to Shensi in the northwest.

May Fourth Movement
A cultural and nationalist revolution of unprecedented diversity centering at Peking University in 1919 and spreading to other urban centers.

May Sixteenth Clique
As of late 1967, a splinter of the May Sixteenth Group initiated by Chiang Ch'ing. Its Ultra-Leftism contradicted her group's original principles.

May Sixteenth Group
Chiang Ch'ing's faction originating with her manifesto of that date in 1966.

Militia
Local defense units trained and equipped by the PLA but responsible to local party organizations. Generally oriented toward Chiang Ch'ing's Cultural Revolution Group, they gained in importance, especially after 1973.

Mukden Incident
Japan's invasion of Manchuria on September 18, 1931.

Newborn Things
Socialist institutions "taking class struggle as the key link." Among those generated during the Cultural Revolution: radical educational egalitarianism; the downward transfer of masses of students to the countryside; the creation of model advanced units in all fields; worker and peasant control of scientific, technical, and cultural affairs; the barefoot doctor movement; revolutionary committees; and the model revolutionary theater.

PLA
People's Liberation Army, a comprehensive term for the PRC military.

PRC
People's Republic of China.

Rectification campaigns
Periodic movements to reform the thought of political personnel in accordance with Mao Tse-tung's line: 1942–1944 and 1957–1958 were the most important.

Red Guards
General term for the millions of young people who wore red armbands, carried red books, and formed numerous organizations in response to Mao's call for support in the summer of 1966.

Resistance War
Waged against Japan from 1937 to 1945.

Revisionism
Chinese exhibition of bourgeois and capitalist traits thought to prevail in the Soviet Union.

Revolutionary committees
New forms of government at provincial and lower levels inspired by Mao and guided by the Cultural Revolution Group from late 1967, commissioned to stabilize power under the new order.

Revolutionary rebels
Generally nonstudent, working-class activists during the Cultural Revolution.

Socialist Education Campaign
A call in the early 1960's for renewal of proletarian class struggle, emulation of the PLA, and cultivation of revolutionary successors; the start of the Cultural Revolution.

Struggle between the Two Lines
Periodic class struggle between the proletarian revolutionary line defined by Mao and that of his opposition, variously denounced as bourgeois, reactionary, revisionist, capitalist roader, right deviationist, etc. Specifically, ten contests between Mao and his rivals.

Tenth Plenum
The CCP Central Committee meeting of September 1962 during which Mao reaffirmed his commitment to collective economy and ideological purity and called for renewed class struggle.

Thought reform
Political reeducation of wayward individuals through programmed criticism and humiliation and reconstruction of political beliefs and personality.

T'ien-an-men
The Gate of Heavenly Peace of the old imperial palace in Peking, facing a huge square where the masses have demonstrated throughout the modern era.

Ultra-Left
The advocacy by some groups during the Cultural Revolution of physical violence over verbal struggle, a priority that Mao's defenders later disavowed.

United Front
Cooperation between opposing classes and political parties against external threats such as Japanese imperialism.

White Terror
The Communists' name for the threatening political climate in the cities held by the KMT during the Nanking Decade, 1927–1937.

Work teams
Groups of officials dispatched by Liu Shao-ch'i and his wife, Wang Kuang-mei, to counteract Mao's offensive of the early Cultural Revolution.

Yang-pan hsi
Revolutionary "model theater," originally a repertory of eight works authorized by Chiang Ch'ing during the Cultural Revolution.

Yenan
The Communists' capital in northern Shensi from 1937 to 1947; the "Yenan Spirit" evokes the revolutionary purity of early days.

Personalities

Chang Ch'un-ch'iao
From the early 1950's active in the government of Shanghai, including its cultural affairs. Long a collaborator with Yao Wen-yuan in ideological journalism. An aggressive and voluble deputy chief of the Cultural Revolution Group from 1966, and close to Chiang Ch'ing thereafter. A vice-premier and major Shanghai Party and propaganda leader at the time he was purged as a member of the Gang of Four.

Chang Keng
Noted drama instructor, critic, and Party leader in the Shanghai underground, the Lu Hsun Academy in Yenan, and the PRC. Unfavorably remembered for personal and political reasons by Chiang Ch'ing, who settled scores against him during the Cultural Revolution.

Chang Ying
Deputy director of propaganda and Chiang Ch'ing's principal confidante during my visit.

Ch'en I
Red Army veteran, mayor of Shanghai in the early 1950's, and foreign minister in the early 1960's.

Ch'en Ming-hsien ("Lao Ch'en")
One of my guides from the Friendship Association.

Ch'en Po-ta
A prolific writer on Marxism who won Mao's trust in the late 1930's, when he was Mao's political secretary in Yenan and at intervals during the 1950's. After heading the Cultural Revolution Group in 1966 and 1967, he was repudiated on the charge of Ultra-Leftism.

Ch'en Yun
Labor organizer for the CCP in the mid-1920's. After training in Moscow, he headed the Party's Organization Department in Yenan in the late 1930's and thus processed Chiang Ch'ing's arrival there.

Ch'i Pen-yü
Editor-in-chief of the Party journal *Red Flag*, who joined the Cultural Revolution Group in 1966 and was removed two years later.

Ch'iao Kuan-hua
European-educated foreign affairs specialist who led Chinese delegations to the United Nations in 1950 and frequently after 1971. Appointed foreign minister in 1975, then dismissed the next year for affiliation with the Gang of Four.

Ch'ien Hao-liang
An actor who committed himself to Chiang Ch'ing; the star of the revolutionary opera *The Red Lantern.* Known throughout China as Hao-liang.

Chou En-lai
Trained in France and the Soviet Union, from the 1930's Chou was one of the three or four most powerful figures in the Communist movement, and the CCP leader best known among world statesmen. Although at various times a Red Army leader, foreign minister, Premier, and Party vice-chairman, he was never a theorist in his own right but was an extraordinary negotiator and skillful manager of changing communities of leaders. He died in January 1976.

Chou Yang
Literary theorist attached to the underground CCP organization in Shanghai, where he advocated the slogan "National Defense Literature" against Lu Hsun's slogan (see Lu Hsun). A major cultural and propaganda authority from the Yenan era to the mid-1960's, he was the symbol of literary and artistic orthodoxy as defined by Mao. His failure to propagate Chiang Ch'ing's proletarian standard and her bitter personal memories of the 1930's caused her to purge him as one of the Four Villains.

Chu Te
Commander-in-chief of the Red Army from 1927, and veteran of all major episodes in the rise of Chinese communism. Until his death in 1976 he was a highly placed though politically inactive representative of the Party founders' generation.

Ch'ü Ch'iu-pai
Moscow-educated writer, Marxian theoretician, and urban CCP leader. The Party's second secretary general (1927–1928). Executed by the Nationalists in 1935.

Ho Tzu-chen
Mao's third wife, from 1930 to 1937.

Hsia Yen
Prolific left-wing dramatist, filmmaker, and film historian who flourished from the 1930's through the early 1960's. As one of Chiang Ch'ing's Four Villains, he was felled during the Cultural Revolution.

Hsien Hsing-hai
Composer of modern and revolutionary music, including the *Yellow River Cantata,* which was created in Yenan and revised under Chiang Ch'ing's aegis during the Cultural Revolution.

Hsu Erh-wei
With Shen Jo-yun, Chiang Ch'ing's major woman interpreter during my visit.

Hsu Hsiang-ch'ien
Vice-chairman of the Military Affairs Commission appointed chief of the Cultural Revolution Group organized within the PLA in January 1967 and thus close to Chiang Ch'ing. Promoted to the Politburo the same year.

Hu Ch'iao-mu
Historian and propagandist who became one of Mao's political secretaries in Yenan after 1937. His *Thirty Years of the Chinese Communist Party* (1951) sold millions and appeared on the required reading list of intellectuals undergoing thought reform. Under Chiang Ch'ing's initiative he campaigned against the critic Yü P'ing-po's "liberal" interpretation of *Dream of the Red Chamber*.

Hua Kuo-feng
Replaced Chou En-lai as Premier in April 1976. After Mao's death he assumed the titles of Party Chairman and chairman of the Military Affairs Commission and made his first order of business the purge of the Gang of Four.

Huang Hua
Student leader of the December Ninth Movement; afterward interpreter for Edgar Snow. In 1971 he was appointed chief delegate to the United Nations and after Mao died in 1976, he was named foreign minister, replacing Ch'iao Kuan-hua.

Jao Shu-shih
Military leader and political commissar from the 1930's. In the early 1950's he headed the East China Bureau and held other top posts in that region, where he also resisted Chiang Ch'ing's intrusions. He and Kao Kang, the head of the Northeast Bureau, were purged in March 1955 for treating their "separate kingdoms" as "private property."

Jen Pi-shih
Soviet-trained member of the Communist Youth League who was elected to the Central Committee in 1927. He was among the top half-dozen Party leaders during the Liberation War.

K'ang K'o-ch'ing
The famous woman warrior of the Long March, who was Chu Te's fourth and final wife. Also a leader of the women's movement from the 1930's on.

K'ang Sheng
Like Chiang Ch'ing, born in Chu-ch'eng, Shantung province. His training in intelligence and security in Moscow won him authority over public security in China, sustained to the end of his life in 1975. A man of broad culture, he served as Chiang Ch'ing's confidant from Yenan days and joined her in the Cultural Revolution Group.

Kao Kang
A key figure in northern Shensi and Yenan after the middle 1930's. From 1949 he was secretary of the Northeast Bureau, which included Manchuria, as well as chairman of the State Planning Commission and a vice-chairman of the Central People's Government Council. Among the charges Mao laid against him and Jao Shu-shih was that of trying to set up an "anti-Party alliance." During his trial Kao Kang committed suicide.

K'o Ch'ing-shih
After 1955, mayor of Shanghai and Chiang Ch'ing's early supporter in the promotion of contemporary and proletarian drama. He died, presumably of an illness, at the start of the Cultural Revolution in 1965.

Lan P'ing
Name used by Chiang Ch'ing in films.

Li Chin
Chiang Ch'ing's original name.

Li Ching-ch'uan
Peasant organizer and Long March veteran who came to dominate Szechwan, serving as chief of the Southwest Bureau. In 1967 he and another Szechwanese, Teng Hsiao-p'ing, were both demoted for associating with Liu Shao-ch'i and the "capitalist roaders."

Li Fu-ch'un
After the Long March, appointed chairman of the Shen-Kan-Ning Regional Party Committee. Although attacked during the Cultural Revolution for having opposed Mao's Great Leap Forward, he was pardoned in 1967 and made a standing member of the Politburo, from which he was dropped two years later. In 1923 he married Ts'ai Ch'ang, the senior leader of the women's movement over the last half-century.

Li Min
Daughter born to Ho Tzu-chen and Mao in 1936 or 1937. Later Chiang Ch'ing adopted her.

Li Na
Daughter born to Chiang Ch'ing and Mao around 1940.

Li Ta-chang
Szechwanese radical who facilitated Chiang Ch'ing's joining of the CCP in 1933.

Li Te-lun
Conductor of the Central Philharmonic Orchestra in Peking before and throughout the Cultural Revolution, during which he learned to direct Chiang Ch'ing's model music.

Li Yun-ho
A name taken by Chiang Ch'ing in adolescence and used on the stage.

Liao Mo-sha
Struggling writer and member of the League of Left-Wing Dramatists in the 1930's. After Liberation, he was appointed director of the United Front Department of the Peking Municipal Party Committee. With Wu Han and Teng T'o he wrote the satirical and politically sacrilegious "Three Family Village," for which they were punished early in the Cultural Revolution.

Lin Piao
Military hero of the Long March, the liberation of Manchuria, and the Korean War. In 1966 he fell heir to Liu Shao-ch'i's title, "Chairman Mao's closest comrade-in-arms," and invited Chiang Ch'ing to wage cultural revolution within the army. Named Mao's successor in 1969, he died in September 1971, after an alleged attempt to murder Mao, Chiang Ch'ing, and other leading comrades who stood between him and immediate accession to supreme power.

Liu Shao-ch'i
In his youth a radical labor organizer, he was an underground Party leader in the North during the Resistance War and a respected ideologue in Yenan of the 1940's. He served as chief of state from 1959 and was Mao's designated successor from 1961 until his purge, along with scores of associates, in 1966 for a suddenly disclosed lifetime of Soviet-style revisionism.

Lo Jui-ch'ing
Long March veteran, minister of public security in the 1950's, and after 1959, PLA chief of staff. He fell from power in December 1965 for contradicting Mao.

Lu Hsun
China's most distinguished modern essayist, short-story writer, and literary historian. He established for his generation and those following a model of left-wing opposition to authoritarian regimes. The Cultural Revolution appreciated his mid-1930's slogan "People's Literature for National Revolutionary War" because of its implication of proletarian class struggle in the arts.

Lu Ting-i
Propagandist for the Red Army, and after 1950 director of the Party's Propaganda Bureau, which controlled the nation's educational and cultural institutions. In 1966 he was accused of being an anti-Party rightist and revisionist. Chiang Ch'ing and her collaborators assumed his vast powers.

Mao An-ch'ing
Mao's second son by Yang K'ai-hui, born about 1921 in Changsha.

Mao An-ying
Mao's first son by Yang K'ai-hui, born about 1920. Educated in the Soviet Union, he worked on a Shansi commune after his return to China in 1948, then entered a Party school. He was killed in Korea on October 25, 1950.

Mao Tse-min
Mao's youngest brother, who worked with him and Liu Shao-ch'i in Hunanese labor organizations in the early 1920's. A Long March veteran, he was arrested and executed by General Sheng Shih-ts'ai of Sinkiang in 1943.

Mao Tse-t'an
Mao's younger brother, also a labor organizer and Long Marcher; killed in action in 1935.

Nieh Erh
A composer of Western-style music who first flourished in Shanghai, where he wrote for films. In the Yenan era, he provided the lyrics for the *Yellow River Cantata*, the Chinese national anthem, and other songs against imperialism and feudalism.

P'an Han-nien
Comintern representative to the CCP who was vice-mayor of Shanghai under Ch'en I from 1949 to 1955. Six years later he was expelled from the Party and imprisoned.

P'eng Chen
Since the mid-1930's a chief Communist leader in North China. From the mid-1950's through the mid-1960's, he was dominant in the National People's Congress and the Peking Municipal Party Committee, serving also as mayor of Peking. Because of his authorship of the February Outline, which blunted the Cultural Revolution's ideological offensive, he was demoted, and his powers were assumed by Chiang Ch'ing's Cultural Revolution Group.

P'eng Te-huai
A long and distinguished military career with the CCP led to his appointment as national defense minister in 1954. He served until 1959, when he lost Mao's favor for say-

ing of the Great Leap Forward: "Putting politics in command is no substitute for economic principles."

Sai Chin-hua
Extraordinary courtesan who was embroiled in the international politics of the Boxer era. Chiang Ch'ing despised her, though eventually she too was charged with "illicit foreign relations" and "national betrayal."

Shen Jo-yun
One of Chiang Ch'ing's female interpreters and our go-between.

T'ang Lung-ping
A vice-chief of protocol at the time of my visit to China, present at most of my meetings with Chiang Ch'ing.

T'ao Chu
Highly positioned during the Resistance War and the Liberation War, and in the early 1950's, the leading Party figure in South China. He became chief of the Central South Bureau in 1962. Subsequently he vied with Chiang Ch'ing for national cultural authority and ideological supremacy. He lost, to be thoroughly discredited by her in 1966.

Teng Hsiao-p'ing
A French- and Soviet-educated member of the founders' generation of Chinese communism, he served as political commissar for the Red Army through the 1940's. In 1955, the year he led the purge of Kao Kang and Jao Shu-shih, he was elected to the Politburo and elevated to its Standing Committee the next year. As secretary general of the Party in the early 1960's, he was involved in making China's case the Sino-Soviet dispute. Red Guards named him Liu Shao-ch'i's chief collaborator. In April 1973 his good name was restored when he became deputy premier and stood in for Chou En-lai until the latter's death in January 1976, after which he was once more disgraced.

Teng Ying-ch'ao
In her midteens a leader of the May Fourth Movement and early member of the CCP. Chou En-lai's wife since 1923. She and Ts'ai Ch'ang, wife of Li Fu-ch'un, guided the women's movement from the time of the Party's founding in 1921 through the next half century. After the deaths of Chou and Mao, she was given the honorific post of deputy chairman of the Standing Committee of the Fourth National People's Congress.

T'ien Han
Distinguished modern dramatist who knew but failed to promote Chiang Ch'ing in her early Shanghai days. One of the Four Villains, he was victimized during the Cultural Revolution.

Ting Ling
China's most famous woman revolutionary writer, whose intellectual and moral independence made her creative life impossible under the Communist regime.

Ts'ao Hsueh-ch'in
Author of the eighteenth-century novel *Dream of the Red Chamber*.

T'ung Hsiang-ling
Actor and early follower of Chiang Ch'ing who earned a starring role in the revolutionary opera *Taking Tiger Mountain by Strategy*.

Wang Hung-wen
In the mid-1960's a politically precocious Shanghai textile worker whom the Cultural Revolution Group aided in seizing power from that city's political establishment. Appointed to the Central Committee in 1969, four years later he was named vice-chairman of the Party and member of the Politburo Standing Committee. Thus, around age forty, he stood as the symbol of the younger generation's prospects of succeeding the aging founders. Purged as one of the Gang of Four after Mao died.

Wang Kuang-mei
Wife of Liu Shao-ch'i, defender of his policies, and like him a casualty of the Cultural Revolution.

Wang Li
In the 1960's an editor of *Red Flag* and a member of the Peking Municipal Party Committee. He turned against Mayor P'eng Chen and his "Black Gang" on the eve of the Cultural Revolution, thus winning a position in the Cultural Revolution Group.

Wang Ming
Leader of the Twenty-eight Bolsheviks who were trained in Moscow in the 1920's. From 1931 to 1935, they governed a Shanghai-based Communist regime rivaling Mao's rural command. After returning to China from Moscow in 1937 Wang Ming implemented the United Front strategy. Mao deplored Wang Ming's "blind worship of foreign [Marxian] dogma," which had little chance of success in China. By 1942 their ideological opposition had hardened into a memorable case of the "struggle between the two lines." At the onset of Sino-Soviet strain in 1956, he returned to Moscow, where he railed against Mao's regime until his death in 1974.

Wang Tung-hsing
Chief bodyguard for Mao and his family from the 1930's, thus Chiang Ch'ing's comrade since Yenan days. Through closeness with Mao an expert in military strategy and history. In 1967 replaced Yang Shang-k'un, who had been purged, as director of the General Office of the Central Committee, and hence was controller of Mao's personal papers and central Party documents. Since the Cultural Revolution headed Army Unit 8341, the "palace guard system" committed to defending Mao and the cultural revolutionaries from coups d'etat and fostering urban militia. Member of the Politburo since 1973. After Mao died, he sided with Hua Kuo-feng and betrayed Chiang Ch'ing by arresting her and her circle and defaming them publicly from the Gate of Heavenly Peace.

Wu Han
Historian, journalist, and dramatist associated with the China Democratic League. With Teng T'o and Liao Mo-sha he wrote the satirical column "Three Family Village." He was also the author of a cycle of historical plays about the Ming official Hai Jui, which Chiang Ch'ing first noticed as allegory slanderous of Mao's regime. Felled during the Cultural Revolution.

Wu Te
Replaced P'eng Chen as Peking mayor in 1966, at which time he assumed other central Party government and military posts. Elected to the Politburo. Largely responsible for quelling spontaneous demonstrations that constituted the T'ien-an-men incident of April 1976. Six months later he turned the leadership and the masses against Chiang Ch'ing, who had supported his general and cultural authority since 1966. In early 1977 he was disgraced, presumably for former ties to Chiang Ch'ing and the cultural revolutionaries.

Yang Han-sheng
In the 1930's author of short stories, plays, and screen scenarios, and a leader in the League of Left-Wing Writers. In 1964 he was attacked as one of the Four Villains for failure to espouse Chiang Ch'ing's new school of class culture.

Yang K'ai-hui
Mao's second wife, daughter of Yang Ch'ang-chi, Mao's revered liberal teacher at Changsha. A liberated young woman, she was twenty-five at the time of her marriage to Mao in 1920. Three sons and ten years later, the Nationalists arrested her for refusing to repudiate Mao or the CCP, and executed her and other members of Mao's family.

Yang Shang-k'un
One of Wang Ming's Twenty-eight Bolsheviks. Soon after Liberation he became director of the General Office of the Central Committee and thwarted Chiang Ch'ing's early rise in that central governing organ. Removed from that post in 1967.

Yao Wen-yuan ·
Literary critic and Marxian ideologue from Shanghai, who served Mao's regime with vigor from the early Cultural Revolution until his purge as one of the Gang of Four in 1976. During the same period he served Chiang Ch'ing personally, casting her ideas into polemic offensives in the Party's major press organs.

Yin Ch'eng-chung
A Moscow-trained virtuoso pianist who found his calling in performing the *Yellow River Piano Concerto*, the model work composed under Chiang Ch'ing's supervision.

Yü Shih-lien
My principal guide from the Friendship Association in Peking.

Abbreviations

CB	*Current Background* (mimeographed; U.S. Consulate General, Hong Kong)
CF	*China Forum, The* (Shanghai)
CL	*Chinese Literature* (Peking)
CNA	*China News Analysis* (Hong Kong)
CQ	*China Quarterly, The* (London)
ECMM	*Extracts from China Mainland Magazines* (mimeographed; U.S. Consulate General, Hong Kong)
HC	*Hung-ch'i* (Red flag; Peking)
HCPP	*Hung-ch'i p'iao-p'iao* (The red flag waves; Peking)
JMJP	*Jen-min jih-pao* (People's Daily; Peking)
JPRS	*Miscellany of Mao Tse-tung Thought 1949–1968*, Parts 1 and 2. Joint Publications Research Service (Arlington, Va.), selections from translation of *Mao Tse-tung ssu-hsiang wan-shui* [Long Live Mao Tse-tung Thought], 1967, 1969 (mimeographed)
KMJP	*Kuang-ming jih-pao* (Enlightenment daily; Peking)
NCNA	New China News Agency (*Hsinhua*; Peking)
PR	*Peking Review* (Peking)
SCMM	*Survey of China Mainland Magazines* (mimeographed; U.S. Consulate General, Hong Kong); later SPRCM
SCMP	*Survey of the China Mainland Press* (mimeographed; U.S. Consulate General, Hong Kong); later SPRCP
SCMPS	Supplement to the *Survey of the China Mainland Press*
Speeches by Chiang Ch'ing	*Chiang Ch'ing kuan-yü wen-hua ta ko-ming ti yen-chiang chi* [Speeches on the Great Cultural Revolution by Chiang Ch'ing] (Macao, 1971)
SPRCM	*Selections from People's Republic of China Magazines* (mimeographed; U.S. Consulate General, Hong Kong)
SPRCP	*Survey of People's Republic of China Press* (mimeographed; U.S. Consulate General, Hong Kong)
SW	*Selected Works of Mao Tse-tung.* 4 vols. (Peking, vols. 1–3, 1965; vol. 4, 1961)

Chapter Notes

1. Encounter

1. With Robert Rinden, *The Red Flag Waves: A Guide to the "Hung-ch'i p'iao-p'iao" Collection* (Berkeley, 1968).
2. CQ 31 (July–September 1967): 128–147.
3. Many of these tales were brought together by Chung Hua-min (pseud.) and Arthur C. Miller in *Madame Mao: A Profile of Chiang Ch'ing* (Hong Kong: Union Research Institute, 1968). The authors warned that the truth of the tales could not be verified.
4. An abbreviated version of that speech appeared in PR 23 (June 2, 1967): 10–16.
5. Nym Wales's superb profiles of Ts'ai Ch'ang, Teng Ying-ch'ao, K'ang K'o-ch'ing, and others appear in *Red Dust* (Stanford, 1952), which has been reissued as Book I of Helen Foster Snow (Nym Wales), *The Chinese Communists: Sketches and Autobiographies of the Old Guard*, 2 vols. (Westport, Conn., 1972). Chiang Ch'ing surely knew of Nym Wales, yet she did not discuss her, perhaps because Nym Wales's interviews with women revolutionaries antedated Chiang Ch'ing's marriage to Mao.

2. Escape from Childhood

1. Dogs and wolves are recurring themes not only in Chiang Ch'ing's life, but also in the art with which she was associated. Literature of the 1930's often alluded to the Japanese invaders as "wolves." Chiang Ch'ing played a starring role in the film *Blood on Wolf Mountain* (1936), which was based on Shen Fu's story "Cold Moon and Wolf's Breath." Set in the 1930's, the film is a parable in which wolves devour isolated members of the community until they stand together in resisting the predatory beasts. See Cheng Chi-hua, *Chung-kuo tien-ying fa-chan shih* [History of the development of the Chinese film], 2 vols. (Peking, 1963), 1: 470–473. In the revolutionary ballet *White-haired Girl*, the female lead is threatened by wolves in her mountain exile.
2. Akira Iriye, *After Imperialism: The Search for a New Order in the Far East, 1921–1931* (New York, 1969), 193–205.
3. For a general account of Tsinan's educational reform, see David D. Buck, "Educational Modernization in Tsinan, 1899–1937," in *The Chinese City Between Two Worlds*, ed. Mark Elvin and G. William Skinner (Stanford, 1974).
4. *Chi-nan chih-nan* [Guide to Tsinan[(Tsinan, 1919), 178–179.
5. *Fen-sheng ti-chih: Shantung* [Provincial directory of Shantung] (Shanghai, 1935), 81–86.
6. Yü Shan was a well-known opera singer and actress when she married Chao T'ai-mou (Edgar Snow, *Red Star Over China*, rev. ed., New York, 1968, 459). Before becoming director of the Experimental Art Theater in Tsinan, Chao had studied at Columbia and Johns Hopkins and had taught at Peking University. See *Shantung sheng chiao-yü t'ing ti-i-tz'u kung-tso pao-kao* [First work report from the Education Department, Shantung Province] (Shantung, 1929); see also Hashikawa Tokio, *Chūgoku bunkakai jimbutsu sōkan* [Biographical dictionary on cultural figures of China] (Peking, 1940), 643, 644, 651, and *Chung-hua min-kuo ta-hsueh chih* [Record of higher education in the Republic of China], 2 vols. (Taipei, 1954), 1: 219–220.

7. Formerly the subordinate of the warlord Feng Yü-hsiang, Han became governor of Shantung in 1930, at the same time switching his allegiance to Chiang Kai-shek. Charged with ineffective resistance to the Japanese, he was tried by a KMT military tribunal and executed in January 1938. See Chalmers A. Johnson, *Peasant Nationalism and Communist Power* (Stanford, 1962), 109–110.

8. Chiang Ch'ing was then a novice at impromptu political theater, yet it had a tradition in China going back three decades or more: at the turn of the century radical young nationalists performed songs and skits to show the evils of foreign imperialism. See Mary C. Wright, ed., *China in Revolution: The First Phase, 1900–1913* (New Haven, Conn., 1968), 9.

9. *Fang-hsia ni-ti pien-tzu.*

10. Although Chiang Ch'ing spoke pejoratively of the May Sixteenth Group in our interview, she was one of the original members of the group, which was set up in May 1966 to discredit the authors of the February Outline, who were identified as supporters of Mao Tse-tung's chief opponent in the Cultural Revolution, Liu Shao-ch'i. One of the May Sixteenth Group's initial goals was to rout out reactionary elements in the regional branches of the PLA, then headed by Lin Piao, Chiang Ch'ing's major patron as of February. According to Chiang Ch'ing's account in our interview, by summer Lin's patronage backfired, for she charged him with secretly triggering "Ultra-Left" attacks on Chou En-lai (whom Chiang Ch'ing always credited as her supporter), herself, and other members of the Cultural Revolution Group identified with Mao. See Barry Burton's analysis based on the published record, which generally does not show Lin Piao to have been a chief Ultra-Left conspirator: "The Cultural Revolution's Ultra-Left Conspiracy: The 'May 16 Group,' " *Asian Survey* 11 (November 1971): 1029–1053.

11. Shen Ts'ung-wen was born into an old military family that lost its fortune during the Boxer Rebellion. When Chiang Ch'ing knew him as a professor and short-story writer, his earnings would have been moderate, but still superior to her own. See Howard L. Boorman and Richard C. Howard, eds., *Biographical Dictionary of Republican China*, 4 vols. (New York, 1967–1970), 3: 107.

3. From Party to Prison

1. Edgar Snow illuminates another dimension of Chiang Ch'ing's introduction to the Party from the point of view of Yü Ch'i-wei (alias Huang Ching, alias David Yü), the chief Communist adviser to the December Ninth Movement, whom he interviewed in 1935. Yü Ch'i-wei told him that he first met Chiang Ch'ing through his sister (or cousin) Yü San (Yü Shan), the wife of Chao T'ai-mou (and a woman whom, as we have seen, Chiang Ch'ing recalled as a "bully"). At that time, about 1933, Yü Ch'i-wei was serving as propaganda chief of the Communist underground apparatus in Tsingtao, in which case he may have been instrumental in putting Chiang Ch'ing in touch with the Party. An uncle of Yü Shan and Yü Ch'i-wei was Yü Ta-wei, minister of defense in the Nationalist government in Nanking, a KMT connection that Chiang Ch'ing would not want to disclose. See *Red Star Over China* (rev. ed., New York, 1968), 459–460, 472.

   Other accounts, of doubtful reliability because they do not cite sources and are also implausible in view of Chiang Ch'ing's recollections, recast her association with Yü Ch'i-wei in sexual terms. They claim that Yü Ch'i-wei and "Miss Li" (Li Ch'ing-yün) of Chu-ch'eng, were married in Tsingtao, where they collaborated in political work and were jointly imprisoned. Released, they sailed together to Shanghai, where Miss Li joined T'ao Hsing-chih's Work Study Troupe. See the entries on Huang Ching in *Hsin Chung-kuo jen-wu chih* [Biographical dictionary of New China], 2 vols. (Hong Kong, 1950), 1: 246; and in Union Research Institute, *Biographical Service* (Hong Kong), 43 (Nov. 27, 1956). See also Chapter 6, note 2. Throughout her narration, Chiang Ch'ing never mentioned Yü Ch'i-wei or his aliases.

2. Included in the Spring and Autumn Drama Society's repertory of the spring of 1933, when Chiang Ch'ing arrived in Shanghai, were some foreign plays in translation and other original dramas on the national resistance theme. Among the foreign plays was Upton Sinclair's *Second Story Man.* Several of T'ien Han's plays written after his swing to the left following the Mukden Incident of September 18, 1931, were also produced, among them *Sister* and *Stirring Bell.* See Kiang Yeh, "Student Groups Give Anti-Japanese Plays," CF 2 (Mar. 27, 1933): 12.

3. Howard L. Boorman and Richard C. Howard, eds., *Biographical Dictionary of Republican China*, 4 vols. (New York, 1967–1970), 3: 267.

4. Lord Marley's arrival was reported in the *North China Herald* (Shanghai), Aug. 23, 1933. Chiang Ch'ing did not mention that Soong Ch'ing-ling, the widow of Sun Yat-sen and a prominent spokeswoman for civil rights causes, led the Chinese reception and was the only Chinese woman pictured in the *Herald* on that occasion.

5. James P. Harrison, *The Long March to Power* (New York, 1972), 231–234.

6. Edgar Snow wrote of Mao as being in similar circumstances and similarly sustained: "After six months I left the school [First Middle School in Changsha] and arranged a schedule of education of my own, which consisted of reading every day in the Hunan Provincial Library. I was very regular and conscientious about it, and the half-year I spent in this way I consider to have been extremely valuable to me. I went to the library in the morning when it opened. At noon I paused only long enough to buy and eat two rice cakes, which were my daily lunch. I stayed in the library every day reading until it closed" (*Red Star Over China*, 144). That intellectual self-reliance and youthful austerity Mao recalled in 1968 in the spirit of Cultural Revolution: "It is much better to study in the library than to attend classes. A piece of cake is enough to take care of a day's meal. The old library attendant became very well acquainted with me." The irony, of course, was that students of the Cultural Revolution generation were no longer allowed to nourish their intellects independently in libraries nor were classes in usual session.

7. Jacques Guillermaz, *La Chine populaire* (Paris, 1959), 226.

8. Israel Epstein, *People's War* (London, 1939), 33.

9. See Nym Wales (Helen Foster Snow), *The Chinese Labor Movement* (New York, 1945), especially 138–139. See also Eleanor Hinder, *Life and Labor in Shanghai* (New York, 1944).

10. In all the modern industrial sectors of the Chinese economy women formed the majority of the labor force. Writing in 1932, Harold R. Isaacs reported that in Shanghai 70 percent of the modern industrial workers were women, and 90 percent of these were employed in the textile industry, particularly in cotton spinning and silk reeling, "though the latter industry is now practically dead and its employees thrown on the scrap heap" (*Five Years of Kuomintang Reaction*, Shanghai, 1932, 55).

11. In her firsthand study of the Chinese labor movement in the 1930's, Nym Wales reported that contract agents for the textile industry went to the countryside to recruit girls for periods of one to three years, after which they were expected to pay each girl's family a small sum. During a girl's time of service in the textile factories the contract agent was obliged to provide her food and shelter, though often he retained over 60 percent of her earnings. See Wales's *Chinese Labor Movement*, 14.

    Harold Isaacs, editor of *The China Forum*, a radical English-language journal published in Shanghai in the 1930's, presented a contemporary view of the contract system (*pao-t'ou*) that corresponds to Chiang Ch'ing's. He reported that the contract system was practiced nationwide in the 1920's and 1930's. Employers delegated the hiring of labor to a middleman who was usually a professional agent or contractor (the *pao-t'ou* man) charged with furnishing a constant supply of labor. Frequently the contractor was appointed concurrently as the factory foreman or supervisor, positions that enabled him to maintain full control over the labor in his hire. Although free workers were paid according to a fixed scale, contract workers were paid a sum less the percentage stipulated for the contractor in the hire agreement. The contract workers' pay was further reduced by "squeeze"—the customary informal service charge taken by the contractor. Thus, the contractor's percentage of the daily wage ranged from slightly less than 10 percent to more than 20 percent.

    The operating practices of the British-American Tobacco Company of Shanghai were typical. The factory's compradore, a Chinese whose job was to mediate between the business and official communities, both foreign and Chinese, was delegated to enlist the aid of a contractor. Thus the compradore was first to rake off a percentage from the workers' wages. If the contractor was recruited through the local criminal gangs, the gang leader also took his rake-off. Sometimes these three functions were performed by one individual acting as compradore, gang leader and contractor, whereby he took the total rake-off. Contractors from the British-American Tobacco Company were known to lend money to workers in their hire at interest as high as 20 percent a month, thus keeping them in perpetual debt. Recruiting workers from the villages, then shipping them en masse to Shanghai, to be temporarily housed and fed until their services were sold to other contractors, afforded contractors still another opportunity for rake-off. (Isaacs, *Five Years of Kuomintang Reaction*, 57–61; also, "Contract Labor at the B.A.T.," CF 2 [May 29, 1933]: 15).

    From an interview with a girl contract worker: "Are we human? Look at our faces. On one a blue bruise. On another a yellow scar. On another a black scar. Marks and lines and sickly pimples and boils. The skin sags on our cheek bones like soggy paper. . . . Here we are, thousands of girls, not one older than nineteen, few older than thirteen — and not one of us untouched by trachoma. . . .

"We work in a Japanese cotton mill for twelve hours a day. We were placed in the hands of contractors who came to our villages, bargained with our parents and took us away. The contractor is supposed to be responsible for us. We pay him $7.00 a month for our board and lodging. All the wages we earn are collected by the contractors, who frown and shrug their shoulders and insist that they are losing money, that they only get $6.00 a month for our wages! No matter what the wages are, the contractor gets them all.

"If some of us are more presentable, he doesn't put us into cotton mills but into brothels to make more money out of us that way" ("Interview with a Girl Contract Worker," CF 2 [Oct. 4, 1933]: 12).

4. Left Wing to Stage Center

1. T'ien Han et al., *Chung-kuo hua-chü yun-tung wu-shih nien shih-liao chi*, 1907–1957 [Collected materials from fifty years of the spoken drama in China, 1907–1957] (Peking, 1958), 13. The play continued to be performed in Shanghai as late as 1963.
2. Ibid.
3. Nym Wales (Helen Foster Snow), *Historical Notes on China* (Stanford, Hoover Institution, c. 1961), 23.
4. In May 1937 Chang Keng wrote favorably of Lan P'ing (Chiang Ch'ing's film name), identifying her as a left-wing actress in popular theater. He quoted her: "When A *Doll's House* was produced I threw myself completely into the part of Nora, but for *Thunder*, a play [by Ts'ao Yü] many times more difficult than A *Doll's House*, I rehearsed only a couple of hours each day." Compared with Lan P'ing, Chang Keng commented, most other actresses were far more self-centered and obsessed with looking pretty ("Some Questions We Face in the Theater Movement," *Kuang-ming tsa-chih* [Enlightenment], [May 25, 1937]: 1494).
5. Composed in 1923, Lu Hsun's analysis of Ibsen's play alerted women to new choices available to them. He observed that in a recent Shanghai production of the play the uncertainty of Nora's future was resolved by making her return home. Yet if Nora were just a bird that had escaped from its cage, he speculated, a hawk or cat could eat her. Or if her wings had withered after years of domesticity, she could not have flown away, and thus would have faced no problems. The most awful experience in life is to awaken from a dream with nowhere to go. People who do not know where to go should not be awakened. And so it should be for the masses. But for modernly educated women, the situation has changed. Just to eat, a woman who leaves home needs money. Although freedom cannot be bought, it can be sold for money. So women of today must fight for their economic rights — their means of exercising power.
6. Sai Chin-hua's extraordinary personal history, so deeply implicated in the struggle between Chinese nationalism and foreign imperialism, nearly obsessed Chiang Ch'ing, who referred to her often, and always vehemently, as if she were still a threat. Sai was born in Soochow, a city legendary for its beautiful and talented women. In the late 1880's she went to Germany, where she became the mistress of the chief of staff of the Prussian army, Count Alfred von Waldersee. During the Boxer Rebellion (1898–1900), the Kaiser, who was incensed by the Boxers' murder of his representative and by the fact that Germany was not invited to participate in relieving the besieged foreign legations in Peking, made the count a field marshal and induced the other foreign powers to accept him as commander of all the Allied troops dispatched against Chinese insurgents.

Sai accompanied the count to Peking, where she tried to persuade him not to murder her countrymen or destroy property in retaliation for losses sustained by the foreigners. She failed. Their exotic liaison conducted openly in Peking spawned numerous literary romances, among them Tseng Meng-p'u's novel *Nieh hai hua* [Flower on an ocean of evil] (1906), a highly successful fictionalized version of Sai's life. After the Manchu dynasty crumbled and Sai had faded — she lived out her years in a dismal section of Shanghai — the writer Liu Pan-nung took down her life story as told to him and published it in 1934 as *Sai Chin-hua pen-shih* [The true story of Sai Chin-hua]. Liu's biographical report served as the nucleus for another spate of stories, novels, and plays about her, and was eventually translated by Henry McAleavy as *That Chinese Woman: The Life of Sai Chin-hua* (London, 1959).

In 1936, Hsia Yen's dramatized version of Liu's work enjoyed great critical acclaim in Shanghai. Sai's part was taken by Wang Ying, one of the most popular actresses of the day. Upon seeing Hsia Yen's play, Chou Yang proclaimed that it "opened a new vista for national defense drama" — for its parallel with the contemporary anti-Japanese theme (*Kuo-fang wen-hsueh lun-chan* [Debates on national defense literature], Shanghai, 1936, 174).

During the Cultural Revolution, Chiang Ch'ing repeatedly and rhetorically raised the question of whether Sai had served or had prostituted the cause of Chinese nationalism; she always argued the latter. By that time, of course, she possessed the requisite power to punish Hsia Yen by destroying his career, ruining his name, and banning his works. See the lengthy diatribe against the play by Mu Hsin in KMJP, Mar. 12, 1966, and in CB 786 (May 16, 1966): 15–36.

7. Japanese fascism and imperialism were the immediate objectives. Soong Ch'ing-ling, the widow of Sun Yat-sen, explained that the National Salvation associations, which were a popular expression of United Front policy in Shanghai, were neither pro-Communist nor anti-government. They endeavored to appeal to all the people regardless of political belief and party affiliation. Their overriding goal was the prosecution of a national war of liberation. ("Statement Issued upon the Arrest of the 'Seven Gentlemen,' " *The Struggle for New China*, Peking, 1952, 85–86.)

In Mao Tse-tung's account of August 1, 1935, the CCP issued a declaration of willingness to establish a national defense government in conjunction with all political parties and other organizations and individuals willing to join the cause of resisting Japan and saving the nation ("Tasks of the Chinese Communist Party," SW, 1: 276).

8. The Women's Association for National Salvation was established in Shanghai on December 22, 1935, just two weeks after the December Ninth demonstration in Peking. According to Soong Ch'ing-ling, on the day of its founding thousands of women paraded through Shanghai chanting slogans that were representative of the general democratic upsurge: "Stop civil war!" "Chinese must not fight Chinese!" "Form a United Front to save the nation!" "Women can emancipate themselves only through participation in resistance!" Association members were teachers, workers, students, and housewives. From the beginning the association was supported by the YWCA. Its publications included *Women's Life*, a monthly; *Women's Masses*, issued every ten days; and *Little Sisters*, appearing fortnightly (*The Struggle for New China*, 155).

Never did Chiang Ch'ing mention to me the name of Sun Yat-sen's widow, Soong Ch'ing-ling, a major leader of the civil rights movement against KMT repression. Although not a Communist Party member, by virtue of her extraordinary intelligence and courage and her husband's role in history, Soong Ch'ing-ling was probably the most prominent woman in leftist politics in Shanghai in the 1930's.

9. John Israel has shown that the protection available from foreign law, especially the rule of extraterritoriality, offering immunity to political and intellectual nonconformists, made Shanghai an attractive center of the National Salvation movement. The Seven Gentlemen were instrumental in the formation of National Salvation associations of women, teachers, dramatists, and filmmakers. Their uncompromising demand for full-fledged resistance to the Japanese at a time when the Communist forces in the Northwest were also calling for a united front led to their harsh punishment by the Nationalist authorities (*Student Nationalism in China*, Stanford, 1966, 132–133).

On December 28, 1936, just two days after Chiang Kai-shek issued a statement, Mao Tse-tung drafted "A Statement on Chiang Kai-shek's Statement," in which he demanded the release of the Seven Gentlemen and all other political prisoners, along with a guarantee of the freedoms and rights of the people (SW, 1: 255–261). Although arrest forced Chiang Kai-shek to adopt, nominally at least, the United Front policy, he was laggard in the release of the political prisoners.

10. For a full account of the Sian Incident, see Lyman P. Van Slyke, *Friends and Enemies: The United Front in Chinese Communist History* (Stanford, 1967), ch. V.

11. Not only "watching," he was writing between 1927 and 1930: *Selected T'ang and Sung Stories* (1928); *Dawn Blossoms Plucked at Dusk* (1928), a collection of reminiscences; *And That's That* (1928), a collection of essays; and he was chief editor of the journal *The Tatler*. In 1930 he grew militant. That year he became a founding member of the China Freedom League, a civil rights organization, and of the League of Left-Wing Writers, the original and most influential of all the left leagues. He wrote numerous short, incisive essays on aesthetics and pieces of

social and political criticism. He also translated A. W. Lunacharsky's *On Art and Literature and Criticism*, G. V. Plekhanov's *On Art*, and other works on literary relations between China and Russia — a phase of his work repressed by his literary executors since the Sino-Soviet rift commencing in the late 1950's.

12. My Shanghai guides described the same meeting between Lu Hsun and Ch'en Keng, adding that Ch'en sketched a map for Lu Hsun describing the military struggles in the base areas. That hand-drawn map was found after Liberation. He also gave Lu Hsun a firsthand report of the revolution of economic and social relations in the Chinese soviets in Kiangsi.

   A year after my interview with Chiang Ch'ing, this incident and others like it were published in a new popular history by Shih I-ko, *Lu Hsun ti ku-shih* [Stories about Lu Hsun] (Peking, 1973), 107–110 passim.)

   Edgar Snow confirmed the anecdote about Ch'en Keng. During the Fourth Encirclement Campaign between the Red Army and the KMT forces in Kiangsi of the fall of 1932, Ch'en Keng was wounded in the leg and went to Shanghai in early 1933 for medical treatment. There he was recognized by the renegade Communist Ku Shun-chang, who turned him over to the Nationalist Police. They failed to talk him into joining the KMT, and he returned to Mao's community in Kiangsi (*Random Notes on Red China* [1936–1945], Cambridge, Mass., 1957, 92–93).

13. In the spirit of bonding Lu Hsun posthumously to the Communist cause, his widow, Hsu Kuang-p'ing, has published reminiscences of their life in Shanghai. Included are notes on their friendship with Ch'ü Ch'iu-pai and his wife, Yang Chih-hua, who were frequent visitors between 1932 and 1934, a period when both writers and their families were aggressively persecuted by the KMT. In January 1934, Ch'ü Ch'iu-pai left Shanghai for Kiangsi to work in the Central Soviet Districts. In June he was captured and executed by the KMT. Lu Hsun is credited with having preserved Ch'ü's writings from loss and destruction during the White Terror. See Hsu Kuang-p'ing, "Lu Hsun and Ch'ü Ch'iu-pai," CL 9 (September 1961): 3–113.

14. Lu Hsun disputed with Chou Yang and T'ien Han on a number of issues, among them the fact that they maligned his literary protégé, Hu Feng, as a spy for the KMT government. *Lu Hsun hsun-chi* [Collected works of Lu Hsun], 20 vols. (Peking, 1938), 6: 540–542.

15. "On New Democracy" (1940), SW, 2: 372.

16. The pertinent part of the letter reads in translation: ". . . The third page of *She-hui jih-pao* [Society daily], at a rough glance, seems to carry essays written by people of unorthodox, mixed lines. These essays appear to have no uniform line in praising or criticizing a particular person. But in fact there exists one consistent line. After reading them continuously for two months, I have not found any single word against Chou Yang and his group, suggesting that there is a [peculiar] 'social relation.' As to the attack on (Wen I-tzu?) and his fellow travelers, this has been the consistent policy [of the paper], and the suspension of *I Wen* is even intended to be used to incite misfeeling. Yet our Mr. Fu Tung-hua is really trying [to fight for us]."

17. "Reply to a Letter from the Trotskyites," *Selected Works of Lu Hsun*, 4 vols. (Peking, 1956–1960), 4: 277–280.

18. *Lu Hsun san-shih nien chi* [A thirty-year collection of Lu Hsun], 30 t'se (Shanghai, 1947), t'se 30: 69–86.

19. The first two essays are in *Lu Hsun san-shih nien chi*, t'se 30: 69–86 and t'se 28: 30–34, respectively; the third is in *Selected Works*, 4: 186–190.

20. See, for example, T. A. Hsia's article, "The Enigma of the Five Martyrs," *The Gate of Darkness* (Seattle, 1968), 163–233, and his other exploratory essays on literary politics of the 1930's.

5. Shanghai Film Afterimages

1. The young Soviet cameraman Roman Karmen arrived in Wuhan in November 1938 to film a news report. In December he went to Chungking and the following May reached the Communists' stronghold in the Northwest. His film report was released in 1941 under the title *In China*. The same year he published in Moscow a diary called *Year in China*. See Jay Leyda, *Dianying: Electric Shadows* (Cambridge, Mass., 1972), 363. The film Chiang Ch'ing mentioned was probably Karmen's *In China*.

2. According to some sources her friend T'ang Na, who possibly became her lover, then her husband, was a film critic on *Ta-kung pao*, where he always reviewed her well.

3. Lan P'ing [Chiang Ch'ing], "Wo-men ti sheng-huo," *Kuang-ming tsa-chih* [Enlightenment], May 25, 1937. The article was reprinted in *Ming-pao* (Hong Kong) 100 (April 1974): 86–88.
4. For a general account in English of the film industry of the 1930's, see Yao Hsin-nung, "Chinese Movies," *T'ien Hsia Monthly* (April 1937): 393–400.
5. Cheng Chi-hua, *Chung-kuo tien-ying fa-chan shih* [History of the development of the Chinese film], 2 vols. (Peking, 1963), 1: 184–185.
6. Ibid., 187.
7. Ibid., 200–201.
8. Leyda, 80.
9. CF 3, no. 2 (Nov. 30, 1933); 3, no. 4 (Jan. 13, 1934).
10. Leyda, 88.
11. The 1930's was an era of snappy professional names for female entertainers — Butterfly Wu and Lily Li (three homophones) were major stars; by comparison Blue Apple was austere. But when the industry started up in the 1920's, film acting was so degrading socially that women disguised themselves with such aliases as Lady Scholar FF or Lady Scholar AA (Kung Chia-nung, *Kung Chia-nung tsung-ying hui-i lu* [Kung Chia-nung's reminiscence on the film], 3 vols., Taipei, 1967, 1: 13).
12. Cheng Chi-hua, 1: 333.
13. Among the authors criticized was Cheng Chi-hua, who wrote the principal source book on the history of Chinese film. See notes 5 and 17.
14. Cheng Chi-hua, 1: 470–472. Another anti-Japanese film in which she appeared was *Lien Hua Symphony*, a medley of eight pieces written by Ts'ai Ch'u-sheng, directed by Ssu-t'u Hui-min, and completed by United Photoplay in 1937. Chiang Ch'ing played in the opening piece, called "Twenty Cents" (Cheng Chi-hua, 1: 473–476, 611–612).
15. Yao Hsin-nung, 399.
16. Lu Ssu, *Ying-p'ing i-chiu* [Reflections on former film criticism] (Peking, 1962), 27–44.
17. Cheng Chi-hua, 1: 473. In Cheng Chi-hua's review of films in which Chiang Ch'ing played, she is cited only as Lan P'ing, her name in film; her subsequent name in revolution, Chiang Ch'ing, and the fact of her marriage to Mao are not mentioned. Cheng corroborates substantially much of what she spoke of allusively, though he also contradicts, perhaps through ignorance or malice, other claims she made of her activities after 1937. For example, he says that in 1938 she was under contract with the Chung Tien Film Company, an organ of the KMT's Central Propaganda Bureau, which, after the dispersal of the Shanghai film industry under the Japanese attack in the summer of 1937, resumed filmmaking in the interior cities of Wuhan and Chungking. Lacking film talent of their own, the KMT lured "progressive" film people to their ranks, among them the skillful director Shen Hsi-ling and a group of actors that included the famous Chao Tan and Lan P'ing. Lan P'ing played in *Chinese Sons and Daughters*, a medley of four stories describing how people of different social classes and living in different parts of China joined the Resistance War. Her part was in the story called "A Peasant's Awakening," about the arousal of patriotic consciousness in the rural areas. Completed in Chungking in September 1938, the film was released in 1939 (Cheng Chi-hua, 2: 59–60).
    But in her narrative in the summer of 1972 Chiang Ch'ing claimed (her vehemence suggesting denial of rumors to the contrary) to have arrived in Yenan directly from Shanghai via Sian in August 1937, which would have made it impossible for her to have made that film according to the schedule Cheng relates. Either Cheng was wrong in fact or wrong in diplomacy. That confusion, as well as his generous praise of Hsia Yen, Yang Han-sheng, and other film talents of the 1930's who were denounced during the Cultural Revolution of the mid-1960's, cannot be dissociated from the fact that in 1966 *People's Daily* attacked Cheng's history for its praise of Hsia Yen and others and for its promotion of the "cult of the films of the 1930's." At the same time Cheng was told that the publication of a third volume, intended to cover the period from 1949–1959, would have to be postponed until he thoroughly revised the first two volumes and submitted them for publication (cf. Leyda, 337, 339). The revision had not been published by the mid-1970's.
18. Cheng Chi-hua, 1: 465–466. Lan P'ing's starring in *Wang Lao-wu* is also mentioned in Yang Ts'un, *Chung-kuo tien-ying san-shih nien* [Thirty years of Chinese film] (Hong Kong, 1954), 172.
19. For example, the film section of the June 15, 1937, issue of *Shih pao* (Shanghai) takes typically inconsequential note of the fact that the evening before Lan P'ing had dined with the son of

the recently divorced actor Chang Min. Asked how she felt after completing the shooting of *Wang Lao-wu* two days earlier, she said, "My spirits are fine!"

20. Cheng Chi-hua, 1: 467.

21. She faulted him mainly on political grounds — for his contentment with the National Defense theme, which did not stress class struggle, and his independence as a leftist artist. He remained in Shanghai after its fall to the Japanese and edited the *National Salvation Daily*, a paper founded by the distinguished writer Kuo Mo-jo, whose good name survived the Cultural Revolution.

22. See T'ien Han's article, "Recollections on Film Affairs," *Chung-kuo tien-ying* [Chinese film] (June 1958): 62–64.

23. Among other films in which Yuan Ling-yü starred were *The Peasant Girl, Morning in the City, Outcry of Women, A Worker in a Match Factory,* and *Girls of the Street.* For short résumés of a life that inspired reams of pulp literature, see Yang Ts'un, 124–130; and Sun Yü, "In Memory of Yuan Ling-yü," *Shang-hai tien-ying* [Shanghai film] 3 (1962): 18–19.

24. Nieh Erh, his pseudonym cleverly composed of four "ear" radicals and nothing else, was a student of Li Chin-hui, the major producer of "yellow music" (popular Western-style) in Shanghai in the 1930's. In 1933 T'ien Han recruited Nieh Erh into the Communist Party and gave him a job at United Photoplay where he composed numerous songs for film soundtracks, radio, and records. Political persecution drove him to Russia, West Europe, and Japan where he drowned in a swimming accident in 1935. Although he and Chiang Ch'ing shared a mentor in T'ien Han, she might not have known Nieh Erh personally (she never mentioned him by name) because her film contract was negotiated the year he died. See Cheng Chi-hua, 1: 385ff; A. C. Scott, *Literature and the Arts in Twentieth Century China* (New York, 1963), 134–135; Kung Chia-nung, 3: 201.

25. Leyda, 96. The transformation of grief to strength — the turning from "bourgeois sentimentality" to revolutionary action — has been a cinematic and literary device in China's proletarian arts since the 1930's.

26. Ibid.

27. The essay, written on May 6, 1935, appears in *Selected Works of Lu Hsun*, 4 vols. (Peking, 1956–1960), 4: 186–190.

28. Edgar Snow says that Chiang Ch'ing returned to Tsinan in 1934, married an actor whose stage name was T'ang Na, and subsequently worked with him in films in Shanghai. In 1937 they were divorced. In view of Snow's other claims about her that contradict her own testimony (e.g., his saying that she arrived in Yenan in 1938, that she and Mao had two daughters, etc. [*Red Star Over China*, rev. ed., New York, 1968, 460]), his note on T'ang Na should be read guardedly. Also, Chung Hua-min and Arthur C. Miller (*Madame Mao: A Profile of Chiang Ch'ing*, Hong Kong, 1968, 24) similarly report, without documentation, that T'ang Na's threatened suicide turned Chiang Ch'ing into a celebrity (though she was a reputed actress before that).

6. Mao's Way in Yenan

1. To give an idea of what our meals were like, dinner the first night at the villa in Canton opened with roasted cashew nuts, tomato and cucumber salad, and thinly sliced smoked ham. Then came three-yellow chicken served with ginger sauce — a Cantonese specialty — and tiny birds, possibly thrushes, which were deep-fried and consumed whole, crackling to the teeth. Two dishes of crab meat, one sweet water and the other saltwater, were turned out in different styles. The chicken congee, which is rice cooked in a rich chicken broth, had edible white jasmine blossoms floating on the surface. Mushrooms and other fresh vegetables were pan-tossed and served without sauce. One striking addition, perhaps in deference to the foreigner, was tall piles of white bread, a plate of butter pats, and a deep bowl of jam. Dessert opened with "pull silk" apples and bananas, prepared by dropping apple and banana slices in caramelized syrup, bringing them hot to the table, and plunging them into a basin of cold water, which made the syrup crystallize into "silk" threads. More unusual was "glass cake," a Cantonese delicacy made of the flour of pulverized water chestnuts. Translucent slices of pineapple and wedges of honeydew and watermelon at the peak of ripeness ended the meal.

Chiang Ch'ing's cooks were versatile — masters of regional Chinese dishes and also skilled in foreign cooking. One most memorable meal was "Western," but presented in the Chinese style. There were the usual ten courses, but each was a meal in itself: a succession of steak and fried potatoes, fried chicken and mashed potatoes, a "curry" and rice, fried fish, a series of overboiled vegetables, and deliberately composed salads. The dessert I have forgotten. Though I was hardly homesick, our aides consumed this exotic feast with chopsticks and obvious relish.

2. Although Chiang Ch'ing did not claim to have traveled to the interior on a KMT cultural mission after 1937, many of her co-workers on stage and in film in Shanghai did join other groups that toured Nanking and Wuhan, some going as far as Chengtu and Chungking, other cities in the Southwest. At each stop they put on National Defense productions.

A Hong Kong source explains Chiang Ch'ing's arrival in Yenan in the winter of 1939 (more than two years after she claims to have arrived) in the company of her "husband" Yü Ch'i-wei (see Chapter 3, note 1). In the winter of 1939 Yü and "Miss Li" went to Yenan and were divorced soon after their arrival. Miss Li entered the Lu Hsun Academy, and Yü departed Yenan to work with the Shen-Kan-Ning Border Region government. After Japan's surrender and the liberation of Chang-chia-kou (Kalgan) he became that city's mayor, and after the Communist government was established in Peking, he became mayor of Tientsin (entry on Huang Ching, *Hsin Chung-kuo jen-wu chih* [Biographical dictionary of New China], 2 vols., Hong Kong, 1950, 1: 246).

In the Communist movement Yü Ch'i-wei was better known as Huang Ching. In 1956 he was elected to the Central Committee and died one and one-half years later. During the 1950's he was married to Fan Chin, a CCP member, prominent journalist, vice-mayor of Peking, and head of *Pei-ching jih-pao* (Peking Daily). In the late spring of 1966, she was singled out as an enemy of the Cultural Revolution and marched before the masses (Donald W. Klein and Anne B. Clark, *Biographical Dictionary of Chinese Communism, 1921–1965*, 2 vols., Cambridge, Mass., 1971, 1: 393).

3. Cheng Chi-hua, *Chung-kuo tien-ying fa-chan shih* [History of the development of the Chinese film], 2 vols. (Peking, 1963), 2: 60. Because the archives of old Chinese films are so poorly maintained and the politics surrounding them so sensitive and divisive, I have not been able to determine independently whether Chiang Ch'ing performed with the Central Film Company in 1938, thus appearing in *Boys and Girls of China*.

4. Around August 20, 1937, some twenty members of the Central Committee met at Lo-ch'uan to formulate a policy for the mounting crisis in the war with Japan. Some of the meetings were enlarged to include Politburo members, heads of various departments of the Central Committee, and key military and political figures, including P'eng Te-huai, Ho Lung, and Lin Piao. Disagreements flared inevitably between Mao, Chang Wen-t'ien (then secretary of the Central Committee), and their followers in one camp, and Chang Kuo-t'ao, who would be driven from Yenan in April 1938, in the other. Mao epitomized his disputes with Chang Kuo-t'ao as one of the "struggles between the two lines": Mao held Chang responsible for strategic errors made during the Long March, for transgressing Party discipline, and for challenging his authority in the Northwest; Chang, for his part, dissented politically, as well as deploring Mao's arrogance and dominance.

At the Lo-ch'uan Conference (as explained later by Chang Kuo-t'ao in exile) plans were drawn up for the Anti-Japanese Military and Political Academy (familiar as K'ang-ta) to train political and military personnel, and for the Party School designed exclusively to prepare Party workers. Another institute, the North Shensi Public School, was planned for developing specialists in technical fields — finance, economics, education, and public health. (Chang Kuo-t'ao, *The Rise of the Chinese Communist Party. The Autobiography of Chang Kuo-t'ao; 1921–1927 Volume One; 1928–1938 Volume Two*, Lawrence, Kan., 1971, 1973, 2: 526, 533–534, 547.)

Not surprisingly, Edgar Snow's view of the background of the Lo-ch'uan Conference leans more toward Mao's side in the dispute with Chang Kuo-t'ao. He wrote that after the Sian Incident of December 1936, which climaxed with the arrest of Chiang Kai-shek, Mao moved his headquarters from Pao-an to Yenan. There, in January 1937, he became chairman of the directorate of K'ang-ta at a crucial point of ideological consolidation. In the capacity of chairman he wrote "On Practice," "On Contradiction" (1937), and "On Protracted War" (1938), three essays first delivered as public lectures at K'ang-ta and attended by the Central Committee.

Reports generally show that at the Lo-ch'uan meeting in 1937 Mao's leadership as Chairman of the Soviet Republic of China was confirmed. Chang Kuo-t'ao was condemned for his "rightism" and made to confess his errors. He did so perfunctorily. The next year he left the

Red Areas for the enemy: Chiang Kai-shek (*Red Star Over China*, rev. ed., New York, 1968, 488).

Mao's report, "Resolution on the Present Situation and the Tasks of the Party," adopted by the Politburo of the Central Committee at Lo-ch'uan on August 25, 1937, deals with the Resistance War in Mao's rhetorical terms: should the KMT and the "bourgeoisie" or the CCP and the "proletariat" lead the United Front in the war against Japan? (SW, 2: 78–71).

5. Chang Kuo-t'ao, 2: 551.
6. The Lu Hsun School had been opened in the summer of 1937 under the temporary direction of Hsu T'e-li, Mao's old and celebrated teacher from Hunan. The next year Mao, Lo Fu, and Ch'eng Fang-wu expanded the school into an academy with several arts departments. For a detailed account, see Ch'i Lu, comp., *Shen-Kan-Ning pien-ch'ü shih-lu* [True record of the Shen-Kan-Ning Border Region] (Yenan, 1939), 147 et passim.
7. For Mao Tse-tung's own account of his early family life and marriages, see Snow, *Red Star Over China*, Pt. IV.
8. Incidentally, the year the poem was written (1957), Mao's wife of eighteen years (Chiang Ch'ing) was deathly ill, exiled in the Soviet Union.
9. *Ch'ing ch'u yü lan erh sheng yü lan*, an expression used with reference to a student whose talents excel those of his teacher. Had Mao paid the compliment to his protégée?
10. Edward H. Schafer, *The Divine Woman: Dragon Ladies and Rain Maidens in T'ang Literature* (Berkeley, 1973), 6–8.
11. The Shen-Kan-Ning Marriage Law proclaimed on April 4, 1939, appears in Wang Chien-min, *Chung-kuo kung-ch'an tang shih-kao* [Draft history of the CCP], 3 vols. (Taipei, 1965), 3: 247–248.
12. CQ 31 (July–September 1967): 148–150.
13. According to Nym Wales (Helen Foster Snow) and Edgar Snow, Mao and Ho, a political worker, were married in the Kiangsi Soviet in 1930, the year his former wife, Yang K'ai-hui, was executed (Nym Wales, *Inside Red China*, New York, 1974, 178; Snow, *Red Star Over China*, 468). Edgar Snow's timing of the divorce corresponds to Chiang Ch'ing's (*Red Star*, 467–468). In *Red China Today* (New York, 1970; first published as *The Other Side of the River*), 174, Snow also cites 1937 as the year of the divorce.

    Han Suyin has written that Mao and Ho Tzu-chen were married in Kiangsi in 1931 and divorced in 1938, though she provides no source (Han Suyin, pseud., *The Morning Deluge: Mao Tsetung and the Chinese Revolution, 1893–1954*, Boston, 1972, 382).
14. According to Snow's information, divorces were freely granted at the registration bureau of the soviet upon the "insistent demand" of either party to the marriage. However, the wives of Red Army men were required to have their husbands' consent before they could apply for a divorce (*Red Star Over China*, 226). That sexist procedure may have conveyed to outsiders that Mao rather than Ho wanted the divorce.
15. In a letter to me dated May 20, 1974, Helen Foster Snow gave additional information about Ho. In 1937 K'ang K'o-ch'ing told her that Ho was the "domestic" type who took personal care of her husband (K'ang K'o-ch'ing, for her part, preferred to delegate domestic tasks to bodyguards so that she could pursue her own revolutionary career). Although Mrs. Snow never interviewed Ho, she knew that Ho despised another American journalist, Agnes Smedley, who openly criticized all thirty Long March women as "feudal-minded" characters and advocated that their husbands divorce them all. Everyone hated Smedley for that, Mrs. Snow added, except the individualist woman writer Ting Ling and Smedley's interpreter Lily Wu, who shared Smedley's hostility to the conditions of marriage among Communist leaders in Yenan.

    When Snow visited Mao in Pao-an in 1936, the year Chiang Ch'ing said was Mao's last with Ho Tzu-chen, he observed of this elusive woman who prepared for Mao and his guest a compote of sour plums: "[Mao] was not the only Politburo member with a wife — women were extremely scarce in that camp — but the only one I noticed whose wife seemed completely under her husband's spell and domination" (*Journey to the Beginning*, New York, 1958, 160, 167).

    Helen Foster Snow, who visited Yenan from May through August 1937 (months when Chiang Ch'ing claims Ho was not in Yenan), wrote of Ho: "Then there was Mao Tse-tung's wife, Ho Tzu-ch'ün [*sic*], a small, delicate woman with a pretty face and a shy, modest manner, who devoted most of her time to caring for her husband — whom she worshipped —and bearing children. She was also an active Communist worker, however, and had been a school-teacher before marrying Mao. She had suffered more than any other woman in the war, for along with having borne several children, she received sixteen shrapnel wounds from an air bomb during the Long March. Ho Tzu-ch'ün was a graduate of Hunan Normal College. She entered the Communist Party in 1927, then joined Mao's first army as a propagandist, and married him after his first wife had been killed" (*Inside Red China*, 178). In correspondence with me of May 1974 Mrs. Snow said that these remarks were made without her actually having seen or interviewed Ho.

16. In the Central Soviet Districts the wives of the Communist leaders had their own contingents of bodyguards apart from their husbands'. In a letter to me dated May 20, 1974, Mrs. Snow remarked that when she visited Yenan in the summer of 1937 Ho's bodyguards were there, although she never ascertained whether Ho was actually among them. However, at that time it was generally known in Yenan that Ho had become extremely sick, and thus it was unlikely, in the judgment of Mrs. Snow, that Ho would have been allowed to languish in Pao-an, where medical facilities and food were much inferior to those in Yenan.

17. Helen Foster Snow (Nym Wales), *The Chinese Communists: Sketches and Autobiographies of the Old Guard*, 2 vols. (Westport, Conn., 1972), 2: 251.

18. Ibid., 252.

19. Ibid., 250; Edgar Snow, *Red Star*, 467–468.

20. Yang Tzu-lieh, *Chang Kuo-t'ao fu-jen hui-i lu* [Reminiscences of Mme. Chang Kuo-t'ao] (Hong Kong, 1970), 333, 334, 338.

21. Mao An-ying was born shortly after the marriage. In 1930 he was arrested along with his mother, and after her execution he was released and taken into hiding in Shanghai by other members of the Mao family who fled from Changsha. During World War II he studied in Russia, returning to China in 1944 (not 1948, as Snow reports). About that time he worked for a few months on a commune in Shansi and went on to a high-level Party school. Trained in the military, he was among the first Chinese to reach Korea, where he was commanding a division when he was killed in action on October 25, 1950 (Snow, *Red Star*, 486).

   Mao An-ch'ing was born around 1921. When his mother was arrested in 1930, he was hidden by friends and later sent with his brother An-ying to Shanghai, and eventually to Russia, where he was educated, reportedly as an engineer. Upon his return to China he worked as a Russian language expert and translated textbooks. In 1965 Mao told Edgar Snow that An-ch'ing and his "two daughters" by Chiang Ch'ing were his only surviving children. Mao also confessed disappointment that his son had not been educated in China (ibid.). Chiang Ch'ing gave no information about Mao An-ling.

22. According to Snow, while in Kiangsi Ho Tzu-chen and Mao had two children, who were left behind with Kiangsi peasants when the parents embarked upon the Long March. The children were never recovered. In Pao-an in 1936 Ho bore Mao a daughter — "Just before I left Pao-an the Maos were parents of a new baby girl" (whom Chiang Ch'ing would bring up as Li Min). When Snow was in Yenan in 1939 he learned that Ho had already gone to Russia, taking their daughter with her (*Red Star*, 91, 467–468).

23. Tillman Durdin reported that in 1944, the year he met Chiang Ch'ing, Mao An-ying, then twenty-four, had just returned from Moscow, where he had gone with "his mother" (actually his first stepmother, Ho Tzu-chen) in 1936. See Durdin's article "Mao Tse-tung ti fu-jen" [The wife of Mao Tse-tung] in *Yenan ti nü-hsing* [Women of Yenan], (n.p., n.d.), 6. The departure date of 1936 corresponds roughly to Chiang Ch'ing's, though it is perhaps as much as one year short. But the more reliable and important date here is 1944, which may establish the time of Ho Tzu-chen's return from Moscow to Shanghai with Mao An-ying and the daughter in tow.

24. Born in 1897, Mao Tse-min became involved in CCP activities in 1922. Three years later he was managing an interurban network of CCP publications. In 1927 he was arrested, then escaped, fleeing to Shanghai. Four years later he became head of the supply division of the Fukien-Kwangtung-Kiangsi Military Region, and in the fall of 1934 joined the Long March. In 1936 he was appointed economic minister in Shansi. Two years later he was transferred to Sinkiang (Union Research Institute, *Mao Tse-tung: A Chronology of His Life*, Hong Kong, 1970, 70, 81, 126, 145, 165, 184). After General Sheng Shih-ts'ai shifted from a pro-USSR to a pro-KMT policy, he arrested Mao Tse-min and other Communists then working in Sinkiang. Chou En-lai's negotiations in Chungking for the release of political prisoners resulted in allowing some of them to go to Yenan. However, Mao Tse-min, along with thousands of others, was executed (or poisoned) in 1943 (HCPP 5: 152–165; 8: 79; 10: 122–155).

   Edgar Snow has written that Mao Tse-tung also adopted and educated the children of his young brother, Mao Tse-t'an, who was killed in action in 1935, as well as children of his youngest brother, Mao Tse-min (*Red Star*, 486–487). Chiang Ch'ing did not mention these earlier adoptions.

25. While Mao Yüan-hsin was a student at the Harbin Military Engineering Institute in July 1964, Mao urged him to analyze the structure of the PLA, in those years upheld as a model for the entire society, and to stress learning from practice rather than from books — the typical weakness of intellectuals. See "Talks with Mao Yüan-hsin (1964–6)" in Stuart Schram, ed., *Chairman Mao Talks to the People: Talks and Letters, 1956–1971* (New York, 1974), 242–252.

26. Mark Selden, *The Yenan Way in Revolutionary China* (Cambridge, Mass., 1971), 180; Harrison Forman, *Report from Red China* (New York, 1945), 73.

27. Yen Te-ming, "Northern Shensi Like Kiangnan," HCPP 16: 134.

28. Nor was the soil always seeded with staples. Earlier, the best lands were planted with opium, the fastest growing cash crop (Selden, 5).

29. Forman, 38–41.

30. Stuart Schram, ed., *Authority, Participation and Cultural Change in China* (Cambridge, Eng., 1973), 33.

31. Yen Te-ming, 134–135.

32. For a firsthand account of the inception of the Nanniwan project in the winter of 1938–39, see Liu Yun-yang, "Starting from Scratch — The Ta Kuang Textile Mill of the 359th Brigade," HCPP 16: 137–147.

33. After Hu Tsung-nan led his Nationalist forces in a blockade of northwest Shansi, conflict between the "New Shansi Army" of indigenous leftists and the more conservative "Old Shansi Army" loyal to the Shansi warlord Yen Hsi-shan ensued, providing further evidence of the crumbling of the united front between Yen and the Communists. Hsiao K'o's 358th Brigade and Wang Chen's 359th Brigade, original parts of the 120th Division, also fought in Hopeh, east and west of Peiping (Peking) respectively. Later, Wang Chen's 359th Brigade withdrew to North Shensi, just before going to Nanniwan (James P. Harrison, *The Long March to Power*, New York, 1972, 298).

34. According to Wang Chen, the women in the Nanniwan project engaged mostly in household tasks, spinning, and weaving (Forman, 67).

35. In the spring of 1962 Chiang Ch'ing published an article, "The Spirit of Nanniwan Will Shine in the Hearts of Soldiers Forever," for *Chieh-fang chün pao* [Liberation Army daily]. Based on a recent visit to Nanniwan, her sentimental and laudatory report on Nanniwan's continuing exemplum of material self-reliance in adversity discloses nothing of her tour of duty there in frontier days. Written in low-level and undistinguished Communist jargon, her report was reprinted in *Chung-kuo ch'ing-nien pao* [Chinese youth paper] (Peking), May 1, 1962; SCMP 2378 (May 5, 1962): 8–10.

7. *Yenan's Popular Culture*

1. Snow, *Red Star Over China* (rev. ed., New York, 1968), 460.

2. Cheng Chi-hua, *Chung-kuo tien-ying fa-chan shih* [History of the development of the Chinese film], 2 vols. (Peking, 1963), 2: 367–369.

3. Roman Karmen, *God v. Kitae* [A year in China] (Moscow, 1941), 108.

4. Tillman Durdin, "Mao Tse-tung ti fu-jen" [The wife of Mao Tse-tung], *Yenan ti nü-hsing* [Women of Yenan] (n.p., n.d.), 3–6.

5. Harrison Forman, *Report from Red China* (New York, 1945), 178–179.

6. David D. Barrett, *Dixie Mission: The United States Army Observer Group in Yenan, 1944* (Berkeley, 1970), 83.

7. Correspondence between the author and John Service, April 23, 1974.

8. Robert Payne, *Mao Tse-tung: Ruler of Red China* (London, 1951), 214.

9. A similar word portrait of tireless intellectualization in a cave appears in the reminiscence of Huo Ch'ing-hua, "Following Chairman Mao on the Way to Yenan," in *Hsing-huo liao-yuan* [A single spark can start a prairie fire], 10 vols. (Peking, 1958–1963), 4: 134–139.

10. The constitution of the Seventh Party Congress of 1945 adopted the thought of Mao Tse-tung and the Marxist-Leninist theory from which it derived as its guiding principle, thereby signifying Mao's victory over Wang Ming's challenge. In 1956, at the Eighth Party Congress, he was reelected to the Central Committee. At this congress, another rival of Mao's, Liu Shao-ch'i,

exercised countervailing power, and the resolution that had been passed in 1945 was not reintroduced. Not until the Ninth Congress in 1969 was it readopted, thereby consolidating the ideological supremacy Mao had won during the Cultural Revolution (James P. Harrison, *The Long March to Power*, New York, 1972, 361).

11. Anna Louise Strong (1895–1970), to whom Chiang Ch'ing accorded Chinese identity on a political standard, was one of few Americans to make a home in the People's Republic in a tumultuous era. She in a sense earned her keep through literary proof of her "friendship." Among her many books are *China's Millions* (1935), *The Chinese Conquer China* (1949), and *When Serfs Stood Up in Tibet* (1960).

12. "On New Democracy" appears in SW, 2: 339–384; "Get Organized!" in SW, 3: 153–161; "On Coalition Government" in SW, 3: 255–320.

13. The reality of the "struggle between the two lines," Mao versus Wang Ming, was apparent to Edgar Snow during his visit to the Communist base in 1936 and 1937. In December 1937 Wang Ming threw down the gauntlet to Mao with his thesis, "A Key to Solving the Present Situation," in which he argued that the Red forces should merge completely with the KMT. Mao's opposing United Front strategy sought to maintain separate CCP command of the Communist armed forces and territorial bases. Though Mao won that argument, Wang Ming stayed in spite of the fact that his Russophile ideas prepared by the Comintern had lost their luster. Young and resilient, he published in 1940 "The Two Lines," in which he advocated marshaling the urban workers to take over the cities before organizing the peasants in the rural areas. Mao advocated the opposite. Snow conjectured that while Wang Ming no longer presented a real threat, Mao may have enjoyed Wang Ming's presence as a focal point for his — Mao's — continuing repudiation of the Comintern line. The "struggle between the two lines," plainly articulated by Wang Ming, led to Mao's rectification campaign, which was designed to eliminate through political persuasion (in contrast to Stalin's bloody liquidations) all vestiges of Russian influence and to assure his own flexible ideological supremacy (*Red Star Over China*, 504–509).

According to official Party history that same polarization between Mao, who claimed to speak for the people and to work out problems in a Chinese way, and the bureaucrats and intellectuals, who acted in sectarian and Soviet style, has been the basis of every major "struggle between the two lines" since the Yenan era. For an early formulation, see Hu Ch'iao-mu, *Thirty Years of the Communist Party of China* (London, 1951). Subsequently, Mao Tse-tung's repudiations of Liu Shao-ch'i (1966) and Lin Piao (1971) were also expressed as major "struggles between the two lines."

The Great Proletarian Cultural Revolution of the mid-1960's spawned a new generation of zealots among the local leaders. When I was in Shanghai (August 1972), a muscle-bound worker representing that city's revolutionary committee treated me to a three-hour harangue in which he claimed that the "struggle between the two lines" underlay all major historical events of China's twentieth century, including the Reform Movement of 1898, wherein the unpopular Empress Dowager Tz'u Hsi was depicted as the antagonist.

14. For a subtle Western analysis based on case studies, see Robert J. Lifton, *Thought Reform and the Psychology of Totalism* (New York, 1961). Allyn and Adele Rickett, two Americans who experienced some facets of thought reform, have written a candid and balanced report: *Prisoners of Liberation* (New York, 1957).

15. For details of the background of the Rectification Campaign, in which competing ideas and personalities were far more complex than Chiang Ch'ing has indicated, see Harrison, ch. 16.

16. Ho Ch'i-fang, *Kuan-yü hsien-shih-chu-i* [On realism] (Shanghai, 1951), 110.

17. Among Chang Keng's writings reflective of this period is *Hsin ko-chu lun-wen chi* [Collected essays on the new musical drama] (Peking: Central Drama Research Academy, 1951).

18. Forman, *Report from Red China*, 87.

19. Ibid., 88.

20. Barrett, 51.

21. Forman, 97.

22. As remembered by the leader of the women's movement, Ts'ai Ch'ang (Nym Wales, *My Yenan Notebooks*, Madison, Conn., 1961, 78).

23. The reprint Chiang Ch'ing handed me, *Wen-hsueh yü sheng-huo man-t'an* [Remarks on literature and life], first appeared in *Chieh-fang jih-pao* [Liberation daily], July 17–19, 1941. In the context of promoting literature reflecting social realities, which Chiang Ch'ing espoused, the phrase she quoted hardly strikes the ordinary reader as seditious.

24. Wang Shih-wei's first piece titled "The Wild Lily" was published in the March 13, 1942, issue of *Chieh-fang jih-pao* [Liberation daily]; additional installments appeared ten days later.

    Wang's essay included the conversation of two girls who complain that in Yenan the sexes are not equal and that certain leaders (none named) wear clothes of "three shades" and eat meals of "five grades" — evidence of hierarchialism disillusioning to young idealists of Yenan.

25. Ma K'o, "Reminiscences of Life at Yenan's Lu Hsun Academy," HCPP 16: 148–166.

26. Li Ch'ing, a woman comrade formerly of Yenan whom I interviewed in Sian, recalled that Chiang Ch'ing also taught painting and other graphic arts (not mentioned to me by Chiang Ch'ing).

27. Chao Ch'ao-kou, who visited Yenan in 1943, corroborates Chiang Ch'ing's recollection of the new drama movement without citing her by name *(Yen-an i yueh* [January in Yenan], Nanking, 1946, 121–132).

28. Another dramatist, Liu Wu, has reminisced cautiously on Mao's attendance of academy performances at the Yang-chia-ling auditorium, close to Mao and Chiang Ch'ing's home. Mao arrived in the company of security chief K'ang Sheng and General Ho Lung, causing excitement and commotion. The ideas exchanged after the show were not elucidated in Liu's report, nor was Chiang Ch'ing's attendance noted ("Under Sun and Rain," in *Hsing-huo liao-yuan*, 6: 34–40).

29. Ma K'o, "Reminiscences."

30. For an account of Wang Ming's "rightist deviation" as recognized by Mao in 1937, see Harrison, 281.

31. Translated in SW, 3: 69–98.

32. V. I. Lenin, "Party Organization and Party Literature," *Collected Works*, 40 vols. (English ed., Moscow: Foreign Languages Publishing House, 1962), 10: 45.

33. "Talks at the Yenan Forum," SW, 3: 70.

34. Ibid., 85.

35. For an intimate portrait of Ting Ling's early years, see Shen Ts'ung-wen, *Chi Ting Ling* [In memory of Ting Ling] (Shanghai, 1934). A more general account appears in Howard L. Boorman and Richard C. Howard, eds., *Biographical Dictionary of Republican China*, 4 vols. (New York, 1967–1970), 3: 272–276.

36. See, for example, Li Ang (pseud.; Chu P'ei-wo), *Hung-se wu-t'ai* [Red stage] (Peking, 1946), 98. Li Ang observed both the personal and political lives of Yenan leaders and was not above gossip.

37. For an extensive account of Ting Ling's buffetings in the world of literary politics, see Merle Goldman, *Literary Dissent in Communist China* (Cambridge, Mass., 1967), passim. Ting Ling's survival in the far north at Heilungkiang is mentioned by Hsu Kai-yu, *The Chinese Literary Scene: A Writer's Visit to the People's Republic* (New York, 1975), 136.

8. On the Road to Peking

1. Among the many personal services rendered by Wang Tung-hsing, a native of Shansi province, was to interpret the Shansi dialect for the Chairman. For more on Wang's early career, see HCPP 3: 357 et passim. After the Cultural Revolution the status of this former leader of Mao's military intelligence soared. In 1974, one year after he became a full Politburo member, the Shanghai journal *Hsueh-hsi yü p'i-p'an* [Study and criticism], which was oriented toward Chiang Ch'ing's interests, celebrated Wang's military heroism during the civil war era (CNA 987 [Jan. 17, 1975]: 7).

2. For multifaceted accounts of this episode of civil war, see General Lionel Max Chassin, *The Communist Conquest of China: A History of Civil War, 1945–1949*, translated from the French by Timothy Osata and Louis Gelas (Cambridge, Mass., 1965); and James P. Harrison, *The Long March to Power* (New York, 1972), ch. 18.

3. Volume 4 of Mao Tse-tung's *Selected Works* in Chinese (1960) and in English (1961), is subtitled "The Third Revolutionary Civil War Period."

4. Snow, *Red Star Over China* (rev. ed., New York, 1968), 172.

5. In his "Circular of April 9, 1947" (SW, 4: 130–131) Mao wrote of the relative troop strength at the time of the temporary abandonment of Yenan: "The Kuomintang troops attacking the Shensi-Kansu-Ninghsia Border Region were more than 230,000 strong, while the Northwest People's Army had only some 20,000 in that region" (130n).

6. According to Jacques Guillermaz, Liu K'an was among several Nationalist generals who committed suicide as a result of battles lost to the Communists in Shensi in the spring of 1948 (*A History of the Chinese Communist Party, 1921–1949*, London, 1968, 403).

7. In an account of the evacuation of Yenan by Yen Ch'ang-ling, one of Mao's bodyguards of those years, he always refers to Chou En-lai of the Liberation War era as Vice-Chairman Chou. Though Chiang Ch'ing never mentioned the fact of his vice-chairmanship, she usually referred to him by his current title, *Tsung-li* (the Premier), or as Chou *Tsung-li*. See Yen Ch'ang-ling, "In His Mind a Million Bold Warriors," and "The Great Turning Point," in *The Great Turning Point* (Peking, 1962), 58–113. This volume is a translation of the original Chinese *Chieh-fang chan-cheng hui-i lu* [Reminiscences from the Liberation Wars] (Peking, 1961).

8. Propriety in costume, especially caps, was symbolic of alternations of cooperation and enmity between the CCP and the KMT. During periods of cooperation, or united front, the Nationalist cap crested with the white sun was worn.

   Mao's former rival Chang Kuo-t'ao reported that after 1937, when the CCP and the KMT effected a reconciliation and agreed to subsume the Red Army into the National Revolutionary Army under central government control, residents of Yenan were free to wear uniforms of the National Revolutionary Army or of the Red Army. Mao possessed two army caps: one of the type of the National Revolutionary Army, and the other his original Red Army cap with the emblem, a five-pointed star. To receive guests from the outside, he put on the former, but donned the latter to attend CCP meetings or to address students at the Anti-Japanese Academy (*The Rise of the Chinese Communist Party*, 2 vols., Lawrence, Kan., 1971, 1973, 2: 530).

9. The same pseudonym for Mao is cited by Yen Ch'ang-ling (*The Great Turning Point*, 69). Slight variations of these two pseudonyms are cited in another revolutionary memoir. Mao is given as Li Te-sheng, in this writing with the character "Te" meaning "virtue" (rather than another meaning "determined"), thus reading "virtuous victory." Chou's pseudonym is written Hu Pi-ch'eng, "certain to succeed" (HCPP 3: 345).

10. For jokes between the leaders and the local people about the disguise of the Central Committee as the Ninth Detachment and Chou En-lai's occasional performances incognito, see HCPP 3: 361.

11. See SW, 4: 130–131.

12. SW, 4: 133–134.

13. Yen Ch'ang-ling made a similar comment on Mao's military genius: "With his thorough grasp of the enemy's ways, Chairman Mao not only commanded our troops, but he also directed the actions of the enemy" (*The Great Turning Point*, 66).

14. For a colorful portrait of the Ma clan, the Moslem satraps of China, see Edgar Snow, *Red Star Over China*, 305–316. Jacques Guillermaz provides details of the engagement with the First Field Army, to which Chiang Ch'ing referred. See *A History of the Chinese Communist Party*, 414, 423–424.

15. Wang's piece was not included in the sixteen volumes of this series of revolutionary memoirs that were available to the editors of the American edition. See Robert Rinden and Roxane Witke, *The Red Flag Waves: A Guide to the "Hung-ch'i p'iao-p'iao" Collection* (Berkeley, 1968). Other portions are possibly sequestered in China. The accessibility of the entire series was curtailed on the eve of the Cultural Revolution, when several authors and many subjects had fallen from favor.

16. The claim of one million troops appears in the title of Yen's essay "In His Mind a Million Bold Warriors" (*The Great Turning Point*, 58–79). In view of the Chinese love of round numbers, this title may be no more than political hyperbole verging on personality cultism. Neither in this essay, nor in the second called "The Great Turning Point," does Yen refer to Chiang Ch'ing's preoccupation with making shoes for the Chairman. Yen says nothing of her matrimonial status and identifies her only in terms of her political post. Like her, he describes the enemy as being at the foot rather than at the top of the mountain during the march from Hsiao-ho to T'ien-tzu-wan (*The Great Turning Point*, 74).

17. Mao's nominal transformation of the Front Committee into an Instruction Brigade led by Chou En-lai is not mentioned in "Strategy for the Second Year of the War of Liberation" (Sept. 1, 1947), as published in SW, 4: 141–146. Chiang Ch'ing's point seems to have been that Mao ordered Chou to instruct all levels of military personnel in Mao's new operational principles. That message is conveyed generally in the essay's eighth and final point.

18. SW, 4: 147–153.

19. Ibid., 155–156.
20. Ibid., 157–176.
21. Mao's comments on this renewal of the Rectification Movement are in "The Present Situation and Our Tasks," ibid.
22. "Tactical Problems of Rural Work in the New Liberated Areas" (Mar. 24, 1948), and "The Work of Land Reform and of Party Consolidation in 1948" (May 25, 1948), SW, 4: 251–259.
23. SW, 4: 247–249.
24. For further details on the three campaigns, see the following reports by Mao: "The Concept of Operations for the Laiohsi-Shenyang Campaign" (September-October 1948; conceived as a telegram; see note 28), SW, 4: 261–266; "The Concept of Operations for the Huai-Hai Campaign (Oct. 11, 1948), ibid., 279–282; and "The Concept of Operations for the Peiping-Tientsin Campaign" (Dec. 11, 1948), ibid., 289–293.
25. At the end of January 1949 General Fu Tso-i, motivated by military weakness and a desire to spare Peking, surrendered the city and his forces, 600,000 to 1,200,000 strong, to Lin Piao, commander of the Liao-Shen campaign.
26. For a list of the eight conditions the Communists set forward at the beginning of peace negotiations, see Mao Tse-tung, "Statement on the Present Situation," SW, 4: 318.
27. Chang Chih-chung arrived in Peking on the first of April; on the fifteenth a peace agreement was handed to the Nanking government but was rejected five days later. Its terms are noted in Mao Tse-tung, SW, 4: 390–396.
28. This may be a reference to telegrams of September and October 1948, titled "The Concept of Operations for the Liaohsi-Shenyang Campaign," addressed to "Lin Piao, Lo Jung-Fuan, and other comrades" by Mao Tse-tung on behalf of the Revolutionary Military Commission of the Central Committee. See SW, 4: 261–266.

9. *The Fifties Incognito*

1. According to the *Agrarian Reform Law* (Peking, 1950), "rich peasants" were lower in status than landlords but higher than middle peasants. A rich peasant was generally defined as one who owned land, plows, and farm implements, but also rented land to others. He took part in labor but also "exploited" the hired labor of peasants poorer than himself. Liu Shao-ch'i's "rich peasant line," or "rich peasant road" as it was also called, meant that rich peasants would remain relatively untouched until the economy's urban sector, to be favored over the rural sector, would be able to provide technological equipment sufficient to make the switch to socialism in the countryside. In the rhetoric of the Cultural Revolution, Liu's "rich peasant line" was denounced as the "capitalist line."

   Mao's policy for rich peasants in the early stages of the land reform movement was the opposite. See the land law drafted on October 10, 1947, at Hsi-pai-p'o, P'ingshan county, Hopeh province, in which Mao calls for the seizure of surplus lands of rich peasants. (Jacques Guillermaz, *A History of the Chinese Communist Party, 1921–1949*, London, 1968, 431). For further calls for confiscation of rich peasant as well as landlord property, see Mao's directives of December 25, 1947 (SW, 4:164) and of February 15, 1948 (SW, 4:201).

   A copy of the Draft Agrarian Law of October 10, 1947, appears in William Hinton, *Fanshen: A Documentary of Revolution in a Chinese Village* (New York, 1966), Appendix A, 615–618.
2. Among them, she said, was Cheng Ch'ien's wife, apparently a recent convert to Communism. Cheng Ch'ien, a native of Hunan, had been a KMT military leader from around 1920, and later became the Nationalist governor of Hunan. Not until August 1949 did he join the Communists.
3. Franz Schurmann and others have written about Kao's and Jao's connections with the Soviet Union (though such links between Chinese and Soviet leaders were common in the early 1950's). Possibly Kao and Jao struck up an alliance of mutual interest in the industrial development of Northeast and East China respectively. Although Stalin could not have hoped to gain control of the political apparatus, which was dominated by the Yenan veterans, he might have sought influence or control over the economic apparatus, and perhaps also the military (*Ideology and Organization in Communist China*, Berkeley, 1966, 334). Chiang Ch'ing represented Kao and Jao as cooperating in the control of major industries, uninterested in rural reform, scornful of Mao's authority, and resistant to investigations by his representatives.

4. Born in Chekiang province, Jao Shu-shih's wife, Lu Ts'ui, studied at Tsinghua University in the mid-1930's, and participated in the December Ninth Movement (1935). In 1946 she and Jao sat in on the Peking peace talks with the KMT under the auspices of General Marshall, the U.S. special envoy. In 1949 she was named to the Standing Committee of the All-China Federation of Democratic Women, the China Peace Committee, and the Sino-Soviet Friendship Association, to which Chiang Ch'ing also belonged. Predictably, her political activities ceased the year her husband was removed from power (Donald W. Klein and Anne B. Clark, *Biographical Dictionary of Chinese Communism, 1921–1965*, 2 vols., Cambridge, Mass., 1971, 1: 411).

5. One *mou* of first-class land or three *mou* of third-class land for all persons over age sixteen; half of those amounts for those under sixteen (Vincent Y. C. Shih, *The Taiping Ideology, Its Sources, Interpretations and Influences*, Seattle, 1967, 83.)

6. Actually, in 1950, a year of revolution and national consolidation, both Mao and Liu were going easy on rich peasants so as not to disrupt production. See Stuart Schram's mention of the controversy in the volume he edited, *Authority, Participation and Cultural Change in China* (Cambridge, Eng., 1973), 38.

   Chiang Ch'ing neglected to point out that 1950 was the first year she took part in the October First celebrations. "The 1st of October celebrations passed off quietly. They started off with a reception by Mao Tse-tung where for the first and last time I saw Madame Mao. She stood at the head of the receiving line, a pretty, youngish woman of about forty, dressed elegantly but in no way different from the rest. With her stood Chou En-lai and his wife, while the Chairman and the Vice-Chairman, including Madame Sun Yat-sen, were inside the hall and received us there" (K. M. Panikkar, *In Two Chinas: Memoirs of a Diplomat*, London, 1955, 109).

7. According to the U.S. Army, 500,000 American soldiers served in the United States forces in Korea. This figure does not include the forces of the U.S. Marines, Navy, or Air Force. The United States forces served as part of the UN forces, which were composed of troops from sixteen member nations. See Walter G. Hermes, *Tent Truce and Fighting Front* (Washington: Office of the Chief of Military History, Department of the Army, 1966), 367 n. 5, 477; Frank A. Reister, *Battle Casualties and Medical Statistics: U.S. Army Experience in the Korean War* (Washington: The Surgeon General, Department of the Army, 1973), 1, 3.

8. Chiang Ch'ing did not elaborate on P'eng's action and its consequences. William Whitson gives an account of P'eng Te-huai's repudiation of Mao's ideological style of warfare, which was prosecuted under Lin Piao's command during the first nine months of the war, but at the cost of tens of thousands of Chinese lives. Taking over from Lin Piao, P'eng Te-huai scorned political commissars and guerrilla strategy in favor of greater military professionalism and the use of much Soviet material. His fifth offensive, which began successfully in the spring of 1951 but ended disastrously, may have been what Chiang Ch'ing mistakenly referred to as the fourth campaign (Whitson and Huang Chen-hsia, *The Chinese High Command*, New York, 1973, 95, 96, 525).

9. As of 1953 the United States had not ratified the convention of the Geneva Conference of 1949, which called for compulsory repatriation of all prisoners of war. A total of 14,234 Chinese prisoners who did not wish to be repatriated were transported to Taiwan through the auspices of the United Nations Command. Hermes, 171, 495–496, 514–515.

10. According to U.S. estimates, American casualties included 33,629 dead, 103,284 wounded, and 5,178 missing or captured, a total of 142,091 compared to Chiang Ch'ing's 400,000. United Nations forces, which included United States forces, suffered more than 500,000 casualties and more than 94,000 dead. United Nations analysts estimated approximately 1.5 million casualties on the North Korean and Chinese sides. Hermes, 501.

11. No reference is made by Chiang Ch'ing to Chinese or North Korean defeats or losses of men and material. According to American Air Force figures, the Far East Air Forces (U.S. Air Force in Korea) lost 1,466 aircraft, the U.S. Marine Corps lost 368, and other UN forces lost 152, making a total of 1,986, significantly different from Chiang Ch'ing's round number of 10,000. (Robert F. Furtrell, *The United States Air Force in Korea, 1950–1953*, New York, 1961, 645.)

12. Roger Boussinot, *L'Encylcopédie du cinéma* (Paris, 1967), 327–328; A. C. Scott, *Literature and the Arts in Twentieth Century China* (New York, 1963), 73–77.

13. Among the functions of the new Cinema Department in an era of cultural reconstruction was the establishment of a cinema academy, its political ethos grounded in Mao's message at the

Yenan Forum. Students were to be drawn from the ranks of the proletariat — workers, peasants, soldiers — rather than from the bourgeoisie or other advantaged classes. *Hsin-wen jih-pao*
[News daily], July 24, 1951; SCMP 150 (Aug. 9, 1951): 22–23.

14. In 1950 Ts'ai Ch'u-sheng, who once directed Chiang Ch'ing in *Wang Lao-wu* (1936), was
serving as head of the Art Committee of the Bureau of Cinema Art of the Ministry of Culture.
Ts'ai had foreseen that the year 1950, when many film experts were released from the People's
Liberation Army, was bound to be important in Chinese film history. That year the state
planned twenty-six full-length feature films emphasizing rural rather than urban themes,
seventeen documentaries, forty reprints of Soviet films with Chinese dialogue dubbed in, and
thirty-six reprints of Soviet education films. Private companies in Hong Kong and Shanghai
were commissioned to produce some fifty new films as well as to arrange reprints of Soviet
films. The overall goal of that formidable production schedule was to wipe out "U.S. film
propaganda" (Ts'ai Ch'u-sheng, "The Chinese Film Industry," *People's China* [June 16, 1950]:
14).

15. See Ch'i Pen-yü, "Patriotism or Treason?" (HC 5 [1967]: 9–23), an expanded version of the
film fracas Chiang Ch'ing described. Composed at the height of the Cultural Revolution, Ch'i
Pen-yü's article points the finger at Liu Shao-ch'i, then dubbed "the top Party person in authority taking the capitalist road." Liu is shown to be the chief promoter of the theme of "patriotism," thus putting him in the same revisionist boat as the Emperor Kuang Hsu and his concubine. The revolutionary spirit of the Boxers was praised, because they (like the Red Guards
of the 1960's) had attacked "foreign imperialists." Ch'i Pen-yü described Chiang Ch'ing as a
member (not the director) of the Cinema Department under the Central Committee, and
added, in the Mao-centered orthodoxy, that the Chairman had led the criticism of the film,
Chiang Ch'ing acting on his instructions.

16. In March 1951 a month-long film festival was held in twenty cities to screen films produced
under the PRC. The most acclaimed were *White-haired Girl, Concentration Camp at Chang-
chao, New Heroes and Heroines, Red Flag over Tsuikang* [?] *Mountain,* and *United for Tomorrow* (Boussinot, 330).

17. Since the founding of the PRC, it has not been unusual for national leaders, except the most
august whose faces were known to the masses, to travel and work incognito in the countryside.
During the Four Cleanups Campaign of 1964 several disguised leaders investigated corruption
in the countryside for extended periods. Among those whose identities were later revealed was
Liu Shao-ch'i's wife, Wang Kuang-mai, who worked incognito in a Hopeh commune (Michel
Oksenberg, "Methods of Communication within the Chinese Bureaucracy," CQ 57 [January-
March 1974]: 1–39, especially 22).

18. Li Ting-sheng, *P'ing Wu Hsun ho 'Wu Hsun chuan'* [Criticize Wu Hsun and "The Story of
Wu Hsun"] (Canton, 1951), 4.

19. Among the laudatory essays contributed on the fiftieth anniversary of Wu Hsun's death were
those by Liang Ch'i-ch'ao, T'ao Hsing-chih, Liu Tzu-tan, and Feng Yü-hsiang. See Liang
Ch'i-ch'ao et al., *Wu Hsun hsien-sheng ti chuanchi* [Biography of Mr. Wu Hsun] (Shanghai,
1948).

20. Chang Mei-sheng, *Wu Hsun chuan* [Biography of Wu Hsun] (Shanghai, 1947).

21. From December 1950 through January 1951 more than forty articles praising the film *The
Story of Wu Hsun* appeared in newspapers and magazines.

22. Photographs of the land titles, the local area, and the persons involved are reproduced in the
formal report of the investigation. See note 25.

23. In 1951 a group of writers went to Shantung to reasearch his life in preparation for a film based
upon it. The film was completed in 1957 (Jay Leyda, *Dianying: Electric Shadows,* Cambridge,
Mass., 1972, 228n). Chiang Ch'ing did not mention that film. However, in August 1967,
some of her supporters in the Cultural Revolution revealed that after completing the Wu Hsun
investigation she tried to write and stage a revolutionary Peking opera on Sung Ching-shih's
life, but Chou Yang canceled the project in its early stages ("Salute to Chiang Ch'ing, the
Great Standard Bearer of the Cultural Revolution," SCMP 3996 [May 25, 1967]: 4).

24. According to Yao Wen-yuan, Mao wrote the editorial in the May 20, 1951, issue of *People's
Daily,* which opened the campaign to criticize the film (HC 1, 1967).

25. The full report of the investigation, of which Li Chin (alias Chiang Ch'ing) of the Ministry of
Culture, Yuan Shui-p'o of *People's Daily,* and Chung Tien-fei, also of the Ministry of Culture, were the joint authors, appears in *Wu Hsun li-shih tiao-ch'a chi* [Record of the investigation of the history of Wu Hsun] (Peking, 1951). From May through August 1951, the distin-

guished cultural authority Kuo Mo-jo, historian and propagandist Hu Sheng, the academic philosopher Fan Wen-lan, and the filmmaker Sun Yü published articles critical of Wu Hsun, in most cases citing the authority of the investigative report. The anti-Wu Hsun campaign culminated on August 8, 1951, when Chou Yang's lengthy condemnation of Wu Hsun appeared in *People's Daily*.

The Wu Hsun affair belonged to a wider movement to promote class analysis on the part of prestigious intellectuals educated in the pre-Marxian era. Although Chiang Ch'ing's former mentor T'ao Hsing-chih was attacked in this context, his stand against Chiang Kai-shek's regime in the 1930's was simultaneously praised (JMJP, May 16, 1951). Under political pressure, surely, the dramatist T'ien Han also denounced Wu Hsun (JMJP, June 10, 1951). Then the case against Wu Hsun was laid to rest until the Cultural Revolution, when for the first time Chou Yang was made the public scapegoat for whatever modest cultural freedom had prevailed during the PRC's first fifteen years. In 1967 Yao Wen-yuan vilified Chou Yang's performance in the Wu Hsun affair. In his extremist language, Yao Wen-yuan charged that "Hsia Yen, another chieftain of the Chou Yan revisionist gang," had completed the unfinished film about Wu Hsun and called upon the proletariat to follow Wu Hsun's "capitulationist" heroism by "surrendering" to the landlord class and the bourgeoisie. He emphasized that the "Investigation of the History of Wu Hsun," which appeared in JMJP, July 23–28, 1951, was drafted by Li Chin, Yuan Shui-p'o, and Chung Tien-fei, and was personally revised by Chairman Mao. Revealing that Wu Hsun was actually a "big landlord, big moneylender, and big loafer" exploded his legend. But Chou Yan's "confession" of August 8, 1951, strove to create the impression that he led the criticism when in fact he only reacted to what Chairman Mao had said. This merely added to the evidence of his "counterrevolutionary double-dealing tactics" ("Criticize Chou Yang, Two-faced Counterrevolutionary Element," HC 1, 1967).

26. Rich peasants were defined as those who employed more labor than they themselves put in; that is, they derived more than half their net income from the manual labor of others. According to William Hinton's report, from which cautious generalizations can be made, rich peasants along with landlords constituted roughly 10 percent of the population and owned 70 to 80 percent of the land and most of the draft animals and farm equipment. Hired laborers, poor peasants, and middle peasants constituted the rest of the population, but held less than 30 percent of the land. Of the latter group the middle peasants comprised some 40 percent of the population, but held less than 30 percent of the land (*Fanshen*, 27, 404, 405). Naturally, proportions varied according to region. The most heated controversies arose over the definition and treatment of the rich peasants — whether they should be lumped with the landlords (Mao's policy before Liberation) or treated more judiciously (Liu Shao-ch'i's "rich peasant line" adopted after Liberation) — and over the definition and treatment of the middle peasants, as Chiang Ch'ing later explained.

27. Restricting herself to her own experience and avoiding, out of personal preference, reporting of carnage, Chiang Ch'ing did not discuss the fact that the land reform campaign of 1950–1951 was among the most violent and bloody stages of the Communist revolution. As many as two million people, mainly landlords, were executed or otherwise died, and millions of others were sent into forced labor. For a citation of numbers of executions and forced labor assignments incurred by land reform, see James P. Harrison, *The Long March to Power* (New York, 1972), 608. A colorful, fictional re-creation of land reform from an ideologically informed viewpoint appears in Ting Ling's novel *Sun Shines Over the Sangkan River* (Peking, 1948).

28. Other reports show illness as explaining Lin Piao's absence from public affairs in the early 1950's (Klein and Clark, 1: 565).

10. Peking and Moscow

1. Konstantin M. Simonov (b. 1915), prolific poet, short-story writer, novelist, and playwright, was chief editor of the leading literary journal *Novy Mir* from 1954 to 1957, years when Chiang Ch'ing was in Moscow. In 1957 he was removed from that post for publishing Dudintsev's novel *Not by Bread Alone* and other dissenting works released during the Thaw. His address on the doctrine of socialist realism presented to the Second Soviet Writers' Congress of December 1954 was cited by Ch'in Ch'ao-yang and Huang Ch'iu-yun, two Chinese writers attacked as "rightists" during the Rectification Campaign of 1957 (Douwe W. Fokkema, *Literary Doctrine in China and Soviet Influence, 1956–1960*, The Hague, 1965, 115).

2. See Donald W. Klein and Anne B. Clark, *Biographical Directory of Chinese Communism, 1921–1965*, 2 vols. (Cambridge, Mass., 1971), 1: 377–379; Merle Goldman, *Literary Dissent in Communist China* (Cambridge, Mass., 1967), 140–146, 149–150.

3. The original Chinese edition, which included 176 articles, was published in three volumes in early 1956. The abridged edition in English (Peking, 1957) included forty-four of the original articles.

4. Probably a reference to the Central People's Government Council, the most powerful state organization from 1949 to September 1954, when it was abolished. Kao Kang, the strong man in Manchuria since its liberation in the late forties, became one of the Central People's Government Council's six vice-chairman under Chairman Mao. In 1953 Kao was officially described as one of Mao's "close comrades-in-arms" (Klein and Clark, 1: 433).

   A resolution adopted by the National Conference of the Chinese Communist Party on March 31, 1955, stated that the "facts" of the Kao Kang case brought to light before and after the Fourth Plenary Session of the Seventh Central Committee held in February 1954 "proved that from 1949 Kao Kang engaged in conspiratorial activities aimed at seizing the power of leadership of the Party and State . . . that he himself should for the time being be General Secretary or Vice-Chairman of the Central Committee of the Party and the Premier of the State Council. After a serious warning was given to the anti-Party elements by the Fourth Plenary Session of the Seventh Central Committee of the Party, Kao Kang not only did not admit his guilt to the Party, but even committed suicide as an expression of his ultimate betrayal of the Party" ("Resolution on the Kao Kang–Jao Shu-shih Anti-Party Alliance," NCNA, Apr. 4, 1955; CB 324 [Apr. 5, 1955]: 4–6). Chiang Ch'ing's reference was probably to his alleged goal of becoming Premier of the State Council.

5. Chiang Ch'ing's language in this passage is strong. "Class enemies at home began to chime in with the Soviet revisionists" establishes an equivalence between Chinese dissenters and Russian revisionist writers allegedly guilty of liberalism, individualism, subjectivism, and other heretical alternatives to the Party's cultural orthodoxy. "Counterrevolutionary opinion" is far more damning than "anti-Party opinion," with which many Chinese dissenters were originally charged.

6. "Realism, The Broad Way" [*Hsien-shih-chu-i, k'uang-k'uo ti tao-lu*] was published under the author's pseudonym Ho Ch'ih in *Jen-min wen-hsueh* [People's literature] 9 (1956): 1–13. Ch'in Chao-yang's essay veered from "socialist realism," which was the Soviet-derived rule of literary orthodoxy, in favor of "realism of the socialist epoch," the liberal alternative that allowed more scope for the author's interpretation. Ch'in also attacked dogmatism in the political control of literature and the arts. For further discussion of this essay and an analysis of the common language and common fund of arguments created among Russian and Chinese writers in the 1950's before and during their contemporaneous "Thaws," see Fokkema, 115 and passim.

   Originally published in the September 1956 issue of *Jen-min wen-hsueh* [People's literature], Wang Meng's story also veered from the narrow path of "socialist realism" to explore a broader range of character and emotion in the manner of "realism of the socialist epoch." Some of the characters are neither all bad nor all good, but are melancholic, romantic, or plain lazy. The young, hankering after what they imagine to be a more liberal Russian literary and musical culture, disparage the stupid bureaucratism of CCP members running a Peking organization department.

7. Chung Tien-fei, Chou Yang's former secretary and Chiang Ch'ing's collaborator in the Wu Hsun investigation, ostensibly wrote this article as a means of extending the Rectification Campaign to the film industry. However, some leaders of the Rectification Campaign, who were displeased with the result, retaliated by dropping him from the editorial board of the leading literary journal, *Literary Gazette*, in November 1957 (Jay Leyda, *Dianying: Electric Shadows*, Cambridge, Mass., 1972, 227; Fokkema, 155n).

8. First published in JMJP, Mar. 24, 1957. For a profile of Fei Hsiao-t'ung's extraordinary career, see A. R. Sanchez and S. L. Wong, "On 'An Interview with Chinese Anthropologists,' " CQ 60 (December 1974): 775–790.

9. Chiang Ch'ing's reference was to the "new cell theory" of O. P. Lepeshinskaya, a female biologist and high-ranking Communist whose postulate that cells may have originated from precellular living matter rejected Virchow's axiom *omnis cellula ex cellulae* (all cells from cells), accepted in the West. Her theory held "that in the process of wound healing new cells are formed not only by way of division of cells . . . but also from living substance in the form of tiniest grains which result from the destruction and disintegration of cells." The new theory,

which repudiated the conventional theory of evolution, was used in the struggles against premature senility and cancer (Gustav A. Wetter, *Dialectical Materialism, A Historical and Systematic Survey of Philosophy in the Soviet Union*, London, 1958, 451–455; Loren R. Graham, *Science and Philosophy in the Soviet Union*, New York, 1972, 276).

10. Chou En-lai's trip to the Soviet Union in the winter of 1957 was provoked by restiveness within the Communist bloc, especially the Polish disturbances in mid-1956 and the Hungarian revolt in the fall. While the Peking leadership supported the principle of Communist bloc solidarity, it disapproved of Khrushchev's methods of restoring order. In mid-November 1956 Chou En-lai toured North Vietnam, Cambodia, India, Burma, and Pakistan. Near the end of the year he was suddenly called back to Peking, arriving in early January 1957. Within a few days he left again, for Moscow, where, from the seventh to the tenth of January, he held talks with Russian, German, and Hungarian leaders. After brief visits to Warsaw and Budapest, he returned to Moscow in mid-January where further communiqués were issued on bloc solidarity. Later that month he resumed his Asian tour to Afghanistan, India, Nepal, and Ceylon (Klein and Clark, 2: 216.) Chiang Ch'ing probably saw Chou during the second week of January, and sensed then the personal tensions between him and Khrushchev.

11. Ch'eng Yen-ch'iu was born into poverty in 1904 and apprenticed into an opera company at age six. After Liberation he was appointed vice-president of the Chinese Opera Research Institute and continued to flourish as an actor who excelled in realistic portrayal of "oppressed women in semi-colonial, semi-feudal society." At a commemoration performance on the first anniversary of his death in 1958 the playwright T'ien Han (one of Chiang Ch'ing's Four Villains) praised Ch'eng Yen-ch'iu's manifestation of the spirit of cultural diversity in the Hundred Flowers Era, while Chang Keng (Chiang Ch'ing's personal adversary since Shanghai days), who succeeded Ch'eng as vice-president of the Chinese Opera Research Institute, noted that during the Japanese occupation of Peking Ch'eng withdrew from the stage and took up farming. The uncertainty of Ch'eng's political status in his lifetime is reflected by the fact that he did not join the CCP until 1957, and then only as a probationary member; full Party membership was awarded posthumously. (NCNA–English, Mar. 9, 1959, reprinted in SCMP 1972 [Mar. 13, 1959]: 9; NCNA–English, Mar. 11, 1958, reprinted in SCMP 1734 [Mar. 19, 1958]: 9).

12. For a balanced account of the border war with India, one of China's major foreign policy disputes of the twentieth century, see Neville Maxwell, *India's China War* (New York, 1970), especially Part III, "The View from Peking," and remarks on maverick General Kaul, passim.

13. For a similar version of the story, see Ting Ch'uan-ching, *Sung-jen i-shih hui-pien* [Collected anecdotes about Sung personalities], 2 vols. (Peking, 1958), 1: 446–447.

11. *Redreaming the Red Chamber*

1. Mao Tse-tung did not escape the fate of being compared with a *Red Chamber* paradigm, even a woman. Li Ang (Chu P'ei-wo), who claims to have known Mao in the 1930's, wrote in a gossipy account that Mao displayed some traits of Black Jade, among them hypochondria (*Hung-se wu-t'ai* [Red stage], Peking, 1946, 97).

2. *Miscellany of Mao Tse-tung Thought*, 2: 391. He meant influenced by the love story.

3. For example, Sun Wen-kuang, "Persist in Using the Class Viewpoint in Studying *The Dream of the Red Chamber*" (HC 11 [Nov. 1, 1973], translated in SCMM 763–764 (Nov. 26–Dec. 3, 1973). Passages in Sun's exegesis are surprisingly similar to Chiang Ch'ing's.

4. Chiang Ch'ing pointed out that *Dream of the Red Chamber*, like other novels, evolved from earlier forms. The original work, called *Breeze Moon Precious Mirror (Feng-yueh pao-chien)*, became *Story of the Stone (Shih-t'ou chi)*. David Hawkes's recent translation of the first third of the novel adopts that title: *The Story of the Stone* (Middlesex, Eng., 1973). Hawkes argues in his introduction that a more accurate rendering of another of Ts'ao's suggested titles, *Hung-lou meng*, is *A Dream of Red Mansions*, though *Dream of the Red Chamber* has become the conventional translation in China and abroad. Only this convention justifies its use here.

The *Precious Mirror–Story of the Stone* sequence explains why the first chapter, originally called "Precious Mirror" (*pao-chien*), came to be known as "Story of the Stone." The Chin edition, copied in 1784, titled *Marriage of Gold and Jade (Chin yü yuan)*, bears many resemblances to the Chih editions — named for the editor Chih Yen-chai whose version appeared with his annotations in 1759, 1760, and thereafter. The Chih edition comes still closer to the *Story of the Stone* edition.

5. For a general account, see Jerome B. Grieder, "The Communist Critique of *Hung-lou meng*," *Papers on China* 10 (1956): 142–168.

6. Yü P'ing-po's "Short Discourse on *Dream of the Red Chamber*" had just appeared in *Hsin chien-she* [New construction] 3 (1954): 34–38. His article was based on his *Hung-lou meng pien* [A discussion of *Dream of the Red Chamber*] (Shanghai, 1923).

7. *Hung-lou meng hsin-cheng* (Hong Kong, 1964).

8. Compare this with Mao Tse-tung's observation: "The class struggle seen *in Dream of the Red Chamber* is very violent, and many scores of people lost their lives, of which only twenty or thirty (someone has counted thirty-three) were from the ruling class, the rest, some three hundred in number, being slaves, such as Yuan-yang, Ssu-ch'i, Yu Erh-chieh, and Yu San-chieh, etc. If one does not discuss history from the point of view of class struggle, his preceptions of history will not be very clear. It is only by using class analysis that it [history] can be analyzed clearly" ("Talk on Problems of Philosophy" [Aug. 18, 1964], *Miscellany of Mao Tse-tung Thought*, 2: 391–392).

9. Compare Mao Tse-tung's remark: "Ts'ao Hsueh-ch'in's *Dream of the Red Chamber* was intended to patch up heaven — the heaven of feudalism. Nonetheless, what Ts'ao Hsueh-ch'in wrote was about the decline of feudal families, and this may be regarded as a contradiction between Ts'ao's world outlook and his creation." ("Talk on Sakata's Article" [Aug. 24, 1964], *Miscellany of Mao Tse-tung Thought*, 2: 401).

   Also Chiang Ch'ing's bête noire Yü P'ing-po wrote, "*Dream of the Red Chamber* is a swan song of the feudal system in China," in his article, titled by the novel, appearing in *People's China* 10 (1954).

10. Translation according to Hawkes, p. 63, who translated the song's title as "Won-Done Song."

11. Translation of this and the following passages of the commentary also adjusted according to Hawkes, p. 64.

12. Conforming to Hawkes's translation, pp. 132–133.

13. Hawkes, p. 133.

14. Hawkes's translation, p. 111, with the names of the families adjusted to the Wade-Giles transliteration system used in this volume.

12. Setting the Stage

1. In later conversation Chiang Ch'ing spoke of concurrent actions on the part of Mao and the Central Committee. Between September 6, 1963, and July 4, 1964, the Central Committee issued nine articles on the subject of the Four Cleanups Campaign (*Ssu-ch'ing*) — cleaning out of corruption in politics, economics, ideology, and organization. See *Nan-fang jih-pao* [Southern daily], Dec. 26, 1964. For the earlier version, which attacked irregularities in accounts, warehouses, workpoints, and supplies, see Richard Baum and Frederick C. Tiewes, *Ssu-ch'ing: The Socialist Education Movement of 1962–1966* (Berkeley: China Research Monographs, No. 2, 1968), 58–71. On July 14, 1965, the Chairman issued the "Twenty-three Point Document on Questions regarding the Socialist Education Campaign in the Countryside." Issues spelled out in that document, she said, included the Four Cleanups, which soon became a widespread movement.

2. Her speech, along with others from the Peking Opera Festival, first appeared in HC 6 (May 8, 1967). The English edition of this collection of speeches with Chiang Ch'ing cited as author, titled *On the Revolution of Peking Opera*, was published by the Foreign Languages Press in Peking in 1968. See p. 309.

3. The "Ten Points" share the theoretic background of a series of directives called the Early Ten Point Document of May 1963, the Later Ten Point Document of September 1963, and the Revised Later Ten Point Document issued by Liu Shao-ch'i in September 1964. They are discussed by Chiang Ch'ing on p. 305. See also Stuart Schram, ed., *Authority, Participation and Cultural Change in China* (Cambridge, Eng., 1973), 76–85; Baum and Tiewes, 15.

4. In August 1946 in Yenan Mao granted an interview to the American journalist Anna Louise Strong in which he said, "All reactionaries are paper tigers. In appearance, the reactionaries

are terrifying, but in reality they are not so powerful. From a long-range point of view it is not the reactionaries but the people who are really powerful" (SW, 4: 100–111). Writings by Mao titled "Imperialists and All Reactionaries Are Paper Tigers" appeared in JMJP, Oct, 31, 1958.

5. Chiang Ch'ing specifically credited Mao for deciding independently to step down as chief of state, in contrast to the common interpreation that he was forced to do so in recompense for miscalculations in the Great Leap Forward.

The main items at the Plenary Session were the national economic plans for 1950 — especially the need to maintain a balance between agriculture and industry and between light and heavy industry, and to develop communes; also the "positive proposal" that Mao not serve as candidate for Chairman of the PRC for the next term. The explanation was that he should have more time for theoretical work (*Documents of the CCP Central Committee, September 1956–April 1969*, 2 vols., Hong Kong, 1971, 1: 113–119, 121–122).

In an unauthorized record of his speech of December 19 at the Sixth Plenum Mao, ironical as usual, commented on his resignation as the Chairman of the PRC: "A formal resolution must be made this time, and I hope my comrades will agree. I ask that within three days, the provinces hold a telephonic conference to notify the regions, counties, and people's communes. The official report will be published three days later, so that the lower levels will not find it a total surprise. Things are really odd in this world! One can go up but not come down. I expect that a part of the people will agree and another part disagree. People do not understand, saying that while everyone is so full of energy in doing things, I am withdrawing from the frontlines. It must be clearly explained. This is not true. I am not withdrawing. I want to surpass the U.S. before I go to see Marx!" (*Miscellany of Mao Tse-tung Thought*, 1: 148).

6. Mao, "The Origin of Machine Guns and Mortars, etc." (Aug. 16, 1959), *Chinese Law and Government* 1 (Winter 1968–1969): 73–74, quoted in Frederic Wakeman, Jr., *History and Will: Philosophical Perspectives of Mao Tse-tung's Thought* (Berkeley, 1973), 37–38.

7. A Hunan native and revolutionary from the early days, Huang K'o-ch'eng served at the center of military and state power to the end of the 1950's. During the final stages of the "offshore islands" crisis (Quemoy and Matsu, between Taiwan and China's southeast coast) in October 1958, Huang was appointed PLA chief-of-staff and the next April reappointed to the National Defense Council. The "crimes" to which Chiang Ch'ing referred were punished in September 1959 by his sudden replacement by Lo Jui-ch'ing as PLA chief-of-staff and his removal from the post of vice-minister of national defense (at which time, Lin Piao succeeded P'eng Te-huai as defense minister). A classified military periodical of the Chinese Communists, *Kung-tso t'ung-hsun* [Bulletin of activities], of 1961 showed that Huang and P'eng Te-huai both had been charged as "modern revisionists" constituting an "anti-Party group" — by implication, relying on the Soviet Union for assistance after that fraternal Communist connection had been severed. See Donald W. Klein and Anne B. Clark, *Biographical Dictionary of Chinese Communism, 1921–1965*, 2 vols. (Cambridge, Mass., 1971), 1: 400.

8. The essence of P'eng's complaint in his "Ten-Thousand Word Letter" came out in the *Peking Review* at the height of the Cultural Revolution. P'eng's letter "painted a pitch-black picture of the present situation in the country. In essence he negates the victory of the general line and the achievements of the great leap forward, and is opposed to the high-speed development of the national economy, to the movement for high yields on the agricultural front, to the mass movement to make iron and steel, to the people's commune movement, to the mass movements in economic construction, and to Party leadership in socialist construction, that is, to 'putting politics in command.' In his letter he brazenly slandered as 'petty bourgeois fanaticism' the revolutionary zeal of the Party and of hundreds of millions of people."

Thus it was necessary to "expose this hypocrite, this careerist, and conspirator, in his true colors and to put an end to his divisive anti-Party activities." P'eng was also said to belong to the Kao Kang–Jao Shu-shih anti-Party alliance. See "Resolution of Eighth Plenary Session of Eighth Central Committee of C.C.P. concerning the anti-Party clique headed by P'eng Teh-huai" (excerpts), PR 34 (Aug. 18, 1967): 8–10.

9. Translated by Willis Barnstone in collaboration with Ko Ching-po, *The Poems of Mao Tse-tung* (New York, 1972), 103. At the height of the Cultural Revolution in November 1967 Chou En-lai first publicized this private exchange between Chairman Mao and Comrade Chiang Ch'ing, presumably because he thought that literary evidence of Mao's affection would enhance her public respect. See *We-ke t'ung hsun* [Cultrual Revolution bulletin] (Canton), Nov. 8, 1967; SCMP 4076 (Dec. 18, 1967): 3.

10. Possibly Ting Wu's Chinese adaptation of 1957 (published in Peking, 1958) of M. Rozental's

and P. Yudin's *Short Philosophical Dictionary*, first published in Moscow in 1939; and revised and reissued for many years thereafter. The Peking adaptation marks the progressive moving away from the Soviet-established terms of Marxism and documents Mao's rising philosophic stature. The extracts from the *Dictionary* published in the Shanghai journal *Hsueh-hsi yü p'i-p'an* [Study and criticism] in the spring of 1974 show the continuation of that Sinocentric process (CNA 992 [March 7, 1974]: 2).

11. Her passing mention of books and commentaries that concerned the Chairman while she was sick and self-absorbed refers to a Soviet work called *Political Economy*, his critiques of Stalin's *Economic Problems of Socialism in the USSR*, and his comments on Stalin's "Reply to Comrades Sanina and Venzher." His unofficially published speech on *Economic Problems* appears in *Miscellany of Mao Tse-tung Thought*, 1: 129–132. Richard Levy's "New Light on Mao; 2. His Views on the Soviet Union's *Political Economy*," CQ 61 (March 1975): 95–117, analyzes Mao's rethinking of the problems of the base and the superstructure, assessment of Stalin's inducement of bourgeois elements to join in the construction of communes, and weighing of the validity of the Soviet model in industrial development in the light of the above publications. Clearly in 1959 Mao was freeing himself and China from the Soviet model.

12. More than Chiang Ch'ing chose to reveal in her narration, Mao was humbled by the disasters resulting from his quixotic scheme of 1959: poor crops, famine, disappointing industrial output, and widespread disorder. On the last day of the Ninth Plenum Mao buckled down to a new empiricism, saying that 1961 was to be a year of "seeking truth from reality." "We have a tradition of 'seeking truth from reality,' but probably as the pressure of official work increased we no longer paid attention to getting to the bottom of things. . . . From now on everybody must do investigation and study and not just run other people down" (*Miscellany of Mao Tse-tung Thought*, 2: 242).

13. Stuart Schram mentions Mao's draft directive presented to the Supreme State Conference on January 28, 1958, titled "Sixty Articles on Work Methods" and dated January 31, 1958 (*Chairman Mao Talks to the People: Talks and Letters, 1956–1971*, New York, 1974, 3; CB 892: [Oct. 21, 1969]: 1–14; Jerome Ch'en, *Mao Papers*, London, 1970, 57–76). This directive must have been an early version of the "Sixty Rules for the People's Commune."

14. The May Sixteenth Circular appeared as an editorial titled "The Intellectuals' Way Forward," HC 10 (May 16, 1962). This reformulation of Mao Tse-tung's talks at the Yenan Forum two decades earlier reminded intellectuals of the perpetual need to "remold" themselves, change their world outlook, and be conscious of whom they serve.

15. A month earlier Liu Shao-ch'i had reasserted himself ideologically by reprinting and distributing widely his memorable essay of the late 1930's, "How To Be a Good Communist," a literary event condemnable only in a society incapable of entertaining simultaneously more than one great man's point of view.

   The precarious parity in the fall of 1962 not only between the political principles of Mao and Liu but also between their wives was never discussed directly by Chiang Ch'ing. By the early 1960's Wang Kuang-mei was recognized internationally for her charm and diplomacy. In the fall of 1962 *People's Daily*, no doubt prodded by Liu Shao-ch'i, broke the convention of keeping screened from the public images of the leaders in the company of their wives. On the second page of the September 25, 1962, issue of *People's Daily* Wang, Liu, and one of President Sukarno's several wives, who was on a state visit, appeared together, and Wang and Mme. Sukarno appeared on the first page the next day. Five days later Mao, Chiang Ch'ing, and Mme. Sukarno appeared on the front page, with Liu, Wang, and Mme. Sukarno on the second. This was the first time since 1949 that a photograph of Mao and Chiang Ch'ing together was officially published. For a Western assessment of political implications see Roderick MacFarquhar, "On Photographs," CQ 46 (1971): 300.

16. "Decisions of the CCP Central Committee on Certain Problems in the Present Rural Work (Draft)," May 20, 1963, *Documents of the CCP Central Committee, September 1956–April 1969*, 1: 735–752.

   Stuart Schram has suggested that the Later Ten Point Document, which opened the Socialist Education Campaign, may have been drafted by Teng Hsiao-p'ing, then secretary general of the Party. A year later Liu published a Revised Later Ten Point Document (Schram, *Authority*, 76–78).

17. As noted by William F. Dorrill, "Power, Policy and Ideology," in *The Cultural Revolution in China*, Thomas W. Robinson, ed. (Berkeley, 1971), 57 n.68.

18. Among such pieces was a laudatory account of a woman comrade named Ch'en Min who first

came into her own at Yenan and Nanniwan, and was still a worthy model twenty years later. Like Chiang Ch'ing, Ch'en Min was married to a man more distinguished politically than herself (political commissar T'an Wen-pang). She was a mother (of nine, five surviving), and commendable for her industriousness and frugality. Already in Yenan she had been elected a "special grade model dependent" (an oblique comment on the restrained feminism of that era). Chiang Ch'ing's article appeared in *Chung-kuo fu-nü* [Women of China] 8 (Aug. 1, 1961); SCMM 277 (Sept. 5, 1961): 18–24.

On August 26 her report, "The Good Traditions of a Red Army Company" appeared in *Chung-kuo ch'ing-nien pao* [Chinese youth]; SCMP 2581 (Sept. 19, 1961): 7–9. That laudatory but bland account of the First Guard Company's loyalty and frugality lacks both the sense of personal and political anguish in her writings of the 1930's and the tough, swashbuckling style she flourished in the later 1960's. Neither article was mentioned in our interview.

19. Speech delivered on Feb. 23, 1964; CB 842 (Dec. 8, 1967): 19.
20. See Yun Sung's article "T'ien Han's *Hsieh Yao-huan* is a Big Poisonous Weed," which appeared in KMJP, Feb. 1, 1966; CB 784 (Mar. 30, 1966): 1.
21. CB 842 (Dec. 8, 1967): 8, 9.
22. Ibid., 17.
23. Ibid., 21.
24. For an account of T'ao Chu's career in the early 1960's see Ezra F. Vogel, *Canton under Communism* (Cambridge, Mass., 1969), 308–309.
25. CB 842 (Dec. 8, 1967): 21.
26. PR 27 (July 3, 1964).
27. See note 2, above.
28. According to Chao Tzu-fan, "His [T'ien Han's] KMT Party Member Card was issued on the third floor of the Mitsui Yoko, a Japanese trading company, on August 7, 1938. In the mid-1930's, he headed the Sixth Division of the Third Department, National Military Council, with the rank of major general, and was in charge of anti-Japanese art publicity ("Left-Wing Chinese Literary and Art Movement in the 1930's," *Issues and Studies* (Taipei) 3 [November 1966]: 27).
29. The February Outline, drawn up on February 7, 1966, was approved by the Central Committee for distribution five days later. After it was revoked by another May Sixteenth Circular, of 1966 (see Chapter 13), both documents were sent to Party committees in all units at all levels for discussion as to which was correct (the successor, obviously). The February Outline is translated in SCMP 3952 (June 5, 1967): 1–4. The other members of the Group of Five were K'ang Sheng, Wu Leng-hsi, Chou Yang, and Lu Ting-i.
30. In the course of a philosophical debate to refute Yang Hsien-chen's principle, "two combines into one," Chou Ku-ch'eng wrote that matter can be undifferentiated with no contradiction. See Ju Hsin, "A Critique of the Philosophical Basis of Chou Ku-ch'eng's Conception of Art," HC 15 (Aug. 15, 1964), and "New Polemics on the Philosophical Front," HC 16 (Aug. 31, 1964), on Yang's theory.

13. *Learn to Swim by Swimming*

1. Franz Schurmann, *The Logic of World Power* (New York, 1974), 334.
2. "Summary of the Forum on the Work in Literature and Art in the Armed Forces with which Comrade Lin Piao Entrusted Comrade Chiang Ch'ing," HC 9 (May 27, 1967), reprinted in PR 23 (June 2, 1967).
3. Interview with Mao in January 1965, published in *The Washington Post*, February 14, 1965.
4. Others among the members of the Cultural Revolution Group were Wang Jen-chung, deputy leader; Kuan Feng, writer; Ch'i Pen-yü, writer; Wang Li, co-author of the Nine Comments against Revisionism; Mu Hsin, editor-in-chief of KMJP and deputy chief director of HC (CB 830 [June 26, 1967]: 4, 27).
5. Speech of Nov. 28, 1966; SCMP 3908 (May 30, 1967): 11.
6 "Excerpts from Talks at Peking University by Leaders of the Cultural Revolution Group under the CCP Central Committee," CB 830 (June 26, 1967): 4.
7. Ibid.
8. The communiqué that gave blanket ratification to decisions on domestic and foreign affairs made by Mao after 1962 was published in JMJP Aug. 9, 1966; its first appearance in English

was in PR 33 (Aug. 12, 1966): 6–11. The Sixteen-Point Decision admonished, "The minority should be defended because sometimes truth belongs to them." Did that mean that the Maoist group did not yet command a majority in the Central Committee?

Richard Baum has pointed out that the Sixteen-Point Decision clarified the complementarity of the Socialist Education Campaign, which was directed toward rural and urban production units, and the Cultural Revolution, which was geared to cultural and educational establishments and Party and government organs. The restriction of Cultural Revolution activities sustained through the late summer and fall was lifted in November and December, when masses of students were ordered to carry the political movement to factories and farms throughout the nation; the result was to bring the nation to the brink of civil war (*Prelude to the Cultural Revolution: Mao, the Party and the Peasant Question, 1962–1966*, New York, 1975, 149–150).

9. CB 830 (June 26, 1967): 26–27. Here and in subsequent passages based upon translated sources I have smoothed the English without altering the meaning.

10. "Chairman Mao Joins a Million People to Celebrate the Great Cultural Revolution (August 18, 1966)," NCNA dispatch in *Carry the Great Proletarian Cultural Revolution through to the End* (Peking, 1966), 15.

11. Ibid., 16.

12. This speech, along with six others (July 1964, at the Peking Opera Festival; Feb. 20, 1966; April 20, 1967; Sept. 5, 1967; Nov. 9 and 12, 1967; Nov. 27, 1967), had been selected by Chou En-lai and was delivered orally to me by her aides in Peking (see Chapter 1). The November 28 speech was never published "officially," Chiang Ch'ing said. However, it appears, much as it was spoken to me, in *Hung-i chan-pao* [Combat bulletin of red arts], Feb. 15, 1967; SCMP 3908 (Mar. 30, 1967): 9–15.

13. SCMP 3908 (Mar. 30, 1967): 9–15.

14. By that time Peking Mayor P'eng Chen, dramatists Wu Han and T'ien Han, and journalist Liao Mo-sha had been arrested. According to Ch'en Po-ta, more than four hundred thousand "enemies of the people" had been exiled from the cities to the countryside. See Douwe W. Fokkema, *Report from Peking: Observations of a Western Diplomat on the Cultural Revolution* (London, 1971), 50.

15. Reported in *Sankei* (Tokyo), Apr. 26, 1967, as cited by Edward E. Rice, *Mao's Way* (Berkeley, 1972), 292–293.

16. "A Counterrevolutionary Record Aimed at the Restoration of Capitalism," CL 6 (1968): 95–100.

17. Translated in CB 786 (May 16, 1966): 15–36.

18. *Wen-hui pao* [Literary Gazette], Sept. 8, 1966; SCMPS 156 (Oct. 7, 1966): 25–29.

19. Rice, 272.

20. Ibid., 273.

21. See, for example, her speech of February 1, 1967, to representatives of film studios, SCMP 3902 (Mar. 20, 1967): 1–7.

22. Mao's verbal adjustment is pointed out in Stuart Schram, ed., *Chairman Mao Talks to the People: Talks and Letters, 1956–1971* (New York, 1974), 15–16.

23. That spring *Red Flag*, then edited by Ch'en Po-ta, published a long article on the Paris Commune (HC 4 [March 24, 1966]).

24. As reported in a JMJP editorial of Jan. 9, 1967.

25. *Hung-wei-ping pao* [Red Guard journal, Peking], Dec. 22, 1966, reprinted in *Speeches by Chiang Ch'ing*, 27–28.

26. *Hung-wei pao* [Red Guard paper] (Jan. 17, 1967), reprinted in *Speeches by Chiang Ch'ing*, 29–33.

27. "Speech to a Revolutionary Rebel Group" (Jan. 17, 1967), *Hung-wei-ping pao* [Red Guard journal, Peking], Jan. 19, 1967, reprinted in *Speeches by Chiang Ch'ing*, 36.

28. Although Chiang Ch'ing's share of the responsibility for setting up Wang Kuang-mei's trial is indeterminable at least one Red Guard publication quoted her as having said on December 18, 1966, "Wang Kuang-mei should be grabbed back to Tsinghua to make a confession" (JPRS, *Samples of Red Guard Publications* [Aug. 1, 1967], 1: 8th item; cited in Rice, 281).

29. For an account of her journal and its later political fallout see Baum, 83–101.

30. William Hinton, *Hundred Day War: The Cultural Revolution at Tsinghua University* (New York, 1972), 101–104. That women are often scapegoats in Chinese history has been observed by many, including Lu Hsun. See his essays "Random Thoughts (40)" and "Women

Are Not the Worst Liars" in *Selected Words of Lu Hsun*, 4 vols. (Peking, 1956–1960), 2: 34–36, and 4: 11–12.

14. Against the Current

1. Canton *Wen-i hung-ch'i* [Literature and art red flag], Jan. 10, 1968; SCMPS 216 (Jan. 26, 1968): 4.
2. Edward E. Rice, *Mao's Way* (Berkeley, 1972), 409.
3. *Hsin Peita* [New Peking University], Feb. 16, 1967; CB 822 (Mar. 23, 1967); Rice, 331–332.
4. For example, Cheng Chi-hua's *Chung-kuo tien-ying fa-chan shih* [History of the development of the Chinese film], and Hsia Yen's *Tien-ying lun-wen chi* [Collected essays on the film] (Peking, 1963).
5. SCMP 3902 (Mar. 20, 1967): 1–7.
6. The editorial, which appeared on January 31, 1967, was titled "Down with the Ego and Forge a Grand Alliance of Revolutionary Rebels."
7. Speech of April 12, 1967, in *Speeches by Chiang Ch'ing*, 1971, 45–61, taken from the original pamphlet titled *Wei jen-min li hsin kung* [Perform new services for the people] (Kunming).
8. JMJP, Apr. 21, 1967.
9. Peking *Ching-kang-shan pao* [Ching-kang-shan journal], May 25, 1967; SCMP 3996 (Aug. 8, 1967): 3. See also the laudatory accounts of Chiang Ch'ing's past, 1931–1964, in Canton *Kuang-yin hung-ch'i* [Printing system red flag], Oct. 29, 1967; SCMP 4089 (Dec. 29, 1967): 1–2; *Kuang-chou hung tai-hui* [Canton red congress], Oct. 28, 1968; SCMP 4306 (Nov. 26, 1968): 1–8.
10. *Hsin Peita* [New Peking University], May 30, 1967; SCMPS 190 (July 6, 1967): 11.
11. PR 24 (June 9, 1967): 24.
12. See, for example, Rice, 396–402, and Jean Daubier, A *History of the Chinese Cultural Revolution* (New York, 1974), 197–204. The *Liberation Army Daily* editorial broadcast by NCNA on July 26, 1967, urged revolutionaries to "take the tiny handful of persons in authority taking the capitalist road within the Army and throw every last one into the trash heap" (SCMP 3993 [Aug. 2, 1967]: 5). Evidently, the summer of 1967 was a low point in the "glorious history" of the PLA.
13. Speech of July 22, 1967; SCMPS 198 (Aug. 18, 1967): 8.
14. See Philip Bridgham, "Mao's Cultural Revolution in 1967," in Richard Baum and Louise B. Bennett, eds., *China in Ferment* (Englewood Cliffs, N.J., 1971), 134–135; Thomas W. Robinson, "Chou En-lai and the Cultural Revolution in China," in *The Cultural Revolution in China*, Thomas W. Robinson, ed. (Berkeley, 1971), especially 239–250.
15. In Chou En-lai's judgment of September 17 the Cultural Revolution by then had entered a second stage. See *K'an chin ch'ao* [Look at today], Oct. 15, 1967; SCMP 4078 (Dec. 12, 1967): 7.
16. First appeared in Canton *Kung-ko-lien* [Work, revolution, alliance], Sept. 18, 1967; reprinted in *Speeches by Chiang Ch'ing*, 68–76; translated from Peking *Ching-kang-shan pao* [Ching-kang-shan journal], Sept. 20, 1967, in SCMPS 209 (Nov. 3, 1967): 1–5.
17. Notably Wang Li, hero of the Wuhan Mutiny, Ch'i Pen-yü, Kuan Feng, and Lin Chich. By September Wang Li was charged with provoking the May Sixteenth Clique to attack Chou En-lai as a "bourgeois reactionary" because, starting in May of that year, he sought to protect veteran leaders, among them Ch'en I, Chu Te, and T'an Chen-lin, against further attacks from the left. Discussed in Daubier, 187–189.
18. *K'an chin chao* [Look at today], Oct. 15, 1967; SCMP 4078 (Dec. 12, 1967): 9.
19. Both incidents are described in Rice, 376–378.
20. Chung-fa (67) 354 (directive of the Central Committee), according to reports in Canton *Wen-i hung-ch'i* [Literature and art red flag], Jan. 10, 1968; SCMPS 216 (Jan. 26, 1968): 1–5.
21. Speech read to me in Peking.
22. *Kuang-chou hung tai-hui* [Canton red congress], Apr. 3, 1968; SCMP 4164 (Apr. 25, 1968): 1–2.
23. *Hung-ch'i* [Red flag; Peking Aviation Institute Revolutionary Committee], Mar. 26, 1968; SCMPS 226 (May 20, 1968): 4–7; also SCMP 4182 (May 21, 1968): 1–12.
24. Canton *Chung-ta hung-ch'i* [Chungshan University red flag] 63 (Apr. 4, 1968); SCMP 4166 (Apr. 29, 1968): 1–4.

25. Events summarized on the basis of contemporary documents in Rice, 437–440.
26. Canton *Chu-ying tung-fang hung* [Pearl River film studio, East is red] 20 (special edition, April 1968); SCMP 4172 (May 7, 1968): 2–7.
27. Canton *Tzu-liao chuan-chi* [Special issue of reference material] 3 (May 1968); SCMP 4196 (June 12, 1968): 4.
28. Peking *Ching-kang-shan pao* [Ching-kang-shan journal] and *Hung-ch'i* [Red flag: Peking Aviation Institute Revolutionary Committee], Mar. 21, 1968; SCMPS 225 (May 14, 1968): 1–14.
29. Canton *Huo-chu t'ung-hsun* [Torch bulletin] 1 (July 1968); SCMM 622 (Aug. 6, 1968): 7–10.

15. Lin Piao the Overreacher

1. Translated as "Lin Piao's Address at the Enlarged Meeting of the CCP Central Politburo (May 18, 1966)," *Issues and Studies* 6 (February 1970): 81–92.
2. For a multifaceted documentary history of Lin Piao's challenge, see Michael Y. M. Kau, *The Lin Piao Affair: Power Politics and Military Coup* (White Plains, N.Y., 1975).
3. At the opening of the case against Lin Piao in the summer of 1972, this exchange between husband and wife was circulated among Party leaders as evidence of Mao's early distrust of Lin Piao, and of Chiang Ch'ing's early warning against him. A translation appears in *Issues and Studies* (Taipei) 9 (January 1973): 94–96.
4. An account of Lin Piao's speech to the Lu Shan Plenum is itemized in the Party's case against him. See Document No. 12 of the CCP Central Committee, in *Issues and Studies* (Taipei) 8 (September 1972): 63–71.
5. Mao's report included a disavowal of nepotism, which by implication paralleled his own situation: "I have always objected to having one's wife serve as director of one's office. In Lin Piao's office it is Yeh Ch'ün who serves as the office director. All four people [Huang Yung-sheng, Wu Fa-hsien, Li Tso-p'eng, and Ch'iu Hui-tso] must first see her in order to seek instructions from Lin. All work must be done personally, read personally and replied personally. We should not rely on secretaries and give them too much power. My secretary only handles reception work; all papers are selected and checked by me. We must do our own work lest some mistakes should occur" (ibid., 71).
6. "Lin Piao's Address" (May 18, 1966), 91.
7. Snow, *The Long Revolution* (New York, 1971), 169. Ruminating among colleagues on the same problem twelve years earlier, Mao, citing Stalin's cult and Khrushchev's demolition of it, distinguished between correct and incorrect "cults of the individual," the incorrect being "simply blind obedience." See "Talks at the Chengtu Conference, March 1958" in Stuart Schram, ed., *Chairman Mao Talks to the People: Talks and Letters, 1956–1971* (New York, 1974), 99–100.
8. See her ardent subscription to Mao's appropriation of Lu Hsun's reputation. Under the Kuomintang White Terror, she reflected in 1967, "Lu Hsun and Chairman Mao were separated by vast distances, but Lu Hsun's heart was with Chairman Mao, beating with Chairman Mao. For Lu Hsun our great Chairman Mao was the reddest red sun in his heart." That was matched by blame of Chou Yang et al. for persecuting her husband and hastening his death (CL 1 [1967]: 36–38).
9. In his report of the Lu Shan Plenum of August 23, 1970, Mao Tse-tung puzzled over a question: "It is also said that I am the founder and leader of the People's Liberation Army but Lin is the personal commander. Why can't the founder be the commander? I am not the only founder either." See Document No. 12 of the CCP Central Committee, 68.
10. Documentary evidence reflects Lin Piao's indulgence in such pronouncements, but starting seven years later. In his speech of May 18, 1966, he remarked: "Every sentence of Chairman Mao's works is a truth; one single sentence of his surpasses ten thousand of ours" ("Lin Piao's Address," 92).

   Mao's recapitulation of Lin Piao's statements at the Lu Shan meeting of August 23, 1970, includes the following: "You overdid it when you talked about 'apex' and 'one sentence worth ten thousand sentences.' One sentence is one sentence. How can it be worth ten thousand sentences? No provision shall be made for state chairmanship and I will not serve as state chairman. I have said so six times. If each time I had made one sentence, there should have been sixty thousand sentences. But they have never listened to me. Therefore my words are not even worth half a sentence; they equal zero" (Document No. 12 of the CCP Central Committee, 68).

11. On June 24, 1968, Li Min mounted a poster entitled "Bombard Nieh Jung-chen," ostensibly a call for class struggle within the Science and Technology Commission (notice made in the Canton *Chung-hsueh hung-wei-ping* [Middle school Red Guards] 8 [July 1968]; SCMP 4236 [Aug. 12, 1968]: 1–2).

16. *Theater of Revolution*

1. Catherine R. Stimpson, "Power, Presentations, and the Presentable," unpublished paper (August 1975).
2. Colin Mackerras, *The Chinese Theatre in Modern Times, from 1840 to the Present Day* (Amherst, Mass., 1975), 92, 97, et passim.
3. *Cosmos and History* (New York, 1954), 32.
4. Mackerras, 163.
5. CNA 1038 (Apr. 23, 1975): 2.
6. See Mei Lan-fang, *Wo-ti tien-ying sheng-huo* [My life in the movies] (Peking, 1962).
7. See, for example, Canton *Kuang-yin hung-ch'i* [Printing system red flag], Oct. 29, 1967; SCMP 4089 (Dec. 29, 1967): 1–13.
8. SCMP 3996 (Aug. 8, 1967): 12.
9. The substance-function (*t'i-yung*) dilemma is provocatively analyzed by Joseph R. Levenson, *Modern China and Its Confucian Past* (Garden City, N.Y., 1964), 82–84 passim.
10. See Jerome B. Grieder's intellectual biography, *Hu Shih and the Chinese Renaissance* (Cambridge, Mass., 1970), 130–131.
11. Speech of November 28, 1966; SCMP 3908 (Mar. 30, 1967): 10.
12. "Chairman Mao's Talk to Music Workers (August 24, 1956)" in Stuart Schram, ed., *Chairman Mao Talks to the People: Talks and Letters, 1956–1971* (New York, 1974), 87.
13. For reflections from the standpoint of the Cultural Revolution, see Mao Chi-tseng, "Traditional Chinese Orchestras," CL 6 (1964): 102–108.
14. Hsiang-shan shih (pseud.; Liang Ch'i-ch'ao), *Yin-ping-shih shih-hua* [Notes on Poetry from the Ice Drinker's Studio] (Shanghai, 1909), *chüan* 2, 1a–1b.
15. Benjamin Schwartz, *In Search of Wealth and Power: Yen Fu and the West* (Cambridge, Mass., 1964); see especially ch. XII, "Some Implications."
16. For an account of Chiang Ch'ing's initial appearances at rehearsals of the Central Philharmonic Orchestra and of Chou Yang, Lin Mo-han, and others' attempted subversions of her work, see CL 3 (1967): 4–8.
17. Hsien Hsing-hai (1905–1945), the son of a Cantonese boat worker and who eventually studied music in Paris, wrote the *Yellow River Cantata* while chairing the Music Department at the Lu Hsun Academy in 1939. Unprecedented in Chinese musical tradition, the *Cantata* incorporated local folk tunes and featured one that represented the voice of an oppressed woman. It was expected that her plaintive voice would heighten consciousness of oppression and yearning for liberation in the listeners. See his personal account, Hsien Hsing-hai, *Huang ho ta-ho ch'ang* [Yellow River Cantata] (Peking, 1951).
18. The *Shachiapang Symphony* was first performed on National Day, October 1, 1965 (HC 8 [1967]); *The Red Lantern* was first orchestrated with piano in July 1967 (PR 30 [1968]: 4–6).
19. For a linguistic analysis of the creation of *yang-pan hsi*, see Hua-yuan Li Mowry, "*Yang-pan-hsi*" — *New Theater in China* (Berkeley: Studies in Chinese Communist Terminology, No. 15, 1973).
20. Widely reproduced, "Chairman Mao Goes to An-yuan" was composed collectively by students from Peking colleges and universities and painted by the twenty-four-year-old son of a poor peasant. Chiang Ch'ing, who promoted the painting during the Cultural Revolution, commended the students' courage in using oil paint (a foreign thing) to project a Chinese image. This cultural synthesis conformed to the style of her model opera, ballet, and symphony. For reference to the painting, see CL 9 (1968): 40–41.
21. Talks at cultural forums, November 9 and 12, 1967, Canton *Wen-i hung-ch'i* [Literature and art red flag], Jan. 10, 1968; SCMPS 216 (Jan. 26, 1968).
22. The terms used by Mao and Chiang Ch'ing here — "typical," "individual," "liberal" — have special meanings in Communist terminology. A "typical" character is a heroic exemplar of

Mao Tse-tung's thought, a model to be emulated nationwide. An "individual" is a character who, in the traditional Chinese manner, spends his life pleasing everyone and offending no one, thereby neglecting Mao Tse-tung's teachings. For literary implications, see Joe C. Huang, *Heroes and Villains in Communist China: The Contemporary Chinese Novel as a Reflection of Life* (New York, 1973), 293–294.

At the Yenan Forum of 1942 Mao said of typicality in a socialist realist context: ". . . Works of literature and art can and ought to be on a higher plane, more intense, more concentrated, more typical, nearer the ideal, and therefore more universal than actual everyday life. . . . Writers and artists concentrate on such everyday phenomena, typify the contradictions and struggles within them, and produce works which awaken the masses, fire them with enthusiasm, and impel them to unite and struggle to transform their environment" ("Talks at the Yenan Forum," SW, 3: 82).

"Liberalism" also has acquired a particular sense in Chinese communism. In his essay of 1937, "Combat Liberalism" (SW, 2: 31–33), Mao defined liberalism extensively as a manifestation of "petty-bourgeois selfishness," of unprincipled compromise, and of tolerance of the political mistakes of others for fear of creating hard feelings. Liberalism — avoidance of active ideological struggle — is exhibited by the "individual" defined above.

23. Though by 1974 Li Hsi-fan, one of Chiang Ch'ing's followers then with the literary section of *People's Daily*, reported that some classical dramas were being selected for foreign dignitaries and in the foreseeable future might be performed publicly once again. See Mackerras, 174.
24. Peking *Hung-ch'i* [Red flag], Mar. 26, 1968; SCMPS 227 (June 4, 1968): 17–18.

17. Heroics in Song and Dance

1. HC 9 (May 27, 1967); SCMM 584 (July 17, 1967): 19.
2. "Summary of the Forum on the Work of Literature and Art in the Armed Forces with which Comrade Lin Piao Entrusted Comrade Chiang Ch'ing," HC 9 (May 27, 1967), reprinted in PR 23 (June 2, 1967): 15.
3. *Hsin Peita* [New Peking University], May 30, 1967; SCMPS 190 (July 6, 1967): 12–13.
4. "Interjections at Conference of Provincial and Municipal Party Secretaries (Collected)" (January 1957), *Miscellany of Mao Tse-tung Thought*, 1: 46, JPRS 61269-1.
5. The unheard-of introduction of the piano into the Peking opera framework of *The Red Lantern* was greeted with a new proletarian pomposity: "Bourgeois musicians claimed that piano playing was an advanced and difficult art, suited only to so-called world-famous compositions of the eighteenth and nineteenth century. This was nonsense. They simply were enamoured of decadent, bourgeois and revisionist stuff. Their high class music serves only to sap the fighting will of the revolutionary people.

"When we saw standing before the piano, not simpering and posturing bourgeois young ladies and gentlemen, but the great images of the workers, peasants and soldiers, and when we heard the powerful notes of the piano and the clear voices of the singers, we were greatly stirred" (CL 9 [1968]: 24–25).
6. On February 23, 1964, Mao ordered actors, poets, writers, and dramatists to leave the cities for the rural areas (CB 842 [Dec 8, 1967]: 19).
7. Chiang Ch'ing's order for Li Yü-ho to walk to the execution ground to the strains of the "Internationale" was squelched by Lin Mo-han, who remarked sardonically at a rehearsal that the "Internationale" played on traditional Chinese instruments "lacked force and sounded like rats squeaking" (CL 3 [1967]: 22).
8. Among the protégés of the former Ministry of Culture was Peking Mayor P'eng Chen, whose impatience with Chiang Ch'ing's new repertory was long-standing. In 1946 he was made secretary of the Party's Northeast Bureau, but in the middle of that year was forced to yield to Lin Piao and his policy of guerrilla warfare, which contradicted P'eng Chen's conventional strategy. Presumably disturbed by a revolutionary drama that by clear implication played up Lin Piao's heroism at the expense of his own, P'eng is reported to have challenged the actors, "Why not perform traditional plays [avoiding modern history]? Don't we still have history courses in universities and colleges?" Rapidly he collected over one hundred eighty traditional dramas, which he forced the troupe to stage in the name of "political and economic tasks." Undaunted, Chiang Ch'ing returned to the troupe and presented them with autographed copies of Mao's *Selected Works*. She told them, "Don't think I'm here to just promote theatrical

performances. I'm here to do battle against feudalism, capitalism, and revisionism" (Peking *Ching-kang-shan pao* [Ching-kang-shan journal], May 25, 1967; SCMP 3996 [Aug. 8, 1967]: 8).

9. A detailed account of the problems of revising *Tiger Mountain* appears in HC 2 (Jan. 30, 1970); SCMM 7002 (February 1970): 36–48.
10. HC 8 (May 23, 1967); JPRS 41,458 (June 20, 1967): 57–64.
11. Ibid., 62.
12. Lin Mo-han, dubbed by cultural revolutionaries the "backstage general manager for the black line on literature and art," "smeared" *Tiger Mountain*, describing it as "lacking the flavor of Peking opera," "just plain boiled water," and "a third-class crop." See Kuan Hsin, "Mao Tse-tung's Thought Guides Us in the Great Revolution of Peking Opera," in Chiang Ch'ing, *On the Revolution in Peking Opera* (Peking, 1968).
13. The "Three Principles of Stress" and other dramatic formulas attributed to Chiang Ch'ing appear in "Let Our Theater Propagate Mao Tse-tung's Thought For Ever," by Yü Hui-yung (named minister of culture in 1975), in CL 7–8 (1968): 107–115.
14. Hsueh Ching, "The Birth of the First Ballet with a Modern Revolutionary Theme," CL 3 (1967): 12.
15. Edgar Snow, *The Other Side of the River* (New York, 1962), 76.
16. The original opera version in six acts appears in *Pai-mao nü* [White-haired Girl], Hu Ching-chih et al., eds. (Peking, 1946).
17. As chief of cultural affairs in Yenan, Chou Yang lauded the story's romantic spirit, realistic basis, demonstration of resistance against Japan, and class struggle (HCPP 16 [1961]: 163).
18. The 1950 version along with its operatic history appears in *Pai-mao nü* [White-haired Girl] (Peking, 1953).
19. Lois Wheeler Snow, *China on Stage* (New York, 1972), 202.
20. *The New York Times*, Oct. 7, 1973.

19. Eleventh Hour

1. Ch'u Lan, "Magnificent Scrolls of Chinese Revolutionary History, On the Achievements and Significance of Revolutionary Model Theatrical Works," HC 1 (Jan. 1, 1974); SPRCM 767–768 (Jan. 21–Feb. 4, 1974): 60–66.
2. Ibid.
3. Ch'u Lan, "Criticism of the Shansi Opera 'San shang T'ao-feng' [Three Visits to Peach Mountain]," JMJP, Feb. 28, 1974; SPRCP 5575 (Mar. 19, 1974): 38–45, especially p. 39.
4. Ibid. See also Wei Ch'ing, "The Shansi Opera 'San shang T'ao-feng' Is a Big Poisonous Weed which Attempts to Reverse the Verdict on Liu Shao-ch'i," KMJP, Mar. 3, 1974; SPRCP 5576 (Mar. 20, 1974): 72–81.
5. See Fang Chin's article in HC 6 (June 1, 1974); SPRCM 778–779 (July 2–8, 1974): 88–92.
6. Chiang Ch'ing's speech of July 5, 1964, was described as "elaborately expounding the brilliant theory of Mao" in JMJP, July 16, 1974.
7. Ch'u Lan, "A Decade of Revolution in Peking Opera," HC 7 (July 1, 1974); SPRCM 784–785 (July 29–Aug. 15, 1974), 80–88.
8. Ibid.
9. "Peking's Rich Repertoire," PR 41 (Oct. 10, 1975).
10. JMJP, Jan. 30, 1974.
11. *Saturday Review World*, May 18, 1974.
12. As observed by an American present at the reception.
13. Ch'u Lan, "Deepen the Criticism of the Bourgeois Theory of Human Nature," HC 4 (Apr. 1, 1974); SPRCM 773–774 (April 22–29, 1974): 63–70.
14. *The New York Times*, Oct. 14, 1973.
15. Four years after Chairman Mao and President Nixon had drawn up the Shanghai Communiqué, and nearly two years after the Watergate debacle, the Chairman invited Mr. Nixon to return to China. Though a disgraced ex-President, he was given the royal treatment. The evening after his audience with Chairman Mao on February 23, Chiang Ch'ing escorted Mr. and Mrs. Nixon to the Great Hall for a cultural program of some twenty-five songs and dances. During the performance Chiang Ch'ing suddenly jumped to her feet and loudly applauded a tenor's song expressing China's determination to "liberate Taiwan" (Peking's sense of the essence of the Shanghai Communiqué). Unaware of the meaning of the Chinese lyrics, Mr.

Nixon started to rise, then caught himself, giving only polite applause. Responding to his cue, Mrs. Nixon had also risen, then sat down with him (*The New York Times*, Feb. 24, 1976).

16. *The New York Times*, Oct. 22, 1973.

17. *International Herald Tribune*, Oct. 26, 1974. Anyone who suspects that Chiang Ch'ing's entertainment of Imelda Marcos was trifling should look to a speech reportedly made by Foreign Minister Ch'iao Kuan-hua in Tientsin on May 20, 1975. He said: "The wife of the president of the Philippines was selected through a beauty contest. She is the product of a corrupt capitalist system, under which capitalists toy with women. From this you can understand what class the president of the Philippines and his wife represent. Nevertheless, in the present international situation, we have to talk with them, as we had to invite Nixon and to talk with him. The brilliance of Chairman Mao consists in this, that he can discriminate between what is important and what is not" (CNA 1036 [Apr. 19, 1976]: 6).

18. For example, James Yen's Ting *hsien* experiment and the KMT's "model counties."

19. *The New York Times*, Dec. 23, 1974, covers Señora Marcos' introduction to the wonders of Hsiao-chin-chuang. KMJP, Oct. 10, 1974, describes the full range of the brigade's cultural enterprises.

20. See, for example, KMJP, Oct. 15, 1974; JMJP, Dec. 7, 1974; HC 12 (Nov. 25, 1975); PR 18 (Jan. 10, 1975). A good general source on the revival of interest in the short-lived Ch'in dynasty and its Legalist example is Li Yu-ning, ed., *The First Emperor of China* (White Plains, N.Y., 1975).

21. See the January 1973 issue of HC, and the discussion in CNA 1059 (Nov. 5, 1976): 3.

22. At the Tenth Party Congress of August 1973, Chou En-lai described the campaign against Confucius as "a continuation and deepening of the campaign against Lin Piao." On February 2, 1975, *People's Daily* proclaimed the turning of that proposition into a mass movement.

23. CCP Central Committee document (Chung-fa) 3 (1974), *Issues and Studies* (Taipei) 10 (August 1974): 110–113.

24. Prominently by the "Iron Girls" team of Tachai. See "We Revolutionary Women Bitterly Hate the Doctrines of Confucius and Mencius," HC 3 (Mar. 3, 1974); SPRCM 771–772 (Mar. 25–Apr. 1, 1974): 36–38; Fu Wen, "Doctrine of Confucius and Mencius — The Shackle that Keeps Women in Bondage," PR 10 (Mar. 8, 1974): 16–18.

25. For new historical comment on matriarchy in primitive society, see Sun Lo-ying and Lu Li-fan, "On Confucian Persecution of Women in History," Hsueh-hsi yü p'i-p'an [Study and criticism] 1 (Jan. 10, 1975); SPRCM 813 (Mar. 17, 1975): 52–57.

26. Lo Ssu-ting, "On Class Struggle during the Ch'in-Han Period," HC 8 (Aug. 1, 1974); SPRCM 787–788 (Aug. 30–Sept. 9, 1974): 15–28.

27. Archaeological digs in Shensi province begun in 1974 yielded great art treasures from the reign of Ch'in Shih Huang-ti (reviewed in *The New York Times*, Nov. 30, 1975). Some one thousand bamboo slips, preserving Legalist laws and documents from the Late Warring States through the Ch'in dynasties (475–224 B.C.), were found in one of twelve tombs excavated in Central China in early 1976 (*The New York Times*, Mar. 29, 1976).

28. Ch'ü T'ung-tsu, *Han Social Structure*, ed. Jack Dull (Seattle, 1972), 60–61.

29. Lo Ssu-ting, "On Class Struggle."

30. For example, see Sun Lo-ying and Lu Li-fan, "On Confucian Persecution."

31. Quoted in Hsueh-hsi yü p'i-p'an [Study and criticism] 1 (Jan. 10, 1975); SPRCM 810 (Feb. 24, 1975): 1. This highly detailed account of Wu Tse-t'ien's career from a Legalist viewpoint is one of several revolutionary revisionist accounts of her reign that began to appear in the fall of 1974. See also "Study the Historical Experience of the Struggle between the Confucian and Legalist Schools," HC 10 (October 1974); SPRCM 795–795 (Oct. 29–Nov. 4, 1974). The HC article was reprinted in JMJP, Oct. 13, 1974.

The redoubtable philosopher Feng Yu-lan published twenty-five politically topical poems in KMJP, Sept. 14, 1974. The eleventh read:

> "The shattered mountains and rivers are reunited.
> Now impoverished families and commoners dominate once powerful clans.
> [Wu] Tse-t'ien, who dared to declare herself sovereign,
> Was a unique heroine for opposing Confucianism."

This is a modified translation based on one that appeared in *Current Scene* 12 (November 1974): 22.

32. Audrey Topping, "China Pushing Drive to Mechanize Farms," *The New York Times*, Dec. 4, 1975.
33. CNA 1019 (Nov. 7, 1975): 5–6.
34. That document, acquired through Taipei sources, is quoted verbatim in CNA 1004 (June 20, 1975).
35. HC 3 (March 1976): 12–16; reprinted in JMJP, Mar. 4, 1976.
36. PR 15 (Apr. 9, 1976): 5.
37. CNA 1054 (Sept. 17, 1976): 4.
38. JMJP, Sept. 12, 1976.
39. PR 44 (Oct. 29, 1976): 14–16.
40. Report by Tiziano Terzani, *Newsweek* (Nov. 1, 1976): 44.
41. *The Washington Post*, Nov. 17, 1976.
42. PR 47 (Nov. 19, 1976): 8.
43. JMJP, Nov. 20, 1976.
44. *The New York Times*, Dec. 4, 1976.
45. PR 46 (Nov. 12, 1976): 6–7.
46. CNA 1056 (Oct. 8, 1976): 6.
47. CNA 1060 (Nov. 12, 1976): 2.
48. JMJP, Nov. 26, 1976.
49. *The Washington Post*, Nov. 17, 1976.
50. JMJP, Nov. 19, 1976.
51. PR 46 (Nov. 12, 1976): 7.
52. Ibid., 7–8.
53. PR 44 (Oct. 29, 1976): 13.
54. *The New York Times*, Oct. 31, 1976.
55. *The New York Times*, Oct. 23, 1976.
56. *The Washington Post*, Oct. 29, 1976.
57. *The New York Times*, Dec. 8, 1976.
58. JMJP, Nov. 10, 1976.
59. JMJP, Nov. 1, 1976.
60. *The New York Times*, Dec. 7, 1976.
61. PR 1 (Jan. 1, 1977): 34.
62. *Manchester Guardian* 115 (Nov. 7, 1976).

[After this book went to press, I discovered a *People's Daily* article of November 26, 1976, which claimed that in the summer of 1974 Chiang Ch'ing had attempted to publish in a Chinese photojournal a landscape photograph and the quatrain that appears as this book's frontispiece, "Han Yang Peak at Lu Shan." Some of her present discreditors believe that she had written the poem herself; the probability of the late Mao's having penned it was not considered. The *People's Daily* critic dissected each line of this "black" poem as an allusive revelation of Chiang Ch'ing's ambition to become a twentieth-century Chinese empress.]

Index

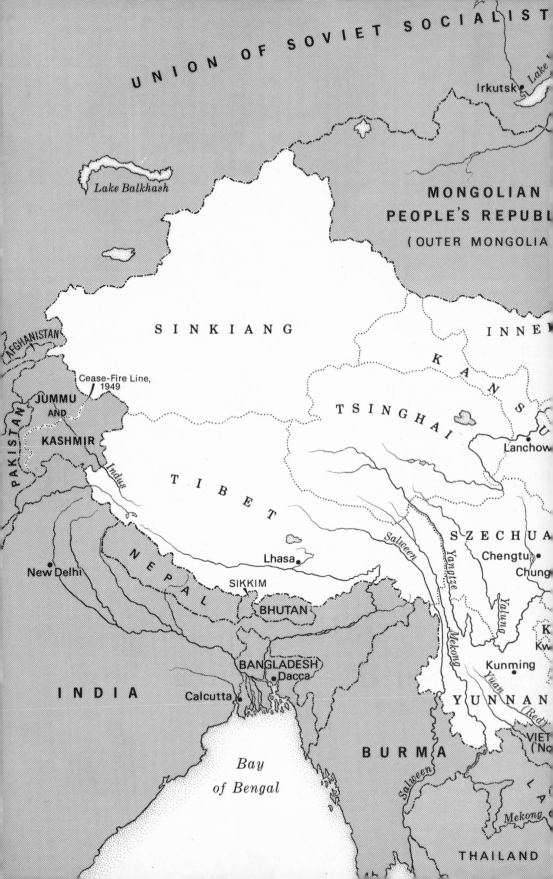